v.2

The American Catholic Parish
A History From 1850 To The Present

Edited by
JAY P. DOLAN

VOLUME II
Pacific States • Intermountain West • Midwest

PAULIST PRESS
NEW YORK • MAHWAH

Book design by Nighthawk Design.

Copyright © 1987 by
Jeffrey M. Burns, Carol L. Jensen
and Stephen J. Shaw

All rights reserved. No part of this book may be reproduced or transmitted in any form or by any means, electronic or mechanical, including photocopying, recording or by any information storage and retrieval system without permission in writing from the Publisher.

The American Catholic parish.

    Includes bibliographies and indexes.
    Contents: V. 1. Northeast, Southeast, South Central—
v. 2. Pacific states, intermountain West, Midwest.
    1. Catholic Church—United States—History—19th century. 2. Parishes—United States—History—19th century. 3. Catholic Church—United States—History—20th century. 4. Parishes—United States—History—20th century. 5. United States—Church history—19th century. 6. United States—Church history—20th century.
I. Dolan, Jay P., 1936–
BX1407.P3A53   1987   282'.73   87-6865

Library of Congress Cataloging-in-Publication Data

ISBN 0-8091-0399-0 (v. 1)
ISBN 0-8091-0400-8 (v. 2)

Published by Paulist Press
997 Macarthur Boulevard
Mahwah, New Jersey 07430

Printed and bound in the
United States of America

Contents

Introduction by Jay P. Dolan   1

I.
Building the Best: A History of Catholic Parish Life in the Pacific States
JEFFREY M. BURNS   7

PREFACE	9
CHAPTER ONE: Introduction	10
CHAPTER TWO: The Missionary Parish	19
CHAPTER THREE: Building and Fund-Raising	25
CHAPTER FOUR: The Spiritual Life of the Parish	33
CHAPTER FIVE: The Organizational Life of the Parish	40
CHAPTER SIX: Ethnic Catholicism on the West Coast	49
CHAPTER SEVEN: The Mexican-American Catholic Community	79
CHAPTER EIGHT: The Post-Vatican II Parish	96
CHAPTER NINE: Conclusion: New Concerns, Old Verities	117
FOR FURTHER READING	119
APPENDIX: The Hawaiian and Alaskan Parishes	121

II.
Deserts, Diversity, and Self-Determination: A History of the Catholic Parish in the Intermountain West
CAROL L. JENSEN   137

PREFACE	139
CHAPTER ONE: The Development of the Church in the Intermountain West, 1539–1960	141
CHAPTER TWO: The Local Church	174
CHAPTER THREE: Religion and Ethnicity	199
CHAPTER FOUR: The Post-Vatican II Period	228
FOR FURTHER READING	269

III.
The Cities and the Plains, a Home for God's People: A History of the Catholic Parish in the Midwest

STEPHEN J. SHAW — 277

PREFACE	279
CHAPTER ONE: The Establishment of Parish Life in the United States, 1604–1914	282
CHAPTER TWO: The Consolidation of Parish Life, 1914–1962	327
CHAPTER THREE: The Reorganization of Parish Life Since Vatican II, 1962–	355
FOR FURTHER READING	380
APPENDIX 1: Catholic Church Statistics in the Pacific States	127
APPENDIX 2: Catholic Church Statistics in the Intermountain West	270
APPENDIX 3: Number of Parishes in the Intermountain West	275
APPENDIX 4: Date When Intermountain States Became More Urban Than Rural	276
APPENDIX 5: Catholic Church Statistics in the Midwest	381
INDEXES	402

Notes on the Contributors

JEFFREY M. BURNS (Pacific States)
Jeffrey M. Burns was born in Lima, Ohio. He received a B.A. from the University of California at Riverside and a Ph.D. from the University of Notre Dame, where he worked for the Cushwa Center for the Study of American Catholicism. He is presently Archivist for the Archdiocese of San Francisco.

JAY P. DOLAN (General Editor)
is professor of history at the University of Notre Dame and director of the Cushwa Center for the Study of American Catholicism. His published books include *The Immigrant Church* (1975) and *The American Catholic Experience* (1985).

CAROL L. JENSEN (Intermountain)
With master's degrees in English Literature and Religious Studies from Indiana University, Carol L. Jensen teaches in Albuquerque, New Mexico, and researches the multicultural religious history of that state.

STEPHEN J. SHAW (Midwest)
Stephen J. Shaw received his Ph.D. from the University of Chicago. Married and the father of two daughters, he is currently teaching in Chicago on the secondary and college level, while pursuing his interests in American religion and ethnicity.

Introduction

This two-volume study of the Roman Catholic parish in the United States is the first major publication of the Notre Dame Study of Catholic Parish Life. The Notre Dame Study was a research endeavor undertaken by a group of scholars from the University of Notre Dame. The goal of the project was to understand more thoroughly the American Catholic parish of the 1980s. The first phase of the project began in 1981 with a general survey of 1,850 parishes, 10% of the nation's total number of parishes at that time. The second phase began in 1982 and concluded in 1985. This part of the study was a more intensive examination of parish life by sociologists, political scientists, theologians, and historians. The final phase of the project is a joint effort by academic scholars and church leaders to interpret the significance of the study's findings for American Catholic parish life. The entire study was made possible by funding from the Lilly Endowment, Inc.[1]

The Notre Dame Study of Catholic Parish Life differed from all previous studies of the parish in a very significant way. It included history in its arsenal of intellectual analysis. At first glance this decision seems quite trivial. But it was hardly a trivial matter. It was a calculated choice made by the directors of the project so that a historical perspective and analysis would become an integral part of the study. Previous studies of the Catholic parish had neglected history and, thus, had unwittingly contributed to the historical amnesia so prevalent in American society.

An understanding of history is critical to a society's development and self-identity. This is so evident in European countries where historical monuments, some dating back more than a thousand years, vividly remind people of their rich cultural heritage. It is naive to believe that a person can understand contemporary English society without understanding the rise and fall of the British Empire. It is equally naive to think that someone can understand the meaning of the American experience without appreciating the cultural and political significance of the American Revolution. To say that 1776 is past history and has no contemporary relevance is to fail to grasp the influence that history has on the development of a people and their culture. To understand English history with its kings and lords, its feudal past, and its age of empire and triumphalism is essential to an understanding of contemporary English society. English people are the way they are because of who they were in ages past. The same is true of Americans. The Revolution of 1776, the settlement of the frontier, the Civil War, and the emergence of the United States as an industrial giant were all phenomena that shaped the American personality. Americans are the way they are because of who they were. The differences between an Englishman and an American are very clear because their histories are so different. People can never understand who they are unless they understand who they were.

Catholics have a peculiar problem with history. They can point to a 2,000-year tradition that touches every continent of the earth. It is indeed an ancient and rich history. But in the nineteenth century Catholics began to believe that somehow, somewhere in the ancient past, history stopped and Catholicism became frozen in time. This view became so prevalent that many people believed that the Catholic religion was immune to the influence of history. This mentality persisted for well over one-hundred years, and only in recent times has it begun to lose its grip on the minds of people. Thus, the paradox—Catholicism has a rich and ancient past, but the Catholic faith is immune to the ebb and flow of historical developments. The Catholic God, in other words, is a God above and beyond history. In such a culture, the study of history is not so central to a person's belief or self-understanding.

This attitude toward history and faith helps to explain the Catholic aversion to religious history. For Catholics, the history of Catholicism is interesting but not personally significant. It really has nothing to do with a person's religion. This is erroneous. History does shape faith, and to think that the faith of a German peasant in the fifteenth century is no different than that of an American astronaut in the twentieth century is to fail to understand the relationship between religion and history.

For Catholics in the United States the problem of history is even more serious. American Catholics have a very brief historical tradition, no more than 200 years old. Compared with Ireland or France, American Catholicism is still in its infancy. Thus, the weight of the past is quite light; it does not leave the imprint on contemporary Catholic culture in the same manner that an ancient Catholic tradition does in a country like Ireland. For this reason, history does not have the same implications for American Catholicism as it does for Irish Catholicism. Nevertheless, the past, however brief it may be, has shaped the present. This is especially pertinent in the 1980s when the American Catholic community is in the midst of a major transformation. For anyone who wants to understand this present era of American Catholicism, an understanding of the past is essential. Catholics will never understand who they are as American Catholics unless they first know who they were.

A key to understanding the history of American Catholicism is the parish. In the ninteenth century, the parish was the central gathering place for the people. This is where they manifested their beliefs and demonstrated their commitment to the Roman Catholic tradition. For many groups, such as the Polish in Chicago and the French Canadians in New Hampshire, even the neighborhood where they lived was named after the parish where they prayed. For these people and for many others the parish was clearly a central neighborhood institution. The spires of parish churches defined the boundaries of the city's neighborhoods. Oftentimes, the neighborhood church took on a size and grandeur that rivaled, even occasionally surpassed, that of the bishop's cathedral. These monuments to the neighborhood God became the people's cathedral, striking reminders to them as well as to their American neighbors of the Catholic presence in the city.

As the Church developed in the nineteenth century, other institutions such as hospitals, orphanages, schools, and colleges were established. Nonetheless, the parish still remained the most important institution in the community. This was where the religion of the people was nurtured and strengthened; nineteenth-century Catholic education is the story of the emergence of the parish school; through their parish organizations, Catholics first learned the lessons of benevolence and social concern. It is no exaggeration to say that in the nineteenth century the parish was the foundation of American Catholicism. Without it everything else would have collapsed.

In other countries where religion and culture were tightly bound together, the parish was not so central to the development of Catholicism. In Ireland, for example, Catholicism has been the religion of the vast majority of the people for over a thousand years. The main vein of the cultural bedrock of Ireland was and still is Roman Catholicism. In such an environment the parish was only one of many cultural institutions that encouraged the religious development of the people. In a country like Ireland the influence of Catholicism was and still remains inescapable. The situation in France, Spain, and Italy was similar. In the United States, however, Protestantism was the main vein of the nation's cultural bedrock. For that reason, Catholics had to establish their own institutions to nurture and sustain their religious tradition. The primary institution established by the people was the parish and in the United States, more so than in other nations, it took on an increased importance.

Because of its central importance in the community, the parish is a valuable analytical tool for the historian. It becomes the historian's magnifying glass and enables him or her to obtain a closeup view of the people and their religion. By focusing on the parish, the historian can begin to sense the pulse of the people and understand more accurately the texture and quality of their lives. For anyone desirous of comprehending the history of the American Catholic people a study of the parish is essential. It was the hinge on which their religious world turned.

By concentrating on the parish community the historian necessarily broadens his or her range of interpretation. Rather than being limited to the lives of noteworthy individuals or important educational institutions, the parish enables the historian to examine a variety of issues that touched the lives of the people. This becomes especially evident in the essays gathered together in this collection.

With the parish community as their focal point, each historian was able to examine a broad range of issues over a century and more of time, from 1850 down to 1980. These issues included such topics as the involvement of laypeople in the establishment and development of the parish community, as well as the religious world of the people. Ethnicity or nationality has been a major theme in American Catholic history, and these essays have examined that issue along with education and schooling, or the various ways immigrants handed on the faith to their children. In addition to the wide range of issues examined, these historical essays also offer the reader the unusual opportunity to compare the development of Roman Catholicism in various regions of the country. Because each essay follows the same thematic framework, valuable comparative perspective is offered. Very few studies can claim this. Moreover, such a perspective should help people in different regions of the nation to understand more thoroughly the growth of Catholicism in their area and how this has differed from other geographical regions. Southeast Catholicism has a very different history than the Midwest; the history of the Western Mountain region is also very unique. Such regional diversity underscores the complexity of American Catholicism and should dispel any lingering belief in the myth that American Catholicism is Chicago or New York Catholicism writ large.

It should also be emphasized that these essays are not histories of a particular parish in a specific region. They examine the historical development in general rather than any one particular parish. Moreover, they use the parish as their focal point of analysis. In a very real sense, these essays represent a major attempt to write a new type of American Catholic history, a history based in a specific geographical region and rooted in the local parish community. In addition, this history is designed to provide a comparative regional analysis, something that has been missing until now.

In his essay on Catholicism in the Pacific Coast region, Jeffrey M. Burns points out how in each age a specific type of spirituality developed in the parish community. He also underscores the great financial pressure that plagued the Church on the West Coast as it sought to keep pace with the rapid population developments of the twentieth century. Upon turning to Carol L. Jensen's essay on the Western frontier, it is striking how different and unique Catholicism was in this region where it was commonplace for parishes to stretch across a territory as vast as any New England state. The boom and bust nature of life in the mining country was a situation that no New York pastor would ever have understood. Stephen J. Shaw's essay on the Midwestern heartland of the United States underlines the unusual ethnic diversity of American Catholicism. He also gives long overdue credit to the indispensable work of priests of various religious orders in establishing Catholicism in the frontier region of the Midwest. In addition, Shaw does a fine job of analyzing the changes that swept through the American Catholic community in the 1960s and 1970s. The Northeast region has been the population center of American Catholicism for decades. It has very rich resources, and Joseph J. Casino was able to use them very effectively. His work in parish financial records was especially revealing because it enabled him to examine the financial priorities of parish communities and demonstrate how central the school was in the parish. The history of Florida is quite different from that of New York or Pennsylvania and the effect of this on Catholicism was stunning. Michael J. McNally emphasizes the destructive effect of the Civil War on Southern Catholicism as well as the damage caused by the economic boom and bust environment of early twentieth-century Florida. The Hispanic transformation of post-World War II Southern Catholicism is also a major interest of McNally. Charles E. Nolan brings different talents and interests to his study of the South Central region. Covering an area that stretches from Kentucky to Texas, he ranges far and wide in his essay. Surely one of the more interesting issues he examined was the effect of twentieth-century suburbanization on such regions as Texas and Louisiana.

These are but a few of the issues examined in the essays of this collection. The essays represent a new departure in American Catholic studies and will, henceforth, ensure that no history of American Catholicism can be complete without the comparative regional dimension that they offer. It is the hope of all of us associated with the Notre Dame Study of Catholic Parish Life that this collection of essays will provide people with a better, more informed understanding of the American Catholic parish, both past and present.

> Jay P. Dolan
> Charles and Margaret Hall Cushwa Center
> for the Study of American Catholicism
> University of Notre Dame
> February 1986

Note

1. For further information on the Notre Dame Study of Catholic Parish Life and the results of this study, consult the bimonthly reports issued by the Institute for Pastoral and Social Ministry, University of Notre Dame, 1201 Memorial Library, Notre Dame, Indiana 46556. These reports are edited by the project's directors, Professor David C. Leege and Monsignor Joseph Gremillion.

PART ONE

Building the Best: A History of Catholic Parish Life in the Pacific States

Jeffrey M. Burns

Contents

Preface	9
CHAPTER ONE: Introduction	10
CHAPTER TWO: The Missionary Parish	19
CHAPTER THREE: Building and Fund-Raising	25
CHAPTER FOUR: The Spiritual Life of the Parish	33
CHAPTER FIVE: The Organizational Life of the Parish	40
CHAPTER SIX: Ethnic Catholicism on the West Coast	49
CHAPTER SEVEN: The Mexican-American Catholic Community	79
CHAPTER EIGHT: The Post-Vatican II Parish	96
CHAPTER NINE: Conclusion: New Concerns, Old Verities	117
For Further Reading	119
APPENDIX: The Hawaiian and Alaskan Parishes	121

Preface

This essay could not have been written without the assistance and kindness of an extraordinary number of people. I want to especially thank Dr. Jay P. Dolan of the Cushwa Center for the Study of American Catholicism of the University of Notre Dame for his continual support, encouragement, and prodding. Special thanks also to my typist and friend, Nancy Rybacki, mother of six wonderful children, who somehow found time to type the manuscript. Her patience and perseverance are remarkable. And finally, thanks to my friend and confidante, Sabina Rybacki, who gave me constant support and encouragement.

Jeffrey M. Burns
San Francisco

CHAPTER ONE
Introduction

Since the mid-nineteenth century, the Pacific Coast has drawn people from all across the United States, and from every nation in the world. Whether attracted by the lush green of Washington and Oregon, or the gold and sunshine of California, people flooded the West Coast in search of a better life. The new arrivals of the 1850s and their counterparts of the 1980s encountered vastly different societies from San Diego to Seattle. In 1850, Washington and Oregon remained distant frontier outposts in America, consisting of scattered white settlements and Indian missions. In California, two distinct cultures were already present. Southern California retained its Mexican ambience and pace, with Los Angeles serving as "Queen of the Cow Counties." Northern California, the beneficiary of the massive influx of peoples brought on by the Gold Rush, consisted of scattered mining towns and the increasingly cosmopolitan San Francisco. San Francisco was an "instant city" where, to borrow Carey McWilliams' phrase, "the lights went on all at once."[1] By 1980, while all the states on the Pacific Coast had to deal with modernization, industrialization, and urbanization, each retained a distinctive culture. The fragmented, freeway culture of the megalopolis of Los Angeles, with its substantial Chicano barrios, differs vastly from the still cosmopolitan "culture of civility" which is San Francisco. Both differ from Washington's and Oregon's mildly progressive culture, which remains rooted in rural and agricultural traditions.

Despite the vast differences in regional culture, Catholics all along the Pacific Coast are united by a common faith and roughly similar parish structures that demonstrate remarkable similarities from state to state. As one San Francisco pastor noted in his annual parish report, "In this respect, the history of all churches is alike—a record of Masses said, Sacraments administered, the instructing of children, visits to the sick and dying, and the burials of the dead."[2] These are the common elements of parish life that unite all Catholic churches wherever they are found. The rhythms of parish life are intimately connected with the life and death of its parishioners. The parish is and has been the basic institution through which the average Catholic has practiced and experienced his or her faith. The parish assists in celebrating or mourning the signal events in the lives of its parishioners—birth, death, marriage, Confirmation. But for the most part, the history of parish life is not caught up with the extraordinary, but records the common, often tedious, experience of parish, priest, and people. As one San Diego pastor succinctly put it in his annual parish report, "Nothing special happened. Same like all the other parishes . . . growing little by little . . . some births . . . some deaths and the survivors each day closer to the end."[3] The parish has provided and continues to provide support and meaning to help its people endure this pilgrimage of life, and to endure the mundane routine of everyday existence.

The history of Catholic parish life in the Pacific states is a story of enormous growth, both numerically and materially. In 1850, the Church was only peripherally present in Oregon and Washington, where just twelve parishes existed. California, which had just been admitted to the Union, and was growing rapidly as a result of the Gold Rush, was not much better off. The remnants of the Spanish missions gave California a Spanish and Catholic demeanor, but as the nineteenth century progressed, the Spanish influence would be eclipsed by the Irish. By 1880, San Francisco was the center of California life, and of Catholic life on the West Coast, and had a very Irish and Catholic cast to it. San Francisco and the Irish would direct Catholic life along the West Coast throughout the nineteenth century.

By 1980, California had lost much of its Catholic demeanor, despite the fact that the Catholic Church in the Pacific states had grown from humble beginnings to its present mammoth size. By 1980, the Catholic Church in the Pacific states totaled over 1,900 churches, over 5.5 million people, accounting for 18% of the state's population, and 52% of all Church members.[4] As the following state by state breakdown shows, California has by far the largest Catholic population, and, excepting Hawaii, it represents the largest percentage of Catholics per total population.

TABLE:
State by State Church Membership Statistics, 1980[5]

	Churches	Catholic Population	% of Total Population	% of Total Membership
California	1,250	4,759,250	20.1	58.3
Alaska	97	39,678	9.9	32.1
Hawaii	64	210,000	21.8	65.6
Oregon	214	320,716	12.2	33.8
Washington	299	380,023	9.2	29.7

Throughout the period from 1850 to 1980, the typical West Coast Catholic parishioner has been ethnic, working class, and urban. Even in 1980 the typical parishioner is ethnic and urban, though a substantial Catholic middle class has developed. Nonetheless, the newer Catholic immigrant groups remain urban and working class.

The enormous growth of the Catholic Church in the Pacific states generated two problems that have preoccupied Catholic parish life throughout the period from 1850 to 1980. First, such growth required massive building programs to provide Catholics with the material facilities for proper worship and the preservation of Catholic culture—church, school, rectory, convent, hall, and the institutions of charity. Much of parish life on the West Coast would center around building programs and fund-raising campaigns. Second, the enormous growth has presented the Catholic Church in the West with its primary task—the assimilation of a wide diversity of peoples. These two problems confronted the Church in all three states, while each state also had unique regional problems and opportunities.

Of the Pacific states, California is the most distinctive, having experienced the greatest growth and ethnic diversity. Wave after wave of immigrants flooded California's Golden Gate, many of them Catholic. From 1850 to 1880, the Irish, Germans, and Mexicans, sprinkled with smaller numbers of French, Chilenos, Peruvians, and Italians, provided the bulk of Catholic immigration to California. Equally prevalent were two non-Catholic groups—the Chinese and Japanese—whose presence would play a significant role in California history. In the late nineteenth century, a large number of Italian immigrants arrived in California, settling primarily in San Francisco and the surrounding farm and wine producing regions. As California industry and agriculture expanded, and the need for a cheap labor supply rose, immigration increased. Between 1920 and 1930, scores of Portuguese, Filipinos, and Mexicans arrived to join in the pursuit of the California Dream. Mexican immigration, which had slowed considerably in the late nineteenth century, rose sharply after 1910 as a result of the dislocation caused by the Mexican Revolution. After 1930, however, many Mexicans and Filipinos were forcefully "repatriated" as a result of the Great Depression. Postwar prosperity and the need for cheap labor would once again bring droves of Mexicans across the California border. In the 1960s and the 1970s, inspired by the liberal immigration law of 1965, California would find itself accommodating a new wave of immigrants—Filipinos, Vietnamese, Koreans, Central and South Americans, Polish, and Mexicans. Besides receiving immigrants from other nations, California has received masses of "Americans" throughout its history—midwesterners and easterners who relocated in California to enjoy the state's gentle climate and economic opportunities. The completion of the transcontinental railroad to San Francisco in 1869, and to Los Angeles in the 1870s, spurred an influx of American migrants that exceeded even the massive influx of the Gold Rush era. In more recent years, between 1930 and 1980, the continual flow of federal moneys to California, particularly on defense related contracts, has insured a constant flow of easterners and midwesterners to California. The presence of so many races and groups has set the stage for numerous racial and ethnic conflicts, but it has also given California an ethnic and cultural richness and complexity.

For the first fifty years of California's existence as a state, San Francisco remained the major city and center of California life. As of 1900, 25% of the state's total population resided in San Francisco. California industry, finance, agriculture, and communications all revolved around San Francisco. Los Angeles remained a Spanish "cow town" that retained much of its pueblo atmosphere. In 1880, Los Angeles had only 11,000 inhabitants, while the Archdiocese of San Francisco boasted 185,000 Catholics alone. By 1900, the Diocese of Los Angeles—Monterey had 51,000 Catholics compared to 225,000 Catholics for the Archdiocese of San Francisco.[6] By 1905, Los Angeles and San Francisco, the state's two largest and influential cities, reflected two very different cultures. San Francisco remained cosmopolitan and Catholic, while Los Angeles had cast off its Spanish Catholic past, and had adopted a midwestern, Protestant tone, as it had been inundated with midwestern Protestants during the last two decades of the nineteenth century. By 1906, Los Angeles was 56% Protestant, compared to San Francisco where only 15% were Protestant; 68% of San Francisco's inhabitants were either first or second generation immigrants, while only 35% of the Los Angeles population were either foreign born or children of foreign born.[7] Also in 1906, San Francisco was devastated by the "Great Earthquake and Fire," and though the city was eventually rebuilt, the twentieth century belonged to Los Angeles. The development of the movie industry and tourism brought large sums of capital to Los Angeles, and spurred the city's enormous growth. By 1920, over half a million people resided in Los Angeles, a figure which more than doubled by 1930. By 1960, Los Angeles county exceeded 6 million people. While San Francisco remained important, the center of industry, agriculture, communications, and finance had moved to Los Angeles. By 1936, when Los Angeles was made an archdiocese, leadership of the Catholic Church in California had effectively moved south. By 1980, California was the most populous and productive state in the Union, with Catholics accounting for over 20% of the population.

California's enormous growth and productivity have presented it with unique problems. As historian Moses Rischin has pointed out, the "single most distinctive fact about California has been the perpetually high proportion of newly arrived immigrants among its inhabitants." The constant influx of new people has prevented California from "consolidating its institutions," or allowed it to firm up its identity, or to establish the "authority of tradition."[8] More than one California bishop and pastor has complained of the organizational strain caused by the state's rapid growth. Constant influx of new peoples also gave rise to an extremely mobile culture, rooted neither in geographical location nor in tradition. Josiah Royce complained that California had an "absence of concern for man's antecedents."[9] As early as 1854, a contemporary observer recorded what would become a quintessentially California characteristic through 1980: "All California is only a sort of theater, where everything goes ahead on the high pressure principle. You can't stand still if you would, and the consequence is that you are whirled around and about until you are apt to get dizzy."[10]

The fluidity of California society, while enabling great social and geographic mobility, was not without its darker side. California's lack of tradition and its highly mobile culture were often sources of a disquieting rootlessness among many residents. From the Gold Rush days to the present, many Californians have fallen prey to feelings of alienation and anonymity. California has long had the highest divorce and suicide rates in the country. In the midst of the frenzied pace of California life, the Catholic parish has attempted to provide an island of order and tradition, offering companionship and relief from the state's dizzying routine. Whether one struck it rich or was trying to recover from shattered dreams, the Catholic parish offered an alternative vision as well as practical assistance.

Oregon and Washington reflected different patterns of growth and culture. For one thing, life there has been more relaxed, less hectic. With each state economy centered in agriculture, lumbering, fishing, and forest related industries, both states have remained predominantly rural. The Diocese of Baker in eastern Oregon, comprising three-fourths of the entire state, is one of the most rural dioceses in America. Only one major city exists in Oregon, and, as of 1980, Portland numbered only 366,000 inhabitants. Portland grew as the "export-import hub" for the San Francisco market, and for inland farmers. It emerged as the main city in the Pacific Northwest until the turn of the twentieth century, when it was surpassed by Seattle. Portland life never achieved the raucous reputation enjoyed (or suffered) by San Francisco and Seattle. In fact, one historian has referred to Portland as an "early to bed town," where a "village mentality flourished."[11]

Washington is more populous than Oregon and more urban, maintaining three major cities—Tacoma, Spokane, and Seattle. Seattle, the largest of the three, has grown from 42,000 in 1890 to 250,000 in 1910 to about 500,000 in 1970. As was the case in California, the emergence of the railroads in the 1890s spurred industrial growth in and immigration to Washington. Seattle grew numerically while serving as "portal to the Klondike" during the Alaskan Gold Rush.[12] Seattle has retained its pre-eminent position as the leading city in the Pacific Northwest due largely to the influx of federal moneys, and the arrival of Boeing industries, during and after World War II. The major city of central Washington, or of the "Inland Empire," as it is called, was Spokane, which served as the central marketplace and distributing center for the expansive wheat culture of central Washington.

The ethnic makeup of both Oregon and Washington, as a whole, has remained relatively homogeneous, consisting mainly of white, Anglo-Saxon, Protestants. The settlers who arrived in Oregon and Washington were predominantly midwestern farmers who came seeking to establish themselves on the land. The majority of immigrants who came to both states—the Scandinavians, the Germans, the English—shared a similar agrarian outlook. Foreigners of different outlook (i.e., Catholics from southern and eastern Europe) were never large enough to make a major impact on the culture of the Pacific Northwest. The lack of ethnic groups and urban centers accounts for the low percentage of Catholics in the two states, 12% in Oregon and 9% in Washington.[13]

The lack of ethnic groups and urban centers may also account for the restful and relaxing style of culture both Oregon and Washington project. Gordon Dodds has dubbed Oregon a "conservative commonwealth," where change comes slowly and never without sufficient reason. An early visitor to Oregon observed, "There is a distinctly Oregonian look about all the natives and old residents which is hard to describe. Certainly they are not an enterprising lot."[14] Despite their relaxed manner, Oregon and Washington led the way in the progressive political reform of the early twentieth century, thereby promoting the image of the Pacific Northwest as being mildly progressive, and progressively practical. One drawback of the region's relaxed ways was decried by the churches—the Pacific Northwest is the most unchurched region in the United States. Many preachers, Catholic and non-Catholic alike, chastised what they perceived as an "indifference to religion."[15] The Church in the Pacific Northwest was faced with the difficult task of inspiring an indifferent people to devotion. In the urban centers, the Church in Oregon and Washington faced the same problems as the Church in urban California though on a smaller scale—the provision of the material facilities for worship and the assimilation of a wide diversity of immigrant groups.

ANTI-CATHOLICISM ON THE WEST COAST

The history of Catholicism on the West Coast has been marred by periods in which anti-Catholicism has been fashionable, though the outbreaks, for the most part, were not as virulent or constant as those encountered in the East. In fact, it is tempting to view the Catholic relationship with Protestant and secular cultures as quite amicable. No less a personage than Archbishop Joseph Sadoc Alemany of San Francisco could assert, "The Catholic Church did not have to face the prejudice in this state which it encountered in other parts of the country,"[16] and another San Francisco clergyman observed in 1878, "a remarkable harmony exists among the clergy of all denominations"; "little invective" found its way into their discourse.[17] Similarly, Gordon Dodds contends that ethnic Catholics in Oregon were "spared from grosser forms of ethnic prejudice."[18] California's Catholic origins did much to foster a greater tolerance for things Catholic. Indeed, the Mission Revival of the early twentieth century made the spirit of Catholicism, at least its aesthetic side, fashionable. In reality, the Catholics who fared better on the West Coast were white, European, immigrant Catholics. The maniacal distrust and hatred of Asians, which obsessed the entire West Coast, diverted concern away from Catholic immigrants. However, Catholic immigrants with darker skin experienced the full brunt of California racism. Mexican, Filipino, and South and Central American Catholics were as poorly treated as any Catholics on the

East Coast. Oftentimes, the racism directed at darker skinned Catholics emanated from within the Catholic community itself.

Despite the greater tolerance for light skinned Catholics, sporadic outbursts of anti-Catholicism did occur. In the early missionary period, battles between Catholic and Protestant missionaries intensified traditionally harsh feelings between Protestants and Catholics in Oregon and Washington. The Indians, caught in the middle, were often left bewildered. In Washington in the 1840s, the conflict reached its peak with the famous Whitman massacre, in which a Protestant minister and his family were allegedly slaughtered by Catholic Indians. When no Indian claimed responsibility for the massacre, a relentless persecution of the Cayuse Indians was carried out by Protestant vigilantes. Finally, five Indians, all baptized Catholic, turned themselves in as being responsible for the massacre. In a poignant scene, one of the condemned Indians reasoned before being put to death, "Did not your missionaries teach us that Christ died to save his people? Thus die we, if we must, to save our people."[19] The incident did little to reduce Protestant fears of Catholic antipathy. In the 1850s in California, outbreaks of anti-Catholicism plagued San Francisco, as the Vigilance Committees singled out Irish Catholics for special chastisement. In the mining towns, Mexican Catholics were abused as much for their race as for their religion. In 1855, a Catholic church was burned down in Drytown, California, as a result of anti-Mexican and anti-Catholic feelings. While anti-Irish feeling would wane, antipathy toward Mexican Catholics has remained strong through 1980.

Another outbreak of anti-Catholicism occurred in the 1890s all along the West Coast with the emergence of the American Protective Association (APA). In San Francisco, the APA launched a bitter media campaign against the Catholic Church. The APA was just as bitterly counterattacked by Father Peter C. Yorke, the brilliant young editor of the *San Francisco Monitor,* the official newspaper of the Archdiocese of San Francisco. The APA and Yorke carried on a prolonged debate, which did little credit to either side.

Perhaps the most serious anti-Catholic outbreaks occurred in the 1920s with the arrival of the Ku Klux Klan (KKK). In Oregon, the KKK gained such power that it was able to pass a law through the state legislature requiring each child in the state to attend a public school. The law was a direct attack upon the Catholic school system and the implementation of the law would have meant the virtual end of Catholic schools in Oregon. In 1925, the Supreme Court declared in *Pierce v. Society of Sisters* that the law was unconstitutional as the primary right of education resided with the parents. Frightened by the growth of the KKK, Catholic Truth Societies and Catholic Evidence Guilds developed to counteract false accusations made against the Church.

Throughout the period from 1850 to 1980, anti-Catholicism broke out at various times on the West Coast. As often as not, the attacks were merged with racial attacks on the non-Anglo Catholic immigrant community.

Introduction 17

Intolerance and racism were only part of the underside of West Coast life. California was also flawed by a rampant materialism and an excessive individualism that made communal and religious life a struggle. Nonetheless, West Coast Catholics remained optimistic about life along the Pacific. Countless clerics endorsed the rhetoric of the American Dream, proclaiming a "new race," and "new people" on the West Coast. Catholics, through the Catholic parish, would help build the new order.

Notes

1. Carey McWilliams quoted in Robert W. Cherny and William Issel, *San Francisco: Presidio, Port and Pacific Metropolis* (San Francisco: Boyd and Fraser, 1981), 9.
2. San Francisco. Chancery Archives of the Archdiocese of San Francisco. (Hereafter referred to as AASF). Parish Files.
3. San Diego. Chancery Archives of the Diocese of San Diego. (Hereafter referred to as ADSD). Parish Files.
4. Bernard Quinn, et al., *Churches and Church Membership in the United States, 1980* (Atlanta: Glenmary Research Associates, 1980), 8.
5. *Ibid.*, 11–13.
6. Statistics taken from the *Official Catholic Directory*. For the pre-1900 period, I have used the *Catholic Directories* published by either D&J Sadlier of New York or M. H. Wiltzius of Milwaukee. In the post-1900 period, I have used the directories published by P. J. Kenedy and Sons of New York.
7. Kevin Starr, *Inventing the Dream: California through the Progressive Era* (New York: Oxford University Press, 1985), 238.
8. Moses Rischin, "Immigration, Migration and Minorities in California," in George H. Knoles (ed.) *Essays and Assays: California History Reappraised,* (San Francisco: California Historical Society, 1973), 65.
9. Josiah Royce, *California from the Conquest in 1846 to the Second Vigilance Committee in San Francisco* (New York: Knopf, reprint 1948, original 1886), 393–394.
10. Joseph B. Crockett, (1854), quoted in Robert M. Senkewicz, S.J., *Vigilantes in Gold Rush San Francisco* (Stanford University Press, 1985), 1.
11. Dorothy O. Johansen, "A Working Hypothesis for the Study of Migrations," *Pacific Historical Review* 36 (1969), 1.
12. Norman H. Clark, *Washington: A Bicentennial History* (New York: Norton, 1976), 75.
13. Gordon Dodds, *Oregon: A Bicentennial History* (New York: Norton, 1976), 185. Also, Quinn, *Church Membership,* 11–13.
14. J. H. Beaddle (1873) quoted in Johansen, "Migrations," 2.
15. The overview of Washington and Oregon was drawn largely from the bicentennial histories written for the American Association for State and Local History by Norman Clark and Gordon Dodds. See above.

16. Archbishop Joseph Sadoc Alemany, O.P., quoted in Francis J. Weber, *California Catholicity* (Hong Kong: Libra Press, 1979), 142.
17. Hugh Quigley, *The Irish Race in California* (San Francisco: A. Roman, 1878).
18. Dodds, *Oregon,* 117.
19. Cited in Clark, *Washington,* 32.

CHAPTER TWO

The Missionary Parish

The period from 1850 to 1880 on the West Coast was characterized predominantly by the frontier mission parish. California, outside San Francisco, remained sparsely populated and unchurched. Even in San Francisco, parish life retained a rugged frontier quality in this early period. Los Angeles and Santa Barbara remained Mexican pueblos, dependent upon the prosperity spawned by the Gold Rush in northern California. Washington and Oregon remained even more undeveloped with Washington continuing to experience Indian wars throughout the 1850s. Prior to 1850, in all three Pacific states, the predominant thrust of missionary activity was the conversion of the Indians. By 1850, however, the Church began to turn its attention to the incoming white settler, placing less and less emphasis on the Indian mission. Historian Leonard Pitt writes of the sorry status of the Catholic Indian community in California. "By the 1850s, the neophytes (Indian converts) remained a demoralized class alternately prey to disease, liquor, violence, submission, and exploitation."[1] The case of the Indians would get worse as many Franciscan missionaries returned to Mexico and were replaced by an "American clergy." In Oregon, the status of the Indian was equally pathetic. Jesuit missionary to the Indians, Pierre Jean de Smet, eulogized, "The poor Indians of Oregon . . . who after having lived peaceably by hunting and fishing during several generations will finally disappear, victims of vice and malady under the rapacious influence of modern civilization."[2] In each state—California, Oregon, and Washington—an explicit decision was made to abandon the Indian, and to attend to the needs of the white Catholic settler.

Attempts were made to provide priests for the Indians, but more often than not, no priests were available. Priests were in short supply even for expanding white settlements. Things were so dire near old Mission Santa Ynez that Archbishop Alemany sent a lay Indian to baptize and minister among the Indian community there.[3] One extraordinary priest who did spend his life serving Indian Catholics (as well as serving mining and frontier parishes) was Father Luciano Osuna. He lived what many of his contemporaries considered to be an "erratic" lifestyle, while others respected him for his piety and saintliness. His great love for the Indians inspired him to dress and live like those to whom he ministered. One contemporary observed of Osuna, "A more dirty, ragged specimen of humanity is rarely seen."[4] Osuna ran afoul of the Methodist federal Indian agent by ignoring federal regulations regarding his visits to Indians on the reservation, but his main crime seems to be that he identified too closely with the Indians. Osuna defended his lifestyle, "I have been with the Indians most of the time; they are sick and hungry, so I am hungry with them."[5] In Osuna's view, the Indians had been poorly used by the Californians and by the federal government. He lamented that the Indians are "prey to all."[6] Osuna lived and served the Indians for many years at St. Turibius Indian Mission in northern California, but there were few priests who served the Indian community with such dedication. The plight of the Indian, Catholic and non-Catholic alike, would remain a sad and disgraceful story.

While Indian missions were neglected, only in San Francisco did regular parish life develop to any extent between 1850 and 1880. In Oregon, only twelve parishes had resident priests by 1880, while the entire state of Washington had only seven parishes with resident priests. In the Los Angeles—Monterey Diocese, Bishop Thaddeus Amat divided his diocese into twenty parish centers, from which all the missions in the diocese were tended.[7] For example, in Orange County, St. Boniface Parish in the city of Anaheim was established as the central parish, serving as Mother Church to all the new mission parishes established in the county during the nineteenth century. This was the general pattern for the missionary parish—a central or "primary" parish would be established at what Alemany called "key points," from which the priest would visit his various missions. This pattern was also employed by Protestant denominations, whose ministers had to confront the same problems as Catholic missionary priests—vast distances with too few clergy to cover the areas adequately.

The lot of the missionary priest was difficult. As ground-breaking historian Father Henry Walsh put it, "The early missionary realized that his ministry was to be carried out in an unbounded parish, made up of rugged hills and isolated gulches and ravines; that his parishioners were constantly on the move, on foot or mule."[8] Due to the vastness of his "unbounded parishes," the life of the Catholic missionary was one of constant travel and incessant demands, which often took their toll. One priest complained in 1863, "Missionary duties are so urgent and oppressive that one can rarely find time for the performance of all the religious duties we were taught to develop at All Hallows."[9]

Besides the hectic pace, the missionary priest might grow discouraged by the crassness and hard-heartedness of his "parishioners." Throughout the missionary era, the parish priest was faced with a general moral laxity and lack of devotional fervor on the part of the Catholics on the West Coast. Public disorder brought the San Francisco Vigilance Committees into existence in the 1850s, and in Los Angeles carnival drinking and fighting were commonplace. In 1856, midnight Mass for Christmas was no longer permitted in Los Angeles because the celebration had become so disorderly. The frontier town of the West remained wild and woolly. Life in the mining towns was worse. The population was primarily young, male, and single, without the tempering influence of established family life. Moreover, the gold seekers were materialistic in the extreme, with little use for religion.

The most successful priests in San Francisco and the mining towns were those who were good preachers and strong men. The Archbishop of San Francisco, in requesting priests from Europe, insisted that they must be good preachers, or they would be lost in California. As early as 1852, a mining town newspaper the *Sierra Citizen* pleaded, "Send us . . . not a weak disciple who will do nothing but vilify Satan . . . but a strong man, with a big heart and cultivated mind; who will tell the story of the Cross with an energy and power and will command respect."[10] Two such preachers were Father James Bouchard and Father Patrick Hennebery, whose fame as preachers spread throughout northern California. Both men were magnificent orators who traveled from town to town conducting "missions," a form of Catholic revival meeting (see below). The fervor inspired by the mission often resulted in the construction of a chapel, or pulled the Catholic community together to at least begin thinking of building a chapel.

Drink and drunkenness were continual problems for frontier pastors and bishops. Frontier life provided as many alcoholic priests as it did alcoholic parishioners. Besides the frantic pace and various discouragements, the life of the missionary was often quite lonely. Separated from people of similar interests or educational background, the priest often turned to drink for comfort. Frontier Bishop Eugene O'Connell of the Diocese of Grass Valley, California, was an impassioned advocate of temperance, urging his priests to "absolute abstinence or strict temperance." In requesting priests for his diocese, O'Connell pleaded, "For heaven's sake, let him be whiskey proof."[11] The Church did try to foster temperance societies during the missionary era, but its efforts met with little success.

The frontier parish remained quite transient. Due to the rapid geographical mobility of the Gold Rush Era, many churches were erected, often at considerable expense, then abandoned as the population moved on. More often than not, however, a makeshift chapel or private home was used as a place of worship until the community became more established.

Another continual problem was the shortage of priests. A parish might enjoy a resident pastor for several years, then go for another stretch with only irregular visits from a circuit riding priest. As there were few native clergymen, All Hallows College in Ireland and other Irish seminaries became the basic suppliers of Catholic frontier priests, providing well over 50% of all the priests working in California during the period from 1850 to 1880. Two distinct groups of frontier priests existed—one group lived long lives and remained at one central parish for thirty or forty years from which they tended their missions. On the other hand, a large group of priests died before they had reached thirty years of age, and still another group died before they reached the age of forty. The high mortality rate (a large number died of tuberculosis contracted before they left Ireland) caused a high turnover rate for most parishes on the frontier. Combined with the transient pastoral situation was the ever present danger of church fire. During the frontier era, virtually every parish experienced the loss of one of its buildings because of fire. Indeed, historian Robert Senkewicz has suggested that the "constant theme" of urban life in the nineteenth century "may well be fire."[12] The transitory nature of priests, people, and buildings made stable parish life difficult to achieve.

Episcopal style was also different in the frontier era. Joseph Sadoc Alemany, O.P., Archbishop of San Francisco, Eugene O'Connell of Grass Valley, and the Blanchets of Oregon and Washington were bona fide missionary priests. Alemany constantly referred to the burden of having to carry out all the regular duties of a parish priest besides taking care of his administrative duties for the archdiocese. All the frontier bishops continued to visit the far reaches of their dioceses. Bishop O'Connell was constantly on the road, having vowed to visit each one of his widespread parishes every two years. And Archbishop Alemany spent so much time in the saddle that he was "accounted one of the finest horsemen of early California."[13] Nor were the living conditions suitable for "princes of the church." Alemany lived in a slum area of San Francisco, populated by poor Chinese and prostitutes. As one contemporary observed of Alemany, "No man is more poorly lodged in the whole city."[14] The modesty and simplicity of episcopal life kept the bishops close to their people. Episcopal aloofness would come when the Church emerged from the missionary period. The modest nature of episcopal dwellings was matched by those of frontier priests. Most priests lived in rented rooms or lodged with families in their parish.

The transitory nature of the frontier parish made parish organizational life somewhat scant. Lay participation was limited, for the most part, to fund-raising. Without the presence of a resident priest, the laity took upon itself the task of raising money for the building of a church. The general process was a subscription drive. Several laymen were given lists of various parishioners, whom they contacted and tried to induce to give donations for the future church. The subscription process was the most significant lay activity in the frontier parish. Once the church was built, the laity would then petition the bishop for a resident pastor. The majority of parishes in the frontier area were begun at the instigation of the laity. This was particularly true of rural parishes (and remained true of rural parishes after the frontier era). Due to the small number of rural families, many rural parishes were dependent upon the donation of land and money for the church from a single donor. The question of who held title to the parish's land often caused conflict between the pastor and the laity. However, conflict on the West Coast never reached the degree of intensity present in the trusteeism controversies of the eastern Church.

The missionary quality of Catholic life lasted well into the twentieth century in parts of Oregon and Washington, and northern California. The Extension Society of America, a national organization begun in the early twentieth century by Father Francis Kelly to assist small missions, played a crucial role in the development of parish life in rural Oregon and Washington. Extension subsidized numerous rural parishes, providing $500 to parishes and missions to build chapels. In 1919, Extension gave the Diocese of Baker $12,500 to assist in the construction of twenty-five new chapels. The most imaginative program initiated by Extension was the "chapel car" program developed to minister to unattended rural parishes and missions in the Pacific Northwest. An old Pullman car was converted into a traveling mission car, complete with chapel, sacristy, confessional, and sleeping quarters for the priest. The chapel car journeyed from small town to small town, staying anywhere from three to ten days at each town. While in the town, the chapel car priest would conduct a mission to inspire Catholics who had grown indifferent from neglect. The mission often inspired the construction of a permanent church in each locale. The chapel car program reached many otherwise isolated Catholic parishioners.[15] After the chapel car left, however, rural parishes were still hindered by a lack of a resident priest. In many priest-less parishes, prayer services and other duties were taken on by the laity. For instance, rural St. William parish in Richland, Oregon, had the luxury of a priest to say Mass only once a month. On the other Sundays, the parishioners would gather for prayer and the Rosary; several of the lay parishioners would also provide religious instruction for the children.[16] At St. William and in other rural parishes, the shortage of resident priests would press the laity into assuming the many responsibilities of parish life. The same story was, and continues to be repeated in rural parishes throughout Washington, Oregon, and California to the present time.

Notes

1. Leonard Pitt, *The Decline of the Californios: A Social History of the Spanish Speaking Californians. 1846–1890* (Berkeley and Los Angeles: University of California Press, 1971), 10.

2. Pierre Jean de Smet, S.J. (1840), quoted in Dodds, *Oregon,* 60.

3. Henry L. Walsh, S.J., *Hallowed Were Those Gold Dust Trails: The Story of the Pioneer Priests of Northern California* (Santa Clara: University of Santa Clara Press, 1946), 23.

4. Quoted in John T. Dwyer, *Condemned to the Mines: The Life of Eugene O'Connell* (New York: Vantage Press, 1976), 150.

5. *Ibid.,* 146.

6. *Ibid.,* 147.

7. Francis J. Weber, *California's Reluctant Prelate: The Life and Times of Right Reverend Thaddeus Amat, C.M.* (Los Angeles: Dawson's Bookshop, 1964), 93.

8. Walsh, *Hallowed Trails,* 19.

9. James Callan, "A Missionary Reports Home, October 30, 1863" in Francis J. Weber, *Documents of California Catholic History* (Los Angeles: Dawson's Bookshop, 1965), 98.
10. Walsh, *Hallowed Trails,* 20.
11. Dwyer, *Condemned to the Mines,* 70.
12. Senkewicz, *Vigilance,* 73.
13. Hamilton Wright and F. Marion Gallagher, "What the Church Has Done for San Francisco, 1907," reprinted in Weber, *Documents,* 212.
14. John J. McGloin, *California's First Archbishop: The Life of Joseph Sadoc Alemany, O.P., 1814–1884* (New York: Herder and Herder, 1966), 231.
15. Most Rev. Francis P. Leipzig, *Extension in Oregon* (St. Benedict, Oregon: Benedictine Abbey Press, 1956).
16. Father Dominic O'Connor and Patrick J. Gaire, *A Brief History of the Diocese of Baker* (St. Benedict, Oregon: Benedictine Abbey Press, 1930, rev. 1966), 193.

CHAPTER THREE

Building and Fund-Raising

From the frontier parish of the early West to the modern, suburban parish of today, the heart and soul of Catholic parish life in the Pacific states has been "building" and "fund-raising" (the two activities are directly interrelated). The common thread running through all the dioceses, from parish to parish, was the continued concern over parish financial solvency. The rapid growth of Catholic life on the West Coast required the continual expansion of old parishes and the creation of new parishes. Both necessitated massive building programs, which resulted in enormous parish debts. The old saw that the Catholic Church was preoccupied with money is firmly grounded in historical truth.

The complaint that pastors have been too preoccupied with money has been a common refrain in parishes throughout the West Coast. One parishioner complained to his bishop, "The only thing we ever hear in Church is finance. Devotion and religion are conspicuous by their absence."[1] The parishioner's complaint, though written in 1923 in San Francisco, is typical of those expressed by parishioners in virtually every era and in every state. The history of the Church in Oregon, California, and Washington is one of continual fund-raisers and subscription drives designed to pay off the parish debt. While the modern churchgoer might scoff at the "sordid" interest the Church took in money, from 1850 to 1960 the struggle to remain in the black had the beneficent side effect of spurring community spirit and action.

THE NEED FOR RESOURCES

Since the frontier era, most parishes on the West Coast have shared a common cycle of building and growth. As parishes stabilized (and at times even before that), suitable places of worship had to be constructed. Bishop Charles O'Reilly of the Diocese of Baker, Oregon, articulated a common outlook, "I know by experience how embarrassing it is to priest and people to be obliged to say Mass in the common room of some country hotel."[2] And so subscription drives were undertaken to pay for the building of the new church. With this accomplished, and a resident pastor obtained, the parish had to concern itself with providing a suitable lodging for the priest. And so the building of the rectory began. In some parishes, education was given top priority, and so the building of a parish school had to be undertaken. With the school building went the convent, necessary for the sisters who staffed the school. In addition, a gymnasium might be built to provide for the school and parish athletic needs. Once all this was completed, a parish hall would be built to provide a community center. At times, the parish hall was built prior to the Church, and served as a temporary site for the Sacraments. Once the "parish plant" was complete, the parish, more than likely, would have outgrown its original church, and a new, bigger church would have to be built, or an expansion of the older one would have to be undertaken. The order in which the buildings were built depended on a given parish's priorities, but the ideal parish would have all the composite parts. The process of building a complete parish plant could occupy a parish for a period of several decades—the entire while saddling the parish with a large debt. As a result, a great deal of time and energy went into the creation and funding of the parish plant.

In Anaheim, California, the parish of St. Boniface reflected the general cycle of building and fund-raising, as it strove to provide its parishioners with a complete parish plant. In 1910, the parish hosted a gala party to celebrate the paying off of the parish debt. In 1911, construction was begun on a new priest's home, and the cycle began anew.[3] So it went in parishes throughout the Pacific Coast.

The drive for the complete parish stemmed from the desire that the Catholic parish be able to provide for all the needs of its people—social, spiritual, and educational, thereby protecting Catholics from the pernicious influences of the public school, Protestant proselytizers, and secular organizations. To provide a completely separate alternative required a completely separate set of facilities and entailed a huge cost. Typical of the protective and separatist building impulse was the request of one San Francisco pastor, in 1921, who wished to build a new parish hall. To justify the expense, he explained, "I have organized a 'social club' among the younger members of the parish so as to keep them away from the dance halls, pool rooms, and decrease their frequent visits to the movies by giving them a meeting place where they can enjoy themselves according to their tastes in an innocent way."[4] The new hall might cost a good deal of money, but it was far less than the unconscionable cost of "losing" the innocence and devotion of Catholic youth.

The protective impulse was not the only reason for Catholic building. To a Catholic population predominantly urban, immigrant, and working class, the beauty and grandeur of the Catholic Church building gave Catholics immense personal satisfaction and fulfillment, in a world in which such qualities were often lacking. As one observer noted, "You know that while Patrick (the Irish) has his nose perhaps in the sewer all week, when he comes on Sunday, he is just as big a man as enters the temple. He is surrounded with objects of beauty and with the incense of worship, and the things are as much for him as for the richest man in the parish."[5] Despite the financial burden, the physical presence of the church proved psychologically supportive. Impressive church buildings could also show the non-Catholic society that Catholics were a group to be reckoned with, and not simply an immigrant rabble. In 1910, the pastor of a Berkeley, California, parish proclaimed, "Berkeley shall boast of a Catholic Church building better than the best. Noble and dignified buildings are a sign of a noble and dignified people."[6] In a culture that placed inordinate stress on the material, Catholics were impelled to provide an adequate material witness to American culture. Substantial church buildings were to be, as one observer noted, "visible tokens of sincerity and zeal"[7] for Catholics, and to the non-Catholic culture. It was a matter of pride and dedication for Catholics to maintain a magnificent physical plant, thereby proving their respectability to the larger community.

Beyond mere respectability, church buildings were to presage the greatness of the Church that was to be on the West Coast. Archbishop Hanna proclaimed in 1916, "We feel the Church of today is little when compared with the glory that is to come."[8] The glory of which Hanna spoke, would not come cheaply.

FINANCING

As a result of its massive building program and dedication to a separate school system, the Catholic parish was constantly in debt. In the mission days, the Church in California had been supported by the Pious Fund, a financial arrangement with the Mexican government. Early California Catholics were unused to paying church fees. In the period from 1850 to 1880, Archbishops Alemany and Amat were continually seeking funds from outside their dioceses, and received a good deal of help from the Society for the Propagation of the Faith in Paris. In Washington and Oregon, outside help in the form of grants from the Catholic Church Extension continued through the 1920s.

Despite the search for revenue from outside sources, Catholic parish life in the Pacific states has been supported, for the most part, by the efforts and sacrifices of its own parishioners. Throughout the nineteenth and twentieth centuries, rich and poor Catholics gave from their earnings to support the massive building programs of the Church. In 1866, one reporter acknowledged, "While the Catholic with the one hand worked and scrambled for wealth, with the other he freely gave to that which is always dearest to his heart."[9] Though the overall generosity of Catholic parishioners has been impressive, to the local pastor, beset by a large and ever present debt, they may not have seemed generous enough. At times his flock may have seemed a little too recalcitrant to give, a recalcitrance born of a lack of charity. At such time, pastoral prodding could be quite harsh. In an editorial, no doubt pleasing to pastors, the *San Francisco Monitor* stated bluntly, "Those who give little or nothing . . . have the spirit of Judas and belong to the genus 'nickel-nurser'. . . . They are the hard boiled eggs of religion."[10]

The constant preoccupation with money and fund-raising often detracted from the pastor's priestly ministry. A parishioner at Most Holy Redeemer in San Francisco complained, "The Pastor never opens his mouth except to mention money; he never makes us feel that his priesthood means more to him than large collections."[11] The debt and building program dictated an agenda of its own. Peter C. Yorke, an advanced churchman, conceded that the typical pastor had little time for extra-parochial concerns: "Even the most zealous pastor, in addition to his spiritual obligations, was charged with expanding and supporting the material edifices for efficient church work."[12] The major task of each pastor was to build a complete parish plant. Pastors who directed building programs and who reduced their parish debt were highly regarded. The second Archbishop of San Francisco, Patrick Riordan, was advanced to the episcopate largely because he had the reputation of being a great builder and good administrator. Another West Coast bishop is reported to have said to his pastors, "I don't care how holy a man is. To be pastor for me a man must be a good administrator." (Even if the story is apocryphal, its message rings true.)[13] Throughout the period from 1850 to 1980, concern over parish finances has deeply influenced both pastoral leadership and parish social life.

Until the 1910s, the most common means of ordinary parish revenue were pew rents and plate collections. Families paid a certain amount for a pew, according to their income. As the income generated was never enough, fairly regular subscription and pledge drives were held to reduce the parish debt. These drives continued to be an integral part of parish financing through 1980.

In the late 1910s and 1920s, a "revolution" occurred in parish financing, as the "Sunday envelope" was introduced. Each registered parishioner was given a set of envelopes. One was provided for each Sunday and Holy Day, thereby encouraging more regular donations. The envelope system also incorporated elements of the pledge drive, as the parishioner was asked to "pledge" a certain amount per week. The Sunday envelope became, and remains, the main source of ordinary parish income.

Despite the various subscription drives, pew rents, and plate collections, the parish annually remained in debt. Large collections were obtained on Christmas and Easter, but the parish remained in constant need of "extraordinary funds." The search for these funds did much to shape parish life and spirit. In order to raise them, each parish hosted an almost endless round of card parties, dinners, raffles, entertainments, picnics, fashion shows, and the ubiquitous game of Bingo, culminating in the greatest of all parish fund-raisers, the annual festival or bazaar. These events did more than just raise money—they created community and friendship by providing the parishioners a chance not only to work together on a common project, but also with a chance to play and recreate together. As one parish historian observed, "The bazaar is a project that annually involves most of the people of the parish. It is an occasion that draws them together as they

Building and Fund-Raising

plan, prepare, and conduct the community event."[14] Moreover, the desire to build and/or pay off the parish debt provided a focal point and purpose to parish social events. One would not only enjoy a dance or raffle, but would also know that he or she was supporting a good cause, making the event doubly enjoyable. The never-ending flow of fund-raisers meant that there was always something going on in the parish. At St. Brigitta's Parish in Portland, Oregon, twenty-three dinners were held in one year.[15] At St. Thomas the Apostle Parish in San Francisco in 1953, thirteen parties, dinners, and entertainments were held, in addition to an annual festival.[16]

The fund-raisers also gave impetus to a number of parish organizations. The Altar Society was listed on the receipt side of each parish financial record in the Archdiocese of San Francisco. Though fund-raising was not its major goal, the Altar Society sponsored whist parties, ice cream socials, and other events to raise money, while at the same time spreading fellowship among the women of the parish. Similarly, the Mother's Club was concerned with raising money for the various school programs. Similar organizations were developed for men.

The greatest event of the year, and the largest moneymaker, was the parish festival or bazaar. In most cases, the festival occurred every year or every other year, depending on the financial condition of the parish. Each parish organization, from the children's sodality to the men's sodality to the St. Anne's married women's sodality and so on, became involved in the festival, operating a booth, preparing food, selling raffle tickets, or operating rides. In all, the festival could account for up to 50% of the total income of a parish for a given year. The benefits of the festival transcended the merely financial. A large bazaar, such as the one held in 1895 at St. Paul's in San Francisco, sent a message to the non-Catholic community as well. As a bazaar bulletin read, "Such then is the object of St. Paul's bazaar (fund-raising and development). It is one which appeals to every member of the parish. Indeed, many of those who do not belong to our faith have generously recognized the power for good which the Church represents,"[17] as a result of the bazaar. As late as 1976, a pastor of an inner-city parish in San Francisco could reflect in his annual report, "The festival, it should be noted, was a great boon to the spirit of the parish."[18]

Despite the beneficent effects of the festivals and other fund-raisers, their proliferation has often caused some anxiety among pastors and church leaders who feared that the Church appeared to be excessively "money-grubbing," and that enormous amounts of energy were being spent on projects that had a low priority on the modern pastoral agenda. In the 1950s and early 1960s, several parishes experimented with "tithing," a system by which each parishioner would give a suitable percentage of the family income (generally 5%). This amount, it was hoped, would put an end to gaudy fund-raisers. A parish in Milwaukie, Oregon, announced in 1963, "At Christ the King we do not believe in professional fund-raising, high-powered financial drives, or trying to support God's work with carnivals, bazaars, or other gimmicks.''[19] The idea of tithing had been suggested as early as the 1920s. St. Cecilia's in San Francisco had pushed "The Idea of Dignified Church Support."[20] In the early 1960s, the Diocese of Oakland attempted to push the tithing idea from the top down, and mounted a concerted (and manipulative) public relations campaign to sell the idea. Tithing never did take hold, and dances, dinners, raffles, Bingo, and festivals remained familiar elements of parish life.

A sampling of the parish financial reports for the Archdiocese of San Francisco shows that, in the period from 1910 to 1920 in about 30% of the parishes, extraordinary revenue exceeded ordinary revenue. In two-thirds of the parishes in which the ordinary revenue exceeded extraordinary (70% of all parishes), two-fifths of the total parish income was from extraordinary sources. In each case, the presence or absence of a festival made a significant difference in parish finance. In the period from 1920 to 1930, far fewer parishes were so dependent on extraordinary income, though the majority of parishes still gained between 25 to 33% of their total income from extraordinary means. The introduction of the Sunday envelope system seems to be the significant factor here.[21]

FINANCE COMMITTEES: LAY INVOLVEMENT

Equally significant, fund-raising was the main area of parish life in which the laity could actively participate in the parish decision-making process. Very few parishes had lay trustees in the manner of eastern Catholic parishes; however, almost every parish maintained a lay finance board, which was in charge of subscription drives and other fund-raisers. In some cases, particularly in rural areas, the finance committee preceded the establishment of the parish. At St. Paul's in San Francisco, a prominent lawyer developed a subscription list, and presented it to the bishop in petitioning for the erection of a new parish in his vicinity of the city. In some parishes, the pastors allowed the finance committee considerable powers, equal to trustees. In the 1920s at St. Cecilia's Parish in San Francisco, Father John Tobin kept a board of twenty-four lay consultors from whom he took counsel before making major financial decisions. Tobin described the group, "These men number twenty-four, taken from every walk of life and from every concern of the parish." These consultors were largely responsible for the "finances of the parish," and, in the case of St. Cecilia's, a number of the consultors were financiers and real estate men.[22] Father Tobin gave great weight to his consultors' advice, and met with them prior to any decision regarding parish expansion, but the final decision resided with the pastor.

Relations between pastors and finance boards were not always so amicable. In 1914 at St. Philip's Parish in San Francisco, the pastor dismissed the lay board for being "incompetent";[23] its incompetence lay in desiring to spend funds in a

Building and Fund-Raising 31

manner different from that desired by the pastor. Again, in a parish in San Diego in the 1940s, parishioners sent a letter to the bishop complaining that the pastor was "nonaccountable" in financial matters. The controversy stemmed from a fund-raiser sponsored by several lay organizations, ostensibly to obtain funds to build a gymnasium and community center. Once the funds were collected, the pastor used them to pay off the parish debt, much to the amazement of his lay workers. Their complaint to the bishop went unheard, as the bishop assured them quite emphatically that the pastor had acted clearly within his right. In a private letter to the pastor, the bishop chastised him for letting his lay parishioners get out of control.[24] What the St. Philip's and San Diego episodes point up is that no matter how involved the laity became, ultimate financial responsibility resided with the pastor.

Nonetheless, fund-raising did provide an important outlet for the laity in a clerically controlled church. In some cases, the enthusiasm and experience gained in fund-raising carried over into other parish activities. Commenting on one parish's "Parish Improvement Campaign" (a campaign designed to raise $100,000), one historian has written, "The literally hundreds of parishioners who worked together in May and June of 1954 gave new injections into lay activity and lay participation in the parish."[25] Throughout the period from 1850 to 1960, parish fundraisers have done more than raise money—they also contributed to lay involvement in parish life and to the creation of parish spirit and community.

PARISH COMMUNICATION

The constant rounds of fund-raisers also made it necessary to develop some form of communication. For special events, special broadsheets and fliers would be printed publicizing these events. For instance, in 1895, St. Paul's in San Francisco began publishing a monthly bulletin a year prior to its major bazaar. At the turn of the century, most parishes published a yearly calendar. The calendar listed the major annual events, feast days, and liturgical seasons. In the 1910s and 1920s, a monthly calendar allowed for greater flexibility in announcing events. In both the yearly and monthly calendars, church regulations on fasting and the like were printed as well as a variety of pious articles. By 1950, practically every parish had adopted the practice of the weekly bulletin that was handed out at the end of each Sunday Mass. The weekly bulletin listed all the significant events for the parish in the upcoming week—spiritual, social, educational, charitable, etc. The Sunday bulletin remains the primary means of communication for the parish.

Throughout the period from 1850 to 1980, the drive to provide a complete parish plant dominated parish life, dictating parish social life and influencing pastoral leadership. The parish, however, was more than the sum total of fund-raisers, buildings, and subscription drives. The spirituality of the parish and its parishioners, and the parish organizational life spoke more directly to the average parishioner's concerns and anxieties.

Notes

1. AASF. Chancery Files. Letter to Archbishop Hanna, March 15, 1923.
2. Charles O'Reilly quoted in Leipzig, *Extension in Oregon,* 19.
3. *The Story of a Parish: Its Priests and People 1860–1960* (Anaheim, Cal.: St. Boniface Parish, 1961), 96.
4. AASF. Priests' Personnel Files. Letter from Father Patrick Heslin to Archbishop Hanna, July 21, 1921.
5. R. A. Burchell, *San Francisco's Irish, 1850–1880* (Berkeley and Los Angeles: University of California Press, 1979), 91.
6. Francis X. Morrison quoted in Harry B. Morrison, "History of St. Joseph the Workman Parish, part VI," 16. This history was published in monthly installments in the parish *Monthly Newsletter* from April 1978 to April 1979. A copy of the history is available in the AASF.
7. Quoted in "California and the Church," *The Catholic World* II (1866), 806.
8. Archbishop Edward J. Hanna, quoted in Frances Weber (ed.), *California Catholicism* (Hong Kong: Libra Press, 1975), 12.
9. "California and the Church," 806.
10. "The Support of Religion," *San Francisco Monitor,* January 10, 1920, 4.
11. AASF. Parish Files. Letter to Archbishop Hanna, March 15, 1923.
12. Peter C. Yorke quoted in James Gaffey, *Citizen of No Mean City: Archbishop Patrick Riordan of San Francisco* (Wilmington, N.C.: Consortium, 1976), 163.
13. This story was told to me by an elderly Salesian priest, who served as pastor in several parishes on the West Coast.
14. *Church of the Assumption of the Blessed Virgin Mary, Ferndale, California, 1878–1978.* (White Plains, N.Y.: Monarch, 1978), 51.
15. *St. Brigitta's Church Diamond Jubilee, Portland, Oregon* (Portland, 1976), 40.
16. AASF. Parish Files.
17. *St. Paul's Parish, San Francisco, California: A Century of Service 1880–1980* (So. Hackensack, N.J.: Custombook, 1980), n.p.
18. AASF. Parish Files.
19. *Christ the King Parish, Milwaukie, Oregon: Handbook and Directory, 1963* (Milwaukie, 1963), n.p.
20. *St. Cecilia's Parish, San Francisco. Golden Jubilee, 1917–1967* (So. Hackensack: Custombook, 1966), n.p.
21. AASF. Annual Parish Financial Reports.
22. *St. Cecilia's Parish Jubilee,* n.p.
23. AASF. Parish Files.
24. ADSD, Parish Files.
25. Morrison, "St. Joseph the Workman, part X," 16.

CHAPTER FOUR
The Spiritual Life of the Parish

Beyond providing a material witness, the primary task of the parish was to provide for the spiritual needs of its parishioners. The parish was, and continues to be, the primary institution through which the average Catholic practices and experiences his or her faith. The spiritual life of West Coast parishes can be divided into two sections: (1) general parish devotions not limited to any specific ethnic group and (2) ethnic piety (which will be treated later). I have divided the general parish devotions into three periods: (1) 1860–1920, the era of sodalities and confraternities; (2) 1920–1950, the era of non-liturgical devotions; and (3) 1945–1960, the era of Catholic Action and retreats. These periodizations are inexact, as sodalities, confraternities, and/or liturgical devotions existed throughout the period from 1850 to 1980. What this breakdown suggests is that the devotions or organizations enjoyed their greatest popularity during that period.

Certain elements of devotional life transcended these periodizations. Between 1850 and 1960 (and even until 1980), the parish mission played an integral part in revitalizing parish spirit. In most parishes, a mission was held yearly, or at least every other year. In the frontier era, bands of traveling preachers journeyed from city to city giving mission after mission. (From time to time in the twentieth century, the traveling mission band has been revived.)

In any case, the parish mission generally followed a similar format from parish to parish. It began with High Mass on Sunday morning when the initial sermon was preached. On Sunday afternoon, the children's mission was begun. Then, on Sunday evening, the major events started with the recitation of the Rosary, followed by instruction and the "big sermon" on salvation. Benediction closed out the evening. During the week, participants in the mission were encouraged to attend Mass as often as possible. Mass was offered three times each morning—early for the workers, later for the housewives, and still later for the children. The children's mission continued with a sermon on Monday afternoon. The next "big sermon" took place on Tuesday night with one on death. Wednesday brought the children's mission to a close with all offered the chance to go to confession. Friday was the day of the mission devoted to the Blessed Virgin Mary. On Friday evening, the Rosary was followed by instruction and then a sermon on Mary. (If the Redemptorists were conducting the mission, consecration would be made to Our Lady of Perpetual Help.) Saturday provided the adults with a chance to go to confession. The number of confessions was used as the criterion for judging the success or failure of a given mission. (A crew in California reported the following statistics for its 1885 mission tour—Los Angeles, two week mission, 1,572 confessions; San Bernardino, nine day mission, 254 confessions; San Diego, one week mission, 265 confessions.)[1] Sunday was the last big day, with the final "big sermon" on perseverance, followed in the evening by the "solemn erection" of the mission cross, a huge cross that was hung on the wall of the church. The mission ended on Monday, "Poor Souls Day," with the mission cross hung high. One last attempt was made to move those in attendance to a sense of contrition for their past sins, and to instill in them a firm purpose of amendment. One last chance for confession was provided and then the mission was officially closed.[2]

Throughout the period between 1850 and 1960, the mission served the parish by revitalizing "indifferent Catholics." It provided a week of intense reflection on the ultimate truths of the Catholic faith. An 1875 mission statement read, "The great object of the mission is to furnish men of business and labor an opportunity for serious attention to those great truths which the bustle of our active civilization is too apt to drive into the dim background."[3] The mission provided lapsed or indifferent Catholics, as well as practicing Catholics, a chance to step outside of their daily routine, to confess their sins, and to receive forgiveness. The mission, it was hoped, would inspire parishioners to be more active, more enthusiastic, and more attentive to the concerns of their faith.

The missions were always well attended because they were regarded as major social events. One held in 1898 at Sacred Heart in San Francisco was reported in this manner, "It (the mission) continued for four weeks with every available space in the church filled. The crowd filled the vestibule, gallery, aisles, sacristy, and sanctuary."[4] The mission flourished in ethnic and non-ethnic parishes alike. In parishes with large foreign born populations, it was common to hold two separate parish missions, one in English and one in the language of the immigrant group. For instance, Corpus Christi Italian Parish in San Francisco would hold a mission in Italian one month, followed by a mission in English the next. Similar practices existed in large German, Chinese, and Spanish speaking congregations.

The quality and style of preaching differed from mission to mission. Particularly proficient in preaching missions were the Dominicans, Jesuits, and Redemptorists. The nature of the mission's subject matter—death and salvation[5]—made for delicate shadings between reason and emotion. One reporter for the *San Francisco Monitor* could write approvingly of the Dominicans in 1873, "The preaching was not of the sensational order, but was characterized by sound reasoning; simplicity, not emotions, was the weapon of these Fathers, and they produced a powerful effect on the minds of the listener, the more likely to be lasting as it was the result of serious conviction."[6] This was the ideal of the mission preacher; however, when dwelling on "the terrible fate of those who die in sin,"

The Spiritual Life of the Parish

the needed balance was oftentimes forgotten. One mother complained to Archbishop Hanna in San Francisco in 1927 about a children's mission. Her child had "awoke in the night screaming that a devil was in the room, hissing and rushing about with ugly red claws. I questioned her and she told me that the Father . . . had told them a story of a wicked man whom God had punished by sending a horrible devil, as described above, to torment him."[7] The need to reach the middle ground was sought, but depended upon the preacher at a given mission. One cannot help but feel, however, that the temptation to frighten people to "salvation" won out as a rule.

In the late 1920s in the Diocese of Los Angeles, Bishop John J. Cantwell inspired a "Mission Revival," from the top down, which posited that the traditional mission formula of "Rosary, sermon, Benediction," no longer appealed to people. Cantwell sought greater participation in the devotions on the part of those attending the mission. He introduced into the mission format the popular liturgical devotions of Father Peter C. Yorke, which emphasized, among other things, congregational singing. Over the course of the year, each parish in the Los Angeles Diocese held a mission, but there is little evidence to indicate that the mission from the top down was any more or less successful than the more traditional type.[8]

Missions continue to the present day, though their tone and format have changed considerably. Many parishes have special sermons on consecutive Sundays, with instruction and discussion periods held during the week. Some parishes still conduct the traditional mission week, but, however it is presented, the modern mission lacks the intensity of the mission in previous eras.

Besides the mission, one other event was shared by most parishes in the Pacific states—the procession of the Blessed Sacrament, particularly the Corpus Christi procession, which was in vogue in California as early as 1850, and was carried on in Washington and Oregon through the 1940s. Typical of this procession was the one held in Verboort, Oregon, in which the Blessed Sacrament was carried from one shrine to another. In the procession came flower girls in white dresses and veils, altar boys in their cassocks and surplices, sodality girls with banners, the Altar Society with banners, followed by the general congregation, the choir, and, finally, the Blessed Sacrament carried beneath a beautiful canopy.[9] A similar ceremony was followed in most parishes on the West Coast, with the various parish societies taking their appropriate parts in the procession. Eucharistic processions grew in popularity in the 1910s and the 1920s throughout the Pacific states. These and other processions were particularly strong among ethnic Catholics.

On a more routine level, Sundays in most developed parishes followed a similar pattern. At least two low Masses were offered early Sunday morning, followed by a Mass for the children. At 10 A.M. or 10:30 A.M., the High Mass was celebrated. It was generally sung by the adult choir of the parish, and then the major sermon of the day was preached. Prior to 1920, the reception of the Eucharist was a rare occasion. Those who did wish to receive Communion generally attended the early morning Masses because, until 1957, a strict fast beginning from midnight the night before was required. The only time Communion was well attended was on Easter Sunday on which close to 75% of the congregation would receive it (largely to fulfill their Easter Duty). In the 1920s, a revolution occurred in which reception of Communion became more widespread. For example, at St. Ignatius Parish in Portland, Oregon, Communions jumped from 330 in 1919 to 14,400 in 1923, despite the fact that the number of parishioners remained the same.[10] On Sunday evenings, Vespers were prayed at most parishes. Then the Rosary was recited and Benediction of the Blessed Sacrament brought the Sunday service to a close.

Besides the weekly Sunday devotions, others were offered at different times of the year. May and October were special months devoted to Mary and the Rosary. The May procession, involving the crowning of Mary with a floral wreath as queen of heaven, became a familiar sight in Catholic schools and churches. June brought special devotions to the Sacred Heart. Lent and Advent brought another whole series of special devotions, disciplines, and observances. In most parishes during Lent, the Stations of the Cross were celebrated each Friday night, and other special devotions and instruction were offered during the course of the week.

The basic units of devotional life of the parish between 1860 and 1920 were the sodalities and confraternities. As the historian for Sacred Heart Parish in San Francisco observed (in a statement that holds true for most parishes on the West Coast), "Sodalities existed from the beginning of the parish, but those of the period of the early 1890s were most active."[11] In a similar vein, Pastor Francis X. Morrison of St. Joseph's Parish in Berkeley, in 1906, believed that the whole "spiritual and social life of the parish" should center around the sodalities.[12] Indeed, most parishes maintained sodalities for married men, married women, young women, young men, boys and girls, single men, and single women. Each was geared for a particular age, sex, and marital status. Most sodalities sought to have their members meet at least once during the month for Mass and Communion, thereby ensuring the reception of Communion at least once a month. Special prayers and devotions were recited at the end of the Mass or at some time during the week. Active sodalities met more often for further devotions and/or social events.

Confraternities also flourished during this period, including the Confraternity of the Blessed Sacrament (each member pledged one-half hour devotion a month before the Blessed Sacrament), the League of the Sacred Heart, the Apostleship of Prayer, the Confraternity of the Rosary, the Angelic Warfare and Blessed Imelda Confraternity (for purity), and the Immaculate Heart Confraternity, to name a few. The majority of these devotional groups were composed of women, who gathered together to pray for various needs. The following description of a prayer at the Immaculate Heart Confraternity in 1875 reflects the all-inclusive nature of

The Spiritual Life of the Parish 37

the prayers of many of the confraternities. "After having prayed for the conversion of a sinner particularly recommended to the prayers of the associates, we must not fail to send supplication also for those who persecute the Church, or who defame her teaching, for Catholics living in sin, for Schismatics, Heretics, Jews, and Pagans, in a word for all those in sin or error, for in Christ there is neither Barbarian or Scythian. All are children of the same father, all brethren, for Christ died for all."[13]

Beginning in the 1920s and increasing through the 1940s and the 1950s, a whole series of non-liturgical and private devotions grew in popularity, particularly Forty Hours' Devotions (which had been popular since the 1890s). Here, the Blessed Sacrament was exposed in the church for adoration for forty hours during which the faithful could come and pray. A similar devotion was that of Perpetual Adoration, where worshipers came at night to keep watch over the Sacrament. Especially popular were the novenas and triduums. Novenas were prayer services held on nine consecutive evenings, generally consisting of the Rosary and other prayers. Triduums were conducted on three consecutive days. Novenas to the Sorrowful Mother, Our Lady of Perpetual Help, St. Jude, and the Sacred Heart were popular. In Portland, Oregon, after World War II, devotions to Our Lady of Perpetual Help flourished, and the Sunday Benediction of the Blessed Sacrament was well attended. The shift in devotion from sodalities and confraternities is significant in that the sodalities urged attendance at Communion and confession (i.e., the Sacraments). The trend in the 1930s was away from the Mass as the central act of worship, to greater stress on private devotions. One pastor reported that the practice of praying the Rosary during the Mass by the faithful continued through the 1950s.[14]

Other devotions flourished as well between 1930 and 1960. In the postwar era, Marian devotions blossomed, spurred on by the Marian year in 1954. One historian has referred to the period from 1940 to 1960 as "the Age of Mary."[15] Devotions to Our Lady of Fatima were held on the first Saturday of each month; devotions to Our Lady of Guadalupe, particularly intense among Mexican parishes, spilled over to non-Hispanic parishes in California. The months of October and May were months of special devotion to Mary, and the Rosary was urged on all Catholics. As stated before, the May procession became a familiar sight in the Catholic parish. Also, the Legion of Mary became quite popular in the 1940s and the 1950s.

The specific devotions adopted by any one parish were often dependent upon the religious order in charge of, or at least present in, the parish. In the 1860s, the sodality of the Blessed Virgin Mary and its attendant devotions flourished in the Jesuit parish of St. Ignatius in San Francisco. In the twentieth century, the Dominicans urged devotions to Our Lady of the Rosary, and, later, devotions to St. Jude. The Jesuits encouraged devotions to the Sacred Heart of Jesus, the Franciscans to St. Francis (through the Third Order), the Benedictines pushed nocturnal adoration, and the Redemptorists sponsored Our Lady of Perpetual Help. These specific devotions enjoyed popularity where these orders were present.

The period from 1945 to 1960 witnessed the emergence of certain elements that were precursors to Vatican II. Several new elements came to the fore in the 1950s, particularly the retreat movement. It became popular for each parish to sponsor, or at least offer, a weekend retreat for its men and women at separate times of the year. Parish organizations also began sponsoring "days of recollection" for those who could not get away for the entire weekend retreat.

Several liturgical changes were introduced during the 1950s. More daring parishes experimented with the Dialogue Mass, and by the late 1950s the use of the English missal was as common as praying the Rosary during the Mass. In 1957, the fast prior to receiving Holy Communion was reduced to three hours, thereby allowing greater attendance at the later Masses.

Organizationally, there were minor inroads made by marriage renewal programs and marriage education programs such as Cana and pre-Cana Conferences, and by specialized Catholic Action groups such as the Christian Family Movement, Young Christian Students, and Young Christian Workers. These programs demanded greater lay involvement, and placed more emphasis on adult education and current affairs. These groups sponsored an "activist spirituality," based on social and community commitment, as opposed to the private devotions of the 1940s.

The programs of retreats, liturgical renewal, and a lay activist spirituality remained subterranean elements in most parishes, practiced by a lay elite. The traditional devotions centering on the Rosary-novena and the adoration of the Blessed Sacrament continued to dominate parish spirituality until the 1960s. The parish organization that demonstrated the greatest growth and vitality in the Pacific states in the postwar era was the Legion of Mary, which had been founded in Ireland in 1921, and introduced to the United States in the 1930s. The majority of parishes saw the Legion of Mary established in their communities on the West Coast between 1945 and 1965. The Legion mixed Marian devotions with old style Catholic Action, emphasizing a program of "spiritual consolation and education."[16] It carried out such tasks as home visitation and visiting the sick and elderly. Despite its usefulness, the Legion of Mary was more a symbol of the 1950s than a harbinger of the new Church.

Notes

1. "Parish Missions in 1885," *Academy Scrapbook* 1 (1950), 19.
2. The specific details presented here are a complete portrait of a typical mission drawn together from several sources. Especially useful is the history, *Holy Redeemer Parish, Portland, Oregon, 1906–1981* (So Hackensack, N.J.: Custombook, 1981).

3. "The Paulist Missions," *San Francisco Monitor*, February 13, 1875, 4.

4. "Sacred Heart Parish, San Francisco," unpublished parish history, AASF.

5. The same concerns continued through the 1950s as a parish in San Francisco reported "The Four Last Things" as the topic for its annual mission. AASF. Parish Files.

6. *St. Dominic's Church, San Francisco: One Hundreth Anniversary, 1873–1973* (San Francisco: James H. Barry Co., 1973), 34.

7. AASF. General Correspondence Files.

8. Francis J. Weber, *John Joseph Cantwell: His Excellency of Los Angeles* (Hong Kong: Cathay Limited Press, 1971), 59.

9. *Visitation of the Blessed Virgin Mary, Verboort, Oregon. Diamond Jubilee Booklet, 1875–1950.*

10. *St. Ignatius Parish, Portland, Oregon: Fifty Golden Years, 1908–1958.*

11. Luke M. Carroll, *Holy Cross Parish and Lone Mountain District in San Francisco* (San Francisco, n.p., 1937), 44.

12. Morrison, "St. Joseph the Workman, part VI.

13. "Immaculate Heart Confraternity in 1875," *Academy Scrapbook* 1 (November, 1951), 173.

14. *St. Mary's Parish, Mt. Angel, Oregon, 1880–1980* (Mt. Angel, Oregon, 1980).

15. *Ibid.*

16. Florentine Schage, "Our Lay Organizations," *Archdiocese of San Francisco Centennial History 1853–1953)* (San Francisco: The Monitor Publishing Co., 1953) 129.

CHAPTER FIVE

The Organizational Life of the Parish

The proliferation of parish organizations, like devotions, went in cycles. Between 1860 and 1920, as frontier life succumbed to the onslaught of modern, industrial culture on the West Coast, devotional and fraternal societies flourished. Indeed, these societies assisted Catholics (and non-Catholics as well) with the transition to the modern era. Historian Peter Decker writes of San Francisco (though the same could be written of any city on the West Coast), "The voluntary associations provided the human cement that transformed San Francisco from a temporary stopover . . . to a permanent, urban community."[1] So prevalent were fraternal associations that one historian has referred to the 1890s as "the Golden Age of fraternity."[2] Between 1920 and 1950, parish organizational life was highlighted by the shift in focus of the fraternal associations. As life became less hazardous and tenuous on the West Coast, these societies shifted their focus from mutual aid to social and charitable concerns. The final decade of the preconciliar era between 1950 and 1960 witnessed the coming of age of Catholics on the West Coast. As a significant Catholic middle class emerged, and as Catholics felt more at home in West Coast society, they joined other Americans in their increasing concern about family life and the proper socialization of their children. For West Coast Catholics, the 1950s was the "decade of the child," as parishes placed special emphasis on the Catholic school and on school related organizations.

Throughout the history of parish life on the West Coast, two societies were established in nearly every parish almost as soon as it was begun—the Altar Society for women and the Holy Name Society (or its equivalent precursor) for men. The Altar Society was given the explicit tasks of providing the altar cloths and vestments for the parish, as well as being responsible for the upkeep of the altar and sacristy area. Besides this, members generally met once a month for Mass and Communion. In addition, the society also provided socials to encourage fellowship among the women of the parish. The socials, which took the form of card parties, luncheons, fashion shows, and so forth, had the secondary motive of raising money to benefit the parish. The Altar Society was the group in which most women participated and was the most active of the female societies.

Similarly, the Holy Name Society was the organization in which most men in the parish actively participated. Like the Altar Society, members met once a month for Mass and Communion. Though the Holy Name Society was not established on the West Coast until the early twentieth century, men were always involved in some form of devotional society, such as the Men's or Married Men's Sodality, which, like the Holy Name Society, received Communion as a group once a month. The Holy Name Society, as it emerged in the twentieth century, had more specific concerns. It was not merely devotional but sought to purify and transform West Coast culture. The society was to be "an association of prayer with praise to God in atonement for the cursing, swearing, and blasphemy of his Holy Name."[3] The main prayer of the society was the "Divine Praises—in reparation for blasphemies," which went, "Blessed be God. Blessed be His Holy Name . . . Blessed be Jesus Christ, true God and true man. . . ." The apostolate took tangible form in anti-pornography campaigns at various times in the twentieth century, as well as in programs for the distribution of good Catholic literature to homes and schools. Beyond these tasks and prayers, the Holy Name organized various parish organizations, ranging from Boy Scouts to athletic programs to parish missions. In the early 1930s, the society sponsored the Catholic sports program in Los Angeles, which served as a forerunner of the CYO in that city. Whatever diverse functions the Holy Name provided, above all it was to provide Christian leaders among the men of the parish for the sake of the parish. The Holy Name was urged by Bishop O'Dea of Seattle to "go forth before the world and win it for Christ and his holy religion by example of good and consistent Catholic living." Members were "to show what Catholic men are."[4] Despite the grandiose rhetoric, in many parishes the Holy Name did provide some type of fellowship and prayer among the male members of the parish, and, it should be remembered, male participation in parish organizational life was always more tenuous than that of women.

Between 1875 and 1910, a series of organizations was established on the West Coast that can best be described as fraternal insurance societies—Young Men's Institute (1883), Young Ladies' Institute (1887), Knights of Columbus (1893, 1902), Catholic Daughters of America (1903), and the Catholic Order of Foresters (1911), and its Ladies' Auxiliary. All six societies had, as one of their original functions, the provision of sick and death benefits to members, reflecting the tenuous quality of life in nineteenth century America. These organizations also represented the "Americanization" of the fraternal society. Prior to their creation, fraternal and mutual aid societies were predominantly associated with a specific ethnic group—the Germans (the Central Verein, which was itself a collection of smaller German societies), the Irish (most significantly, the Ancient Order of Hibernians), the Italians, the Portuguese, and other ethnic groups all had a separate network of fraternal societies. The new fraternal organizations were non-ethnic in character, appealing to all the Catholic ethnic groups for membership. Not surprisingly, these societies were strongly patriotic, urging Catholics to be good citizens and good parishioners. For instance, the motto of the Young Men's Institute was "Pro Deo, Pro Patria." Many of the activities of these groups were geared to reduce the gap between Catholics and America, and to protect Catholic interests in America. In the 1920s, the Knights of Columbus printed pamphlets and distributed literature to counteract the Ku Klux Klan.

While these societies were never solely mutual aid societies, between 1920 and 1950 they functioned primarily as social and charitable organizations. The Young Men's Institute (YMI), the earliest of these groups, was founded at St. Joseph's Parish in San Francisco in 1883, and enjoyed great popularity throughout the West Coast. Though initially started for young Catholic men beginning life in the world, to "shield (them) from secret and Masonic organizations,"[5] it came to include Catholics of all ages. Besides supplying sick benefits, the YMI wished to provide for the "intellectual, social, physical, and spiritual" development of its members. The Young Ladies' Institute (YLI) was begun three years later, and followed a similar pattern.

Besides these two local groups, two national groups were established in the first decade of the twentieth century in Washington, California, and Oregon, and enjoyed wide popularity—the Knights of Columbus for men and the Catholic Daughters of America for women. (The groups were not connected in any way.) By 1920, all four groups were participating in what would soon be called "Catholic Action." Hospitals and homes for the aged were visited, and seminary scholarships were provided. The Knights were especially active in providing scholarships to Catholic students for high school. The Catholic Daughters often reinforced the work of the Altar Society, raising funds for a new organ, or for school library acquisitions. Both the Knights and Catholic Daughters sponsored many social activities, such as dances and athletic programs for high school students. The various charitable activities gave the groups a purpose beyond the merely social, which served to make their social gatherings (and there were many) quite convivial.

While the fraternal-charitable organizations provided a wide variety of services, the nitty gritty of Catholic charity at the parish level fell on two organizations—the St. Vincent de Paul Society and the Catholic Ladies' Aid Society. The parish, as an institution, expended little if any time and money on charitable endeavors. Parish reports listed few funds allotted to charity outside of the yearly collection for the diocesan Catholic Charities. In rare instances, the demands of the parish environs were so dire that relief was undertaken by the parish itself. Two inner city parishes in San Francisco sponsored such direct relief. In 1927, St. Patrick's Parish began a shelter for homeless men, and in 1950 the German parish of St. Boniface began a soup kitchen, named St. Anthony's Dining Room. In both cases, the presence of an extraordinary priest initiated the parish programs. For the most part, major charitable endeavors were left to the diocese, and,

The Organizational Life of the Parish 43

at the parish level, to the Saint Vincent de Paul Society and the Catholic Ladies' Aid Society.

The St. Vincent de Paul Society was a national organization that operated through parish conferences. In the parishes on the West Coast, the society provided direct relief to the needy, as well as spiritual consolation. Society members visited the poor in their homes, bringing families what they needed—clothing, food, etc. The society was not concerned with structural reform, but sought to provide relief at a personal level. In Los Angeles during the 1950s, it expended more than $42,000 annually.[6]

Besides providing spiritual and material relief to the needy, the society assisted poor families in sending their children to Catholic schools. It also learned a hard lesson of Catholic parish life—expenses had to be met, and, like other parish organizations, the society often went begging. Also, like other parish organizations, it sponsored socials and bazaars. One of its major projects, pursued at a supra-parish level, was that of a salvage and thrift store. Discarded items that could be repaired and reused were solicited and collected. The Salvage Bureau provided the poor with inexpensive goods, some income for the society, and some work for the unemployed. Throughout its history, the society strove to remain true to its motto, "no work of charity is foreign to us."

The Catholic Ladies' Aid Society was begun in 1887 at St. Mary's Parish in Oakland, California, and rapidly spread to St. Charles' Parish in San Francisco, and elsewhere. The female counterpart to the St. Vincent de Paul Society also provided direct material relief to the needy. Special emphasis was placed on protection of the young in general, the young woman in particular. Several homes for young working girls were sponsored by the Ladies' Aid. At the parish level, "personal service" to the poor was stressed; acts of "hidden charity" were pursued, such as the collection and distribution of food and clothing. To assist the clothing program, a series of parish sewing circles was established.

Though parish charity on the West Coast rested on these two organizations, the other fraternal societies provided great support to them in their various endeavors. One element lacking from the two charitable societies, but stressed in the fraternal societies, was an emphasis on patriotism. The two charitable societies conducted their works of mercy withdrawn from the world of politics and public controversy.

Catholic charity demonstrated a noticeable lack of enthusiasm for structural reform until the 1960s. The Progressive reformers, who achieved so much success in the early twentieth century in Oregon, Washington, and California, enjoyed only sporadic and isolated Catholic support. Catholics in general were "skeptical of reform," as Kevin Starr suggests, because Progressive reform had little to do with the Catholic immigrant group's "social identity" or "self-interest."[7] Progressives were depicted as middle class Protestants, a group for which the Catholic working class had little use. The reformist mentality also conflicted with the Catholic view of the world, which rejected the Horatio Alger rags-to-riches myth that pervaded American and West Coast culture. To Catholics, the notion that "God helps those who help themselves" was simple heresy. Catholics observed that "poverty was an unavoidable part of the human condition."[8] There was no such distinction as deserving and undeserving poor. As such, Catholic charitable organizations were content to provide direct relief to the poor and needy, and were reluctant to join reformist crusades.

THE 1950s: THE DECADE OF THE CHILD (THE SOCIALIZATION OF CHILDREN)

The correct socialization of its children has always been a top priority of Catholic parishes in the West, but this concern took on a special intensity in the 1950s. The institution most heavily burdened with the task of socializing the children outside of the family was the parish school. Here, the child was immersed in an entirely Catholic environment that prepared it for its encounter with the hostile American environment. Where parish schools were impractical, weekly and sometimes biweekly Catechism classes were taught to provide the cultural antidote. In both educational endeavors the task of socializing the young was carried out by orders of teaching sisters; *indeed,* without the sisters the separate Catholic school system would never have existed. In most cases, the establishment of a Catholic school in a parish depended on the prior procurement of an order of teaching sisters. As late as 1950, teaching sisters outnumbered lay teachers in Washington Catholic schools 7 to 1, in Oregon 6 to 1, and in California 5.5 to 1.[9] The largest orders on the West Coast were the Sisters of the Immaculate Heart, the Sisters of St. Joseph of Carondolet, Sisters of the Holy Name, the Dominican Sisters, the Sisters of Charity, the Presentation Sisters, and the Sisters of Mary, to name a few. Los Angeles alone had twenty-four different teaching orders in 1940.[10] The main order in charge of the catechetical instruction of public school children was the Sisters of the Holy Family, which was founded in San Francisco in 1872 to fulfill this precise role. The task of the religious socialization of children was largely the task of religious women from 1850 to 1960.

Between 1950 and 1960 was the decade of the Catholic school and, therefore, of the child. In Oregon, the number of parish schools increased by sixteen, despite the fact that the total number of parishes increased by only seven. In Washington, the total number of Catholic schools was up thirty-eight. In California, the Archdiocese of San Francisco was up seventy-two to a total of 159 of 243 parishes (65% of all parishes), and in Los Angeles schools were up 105 for a total of 238 of 291 parishes (over 80% of the parishes).[11] The same decade saw the rapid expansion of the Confraternity of Christian Doctrine (CCD—the updated name for Catechism). As of 1934, only 30,000 public school students were being instructed in religious education in the Los Angeles Archdiocese. By 1952, this number had shot up to 70,996 and to 195,000 in 1965. In San Francisco, 29,424 CCD students were being instructed in 1952, while the number shot up to 91,000 in 1965. Similarly, Seattle was instructing 41,000 public school students in 1965. Of the major cities on the West Coast, only Portland showed a decided lack of enthusiasm for CCD, as its program increased from 2,965 public school students in 1952 to only 7,182 in 1965.[12]

Despite the large sacrifices made by lay volunteers to staff CCD programs, the one hour a week remained a largely ineffective means of socializing children. Even in the best of parishes, the CCD student remained a second class citizen, an outcast from the public school, unfit to mingle with the elect Catholic school child. Attendance at CCD was at best sporadic, and regular attendance came about only during sacramental preparation years.

The Catholic school and CCD craze peaked in the 1950s. Between 1960 and 1980, the number of parish schools decreased in the Archdiocese of Portland by twenty, despite an increase of thirty-four parishes. Similarly, in California commitment to the maintenance, much less the building of new schools, declined considerably. CCD also declined. Los Angeles dropped from 195,000 CCD students in 1965 to 108,000 in 1980, San Francisco dipped from 91,000 to 38,000, and Seattle dropped from 41,000 to 24,000.[13] The golden age of Catholic school expansion had ended.

Nonetheless, the 1950s was a period of great enthusiasm for the Catholic school. Three organizations benefited from the school craze—the Mother's Club, the Men's Club, and the Parent-Teacher Guild. The main intent of the Mother's Club was to raise money for the benefit of the school. The Men's Club was in charge of directing the school's athletic program, and the Parent-Teacher Guild sought better relations and understanding between parent and teacher. All three groups flourished in the 1950s.

The Catholic school child was socialized in a three-pronged manner—in the faith, in citizenship, and in athletics. The child generally belonged to a sodality, such as the Children of Mary, which introduced him or her to a myriad of devotions. In addition, the school observed all the feasts and Holy Days with their appropriate devotions. The student was also urged to be both a good Catholic and a good citizen. As a publication from an earlier period noted, "The young are exhorted to obey the law of God and country, and by honesty, sobriety, truthfulness, courage, and justice, to prepare themselves for the high duty of citizenship. All are instructed in these principles of obedience to law and devotion, which makes a community progressive, prosperous, and patriotic."[14] The effort to be good citizens was furthered by the growth of the Boy and Girl Scouts in the 1950s.

Scouting strove to become a partner of the Catholic school and parish. Finally, athletics played an important role in the socialization of the Catholic school child, and elaborate sports programs were developed around the parish and school. The ideal Catholic child would blend all three areas—faith, sports, and citizenship, God, team, and country. One such child, Sylvia Volpi of Petaluma, California, was selected "Prep of the Week" in 1955, and held up as a model for other children to follow. The headline of the archdiocesan newspaper read, "She Leads Sodality and Team, Too."[15] Sylvia was president of her sodality, captain and star of her basketball team, as well as being a model citizen. In short, she was the ideal.

Despite the widespread enthusiasm for Catholic schools, not all Catholic school age children attended, and even fewer went to Catholic high schools. Combined with the lack of Catholic high schools is the fact that CCD at that level was even more hopeless than the grade school program. The problem of reaching teenage Catholics has been a perennial one for the Catholic Church on the West Coast. Between 1890 and 1910, teens, like other age groups, were brought into the Church through participation in sodalities. One for ages 12–17 and another for ages 17–25 sought to maintain the teenager and young adult's devotional life. The sodalities also sponsored socials to allow Catholic boys to meet Catholic girls in a proper setting. In later years, the sodality would be replaced by such groups as the Junior Holy Name and Junior Altar Society.

In the 1910s and the 1920s, teenage clubs enjoyed modest popularity. Teen clubs sponsored outings, dinner-dances, and lectures; particularly popular were the teen drama clubs. As many as three or four "entertainments" a year were sponsored by the parish drama club. The entertainments, besides providing a social event for the parish in the pre-television age, were also used to raise money for the teen club. One historian has noted that teen and drama clubs "made a real effort to integrate not only graduates of the parish schools, but also other young people and newcomers into the social and religious life of the parish community."[16] The success of teen clubs varied from parish to parish, but the overall record was not very good.

Whatever the designated purpose or activities of a teen club, an underlying purpose of all young people's clubs was to encourage young Catholic men to meet young Catholic women in a wholesome setting. The fear of mixed marriage necessitated a separate Catholic social life, to complement the separate Catholic devotional, educational, and charitable establishments. The grouping of young Catholic adults did achieve the desired effect, and in one parish the young people's club was affectionately known as "Father Brennan's Matrimonial Society."[17] However, the limited success of Catholic teen clubs was reflected in the growing incidence of mixed marriage as the twentieth century progressed.

Another means of involving teenagers was athletics. Each parish sponsored various sporting events, ranging from boxing tournaments to basketball and baseball leagues. The Salesian Boys Clubs epitomized this type of organization, but the best known sports program was the Catholic Youth Organization. The CYO was enormously popular in the 1930s and grew through the 1950s. It was not limited to parochial school students, but was open to all parishioners who wished to participate on CYO teams. Great energy was spent by parishioners in supporting these teams financially, in terms of volunteer time, and in rooter support. One parish historian noted, "Athletics play a very prominent part in the life of the parish."[18] The athletic program not only involved the parish youth, but provided a focus for parish spirit. In the 1950s, the success and popularity of the Men's Clubs, which ran the parish athletic program, were attributable to the fact that men who had hitherto been reluctant to join pious church societies now had a group they could actively support.

Despite the various efforts to engage the teenage and young adult set in parish life, real integration seldom occurred. Public school children, in particular, were hard to incorporate. An even bigger lacuna existed in the Church's program for young single adults, ages 19–30. In the 1940s and 1950s, the realization that young Catholics were being lost spurred the development of two specialized Catholic Action groups—the Young Christian Students (YCS) and the Young Christian Workers (YCW). Neither group made a significant impact on the West Coast, though in various parishes they were quite active.

Earlier efforts had been made to address the problems of Catholic youths at non-Catholic colleges and universities by the development of Newman Clubs, which are now attached to virtually every major college in California, Oregon, and Washington. Despite their success, they often provided an "unreal setting" that made reintegration into regular parish life difficult for many Newman alumni.

In any case, integrating Catholic teenagers and young adults into parish life remains a problem to the present day.

CONCLUSION

Throughout the period from 1850 to 1980, organizations were created to meet the various needs of the parish and its parishioners. The social, educational, spiritual, financial, and even the material interests of its parishioners were looked after through a well-developed organizational life. However, this was not limited to the organizations cited in this chapter. Parish life and parish organizational life were greatly enhanced by the rich associational life of the many and diverse groups of Catholic immigrants that made up Catholicism on the Pacific Coast. The immigrant groups, and their impact on parish life, are the subject of the next chapter.

Notes

1. Peter Decker, *Fortunes and Failures: White Collar Mobility in Nineteenth Century San Francisco* (Cambridge: Harvard University Press, 1978), 107.
2. Gaffey, *Riordan*, 180.
3. *St. Dominic's Church: 100th Anniversary 1873–1973* (San Francisco: James H. Barry Co., 1973), 70.
4. "Lay Organizations," *Centennial of the Diocese of Seattle (1850–1950)* (Seattle: Northwest Progress, 1950), 41.
5. Gaffey, *Riordan*, 82.
6. *Centennial of the Archdiocese of Los Angeles 1840–1940* (Los Angeles: The Tidings, 1940), 170.
7. Starr, *Inventing the Dream*, 239.
8. Cherny and Issel, *San Francisco*, 91.
9. Statistics drawn from *Official Catholic Directory 1950*.
10. "Religious Orders of Women," *Los Angeles Centennial*, 143 ff.
11. *Official Catholic Directory 1960*.
12. *Official Catholic Directory 1934, 1952, 1965*.
13. *Official Catholic Directory 1980*.
14. Jill F. Villadares, "St. Paul's Legacy" unpublished manuscript. AASF. Parish Files.
15. "She Leads Sodality, and Team, Too," *San Francisco Monitor*, January 28, 1955, 8.
16. Morrison, "History of St. Joseph, part IX," 16.
17. *Ibid.* part VII, 7.
18. AASF. Parish Files.

CHAPTER SIX

Ethnic Catholicism on the West Coast

The Catholic Church on the West Coast, like the Catholic Church throughout the United States, is a church of immigrants, and like the Church elsewhere, the parish has played an integral role in the immigrant community, religiously and socially. Unlike the Church in the eastern United States, however, bishops on the West Coast were reluctant to establish ethnic national parishes. In 1921 and again in 1946, Archbishop Cantwell of Los Angeles articulated the standard West Coast response to the national parish. "The Holy See," he opined, did not want "to encourage," and wanted to "dispense with" the national parish.[1] National parishes did develop, but not to the extent they did in the East. The largest number of national parishes in any one city on the West Coast for any one period never exceeded fifteen. Of all the ethnic groups on the West Coast, the Italians were more likely to have a national parish than any other ethnic group (except the Mexicans in southern California in the 1940s and 1950s). Though Archbishop Alemany of San Francisco was not averse to establishing national parishes (he established Notre Dame des Victoires for the French in 1856, St. Boniface for the Germans in 1860, and Our Lady of Guadalupe for the Spanish speaking in 1875), he initiated a policy that came to be the standard procedure in dealing with ethnic Catholics—a priest who spoke the language of the immigrant group was contracted to minister to that group within the structure of the territorial parish. In the early 1850s, as the Chinese population increased in San Francisco and the mining regions, Alemany obtained the service of a Chinese priest, Father Thomas Cian, to minister to his countrymen. This became the dominant pattern of dealing with ethnic groups throughout the West Coast; however, there were never enough foreign-language-speaking priests to serve the many immigrant communities. The procurement of enough ethnic priests was a major problem for the Church in the Pacific states. Ethnic national parishes were turned to only as a last resort, and were often regarded as temporary institutions. The *San Francisco Monitor* pronounced a commonly held West Coast attitude: "The national churches are all temporary by their very nature. They will eventually cease and become part of the ordinary system of the Archdiocese."[2] Once the national parish had outlived its usefulness, it was to be converted into a territorial parish. For instance Corpus

Christi Parish in San Francisco began as an Italian national parish in 1898, but was turned into a territorial parish in 1926. Almost all national parishes resulted from lay petitions to the bishop.

For the most part, ethnics on the West Coast learned to get along with one another inside the territorial parish. The historian of St. Joseph the Workman Parish in Berkeley, California, reports of the post-World War II period: "As Berkeley's population became more diverse and many different ethnic groups gained in numbers . . . the parish did not encourage separate ministries or special attention to meet the needs of the individual groups. Rather, all Catholics, of whatever race or nationality, were offered the traditional organizations, services, and school of the parish for their spiritual welfare. . . . For many years Mexicans, Filipinos, blacks, Asians, and others would share and be welcome in the life of (the parish) as they participated in the heretofore white, Anglo mainstream of the parish, which dominated every aspect of parish life."[3] More often than not, "Anglo" meant "Irish," as it was the Irish who set the tone for the Church on the West Coast. This is not to say that ethnic Catholicism did not flourish on the West Coast. Ethnicity played and continues to play an integral part in Catholic parish life as evidenced by the many ethnic festivals, processions, and societies. The coexistence of ethnic communities and the dominant "orthodox" Catholic community provided grounds for numerous conflicts, but also served to greatly enrich parish life.

The reluctance to establish national parishes reflected a fear in the Catholic community of appearing too foreign to the American host society. A recurring theme in West Coast parish life was that the foreign, "exotic" expressions of faith of the newly arrived immigrants would isolate or bring opprobrium upon the Catholic community as a whole. From the early Californians being embarrassed by the newly arrived Mexicans, to the Irish being ashamed of the miscreant Italians, to the recent conflicts of the Filipino community, there has always been the fear that being too ethnic would be detrimental to the Catholic community in the West. (Catholic sensitivity to criticism from the host culture may have stemmed from the realization that Catholic ethnics had done better economically on the West Coast than their brethren had done in the East.)

Whether a national parish was created, or whether the immigrant group was ministered to from within a territorial parish, the parish remained the central mediating institution between the immigrant and American culture. The parish sought to make good, practical American Catholics out of the immigrant. As Archbishop Cantwell noted, "In making better Catholics of them, we shall be making better citizens of them."[4] By becoming better Catholics, and better Americans, the Church could deflect needless hostility from the host culture.

The parish was also the key unifying agent for the immigrant group. Several of the Catholic immigrant communities were split apart by a severe regionalism. Loyalties were to the city or region from which the immigrant had come. The

Church provided an interest and reality that transcended regional loyalty, and gave immigrants from diverse regions a common goal and purpose.

Besides being a mediating and unifying institution, the parish helped the immigrant group to preserve its ethnic heritage. In an alien and unfamiliar culture, the Church provided familiar rhythms, routines, and symbols. Familiar saints and devotions reminded the immigrant of the land he or she had left. And as the ethnic community entered its third and fourth generations, the parish continued to be the key preserver of the immigrant's past and culture.

The parish, then, was mediator, unifier, and preserver, all of which assisted the immigrant and the immigrant community with the transition to American life. The parish assisted in a triple assimilation—to American life, to American Catholic life as it existed on the West Coast, and to the immigrant community in America. For instance, the Portuguese immigrant not only had to adapt to American culture, and to the Irish flavor of West Coast Catholicism, but he or she also had to adapt to the Portuguese-American community, which was no longer "Portuguese." The parish was the principal institution in assisting with the triple assimilation.

As stated earlier, Washington, Oregon, and California demonstrated different patterns of ethnic growth. Historian Gordon Dodds describes the state of Oregon as being "ethnically homogeneous,"[5] and the largest city in Oregon, Portland, as having "few ethnic enclaves."[6] The period from 1870 to 1920 witnessed a large influx of immigrants to Oregon, but these immigrants were, with few exceptions, white, Anglo-Saxon Protestants—English, Scots, Swedes, Irish, Canadians, and Germans. A few eastern European immigrants arrived to provide menial labor, but never came in very significant numbers. The expansion of the railroads brought an influx of Italians, and in 1901 St. Michael's Italian Parish was begun in Portland, Oregon. On the whole, the non-urban, agricultural environment of Oregon has tended to limit ethnic diversity. The small number of ethnics may account for the low percentage (12%) of Catholics in the state. Since the 1920s, the Catholic population in Oregon has added increasing numbers of Mexicans, who have come as migrant, agricultural workers. Mexican Americans now make up the largest minority group in Oregon and have undergone significant changes over the last half century. In 1930, a high proportion of Mexicans were rural, seasonal workers. By 1980, the majority of the Mexican-American population in Oregon was urban, providing a new array of challenges for the Church and society.

Washington is considerably more ethnic than Oregon, owing to the greater urbanization and industrialization in the state. Washington has three major urban centers—Seattle, Spokane, and Tacoma. The urban centers, plus available work on the railroads and in the coal mines, attracted a more diverse populace. N. H. Clark provides the following description of immigrant life in Washington at the turn of the century: "For the European immigrant there were neighborhoods predominantly Scandinavian or German or Italian or English, and antecedents where the native language church, the fraternal organizations, and the national social clubs embraced the newcomer and carried him into a rich fabric of new associations."[7] (However, Dodds has suggested that immigrant associations seldom lasted more than one generation in the Pacific Northwest.) The major Catholic immigrant groups were the Irish, Germans, Italians, Slovaks, Slavs, and Polish, but overall these groups represented a small proportion of the total Washington population. As in Oregon, the ethnic composition was predominantly white, Anglo-Saxon, Protestant. Though national parishes were present in Oregon and Washington, particularly in the urban centers of Portland, Seattle, Tacoma, and Spokane, they were never very numerous.

In contrast to Oregon and Washington, California has experienced immense ethnic diversity. Practically all the nations of the world have sent citizens to California. At its admission to the Union in 1850, California was bi-cultural. The cosmopolitan character of California, in general, and San Francisco, in particular, boomed with the enormous immigration occasioned by the Gold Rush of the 1850s. Irish and German Catholics were the two largest Catholic groups to arrive during this period. Italians did not begin to arrive in any great numbers until the turn of the twentieth century. Mexican immigration to California had remained steady over the course of the nineteenth century, but boomed in the period after 1920. In recent years, California has experienced another wave of Catholic immigrants, this time the Vietnamese, Polish, Mexicans, South and Central Americans, and Filipinos. The following groups and their relationship to Catholicism will be examined in the ensuing sections: the Irish, Germans, Italians, Japanese, Chinese, Portuguese, Filipinos, Polish, blacks, and Mexicans. These do not represent all the ethnic Catholics on the West Coast, but only the largest and most significant Catholic immigrant groups. Notable exceptions are the Maltese, who have their own national parish, St. Paul of the Shipwreck in San Francisco, and the Slavs, who have the Church of the Nativity in San Francisco.

Three distinct types of Catholic immigrants arrived on the West Coast. First came the Germans and Irish, who were "practical" Catholics. They supported parish life and parish schools, attended the Sacraments regularly, and developed a diverse devotional and social life around the parish. The Irish came to dominate the leadership roles, both clerical and lay, within the Western Catholic community, and dictated the style and direction of Pacific Catholic culture. The Germans provided a model of devotional and associational life.

In contrast to the Germans and Irish was the second type of immigrant—the "cultural Catholic," who initially operated on the periphery of parish life, and was noted for his lack of practicality and reluctance to participate in the formal, sacramental life of the parish. Such were the Italians, Portuguese, Filipinos, and Mexicans. These immigrants came from "Catholic" countries where over 90% of the population was Catholic, and where the Catholic "religion was enmeshed

TABLE:
Major Catholic Immigrant Groups in California Decade by Decade*[8]

Group Decade	Irish	German	Italian	Portuguese	Mexican	Polish
1850	2,452	3,084	229	109	6,454	0
1860	33,147	20,919	2,987	1,495	9,158	730
1870	54,541	29,701	4,660	2,508	9,339	804
1880	62,962	42,532	7,537	4,705	8,648	1,026
1890	63,138	61,472	15,495	9,859	7,164	914
1900	44,476	72,449	22,777	12,068	8,086	1,320
1910	52,475	75,832	63,601	22,427	33,444	3,542
1920	56,308	67,180	88,502	24,517	86,610	7,082
1930	34,493	81,840	107,249	22,711	199,165	14,290
1940	27,631	71,727	100,911	18,944	134,312	14,735
1950	28,405	70,791	104,215	15,134	162,309	23,776

*All figures refer to the foreign born population present in given year. The figures do not account for second and third generations. Also, the figures are not exclusively of Catholics, but represent all the immigrants of that specific group regardless of faith.

in the culture."[9] Nonetheless, the cultural Catholic was unschooled in the formal doctrines of the Church, and showed little inclination to support parochial schools or regular parish societies. Eschewing formal church practices, which seemed too cold and distant, the cultural Catholic reveled in a warm, festive "folk Catholicism," which enjoyed non-liturgical devotions to saints, popular stories and legends about the saints, festivals, and processions. Religious events were family events, which were celebrated within an intimate and intricate extended family network. The cultural Catholics have also been pushed to the periphery of parish life by the racism they have encountered, both inside and outside the Catholic community. They have often been the victims of either rejection or neglect by the official Church. As a result, they have long been prey to the aggressive evangelization efforts of the Protestant churches. Fear of Protestant proselytism spurred Church efforts on behalf of the cultural Catholics. Despite less than perfect conditions within the Church on the West Coast, the cultural Catholics have remained extraordinarily faithful to the Catholic Church in the Pacific states.

The third group of Catholic immigrants was the "mission Catholic." They were from predominantly non-Catholic cultures—the Chinese and Japanese. The Church had made slight inroads among these peoples, and the majority of mission Catholics were either converts or children of converts. Parish life in these communities centered around evangelizing the non-Catholic, and supporting the convert. Ministry to these groups was generally performed by a religious order—Maryknoll, Paulist, Divine Word, or others.

THE IRISH

The Irish were the first major Catholic immigrant group to establish themselves on the West Coast, and they immediately set about establishing their hegemony in politics and in the Church. In the first decade of California's history, two Irish-American Catholics rose to the top of political life in the state—John G. Downey became Governor, and David Broderick became a U.S. Senator. By 1860, 33,147 foreign born Irish resided in California, up from 2,452 in 1850. (See the Table.) In 1870, the total foreign born Irish population had reached 54,421, and peaked in 1890 at 63,000. Large numbers of Irish flocked to San Francisco; 6,000 foreign born Irish accounted for 12% of the city's total population in 1856, growing to 9,363 by 1860 (16%), and 30,178 in 1870 (10%), declining to 15,963 in 1900. These figures represent the first generation of Irish, which, when coupled with second and third generation Irish, gave San Francisco a very Irish cast. By 1880, about 33% of the city (and 27% of the work force) were either Irish born or of Irish descent.[10]

Most Irish immigrants did not arrive directly from Ireland, but were generally transplants from Irish enclaves in the eastern United States. Historian of Irish immigration, Patrick Blessing, acknowledges that while Irish immigrants who came west were "more likely to be literate and from the higher ends of the occupational ladder than those who remained in the East, the great majority were from the lower rungs of the occupational ladder." Two distinct types of Irish headed west—"educated and modern-minded" Irish, who mixed easily with the larger society, and "unskilled Irish" of "limited means and ambition," who generally kept their distance from the native whites.[11]

Two recent studies of the Irish status in early San Francisco have arrived at conflicting conclusions. R. A. Burchell's study sees the rise of the Irish in San Francisco as coming about amicably, whereas Patrick Blessing sees the Irish culture as clashing with the predominantly Protestant cultural values of San Francisco society, at least during the 1850s. Both historians acknowledge that the immigrant Irish rose more quickly on the occupational ladder in San Francisco than in any other American city. Likewise, both acknowledge Irish success in city politics. However, Blessing describes the violent actions of the San Francisco Vigilance Committees in the 1850s as actions directed specifically against the immigrant Irish. Blessing contends that the Protestant social elite used the Vigilance Committees to control Irish advancement, spurred on by both anti-Catholic and anti-Irish sentiments. Burchell places little emphasis on the clash of culture.

Another area where Burchell and Blessing disagree is over the nature of Irish Catholicism. Blessing focuses on the "peasant," who, while remaining loyal to Catholicism, did not actively participate in the devotional life of the Church. He writes: "Not until the late nineteenth century did the Irish Church (or the American Irish Church for that matter) succeed in making practicing Catholics out of nominal Catholics."[12] A sense of the supernatural pervaded peasant lives, as they depended on "charms" and the intercession of saints to provide for good fortune. A variety of "pre-modern" rituals and devotions was practiced by the Irish peasant immigrant who had resettled in the West. (These were the same traits the more established Irish would criticize in newer immigrant groups in the late nineteenth and early twentieth century.)

Equally important to the Irish immigrant were two communal values that conflicted with the rugged individualism of Protestant, frontier San Francisco. The Irish peasant was motivated by "comhair," which Blessing translates as "reciprocal cooperation"[13]—used to describe assistance to kin and neighbors. Meagre material goods were to be shared with the less fortunate. Second, the Irish peasant scorned the ambition of "getting ahead." The peasant believed that a move up the social ladder could only be accomplished at the expense of family and neighbors. These two communal impulses brought the Irish into direct conflict with the dominant culture.

A different picture of the early Irish immigrant community is provided by R. A. Burchell (though the difference between Blessing and Burchell lessens for the period after 1860). According to Burchell, the Catholic Church played an integral role in fashioning a contented Irish immigrant community. The Church was an "integrating force" that "functioned daily to meet the needs of the Irish."[14] The Church on the West Coast took on a decidedly Irish cast as the Irish shouldered the financial burden of early Church development. The erection of parishes in San Francisco followed the development of the Irish in the city: St. Francis (1849), St. Patrick's (1851), St. Mary's (1854), St. Joseph (1861), and St. Brigid's (1863) were all substantially founded and funded by the Irish. The financial partnership of the Irish and the Catholic Church established the "unshakable hegemony" of the Irish within the Church.[15] The building of magnificent church buildings served as a psychological support to the Irish immigrant community.

The Church also acted as chief meeting place and social center of the Irish community. Burchell writes: "The Church itself recognized its social roles that ran beyond its religious one and symptomatically became the center of a system of associations that revolved around it," beyond the Sacraments.[16] Sodalities and other devotional societies prospered among the Irish—the Sodality of the Blessed Virgin Mary, begun in 1861, had 600 male members and 250 female members by 1880.[17] Seven other societies provided social services through the Church to the Irish community. Several benevolent societies were begun around 1860—St. Mary's Ladies' Society and St. Joseph's Benevolent Society for men. Both were primarily religious societies by 1880. The Irish community also supported a number of fraternal insurance or mutual aid societies. The most significant of these was the Ancient Order of Hibernians founded in 1875 in San Francisco. By 1900, the AOH had the "largest membership and strongest financial standing of any Catholic organization in southern California,"[18] reflecting the growth and development of the Irish Catholic community in Los Angeles. The AOH continues to function as of 1980.

The Irish also provided considerable support to the Catholic school system in San Francisco. The parishes of St. Francis and St. Patrick combined to begin a Catholic school by 1853. By 1854, 900 students were in Catholic schools, rising to 1,421 by 1856.[19] Nonetheless, by 1869, only 2,000 students out of a possible 8,000 to 10,000 Catholic school age children were in Catholic schools. The Irish never were the Catholic school enthusiasts the Germans were.

Burchell portrays the relationship of the Church and the Irish to be intimate from 1849, unlike the non-practical Irish peasant portrayed by Blessing. Burchell concludes: "The combination of private stability of the family, the institutional strength of the Church, and the functional vitality of associations (were responsible) in producing Irish satisfaction."[20] The institutional strength of the Irish Church seems to belie Blessing's portrayal. However, "the educated, upper class" immigrants may have supported the Church to counteract the damage done to their image by the Irish rabble. By sponsoring impressive Church buildings, the Irish could show their stability and respectability. On the other hand, the Irish in San Francisco were not arriving directly from Ireland, but arrived via eastern urban centers. The Irish immigrant in the West had already been exposed to Catholicism U.S. style. Though elements of Irish peasant religion undoubtedly remained, their days were numbered.

In any case, by 1880, Irish-American parish life was thriving on the West Coast. At the center was the irrepressible Irish pastor, who has grown to mythic proportions in recent times. He acted as a "cultural broker," the equivalent of the ward boss in politics, mediating between the Irish community and the American host culture on a highly personal level.[21] Not only did the pastor celebrate religious events, he also dispensed political and economic advice, and resolved neighborhood conflicts. The Irish pastor and the Irish sisters and nuns were revered by the community as people who "spared no effort to aid their flock,"[22] especially the sick and poor. The image of the domineering Irish pastor who tyrannically ruled his parish is an image that developed over the course of the twentieth century. In contrast to the domineering pastor, Thomas Quigley in his study, *The Irish Race in California* (1878), reviews the lives of Irish clergymen working in California in the nineteenth century. All are depicted as selfless, modest, hardworking priests, committed to poverty and the care of the sick, the orphan, the widow, and the destitute.[23] Whether Quigley's portrayal is historically accurate or not (and in a number of cases it was accurate), his observations reflect the ideal of the priest held by the Irish-American community on the West Coast. In time of trouble, the pastor was the one to go to.

The Irish Catholic community, like other immigrants, demonstrated an intense interest in the events in their homeland, particularly the Irish struggle for nationhood. Irish nationalism flourished on the West Coast. Father Peter C. Yorke of

San Francisco gave fiery speeches in front of large crowds in support of Irish freedom. Textbooks in Catholic schools were full of stories about Irish history and culture. The *San Francisco Monitor,* the archdiocesan newspaper, devoted considerable space to Irish news and political developments. Blessing suggests that the nationalistic fervor was designed "to counter the image of the Irish immigrants as poor relatives of a conquered, henceforth, inferior people."[24] In any case, a firm emotional bond was established between the Irish Americans on the West Coast, and their former homeland, a bond that erupted into gala celebrations each St. Patrick's Day.

Though life on the West Coast was better for the Irish than life in the East had been, they were still subjected to rather severe outbreaks of anti-Irish sentiment. At a St. Patrick's Day celebration in 1860 in San Francisco, some anti-Irish hecklers hanged St. Patrick in effigy across the street from the celebration, prompting the Irish to cut the pole down, "freeing" St. Patrick. Serious violence was narrowly avoided.[25] Of course, these events were nothing compared to the anti-Irish violence of the Vigilance Committees. Incidents of violence against the Irish were not uncommon in the Pacific states in the nineteenth century.

A favorite target of anti-Irish forces and of Progressive and Protestant reformers was the Irish predilection for drink. The city of San Francisco had the highest number of saloons per capita of any city in the United States, including 440 saloons in the sixty-four square block, Irish working class area, south of Market district.[26] For the working class Irish, the neighborhood saloon served as a social club, a "working-man's club,"[27] where the worker could relax and socialize; temperance efforts were generally unsuccessful. In the Progressive mind, the saloon became associated with "Roman Catholic subversion."[28]

To counteract this negative image, the Church sponsored several temperance societies, the most important being the Catholic Total Abstinence Union. Another aggressive program directed at Catholic youth was begun in the Irish parishes of St. John's and St. Peter's in 1886 and 1887 in San Francisco—the League of Cross Cadets. The league was a paramilitary organization aimed at young men in their late teens, who, through discipline and comradery, would avoid the perils of the saloon. Each member was required to take the pledge, "I will abstain from drinking intoxicating drink, and from visiting places where liquors are sold, until the age of twenty-one, and I will discourage . . . the habit of drinking in saloons."[29] At the same time, Archbishop Riordan of San Francisco introduced a similar pledge into the rite of Confirmation, a practice that continued in California through the 1960s.

The Irish sensitivity to public opinion did more than spur the creation of Irish temperance societies. By 1920, as Irish immigration continued to decline, the Irish-American community was the firmly established leader of West Coast Catholicism. Though many Protestant Americans might have been skeptical, the Irish-American community "perceived itself as a conservative force, ready to rescue and perfect American society."³⁰ As the new "defenders of American innocence," the Irish felt it was their duty to make sure that the many newly arrived immigrant groups (i.e., the Italians) would be assimilated into American life with the least amount of conflict or friction with the host culture. The Irish efforts often generated a good deal of animosity between themselves and the new immigrants, who rejected the Irish's good intentions. The emergence of the Ku Klux Klan on the West Coast in the 1920s suggests that the Irish efforts were not too successful.

In any case, the bond established between the Catholic Church and the Irish continued to influence the Catholic Church in the West through the modern era. As Burchell put it, the Church took on an "Irish cast,"³¹ one it maintained until the post-Vatican II era. The appointment of the Irish to California Bishoprics, such as Patrick Riordan in San Francisco and James Francis McIntyre in Los Angeles, did much to reinforce the Irish cast. The vestiges of Irish hegemony remain. In 1976, St. Patrick's Parish published its history. Like many inner-city parishes, it has become predominantly Hispanic and Filipino. Nonetheless, three-fourths of its commemorative booklet is spent describing the counties and patron saints of Ireland. Little attempt was made to describe the Hispanic and Filipino community. The back cover of the book was graced with a lovely map of Ireland.³²

THE GERMANS

If the Irish became the leader of ethnic Catholicism on the West Coast, then the Germans provided its heart and soul. Of all the ethnic groups, the Germans demonstrated the richest devotional and associational life. The German parish centered around worship, family, and school. Parish schools were often established as soon as the parish was founded. St. Boniface school was established in 1861 in San Francisco, the year after the first German national parish on the West Coast was established. Sacred Heart German Parish in Seattle, Washington, established a parish school two years after the parish was erected (1889), despite an "unmanageable debt."³³ Besides protecting the Catholic child from a hostile, Protestant environment, the German Catholic school was spurred by the dictum, "language saves faith." St. Boniface school in Anaheim conducted classes in both German and English, as was typical in German Catholic schools. German parishes in the nineteenth century also enjoyed vital sodalities and mutual aid societies. The latter were unified into the German Catholic Central Verein, and the women's benevolent associations were bound together in the Catholic Women's Union. One function of the benevolent societies was to promote a greater understanding between Catholics from different regions of Germany. Overall, Germans were the most practical of Catholics and their organizations inspired a "virile Catholicity."³⁴

Germans began arriving in California as early as 1850 in response to the Gold

Rush. German immigration remained steady throughout the course of the century from 1850 to 1950. The following table presents the number of foreign born Germans present in California, and the percentage of the total foreign born population they account for.

TABLE:
Foreign Born Germans Residing in California Decade by Decade[35]

Decade	German Foreign Born	Percent of Total Foreign Population
1850	3,084	14.1
1860	20,919	14.3
1870	29,701	14.2
1880	42,532	14.5
1890	61,472	16.8
1900	72,449	19.7
1910	75,832	14.7
1920	67,180	9.9
1930	81,840	8.2
1940	71,727	8.2
1950	70,791	7.2

German growth was particularly rapid in the last half of the nineteenth century. As with other immigrant groups, the greatest number settled in San Francisco in the nineteenth century, but from 1910 on, larger numbers of Germans settled in Los Angeles. Unlike several of the other Catholic immigrant groups, the German immigrant community was only about one-third Catholic. The German community consisted of Reformed Lutherans, Evangelicals, Jews, free-thinkers, and others. This made for an interesting relationship between the German Catholic community and the entire German immigrant community, which other Catholic immigrant groups did not face.

Ministry to the German Catholics on the West Coast began in 1852 in San Francisco as Rev. Florian Schweninger, O.S.B., was sent to minister to his countrymen. In 1856, lay members of the German community founded a building society, and began soliciting funds for the erection of a German church. Their petition to Archbishop Alemany was approved, and in 1860 St. Boniface Parish was opened as the first German national parish on the West Coast, with Father Sebastian Wolf as pastor. The Germans seemed content to lead a separate, ecclesiastical life, causing Alemany to grumble about their lack of generosity.[36] They were supportive of St. Boniface, however. Several other German national parishes were established in the late nineteenth century in the Pacific states—Sacred Heart in Seattle (1889), St. Elizabeth in Oakland (1892), and St. Anthony in San

Francisco (1893). Benevolent and fraternal societies flourished in all these parishes.

The German parish, between 1920 and 1960, represented what an ideal Catholic parish should look like. Germans enjoyed an active laity—they were more likely to have an active board of trustees than other groups, and their charitable, benevolent, and insurance societies had a tradition of lay participation. What distinguished the German parish from others was an intensely active devotional life. Missions were commonplace in the German parish, but more common were the endless round of novenas, triduums, Rosary nights, and devotions to the Blessed Sacrament. St. Boniface German Parish in San Francisco provides a good example of the devotions in the German parish. Besides the missions, novenas, and triduums, St. Boniface provided Stations of the Cross, a Holy Hour, and Benediction every Friday throughout the year. Solemn exposition of the Blessed Sacrament took place each day from 12 noon to 5:15 P.M. and was followed by Benediction. Each first Saturday, twenty-four hour exposition of the Blessed Sacrament was observed beginning Friday at midnight. During the 1950s, the exposition of the Blessed Sacrament was merged with devotions in honor of Our Lady of Fatima. Forty Hours' Devotions were provided at regular intervals throughout the year. During Lent, Stations of the Cross were observed each evening, and a second time on Friday evening. Each Wednesday night in Lent, a sermon was offered, followed by Benediction. May and October devotions consisted of Rosary, prayers, and Benediction each evening. In no other parish was the same degree of devotional practice present.[37]

The German community was also receptive to various marriage education and family programs. St. Boniface Parish sponsored the St. Francis Guild designed to foster the Catholic teaching on marriage and the family, to oppose birth control, and to provide material assistance to young Catholic families. It sought "to help solve the spiritual and economic problems of raising a truly Christian family in a modern, pagan world."[38] In 1949, a Maternity Guild was established to assist young parents with maternity expenses, and several parishes established "well baby clinics" to provide inexpensive medical care for the newborn infant and young child. The German community was also actively involved with the Cana and Pre-Cana Conferences and the Christian Family movements. The family provided the integral unit of German community life, so church programs in support of the family were vigorously endorsed by the German Catholic Community.

By 1970, a distinctive German Catholic presence on the West Coast was on the wane. As one historian of German immigration put it, "German Catholics gradually became simply Catholics."[39] In 1971, St. Boniface was made a territorial parish as well as being the German national parish. In the same year, the traditional noon Rosary betrayed the changing times as the Rosary was now offered for "peace and justice."[40] Even German devotionalism was becoming relevant. In Oakland, St. Elizabeth's Parish, originally a German national parish, is now a Latino parish, offering several Masses in Spanish but none in German. The transfer of old immigrant parishes to new immigrants is a familiar phenomenon in West Coast parish life.

THE ITALIANS

The third largest Catholic immigrant group arriving on the West Coast was the Italians. Unlike the Germans and Irish, large numbers of Italians did not begin to arrive on the West Coast until the 1880s. The number of foreign born Italians in California jumped from 7,537 in 1880 to 22,777 in 1900 and 107,249 in 1930.[41] Like other ethnic groups, the Italian immigrant settled largely in urban centers—Seattle, Tacoma, Portland, Los Angeles, and particularly San Francisco. California did have several significant Italian immigrant agricultural communities, particularly in the wine regions. (The names of Ernest and Julio Gallo represent not only "all the best," but also the Italian Catholic vineyard owners who made good. They also symbolize the continuing conflict between different generations of Catholic immigrant groups, as the Gallos would later exploit their Mexican Catholic brothers in faith in the grape fields of California.) The largest Italian center was the city of San Francisco, where 5,212 settled in 1880, another 7,508 by 1900, and another 16,918 by 1910.[42] By 1930, Italians of first, second, and third generations accounted for close to 20% of the entire population of San Francisco.[43] A significant feature of Italian immigrant life was the "birds of passage" phenomenon. Many Italians came to the United States (and to the West Coast) with no intention of settling. They came to make money and return to Italy. In San Francisco, the returnee rate was quite large, reaching as high as 50% of the number of incoming immigrants in certain years.[44] The high turnover rate in the Italian Catholic community presented interesting pastoral problems, and may account for the fact that Italians were granted more national parishes than any other ethnic group.

Despite the high returnee rate, life on the West Coast was good for the Italian community. They worked a variety of professions, with the majority involved in domestic and personal services, one-fourth in trade and transport, and others in manufacturing and in fishing.[45] The Italians demonstrated good upward mobility across the generations with banking (particularly the Giannini family of the Bank of Italy, and later the Bank of America), small industry, and fishing providing paths to the upper echelon of San Franciscan society. As one historian assesses, "The San Francisco Italian community contained the most prosperous groups of Italians in the United States."[46] No padrone system ever developed on the West Coast as it had in the East.

Besides the pastoral problem of a community that was geographically very mobile, the Irish-led Catholic Church had difficulty coming to terms with the peculiarities of Italian Catholicism, or what one pastor referred to as the "devotions of pagan Mediterraneans."[47] Italians were generally unfamiliar with the official teaching and rituals of the Church and showed little interest in learning about them. One pastor in Washington complained that the Italians were not fervent; they were "not practical," with less than 25% attending Sunday Mass regularly.[48] The formal observances of the institutional Church seemed cold and distant to the Italians who preferred the warm, emotive family celebrations associated with baptisms, weddings, and burials.

Men rarely went to church, as church observance was left to the women. Male detachment had been further increased by the Church's ill-fated opposition to Italian unification in the mid-nineteenth century. In contrast to the Irish community, where nationalism reinforced loyalty to the Church, Italian nationalists felt alienated from the Church. In the 1870s, Italian republican clubs and Masonic societies, both virulently anti-Catholic, emerged in San Francisco and attempted to seduce Italian Catholics away from the Church, promising greater equality in the Protestant churches, and greater opportunities for economic advancement outside the Catholic Church. In the 1920s, the Italian church in San Francisco was bombed on three separate occasions by anti-Catholic forces. Though most Italian men did not go to such extremes, a significant anti-clericalism did develop among them. While the vast majority of Italian men remained loyal to the Catholic faith, they exhibited an intense aversion to the institutional and clerically controlled Church. The Irish Catholic leaders interpreted Italian anti-clericalism as anti-Catholicism, unable to appreciate the essential Italian loyalty to Catholicism despite their anti-clerical leanings.[49]

Ministry to the Italian community began in San Francisco in the 1850s with Italians attending St. Francis of Assisi Parish. A Portuguese priest, Father Valentin, was appointed to care for the Italians. Valentin was "tolerant of the casual attitudes of Italians toward their religion," and the relationship between parish and Italians remained amicable. From 1875 to 1884, the Italians shared the Spanish national church, Our Lady of Guadalupe, with the Spanish-speaking community. An Italian priest, Father Carlo Franchi, was assigned to their care. On Sundays, an Italian Mass at 9 A.M. would be followed by a Spanish Mass at 10 A.M. The Italians were finally allowed to establish their own church, SS. Peter and Paul, in the North Beach district of San Francisco in 1884. In 1898, a second Italian parish, Corpus Christi, was begun in the Mission district, and in 1912 the third Italian parish, Immaculate Conception, was established. In Los Angeles, St. Peter's Italian Church was erected in the early 1900s. As was the case with many foreign language groups, ministry was hindered by a shortage of Italian-speaking priests. This problem was eased somewhat in the late 1890s with the arrival of the Salesian Fathers on the West Coast to operate their special ministry to the Italian Catholic community.

Italian immigrants demonstrated a strong attachment to their fellow Italian immigrants. More than any other immigrant group, they tended to marry their own. As of 1920, 97% of Italian marriages were Italians marrying Italians, compared to 62% for the Irish and 42% for the Germans.[50] In the nineteenth century, however, Italians had no sense of being "Italian," but congregated with people from their own region. A whole network of mutual aid societies developed based on regional loyalties. These societies provided the usual medical, unemployment, and burial benefits, but they also served as social and religious centers. Each regional society had its own patron saint, and every year the feast of the patron saint was celebrated by a festive procession on Sunday afternoon. As a result of the many societies, the Italian community had a procession virtually every weekend. The folk quality of these celebrations and their lack of "decorum" offended the Irish clergy largely because they felt that the celebrations made Catholics seem too "foreign" to Americans. An attempt was made to collect all the statues of the various patron saints at one church, in order to reduce the number of processions and to get the Italians to join more "orthodox" groups like the Holy Name Society. These attempts to make Italians "more regular" Catholics met with little success, though by 1890 the Italian parish numbered 400 members in the Legion of the Sacred Heart, 200 in the Altar Society, 125 in the Holy Angels Sodality, and 100 in the Holy Childhood.[51]

Even as the Italians became more "American" and "orthodox," a warm, devotional processional piety continued to flourish, devoted especially to the Blessed Mother. Of the five most popular societies, four were dedicated to Mary—Madonna Doloratta, Madonna della Grazie, Madonna del Lume (Sicilian), Madonna della Guardia (Genoese), and Santa Genna Gargagni (Tuscan).[52] Despite the regional differences, all five groups, over a period of time, came to participate in one another's processions, carrying banners and the sacred image of their special devotion. All marched in the Italian communal celebration on Columbus Day. One procession, the blessing of the fishing fleet, originally a Sicilian celebration, and celebrated in San Francisco, Bodega Bay, Monterey, and San Pedro in California, has now achieved the status of a civic celebration in San Francisco with much of the religious content lost. However, Italian processions have always had two elements—the private and the public.[53] The public was the open display, the procession, which everyone, Catholic and non-Catholic, Italian and non-Italian, could enjoy and join in celebrating. The private side united the Italian with a heritage and faith that was impenetrable to the outsider. The blessing of the boats originated in twelfth century Sicily where, as legend has it, a picture of the Madonna sent out a beam of light, rescuing a fishing fleet floundering in the fog. The celebration, perpetuated by the Madonna del Lume Society, was more than a civic event; it also reminded and reassured the Italian-Americans of the loving care and protection of the Blessed Mother.

Increased economic success plus the arrival of the Salesians contributed to the Americanization of the Italian parish. Regional loyalties were transcended, albeit reluctantly, as Italians strove to become "good citizens" and good Catholics. Integral in and to the development of the Italian community was the parish. According to historian D. P. Gumina, "The parish kept the Italian Colony together as an ethnic whole and enabled a gradual program of assimilation to penetrate the colony," and again, "the parish was the most important agency and social center for the entire Italian Colony of San Francisco."[54] The parish sponsored a number of societies, ranging from devotional to mutual benefit societies. A Salesian Young Men's Institute was established in 1901 and maintained 400 members by 1920, including 100 members in its reading circle.[55] The parish also provided classes in English and citizenship, to assist the immigrants in becoming U.S. citizens. The parish leaders stressed the need for Italians to learn English for their children's sake; nonetheless, most parents preferred to speak their own regional dialect.

One of the strongest aspects of Italian parish life, as run by the Salesians, was their youth program. Italians showed little inclination to support a separate school system, and lagged behind other ethnic groups in establishing parish schools. By 1924, only seven classes had graduated (somewhat sporadically) from SS. Peter and Paul parish school (girls were not admitted until the 1950s). As a result, the majority of Italian children attended public schools. In an attempt to reach the Italian youth, the Salesians sponsored an aggressive youth program designed to keep the children "far from the dangers of the streets and bad companions."[56] In 1921, the Salesian Club for young men was established, thus formalizing the work the Salesians had been doing for years. By the 1940s, the club had over 2,000 members. The club sponsored socials and lectures, but the greatest emphasis was placed on the sports program. A girls' auxiliary was also established, meeting twice a week and stressing the more feminine pursuits of "sewing, music, reading, and personal hygiene."[57] The Salesian Boys Club continued to flourish through 1980.

One of the most significant symbols of Italian Americanization was the establishment of the parish based Italian Catholic Federation (ICF), an organization that transcended regional loyalties. General Italian societies with no specific regional attachment had enjoyed little success in the Italian Colony during the nineteenth and early twentieth centuries. In the nineteenth century, the Society Italiana di Mutua Beneficienza had attempted a "national" organization, but gained little support. Similarly, the ICF, begun in 1924 in San Francisco and Stockton, met with little support. One history of the ICF reports: "The foundation of the Federation had anticipated a certain amount of difficulty in promoting a new society among its people—and they were not disappointed. Often they met with opposition and at times the appearance of their banners on the streets of a town called forth derisive comment."[58] As late as 1940, the historian for the Archdiocese of Los Angeles could express doubts about an organization claiming to be Italian, Catholic, and American. "It is beyond a doubt that the Italian spirit is essentially

Catholic but there are many factors which at times have militated against active realization of the spirit."[59] Language was listed as one of the problems, but one can assume that Italian anti-clericalism and folk religion were not far behind.

Nonetheless, the ICF was founded by an Italian-American layman and brought to fruition by two priests for the express purpose of affecting "the greatest possible unity between the Italian population and the Church."[60] Unlike other fraternal societies that were limited to either male or female, the federation was open to the entire family, with both husband and wife being allowed to join as members. Initially, the federation provided death and sick benefits, but it rapidly began to emphasize spiritual and social activities. Each parish branch of the ICF was initiated with a mission. From then on, general Communions were regular monthly events. Socially, the ICF was also active, sponsoring dinners, dances, picnics, and, in some parishes, actively supporting the parish athletic programs. Though initially unpopular, the ICF grew in membership throughout the 1940s and the 1950s and continues in less vigorous form to the present day.

Processions continue to play an important part in the religious life of the Italian Catholic community. The blessing of the fishing fleet, the Columbus Day parade, and other processions and festivals remain major communal events that merge Italian, American, and Catholic elements. The Italian parish continues to live on in San Francisco, but its primary function is no longer active service to an immigrant community. The symbols used in the processions and festivals, represent "not so much group solidarity, but group heritage."[61]

THE PORTUGUESE

The Portuguese Catholic community on the West Coast exhibited many of the traits that were present in the Italian and other "culturally Catholic" immigrant groups. Though over 95% of the Portuguese were at least nominally Catholic, they had to be assimilated into the formal practices and structure of the American Catholic Church in the Pacific states. Portuguese Catholics were present from the earliest days of California, but did not start arriving in large numbers until the 1880s. California had 4,705 foreign born Portuguese in 1880, jumping to 12,068 in 1900, and peaking at 24,517 in 1920.[62] Like the Italian community, the Portuguese immigrants came from different and competing regions of Portugal, including the various mainland regions and the islands, Cape Verde, the Azores, and Madeira. The majority came from the Azores, but prior to coming to California most Portuguese immigrants spent some time in New England or New York. The majority settled in northern California in the areas around Oakland, San Jose, and Sacramento (81%), where they worked mainly as ranchers and farmers. Another significant Portuguese community settled in San Diego as fishermen.

The parish served as the focus of Portuguese community life, providing a social and devotional center. As with most "cultural Catholics," the early Portuguese community did not actively participate in formal church observances—Mass attendance was low and sporadic, and they provided only minimal support for parochial schools. The parish, nonetheless, provided the Portuguese immigrant with a feeling of security—it was a familiar institution, which housed the familiar and popular Portuguese saints. The parish priest was an important figure in Portuguese community life, though a mild anti-clericalism was present among Portuguese men, who believed that the pastor tended to be overly concerned and involved with "worldly affairs."[63]

Like other immigrant groups, the Portuguese community was constantly in search of priests who spoke their native tongue, and there was always a shortage. One Portuguese immigrant to California, Manuel Francisco Fernandes, after working as a shepherd and in the mines, and observing the need for Portuguese priests, returned to the Azores to study for the priesthood. He returned to Santa Barbara to be ordained, and, along with Father Joao Manuel Tavares, was the earliest priest working among the Portuguese in the Oakland area. In 1892, Father Fernandes founded the first national parish for the Portuguese, St. Joseph's in Oakland. In 1909, a Portuguese national parish was opened in Sacramento under the patronage of St. Elizabeth. In 1914, Five Wounds national parish was opened in San Jose for the Portuguese (the five wounds of Christ appear in the Portuguese heraldic symbol).[64] Other parishes in northern California were begun by Portuguese, but did not become national parishes. The lack of Portuguese speaking priests, plus the general West Coast reluctance to establish national parishes, prevented the creation of more Portuguese national parishes.

At the heart of Portuguese religious life was the festival, complete with procession and special devotions. The festival was important in unifying the diverse elements of the Portuguese community, celebrating a common faith and heritage. One historian noted of an early festival: "The initial purpose of introducing the festival along the Pacific slope was that of uniting all the Portuguese people of California into a more cohesive community."[65] Festivals were also popular among Portuguese men, as the celebrations were not exclusively under the control of the local pastor. Each Portuguese festival had the usual components of Mass, procession, festive dancing, and dining.

Traditionally, the major celebration of the Portuguese community was the Festival of the Holy Ghost. It was begun in California in 1871 at Half Moon Bay, and has been celebrated faithfully every year since then. The festival celebrates the intercession of the Holy Ghost on behalf of the Azores islanders, who were beset by famine in the fourteenth century. When Queen St. Isabella learned of the miraculous intervention, she organized a solemn procession in honor of the Holy Ghost. Accompanied by her maids, she carried her crown through the streets of

Lisbon to the Cathedral, where she left the crown in thanksgiving to the Holy Ghost.[66] The tradition, transplanted in California in 1871, re-enacts the queen's procession.

The events of the festival have remained virtually unchanged over the course of the century. It begins on the eve of Pentecost Sunday. A procession carries "Isabella's crown and scepter" to the church to be blessed. On Pentecost Sunday morning at 10 A.M., a large procession leads the congregation to High Mass. The crown and scepter are placed on the altar, where they remain for the three days of the festival. At noon, a great barbecue begins, followed by the Chamarita Dance (a traditional and complex Portuguese folk dance). The following two days are filled with folk dancing and fund-raising auctions.

Though the Holy Ghost festival was the major celebration, equally festive celebrations were held in honor of "Senhor Santo Cristo dos Milagres," an Azorean festival that celebrated Christ standing before Pilate. A haunting image of Jesus, entitled "Ecce Homo" ("Behold the Man"), is carried in the procession. The Festo do Menino Jesus (the Feast of the Child Jesus) is celebrated on Christmas Eve, with the Christ child "serenaded" in the streets by people on the way to Midnight Mass. After the Mass, a festive meal is served. In Gustine, California, the Festo do Nossa Senhora dos Milagres (Our Lady of Miracles), is celebrated; an annual novena is held each September in which the images of sixteen saints are decorated with "satins, flowers, and laces." The novena culminated with a procession, featuring the sixteen saints and Our Lady being paraded through the town. A large fiesta followed. In 1917, in Los Banos, California, the first festival and devotions in honor of Mary's recent apparition at Fatima were celebrated. The festival included bullfighting and dancing, though the latter manifestations were quickly suppressed. Devotion to Our Lady of Fatima continued to grow in the Portuguese community, and eventually transcended the Portuguese community and became popular all along the West Coast in the 1940s and 1950s.[67]

The Portuguese parish also served as the center of a rich associational life. The two most important societies were the Brotherhood of the I.D.E.S. (Irmandade do Divino Esanto: Society of the Divine Holy Spirit), founded in 1889 at Mission San Jose for men, and the Sociedade Portuguesa Rainha Santa Isabel, begun in 1898 in Oakland for women. Both societies provided mutual aid benefits and charitable services, but more importantly they promoted Portuguese culture and the Catholic faith. A main task of the societies, particularly the I.D.E.S., was to prepare for the annual Holy Ghost festival. In the late nineteenth century, I.D.E.S. members began the tradition of attending Mass before each meeting to offset accusations that the society was Masonic.[68]

Both associations and the parish assisted the Portuguese immigrants' assimilation into mainstream American life, while preserving and deepening the community's Catholic faith and Portuguese heritage.

THE FILIPINOS

The Filipinos are one of the newer, but fastest growing, immigrant groups on the West Coast and are the most Catholic, Asian immigrant group, the Philippines having been colonized by the Spanish in the sixteenth century. Though nominally Catholic, the Filipino immigrant community has exhibited traits similar to those of the "cultural Catholic" group. The Filipinos arrived in the Pacific states in three waves—(1) the 1920s, (2) post-World War II, and (3) 1965 to 1985. Their California community has grown from less than 3,000 in 1920 to 40,000 in 1950 to 357,000 in 1984.[69] The years from 1975 to 1985 have been the period of most intense immigration. The early Filipino immigrants were almost exclusively male; it was not until the 1970s that family immigration became the norm. San Francisco and its environs have been the hub of Filipino life in the Pacific states, though large Filipino communities have developed around Los Angeles and Seattle. The majority of Filipinos worked in agriculture, domestic and personal services, and in the fishing industry. One historian has written that the Filipinos "with the Mexicans have constituted the backbone of the California agricultural force."[70]

Ministry to the Filipinos began in the 1920s in Seattle, as Archbishop O'Dea was asked by the Archbishop of the Philippines to assist the growing Filipino community in his archdiocese. O'Dea placed the Filipinos under the care of the Maryknoll Fathers at Our Lady Queen of Martyrs, the Japanese national parish. Ministry to the Filipinos was assisted by the Young Ladies' Institute and the Knights of Columbus. By 1928 in Seattle, there was a Filipino study club, a Filipino Legion of Mary, and the Catholic Filipino Club (which flourished throughout the West Coast). In 1929, a small hall at the church was given to the Filipinos, which became the center for their monthly business meeting and social affairs. In the 1930s, they actively participated in the St. Vincent de Paul Society.[71] Throughout the 1930s, they struggled to obtain a separate parish, which brought them into conflict with their Japanese co-parishioners. One report stated: "There was an incredible amount of tension between Japanese and Filipinos about who the church 'belonged' to."[72] Nonetheless, the Filipinos were never granted a separate parish. In Los Angeles in 1942, a community of 9,000 Filipinos was present in the city, and St. Columban's was established to serve them.[73] Despite the activity in Our Lady Queen of Martyrs in Seattle and in various California communities, the majority of Filipinos were never fully integrated into Catholic parish life. They enjoyed a strong family life and a tightly knit community, falling back on the traditional Filipino values of "reciprocity, obligation, loyalty, and unity."[74] The major religious events were family celebrations centered around baptisms and burials and incorporating an extensive system of "Godparentage" (compadrazgo). The close family and community life was not successfully able to be grafted onto parish life. One sociologist attributes Filipino reluctance to become involved in parish life in America to the Catholicism most experienced in the Philippines, where there were no Sunday collections and no tradition of parish support existed. Parishes were large and impersonal with the priest-to-people ratio being about 1 to 10,000. Registering in a parish was unknown to the Filipino, and little involvement in parish life occurred beyond Sunday Mass.[75] In addition, the Filipino community had been inadequately evangelized by their Spanish colonizers. The Filipino bishops acknowledge that the Filipino Catholic has received "no adequate, systematic instruction in the faith."[76] As a result, a folk Catholicism arose, centered on devotions, not liturgy. The Filipino community felt Christ's presence in the fiesta, not in the liturgy. "Fiestas, processions, pilgrimages, novenas, innumerable devotional practices"[77] form the heart of Filipino Catholicism.

Besides the ethnic baggage, the Filipino community had been driven in upon itself by strong anti-Filipino sentiment on the West Coast, which erupted in riots in Exeter, Tulare, Watsonville, and Monterey in the late 1920s. In 1935, with the passage of the Repatriation Act, Filipinos were forceably returned to their homeland. In the same year, a San Francisco pastor reported: "The Filipinos are practically exiles in a foreign and unsympathetic land."[78] Though efforts were made to provide a ministry to the Filipinos, their community was isolated within American society and within the Church. One historian observes: "The institutional Catholic Church's commitment to the Filipino American is one of indifference . . . if not benign condescension."[79] Protestant missions, sponsored by such groups as the YMCA, attempted to assist the Filipinos, and raised fears in Catholic circles that the Filipino was being lost to the Protestants. The Filipino Catholic Center was established in the 1920s in San Francisco to counteract Protestant influence. The different style and focus of Filipino Catholicism, along with a strong sense of family, mixed with the racist attitudes they encountered, kept the Filipino community isolated and detached from parish life. Nonetheless, they remained Catholics.

Like many immigrant groups before them, Filipinos took special delight in religious processions. In Seattle, Rizal Day was the occasion for a large procession and festival. In May, the "Flores de Mayo" was celebrated, as flowers were offered to the Blessed Mother. On Christmas Eve, a couple dressed as Mary and Joseph would lead a procession from house to house, seeking shelter, on the way to Midnight Mass. The community also celebrated the "Simbang Gabi," a series of Masses held at dawn the eight days prior to Christmas. In San Francisco, since 1969, a major procession and fiesta have been held to honor "Santo Niño de Cebu." The festival dates back to the sixteenth century in the Philippines, centering on a sacred statue of the child Jesus that is supposedly the source of countless miracles. The fiesta includes a procession with the "enthronement" of a replica of the Santo Niño statue on the altar. Mass and a novena of prayers follow the procession. After the Mass, a large banquet was enjoyed, followed by a ball where traditional Filipino dances were performed. The entire festival served to merge religious and communal values. As one brochure read: "The devotion to the Santo Niño is a means of inspiring the highest values in upholding Sacred Traditions of Philippine Culture and Heritage."[80] As was the case with previous ethnic devotions, the Santo Niño has met opposition, but the celebration continues.

The opposition to the Santo Niño celebration has intensified in recent years with the appointment of a Filipino priest to St. Joseph's Parish in San Francisco, where the statue resides. Ironically, the Filipino celebration flourished while the parish was attended by an old Irish pastor; however, the new Filipino pastor has sought to remove the shrine from the church. He argues that the procession and celebration are "un-American," and serve only to increase alienation between the Filipino and American communities. In addition, he claims that the devotion is not in the spirit of Vatican II, and that the presence of the statue on the altar is a clear violation of proper liturgical practice. Opposing the pastor are members of the Filipino community who see the festival as being an enormous boon to the vitality and spirit of the Filipino community.[81] The battle between the American Church and the folk Church continues to the present day.

THE CHINESE AND JAPANESE

Two of the largest immigrant groups in the West were the Japanese and Chinese, a fact that has presented a major problem of evangelization for the Church. A very small percentage of the Chinese and Japanese population is Catholic. In Japan, Catholics make up less than 1% of the total population. Though there are more Chinese Christians (15%), only one-third of these are Catholic. Unlike other Catholic immigrant groups, Japanese and Chinese Catholic communities contained a large number of converts, or children of converts. As a result, parish life developed along American lines. Little that was distinctively Japanese or Chinese penetrated the Japanese or Chinese Catholic parish, at least in terms of devotional practices and parish societies.

Both the Japanese and Chinese were subjected to a bitter and violent racism on the West Coast. The Chinese were excluded in 1882, and the number of Japanese immigrants was "voluntarily" reduced with the Gentlemen's Agreement of 1908. Chinese immigration to the Pacific states began earlier than Japanese immigration, which did not reach significant amounts until the 1880s. Though Americans might make little distinction between Japanese and Chinese, the intense national competition between the two peoples prevented cooperation or joint ventures in Japanese-Chinese parishes.

Ministry to the Chinese began in 1854, as Archbishop Alemany procured a Chinese priest, Father Thomas Cian, to minister to his exploited countrymen. What Cian encountered was a few Chinese Catholics widely scattered (some fifty or sixty in San Francisco and the mining regions), and a hostile, racist environment (many Catholics on the West Coast had difficulty believing Cian was a priest because he was Chinese). Cian wrote in 1855: "I cannot see much prospect of doing much good here."[82] The Chinese seemed hard-hearted. He petitioned to build a small chapel for Chinese Catholics in San Francisco, as he witnessed the inroads being made by Protestant clergymen among the "heathen" Chinese. No chapel was ever built. At the heart of Cian's difficulty was that he did not speak the same dialect as the majority of the Chinese in San Francisco. (The problem of dialect would continue through the 1960s in Chinese ministry.) Discouraged by his lack of success, Cian returned to China via Italy in 1865.[83]

From 1865 to 1902, the Chinese community was neglected until Paulist Father Ignatius Stark initiated the first (and at the time only) Chinese mission on the West Coast. It was begun in San Francisco in 1902 as part of the Paulist Fathers' ministry in Old St. Mary's Parish, located in the heart of Chinatown. Sunday school was offered to the children, but the parish's largest draw was the courses in English taught there. Two Chinese sisters arrived in the early 1900s to assist in the founding of a Catholic school for Chinese children. Paulist Father Charles Bradley served the Chinese community from 1910 to 1927, and was dubbed the "Apostle to the Chinese."[84] Bradley had difficulty with the intricacies of the Chinese dialects, and so brought a native, lay catechist, Anthony Chan, from Canton, to preach to the Chinese of San Francisco.[85] In 1921, St. Mary's Chinese Mission was officially erected and renamed Holy Family Mission. The same year also marked the completion of Holy Family parochial school for the Chinese. The Chinese Language School, as it was called, taught the Chinese language and writing, Chinese traditions and Chinese history, as well as the fundamentals of the Catholic faith. Conversions increased to a steady fifteen or twenty a year. In the 1920s, a number of active social clubs developed among Chinese Catholics spurred by the creation of the Chinese Catholic Social Center in 1921. Youth clubs grew, reflecting the typical concerns of Catholic youth groups—athletics, drama, music, and dance. In 1927, the mission sponsored a festival, in the great tradition of Catholic parishes on the West Coast, to raise funds. In the 1920s, a social service bureau was established to help with the needy, the unemployed, and the sick.[86] By the 1940s and the 1950s, the Chinese parish was operating much like other parishes, maintaining a branch of the Catholic Daughters of America, Boy and Girl Scouts, a Glee Club, PTA, the Legion of Mary, Men's Club, Boys Club, and various youth clubs (including the famous Drum Corps). Like other parishes, the Chinese hosted the usual rounds of missions, picnics, bazaars, May Crownings, and even fashion shows.[87] In Los Angeles, a Chinese Catholic Center was established in 1942, serving the Catholics in Los Angeles' Chinatown. Symbolic of the merging of Chinese, Catholic, and American elements was the participation of the Holy Family Drum Corps in the inaugural parade of the first Catholic president, John F. Kennedy, in 1960. The 1960s marked the beginning of a special Chinese New Year Mass. In the late 1970s, the Chinese parish assisted in the relocation and assimilation of Vietnamese Catholic refugees.

Ministry to the other large Asian community, the Japanese, did not begin in earnest until 1913. At that time, a Japanese Catholic in Los Angeles named Leo Hatekeyama, wishing to receive the Sacrament of Penance, could find no priest in Los Angeles who spoke Japanese. He wrote to the Bishop of Japan, asking to send his confession by registered mail, and requesting his penance and absolution to be returned the same way.[88] The incident sparked concern for Japanese Catholics on the West Coast, and soon Japanese missions and parishes were established in San Francisco in 1912, Los Angeles in 1913, and Seattle in 1922. As with the Chinese Catholics, the Japanese Catholic parish developed along American lines because there was little Japanese Catholic tradition on which to draw.

In Los Angeles, Father Albert Breton arrived in 1913 to work among the Japanese. In 1915, a group of Japanese sisters arrived in the city and opened an orphanage and a school for the Japanese. In 1920, the Maryknoll Fathers took over the Japanese ministry, and by 1933 St. Francis Xavier chapel was dedicated. In 1938, a permanent church was erected for the Japanese of the city.[89]

In San Francisco, St. Francis Xavier Mission was established in 1912, with the Jesuits in charge until 1925, when they were replaced by the Divine Word Fathers. A kindergarten was established soon after the mission was founded. A complete elementary school called Morning Star was not established until 1930, at which time it was run by the Daughters of Mary and Joseph. The separate Japanese mission was a necessity not only because of language difficulties, but because of the intense racial prejudice and hatred of Asians, which had long been a problem on the West Coast. One pastor reports: "Americans will leave if a Japanese comes in their pew."[90] As with the Chinese, an important part of the Japanese mission was the language school, which not only taught the Japanese English, but also introduced the Japanese to American culture and prepared them for citizenship.

Between 1913 and 1941, the Japanese parish developed like other American parishes. In 1917, a Mission Club was established at St. Francis Xavier. The club had three purposes. First, it encouraged spiritual devotions among the Japanese. Second, it studied and contrasted the customs and culture of Japan with those of America, thereby helping the Japanese to assimilate. Finally, the club was social, providing for fellowship among Japanese Catholics, and a sense of group unity and identity.[91]

In Seattle, Washington, Our Lady Queen of Martyrs was established in 1922 for Japanese and Filipino Catholics, though the Japanese outnumbered the Filipinos four to one. The parish was conducted by the Maryknoll Fathers, who immediately began a Sunday school, followed by a kindergarten, and then three grades of primary school (1928). As had been the case with the Chinese, the Japanese parish established the traditional societies—St. Vincent de Paul, Legion of

Mary, Holy Name Society, YLI, and the Boy and Girl Scouts. Similar patterns were followed in the Los Angeles and San Francisco Japanese parishes.

In 1941, World War II brought regular parish life to a halt, as Japanese Americans were herded into relocation camps. Significantly, Father William Stoeke, S.V.D., pastor of St. Francis Xavier, accompanied his parishioners to the relocation camps. The sadness of the situation is captured in the succinct annual report of St. Francis Xavier in 1944: "Because of the evacuation of parishioners, no special activities or events took place."[92] By 1954, regular parish life had returned, as the annual report notes a bazaar, days of recollection, novenas and triduums, and a variety of children's programs.[93] Through 1980, the Japanese parish continued much like any other parish.

MINOR IMMIGRANT GROUPS

A large number of smaller ethnic groups also arrived on the West Coast—the Polish, the Slovaks, the Slavs, the Croatians, the French, the Maltese, the black community, and others. The Poles did not arrive in any significant number until the 1920s, and even then the foreign born population never exceeded 15,000 until 1950.[94] The only Polish national parish on the West Coast was erected in Los Angeles. In 1908, a committee was formed to collect funds to build a Polish church. Two Polish priests served the Polish community from 1908 to 1916, and several fraternal and social societies were developed. From 1916 to 1925, services in Polish were discontinued. In the mid-1920s, the Poles once again formed a committee to build a church. In 1926, the new church was opened and named El Cristo Rey (Christ the King). By 1930, 13,872 Poles were residing in Los Angeles. A flurry of parish organizations developed over the course of the next two decades, including the Altar and Holy Rosary Societies, Society of the Holy Name of Jesus, Queen Jadwiga and St. Stanislaus Club. In 1940, a Polish parish school was established. In 1956, the new church was dedicated to Our Lady of Bright Mount. The Polish Catholic community maintained a strong devotion to the Blessed Virgin Mary, particularly Our Lady of Czestochowa. In 1966, the parish received its first resident pastor after having been attended from other parishes.[95] Polish missions were established in San Francisco and San Diego in the post-Vatican II era.

The only Slovak parish on the West Coast was St. Joseph's, erected in the 1910s in Tacoma, Washington. Like most ethnic parishes, the Slovak laity petitioned its bishop to have its own parish, and a series of fraternal associations and social clubs was developed around the parish.[96]

The French accounted for a large enough population in San Francisco (8,000) in 1856 to merit their own parish, Notre Dame des Victoires. In 1892, the Marist Fathers took over Notre Dame. The French church has served as the center of

French cultural and social life. As the historian of the French community put it, Notre Dame is "more than a church," it is a "place where the soft sounds of French are spoken, where friends could gather, and where the customs are familiar."[97] To draw back indifferent French Catholics, the Marist Fathers opened the church to various non-church societies. The church remains the center of French life, preserving its French culture and Catholic faith, as well as assisting French assimilation to American life.

A related group, the French Canadians, settled in significant numbers in the Willamette Valley in Oregon, and established French-Canadian Catholic life there.

Ministry to the black community has presented a major pastoral problem for the Church on the West Coast. The black community is principally urban and non-Catholic and has grown in areas formerly populated by Catholic ethnics. In San Francisco, the black population grew from 5,000 in 1945 to 75,000 in 1953, with the majority residing in the inner city. Many inner-city parish schools face the problem of being black and non-Catholic, and to close the school may appear to be an abandonment of both the black and the inner city. Inside the Church, the black Catholic, like the Japanese, Chinese, and Mexican Catholics, has had to contend with racism. A quite candid comment by the pastor of a major San Francisco parish in 1953 reflects a common problem: "Due to a great influx of Negroes in this section a large number of parishioners are selling their homes and moving elsewhere."[98] In Los Angeles, a center for black Catholics was established under the protection of St. Victor in 1922. In 1927, St. Odilia was erected to serve black Catholics.[99] A separate parish was established for blacks in San Francisco in 1938, St. Benedict the Moor. Outside of being black, parish life at St. Benedict followed a pattern similar to other parishes with the usual devotional, fraternal, and charitable societies developing, and the usual devotions sponsored. In 1957, the separate church for blacks was phased out as the Church feared it was becoming an instrument that was perpetuating segregation, a concern expressed earlier by Archbishop Cantwell of Los Angeles. Despite this enlightened view, ministry to the black community remains a problem.

CONCLUSION

Since 1850, the Catholic Church in the Pacific states has accommodated an almost endless stream of immigrants. Despite the reluctance of West Coast bishops to establish national parishes (far fewer ethnic parishes were established in the West than in the East), and despite the assimilationist mentality of the American Church, ethnic Catholicism flourished on the West Coast, demonstrating a rich devotional and associational life. Although the Irish quickly established their hegemony over the West Coast Church, and attempted to dictate its style and direction, the Church in the Pacific states has never been a monocultural, monolithic institution. Since San Francisco's earliest parish, St. Francis of Assisi, offered sermons in Italian, Spanish, French, and English, Catholic parishes in the West have learned to accommodate a varied flock. This is not to say that conflict did not occur; often it did. But, conflict and all, the parish acted as mediator, preserver, and unifier—mediating between the immigrant and American culture, preserving the group's heritage, and unifying diverse elements of both the immigrant community and the Catholic community. The parish, however, was not always able to fulfill these roles with each group. The largest immigrant group on the West Coast (the Mexicans) was often detached from parish life; the effort to integrate the Mexicans into normal parish life is the subject of the next chapter.

Notes

1. Archbishop John J. Cantwell, quoted in Weber, *Cantwell*, 125, 127.
2. *San Francisco Monitor*, January 23, 1904, quoted in Antonio Soto "The Chicano and the Church in Northern California, 1848–1978" (Ph.D. dissertation, University of California, Berkeley, 1978), 96.
3. Morrison, "History of St. Joseph, part X," 14.
4. Weber, *Cantwell*, 105.
5. Dodds, *Oregon*, 185.
6. *Ibid.*, 117.
7. N. H. Clark, *Washington: A Bicentennial History* (New York: Norton, 1976), 62.
8. Warren S. Thompson, *Growth and Changes in California Population* (Los Angeles: The Haynes Foundation, 1955), 70.
9. Rose Doris Scherini, *The Italian American Community of San Francisco: A Descriptive Study* (New York: Arno Press, 1980), 160.
10. Thompson, *Growth and Change,* 70; Burchell, *San Francisco's Irish,* 8.
11. Patrick Blessing, "Culture, Religion and the Activities of the Committee of Vigilance, San Francisco, 1856." Working Paper Series, Cushwa Center for the Study of American Catholicism, Notre Dame, Indiana, Series 8, Number 3, Fall, 1980, 15.
12. *Ibid.,* 13.
13. *Ibid.,* 10.
14. Burchell, *San Francisco's Irish,* 87.
15. *Ibid.,* 89.
16. *Ibid.,* 91.
17. *Ibid.*, 91.
18. Francis Weber, *Thomas James Conaty: Pastor-Educator-Bishop* (Los Angeles: Westernlore Press, 1969), 23.
19. Burchell, *San Francisco's Irish,* 161–166.
20. *Ibid.,* 95.

21. Patrick Blessing, "Irish," in Stephen Thernstron (ed.), *Harvard Encyclopedia of American Ethnic Groups* (Cambridge and London: Harvard University Press, 1980), 534.
22. *Ibid.*, 534.
23. Thomas Quigley, *The Irish Race in California and on the Pacific Coast* (San Francisco: A. Roman and Co., 1878).
24. Blessing, "Irish," 533.
25. "Just Thirty Years Ago," *San Francisco Monitor*, April 23, 1890, 5.
26. Starr, *Inventing the Dream*, 245.
27. Cherny and Issel, *San Francisco*, 91.
28. Starr, *Inventing the Dream*, 243.
29. Quoted in Francis Weber, *California Catholicity* (Hong Kong: Libra Press Ltd., 1979), 180.
30. Robert M. Senkewicz, "American and Catholic: The Premature Synthesis of the San Francisco Irish," in David Alvarez (ed.), *The American Church: Essays on the Americanization of the Catholic Church* (St. Mary's: Moraga, Cal., 1979), 146.
31. Burchell, *San Francisco's Irish*, 10.
32. *The History of St. Patrick's Parish and Church, San Francisco, 1851–1976* (So. Hackensack, N.J.: Custombook, 1976).
33. Seattle, Washington. Chancery Archives of the Archdiocese of Seattle (hereafter referred to AAS). Parish Files.
34. "St. Anthony's Parish History, San Francisco," unpublished history. AASF. Parish Files.
35. Thompson, *Growth*, 70.
36. Gaffey, *Riordan*, 191.
37. Overview based on St. Boniface Annual Reports, 1943–1983. AASF. Parish Files.
38. Alfred Boeddeker, O.F.M., *100th Anniversary St. Boniface Parish* (San Francisco: James H. Barry, 1960), n.p.
39. Kathleen Neils Conzen, "Germans," in Thernstrom, *Harvard Encyclopedia*, 419.
40. AASF. Parish Files.
41. Thompson, *Growth*, 70.
42. Four recent studies describe the Italian immigrant experience in San Francisco and California: Dino Cinel, *From Italy to San Francisco: The Immigrant Experience* (Stanford: University of Stanford Press, 1982); Deanna Paoli Gumina, *The Italians of San Francisco, 1850–1930* (New York: Center for Migration Studies, 1978); Rose Scherini, *The Italian American Community of San Francisco* (New York: Arno Press, 1980); Michaela di Leonardo, *The Varieties of Ethnic Experience: Kinship, Class and Gender Among California Italian Americans* (Ithaca: Cornell University Press, 1984).
43. Cinel, *From Italy*, 18–19. See also Humbert Nelli, "Italians," in Thernstron, *Harvard Encyclopedia*, 531.
44. Cinel, *From Italy*, 46–47, 101.
45. *Ibid.*, 137.
46. Nelli, "Italians," 550.
47. Cinel, *From Italy*, 207.
48. AAF. Parish Files.
49. Gumina, *Italians*, 169.
50. Cinel, *From Italy*, 177.

51. Gumina, *Italians*. 173.
52. Scherini, *Italian Americans*, 167.
53. *Ibid.*, 180.
54. Gumina, *Italians*, 181, 183.
55. *Ibid.*, 177.
56. *Ibid.*, 179.
57. *Ibid.*, 179.
58. *San Francisco Centennial*, 126.
59. *Los Angeles Centennial*, 181.
60. *Ibid.*, 181.
61. Scherini, *Italian Americans*, 181.
62. Thompson, *Growth*, 70; Francis M. Rogers, "Portuguese," in Thernstrom, *Harvard Encyclopedia*.
63. Sandra Wolforth, *The Portuguese in America* (San Francisco: R and E Associates, 1978), 113.
64. Leo Pap, *The Portuguese Americans* (Boston: Twayne Publishers, 1981), 180.
65. Francis Weber, *California's Catholic Heritage* (Los Angeles: Dawson's Bookshop, 1974), 153.
66. A variety of legends exist concerning the origins of the Holy Ghost festival. I have chosen the story related in the Centennial Yearbook, *Holy Ghost Festival Centennial Year, 1871–1971 Commemorative Booklet* (Half Moon Bay, Cal.: I.D.E.S. Society, 1971).
67. For the Festivals, see Pap, *Portuguese Americans*, 194–202.
68. Pap, *Portuguese Americans*, 169. See also August Mark Vaz, *The Portuguese in California* (Oakland: I.D.E.S. Supreme Council, 1965).
69. Sonia Wallouts, "Filipinos in California" (Master's thesis, University of Southern California, 1966), 80.
70. H. Brett Melendy, "Filipinos" in Thernstrom, *Harvard Encyclopedia*, 359.
71. AAS. Report on Our Lady Queen of Martyrs, Filipino-Japanese National Parish, Seattle, Washington, compiled by Christine Bauer, archivist. AAS.
72. AAS, Parish Files.
73. Weber, *Cantwell*, 129.
74. Melendy, "Filipinos," 360.
75. AASF. Parish Files.
76. Filipino bishops, quoted in Anthony McGuire (ed.), *Light of Nations: A Resource Directory for Ministry to Ethnic Groups* (San Francisco: Archdiocese of San Francisco, 1985), F-3.
77. *Ibid.*, F-3.
78. AASF. "Report from Catholic Filipino Club, 1935."
79. Fred Cordova (ed.), *Filipinos! Forgotten Asian Americans* (Dubuque: Iowa: Kendall Hunt, 1983), 171.
80. *First Decade Filipino Fiesta: Santo Niño de Cebu Week: Commemorative Booklet* (San Francisco: Cebu Association, 1979).
81. Warren Hinckle, "The Priest and the Philippine Saint," *San Francisco Chronicle*, February 27, 1984, 5.
82. John B. McGloin, S.J., "Thomas Cian: Pioneer Chinese Priest in California," *California Historical Society Quarterly* XLVIII (1959), 50.

83. *Ibid.*
84. Deanna Paoli Gumina, *Old St. Mary's: Crossroads of the World* (San Francisco: Old St. Mary's, Paulist Center, 1978), 41.
85. *Ibid.*, 40.
86. *Ibid.*, 40–44.
87. AASF. Parish Files.
88. Tony Matsuda, "St. Francis Xavier Mission," *Academy Scrapbook* 2 (January, 1952), 233–238.
89. Weber, *Cantwell*, 129.
90. AASF. Parish Files.
91. AASF. Parish Files.
92. AASF. Parish Files.
93. AASF. Parish Files.
94. Thompson, *Growth*, 70.
95. Jacek Przygoda (ed.), *Polish Americans in California, 1827–1977 and Who's Who* (Los Angeles: Polish American Historical Society—California Chapter, 1978).
96. Chris DuBois, "The Church in Tacoma: 100 Years of Faith, Hard Work, and Stubbornness," *The Seattle Progress,* June 16, 1983, 13.
97. Terry O'Neill, "The French Colony of San Francisco, 1900 to 1920," (Master's thesis, University of San Francisco, 1976), 90.
98. AASF. Parish Files.
99. Weber, *Cantwell,* 120–125.

CHAPTER SEVEN
The Mexican-American Catholic Community

The Mexican-American Catholic community has the unique distinction of being the oldest and newest immigrant group in California, as well as being the largest Catholic immigrant group in the state. Despite this distinction, the history of the Mexican-American Catholic community has been largely neglected. Three recent studies by Albert Camarillo, Richard Romo, and Richard Griswold del Castillo[1] have done much to delineate the contours of Mexican-American society in southern California, but none adequately describes the religious dimension of Mexican-American life. As the study, *The Mexican American People: The Nation's Second Largest Minority,* asserted in 1970, "Despite the importance of this group (the Mexican Americans) to the Church (and vice versa), no literature exists on the role of the Church among the Mexican-American population."[2] Outside of several recent dissertations[3] the Grebler assessment remains true as of 1980.

California had been a Mexican province until 1848, when it was ceded to the United States in the Treaty of Guadalupe Hidalgo. As of 1850, when California was admitted to the Union, the remnants of the Franciscan mission tradition remained highly visible. Though the common perception has been that the California Church had collapsed with the secularization of the missions, and later with the transfer to American rule, regular Church life was maintained in California through the careful ministrations of Franciscan Father Gonzalez Rubio, administrator of the California Catholic Church from 1846 to 1850. Fifteen of the twenty-one missions still had resident pastors as of 1850, and the other six were visited frequently by missionary priests. Also, resident pastors were present at the pueblos of Los Angeles and San Jose.[4] The Hispanic cast of the California Church, however, was on the wane as the Gold Rush brought hordes of non-Mexican immigrants to California. San Francisco was quickly transformed into an "American city," with the Spanish speaking population assuming a decidedly minority position. In Santa Barbara and Los Angeles, the transfer of cultural hegemony from the Mexican community to the "American Anglo" community was not completed until 1880. Nonetheless, the importance of the Spanish community to the California Church was reflected in the appointment of two Spaniards, Joseph Sadoc Alemany, and Thaddeus Amat, as the first bishops of American California.

Though California experienced a burst of Mexican immigration in the 1850s as a result of the Gold Rush, Mexican immigration slowed considerably during the last half of the nineteenth century. As of 1900, the foreign born Mexican population numbered less than 10,000.[5] The twentieth century brought increasingly large numbers of Mexican immigrants to California. In 1910, the foreign born Mexican population had risen to 33,444, jumping to 86,610 in 1920, and, amazingly, to 199,165 by 1930.[6] The rapid increase was due in large measure to the dislocation created by the Mexican Revolution, but it was also spurred by the expanding economy of southern California, which was desperately in need of a cheap labor supply. Immigration declined between 1930 and 1950, and, in fact, an aggressive drive was launched in the 1930s to "repatriate" the Mexican immigrant. The Great Depression had made jobs scarce, and the Mexican, who was at best minimally accepted when his labor was needed, was now forcefully driven from the state. Mexican immigration again increased as postwar prosperity came to California. As many as 5,400 Mexicans entered California each month during the 1950s, with about 350,000 entering California legally between 1953 and 1959. By 1964, over 2,000,000 Spanish speaking were in California with over 700,000 residing in the Los Angeles metropolitan area, accounting for about 20% of that area's total population.[7] By 1970, 50% of all Mexican Americans living in the Southwest United States resided in California, up from 30% in 1950.[8] Significant to the Church in California was the fact that nearly 90% of these immigrants were at least nominally Catholic, thereby posing enormous pastoral problems for the California Church.

The Catholic Church's care for its Mexican faithful has been termed by one historian as "a history of neglect."[9] While this assertion may be true for the period between 1880 and 1980, it is less true for the period from 1850 to 1880. The early Mexican community was made up of two distinct groups—newly arrived immigrants, and those who had resided in California for several generations and referred to themselves as "Californios," to distinguish themselves from the new arrivals. The Californios remained the social and political elite in southern California until 1880 when the Yankee hordes overtook them and stripped them of their land and power. The newly arrived Mexican immigrants clustered, from the beginning, at the bottom of the socioeconomic realm, and were referred to by the Californios as "cholos" (scoundrels), as the Californios wished to keep a separate identity. The Yankees made no such distinction and the Californios would soon join the "cholos" at the bottom of American society.

Despite their loss of power in San Francisco in the early 1850s, a significant group of Spanish-speaking Catholics continued to reside in the city, and the first Archbishop of American California, Joseph Sadoc Alemany, O.P., adopted a conciliatory attitude toward the recently displaced Spanish speaking and the newly arrived Mexican immigrants. Ministry was provided initially at St. Francis of Assisi Parish in San Francisco, where a sermon in Spanish was provided at the 8:30 A.M. Mass on Sunday mornings. In addition, Franciscan Mexican priests, Prudencio Santillon and Jose Maria Suarez del Real, remained at Mission Dolores and Mission Santa Clara, respectively, in the early 1850s, ministering to the surrounding Mexican communities. In 1865, Father Gabriel Serrano was appointed by Alemany as "pastor hispaniorem" for the city of San Francisco.[10] Despite the ongoing ministry, by 1871 the Spanish community was in sad disarray. A group of Spanish leaders circulated a petition asking Alemany for a Spanish national parish for San Francisco "to reestablish . . . the splendor, brilliance, and influence of our race." The petition reports that all other organizational efforts—political, philanthropic, and social—had failed to unite the Spanish community, and that the Church alone was powerful enough to provide unity.[11] Alemany acceded to their request. In 1875, Our Lady of Guadalupe Parish (Nuestra Señora de Guadalupe) was established as a Spanish national parish, to provide better pastoral care for the Spanish-speaking residents of San Francisco, and to unite the Spanish community.

Alemany did not limit his attention to the Spanish community in San Francisco. Further south in the archdiocese, large Hispanic communities remained around Mission San Jose and Mission San Juan Bautista. In southern San Mateo County, another special parish for the Spanish speaking, Our Lady of the Pillar (Nuestra Señora del Pilar) was established in 1868. Alemany also provided a Spanish speaking priest for the Mexican gold miners who lived in Sonora, California, in the 1850s. Furthermore, Alemany decreed, in the early 1850s, that the Mexican population could request a priest of their own nationality to perform their weddings, regardless of the parish they were in. As historian Michael Neri asserts, "Such a decree indicated Alemany's high regard for the Spanish speaking Catholics in California."[12]

However, the institutional Church did not enjoy such amicable relations with the larger Mexican communities at Santa Barbara and Los Angeles. From the time of his appointment as Bishop of Monterey and Los Angeles in 1853, Bishop Thaddeus Amat, C.M., a Spaniard like Alemany, demonstrated little sympathy for the Mexican Catholicism he found in his diocese. Amat set out to monitor the religious orthodoxy of his Mexican faithful and to bring them into closer conformity with the American Church. His efforts won him little popularity with his Mexican flock. In one of Amat's earliest pastorals, he chastised the people for their careless attitude toward religious observances and the laxity of their moral behavior. To many in the Mexican community, used to the easy-going ministrations of the mission padres, the bishop's tone sounded judgmental and threatening rather than paternal. Furthermore, Amat had little patience with Mexican folk Catholicism. He prohibited many fiestas because he believed that their disorderly quality left the Church open to ridicule from Americans. Nonetheless, several fiestas were continued without official approbation. Other folk practices such as the rituals of the "curanderas," or "folk-healers," were rigorously discouraged. In Santa Barbara in 1858, Amat suspended the Mexican Franciscans for (among other things) "fomenting superstition."[13] Their crime was that they tolerated Mexican folk customs, among which was the selling of burial shrouds. Amat contended that such practices amounted to attempts to "purchase heaven." The ancient Indian practices were lost on him. Central to his objections was the fear that the "ceremonies, cults, and devotions of corrupt Catholicism" (a phrase used by one of Amat's priests in describing Mexican Catholicism)[14] would discredit the Church in the eyes of the increasingly predominant Anglo-American society. Amat's fears were not without substance. In 1855, a Protestant minister was aghast at the Sunday "observances" of Los Angeles Catholics. "What a spectacle. . . . Here in Sunday horse-racing is seen the fruits of Popery."[15] Similarly, a Protestant superintendent of the New Almaden mines described a Mexican religious festival celebrated at the mines as a "pagan riot."[16] To a Catholic churchman trying to show the compatability of Catholicism and Americanism, the Mexican festivals may have seemed excessive.

At the center of the conflict, then, was the difficult switch from a Mexican to an American Catholic Church. The situation was aggravated by Amat's seeming lack of understanding of the social and historical context of post-Mexican California. His Spanish speaking faithful "saw themselves as victims of American expansionism, who were being disenfranchised socially, culturally, politically, and economically under the new American regime."[17] Amat's policies and attempts to enforce strict discipline seemed like more of the same.

As late as 1940, there seemed to be little room for Mexican practices within the institutional Church because they were offensive to Americans, and American Catholics as well. Bishop Charles Buddy of San Diego wrote to the Apostolic Delegate in 1940, ". . . we have indulged and tolerated their (the Mexicans) customs which would not hurt the cause of religion. But some of their customs we could not permit because they are a source of scandal and could easily weaken the faith of the people. For example, girls dancing in the church on the feast of Our Lady of Guadalupe and the dances held before processions of the Most Blessed Sacrament."[18] Buddy canceled several outdoor processions as well, confiding to the Cardinal Prefect of the Propagation of Faith, "After all, this is America, and we must protect the faith of our own people."[19] Throughout the period from 1850 to 1980, a conflict would exist between institutional Catholicism and the folk customs of Mexican Catholicism.

Despite the conflict with Amat, religion continued to permeate the daily life of the Mexican-American community throughout the nineteenth century. In the 1850s in Los Angeles, Mexican community life centered around the Plaza Church located in downtown Los Angeles. Little distinction was made between "religious" and "secular" life. As one historian has noted, "It (the Plaza Church) was the place where the community celebrated its traditional secular and religious fiestas, events which had a collective significance unifying the town and reaffirming traditional loyalties."[20] The numerous fiestas in Los Angeles were legend; central festivals focused on Holy Week, the Feast of the Assumption, and numerous feasts in honor of Mary. One major fiesta, the Feast of Corpus Christi, was celebrated forty days after Easter, and was described by a contemporary in the following manner: "On Corpus Christi Day, there was a procession around the Plaza. In front of their homes the wealthier families erected altars, many of which were decorated with satin, lace, and even costly jewelry. The procession started from the church after the four o'clock service and halted at each one of the altars in turn for formal worship, the procedure requiring not less than two hours, one feature being twelve men, who represented the apostles, carrying great candles."[21] Most fiestas included bullfighting, dancing, and general feasting, all of which contributed to the general good spirits of the Mexican community. Despite the active fiestas and ceremonies, by the end of the nineteenth century formal religious participation was in serious decline among the Mexican community.

The final two decades of the nineteenth century witnessed the first generation that had to face the reality of being "Mexican in an Anglo society."[22] During this period, the Mexican-American community became socially and residentially isolated from the Anglo community, and relegated to the bottom rung of the socio-economic ladder in California—a process that historian Albert Camarillo has termed barrioization. This barrioization coincided with increasing neglect and isolation from the mainstream Catholic Church in California. By 1900, few Mexicans were attending the formal worship services of the Church. As one historian concludes, "For most Mexican Americans, the Church's symbolic and spiritual meanings were more important than its hierarchy" and formal services.[23] The most important rites of passage—baptism, marriage, Confirmation, and burial—continued to be celebrated in the church, but more daily devotions remained detached from parish life. In Los Angeles, the growing sense of religious isolation felt by the Mexican community from the Anglo community was made complete with the opening of St. Vibiana's Cathedral in 1876. The Hispanic community continued celebrating at the Plaza Church in downtown Los Angeles, while the Anglo community moved to the more fashionable Cathedral Parish. In Santa Barbara, "By the 1880s there was little other than tradition that attracted the Chicanos to the Church. Importantly, after 1883, a Spanish surnamed priest was seldom resident at the parish or mission."[24] In San Jose, no Mexican pastor was appointed from 1852 to 1962 despite the large Mexican community in San Jose.[25]

As the Church entered the twentieth century in California, the history of ministry to the Mexican American did seem to have become "a history of neglect." In 1913, an article in the *San Francisco Monitor* describing the Church's care of the Mexican immigrants was titled simply, "A Sad Story of Neglect."[26] Despite their vast numbers, Mexican Americans have often seemed invisible to the American Church. Their recurrent neglect has been attributed to a chronic shortage of Mexican priests. The Chancery Archives of San Diego, Los Angeles, and San Francisco are full of requests for "Mexican priests" from Mexican-American parishioners.[27] The problem was that few priests were imported from Mexico and priestly vocations from among the Mexican-American community were virtually nonexistent. A common mistake made in the ministry to Mexican Americans was the belief that all that was necessary was Spanish speaking priests. In Los Angeles, the Spanish Vincentians and Spanish Augustinians were imported to minister to the Mexican community. However, a wide gap existed between Spanish and Mexican mentalities. One pastor, in the 1930s, noted that Spanish priests have difficulty in understanding "the psychology, manner, religious feeling, and educational problems of the Mexican."[28] The Spanish priests were often criticized for remaining too aristocratic and aloof. Many Mexican parishioners complained that the Spanish pastor was too "regañon" (too scolding), and too authoritarian.[29] The simple importation of Spanish priests backfired at times because the Spanish priest aggravated the isolation of the Mexican American from parish life.

Central to the "Mexican problem," as it was referred to in Chancery circles, was the inability to develop strong ties between the Mexicans and their parishes. They were repeatedly accused of making only limited economic sacrifices for church maintenance. They seemed content to take over churches built by previous ethnic groups, and showed little interest in the American Catholic passion for building the "parish plant." In addition, pastors from San Diego to San Francisco complained about the infrequency with which Mexicans attended the Sacraments. One pastor noted that for most Mexicans, "confession once in a lifetime is sufficient."[30] Estimates suggest that only 20% to 33% of Mexican Catholics attended Mass regularly. In addition, the Mexican was regarded as uninstructed in his faith and superstitious in his devotional life, and, what was most frustrating to the American clergy, the Mexican American showed little interest in changing. Parish societies achieved limited success, and what parish life did exist was limited to Mexican women. Societies for men were nearly impossible to maintain.

The lack of practicality of Mexican Catholics was of great concern to pastors who feared that Mexican immigrants would be lost to Protestantism. However, although there were over twenty Protestant missions to Mexicans in Los Angeles in 1920,[31] as well as aggressive Protestant campaigns elsewhere, few inroads were made by the Protestants as the Mexican American remained staunchly loyal to the Catholic Church. Lawrence Mosqueda points out that Mexican loyalty to Catholicism was not simply a result of deep piety. To convert to Protestantism meant more than simply adopting another form of Christianity; it meant "denying his heritage, culture and . . . family."[32] Few Mexicans could overcome these pressures. Nonetheless, the presence of small, evangelical Mexican churches created a fear that the Mexican was being "lost" to the Church.

Strategies for ministry differed in northern and southern California, but neither seemed to make the Mexican a practical Catholic. In the north, a separate ministry to the Mexican American was discouraged. As late as 1953, a request by the Mexican community of San Jose for their own parish was turned down. Instead, Our Lady of Guadalupe Chapel was established as a mission of St. Patrick's Parish. The goal of the northern practice was to integrate all parishioners into one parish community. The result was that the Mexican was often forgotten. In mixed parishes, pastors tended to concern themselves with their more regular and financially generous parishioners than they did with their erratic Mexicans. In the south, as many as twenty-four Mexican national parishes and missions were created in Los Angeles and San Diego, but these proved too few to incorporate all the area's Mexicans, and had the untoward effect of creating a less effective ministry to the Mexican community. One observer complained, "Some pastors waive responsibility to the Mexican Americans because of the national parish."[33] In other words, the Mexican Americans were sent to the national parish, despite the fact that not enough Mexican national parishes existed to meet their needs.

Central to the failure of ministry to Mexican Americans was a continual lack of resources, but racial prejudice seems to be another reason for their neglect, or at least for their isolation. A parishioner in San Diego lamented, "We who because we are Mexicans are treated as accursed and despised by him (their pastor) who . . . should defend us."[34] This is not an isolated complaint. In every official report concerning the condition of the Mexican Catholics between 1940 and 1960, racism is acknowledged. Bishop Buddy writes in 1940 that when he opened the parochial schools to Mexican children, "Some American Catholics became enraged to the point of withdrawing their children . . . because they refused to have them associate . . . with Mexicans."[35] And a report on Mexicans in Oakland in the 1950s states that they were "treated as unwanted and unwelcome intruders."[36] Widespread racism reinforced their sense of isolation from American parish life.

As had been the case with previous immigrant groups, at the heart of the "Mexican problem" was a conflict over what it meant to be Catholic. Mexican Americans resisted attempts to be regularized and Americanized. The Mexican faith has thrived on non-liturgical devotions of a popular nature, which have not always been approved by the official Church. Strong among Mexican Americans was their devotion to Mary, especially to Our Lady of Guadalupe. The majority of Mexican churches are devoted to Our Lady. Most Mexican homes maintain small shrines and altars in her honor. The intense devotion to Our Lady of Guadalupe ("La Morenita") developed from Mary's appearance before a young Indian boy, Juan Diego, in 1531 in Mexico. In the guise of an Indian maiden, she offered comfort to a suffering and exploited people: "I am thy merciful mother . . . I shall listen to your sorrows, and free you from all your misery, grief, and anguish."[37] To the Indian and mestizo population, Mary became a symbol of personal dignity against the affronts of the Spanish colonizers. She was not only a religious figure but a national symbol, one who gave birth to the Mexican faith and people. Richard Rodriguez captures the importance of Our Lady of Guadalupe to the Mexican Catholic community: "Above all mediators there was Mary, Santa Maria, the Mother. Whereas at school the primary mediator was Christ, at home that role was assumed by the Mexican Virgin, Nuestra Señora de Guadalupe, the focus of devotion and pride for Mexican Catholics. The Mexican Mary 'honored our people,' my mother would say, 'she could have appeared to anyone in the whole world, but she appeared to a Mexican,' someone like us. And she appeared, I could see from her picture, as a young Indian maiden—dark just like me."[38] The intense devotion to Our Lady made some Anglo clergy fear that Mary had superseded Jesus in Mexican Catholicism. With or without approval, devotion to the Mexican Virgin prospered. Appropriately, one of the most active Mexican religious societies at the parish level was the Sociedad Guadalupana, which attempted to utilize Mexican devotion to Mary as a cornerstone for drawing them into more active participation in parish life.

The Marian devotion served as the basis for many fiestas and processions. (Fiestas and processions remained integral parts of Mexican Catholicism throughout the twentieth century.) One observer of the Mexican community has assessed, "The Mexican Catholic loves ceremonials so much that his life may be said to center around certain Church rites."[39] Particularly popular was the procession and fiesta surrounding the feast of Our Lady of Guadalupe, including the popular Marian ritual called "mañanitas." Here, the people rose early in the morning, arrived at the church prior to the first Mass, and proceeded to "serenade" the Blessed Virgin. The love of procession and ceremonial also informed two traditional Christmas processions, Las Posadas and Los Pastores. In Las Posadas, two parishioners dress up as Mary and Joseph, ride a burro, and lead a procession from house to house in the parish in "search of lodging." The procession ends with a large party. Similarly, in Los Pastores, twelve parishioners dress up as shepherds, and lead a procession from home to home.

The Mexican reluctance to participate in formal parish life has stemmed in part from the strength of the Mexican extended family. The religious socialization of the Mexican child took place largely within the home, as traditional teachings and devotions were passed on within the family. This tradition is called "religion casera."[40] As one observer explained, "The greater part of one's faith life and devotional life is learned from mothers and grandmothers who make use of novenas, prayers, and *imagenes* to communicate the religious sense and to foster a personal and family spirituality. This whole strain of religiosity has been developed without the need for the presence of priests and is generally unrelated to the official liturgical life of the Church."[41] The family nature of religious life is further emphasized by the system of Godparents or "compadrazgo" (literally "co-parenthood").[42] Godparents are chosen for the child's baptism, First Communion, Confirmation, and marriage, making it possible for one child to have as many as eight Godparents. The role of the Godparents is taken as a serious responsibility, which incorporates them into the family in an integral way. Ironically, the functions the Church provided created an even more extensive Mexican family network, which, in turn, increased Mexican distance from the parish.

One last element of the popular religiosity of the Mexican-American community is the celebration of and devotion to "patron saints." Families celebrated the feast days of their patron saint, but the communal celebration of saints' days could also incorporate the family into the life of the larger community. Towns and villages would hold elaborate celebrations in honor of their patron saints. Celebrations might last as long as a week, consisting of "processions, pilgrimages, novenas, triduums, missions as well as fireworks, fiestas, dances and social gatherings."[43] The celebrations did much to develop the spirit of the community. Ironically, in Montecito, the celebration of the town's patron saint's day, which had served to integrate the entire community in the nineteenth century, came to be symbolic of the Mexican community's isolation from the Anglo community. Anglos viewed the celebration as a "romantic diversion," while to the Mexican community it remained an important communal celebration.[44]

Besides being out of touch religiously with the American Church, the Mexican American has found other elements of American culture difficult to accept. The Mexican sense of alienation has been increased by his or her inability to relate to the American work ethic. Nor was the ambition to succeed highly prized. Satisfaction was found in one's family and friends. To outsiders, this was often interpreted as sloth. The lack of initiative made many Anglos assume that the Mexican was best suited for menial labor. Neither did the Mexican family place much emphasis on formal education. Reports in 1929 and 1963 to the Archdiocese of Los Angeles complained of Mexican-American children who came to school or Catechism with little previous instruction in the faith. One report reads, "There are hundreds of little children in the parish who didn't even know God."[45] The Catholic school and the Confraternity of Christian Doctrine (CCD) were seen as "solutions" to the Mexican problem, but Catholic schooling never really took hold to any significant degree, and education remained rooted in the family.

In the 1920s in Los Angeles, under the tutelage of Archbishop John J. Cantwell, a strong push was made to Americanize the Mexican immigrant, a task that was seen as "pre-eminently a Catholic undertaking."[46] Supraparochial organizations, such as the National Catholic Welfare Conference and the Knights of Columbus, organized citizenship classes for the Mexicans. To draw the Mexicans into American life, these groups promoted athletic programs (especially baseball), classes for mothers, and sewing classes and picnics for young girls. The

Knights published a Spanish Language *Civics Catechism,* which discussed the rights and duties of U.S. citizens,[47] and was enormously popular. Despite the intense efforts of Church and civic agencies, few Mexicans filed for citizenship. As a Los Angeles priest observed in the 1920s, "As long as Americans treat Mexicans as an inferior race, under-value their work and mistreat them in general, Mexicans would show little interest in becoming American citizens."[48] Americanization of both a religious and civic nature had also been frustrated by the constant influx of Mexican immigrants. In 1970, 24% of the Mexican population in Los Angeles remained first generation, and the influx of immigrants from Mexico has increased since 1970.

While the Archdiocese of Los Angeles tried to Americanize the Mexican immigrants, it also devoted considerable resources to their temporal and spiritual care. Historian Francis Weber has dubbed Archbishop Cantwell the "Irish born Champion of the Mexican Americans."[49] And, in fact, aside from Archbishop Robert Lucey of San Antonio, Cantwell was one of the few members of the hierarchy who seriously addressed the "Mexican problem." Under Cantwell, the archdiocese sponsored several settlement houses and recreation centers for the Mexican Americans. Several health clinics were set up in the poorer neighborhoods, which primarily benefited the Mexican community. In the 1920s, over 50% of the expenditures of the archdiocese's Catholic Welfare Bureau were devoted to the Mexican community. Despite these efforts, the temporal and pastoral needs of the Mexican remained overwhelming, and Cantwell's efforts were inadequate. To the modern scholar, Cantwell's attitude toward the Mexican may seem too paternalistic, and even somewhat overly concerned with the Americanization of the Mexican immigrant. Despite his efforts, the Mexican remained isolated from the institutional Church. Cantwell's successor, James Francis McIntyre, like his predecessor, spent large sums of money on the Mexican community. McIntyre redirected funds gathered by Cantwell for the construction of a cathedral, and used them to build parochial schools in Mexican parishes.[50]

Another reason for the failure of Mexican Americans to be integrated into the American system is that they had remained at the bottom of the socioeconomic heap. As late as 1970, 77% of the Mexican work force in Los Angeles were among the laboring classes.[51] Reports from Mexican parishes in San Diego in the 1940s, the 1950s, and the 1960s repeatedly refer to the "economic decline" of their parishioners.[52] Little upward social mobility continues to be a problem for the Mexican-American community.

If the urban Mexican has suffered from poverty and neglect, the plight of the rural Mexican community has been worse. In 1940, the Mexican was the most rural of the ethnic minorities (though still over 65% urban). Mexican Americans provided the "backbone of California agriculture," working as migrant and seasonal laborers. In 1942, the "guest worker" or "bracero" program began, bringing in Mexican Nationals to work on California farms. By 1946, 21,000 braceros were at work in California. Ministry to the braceros and to migrant Mexican-American Catholics was nonexistent at times, and at most consisted of a priest occasionally visiting the workers at their camp. Father Patrick Browne of St. Boniface Parish in Anaheim, California, had set up four mission chapels that he tended, to serve the migrant workers in Orange County in the 1920s. Around Los Angeles, the Columban Fathers visited the bracero camps in the 1940s every Friday, praying the Rosary, the litany of saints, and offering the workers a chance to go to confession. In Oakland in the 1940s, Father Charles Philipps, pastor of St. Mary's Parish, took special care of the migrant workers, and inspired four young priests of the Archdiocese of San Francisco—Fathers Donald McDonnell, Thomas McCullough, Ralph Duggan, and John Garcia—into migrant ministry. These four were commissioned by Archbishop John Mitty in 1949 as the Spanish Mission Band.[53] The priests were not attached to any parish, and were given as their primary responsibility the care of migrant Catholics, whose constant mobility and distance from parish centers made ministry to them difficult. The Mission Band was to travel to wherever there were Mexican Catholics, and attempt to re-integrate the migrants into regular parish life. The Mission Band went from Mexican center to Mexican center, giving missions, saying Mass, administering the Sacraments, and so on. Week by week service to the agricultural worker remained irregular.

In 1951, one Mission Band member, Father Garcia, reported his endeavors to the archbishop. Garcia noted several semistable Mexican communities around Richmond and Berkeley, but observed that Mass attendance and knowledge of the faith were low. He cited as causes, "lack of personal contact with priests," a situation caused by language difficulties as much as anything,* and also the large distances Mexicans were required to travel in order to attend Mass. Garcia began a home visitation program, emphasizing the recitation of the Rosary in the home. He complained of financial problems and the need for more personnel. Missions offered in these areas had good attendance (averaging 300 per mission). Garcia then lamented the difficulty of working with the Mexican migrants as they were continually on the move. He reports, "Lately, I have been concentrating more on the camps. Around Brentwood during peak season, lasting about six months, there are about 1,000 men to say nothing of women and children. These are practically all Catholic and there are many more between Brentwood and Stockton, a distance of thirty miles. . . . I have been going to camps in the evenings, saying the Rosary, giving talks, hearing confessions, and saying Mass in the morning before they go to work. . . . Perhaps something could be worked

---

* Garcia's report reiterated the findings of a report made by Father Charles Philipps in 1942. Philipps contended that the American clergy's meagre knowledge of Spanish kept the Mexicans at a distance. While the priest often knew enough Spanish to hear confession, he was unable to offer counsel and advice.

out with other dioceses to keep following the migratory worker. They keep moving from one diocese to the other, yet they still remain Catholic and in need of a priest."[54] In short, personnel, resources, and, above all, planning were needed if the Mexican-American farmworkers were going to be properly cared for.

One effect of the intimate knowledge of the farmworkers' plight gained by the Spanish Mission Band was the move toward a more strident demand for social justice. Protestants had spoken out much earlier about the abuse of Mexican farmworkers in Oregon and California. While the Protestants concerned themselves with social justice and material matters, Catholics had limited their concerns to the spiritual. Even as the mission priests became more political, they were reminded that their tasks were primarily spiritual. Nonetheless, the mission priests became involved in the efforts to provide unions for the farmworkers, and Fathers McDonnell and McCullough testified before state and federal congressional hearings about the abuses perpetrated by the growers and farmowners. The work of McDonnell and McCullough inspired two future United Farm Worker leaders—Cesar Chavez and Dolores Huerta.

The activities of the mission priests brought increasingly hostile complaints from Catholic growers, who saw the priests as "trouble makers" and "rabble rousers." In 1962, the Spanish Mission Band broke up, in part because it had grown too political, in part because it had outlived its usefulness. The end of the Mission Band began in 1959 with the creation of the Catholic Council for the Spanish Speaking for the Archdiocese of San Francisco. The council, realizing the highly urban quality of Bay Area Hispanics, sought to encourage Hispanic ministry at the parish level. The extra-parochial nature of the Mission Band would be terminated; nonetheless, it had done much to alert the Church to the plight of the farmworker. The fruits of its labors would be seen in the Church support of the farmworkers' struggle in the 1960s and the 1970s.

The priests in the Mission Band were also ready to move on. Several had become involved with the *Cursillo* Movement. Begun in Mallorca, Spain, in the 1940s, transported to the United States in the 1950s, and first offered at St. Mary's Parish in Stockton, California, in February of 1961, it made a major impact on the Hispanic community. The *Cursillo* was a three day weekend that provided "in depth discussions" about the "fundamentals of the Christian faith and its relation to the modern world."[55] It was conducted in Spanish and utilized the Mexican culture in getting its point across. The *Cursillo,* it was hoped, would draw back the nonpracticing Mexican Catholic. The movement spread rapidly and was instrumental in the formation of many lay Mexican leaders in the 1960s. The *Cursillo* was translated into English in the mid-1960s, and its influence was no longer confined to the Hispanic community.

In Oregon, the Mexican Americans had become the largest immigrant group in the state. The first migrants began arriving in the 1920s,[56] but concern and care for them did not begin in earnest until much later. In the 1950s, the Archdiocese of Portland began bringing in priests from Mexico to serve the migrant workers during the summer. Over a period of time, Hispanics settled in increasing numbers in Oregon. Thousands more came to harvest the seasonal crops, reaching as many as 20,000 migrant workers in the Willamette Valley alone (1983). In the late 1970s, the archdiocese set up five missions or "quasiparishes," which covered enormous areas. Sunday Masses in Spanish were offered in ten locations each week, but many were still required to travel long distances to attend Mass. The mission also provided various other services to the migrants. One major problem facing the Mexican-American community in Oregon was a "lack of lay leaders," according to one pastor.[57] Though problems remain, current efforts to care for the migrant worker far surpass anything done in the past.

The common perception of the Mexican-American Catholic community between 1962 and 1980 is that it has moved increasingly into the social justice arena. Church support of Cesar Chavez and the farmworkers' protests of the 1960s and the 1970s was seen as a watershed for the relationship of the Church and the Mexican-American community. Unlike many of the more radical Chicano movements, which saw the Church as "irrelevant,"[58] Chavez made explicit use of Catholic symbols and rhetoric. Present at all Chavez's protests was a large banner of the Virgin Mother of Guadalupe. Besides its newly found support of the Mexican farmworker, the Church also became active in neighborhood organizing among the Mexican-American community. As early as the 1940s, the churches in San Jose and Los Angeles had assisted in the operation of the Community Service Organization. In the late 1950s, Our Lady of Guadalupe Chapel of San Jose sponsored the Opportunities Industrialization Center, and, later, the Center for Employment Training.[59] All these groups were locally based self-help organizations.

In East Los Angeles, the Church was instrumental in the formation of the UNO (United Neighborhoods Organization), which is an action group centered in the area's parishes. The Church's support of Chavez and of organizations such as the UNO, as well as various episcopal pronouncements, indicates an increasing commitment to social justice on the part of the Church.

While the Church's more agressive stance has proved attractive to many young Chicanos, the primary problems confronting the Mexican-American community remain the same—a lack of priests who can speak Spanish and a lack of funds to provide for the proper pastoral care of the Mexican community. The pastor of a parish in Riverside, California, expressed a common lament in his annual report of 1975: "The parish is badly in need of an associate; great potential is going down the drain, and what could become an alive Catholic community is becoming another neglected Mexican barrio."[60]

Successful ministry to the Mexican-American Catholic community requires more than just money and priests; it also requires a fundamental restructuring of expectations and a greater acceptance of Mexican culture. Happily, with the appearance of the recent pastoral on Hispanics issued by the U.S. Bishops, which is entitled "The Hispanic Presence: Challenge and Commitment," a more open attitude to Mexican culture would seem to be in the offing. The pastoral challenges Catholics "to be more 'catholic,' more open to the diversity of religious expression." It also encourages study of Hispanic prayer forms and Hispanic culture, an appreciation of the familial quality of Mexican religiosity, and an appreciation of the "popular Catholicism" manifest in the Hispanic community. In short, the pastoral suggests a greater acceptance and tolerance of Hispanic culture and practices,[61] a policy that represents a sharp break with the Church's century-long policy of Americanization.

The shift in Church policy has resulted in some confusion and contradiction. In a recent forum on Hispanic ministry in the Diocese of Orange, the same complaints that have been circulating for over one hundred years once again resurfaced. Participants complained that the Mexican American did not attend the Sacraments regularly, and that Mexican knowledge of the faith was poor. More fundamentally, one speaker complained, "I note a lack of incentive among Hispanics. There is a need to convince them to strive for a better life."[62] Ironically, not long after the forum, the leading spokesman for the Diocese of Orange on Hispanic matters was quoted as saying, "It is the Church's conviction that Latinos should become critical of the Americanization process."[63] The bishops' pastoral warns Hispanic youth of "self-seeking values" and "dreams of success at any price" which seem to be such a fundamental part of the American system.[64] At the heart of the new policy toward the Hispanic community is a new attitude toward what "a better life" consists of. It is no longer assumed that the American way is best. It is now conceded that the American community may learn much from the attitudes and values of the Mexican-American Catholic community. Though this attitude is a long way from being accepted at a popular level, it marks a switch on the part of the hierarchy away from the aggressive Americanization policies that have characterized Church and Mexican-American relations for over a century.

Notes

1. Albert Camarillo, *Chicanos in a Changing Society: From Mexican Pueblos to American Barrios in Santa Barbara and Southern California* (Cambridge: Harvard University Press, 1979); Richard Griswold del Castillo, *The Los Angeles Barrio 1850–1890: A Social History* (Berkeley and Los Angeles: University of California Press, 1979); Richard Romo, *East Los Angeles: History of a Barrio* (Austin: University of Texas Press, 1983).

2. Leo Grebler, et al., *The Mexican American People: The Nation's Second Largest Minority* (New York: The Free Press, 1970), 456–457.

3. Michael C. Neri, "Hispanic Catholicism in Transitional California: The Life of Jose Gonzalez Rubio, OFM (1804–1875)" (Ph.D dissertation, Graduate Theological Union, Berkeley, Cal. 1974); Lawrence J. Mosqueda, "Chicanos, Catholics and Political Ideology" (Ph.D. dissertation, University of Washington, 1979); Antonio Soto, "The Chicano and the Catholic Church in Northern California, 1848–1978: A Study of an Ethnic Minority Within the Roman Catholic Church" (Ph.D. dissertation, University of California, Berkeley, 1978); Patrick McNamara, "Bishops, Priests and Prophecy" (Ph.D. dissertation, UCLA, 1968), and Josephine Kellogg, "The San Francisco Mission Band, 1948 to 1961" (Master's thesis, Graduate Theological Union, Berkeley, 1974).

4. Harry B. Morrison, Report to the Bishop on the History of the Mexican American in California. Archives of the Diocese of Oakland. (Hereafter referred to as ADO.)

5. Thompson, *Growth*, 70.

6. *Ibid.*, 70.

7. Castillo, *Los Angeles Barrio*, 4.

8. Carlos Cortes, "Mexicans" in Thernstrom, *Harvard Encyclopedia*, 711.

9. Castillo, *Los Angeles Barrio*, 169.

10. See Soto, "Chicano in Northern California," 59, 63, 96.

11. "Lo que puede y necesita la raza española en San Francisco" (San Francisco: 1871). Copy in Bancroft Library, Berkeley, California.

12. Neri, "Hispanic Catholicism," 110.

13. Francis Weber, *California's Reluctant Prelate: The Life and Times of the Right Reverend Thaddeus Amat, C.M.* (Los Angeles: Dawson's Bookshop, 1964), 56.

14. Father Blas Raho quoted in Neri, "Hispanic Catholicism," 174.

15. Starr, *Inventing the Dream*, 14.

16. Soto, "Chicano in Northern California," 80.

17. Neri, "Hispanic Catholicism," 136.

18. ADSD. Letter from Bishop Charles Buddy to Apostolic Delegate Amleto Cicognani, February 24, 1940.

19. ADSD. Letter from Bishop Charles Buddy to Cardinal Fumasoni-Biondi, Prefect of the S. Congregation de Propaganda Fide, April 10, 1940.

20. Castillo, *Los Angeles Barrio*, 17.

21. Francis Weber, *The Old Plaza Church: A Documentary History* (Hong King: Libra Press, 1980), 182.

22. Camarillo, *Chicanos in a Changing Society*, 78.

23. Castillo, *Los Angeles Barrio*, 168.

24. Camarillo, *Chicanos in a Changing Society*, 63.

25. Soto, "Chicano in Northern California," 63.

26. "A Sad Story of Neglect," *San Francisco Monitor*, September 20, 1913, 1.

27. For example, a letter in the Parish File for Our Lady of Guadalupe, San Francisco, in the Chancery Archives of the Archdiocese of San Francisco, written by a parishioner to the Archbishop in 1956 states: "It is imperative for us Mexicans to have a good Mexican priest in our Church instead of the actual priest now in charge." This letter is quite typical.

28. ADSD. Parish Files.

29. Soto, "Chicano in Northern California"; 177; also Buddy, ADSD, "Letter to Fumasoni-Biondi."
30. ADSD. Parish Files.
31. G. Bromley Oxnam, *The Mexican in Los Angeles* (Los Angeles: Interchurch World Movement, 1920).
32. Mosqueda, "Chicanos, Catholics, and Political Ideology," 108.
33. ADSD. Parish Files.
34. ADSD. Parish Files.
35. ADSD. Buddy to Cardinal Fumasoni-Biondi.
36. Kellogg, "Spanish Mission Band," 59.
37. Alfredo Mirande, *The Chicano Experience: An Alternative Perspective* (Notre Dame: University of Notre Dame Press, 1985), 123.
38. Richard Rodriguez, *Hunger of Memory: The Education of Richard Rodriguez* (New York: Bantam, 1982), 85.
39. Samuel Ortega, "The Religious Status of the Mexican Population in Los Angeles" (Master's thesis, USC, 1932), 18.
40. Rev. Rigoberto Calcoa-Rivas, "U.S. Hispanics and the Catholic Church," *The Oakland Catholic Voice*, September 26, 1983, 18.
41. *Ibid.*, 18.
42. Castillo, *Los Angeles Barrio*, 97; Rev. George Crespin, "Understanding the Hispanic Family," *The Oakland Catholic Voice*, October 3, 1983, 10.
43. Calcoa-Rivas, "U.S. Hispanics," 18.
44. Camarillo, *Chicanos in a Changing Society*, 63.
45. ADSD. Parish Files.
46. Grebler, *Mexican American*, 457.
47. Romo, *East Los Angeles*, 145.
48. *Ibid.*, 147.
49. Weber, *Cantwell*, 133.
50. Mosqueda, "Chicanos, Catholics, and Political Ideology," 123.
51. Castillo, *Los Angeles Barrio*, 175.
52. ADSD. Parish Files.
53. Kellogg, "Spanish Mission Band."
54. ADO. Parish Files.
55. Soto, "Chicanos in Northern California," 199–200.
56. See Richard Slatta, "Chicanos in the Pacific Northwest: A Demographic and Socioeconomic Portrait," *Pacific Northwest Quarterly*, 70 (1979), 153–162; Erasmo Gamboa, "Mexican Migration in Washington State: A History, 1940–1950, *PNQ*, 72 (1981), 121–131.
57. Ron Karlen, "Church Gears Up To Meet Spiritual Needs of Farmworkers," *Portland Catholic Sentinel*, June 24, 1983, 1, 9.
58. Maxine Sitts, "La Raza Leader Calls Church 'Irrelevant,' " *San Francisco Monitor*, February 3, 1972, 7.
59. Soto, "Chicano in Northern California," 183, 211; Kellogg, "Spanish Mission Band," 94.
60. ADSD. Parish Files.

61. U.S. Bishops, "The Hispanic Presence: Challenge and Commitment," *Origins: NC Documentary Service,* 13 (January, 1984), 530–541.

62. "Hispanic Leaders Express Concerns for Young Adults," *The Diocese of Orange Bulletin,* July, 1983, 7.

63. David Reyes, "In Pursuit of the Latino Dream," *Southern California's Latino Community* (Los Angeles: Los Angeles *Times,* 1983) 14.

64. U.S. Bishops, "The Hispanic Presence," 536.

CHAPTER EIGHT

The Post-Vatican II Parish

Popular wisdom has it that parish life on the West Coast has undergone a profound change since Vatican II. If the new rhetoric is any indication, a new model of the parish has emerged. St. Michael's Parish in San Francisco in the 1970s asserted, "The Church exists to make Christ effectively present as the sign of God's redemptive love."[1] And St. Elizabeth's Parish in San Francisco described its purpose in similarly grand rhetoric: "The vision of Jesus Christ, the vision of the Catholic Church, the vision of St. Elizabeth's Parish is to gather the whole world and therefore that section of the world known as St. Elizabeth's Parish, into a community of Believing People, who will proclaim the Gospel of Jesus Christ and who will love and care for one another, and who will bring the good news of God's saving love to others."[2] The emphasis in parish life had shifted from the provision of the Sacraments and the construction of a parish plant, to a stress on a community of faith that must provide a witness to its faith in God's love through service.

One fundamental change in parish life on the West Coast brought on by the shift in parish focus has been the creation of lay parish councils. Practically every parish in the Pacific states has at least experimented with a parish council since Vatican II. Some parishes erected elaborate structures with a variety of ministries and committees such as religious education, finance, liturgy, social concerns, youth, family life, social events, and so on. In the Cathedral Parish in Oakland, California, St. Francis de Sales, a series of "task forces" are maintained. Each task force has a lay chairperson, who has been elected by the task force members. Each task force member, in turn, represents a specific ministry. For instance, the Religious Education Task Force is made up of representatives from adult education, Sunday school, grade school programs, sacramental preparation, and the catechumenate, along with several others. Overseeing all the task forces (religious education, community action, liturgy, administration and finance, youth, senior citizens, and social events) is a general chairperson, a lay man or woman who has been elected by the entire parish. The chairperson presides over the "executive committee" of the parish council, which is made up of the chairpersons of the various task forces, and the Cathedral staff. Each task force operates with a great deal of autonomy in creating parish programs in its specific area. The adult education committee determines which topics adult education will examine; the community action task force determines which social justice concerns the parish will pursue; and the liturgical task force plans the weekly Sunday liturgy. The pastor maintains a loose control over the entire parish council, but generally allows his task forces to run the parish. (Of note in this regard, St. Francis attracts a highly educated white-collar congregation that comes mainly from outside the parish's territorial boundaries. Inside the boundaries, the parish is poor, transient, black, brown, and elderly, and faced with typical inner-city problems. The freedom and the responsibility granted the task forces attract people from throughout the Bay Area.)

At the opposite extreme is the parish council that merely serves as a rubber stamp for the pastor. In other words, the council is mere window dressing, with authority remaining in the rectory. For instance, in a transitional parish in East Oakland, a parish council exists, but the resident pastor, an aging monsignor who has been at the parish for decades, is in complete control. The parish council can advance only what it knows to be the monsignor's desires, and the monsignor can thwart programs on the basis of personal whim. Though this style of leadership is generally associated with an older, entrenched clergy, a recent phenomenon on the West Coast is the appearance of a "new clericalism," in which young priests are adopting the older trappings of priestly authority, which had been abandoned in the decade after Vatican II. The new clericalism provides interesting problems for the future of lay initiative and clerical authority.

In the middle ground, between the task force model and the clerically controlled parish, is the parish which has a lay council that works in close cooperation with the pastor, where give and take is the rule. At a large suburban parish in Orange, California, the parish is divided into twelve geographic regions. Each region is named after an apostle, and each has a lay couple serving as community leaders and representatives to the parish council. These representatives are appointed by the pastor. Each regional leader hosts social events, home Masses, and is required to provide workers for different parish functions and services. The twelve couples have free reign in the social arena but are merely consultants when it comes to crucial parish decisions. Nonetheless, the laity is consulted prior to most parish decisions, though the pastor has the final word.

Increased lay participation has not always been successful or greeted joyfully by pastors. One San Diego pastor lamented in 1974, "I have allowed the council to lie dormant until parishioners do more study: some wanted to run the parish, make decisions, dictate policy without any work and without any Christianity."[3] Inner-city parishes faced with a highly transient population found stable lay leadership difficult to attain.

The laity was not always the problem. Some pastors refused to relinquish any authority, which created conflicts with an increasingly militant laity. A letter from a parish in San Francisco to the archbishop attacked the resident pastor as "not being right for the parish." He was "more a divisive factor than unifying." The pastor used his position "not in a fatherly and kind way but with the old, negative 'only I know best' attitude."[4] The letter went on to urge the pastor's removal for his sake and the sake of the parish.

The pastor in the post-Vatican II parish has remained the central authority, but his authority has been more subtle. Despite the shift to greater lay participation, the pastor remains the chief determinant of a parish's spirit. This is true whatever the setting—rural, urban, or suburban. In the six Washington and Oregon parishes selected for the sociological field studies of the Notre Dame Parish Life Study, each field report reflects the pastor's importance. Where the laity is given a great deal of power in the decision-making process, this power is dependent upon the pastor, and could just as easily be revoked by a less flexible priest. In Sacred Heart Parish, Battle Ground, Washington, 1977 to 1983 were years of conflict with the parishioners attributing "the majority of conflict to a recent priest." The pastor had had continual confrontations with various parishioners and used the parish council as a scapegoat. As a result, the report notes, "In recent years, the parish had problems recruiting people to run for the parish council or any other leadership position." With the removal of the pastor, and the arrival of one who was more flexible, "many reported an increased sense of parish community."[5] Similarly, in St. John Vianney Parish, Kenmore, Washington, the parish experienced discord as a result of the associate pastor who had several "personality clashes with the laity" that resulted in alienating many parishioners.[6] In both cases, lay involvement depended on an appropriate style of pastoral leadership. Where the pastor exercised his authority arbitrarily, lay involvement and the parish spirit lagged. Where the pastor involved the laity, parish spirit flourished.

At the other extreme is Sacred Heart Parish, Tekoa, Washington, a rural parish that shares its pastor with the neighboring community of Rockford (he alternates weeks between parishes). The parish maintains an active parish council, which organized and developed various parish committees, and drew up the year's budget while its pastor was absent. One field reporter assessed enthusiastically, "This is not the type of parish where the pastor's theological or liturgical positions/preferences might create debilitating conflict."[7] The reporter's statement curiously neglects the recent history of the parish. The other field report on Sacred Heart notes, "Until the mid-1970s, the parish was low in membership and enthusiasm; and since the mid-1970s enthusiasm and lay involvement have been on the increase. The parishioners charted most of these changes by the *presence or absence of a particular priest*"[8] (emphasis mine). The field report also tempers the reported autonomy the laity enjoys; "Though the church is organized and run by the laity" (the reporter notes), it does so only "with the blessing of the priest."[9] The implication is clear—lay involvement and power depend on the current pastor.

The norm for lay involvement, vis-à-vis the pastor, is represented at St. Michael's Parish, Snohomish, Washington, and St. Thomas More Parish, Spokane,

Washington. In each parish, there is an active parish council with active lay committees, which contribute significantly to the life of the parish. In both parishes, however, "the priest is the center of the decision-making process."[10] In both cases, the pastor recruits the lay leaders, and then gives them significant amounts of freedom and responsibility. The leaders in one parish report, "Father gives them a lot of freedom with their programs, and he does not try to make their decisions."[11] However, in the assessment of the field reporter at St. Thomas More, "The priest has either direct or indirect influence in every major decision made in the parish."[12] The case of St. Thomas and St. Michael points up an important lesson in modern pastoral leadership—while the pastor retains ultimate control, he must do so subtly, giving his lay leaders the sense that they are being listened to and that their efforts and observations do have impact in parish policy. Pastoral leadership that attempts to ignore lay participation in the decision-making process runs the risk of depressing parish spirit. At the other extreme, the pastor must support and direct the laity, or the parish may drift aimlessly. An example of the latter case is St. John Vianney Parish, Kenmore, Washington, where the pastor adopted a "laissez-faire" administrative style. "He does not want to interfere with the decisions made by the parish council or his staff, and he does not want to be held responsible for their decisions."[13] The result was continual conflict between committees, contradictions and duplications in policies and tasks, and a general parish aimlessness. Again, what St. John's points up is the need for effective pastoral leadership, without robbing the laity of its initiative and enthusiasm.

What all the parishes demonstrate is that a definite shift has taken place in what people expect of a post-Vatican II pastor. Prior to Vatican II, the successful pastor was often the one who was sympathetic to his people's needs and who used subtle machinations to direct his parish; however, a stereotype that often recurred depicted the pastor as an absolute authority who ruled his parish arbitrarily and unilaterally. It was the duty of the parishioners to put themselves in line with their pastors, not vice versa. In the post-Vatican II era, with the heightened rhetoric of the laity's "co-responsibility" in Church affairs, a pastor may still use his authority arbitrarily, but he will now face stiff opposition and unrest among his parishioners, or his unhappy parishioners will simply attend another parish. The pastor is now expected to consult his parishioners prior to important parish decisions. The stereotype of the domineering pastor is a thing of the past even if the reality is not. The pastor must at least make his parishioners feel that they are being listened to. What has occurred is a dramatic shift in the way people expect pastors to manage their authority.

Beyond the rhetorical impulse and behind the shift in pastoral authority is the practical reality of fewer priests. As the number of priests continues to decline, the laity will be required to bear more and more of the responsibilities of parish life. The shortage of priests has already had significant impact on rural parishes in the West, where many no longer enjoy the luxury of a resident pastor. Rural Sacred Heart Parish, Tekoa, Washington, shares a priest with neighboring Rockford. As pointed out earlier, Sacred Heart's lay council planned the annual parish budget, and managed much of the day-to-day functions of the parish. Another alternative proposed as a solution to the lack of priests is the appointment of women religious as administrators of parishes. The Diocese of Spokane already has one sister who is operating as a "full-fledged pastor and another who is co-pastor with a priest."[14] The Bishop of Oakland has announced that the shortage of priests will make it impossible for him to provide a resident pastor for each parish and that a woman religious will be sent to administrate parishes. If the decline of priests continues, it is inevitable that more and more responsibility will be bestowed upon lay parishioners.

LITURGY

The most noticeable change in post-Vatican II parish life has been the liturgical renewal. Manifestations of renewal have been varied, and include Mass in the vernacular, reduction to one hour of the pre-Communion fast, greater stress on community participation in the liturgy symbolized by having the priest face the congregation during the Mass, the sign of peace and the prayer of the faithful, reception of Communion in the hand, face to face confession (now called the Sacrament of Reconciliation), increased celebration of the Sacrament of the Anointing of the Sick (no longer called Extreme Unction and no longer reserved for the dying), communal penance services and liturgies, the introduction of a Saturday evening Mass that satisfies the Sunday obligation, the introduction of folk and guitar Masses, baptismal ceremonies incorporated into the format of Sunday Mass, lay Eucharistic ministers, female extraordinary ministers, lay lectors, and so on. Besides greater communal participation in the Sacraments, an emphasis was placed on providing the laity with a better understanding of the Sacraments. This shift is particularly evident with baptism and Confirmation. Most parishes require the parents of prospective baptismal candidates to attend several classes of instruction before their child is baptized. One result of this has been later baptisms, indicating a revision of the popular theology of infants and salvation. For instance, a parish calendar in Eugene, Oregon, in 1907, expressed a typical viewpoint, "Parents must not delay to have their children baptized. A newborn infant while unbaptized is under the power of darkness."[15] Limbo belongs to the pre-Vatican Church. In a similar vein, Confirmation in many parishes has been pushed back to 16 years of age, so that the confirmands can be better instructed and have a clearer notion as to what they are committing themselves. Greater emphasis is placed on what the Sacrament is, and on what its symbols mean. Conservative Catholics lament that the overemphasis on understanding robs the

Sacrament of its essential mystery. Another result of the emphasis on understanding is that the celebrant spends much of his time during the sacramental ritual explaining different symbols and procedures, thereby robbing the ritual of much of its impact. The notion that the impact and efficacy of the Sacrament is not dependent upon total understanding is often overlooked.

Historically, what is most significant about the post-Vatican II Church is the shift from an emphasis on the Rosary-novena, non-liturgical devotion of the 1950s to a stress on Scripture and liturgy in the 1960s. In rhetoric typical of the post-Vatican II Church, St. Dominic's Parish in San Francisco asserted, "The most important events at St. Dominic's are the liturgical celebrations of the Sacraments."[16] The old devotions continue in many parishes, particularly where the parish population is elderly. In some parishes, the old novenas have been updated to bring them into conformity with the elusive "spirit of Vatican II." At St. Gabriel's Parish in San Francisco during the 1960s, a "social action thrust" was given to the traditional novena.[17] At St. Boniface German Parish in San Francisco, the traditional daily Rosary was offered for "peace and justice" (1971). At Holy Redeemer Parish, Portland, Oregon, old devotions were given a "new scriptural and liturgical form."[18] Overall, the post-Vatican II parish on the West Coast has witnessed a marked decrease in non-liturgical devotions.

In most parishes, a generational conflict appears to have developed in regard to the adoption of the new liturgy. At Star of the Sea Parish in San Francisco, the pastor reports that while children and young adults are enthusiastic about face to face confession and Communion in the hand, less than 25% of the older parishioners receive Communion in the hand, preferring to receive it on the tongue, and that even fewer take advantage of face to face confession.[19] At Holy Redeemer Parish in Portland, the elderly parishioners were disgruntled by the new scriptural and liturgical novenas. As the parish historian reported, "A reduced collection ($1,050 to $600) suggested the people's lack of enthusiasm with the new format."[20] In 1967, however, the same parish instituted a folk Mass that attracted participants from all over the city of Portland, resulting in "standing room only." What is especially significant in terms of the future of the Church is that young people who are now college age or slightly older have known no other Church than that of post-Vatican II. To these Catholics, the devotions of the 1940s and 1950s seem strange and mysterious, or remain something their mothers might observe. To this generation, there is no "crisis of change." Whereas to the older generation, the Church might seem to be teetering on the brink of destruction, to Catholic youth the Church remains bright with promise.

One of the major new forces in parish life in the 1960s and 1970s was the parish liturgical committee. This lay committee plans the weekly and other special liturgies. Its responsibilities range from selecting appropriate music for the liturgy and providing lectors for the readings, to providing an "offertory family" to bring up the gifts to the altar at the offertory (besides bread and wine, other symbolic gifts, as well as the Sunday collection, are brought to the foot of the altar). In all, the liturgical committee lends itself to greater participation of the laity in the planning and execution of the liturgy.

One offshoot of the liturgical committee has been various kinds of Masses. One parish may offer as many as four or five different types of Masses that appeal to the varying sensibilities of its parishioners. For instance, it might have a folk Mass aimed at its teenage flock, as well as a more staid mass with traditional hymns and a more subdued tone and quality for its elder parishioners. Or, a special children's liturgy might be planned, or a family oriented Mass. Many parishes maintain the equivalent of what used to be called the High Mass in which the parish choir leads the singing. In addition to the various styles of Masses, those which celebrate various folk traditions have become popular. Black culture and Hispanic culture Masses have all become familiar occurrences in post-Vatican II parishes on the West Coast.

St. Julie's Parish, San Jose, California, serves as a good example of the new parish. Founded in 1974, the very familiarity of its name indicates a new spirit. St. Julie's is in the heart of an expanding, high-technology area, and maintains a white, educated, middle-class clientele, as well as a large number of Spanish speaking parishioners. As the parish historian asserts, "The 'new' liturgy is 'old' to this parish."[21] The original five Masses called for two folk Masses, and one Mass in Spanish. The rhetoric and impetus of the new parish are thoroughly post-Vatican II, stressing communal participation, experience, and understanding. This is how the religious education program for children is described: "Lessons are not merely training in religious presentation, but are experiences aimed at deepening the children's appreciation of their faith and liturgy."[22] A teen program entitled J.O.Y. (Jesus Over You) attempts to give young adults the "same type of experiential insight." In the first year of the parish, a liturgical committee called the Parish Worship Committee supervised the community's liturgies, including one for children. "Through it, the youngsters were helped to understand the joy and the love of the Eucharistic celebration and enter into other forms of community prayer, each according to his or her own age."[23] Besides a children's liturgy (which is held once a month), twice-a-month paraliturgical prayer services (non-sacramental) are prepared for first, second, and third graders. The liturgy planning commission is at the heart of St. Julie's. "Worship in a parish community is at its best when it is planned and carried out by those who share in congregational praise and thanksgiving to God."[24] Each month, the liturgical committee meets to discuss the scriptural readings for the following month's Sunday Masses. A scriptural theme is planned for the Sunday Mass, to be presented through "music, visual aids, the homily, and other elements of the celebration of the Mass."[25] The committee writes thematic introductions to the various parts of the Liturgy of the Word, as well as preparing petitions for the Prayer of the Faith-

The Post-Vatican II Parish

ful and a meditation after Communion. St. Julie's is typical of the new liturgical emphasis on community and experience.

NEW CONCERNS IN THE 1960s

Besides the liturgical revolution, the post-Vatican II parish has become increasingly concerned with matters of social justice. Specific issues such as poverty, racial discrimination, war, and peace began to occupy the attention of parish groups much as they did Catholics at a national level. In the Archdiocese of San Francisco in the mid-1960s, the majority of parishes established social justice committees, to direct parish social justice activities. At St. Peter's in San Francisco, an anti-poverty program was begun, featuring a job procurement plan.[26] In Portland, Holy Redeemer devoted specific Sundays to the raising of people's awareness of such problems as hunger and poverty. The Sundays were dubbed "Hunger Sunday" and "Poverty Sunday" (1975).[27] Inner-city parishes increasingly concerned themselves with social action programs as their constituencies became predominantly poor, minority, and elderly. In many California parishes, social justice committees focused on the attempt to unionize California farmworkers by Cesar Chavez, and the ensuing boycott of grapes and lettuce. Parish committees publicized the boycott, as well as providing spiritual and material supports to the striking farmworkers. In the 1970s, appealing to a more conservative constituency, parish Right to Life groups became increasingly active in their opposition to abortion, sponsoring constant picketing of abortion clinics and other such activities.

The increased social awareness of the parish community was not only directed outward toward the society, but also was focused inward toward the disadvantaged inside the Church. Special programs were developed for the handicapped, shut-ins, the sick, and the elderly. Special lay Eucharistic ministers were commissioned in many parishes to carry the Eucharist to people who were in hospitals or otherwise unable to attend Mass. The Marian Visitors (not to be confused with the Legion of Mary) flourished in several parishes, having as their apostolate the visitation of the sick and elderly. The 1960s and the 1970s saw an increased awareness of the plight of the elderly. When St. Paul's parish in San Francisco established a Senior Center in the 1960s, it was only the second parish in the city to do so.[28] As the divorced Catholic population grew, support groups for divorced and widowed Catholics grew also. All these groups had traditionally been neglected by parishes and left to the care of individual families. Now they became parish concerns.

The 1950s had seen the growth of many family enrichment programs within the Church. With the 1960s, the Christian Family Movement had begun to decline, but by the early 1970s a new family movement was thriving—Marriage Encounter—a retreat weekend for couples that stressed the need for openness between marriage partners. The 1970s saw many other family programs created; one of the most interesting was family First Communion. Rather than receiving his or her First Communion with the traditional First Communion class, the child received it with his or her family. Religious education, in general, came to stress the need for parental participation in the religious socialization of their children.

The two most popular spiritual movements in the 1960s and the 1970s were the *Cursillo* Movement and the Catholic Charismatic Renewal. The *Cursillo,* the short course in Christianity, was a retreat for adults, made once in a lifetime, but whose spirit is perpetuated by recurrent follow-up meetings of *cursillistas.* In keeping with the "spirit" of Vatican II, the *Cursillo* stresses the "experiential" side of faith. Similarly, the Charismatic Renewal centers around parish groups that pray for the Holy Spirit to bestow on them the gifts of the Spirit. Part of the process entails experiencing a "second birth" that is called being "slain in the Spirit." Here, again, the emphasis is on personal spirituality, not social justice commitment. The Charismatic Renewal has enjoyed enormous popularity throughout the West Coast.

Though all three movements—Marriage Encounter, *Cursillo,* and the Charismatic Renewal—draw on parish communities, their ties to the traditional parish have been tenuous. The emphasis of the three groups has been on personal spirituality and personal renewal as opposed to parish spirituality and parish renewal (though the latter often benefits from the former). All three groups are supra-parochial, with diocesan and national structures informing and directing the movements. For instance, the Charismatic Renewal in southern California is guided by the Southern California Renewal Conference (SCRC), which provides literature and organizes conferences and days of renewal in an effort to provide cohesiveness to the movement. Equivalent organizations exist throughout the Pacific states, and several dioceses have appointed priests or commissions to oversee the movement in that diocese. *Cursillo* and Marriage Encounter have been introduced to parishes in the Pacific states from the outside. The central event for both groups is a weekend retreat that draws participants from many different parishes. The leadership is not grounded in the parish and looks beyond parish life. The parish is the location for Marriage Encounter and *Cursillo* "follow-ups" and support groups, but even these follow-ups draw participants from several neighboring parishes. Moreover, these groups look to the movement's leaders for direction, not their pastors. At St. Michael's Parish, Snohomish, Washington, the field report observes that the parish Marriage Encounter group operates "independent of priest and parish council."[29] The same is often true of *Cursillo.* In all three cases, Marriage Encounter, *Cursillo,* and the Charismatic Renewal, there is a danger of creating an "elite" group, which, while providing impetus and support to many parish activities, may also be the source of many parish conflicts.

This divisive quality was particularly true of the Charismatic Renewal in the early and mid-1970s and may account for the need to appoint diocesan directors and clerical moderators. Charismatics, who had undergone baptism in the Holy Spirit, felt that it was their duty to direct parish life. Those outside the movement resented what they perceived as the "arrogance" of the charismatics—conflict often ensued. For many traditional Catholics, the Pentecostal style of Catholic charismatics was troublesome. One observer noted, "They clap their hands and sway while in song, they cry while praying with uplifted hands, they shout out 'hallelujahs' during the sermon and occasionally they speak in the 'tongues of the Holy Spirit.' Except for the manner in which Communion is administered at the end of the service, it could easily be mistaken for a Pentecostal service."[30]

The basic unit of the Charismatic Renewal is the prayer group, but a hallmark of the movement since its earliest days has been large gatherings of charismatics from a wide area. In Los Angeles in the early and mid-1970s, Loyola-Marymount served as the center for a Wednesday Mass and prayer meeting that was attended by as many as 1,000 charismatics. Blessed Sacrament Parish in Orange County hosted large Friday night meetings. In East Los Angeles, a group called "Charisma in Missions" holds monthly meetings at the Olympic Auditorium, which attracts between 5,000 and 7,000 Catholics. Again, the impulse here is to transcend parish boundaries, often making charismatic attachment to the parish tenuous. The Charismatic Movement boomed in the Pacific states in the early and mid-1970s, but its overall popularity has waned in recent years. The movement has become increasingly popular with Latino Catholics. As of 1982, 140 Spanish-speaking charismatic prayer groups are in the Archdiocese of Los Angeles alone. The ever increasing number of Latinos in the Pacific states suggests that the Charismatic Renewal will remain popular for at least the next several years in California.

Another area of concern for the parish has been ecumenical outreach. Spurred by the "spirit of Vatican II," parishes have attempted to establish bonds with their "separated brethren," as the Protestant churches were often called in an earlier era. Many parishes joined with non-Catholic Churches for ecumenical prayer services, particularly around Thanksgiving and Christmastime. In the Archdiocese of San Francisco, a week of prayer for Christian Unity is observed in January, marked by numerous interfaith services. Overall, joint prayer services have become common events. In a number of parishes, congregations have exchanged pulpits—Protestant ministers are invited to give sermons at Catholic parishes with Protestant churches reciprocating by opening their pulpits to Catholic priests. For instance, at St. Francis de Sales Parish in Oakland, the neighboring Baptist minister gives a sermon once a year at St. Francis Church, and the St. Francis priest returns the favor for the Baptist congregation. In addition, once a year each congregation attends Sunday service at the other's church. Many of the ecumenical efforts place their emphasis on explaining the various traditions and on stressing what is common between the faiths. In the Diocese of Orange, several parishes host an annual "progressive ecumenical dinner," in which a different course is served at each church. Prior to the course being served, the host church briefly explains its traditions. Despite the various efforts, for most parishes on the West Coast, ecumenical concerns remain peripheral and have not yet penetrated the parish deeply. The most common ecumenical occurrence is the "ecumenical" wedding service, in which both a Protestant minister and Catholic priest witness the couple's marriage vows. This practice has become quite common.

The area of greatest cooperation between Catholic parishes and Protestant congregations has been in community and social services. Catholic and Protestant have increasingly joined in "non-denominational" programs that contribute to the common welfare of their community. In the early 1970s in San Francisco, many parishes actively supported the "Summer of Love" program, which provided day camping for Catholic and non-Catholic inner-city youth. In Tekoa, Washington, Sacred Heart Parish and the local United Church of Christ both contribute to a "joint emergency fund for the community."[31] In Santa Ana, California, the Southwest Community Center is supported by various Christian Churches, which take turns in providing for the center's soup kitchen. In these and many other parishes, Catholics have strayed outside the parish fold to assist in ecumenical projects that provide community service. Though ecumenical inroads remain limited, the Church has made major strides, considering that as late as the 1950s it was considered dangerous for a Catholic to even attend a Protestant service.

The concerns of the post-Vatican II Church are somewhat balanced between social justice issues and an increasingly personal, experiential style of spirituality. In most parishes, the older, more traditional parish groups, such as the Altar Society, the Men's Club, the PTA, and various devotional groups, continue to plod on, but without the fanfare of the newer movements.

CATHOLIC EDUCATION IN THE POST-VATICAN II PARISH

The 1950s had been a time of enormous parochial school building and expansion. The period between 1960 and 1980 brought a virtual freeze to that expansion. In Oregon, while the number of parishes increased by nineteen, the total number of parish schools declined by twenty. In Washington, the number of parishes increased by forty-four but the number of parochial schools declined by eight. In California, parochial schools increased by thirty-six, but did not keep pace with the increase of 154 parishes during the same period.[32] The rapid increase of the 1950s was over. During the same period (1960 to 1980), enrollment in CCD programs declined in the major archdioceses of Los Angeles, San Francisco, and

Seattle.[33] The only area committed to the building and sustaining of new parish schools was the newly developing suburban parishes. More and more inner-city parish schools were closed, as their former parishioners fled to the suburbs. The inner-city school became the preserve of blacks, Hispanics, and other "new" immigrant groups who were either unable or unwilling to foot the bill for the separate school system. The irony is that in some inner-city parishes, non-Catholic students outnumbered Catholic students. The Church is faced with tough decisions in the inner city. If the schools are closed, the Church may be accused of abandoning the inner city and its poor; on the other hand, is the enormous expense needed to keep the schools open worth it?

The crisis of the schools has been brought on by more than a demographic shift. Vatican II had an unsettling effect on women religious, the foundation of Catholic education in the West. As late as 1960, women religious provided better than 67% of the Catholic teaching force in California, Washington, and Oregon (ratios of 2:1, 2:1, and 5:2, respectively). By 1980, with the sisterhood in serious disarray, lay teachers made up over 70% of the Catholic teaching force, with lay outnumbering religious 5 to 1 in Washington, 2 to 1 in Oregon, and 3.5 to 1 in California.[34] The impact of this shift meant more than the turning over of the religious socialization of the children to the laity. The increase in Catholic school budgets, as a result of paying for a lay faculty, is the single biggest increase in the parish budget in the post-Vatican II era. When the schools were run by the teaching sisters, the sisters were paid only nominal wages, allowing the Catholic schools to run for practically nothing in terms of salaries. With the increased presence of lay teachers who required a "living wage," school budgets soared. For most schools, teachers' salaries became their single largest expense.[35] The result has been that Catholic school teachers have received less than adequate wages, as pastors wrestled with the psychological adjustment of expending the required amounts of money on the school. To perpetuate the separate system of Catholic schools will require a major financial commitment, which many parishes may be unwilling to make.

Another cause for the freeze in Catholic school expansion has been the stress on adult education since Vatican II. Catholic educational concerns had long focused on children at the expense of adults. As more and more emphasis was placed on the parents' role in the religious education of their children, it also became necessary to provide continuing education for adults. Many had not progressed beyond the childhood notions of the faith they had learned in grade school; adult education sought to provide parents and adults with a more mature understanding of the faith. A debate has ensued—should the limited resources of a parish be put toward grade school or adult education? Most parishes have sponsored various adult education courses on such topics as sacramental life, the Church's social teachings, Church history, canon law, family life, and so on. In a number of parishes, adult study clubs have developed around a variety of topics. In any case, the new stress on adult education represents a shift from the child centered parish of the 1950s to a more adult oriented parish in the 1970s.

THE DEMOGRAPHIC SHIFT: THE INNER CITY AND SUBURBAN PARISH IN THE 1970s

The 1960s and the 1970s witnessed the development of two distinct types of parish—the inner city and the suburban. Catholics continued to climb the economic ladder, so that by the 1960s a distinct Catholic middle class existed. With Catholic economic success came the attendant flight from the city to the suburb. As the older ethnic groups, such as the Irish, Germans, and Italians, moved out, newer ethnic groups moved into the inner city—Mexican American, black, Asian, and Filipino. The inner city also had a large elderly population, people who were "trapped" there by escalating rents. Other elderly people had lived in the inner-city all their lives and were not about to move. The inner-city parish, then, became an interesting blend of the new ethnics, the elderly, the down-and-out, and the transient. Inspired by the social justice concerns of the post-Vatican II Church (oftentimes, even prior to Vatican II), it committed itself to a dizzying variety of apostolates, including providing housing for the homeless, the elderly, and the handicapped, soup kitchens, recreational programs for inner city youths, etc. The parish was forced to confront the problems of inner-city life—alcoholism, violence, poverty, and despair. In addition, with a predominantly poor working-class parish, and with more successful parishioners having departed, the inner-city parish was in a constant state of financial crisis. Fund-raising once again became central in Catholic parish life—not for the brick and mortar programs of previous years, but for bread and butter programs. Devotionally, many inner-city parishes maintained the traditional life popular in the 1950s, as a high percentage of parishioners were elderly, and still adhered to the old practices. In addition, the new ethnic groups were more devotionally than liturgically oriented.

An example of modern inner-city parish life is St. Patrick's in downtown San Francisco. Originally an Irish parish, it is now predominantly Hispanic, Filipino, and elderly. St. Patrick's ministries involve direct charity—each month the parish gives meal tickets to over 1,200 men. Lodging is provided for the homeless in two nearby "hotels," and clothing is distributed to those who need it. Approximately half of St. Patrick's $57,000 yearly budget is expended on "people needs." The parish is funded by the generosity of former parishioners and other benefactors. It has had the benefit of one wealthy "guardian angel" who has picked up the parish deficit to the tune of $10,000 a year. The parish has a core of about 250 families who carry on the normal rounds of parish life. The Legion of Mary is active in the parish, primarily providing home visitation to the elderly.

One branch of the Legion of Mary has named itself "Our Lady of the Inner City" and seeks to inspire Marian devotions in the heart of the city. For its young families, the parish sponsors a "well baby" clinic and a day care center. A teen club named "Pag-Asa" (which means hope in Tagalog, the language of the Philippines) emphasizes singing: singing at Mass and at senior citizens' centers.

The senior citizens of the parish are provided with a number of programs. In the early 1970s the parish, in conjunction with the St. Vincent de Paul Society, sponsored a monthly outing for the elderly. This program has been discontinued because of a lack of funding. More significantly, the parish, assisted by government subsidies, constructed a low cost housing project for the elderly and handicapped. The parish also provides senior citizens with interest free loans. Spiritually, the parish remains very traditional. St. Patrick's is the only parish in the city to offer a Latin Mass. Statues of patron saints, novenas, and Benediction of the Blessed Sacrament remain popular. Tuesday noon Mass is followed by devotions to the Blessed Virgin. In addition, the noon Mass is well attended by downtown office workers from the nearby business district. In all, St. Patrick's represents a typical inner-city parish, providing for the social needs of its parishioners, while continuing to provide the traditional spiritual and devotional life.[36] The problems confronted by St. Patrick's are encountered in all the major urban centers on the West Coast—Los Angeles, San Diego, Oakland, San Francisco, Seattle, Spokane, and Portland, as well as smaller cities.

In the suburbs, life was quite different. Finances remained a worry, but for the more traditional reason of funding a complete parish plant. The suburban church's financial basis was much more secure. The parish school continues to be central to the suburban parish.

At St. Thomas More Parish in a suburb of Spokane, Washington, the field reporter observes, "The school is the definite rallying point of parish life."[37] In addition, CCD programs seem to be most active in suburban parishes. At Sacred Heart Parish, Battle Ground, the field reporter cites the CCD program as one of the activities around which the parish "revolves."[38] Many of the new suburban parishes are populated by young, upwardly mobile, Catholic couples who are just beginning their families. The field reporter at St. John Vianney Parish, Kenmore, Washington, observes, "The parish is young and filled with children."[39] As a result, time and energy are focused on "youth" activities, children's liturgies, (such as those described at St. Julie's in San Jose), and the like.

School organizations, such as the Men's Club, Women's Club, and the PTA, continue to center their attention on the child and school. However, the suburban parish is "modern" and its parishioners are deeply imbued with the spirit of Vatican II. Social services, such as care of the elderly, the poor, and minority groups, are attended to as a matter of course. Adult education classes and lectures are frequently offered, though attendance is sporadic.

Lay involvement in the suburban church is high, but many times involvement is limited to a small elite of parishioners. One drawback of the suburban parish is its large size, making relationships between clergy and parishioners somewhat distant. One outcome has been the creation of the "filling station mentality."[40] Parishioners come to the church to receive various Sacraments, to be refueled, but they remain on the periphery of parish life. The central problem of the suburban parish remains that of inculcating in its parishioners a sense of community; bonds of ethnicity and ghetto Catholicism (that is, unity brought on by a hostile culture) no longer pertain, and nothing has yet filled the gap. In the atomized void of modern suburbia, the Church must forge a unity of many diverse and private individuals.

A typical suburban parish is St. Charles Borromeo, Tacoma, Washington. Founded in 1956, St. Charles is the largest parish in Tacoma, consisting of 1,627 families as of 1983. It was established in response to young families who had moved to the suburbs. The parish plant is typical of the large, suburban parish, consisting of church, grade school, junior high, gymnasium, convent, rectory, and "hundreds of square feet of black topped parking lots."[41] In 1983, the parish was made up primarily of young, well-to-do professionals. Baptisms outnumbered funerals in 1982 by more than three to one. One observer noted, "The focal point of parish life is the school."[42] The parish school has few financial problems. Ninety percent of the eighth graders go on to a college prep school, Bellarmine. A recently completed school fund drive, called PEP—the Parish Education Plan—"asked school families to donate to the school the difference between what it cost to educate the child and what they were actually paying (donations are tax deductible, tuition isn't)."[43] Older parishioners were asked to "adopt a child" from a low-income family and pay his or her tuition. As with most suburban parishes, community spirit has been slow in coming. Nonetheless, thirty different groups are operating in the parish, ranging from the St. Vincent de Paul Society to Bible study groups to Cub Scouts. But for all the diverse activity, the parish remains disjointed. It enjoys a large number of lay volunteers who act as Eucharistic ministers and lectors, take Communion to the sick and elderly, and provide marriage education courses. Unlike the inner-city parish, the devotional life is more modern, with greater emphasis placed on the liturgy and on lay involvement in the liturgy.

One recent development that has had significant consequences for both the suburban and inner-city parish is the rise of what are called "magnet parishes." These are parishes that attract people from beyond their territorial boundaries, people who are unhappy with their own parishes for one reason or another—the pastor is too autocratic, liturgies are tedious, the parish has few activities, etc. A suburban parish may attract scores of young people as a result of a lively folk Mass, while an inner-city parish may draw socially concerned parishioners to its social justice activities. Elderly parishioners may be attracted to parishes that have maintained the old traditions. In any case, magnet parishes are on the rise, particularly among suburban Catholics who are seemingly less connected with their neighborhoods and communities than inner-city Catholics. Traditionally, Newman Centers attached to secular colleges and universities have attracted "progressive" Catholics from neighboring parishes. St. Andrew's Newman Center, attached to the University of California, Riverside, was in continual conflict with its neighboring parish, which accused the Newman Center of stealing its parishioners. However, now the phenomenon of the magnet parish is no longer limited to Newman Centers. In Oakland, the Cathedral Parish is located downtown in the midst of a neighborhood that is predominantly Black, Hispanic, transient, and elderly. A high-rise for the elderly is located right down the street from the parish, and in the plaza, directly in front of the church, the transient and homeless are ever present. While blacks, Hispanics, and the elderly are represented in the parish, a large number of parishioners are white, middle-class, educated Catholics who have been attracted from neighboring city and suburban parishes. The open democratic style of the parish, innovative liturgies, and effective preaching draw Catholics from throughout the area. The increase of what Andrew Greeley has termed "communal Catholics"—that is, Catholics who are selective in the aspects of Catholicism they accept or reject—will make magnet parishes a common phenomenon in the upcoming years. The pastoral implications for both inner-city and suburban parishes are enormous.

THE NEW IMMIGRANTS

The demographic shift of the 1960s and the 1970s consisted of more than the urban-suburban relocation. In 1965, a liberal federal immigration law was passed overturning the national origins' quota system that had governed U.S. immigration since 1924. Immigrants from European countries were no longer given special preference, and millions poured into the United States from Asia and the Western Hemisphere countries, with many settling on the West Coast. Between 1970 and 1980, California received 1,868,000 new immigrants,[44] giving it the largest foreign born population of any state in the Union,[45] and causing one wag to dub California the "new Ellis Island." The new immigrants came, not from Ireland, Germany, and Italy as in the old days, but from Vietnam, Korea, China, Cambodia, Laos, the Philippines, Nicaragua, El Salvador, Costa Rica, Honduras, Guatemala, and, above all, from Mexico. (Close to half of the immigrants to California in the 1970s came from Mexico.) Like the old immigrants, the new ones settled predominantly in urban areas.

Of special concern to the Catholic Church on the West Coast was that 70% to 75% of the new immigrants were Catholic. Mexico, the Central and South American countries, and the Philippines were all nations where over 90% of the populace were Catholic. Even the Vietnamese refugee immigrants, who began arriving in large numbers after the unhappy conclusion of the war in 1975, were largely Catholic (surprisingly, over 40%, a disproportionately high number, considering that Vietnam had been less than 10% Catholic). This is explained by the fact that the majority of Vietnamese immigrants to America had also migrated from North to South Vietnam after the Communist takeover of the North in 1954. These immigrants were mainly Catholic and staunchly anti-Communist. Their move to America was their second migration experience.[46]

The enormous influx of new immigrants presented the Church in the Pacific states with enormous pastoral problems. Once again, it has had to accommodate a wide variety of cultures and styles of Catholicism. The Church has answered the pastoral problem once more by providing priests who speak the immigrants' language, or who are immigrants themselves, to minister to the communities. When necessary, special missions are established for a specific group, but for the most part the new immigrants are provided care through the traditional territorial parish. The Vietnamese Catholic community, which has grown significantly in Orange County, Los Angeles, San Francisco, and Portland, was fortunate in having a significant number of priests join their flight to America. These priests now minister to their own countrymen. A priest in Orange County observes of the Vietnamese, "We don't have many faith problems here in Orange because the Vietnamese priests are here to say Mass, hear confessions, and even teach the young to sing Vietnamese songs."[47] Other new immigrant groups have not been as fortunate and the perennial problem of finding enough foreign language priests remains a pressing problem for the Church in the Pacific states.

Ministry to the new immigrants is also complicated by the large number who have entered the country illegally. Of the 900,000 Mexicans who entered California in the 1970s, over 70% did so illegally.[48] Many more illegals have arrived from Latin American countries, with an estimated 60,000 in the San Francisco Bay Area. The illegals live in constant fear of being deported, are mercilessly exploited, and live near or below subsistence level. Ministry to this group remains difficult, and presents a major challenge to the Church in the Pacific states in the 1980s.

While the Church and the new immigrant groups continue to face many of the same problems that previous groups encountered, the social and ecclesial environments in which these problems will be encountered have changed dramatically. The rise of the new immigration coincided with one of the most turbulent decades in American history. Historian Philip Gleason writes of the decade between 1965 and 1974, a period rocked by the Vietnam war, civil rights protests, race riots, and Watergate, "The decade witnessed a severe weakening of confidence in the American system—in the principles on which it was based, in the integrity of those who espoused such principles and in the efficacy of its institutions."[49] The loss of confidence in America made the system dubbed "Americanization" seem a dubious policy to employ in relation to the new immigrants.

This attitude was reinforced by the ethnic revival of the 1970s in America, which stressed pride in one's distinctive ethnic heritage. Americanization was viewed as an attempt to force the immigrant to conform to a suspect WASP culture, and so was to be rejected.

While American society was undergoing a profound shift, American Catholicism was similarly being transformed. By the 1970s, the Catholic Church in America and on the West Coast had come of age, casting off its compulsive need to prove its compatability with and loyalty to American ideals, while growing increasingly critical of American society. In addition, the Vatican Council II had stressed a new openness toward cultures, and the "spirit of Vatican II" demanded a reassessment of the Church's relation to the new immigrants. As a result, the old Americanization model of immigrant assimilation was replaced by "cultural pluralism" as the new paradigm for accommodating immigrant groups within the Church and within society. In their recent pastoral on Hispanics, the U.S. Bishops clearly articulated the new policy: "Respect for culture is rooted in the dignity of people made in God's image. The Church shows its esteem for this dignity by working to assure pluralism, not assimilation and uniformity, as the guiding principle in the life of communities in both the ecclesial and secular societies. All of us in the Church should broaden the embrace with which we greet out Hispanic brothers and sisters and deepen our commitment to them."[50] "Broadening the embrace" was not limited to Hispanics, but was to be offered to all the new immigrant groups. The broader embrace entails a new respect for folk customs and popular devotions. Unity and understanding between peoples was to be stressed, not uniformity. The Church was to be a "community of communities."

St. Andrew's Parish in the Archdiocese of San Francisco is offered as a textbook example of cultural pluralism in action by the archdiocese's resource book for ethnic ministry. Located in Daly City, the parish consists of a variety of new immigrant groups. In order to promote greater understanding of and between the various cultures and nationalities present in the parish, a Cultural Exchange Committee was formed consisting of twenty-two parishioners who represent eight different nationalities. The Committee's Mission Statement, drawn from the work of Father Virgil Elizondo, proclaimed, "We want to create . . . a church that will not only accept but welcome difference." The resultant diversity would ultimately "come together joyfully in the unity of the Fatherhood of God."[51] The committee then planned a series of liturgical and social events, designed to reflect the history and culture of the different immigrant groups. In one year, the parish sponsored five different ethnic celebrations and information nights, including Flores de Mayo (Filipino), Guadalupe Fiesta (Mexican), Polynesian Night (Samoan), Honduran Information Night, and Octoberfest (Polish, northern and eastern European). Each celebration was intended to provide parishioners with a greater knowledge of their co-parishioners' culture, and to create a spirit of harmony and cooperation between all the ethnic groups in the parish.[52]

Unfortunately, the reality of seeking to attain unity, while allowing for the greatest cultural diversity, has often resulted in parish conflict and disharmony. Some parishioners are jealous of the special treatment the new immigrants receive. Others complain that the new immigrants remain too separate from parish life and tend to form a parish within a parish. Even within ethnic communities, conflict continues over how best to adapt to life in America. The Filipino community in San Francisco has clashed over the place of a popular Filipino devotion in the life of the parish. The Filipino pastor wishes to de-emphasize the devotion and accompanying festival, claiming that it prevents Filipinos from entering mainstream American Church life, while the devotees argue that the devotion provides unity for the Filipino community. Conflicts will continue as long as the Church on the West Coast espouses a policy of openness and non-coercion toward all its ethnic groups.

Despite the conflicts, the post-Vatican II Church in America and on the West Coast is committed to a new policy toward its immigrant communities—cultural pluralism, not Americanization, is the order of the day. The new openness of the Church will be put to the test in the next decades as new immigrant communities continue to grow and develop.

One final problem the Church on the West Coast will face is the presence of an intense anti-immigrant feeling, a feeling expressed by elements in both the Catholic and non-Catholic communities. The new immigrant groups come primarily from Asia, Mexico, Central and South America, and the West Coast has a long tradition of hostility toward these peoples. Beyond their different customs and manner of speaking, the darker skin of the new immigrants will easily separate them from white America and subject them to racism, American style. An equally insidious attitude is prevalent among older immigrant groups, who now consider themselves "American." These people seem to have forgotten their immigrant past, and espouse the simplistic (and inaccurate) dictum, "My people made it by themselves, why can't they (i.e., the new immigrants)?" The attitudes of racism and forgetfulness provide major challenges to effective Church ministry to the new immigrant groups of the 1980s.

Notes

1. AASF. Parish Files.
2. AASF. Parish Files.
3. ADSD. Parish Files.
4. AASF. Parish Files.
5. Roger Finke, Field Report—Sacred Heart Parish, Battle Ground, Washington (Notre Dame Parish Study, 1983).

6. Roger Finke, Field Report—St. John Vianney Parish, Kenmore, Washington (Notre Dame Parish Study, 1983) 5.

7. Michael Ball, Field Report—Sacred Heart Parish, Tekoa, Washington (Notre Dame Parish Study, 1983) 7.

8. Roger Finke, Field Report—Sacred Heart Parish, Tekoa, Washington (Notre Dame Parish Study, 1983) 5.

9. *Ibid.*, 6.

10. Roger Finke, Field Report—St. Michael's Parish, Snohomish, Washington (Notre Dame Parish Study, 1983) 5.

11. *Ibid.* 5.

12. Roger Finke, Field Report—St. Thomas More Parish, Spokane, Washington (Notre Dame Parish Study, 1983). 5.

13. Finke, St. John Vianney, 7.

14. Ball, Sacred Heart, 3–4.

15. *St. Mary's Catholic Church, Eugene, Oregon, Twentieth Jubilee History* (Eugene, 1907).

16. AASF. Parish Files.

17. AASF. Parish Files.

18. *The Story of Holy Redeemer Parish, Portland, Oregon, 1906–1981* (So. Hackensack, N.J.: Custombook, 1981).

19. AASF. Parish Files.

20. *Holy Redeemer*, 185.

21. *St. Julie's Parish, San Jose, California* (So. Hackensack, N.J.: Custombook, 1976). n.p.

22. *Ibid.*, n.p.

23. *Ibid.*, n.p.

24. *Ibid.*, n.p.

25. *Ibid.*, n.p.

26. AASF. Parish Files.

27. *Holy Redeemer*, 185.

28. *St. Paul's SF*, n.p.

29. Finke, St. Michael's, 5–6.

30. Julio Moran, "Latinos Renewing Bonds with Religion" *Southern California's Latino Community*, 106.

31. Finke, Sacred Heart, Tekoa, Washington, 2.

32. *Official Catholic Directory 1980*.

33. *Ibid.*

34. *Ibid.*

35. AASF. Annual Financial Reports.

36. Robert Mendeica, "Salvation in the Inner City," *Columbia Magazine* (March, 1975), 13–19.

37. Ball, St. Thomas More, 2.

38. Finke, Sacred Heart, Battle Ground, Washington, 3.

39. Finke, St. John Vianney, 5.

40. Du Bois, "The Church in Tacoma," 19.

41. *Ibid.*, 13.
42. *Ibid.*, 13.
43. *Ibid.*, 19.
44. "Review of The Fourth Wave: California's Newest Immigrants," *Wilson Quarterly*, 8 (1984), 47.
45. Bryant Robey, *The American People* (New York: E. P. Dutton, 1985), 103.
46. Mary Bowen Wright, "Indochinese" in Thernstrom, *Harvard Encyclopedia*, 510.
47. Julie Sly, "America's Vietnamese: Preserving Their Heritage in a New Land," *St. Anthony's Messenger* (February, 1985), 36.
48. "California's Fourth Wave," 47.
49. Philip Gleason, "American Identity and Americanization," in Thernstrom, *Harvard Encyclopedia*, 55.
50. U.S. Bishops, "The Hispanic Presence," 531.
51. McGuire, "Light of Nations," C-7.
52. *Ibid.*, C-7, C-8.

CHAPTER NINE

Conclusion: New Concerns, Old Verities

The Irish immigrant who arrived on the West Coast in 1850 seeking gold encountered a vastly different world and Church than the Mexican who arrived in 1980 seeking to become part of the ever elusive American Dream. From the scattered Spanish missions in California to the struggling mission churches in Washington and Oregon, a Church of enormous wealth and power has emerged whose presence is evident by the number of impressive church structures dotting the Pacific coast. Besides its obsession with building the complete parish plant, the major task of the Church in the Pacific states has been the assimilation of a wide diversity of peoples and cultures. The primary institution in the assimilation of this diverse flock has been the parish.

As the Church in the Pacific states deals with the 1980s, one of its primary undertakings remains the assimilation of its latest wave of immigrants, (as evidenced in the last chapter). The Church's treatment of one group of immigrants—those from Nicaragua, El Salvador, Guatemala, Honduras, and other Latin American countries, who have entered the United States illegally, fleeing their strife-ridden countries—is symbolic of its new stance in relation to American society. The Latin American immigrants have been denied political refugee status by the United States government, despite the reality that returning to their countries might mean death, and would certainly involve suffering. In light of this reality, a number of parishes on the West Coast have joined the growing movement that provides the illegal immigrants with sanctuary—protection from immigration officials, a place to live, and material and spiritual sustenance. Though threatened with legal action by U.S. Immigration officials, these parishes have risked caring for the immigrants. What is significant here is not just the care of the immigrant. More importantly, the Sanctuary Movement is a knowing violation of U.S. law, and indicates a rejection of the present U.S. Central American policy. Participation in civil disobedience by entire West Coast parishes represents a major break with the pre-Vatican II parish, which limited its vision to spiritual concerns and avoided politics at all costs. The post-Vatican II parish is no longer so worried about proving its loyalty to America, and some parishes now knowingly set themselves up in direct conflict with the stated policies of the U.S. government. The shift in concerns is reflected at the national level in the U.S. Bishops pastorals on peace and on the economy, which are both highly critical of present U.S. society.

Despite the new attitudes toward American society, and the broadening vision of the parish, the more mundane tasks of providing pastoral care for the latest influx of immigrants remain, and will remain, a major concern of the Church in the Pacific states throughout the 1980s.

At the same time, the Sanctuary Movement suggests that a new agenda has been presented to the parish in the post-Vatican II era. Symbolic of the shift in priorities since Vatican II was the extended controversy over the building of a new cathedral in San Francisco. After St. Mary's Cathedral burned down in 1962, Archbishop Joseph T. McGucken began an aggressive fund-raising campaign for a new cathedral. By 1965, however, the building of magnificent churches, once an unquestioned part of parish life, had been brought under close scrutiny. Historian James Gaffey describes the San Francisco Church as split into two factions—those "who would first nourish and clothe the body" and the "institutional leadership which would create a feast for the soul."[1] Opposed to the cathedral were those who believed the money that had been raised should be used to assist the poor, arguing that a large and expensive church building was a scandal to the poor and the oppressed. Mexican leader Cesar Chavez wrote, "We don't ask for more cathedrals; we don't ask for bigger churches or fine gifts. We ask for the Church's presence among us. We ask for the Church to sacrifice with the people for social change, for justice, for love of brother."[2] The pastoral agenda of the Vatican II parish differed dramatically from that of the nineteenth century Church, which saw the building of large churches as a sign of respectability in America.

In a similar situation in Los Angeles, Cardinal James Francis McIntyre faced protests for building St. Basil's Church at a cost of $4 million as a showcase for the archdiocese. On Christmas Eve of 1979, a group of Chicano Catholics calling themselves "Catolicos por la Raza" led a candlelight march against the cardinal, which turned into a violent encounter with police and FBI agents. The Chicanos' complaint—abundant money was available for church buildings but none for social programs. Both the San Francisco and Los Angeles incidents indicate a new model of the Church emerging. Many now sought to create a Church that emphasized people and service rather than pride in its buildings. The shift went beyond the simple question of how resources were to be allocated. New concepts, such as the "shared responsibility of the laity," "fiscal accountability," and the right of priests and laity to protest ecclesial abuses, came to the fore. Though, as of 1980, these concepts remain far from achieving universal application, they do represent a new rhetoric of what people increasingly expect the Church to be.

One final element that will influence parish life in the 1980s is the increasing presence of massive diocesan and archdiocesan bureaucracies. In all the major dioceses, centralization has increased to the point that parishes are inundated with directives, programs, and appeals from the central office. In some dioceses, as many as ten "second" collections are undertaken in the parish for the benefit of the diocese. Many pastors have opposed what they see as a desire for increased control and systemization stemming from the Chancery Office. The difficulty of increasing centralization is that it ignores the genius of parish life, which is to respond to its unique problems at a pragmatic level. Parish community must grow intrinsically; it can not be imposed from outside or from the top down.

Despite all the changes in parish life, despite all the new apostolates and rhetorical imperatives, the task of the parish remains essentially the same: to provide its people with solace and understanding in the face of suffering and death, to assist families in raising their children, to provide community in the midst of an increasingly isolated society, and to participate in celebrating its peoples' joys and triumphs—births, weddings, Confirmations, etc. The parish is still the fundamental institution through which most Catholics encounter and practice their religion, and it is the chief institution in determining their satisfaction or disaffection with the Church. A recent study by Andrew Greeley and the National Opinion Research Center has concluded, "Warm images of God, Jesus, and Mary are typical of persons within a church community. 'Cold' images characterize the feelings of those persons who are estranged from the Church. . . . The more that the Church is seen as 'mother'—warm, welcoming, comforting, affectionately strong—the more those who have left the Church will want to return."[3] Historically, and at the present moment, it has been and continues to be through the parish and the community of love, which the good parish creates, that most Catholics have and will experience the Church as "mother." It is in the creation of such warm and loving parish communities that the future success of Catholic life on the West Coast resides.

Notes

1. James P. Gaffey, "The Anatomy of Transition: Cathedral Building and Social Justice in San Francisco, 1962–1971," *Catholic Historical Review,* 70 (1984), 84.
2. *Ibid.,* 72.
3. Andrew Greeley, et al., *Young Catholics in the United States and Canada* (Los Angeles: Sadlier, 1981), 31.

For Further Reading

Though few books deal specifically with parish life, I have chosen the following books for their insight into religious life in the Pacific states in general.

R.A. Burchell, *The San Francisco Irish, 1848–1880* (Berkeley and Los Angeles: University of California Press, 1980).

Albert Camarillo, *Chicanos in a Changing Society: From Mexican Pueblos to American Barrios in Santa Barbara and Southern California* (Cambridge: Harvard University Press, 1979).

John T. Dwyer, *Condemned to the Mines: The Life of Eugene O'Connell, 1815–1891, Pioneer Bishop of Northern California and Nevada* (New York: Vantage Press, 1976).

James P. Gaffey, *Citizen of No Mean City: Archbishop Patrick Riordan of San Francisco* (Wilmington, N.C.: Consortium, 1976).

Deanna Paoli Gumina, *The Italians of San Francisco, 1850–1930* (New York: Center for Migration Studies, 1978).

John B. McGloin, *California's First Archbishop: The Life of Joseph Sadoc Alemany, O.P., 1814–1888* (New York: Herder and Herder, 1966).

Kevin Starr, *Inventing the Dream: California Through the Progressive Era* (New York: Oxford University Press, 1985).

Henry L. Walsh, *Hallowed Were the Gold Dust Trails: The Story of the Pioneer Priests of Northern California* (Santa Clara: University of Santa Clara Press, 1946).

Francis J. Weber, *Documents of California Catholic History* (Los Angeles: Dawson's Bookshop, 1965).

Francis J. Weber, *John Joseph Cantwell: His Excellency of Los Angeles* (Hong Kong: Cathay Limited Press, 1971).

Francis J. Weber, *California's Reluctant Prelate: The Life and Times of Right Reverend Thaddeus Amat, C.M. (1811–1878)* (Los Angeles: Dawson's Bookshop, 1964).

APPENDIX
The Hawaiian and Alaskan Parishes

The Hawaiian and Alaskan parishes reflect rather different development from parishes in California, Oregon, and Washington. Both Hawaii and Alaska have only recently been admitted to the United States, and though contemporary parish life is not radically different from the other Pacific states, both states were primarily missionary endeavors until well into the twentieth century. For that reason, Hawaiian and Alaskan parishes will be treated separately and presented in this chapter.

THE HAWAIIAN PARISH

Catholicism was introduced to Hawaii in 1827, seven years after the first Protestant missionaries had arrived on the islands. For much of the nineteenth and early twentieth centuries, Hawaii remained a mission country. In the early days, successful evangelization in Hawaii depended on gaining the favor of the native tribal leaders, a task that eluded the earliest Catholic missionaries. In 1831, Catholic priests were banned from Hawaii. In 1839, religious liberty returned and so did the Sacred Hearts Fathers (SS.CC.), who would be the primary evangelizers on the Hawaiian Islands. Protestant "correctness" had caused Protestantism to lose favor with the tribal chiefs, who came to prefer the Catholic priests who allowed them to smoke, drink, wear leis, and, most importantly, allowed them to enjoy their traditional luaus. In 1843, the Cathedral of Our Lady of Peace was erected in Honolulu. The cathedral would serve as the central parish in Hawaii for the next three-quarters of a century.[1]

Regular parish life in Hawaii was not established until well into the twentieth century. During the missionary period, a central parish would be established on each major island, from which the missionary priest would make his way from village to village, celebrating Mass, baptizing, instructing, and providing the other Sacraments. On the main island, Oahu, all the priests lived at the cathedral rectory until the mid-1920s, servicing the other "quasi-parishes" from the cathedral. No other parish had a resident pastor until 1908.

The period between 1850 and 1880 was a time primarily of missions to the native tribes, an endeavor that brought about the inevitable conflict of Western priest and native culture. In 1857, a missionary priest, Father Roualt SS.CC., tried to establish one central parish on the Island of Hawaii, to which people from all the villages would come, thereby freeing him of the need to visit each small village. The result: no one came to Mass, and Father Roualt once again found himself riding from village to village to celebrate Mass in grass huts. On a typical missioner's day, the morning was spent at the central parish celebrating the sacred devotions, instructing the children in doctrine, receiving people with problems, and visiting the sick. Then, in the afternoon, he would visit two villages.[2] The spread of faith was slow, and never took much hold among the native Hawaiian population. By 1926, Hawaiians accounted for only 14,830 of the 105,000 Catholics in Hawaii.[3]

Two elements of Catholic life did appeal to the native population. First, the Hawaiians participated enthusiastically in the singing at the various rituals and liturgical celebrations. One missionary claimed that he "could always rely on the Hawaiians to enhance the divine services by their beautiful singing of polyphonic Masses as well as the Church's plain chant," and "There was nothing the Hawaiians liked better than to sing God's praises on all occasions."[4] The songs were often Western in origin. On Christmas eve of 1899, the congregation sang "Alma Redemptoris Mater." Second, the major celebration of the Hawaiian Church was the Corpus Christi procession. The celebration began with Mass, followed by a procession of the Blessed Sacrament, and then Benediction. The religious ceremonies were followed by a festive luau. The Corpus Christi celebration successfully merged Hawaiian cultural traits with Catholic worship. Other devotions were less successful. The Sacred Hearts Fathers particularly pushed the devotion of perpetual adoration to the Blessed Sacrament, but it never enjoyed widespread popularity.

The role the laity has played in the history of the Hawaiian Church is also instructive. As the missions had few priests, great responsibility was placed on the laity, particularly in the outlying islands. On the Island of Hawaii, a "league of catechists" was formed of the laity to instruct the faithful in the absence of the priest. More radically, the Catholic faith was introduced to the Island of Maui exclusively by lay preachers, not by priests. The lay catechists were sent out after having been instructed by Sacred Hearts priest, Father Bachelot. The catechists would not perform baptisms, however. They would instruct the people, then present their catechumens to the priest for examination and baptism. Significantly, the chief catechist was many times a woman, and various women assumed the role of unofficial "prophetesses." The faith preached by these "prophetesses" was quite traditional; one advised, "Quit sinning, receive the Sacraments, and pray the Rosary."[5] The other main function left to the laity was the building of the church, often done while the priest was gone. Overall, the laity was integral to the spread of faith in Hawaii. One historian notes, "History records . . . lay participation in the beginnings of all parishes."[6]

The limited success in numbers among the Hawaiians is tempered by the fact that the native Hawaiian population suffered a severe loss of population after the whites arrived. By 1900, the Hawaiian race had declined severely. The decline was the result of disease, immigration, and "a lack of the will to live."[7] The imposition of Western culture, epitomized by the overthrow of the native monarchy, and the establishment of a planter's republic in 1895, dealt a death blow to the native Hawaiian culture, and indirectly to the native population.

Hawaiian society and the Hawaiian Catholic Church began to change most drastically in the 1880s, with the boom in the pineapple and sugar industries. As these industries grew, immigration rose. Native Hawaiians resisted working on the plantations so the work fell instead to Chinese, Portuguese, and Filipino immigrants. The influx of immigrants provided the Catholic Church with a host of new problems, and effectively changed the face of Hawaiian Catholicism. By 1926, the two major groups of Catholics in Hawaii were the Filipinos, who numbered 48,000 or 45% of the entire Catholic population, and the Portuguese, who numbered 27,170 or 28% of the total Catholic population.[8] The pastoral care of these groups became the main concern of the Hawaiian Church. In 1903, a Portuguese priest was commissioned from San Francisco to minister to the growing Portuguese population. In the early 1900s, sermons in Honolulu were being preached in Hawaiian, English, and Portuguese.

Ministry to the plantation workers operated in a manner similar to the mission "quasi-parish" system. Each plantation formed its own community and maintained its own chapel. Each plantation was tended by a circuit riding priest. Again, heavy responsibility was placed upon the laity in the maintenance of the Catholic community.

The Filipino community presented an interesting problem for the Church. Filipino Catholics arrived in Hawaii poorly instructed in their faith and with little practice in observing Church law. The Filipinos did have their children baptized and confirmed. Moreover, like the native Hawaiians, the Filipinos loved processions and celebrations. The Filipino community was also enthusiastic in its celebration of Mass for its departed relatives, and saints, making some clergy uneasy about the apparent "ancestor worship."

The missionary quality of Hawaiian Catholic life made the establishment of Catholic parochial schools somewhat precarious. By 1930, only eleven of thirty-three parishes maintained their own schools, and, by 1950, only eighteen of fifty-one parishes had schools,[9] rising to twenty-five of sixty-one by 1960. Here, as elsewhere, parochial education depended on the efforts of religious orders of brothers and sisters.

In 1941, the missionary status of Hawaii was lifted, and the Diocese of Honolulu officially erected. Parish life became more stable, particularly in Honolulu. Nonetheless, by 1950 mission chapels still outnumbered regular parishes fifty-nine to fifty-one. As regular parishes were established, the traditional parish organizations began to appear. By 1940, such societies as Catholic Women's Aid, the Young Ladies' Institute, the Young Men's Institute, the CYO, Sodalities of the Blessed Virgin Mary, Holy Name Society, Sacred Heart League, and various ethnic societies had come into existence. By 1956, the Confraternity of Christian Doctrine was established in Hawaii, and, by 1960, 27,613 students were being educated.

The 1940s and the 1950s also witnessed the growth of the American military presence in Hawaii. Holy Family Parish was devoted entirely to military personnel, and was a mission until 1950. By 1955, a parochial school was operating, as well as a Sodality to Our Lady of Good Counsel, an altar society, a Holy Name Society, and, by 1960, a CCD program. The military parish reflected the typical development of a mainland parish.

Parishes in Hawaii in 1980 face many problems similar to Catholic parishes in the other Pacific states. Immigration has continued in the 1970s with large groups of Samoans, Filipinos, Koreans, and Vietnamese Catholics entering the Islands. By 1980, 85% of all Catholics lived on the islands of Oahu and Hawaii (over 70% on Oahu, where Honolulu is located).[10] The missionary quality of Hawaiian Catholicism has lessened with sixty-four parishes with resident pastors and only thirty-six mission stations; twenty-eight of the sixty-four parishes (44%) now maintain parochial schools. Diocesan priests are still greatly outnumbered by religious order priests (112 to 43), but the number of diocesan priests is increasing while the number of order priests is decreasing. The 1970s also witnessed the introduction of the various changes occasioned by Vatican II. In 1974, a Korean Mass was instituted for the Koreans, a Spanish Mass for the Hispanics, and, in 1975, a Hawaiian sung folk Mass was begun. Other organizations like the CYO and pro-life groups continued to expand, and newer groups such as *Cursillo* and Marriage Encounter were introduced.

As the Hawaiian parish confronts the 1980s, it will face problems similar to those discussed in the general section on the post-Vatican II parish.

THE ALASKAN PARISH

The Catholic Church in Alaska remains the youngest and most missionary of the Catholic Churches in the Pacific states. Historian Vincent A. Yzermans writes as late as 1979, "In Alaska, the Catholic Church is still a young and primitive church."[11] The youthfulness of the Alaskan Church reflects the youthful quality of the Alaskan populace—as of 1980 the median age for Alaskans was 22. As of 1980, Alaska registered only ninety-seven churches to care for its 39,678 Catholics. Catholics make up only 9.9% of the total population and 32.1% of all church members.[12] Mission parishes and mission stations continued to outnumber parishes with resident pastors, sixty-nine to forty-nine.[13] The vast majority of Catholics live in the three major urban centers—Anchorage, Juneau, and Fairbanks, where regular parish life has been established.

The early apostolate in Alaska was undertaken exclusively by the Jesuit order. Like other mission parishes, Alaskan missions were confronted with the usual mission problems: chronic shortage of priests, large distances for the priests to travel, poor communications between mission outposts, and, in the gold mining frontier towns, the usual "laxity of morals." One pastor described his congregation of the early 1900s in the following manner; his congregation was made up of "indifferent, non-practical, or apostate Catholics . . . a queer congregation. . . . One more hopelessly corrupt and unmanageable it would be difficult to find."[14] In eastern Alaska, the quality of Catholic life was little better. Of the town named Wrangell, one pastor wrote that of the 500 townspeople, 200 were Catholic "whether they knew it or not."[15] Despite the drawbacks, by 1917, the Alaskan Church had developed around twenty-five stable mission centers that operated as "quasi-parishes."

Where stability was provided, Alaskan parishes developed along lines similar to other parishes in the Pacific region. The absence of priests left lay parishioners with a good deal of responsibility, particularly in terms of raising funds for church building. Alaska, too, reflected the Catholic penchant for building the complete parish plant, and, as a result, fund-raising was also a common feature of Alaskan Catholic parish life. By 1895, the parish in Juneau, then the "metropolis of Alaska," maintained a church, a rectory, a school, and a hospital. In Fairbanks in 1905, two entertainments were sponsored to raise money for the new church. At St. Joseph's Parish in Nome, an Altar Society was formed by 1903 (two years after the parish was established), and the society hosted a series of banquets, balls, and entertainments. In Alaska, as elsewhere, fund-raising and building provided the focus of Catholic parish life.

An interesting aspect of Alaskan parish life in the nineteenth century was its ecumenical bent. St. Rose Parish in Wrangell reported working closely with Protestant groups. At St. Joseph's Church in Nome, a Miner's Home Club was established in 1903. The club was open to Catholics and non-Catholics alike, and sponsored a reading club, lectures, games, and entertainments. The club flourished in the early 1900s until the arrival of a less flexible pastor. The new pastor established separate Catholic societies, such as the Catholic Library

Club, to protect Catholics from Protestant influence. Nonetheless, the isolated quality of frontier life in Alaska often gave rise to *de facto* ecumenism.

The largest native ethnic group serviced by the Church in Alaska was the Eskimos. The first permanent mission center for the Eskimos was established at Mary's Igloo, just north of Nome in the early 1900s. Nome became the center of Eskimo mission activity, as it served as home base for Father Bellarmine La Fortune, S.J., the premier missionary to the Eskimos. La Fortune was critical of attempts to "domesticate" the Eskimos, and sought to preserve their culture through a separate parish structure for Eskimos. As he put it, "We do not at all want to make white people out of the natives."[16] In Nome, separate Eskimo parish organizations were established, such as the St. Joseph's Society, which attempted to improve the spiritual and temporal circumstances of the Eskimo. Regular Catechism classes were held at the various mission centers, using the *Baltimore Catechism* as the basic textbook. Complete separation was never entirely achieved. The Eskimos had their own choir, and the 7 A.M. Mass was for them, but whites were not excluded. Still, the more detrimental elements of white culture were avoided. In 1925, the Native Building was open for native dancing to counteract the Hunter Saloon Dancing Hall, where "the scum of the white population" congregated. Whites were welcomed, but had to agree to the house rules of "no boozing" and "no familiarities between the sexes."[17]

The Eskimos were described as an "intensely superstitious" people,[18] who were attracted to the rituals of the Catholic Church. One sociologist has pointed out the confluence of Eskimo and Catholic values. "A greater harmony exists between Catholic and Eskimo values than between traditional Eskimo values and the success ethic."[19] The Catholic stress on responsibility to others and the mitigation of self meshed well with the communal values of Eskimo culture. Also, the worth of the person was not defined in terms of achievement, but in terms of personal qualities. Beyond these communal values, the Eskimo culture remained largely premodern. La Fortune described his parishioners in the following manner: "My people are good, but they don't know the meaning of discipline. Their clock is the sun . . . they confess at all hours of the day. The women come to church with babies on their back. The men and women are dressed in typical Eskimo fashion, and they have no fear whatever of kneeling at the Communion rail next to a white lady dressed in silk."[20]

The Eskimo parishes did provide some unique problems for La Fortune, namely the continued influence of shamans, wife-swapping and wife-beating, and the more common problem of excessive drinking among the natives. La Fortune established an adult education program, run much like town meetings, which tried to address these problems.

As of 1980, Alaska still remains a missionary Church, but in the major cities of Anchorage, Juneau, and Fairbanks parish life confronts problems typical to other parishes in the Pacific region.

Notes

1. *The Tree Has Grown: The Church in Hawaii, 1827–1977* (Honolulu; 1977).
2. Robert Schoofs, SS.CC., revised by F. W. Midkiff. Edited, published by Louis Boegmaens, *Pioneers in Faith: History of the Catholic Mission in Hawaii, 1827–1940* (Honolulu, 1978), 131.

3. Reginald Yzendoorn, SS.CC., *History of the Catholic Mission in the Hawaiian Islands* (Honolulu, 1927), 244.

4. Schoofs, *Pioneers in Faith*, 167.

5. *Ibid.*, 225.

6. Maggie Bunson, *Faith in Paradise: A Century and a Half of the Roman Catholic Church in Hawaii* (Boston, 1977), 179.

7. Schoofs, *Pioneers in Faith*, 168.

8. Yzendoorn, *Catholic Mission*, 244.

9. *Official Catholic Directory 1930, 1950,* and *1960*.

10. Bernard Quinn, et al., *Church and Church Membership in the United States, 1980* (Atlanta, 1980).

11. Vincent A. Yzermans, *St. Rose of Wrangell: The Church's Beginnings in South East Alaska* (St. Paul, Minnesota, 1979), x.

12. Quinn, et al., *Church and Church Membership*, 10.

13. *Official Catholic Directory 1980*.

14. Louis L. Renner, S.J., *Pioneer Missionary to the Bering Straits Eskimos, Bellarmine La Fortune, S.J.* (Portland, Oregon, 1979), 25.

15. Yzermans, *St. Rose*, 22.

16. Renner, *Pioneer Missionary*, 31.

17. *Ibid.*, 59.

18. M. Balcom, *The Catholic Church in Alaska* (Chicago, 1970), 10.

19. Judith S. Kleinfeld, *Eskimo School of the Andeokskeag: A Study of Effective Bicultural Education* (New York, 1979), 61.

20. Renner, *Pioneer Missionary*, 75.

APPENDIX 1
Catholic Church Statistics in the Pacific States

CALIFORNIA
Diocese of San Francisco

	1850	1880	1900	1930	1950	1960	1980
Parishes	—	115	82	168	190	243	153
Parishes without Priests (i.e., Missions)	—	—	53	53	42	49	15
National Parishes	—	3	10	15	15	16	13
Parish Schools	—	11	32	87	87	159	97
Diocesan Priests	—	65	125	330	425	483	253
Religious Order Priests	—	83	101	209	396	635	530
Women Religious	—	—	—	882	2,315	2,964	1,617
Catholic Population	—	185,000	225,000	350,000	650,000	1,093,595	629,336
Total Population (if available)	—	—	—	—	—	4,181,440	2,694,200

CALIFORNIA
Diocese of Los Angeles

	1850	1880	1900	1930	1950	1960	1980
Parishes	—	30	42	212	234	291	278
Parishes without Priests (i.e., Missions)	—	36	34	61	43	51	30
National Parishes	—	0	2	—	9	13	5
Parish Schools	—	8	24	79	133	238	226
Diocesan Priests	—	28	66	340	392	536	488
Religious Order Priests	—	11	26	150	300	600	654
Women Religious	—	—	—	—	2,175	3,520	2,545
Catholic Population	10,000–20,000	21,000	51,000	301,775	832,375	1,348,104	2,069,682
Total Population (if available)	—	—	—	—	—	7,110,796	7,908,300

Appendix: Church Statistics in the Pacific States

CALIFORNIA
Diocese of Sacramento

	1850	1880*	1900	1930	1950	1960	1980
Parishes	—	35	33	54	68	85	91
Parishes without Priests (i.e., Missions)	—	70	49	79	72	77	49
National Parishes	—	0	0	—	2	2	—
Parish Schools	—	0	9	11	19	34	41
Diocesan Priests	—	31	40	87	115	162	156
Religious Order Priests	—	—	2	5	19	46	76
Women Religious	—	—	—	—	274	434	327
Catholic Population	—	14,000	30,000	60,315	202,475	219,000	228,734
Total Population (if available)	—	—	—	—	—	1,177,485	1,355,814

*Diocese of Grass Valley became Sacramento in 1886.

CALIFORNIA
Diocese of Monterey

	1850	1880	1900	1930	1950	1960	1980
Parishes	—	—	—	53	73	101	43
Parishes without Priests (i.e., Missions)	—	—	—	23	28	48	12
National Parishes	—	—	—	—	1	—	—
Parish Schools	—	—	—	17	26	43	12
Diocesan Priests	—	—	—	80	120	164	62
Religious Order Priests	—	—	—	14	46	77	31
Women Religious	—	—	—	—	367	558	203
Catholic Population	—	—	—	76,800	187,767	371,007	95,000
Total Population (if available)	—	—	—	—	—	1,407,958	484,365

CALIFORNIA
Diocese of San Diego

	1850	1880	1900	1930	1950	1960	1980
Parishes	—	—	—	—	116	156	87
Parishes without Priests (i.e., Missions)	—	—	—	—	38	40	17
National Parishes	—	—	—	—	8	5	—
Parish Schools	—	—	—	—	34	74	41
Diocesan Priests	—	—	—	—	152	285	183
Religious Order Priests	—	—	—	—	78	111	67
Women Religious	—	—	—	—	444	454	565
Catholic Population	—	—	—	—	160,000	387,234	345,000
Total Population (if available)	—	—	—	—	—	1,914,898	1,851,350

CALIFORNIA
1980*

	Fresno	Oakland	Orange	San Bernardino	Santa Rosa	Stockton
Parishes	85	—	87	49	87	38	31
Parishes without Priests (i.e., Missions)	42	—	3	7	11	24	13
National Parishes	—	—	1	—	1	—	—
Parish Schools	24	—	57	33	29	12	12
Diocesan Priests	91	—	117	103	124	71	43
Religious Order Priests	54	—	229	104	56	24	32
Women Religious	177	—	607	475	222	127	93
Catholic Population	307,000	—	380,000	240,570	228,734	88,660	112,610
Total Population (if available)	1,377,500	—	1,718,500	1,872,000	1,355,814	558,102	628,960

*All these dioceses were founded after 1960.

Appendix: Church Statistics in the Pacific States

OREGON
Diocese of Portland[1]

	1850	1880	1900	1930	1950	1960	1980
Parishes	12	18	39	85	97	104	123
Parishes without Priests (i.e., Missions)	7	—	30	66	43	44	29
National Parishes	—	0	2	2	2	2	3
Parish Schools	—	6	23	52	54	70	50
Diocesan Priests	—	—	43	83	119	157	152
Religious Order Priests	—	—	24	95	156	263	235
Women Religious	—	71	—	—	1,149	1,095	869
Catholic Population	10,000	20,000	34,000	50,000	92,378	186,560	294,952
Total Population (if available)	—	—	—	—	—	1,503,523	2,195,800

[1]The Diocese of Portland was originally the Diocese of Oregon City; name changed to Portland in 1928.

OREGON
Diocese of Baker[1]

	1850	1880	1900	1930	1950	1960	1980
Parishes	—	—	—	18	23	29	29
Parishes without Priests (i.e., Missions)	—	—	—	38	—	32	31
National Parishes	—	—	—	0	0	—	—
Parish Schools	—	—	—	0	2	2	1
Diocesan Priests	—	—	—	19	31	41	36
Religious Order Priests	—	—	—	9	8	8	11
Women Religious	—	—	—	—	130	120	95
Catholic Population	—	—	—	7,851	14,729	21,528	25,361
Total Population (if available)	—	—	—	—	—	265,182	300,500

[1]Baker became a separate diocese in 1903.

WASHINGTON
Diocese of Seattle

	1850	1880*	1900*	1930	1950	1960	1980
Parishes	—	24	45	86	108	110	130
Parishes without Priests (i.e., Missions)	—	—	52	74	58	48	36
National Parishes	—	0	1	5	5	5	4
Parish Schools	—	0	17	41	45	59	58
Diocesan Priests	—	11	40	98	121	161	173
Religious Order Priests	—	5	80	115	176	253	232
Women Religious	—	52	300	842	1,008	1,162	895
Catholic Population	—	11,000	42,000	91,000	183,000	239,462	358,460
Total Population (if available)	—	—	—	—	—	—	—

*Diocese of Nesquilly became Diocese of Seattle in 1907.

WASHINGTON
Diocese of Spokane

	1850	1880	1900	1930	1950	1960	1980
Parishes	—	—	—	43	48	56	58
Parishes without Priests (i.e., Missions)	—	—	—	56	52	26	24
National Parishes	—	—	—	0	1	0	0
Parish Schools	—	—	—	19	20	27	19
Diocesan Priests	—	—	—	44	62	81	75
Religious Order Priests	—	—	—	39	86	103	102
Women Religious	—	—	—	—	420	569	488
Catholic Population	—	—	—	28,819	44,101	66,608	73,649
Total Population (if available)	—	—	—	—	—	470,462	610,100

Appendix: Church Statistics in the Pacific States

WASHINGTON
Diocese of Yakima

	1850	1880	1900	1930	1950	1960	1980
Parishes	—	—	—	—	—	27	39
Parishes without Priests (i.e., Missions)	—	—	—	—	—	13	7
National Parishes	—	—	—	—	—	—	—
Parish Schools	—	—	—	—	—	6	7
Diocesan Priests	—	—	—	—	—	55	50
Religious Order Priests	—	—	—	—	—	5	13
Women Religious	—	—	—	—	—	95	61
Catholic Population	—	—	—	—	—	45,466	56,200
Total Population (if available)	—	—	—	—	—	343,215	387,000

HAWAII
Diocese of Hawaii

	1850	1880	1900	1930	1950	1960	1980
Parishes	—	—	—	33	51	61	64
Parishes without Priests (i.e., Missions)	—	—	—	—	59	55	36
National Parishes	—	—	—	—	—	—	—
Parish Schools	—	—	—	11	18	25	28
Diocesan Priests	—	—	—	2	6	17	43
Religious Order Priests	—	—	—	50	115	132	112
Women Religious	—	—	—	227	363	476	383
Catholic Population	—	—	—	116,000	145,000	200,000	210,000
Total Population (if available)	—	—	—	—	—	621,319	896,000

ALASKA
Diocese of Alaska

	1850	1880	1900[1]	1930	1950	1960	1980
Parishes	—	—	5	20	48	18	—
Parishes without Priests (i.e., Missions)	—	—	5	30	22	3	—
National Parishes	—	—	—	—	—	—	—
Parish Schools	—	—	4	4	3	0	—
Diocesan Priests	—	—	0	4	9	2	—
Religious Order Priests	—	—	13	23	26	31	—
Women Religious	—	—	28	49	76	46	—
Catholic Population	—	—	2,000	9,500	10,833	15,500	—
Total Population (if available)	—	—	40,000	—	—	81,915	—

[1] Alaska was still a prefecture as of 1900.

ALASKA
Diocese of Juneau

	1850	1880	1900	1930	1950	1960	1980
Parishes	—	—	—	—	—	11	10
Parishes without Priests (i.e., Missions)	—	—	—	—	—	7	4
National Parishes	—	—	—	—	—	—	—
Parish Schools	—	—	—	—	—	2	1
Diocesan Priests	—	—	—	—	—	10	10
Religious Order Priests	—	—	—	—	—	19	1
Women Religious	—	—	—	—	—	27	14
Catholic Population	—	—	—	—	—	20,000	5,272
Total Population (if available)	—	—	—	—	—	145,000	47,300

Appendix: Church Statistics in the Pacific States 135

ALASKA
Diocese of Fairbanks

	1850	1880	1900	1930	1950	1960	1980
Parishes	—	—	—	—	—	—	27
Parishes without Priests (i.e., Missions)	—	—	—	—	—	—	20
National Parishes	—	—	—	—	—	—	—
Parish Schools	—	—	—	—	—	—	1
Diocesan Priests	—	—	—	—	—	—	4
Religious Order Priests	—	—	—	—	—	—	36
Women Religious	—	—	—	—	—	—	51
Catholic Population	—	—	—	—	—	—	14,000
Total Population (if available)	—	—	—	—	—	—	117,000

ALASKA
Diocese of Anchorage

	1850	1880	1900	1930	1950	1960	1980
Parishes	—	—	—	—	—	—	18
Parishes without Priests (i.e., Missions)	—	—	—	—	—	—	9
National Parishes	—	—	—	—	—	—	—
Parish Schools	—	—	—	—	—	—	1
Diocesan Priests	—	—	—	—	—	—	15
Religious Order Priests	—	—	—	—	—	—	20
Women Religious	—	—	—	—	—	—	38
Catholic Population	—	—	—	—	—	—	20,038
Total Population (if available)	—	—	—	—	—	—	195,000

PART TWO

Deserts, Diversity, and Self-Determination: A History of the Catholic Parish in the Intermountain West

Carol L. Jensen

Contents

Preface	139
CHAPTER ONE: The Development of the Church in the Intermountain West, 1539–1960	141
CHAPTER TWO: The Local Church	174
CHAPTER THREE: Religion and Ethnicity	199
CHAPTER FOUR: The Post-Vatican Period	228
For Further Reading	269

Preface

The history of Catholic parish life in the Intermountain West is a story of struggle. It is the drama of a diverse people searching for authentic ways to acknowledge God's Presence in a sparsely settled land. It is the tale of individual and communal wrestling with the resistant forces of nature, with a dependent economy, with the multiple traditions of an indigenous non-Christian culture, with evangelical Protestants and a militant Mormon society, and with contrasting forces within Catholicism itself. Such a history considers concrete evidence of the geographic struggle (physical, political, and economic). It describes the ethnic struggle of Native American and Hispanic minorities with the dominant society and with each other, as well as the multi-cultural conflicts of nationalistic European immigrants. It listens to the experiences of other religions as they encounter Catholicism. It strives to understand the interplay of complementary but often conflicting principles within the Church itself: hierarchical order and the prophetic principle, an organizational style and an expressive one, the "great tradition" and the "little tradition," the communal impulse and personal needs. It also raises a series of questions: Is there some way in which regional sensitivity can enliven one's Catholicism? What spiritual and social needs of parishioners have not been met, are not now met, or cannot be met by existing parish structures? What can we learn from the religious experience of Native American and Hispanic Catholics? Can the use of regional imagery help integrate one's religious affiliation with the realities of daily life?

Since the 1970s, the eight states that comprise the Intermountain West (Idaho, Montana, Wyoming, Nevada, Utah, Colorado, Arizona, and New Mexico) have become increasingly aware of the common bonds that make them "other than" Eastern. Not properly sectionalism (as it does not seek separation or isolation), this spirit of diversity in unity finds parallels in such concepts as the United States or the Mystical Body of Christ. One's concern is with the free development of each member for the greater good of all. Perhaps a clearer profile of Catholic parish life in a particular region, and the dynamic interplay of contrary forces within specific sections of that region, can contribute creatively to a deeper understanding and richer expression of the total American Catholic experience.

The telling of the story is itself a sort of creative struggle with a wide variety of sources. With ecclesiastical histories of institutional structures providing only a portion of our Catholic past, it is important to look also at sociological statistics and folk traditions, some of the broader strokes of secular history and the personal perspectives found in diaries, letters, autobiographies, and interviews. Finally, the inclusion of regional characteristics reminds us that in an area where literacy was for so long a luxury, oral tradition counts for a great deal.

The story brings together for the first time a wide variety of related facts about Catholics in the Intermountain West; it attempts to point out some common concerns for an entire region of great geographical, cultural, and religious diversity; and, finally, it dares to suggest the unexplored potential of regional, multi-cultural, and deeply held religious values in the further development of American Catholic life.

It begins with a general chronology of the development of the Church in the Intermountain West, moves in for a close look at the actual functioning of parish life in those eight states, considers in some detail the particular ethnic influences on the region's self-understanding, and discusses some of the changes in Intermountain Catholic life wrought by both ecclesiastical and economic determinants during the past twenty-five years. If more questions than answers arise as a result of this effort, the author will be satisfied.

CHAPTER ONE

The Development of the Church in the Intermountain West, 1539–1960

A sense of geography (physical, political, and economic) is basic to an understanding of the Intermountain West and its people. The very immensity of the region, a variety of imposing land forms, and pervasive dryness have created awesome obstacles to the civilizing tendencies of humankind. The late establishment of both civil and ecclesiastical jurisdiction caused considerable confusion and delayed the development of organized Church life. Thus, the first Catholic parishes in the northwestern and southwestern parts of this region were often the offspring of Indian missions established by Jesuits or Franciscans. As later settlements were formed around agricultural enterprises, mining camps, or railroad activities, frontier Catholics sought visible religious communities where they could fulfill their religious duties and celebrate the important events in their lives. In an area filled with Protestant evangelizing efforts and a militant Mormon presence, the official establishment of Catholicism often contributed to inter-religious tensions. The lack of early industrialization in the region, along with the boom and bust phenomena related to mining and the shifting populations of relocated railroad junctions, delayed stabilization of the population and its movement from rural to urban settings. These geographic and demographic conditions contributed to a sort of economic colonialism from which the region is only recently emerging. Thus, despite the later development of a handful of significant urban centers (Denver, Phoenix, Tucson, Salt Lake City, and Albuquerque), Catholic parish life in this region has generally retained a rural missionary character.

The importance of physical geography in determining the locale of Catholic parishes in the Intermountain West is clear if one looks at the vast spaces involved and the natural barriers that forestall movement through those spaces. When Pierre J. De Smet, S.J., wrote of his journeys through this territory in 1841, he described the land between the South Platte River and the Rocky Mountains as a

> vast solitude completely uninhabited. . . . Here and there are heaps of stones, piled confusedly like ruins; ridges of rock, which rise up before you like impassible barriers, and which interrupt, without embellishing, the wearisome sameness of these

solitudes. . . . This desert of the West, such as I have just described it, seems to defy the industry of civilized man. Some lands, more advantageously situated upon the banks of rivers, might, perhaps, be successfully reduced to cultivation; others might be turned into pastures as fertile as those of the East—but it is to be feared that this immense region forms a limit between civilization and barbarism.[1]

De Smet's sense of the defiant character of the land is accompanied by the desire to dominate what is considered of lesser value: geographic barriers and barbarism.

A sense of immensity and isolation is still possible in many parts of the region. While the eight states constituting this area contribute nearly one-fourth of the nation's contiguous land area, they contain less than 5% of its population. "Altogether there are 863,524 square miles in this vast expanse of sagebrush and mountain, thirteen times as large as New England, five times as large as California, the equivalent of the combined area of thirteen European nations."[2]

Montana, the largest state in the region, has an area of 147,046 square miles and is the fourth largest state in the union. It is followed by New Mexico, Arizona, Nevada, Colorado, Wyoming, Utah, and Idaho, which rank fifth, sixth, seventh, eighth, ninth, eleventh, and thirteenth, respectively.

The region's low population density is characterized by the predominance of rural communities and isolation created by the great distance between urban centers. With Catholics representing a small percentage of that population, it is no wonder that the majority of Intermountain parishes are rural rather than urban. (See Appendix 3.)

Significant natural barriers in the region include the Rocky Mountains, the Great Basin, and desert-like terrain throughout. The Rocky Mountains are a 3,200-mile-long chain stretching from Alaska to New Mexico. Parts of these more than twenty separately named ranges can be found in five of the region's eight states. Some of the most familiar of these segments are the Teton Range and Bighorn Mountains in Wyoming and the Wasatch Range in Utah. The Rockies' highest peak, Mount Elbert in the Sawatch Mountains of Colorado, reaches 14,331 feet. In this southern segment of the Rockies, the absence of low mountain passes has made the area one of the last in the country to be settled. The land intervenes. It imposes itself upon living creatures; one is forced to reckon with it. The Rocky Mountains separate Montana, Wyoming, and Colorado each into geographically distinct regions with mountainous terrain in the west and high plateaus or plains in the east. In Montana, these geographically distinct regions gave rise to culturally distinct Indian tribes and, thus, were instrumental in bringing Catholic missionary efforts to one locale rather than to another. While the plains Indians of the east remained mobile and independent, the less powerful mountain Indians of the west were eager to receive missionaries.

Early visions and tales of black robes among Rocky Mountain Indians prepared the Salish Flatheads of Montana's Bitterroot Valley for conversion by a Catholic

Mohawk-Iroquois layman in 1820. Ignace La Mousse and his band, which had migrated west in the fur trade, taught the Flatheads Catholic prayers, baptized their children, and urged them to obtain black robes for themselves. In a dramatic gesture, La Mousse raised a simple, hand-hewn wooden cross and proclaimed, "This is the only way to heaven. The words I speak to you are nothing; they are like dry buffalo bones with no meat on them, compared to what the black robes know."[3] This testimony convinced the Flatheads to act, but it took four separate delegations to St. Louis before help came in the person of Father Peter J. De Smet, S.J., in 1840. The Flatheads and other mountain tribes welcomed the black robes with their mysterious promise of eternal life as they had earlier welcomed the mountain men, who traded manufactured goods for furs and joined them in battle against enemy tribes. It is hard to tell from this point in time just what religious principles motivated La Mousse and the Flatheads. Were they intellectually convinced of the superiority of one form of religion over another, or did they see the practicality of "eternal life" sustaining them in battle against their enemies?

Second in prominence to the Rocky Mountains as a natural barrier in this region is the Great Basin. This immense interior depression, bounded on the east by Utah's Wasatch Range and on the west by California's Sierra Nevadas, covers more than 200,000 square miles. Much of Utah and Nevada, with small parts of Wyoming and Idaho (as well as parts of California and Oregon), lies within it. An arid sagebrush desert punctuated by isolated mountain ranges, the Great Basin has long been considered "the most desolate, the most inaccessible, the wildest" portion of the region.[4] It is within this relatively unproductive area that the Mormon Kingdom of Deseret and the Nevada gambling casinos have flourished, while a widely dispersed Catholic population rose and fell with the fortunes of the mines. When Rev. James B. Foley was sent to Salt Lake City in 1868 as the city's first resident pastor, his parish included the entire state of Utah as well as the mining towns of eastern Nevada, an area larger than 84,899 square miles.

Clearly, nature has created in the Rocky Mountains and the Great Basin magnificent obstacles and seemingly endless spaces conducive to human humility and to an appreciation of the spiritual power inherent in the land. A third condition of this region's physical geography creates an even more pervasive image—aridity and its antidote, water. Western analysts have described this region as a series of deserts and semi-deserts separated by magnificent snow-covered mountains. The spring runoffs from these mountains, an unpredictable rainfall, and a limited supply of underground water make life possible for the living creatures of this desert.

The Papago Indians of Arizona's Sonoran Desert know this arid condition from centuries of day-to-day observations. Among them, a cultural tradition that respects rain and perceives its place in desert life, that does not diminish non-humans in an interdependent creation, has linked itself to the ancient principle in Catholic spirituality that believes in the power of prayer and in ritual. When desert dryness seems to deny the possibility of planting summer crops, the Papago gather for the *nawait* ritual in which saguaro fruit wine is drunk with symbolic gesture and prayer.

But theirs is not the only regional example of a Catholic spirituality that has remained one with its surroundings. Another group in this desert environment that invests spiritual energy in obtaining the necessary blessing of rain is the Hispanic Catholic ranching community of eastern New Mexico. When Fabiola Cabeza de Baca Gilbert recalls her childhood on the Llano southeast of Las Vegas, New Mexico, she says:

> Money in our lives was not important. Rain was important. We never counted our money; we counted the weeks and months between rains. . . . From childhood we were brought up to watch for signs of rain. . . . As a child, prayer was the only solution to the magic of rain. . . . On reaching middle age, I am still praying for rain.[5]

These two examples of the Southwesterners' spiritual sensitivity to water represent the minority of faith-filled people who could wait and pray for rain. The majority could not, and settled near rivers seasonally swelled by spring runoffs. Early settlements near these water sources led to the later development of a sophisticated system of dams and irrigation projects intended to solve a whole complex of problems: storing water for drinking and farming, providing flood control, generating electric power, and providing recreational water playgrounds.

But, perhaps, the Intermountain West cannot solve its water problems through federally subsidized reclamation projects alone. As contemporary objections from conservationists, competing farmers outside the region, and federal taxpayers throughout the country increase, the citizens of this desert will have to become more involved in the geographic, ecological, economic, and political issues regarding water. Is there a role for the Intermountain Catholic in this crisis? Can the prayerful and prudent traditions of the Papago farmers and Hispanic ranchers, combined with a realistic awareness of the limited benefits of federal reclamation projects, and the Church's own rich tradition of water imagery be a source of regional spiritual energy contributing to the solution of one of the fundamental problems of life in this region? Is Catholic parish life an appropriate arena in which to struggle with this vital concern?

In addition to physical geography, political geography plays an important part in the drama of Intermountain Catholic history. The relatively late determination of civil boundaries contributed to the rural character of parish life in this region. The Louisiana Purchase of 1803, which doubled the size of the existing United States at that time, added parts of Montana, Wyoming, and Colorado to the Union. The Oregon country was not freed from joint occupation by both Great Britain and the United States until an 1846 treaty made it the Oregon Territory of the United States. It was from this land that Idaho and western Montana were carved.

In 1847, Father Pierre J. De Smet, who had been asked by Bishop Rosati of St. Louis to minister to Catholics in the Oregon Territory, wrote of the promise of this newly acquired land:

> The political discussion, which has been going on for years between the British government and that of the United States, in regard to the boundary which defines their respective portions of the Oregon territory, has turned upon this distinct region a large share of public attention, and has won for it an interest which will increase in proportion to the advances of civilization and commerce within its borders.[6]

Only six years after his description of the Rocky Mountains' eastern slopes as a barrier between "civilization and barbarism," De Smet expressed a vision of economic and religious growth beyond that barrier.[7]

In 1848, the Treaty of Guadalupe Hidalgo increased the size of the United States by about 17% in adding Nevada, Utah, and California, as well as parts of Arizona, New Mexico, Colorado, and Wyoming. In 1850 the United States purchased portions of New Mexico, Colorado, and Wyoming from the Republic of Texas. Finally, in 1854 the Gadsden Purchase acquired from Mexico the southern portions of Arizona and New Mexico, which would later become parts of the dioceses of Tucson and Las Cruces, respectively. Negotiating these several acquisitions and creating subsequent subdivisions into territories of the United States forestalled settlement in the area and, thus, delayed the development of formal Catholic parish life.

Just as civil boundaries in the Intermountain region remained unsettled into the second half of the nineteenth century, so too did ecclesiastical boundaries. Decisions made in Rome about the boundaries of a mission area, Vicariate Apostolic, or diocese often did not correspond with U.S. state or territorial boundaries. Furthermore, shifting ecclesiastical jurisdiction often created confusion over just who was responsible for a given area. Sometimes, even when a new ecclesiastical area was named and assigned an administrator, the reluctance of that administrator to "civilize" wild, isolated areas resulted in lack of consistent care for some years. After an initial three decades of settlement, several areas in this region became dioceses. Others, however, did not attain that status until well into the twentieth century.

In 1850 New Mexico, the only Vicariate Apostolic in the region included the territory conceded to the United States by the 1848 Treaty of Guadalupe Hidalgo, except for the towns of Doña Ana and Las Cruces whose names were somehow omitted from the document, and which remained under the jurisdiction of the bishop of Durango, Mexico, until their annexation to the vicariate in 1858.[8] Congressman Truman Smith of Connecticut spoke on the floor of the House of Representatives about the difficulty of defining this boundary, quoting from the letter of an Army officer:

> The boundaries of the territory have never been very exactly defined, as a great share of the line lies over desert countries, where very little importance can attach to an exact location. Whilst in Santa Fe I endeavored to ascertain the exact southern boundary of the territory, but I found that various lines had been claimed both by New Mexico and Chihuahua.[9]

When Bishop John Baptist Lamy journeyed from Santa Fe to Durango in 1851 to clarify for New Mexico's Hispanic clergymen his official appointment as their vicar, the definition of territorial limits was an issue as well.

At the same time, eastern Montana and Utah (which had been under the jurisdiction of the Archdiocese of San Francisco through 1859) were given to the Santa Fe Diocese. Nevada, perhaps the most shifting of all the Intermountain ecclesiastical jurisdictions, was divided in 1860, leaving that portion south of the 39th parallel in the San Francisco Archdiocese and placing that part north of the parallel in the Vicariate Apostolic of Marysville. Father John Baptist Raverdy's attempt on behalf of the Dicoese of Santa Fe to minister to eastern Montana resulted in a letter to Bishop O'Gorman of the Nebraska Vicariate, in 1864, explaining the difficulty of ministering to that area from Denver and requesting that O'Gorman look after it.

The New Mexico Vicariate also included most of Arizona. On July 19, 1850 (the same day that New Mexico was named a Vicariate Apostolic), Pope Pius IX erected the Vicariate Apostolic of the Indian Territory, sometimes referred to as the Vicariate of the Rocky Mountains, which included those parts of Montana and Wyoming that lie east of the Rocky Mountains, and that part of Colorado obtained by the Louisiana Purchase. Meanwhile, Idaho and western Montana were under the jurisdiction of the Archdiocese of Oregon City, while Utah and Nevada were included in the Diocese of Monterey, California.

In 1853, changes in jurisdiction included raising the New Mexico Vicariate Apostolic to the Diocese of Santa Fe and creating the Archdiocese of San Francisco, which included Utah and Nevada.[10] In 1857, the Vicariate of Nebraska (including parts of Montana, Wyoming, and Colorado) was carved out of the Vicariate Apostolic of the Indian Territory. In 1859, those southern portions of Arizona and New Mexico ceded to the United States by the Gadsden Purchase of 1854 were annexed to the Diocese of Santa Fe. In the following year, Bishop Miege, temporary administrator for the new Vicariate of Nebraska, visited Colorado, decided that it should be annexed to Santa Fe, and requested the transfer of dominion from Rome.[11]

In 1865, despite the conclusion of the 1854 Gadsden Purchase clarifying civil jurisdiction over Doña Ana County, and the 1858 annexation of the towns of Doña Ana and Las Cruces to the Diocese of Santa Fe, Lamy was still striving to settle ecclesiastical jurisdiction of the county. He wrote to Alessandro Cardinal Bernabo, Prefect of the Propagation of the Faith, in Paris:

> In your letter of November 8, 1894, you gave me hope that the affair . . . of Doña Ana County would soon be decided. Last December I visited our possessions in this country, but as half is under the jurisdiction of Durango, I saw there were difficulties arising from policy differences, especially for marriages.[12]

Lamy cites difficulties between American civil authorities and Durango diocesan priests in that area as another urgent reason for a prompt settlement of jurisdiction over Doña Ana.

In 1868, Colorado and Utah were removed from the Santa Fe Diocese and erected into a single Vicariate Apostolic, but the union lasted only three years; in 1871, Utah was transferred once again to the jurisdiction of San Francisco. Is it possible that this pattern of shifting ecclesiastical jurisdiction imparted to Intermountain Catholics a sense of marginality until the Church was officially established among them? Did this exclusive way of defining a community's status in the Church contribute to a regional self-image of dependence on outside recognition and support? How dependent was the faith of the Catholic community on hierarchical order for its growth?

This early period of ecclesiastical shuffling included some successful attempts to bring stability and mark progress. In 1868, Arizona and the southern counties of New Mexico became a vicariate; and the Vicariate Apostolic of Idaho (including all of Idaho and western Montana) was created. However, the general tide of changing jurisdiction was more common during this period. The northern part of Nevada was transferred once more, this time to the Diocese of Grass Valley. And although a Vicariate of Montana was established by Pius IX on the same day as the establishment of the Vicariate Apostolic of Idaho, Father Augusting Ravoux, who was named administrator, declined the honor because of poor health, and so eastern Montana remained under the jurisdiction of the Vicariate of Nebraska.[13] In 1875, the resignation of Bishop Lootens of the Idaho Vicariate Apostolic resulted in the return of Idaho and western Montana to the jurisdiction of Oregon City. It is no wonder that there was some confusion about under which jurisdictions the traditionally separate segments of Montana fell. Perhaps through some agreement with Archbishop Francis Blanchet of Oregon City, Bishop James O'Connor extended his administration to those portions of Montana and Wyoming lying west, as well as east, of the Rocky Mountains. Because Montana had been united as a U.S. territory in 1864, the continuation of dual ecclesiastical jurisdiction seemed to many to hinder the spiritual welfare of the people and the development of parish life at that time in the territory.[14]

A further example of shifting ecclesiastical status and episcopal responsibility occurred in 1887 when Rev. Maurice F. Burke was appointed the first Bishop of the Diocese of Cheyenne. After assessing the size of his territory, Father Burke concluded that the erection of the diocese had been premature and requested its suppression by Rome.[15] His proposal was rejected, and so the diocese remained without episcopal direction until 1897.

The need for more comprehensive and effective jurisdiction ushered in a seventeen-year period during which six new dioceses joined the Santa Fe Diocese (until 1884, the only diocese located in the region). In 1883, at the urging of Archbishop Seghers of Oregon City, the Vicariate Apostolic of Montana was erected, uniting eastern and western Montana ecclesiastically for the first time.

A letter from Bishop O'Connor, Vicar Apostolic of Nebraska, to Bishop John B. Brondel, newly appointed Vicar Apostolic of Montana, suggests the legacy of difficulties resulting from the jurisdictional problems imposed by great distances and frontier life.

> On my return from Philadelphia yesterday I received the formal notification . . . of your appointment to Montana. This news was a great relief to me, and I rejoice to think that the charge of that territory has been given to one well-acquainted with Western life, and who will not shrink from the hardships . . . the trials and privations of such a place. . . . In a short time, no doubt, your difficulties will be overcome, but for four or five years, "you will have distress."[16]

A year later, this vicariate was raised to the Diocese of Helena. Shortly thereafter, in 1886, the Vicariate of Utah (including the six counties of Nevada, which, with Utah, had been under the jurisdiction of San Francisco) was created. In the same year, the northern counties of Nevada were transferred from the Diocese of Grass Valley to the Diocese of Sacramento. And the following year, both the Diocese of Cheyenne and the Diocese of Denver were erected. These decisions gave a greater stability to Church leadership in the Intermountain region and led in less than a decade to the erection of the Diocese of Salt Lake City in 1891, the Diocese of Boise in 1893, and the Diocese of Tucson in 1897. In Nevada, however, the situation was still one of shifting jurisdiction. In 1891, the creation of the Diocese of Salt Lake City divided Nevada again, taking several eastern and southern counties with it and leaving others with Sacramento.[17] By 1893, with the erection of the Diocese of Boise, each of the Intermountain states, except for Nevada, had its own diocese. From then on, jurisdictional changes occurred only every ten or twenty years.

Clearly, the initial conflicts necessary in gaining possession of this region marked only the beginning of the struggle to develop it and to establish official institutions for the religious care of its people. Problems resulting from the great distances involved and the harsh living conditions often discouraged ecclesiastical leaders in their attempts to impose order on wilderness Catholicism.

In this setting determined by physical and political geography, a limited number of economic opportunities determined settlement patterns and, thus, the development of Catholic parish life. The eras of early adventurers and fortune seekers in both the Southwest and the Northwest were short-lived; but this did not deter the more purposeful efforts of religious order priests to establish Indian missions in those areas. It was out of these frontier institutions, and the agricultural/pastoral settlements that developed near them, that the region's first Catholic parishes came into being.

In the Southwest, not only was Catholic settlement initiated nearly 250 years earlier than in the Northwest, but because its impetus came from Spain, rather than from the United States, the Southwest's frontier economy developed differently as well.[18] Spanish explorers looking for mineral wealth and the legendary Seven Cities of Cibola came as early as 1539 accompanied by Franciscan Friars. Both were official representatives of the Two Majesties, God and the King of Spain, and both were supported by the national treasury.

Despite initial disenchantment at the empty promise of quick riches, colonizing expeditions followed the explorations of *conquistadores,* as the Spanish church and state attempted to civilize and protect New Spain's far northern frontier. The friars developed a mission system for Christianizing Indians while laymen manned military outposts and developed a subsistence economy. Although church/state cooperation did not always match in practice the ideals outlined by the Spanish crown, such an intent was clearly stated in specific instructions issued by the central government. An example of this policy is contained in the instructions given by Luis de Velasco, the king's chief political official in New Spain, to Don Juan de Oñate, appointed in 1595 to colonize New Mexico.

> You should try to bring the natives of these provinces to you and to induce them to hear the word of the holy gospel, that they may receive and accept it, converting them to our holy Catholic faith. . . . You shall arrange all things . . . wisely and harmoniously, always ordering everything for the glory of God and the increase of our holy Catholic faith.[19]

In the spirit of this policy, San Juan Bautista was erected as the first church in New Mexico on August 23, 1598, with an accompanying garrison erected on September 7, 1598. Later, Nuestra Senora de Guadalupe de Zuñi in New Mexico, and San Bernardo at the Hopi village of Awatovi in Arizona, joined a growing network of Franciscan missions in New Spain. However, a widespread Pueblo Revolt in 1680 nearly destroyed this early work. Those friars who returned with Captain General Diego de Vargas in 1692 to reconquer New Mexico established the mission system among the Rio Grande Pueblos, but subsequent efforts among the Hopi in Arizona were doomed. Hopi resistance to Spanish reconquest resulted in Indian destruction of the entire Catholic village of Awatovi and of all other Catholic mission structures among that tribe. The imposition of a foreign faith deemed superior by the conquerors enraged the subjugated Hopi. But many of the original missions at New Mexico Pueblos, including San Juan and Zuñi, developed self-supporting agricultural enterprises and have active Catholic parishes today.

In Arizona, it was the early work of the Jesuits, particularly the work of Padre Eusebio Francisco Kino, which laid the most lasting foundations of Catholic parish life. For twenty-four years, Kino the missionary also served as Kino the explorer, mapper, ranchman, and writer in the desert wilderness of Sonora, Mexico. From his first mission in this province, Nuestra Señora de los Dolores at the Indian village of Cosari 150 miles south of Tucson, the Padre on Horseback traveled thousands of miles between the years 1687 and 1711, supervising native groups of carpenters, brick layers, and cowhands in the establishment of several missions among the Pima, Papago, Yuma, and Sobaipuri Indians. The most famous of these foundations within U.S. territory, San Xavier del Bac, the "White Dove of the Desert" (founded in 1700), functions today as an active city parish and Papago Indian mission in Tucson. At Kino's time, this was the site of an opulent Pima village, the most populous settlement in all Primeria Alta. His desire to relocate headquarters at San Xavier del Bac and his request for a replacement at Dolores Mission were never fulfilled. But the Italian-born ascetic's humility and zeal remained undaunted, inspired in particular by his patron, St. Francis Xavier, to whom he attributed his youthful recovery from a serious illness, his entry into the Society of Jesus, and the pursuit of his missionary dream. In the Prologue to his historical memoirs of Primeria Alta, the *Favores Celestiales,* Kino expresses this sense of gratitude for his ministry:

> Let thanks, then, be given to the Most Holy Trinity, thanks to Jesus and most Holy Mary, thanks to the most glorious apostle of the Indies, San Francisco Xavier, and to all the celestial court for all the celestial favors that we have received and are receiving in these new spiritual and temporal conquests and conversions.[20]

Although Kino uses the hierarchical language of heavenly courts and earthly conquests, it appears that his ministry was one based on inclusive principles. Motivated spiritually by a sense of mutual support and by an appreciation for the people and the physical environment surrounding him, the Jesuit missionary succeeded in making a substantial contribution to the economic development of Primeria Alta. Western historian Eugene Bolton lauds the padre as the cattle king of his day and region:

> From the small outfit supplied him from the older missions to the east and south, within fifteen years he established the beginnings of ranching in the valleys of the Magdalena, the Altar, the Santa Cruz, the San Pedro, and the Señorita. The stock-raising industry of nearly twenty places on the modern map owes its beginnings on a considerable scale to this indefatigable man.[21]

The accomplishments of Padre Kino and his Jesuit co-workers in Arizona occurred during a peaceful episode between the Pueblo Revolt of 1680 and the Pima rebellion in 1751. The loss to the Church in the Southwest suffered by these two uprisings was increased by the loss of Jesuit services altogether when, in 1767, Charles III expelled the Society of Jesus from New Spain and Pope Clement XIV subsequently suppressed their order. The isolation of these southern Arizona missions, the continual threat of marauding Apaches, and the need for ecclesiastical reorganization of the province hindered further missionary experiments in that area. Consequently, the New Mexico missions developed more consistently than those in Arizona.

Despite the heroic efforts of Franciscans and Jesuits to bring Christianity and "civilization" to the Indians of the Southwest, New Spain was unable to establish for Hispanic settlers an economically independent colony on its far northern frontier. A lack of mineral wealth, Spanish regulation forbidding trade with any foreign power, geographic isolation of the separate Spanish provinces in America, and the brief, unsuccessful use of the *encomienda* system among the Pueblos contributed to a situation characterized for the most part by poverty and continued dependence on the crown for financial and ecclesiastical assistance. Still, reluctant to continue supporting an unproductive colony, Spain turned a deaf ear to the repeated requests of colonists for aid. Fray Alonzo Benavides, early Father custodian of the Franciscans in New Mexico, met no favorable response at Madrid and at Rome between 1630 and 1636 in his pursuit of a bishopric for New Mexico. In 1811, when Don Pedro Bautista Pino was sent from New Mexico to Spain to represent the people at the First Constitution of Spanish Cortes in Cádiz, his plea for financial aid as well as a bishopric cited more than two hundred years of neglect and its deplorable results:

> Agriculture, industry, and commerce are the three bases of all prosperity. The province of New Mexico has none of these because of its location, because of the neglect with which the government has looked upon it up to this time, and because of the annual withdrawal of the small income that it is able to derive from its products and manufactures. . . . This income is so small, as we have previously stated, that until recently the majority of its inhabitants had never seen money.[22]

Such neglect had religious as well as economic results. Not only had the majority of New Spain's inhabitants not seen money, they had also not seen a bishop. Pino lamented the abuses that resulted: "It is truly grievous that in spite of the fact that from 9,000 to 10,000 duros are paid by that province in tithes, for fifty years the people have not had an opportunity to see the face of their bishop. I, an old man, did not know how bishops dressed until I came to Cadiz."[23] The energetic appeals of both Benevides and Pino seem to suggest that without the official hierarchical establishment of a bishopric in the Southwest, the faith would shrivel and die. But did it? Instead, the Spanish Catholics and their Indian converts seem to have been urged by necessity to preserve and pass on the faith themselves.

The sense of isolation from the center of civil and ecclesiastical government, in addition to a constant fear of marauding nomadic tribes, may have contributed to a sense of Southwest regional unity begun, some suggest, as early as 1776 with the separation of the northern provinces from the Viceregency of New Spain.[24] Nevertheless, among the Spanish of the Southwest this regional identity was characterized by the economic colonialism and apparent dependence on outside support that have continued to plague the entire Intermountain region until recently.

Unlike the Spanish political/religious colonization of the Southwest that preceded it by two centuries, Anglo settlement of the Northwest was a haphazard affair.[25] Individual initiative characterized the arrival of early trappers, miners, and yeoman farmers whose geographical discoveries, construction of forts, and establishment of trade with the Indians were only incidental to their main objective, adventure and personal economic gain. From the date of the Louisiana Purchase and the consequent explorations of Lewis and Clark at the beginning of the nineteenth century, until the arrival of both Catholic and Protestant missionaries in the 1840s, only a few U.S. citizens had penetrated the Northwestern part of the Intermountain region, and these had no official commitment to the spreading of the Gospel or the establishment of churches. Unfortunately, their legacy to the Indians was not so disinterested. Although they came neither to claim land nor change the lifestyle of the natives, the mountain men contributed to the decline of Indian self-sufficiency with their introduction of manufactured goods, and to the decline of Indian health by spreading cholera, smallpox, measles, and other diseases. It was into this unhappy situation that Father De Smet and his Jesuit companions came in the 1840s. The Jesuits in the Northwest, representing no foreign imperial power, but, instead, the spirit of their own founder, entered the wilderness in response to Native American initiative. Once there, like their missionary counterparts in the Southwest, these dedicated men laid the foundation for Catholic parish life in Idaho, Montana, and Wyoming. The first Jesuit mission in the Northwest was established by Father De Smet in Montana's Bitterroot Valley on September 24, 1841. This was St. Mary's Mission for the Flatheads fifty miles south of present-day Missoula. A legend related to the establishment of this mission tells of a baptized Flathead child named Mary who had died some time before the construction of the mission church. " 'I see Mary, our Mother!' she had exclaimed to Peter, the Iroquois who had baptized her. 'She says a house of prayer will be built here.' "[26] It is said that St. Mary of the Rocky Mountains Church was built on the very place where little Mary saw the vision, died, and was buried. It is also said that word of this event traveled, and, soon, Indians from twenty-four tribes came to St. Mary's asking for black robes.[27] It is clear that in this case the propagation of the faith did not depend on an official establishment.

During the half century that St. Mary's served the Flatheads, it also contributed to the early economic life of Montana, providing the state with its first flour and lumber mills, the first oat and wheat fields, the first cattle, hogs, and chickens bred.[28] At a later date, this mission also provided Indians and Anglo settlers with the medical services of Father Anthony Ravalli, Montana's first doctor. The closing of St. Mary's Mission in 1891 coincides with the final migration of the Flatheads from their traditional land to the Jocko Reservation.

St. Ignatius Mission, the second in Montana, and the fifth established by Jesuits in the Pacific Northwest, was first established in 1845 on the Bay of the Kalispels on Pend d' Oreille River in what is now Idaho. The location proved undesirable, however, because of the runoffs from heavy snows in the mountains, a common problem in the establishment of many Intermountain missions and settlements. In its second locale (established by 1845), this mission for Flatheads, Kalispels, Kootenais, and Pend d' Oreilles became a cradle of civilization in Montana as well as a model mission presented as an ideal in both Europe and the United States. The mission eventually gave its name to a town with its own parish.

In 1843, the first Indian mission in Idaho was established on the St. Joe River. One year later, the new Coeur d' Alene Indian village near the mission boasted more than a hundred Christian families, but, by 1847, it was moved to the present town of Cataldo on the Coeur d' Alene River, where work on the more stable Sacred Heart Mission Church was begun in 1851.[29] Today, this mission is a parish within the Diocese of Boise.

Despite the multiple moves of many Northwest missions from one locale to another, the pioneering achievements of the Jesuits in the area and the settlement of French Canadian trappers and traders even before the arrival of the priests created a Catholic atmosphere conducive to the beginnings of parish life. Throughout the region, if it had not been for the missionary efforts of religious order priests, particularly the Jesuits and Franciscans, and for their willingness to serve white settlers, parish life in this region would have developed even more slowly.

Those parishes in the Intermountain region, which did not spring from previously established Indian missions, began often as agricultural/pastoral settlements near valuable water sources. Early agricultural (sometimes also military) settlements of New Mexico's Spanish colonizers were located in the Rio Grande Valley.

Churches built at the Hispanic villages of Santa Fe and Santa Cruz in the Rio Arriba area (upstream) and a third at Albuquerque in the Rio Abajo area (downstream) were the first in New Mexico to be built by the Hispanic people at their own (rather than royal) expense, manned by secular priests, and supported by local collections. The Santa Fe parish begun in 1606 became the diocesan cathedral in 1850. The Santa Cruz parish celebrated its 250th anniversary in 1983, and the Albuquerque parish of San Felipe de Neri, erected in 1706, today is one of twenty-six parishes in New Mexico's most populous area. At places like Taos, New Mexico, the Pueblo church of San Geronimo served both the Indians and the Spanish settlers, even after its restoration following the reconquest in 1692, and it was not until 1802 that the people of La Plaza de Don Fernando de Taos had their own church.[30]

In Arizona, despite isolation and the constant threat of Apache raids, a small number of Spanish colonists settled in the Santa Cruz valley as farmers, cattlemen, and miners. These separate gatherings of extended families were referred to, respectively, as *haciendas de labor, ranchos,* and *reales de minas*.[31] At the Presidio de los Espanoles established at Tucson in 1776, military men and their families worshiped in their own church separate from the pre-existing church of the Indians at Pueblito del Tucson. The Spanish church eventually became San Augustine Cathedral for the Tucson Diocese.

At mid-nineteenth century, most Intermountain Catholics maintained a subsistence economy based on agricultural and pastoral pursuits. In the Southwest, along the Rio Grande watershed of New Mexico, Hispanics and Pueblo Indians were served by Spanish and Mexican priests prior to the arrival of U.S. military forces in 1846. When the Army of the West took possession of Santa Fe in May of 1846, General Stephen Watts Kearney addressed its citizens with promises he would never be able to keep:

> New Mexicans! . . . We have come with peaceable intentions and kind feelings toward you all. . . . In taking possession of New Mexico we do not mean to take away your religion from you. . . . Every man has a right to serve God according to his heart.[32]

Despite the "peaceable intentions" and belief in religious freedom voiced by the general, the complexion of Catholic life for 75,000 Spanish-speaking people and thousands of nominally Catholic Indians would be dramatically altered by this change in government. As we shall see later, the modernizing tendencies of the civil government of the United States were reflected in the Americanizing policies of the U.S. Church as well. Cultural and religious toleration clearly had limits.

In Colorado, settlement of the San Luis Valley marked the final colonizing effort of Hispanics in the American Southwest. Although an attempt to populate the area in the early 1840s was thwarted by Indians, in 1854 a group of colonists settled themselves on the north side of the Rio Conejos, supported this time in their conflicts with Indians by the U.S. government. Like the settlers at Santa Cruz in New Mexico, and the Indian missionaries of the Northwest, they soon realized that spring flooding regularly disrupted village life, so they moved downstream, founded the *plaza* of Conejos, and, in 1857, built Our Lady of Guadalupe, the first church in Colorado.

Changes in lifestyle at Conejos brought on by political and physical geography affected parish life as well. Suppression of nomadic Indian raids by U.S. forces in conjunction with stipulations for land acquired under the Homestead Act encouraged settlers to move closer to their lands and pastures and out of the protective *plazas* in which they had originally resided. In 1874, Father Salvatore Persone, pastor at Conejos, remarked on the pastoral results of such dispersal:

> This condition is the cause of the long journeys that we are obliged to make, because the families, since they have to live each on its own land, cannot form large towns. Since they are scattered here and there, we ourselves are obliged to run about a lot if we want to visit them. Our parish then . . . composed of . . . little more than 3,500, nevertheless is spread out in twenty-six little towns. When we go for confessions, we have to resign ourselves to go from house to house and confess them where they are to be found. We say Mass in private houses except in two places where there are small chapels. This necessity of going from house to house causes very great fatigue and makes us lose a great deal of time.[33]

Today, Our Lady of Guadalupe at Conejos remains a rural parish without a resident pastor.

In 1859, when the territory of Arizona was annexed to the diocese, the Very Rev. Joseph Priest Machebeuf was sent to Arizona to assess the condition of the Church there. Tucson, numbering about 600 Hispanics, was the most important center of population at this time; the old mission founded by Father Kino, San Xavier del Bac, housed about two hundred Papago Indians; Tubac was a military post with thirty Hispanic families; and Yuma had only a small population.[34]

Between Rev. Machebeuf's visit to Arizona in 1859 and the arrival of three priests and a lay teacher from Santa Fe in 1886, only two Jesuits and a former Franciscan had served the Church there. A lack of available clergymen and the danger of roaming Apaches between Santa Fe and Tucson had prevented earlier parties from making the trip.

Most of the early Catholic agricultural or pastoral settlements in the Intermountain region were founded in the Southwest by Hispanic peoples who had received land grants from Spain or Mexico. Somewhat later, the Homestead Act of 1862 placed new stipulations on those same lands and encouraged whites coming west to settle and work the land. The opening of the Mullan Road from Fort Benton, Montana, to Walla Walla after 1860 was responsible for the influx of growing numbers of whites in the Northwest. Because of this road, Idaho was populated by immigrants from other Western states.[35] In Montana, two white settlements came into existence with the opening of this government road. Both Hell's Gate and Frenchtown were located within forty miles of St. Ignatius Mission and on the mission road taken by the Jesuits in their travels from one Indian mission to another. The Hell's Gate Church, built in 1863, was the first church for whites in Montana.[36] The following autumn, the church at Frenchtown was built. Within seventy-five years, St. Louis Church had developed into eight parishes.[37] Today, the rural parish at Frenchtown is part of the Helena Diocese.

Mining was more erratic but perhaps more effective than agriculture in attracting Catholic settlers to the Intermountain region. The promise of quick riches appealed to many, and the prospect of work attracted others, especially European immigrants whose ties to home and economic stability were already broken. But shifting economic and demographic conditions made the establishment of Catholic parishes in particular locations a very unstable enterprise.

Although some mining activity was important in settling the Gallup and Silver City areas of northwèstern and southwestern New Mexico, and the area around the present town of Douglas, Arizona, Colorado offers the best early example of the influence of mining on ecclesiastical growth. With the 1858 Cherry Creek gold strike, Denver soon became the center of mining activities in the territory.

Rev. J. P. Machebeuf and his assistant Rev. J. B. Raverdy, representing the Diocese of Santa Fe, arrived in Denver, Colorado, in the fall of 1860 to serve between thirty and forty Catholics, who had been visited earlier in the year by Bishop Miege representing the Vicariate of the Indian Territory.[38] The Catholics of Denver were an energetic group who did not wait for clerical initiative to gather a worshiping community. Father Machebeuf tells us:

> As the few Catholics of the town had received news that a priest was coming from Santa Fe, they expected us in summer, and becoming impatient, they obtained a donation from the express company of two lots, worth about $15.00 each, and had formed a committee and had given the contract for the erection of the building which was 50 × 30 feet.[39]

This church became St. Mary's Cathedral in 1868 when Machebeuf became bishop of the Utah and Colorado Vicariate Apostolic.

Outside of Denver, at least eleven other mining camps had several Catholics each. But, the growing populations based on mining could just as quickly decline. At Breckenridge, born with the first gold strike on the western slopes in Denver in 1859, the population dropped from 8,000 during the 1860s to about 500 by 1866.[40] When Father Henry Robinson was assigned to Park, Summit, Lake, and Chafee counties in 1874, there were approximately one-hundred Catholics in his 4,000-square-mile district.[41] Subsequent gold rushes dramatically altered that number, and the consequent pattern of boom and bust affected the development of parish life.

Mining enterprises in Idaho, Montana, Utah, and Nevada brought large numbers of Catholics who began to build congregations and churches. Discoveries of gold in southern Idaho brought 1,200 people to Lewiston by 1861 and encouraged the naming of Idaho as a U.S. territory in 1863.[42] In that year, the joint efforts of Rev. Toussaint Mesplie, an Indian missionary, and Father A. Z. Poulin, a Canadian, succeeded in erecting the first churches for white people in Idaho City, Placerville, Centerville, and Pioneer. It was at Lewiston that St. Stanislaus, the first church for whites in northern Idaho, was built in 1868. By 1864, Boise had outgrown Lewiston and was named the new capital. However, Idaho's boom towns, too, had their busts. By 1870, the state's population had decreased from 32,342 in 1863 to 14,999.[43] Although St. Patrick's, the first Catholic church in Boise City, burned to the ground three weeks after its dedication in 1871, the church rebuilt on that spot became the cathedral for the Diocese of Boise in 1894.

Miners and merchants were prominent among those who came into the upper Wood River Valley in the spring of 1881. Of the many miners who filed claims around Hailey, half were Irish Catholic. Thus, when Archbishop Charles John Seghers visited Hailey in 1882, he recognized the need for a priest and sent one. A small church was built and dedicated a year later, the first church of any denomination in the Wood River Valley. Today, St. Charles of the Valley flourishes as a rural Idaho parish.

Mining influenced the settlement of Montana, too. In 1862, when gold was discovered in both Deer Lodge and Beaverhead counties, white immigration to Montana began. In the same year, mining began at Bannack, Montana's first capital; in the following year at Virginia City; and, in 1864, at Silver Creek in Helena. The first church in Helena, completed in 1864, was torn down when miners left Silver Creek.[44] But, the second church there became the first cathedral in Montana in 1884.

Because of the great distance between these many mining towns, pioneer priests had no choice but to ride circuit. Father Cyril Pauwelyn, the first diocesan priest ordained in Montana for its people, was, on the day after his ordination in 1885, put in charge of all the white population outside of Helena. Father Pauwelyn described his new ministry in this way:

> It is a month today since my ordination, and I have not spent two consecutive days in Helena. Yesterday I returned from a mining camp, Marysville; the day after tomorrow I shall leave again. Every Sunday for eight consecutive weeks I am booked for another place, and when the first merry-go-round will be over, it will have to be repeated.[45]

In 1886, White Sulphur Springs boasted six or seven Catholic families involved in mining.[46] As the population at those mines dwindled, many settlers left the area, but others who planned to stay dreamed of creating a health resort around their mineral springs. They succeeded in building a town, and today St. Bartholomew's at White Sulphur Springs endures as a rural parish.

In Utah, where Mormon settlement was the dominant pattern, Park City, a Gentile (non-Mormon) camp, had St. Mary's as its first church. Utah clergymen were more often on the road visiting remote mining camps and towns than they were in the rapidly growing Salt Lake area. On November 30, 1868, when Bishop Machebeuf visited Salt Lake City, three Catholic families were living there.[47] But by 1873, when Rev. Lawrence Scanlon became pastor of the entire Salt Lake parish, ninety of his 800 parishoners were in Salt Lake and Ogden.[48] Although there were more Catholics dispersed in rural areas than there were in urban centers at that point in Utah's history, today, of those early mining towns, only Eureka, together with Park City, maintains its own parish.

The mining communities in Nevada gave the most dramatic evidence of the boom and bust pattern that characterized many of the early mining towns and, consequently, their churches. Catholic parishes were established in western Nevada during the great mining boom of the late 1850s and 1860s. But the 1870s ushered in a series of mining busts in Nevada. As populations decreased, Catholic congregations decreased or disappeared. In 1870, Hamilton, with a population of 3,913 became the county seat and headquarters for SS. Peter and Paul Parish.[49] Within a few years, however, the parish mission at Cherry Creek and stations at Treasure Hill and Piedmont were largely abandoned, and, by 1880, the 203 people remaining in Hamilton were reason enough to downgrade the parish to a mission.[50] A similar fate befell St. Lawrence Parish at Pioche, which decreased from 1,140 people in 1870 to 745 in 1880, 646 in 1890, and 240 in 1900.[51] The continuing decline in mining caused the state to lose one-third of its population between 1880 and 1900.[52] "That pattern of mining boom, population explosion, chapel building, stabilization, and sometimes decline became a model for pioneer Catholicism in the eastern and southern counties," as well as in several other sections of the Intermountain region.[53] Under these conditions, Catholic congregations seemed grateful for the stabilizing influence of church order.

Second only to mining, the building of railroads was responsible for bringing immigrant Catholics to the Intermountain West. Eager to lure European immigrants out west, the federal government devised a land-grant subsidy program through which six alternate sections of land per mile of track were given to railroad companies that would build across the barren plains, the Rockies, and the vast deserts of the West.[54] The railroads could then sell the granted land to settlers and build up commerce along their routes. The earliest transcontinental line, covering 1,800 miles of plains, Rockies, and desert, was completed on May 10, 1869, with the driving of a golden spike at Promentory Point, Utah. While the railroads made mining more profitable, gave a new impetus to agriculture and stock raising, and helped to stabilize the population at many places, they were also responsible for some demographic changes, and for contributing to the pattern of exploitation whereby Eastern and Midwestern businessmen profited as processors of the raw materials plundered from Intermountain suppliers. Federal ownership of almost half the land of the Intermountain West encouraged federal spending in the area and provided a basis for employment and development, but it did not make these eight states less economically dependent on outsiders.

Although Wyoming's first permanent settlement at Fort Laramie was built as early as 1835 by one of the fur trading companies, it was only with the construction of the Union Pacific Railroad in 1867 that an influx of settlers made their way to that territory. In that same year, Bishop O'Gorman of Nebraska sent Father

William Kelly (the first resident pastor of Cheyenne) to organize the Catholics and build up a parish that extended from Sidney, Nebraska, to the Wasatch Canyon in Utah.[55] Within one year, a frame church built on lots donated by the Union Pacific was dedicated. First called St. John the Baptist, then St. Mary's of the Plains, this church would become St. Mary's Cathedral. As cities sprang up along the railroad route, the town of Rawlins gathered a Catholic congregation at St. James in 1867, and, by 1871, St. Lawrence O'Toole at Laramie was elevated to a parish. Both function today as small city parishes in the Cheyenne Diocese.

By the time the Union Pacific reached Utah in 1869, it was responsible for bringing the first Catholic families to Ogden. Soon, they were visited regularly by a priest, and, by 1877, Holy Family was a parish. Today, it operates as a city parish in the Salt Lake Diocese. Although the town of Corinne was the home of Utah's first Catholic parish outside Salt Lake City, a change initiated by the railroad completely eclipsed the town's promising future. As a railroad construction camp northwest of Ogden, Corinne might have become the Gentile capital of Utah as a junction for transcontinental and state traffic. It was the center of Protestant activity in Utah, the locus of the Liberal Party's formation, a center for journalism, and the home of many Catholics. In 1872, Father Patrick J. Dowling was sent as resident pastor to Corinne. But, when Ogden became the railroad junction, Corinne's population dwindled, Father Dowling returned to San Francisco, and, by 1880, only 272 inhabitants remained.[56] Railroad towns, like mining camps, could have fluctuating populations, and, thus, what might have been the beginning of a thriving parish could even more quickly be abandoned. Today, Corinne has no Catholic church.

Construction of the Central Pacific Railroad across Nevada brought a new kind of settler to Battle Mountain, Carlin, and Elko in 1869 and 1870. These towns became discharge points for people heading to the White Pine mining districts. Because of the sale of railroad land to settlers and the increased demand for beef and sheep, Elko County became a grazing and agricultural center with a more stable population than most of the mining towns.

Elko had its own church by 1890, but it was 1897 before Bishop Scanlon of Salt Lake City founded Sacred Heart Parish for Battle Mountain and Carlin. Today, St. John Bosco at Battle Mountain and St. Joseph's at Elko serve as small town parishes, while Sacred Heart at Carlin remains a rural parish. Las Vegas owed its beginnings to the building of a railroad from Salt Lake City to Los Angeles, and later found that serving the supply and freight needs of the mining communities made for continued growth. St. Joan of Arc Parish was established in 1908 by Father E. V. Reynolds, chaplain to the workers on the San Pedro, Los Angeles, and Salt Lake Railroad.

In Montana, the railroad was responsible for the growth of Billings, where Mass was held in a private home as early as 1883. By 1885, parishioners had rented a building from the Gazette Publishing Company for their church, and, by

1887, a new church building was blessed. In 1908, because of the increased population, this building was replaced by a larger church dedicated to St. Patrick. In Havre, the first Mass was celebrated in a Great Northern Railroad section house in 1887, but a church was built in 1894. Today, St. Jude Thaddeus is a small city parish in the Great Falls-Billings Diocese.

In 1877, Bishop O'Connor of Nebraska made a visitation to the outlying districts of his diocese. At that time, the population of Cheyenne, Wyoming, was about 4,000, and the Catholic population was about forty-five Catholic families with about forty unmarried adults.[57] The establishment of towns and churches often coincided as the railroad penetrated the Intermountain West.

The struggle of Intermountain Catholics to build a religious community, as well as a society, on this region's nineteenth-century frontier did not take place in isolation from larger national issues, both secular and religious. The Compromise of 1850, the war between capital and labor, and Protestant evangelicalism resulting from the Second Great Awakening made their marks on the region.

In 1848, the deepening rift between North and South was aggravated by the Mexican Cession and the possible extension of slavery into that area. But physical and economic geography had predetermined that slavery would not be profitable there, and so the Compromise of 1850 provided for the admission of California as a free state, and for the establishment of territorial governments for the rest of the acquired land with no congressional action for the introduction or exclusion of slavery there. Henry Clay, in support of the compromise, assured the North, "You have nature on your side—facts upon your side—and this truth staring you in the face, that there is no slavery in those territories."[58] Daniel Webster, too, recognized the persuasive argument of geography. "I would not take pains to reaffirm the ordinance of nature, nor to reenact the will of God."[59]

The region was not significantly involved in Civil War action. Confederate forces invaded New Mexico from Texas, held a handful of towns in the southeastern part of the territory for a time, and occupied Santa Fe briefly. But Union forces met and defeated the Southerners near Glorieta Pass in a battle often called "The Gettysburg of the West."[60] Most Intermountain Catholics remained loyal to the Union in solidarity with their region, just as Northern and Southern Catholics chose regional alliance over adherence to a single Catholic policy toward the war. Such is the influence of geography over religious affiliation.

Perhaps because of their foreignness, perhaps because of their working class status, most American Catholics were not divided, as were American Protestants, in their official response to the rise of science, particularly as a challenge to religious tradition. A general Catholic indifference to the theories of Charles Darwin, Henry James, and the new biblical scholars was even more characteristic of the rural Intermountain Catholic whose lifestyle of hard physical labor saw education as a luxury and intellectual argument as a distraction from the necessary tasks of taming a wilderness, settling a frontier, and establishing a God-fearing society.

In contrast to their indifference toward the scientific challenge to faith, the role of American Catholics in the national conflict between capital and labor was one of intense involvement, and Intermountain Catholics, many of them immigrant miners and railroad workers, found themselves on the disadvantaged side. A rare example of a Catholic laborer achieving economic success is the story of Marcus Daly, an Irish immigrant and miner who bought the Anaconda copper mine for $30,000 in 1880, thinking that he was buying a silver mine.

> Three years later it shipped more than 25,000 tons of copper to Swansea Wales, for smelting at a gross profit of $1,702,400. By 1890, copper led silver and gold with a value of $17,625,020. . . . In the same period, the population of the state increased from 40,000 to 143,000.[61]

The establishment of Catholic parishes for whites in the Intermountain West coincides with the renewal of home missionary concern among American Protestants in the post-Civil War years. A century earlier, the First Great Awakening (1740–1776) had produced a Protestant vision of Christianizing a continent through evangelical zeal. This interdenominational movement, based on a belief in the necessity of a conversion experience and a consequent need to bear witness to it, was supplemented by a general sense of Manifest Destiny. By the time of the Second Great Awakening (1780–1830), a growing fear of barbarism on the rapidly developing Western frontier, as well as this desire to create a righteous empire, spurred Eastern churchmen to establish churches and provide a ministry to these new settlements.

> The great fear was that people of the West, being far removed from the civilizing and Christianizing influence of the settled communities of the East would revert to "barbarism" and subvert the moral order of society.[62]

Even Eastern Catholics recognized the potential threat to an orderly and moral nation. Speaking for them, Bishop John England of Charleston, South Carolina, declared, "Give us the West, and we shall take care of the East."[63] Although the population of the West was younger and less inhibited by social convention than that of the East, the barbarism so feared did not develop. Nevertheless, a sort of elitism and condescension on the part of Eastern ecclesiastical leaders often characterized their initial approach to the unrefined condition of Western congregations, an attitude not totally absent in East/West church relations today.

This belief in the superiority of American Protestantism over Catholicism, and even of one form of Catholicism over another, characterized much of the religious conflict in the Southwest at mid-nineteenth century. Hispanic Catholics, both priests and people, had become accustomed to a sort of religious autonomy during three centuries of isolation and neglect. Bishop Lamy's formal arrival in Santa Fe in 1851 aroused the suspicion of both laity and clergy.

> Since the Americans had come to New Mexico, people and priests had noticed that among the newcomers were many Protestants, Jews and *quien sabe que* (who knows what else), so that when they heard that a new bishop had come, without having been previously announced, their first impression was that he might very well be anything but a Catholic dignitary.[64]

This fear of strangers, especially of Anglos and their foreign religions, soon gave way to a sort of ethnic resignation to the inevitable, but 300 years of isolation from the centers of Catholic orthodoxy, followed by the aggressive reorganizing effort of an imported American hierarchy, left enough discontent among the people to make them potential converts to Protestantism. With American occupation came Baptists, Methodists, Presbyterians, Congregationalists, and other Protestants. At first concerned with Anglo settlers, they eventually designed a plan to deliver Hispanics from the "ignorance and superstition" of their Catholic faith. Primarily through the dispersal of Spanish Bibles, these evangelists encouraged Hispanics to question Catholic tradition. A follow-up program of tracts to supplement Bible reading confirmed a growing conviction for many that Roman Catholicism was truly in error. A Protestant history of its ministry among New Mexico Hispanics presents the following example of the necessary price for rejecting "superstition":

> In the 1870s near Las Vegas, New Mexico, José Inéz Perea previously awakened by contact with the Bible . . . protested to his mother that the wooden image of the Virgin Mary which hung in a prominent place in the house should be removed. During a quarrel which ensued, Perea, in dramatic display of iconoclastic zeal, put a bullet through the statue. For this deed he was banished from his home and cut off from his family.[65]

Clearly, one's conversion from Catholicism to Protestantism was not easy. But, in New Mexico, some think that the way had been paved by the public conflict between Bishop Lamy and the popular, secular clergyman from Durango, Padre Antonio José Martínez. Some Protestants even boast of him as the "forerunner and foundation layer of Protestant missions in New Mexico," particularly in the Taos area, where Presbyterians gained many converts among the Martínez family.[66]

To further capitalize on their gains, and in response to the dramatic neglect of education in the Southwest, Protestants set up more than sixty schools in New Mexico and southern Colorado between 1879 and 1891.[67] The Catholic response was more negative.

> Many of them were frankly educational institutions for the betterment of the people. . . . But others, those called "Spanish Mission Schools," went all out under the

guise of education to take away the faith of the poor and ignorant by offering them an education which the Church at the time could not afford. Their procedure was to blacken Catholicism in the eyes of simple folk. . . . What these sects did effect too well was to confuse souls; they took away the faith of many and left them not Protestants, but infidels and scoffers.[68]

In addition to their disdain for Protestant schools, many Intermountain Catholics also feared public schools. This attitude was common among nineteenth-century American Catholics and was related, in part, to the mandate of the Third Plenary Council of Baltimore for more parochial schools. In Albuquerque during the 1890s, the Jesuits watched carefully to see who would be appointed as public school teachers; if a teacher should speak out against Catholicism, the priests were quick to direct a Sunday sermon against him.[69] Competition for pupils is evident in the Jesuit diary notation of 1896 that forty children had been lured away from the Protestants.[70]

Three hundred years of Southwestern Catholic presence before the arrival of American modernization and Protestant evangelicalism made for poor inter-faith relations in that area during the nineteenth century. In the Northwest, Protestant missionaries preceded Catholics by less than a decade. There, the lack of any previous Christian tradition provided a missionary field vast enough to accommodate several separate enterprises simultaneously. Sponsored by the American Board of Commissioners of Foreign Missions, the Methodist missionaries Jason and Daniel Lee, Samuel Parker, and Marcus Whitman combined their ministry to the Indians with pioneer settlement projects in the Oregon territory in 1834 and 1835. In Idaho, Rev. Henry Spalding and his wife built the Lapwai Mission for the Nez Perce, near Lewiston, in 1836. Just as Jesuit missionaries were first in establishing many economic and cultural institutions in Montana, so, too, the Spaldings were responsible for the first sawmill, flour mill, church school, and printing press in Idaho.[71] The Protestant missionary approach to the Indians during this period was to teach them English so that they could read the Bible and be taught more easily how to farm. In contrast, the Catholic missionary approach was to learn the Native American language for the purpose of teaching doctrine, to use concrete symbols in a multi-sensory approach, and to emphasize religious celebration. While the latter approach, with less emphasis on literacy, seems more clearly linked to pre-existing Native American tradition, and the former more hierarchical in that it presumes the superiority of one religion and culture over another, both missionary groups were instrumental in developing the area economically, and influential in heightening American demands for the acquisition of Oregon in 1846.

The Church of Jesus Christ of Latter-Day Saints (the Mormons) has received, perhaps, more notice than any religious group in the Intermountain West. Its 1847 arrival in Utah under the leadership of Brigham Young preceded that of both Catholic and Protestant churches. In his desire to create a religious empire separate from U.S. social, political, and economic restraints, Young discouraged his followers from participating in mining or railroad enterprises. Instead, he insisted on an efficient agricultural system of separateness. "By the very nature of its teachings, Mormonism awakened antagonism. The hegira to the barren valley of Utah merely afforded the sect an opportunity to consolidate its forces against the threat of national disapproval."[72] National disapproval came to Utah not only in the form of U.S. military force, but also in the form of moral outrage and militant Protestant evangelization. Although Catholics were numerically the largest of the Gentile religious groups, they, like the Episcopalians in the territory, took little part in that conflict. The main concern of these two sacramentally focused churches was to provide for the spiritual welfare of their own members, not to proselytize.

In this, the Catholics seemed more tolerant than the Protestants. Early explorations through the territory by the Franciscan friars Francisco Atanasio Dominguez and Silvestre Velez de Escalante (1776–1777), and by the Jesuit missionary Peter De Smet (1840), resulted in favorable reports about the terrain that supposedly influenced Brigham Young in his search for a Zion. During the 1850s and the 1860s, traveling clerics periodically stopped to minister to Catholic military men and their families. Because of jurisdictional changes, these clergymen represented, at one time, the Archdiocese of San Francisco and, at another, the Archdiocese of Santa Fe. In 1866, Rev. Edward Kelly was sent from San Francisco to Salt Lake City; he celebrated Mass in an old assembly hall of the Mormons, "which was courteously placed at Father Kelly's disposal by the President and Elders of the Mormon Church."[73] In a subsequent series of social and economic negotiations, Father Kelly was publicly supported by Brigham Young, until the priest was recalled a few months later. In 1868, when Utah became part of the Vicariate Apostolic of Colorado and Utah, Bishop Joseph P. Machebeuf sent Rev. James P. Foley to Salt Lake City as pastor. There is no record of Father Foley's interaction with Mormons or Protestant churchmen before his return to Denver two years later, when Utah was again placed under the jurisdiction of the Archdiocese of San Francisco. Under the pastorate of Father Patrick Walsh in 1871, Utah Catholics built their first church, St. Mary Magdalen, in Salt Lake City, financed in part by generous contributions from non-Catholics. It is most probable that this non-Catholic support came from Protestants, rather than Mormons. Congregationalists, Methodists, Presbyterians, and other denominations caught up in the evangelical fervor of the times regarded Mormonism (and especially the practice of polygamy) as a challenge to American social and political morals.[74] Ultimately, their crusade to conquer Mormonism as a faith and as a political power failed, but their public denunciations from pulpits during the 1870s to the 1890s, and their purposeful organization of the Liberal Party to defeat Mormon power, resulted in upsetting Utah's early bid for statehood and in federal legislation against polygamy. Because of the transient character of their lifestyle, the Gentiles in the mining camps of Utah did not figure prominently in these controversies, but the merchants, traders, and representatives of transportation and communication companies did.

Rev. Norman McLeod began his evangelical crusade in Utah in January of 1865 under the direction of the Home Missionary Society of the Congregational Church. His establishment of a Sunday school for children and his well-publicized attacks on Mormon theology earned him harassment and physical retaliation. During a six year absence from Utah, McLeod lectured in Nevada and California to raise money for the construction of a chapel, later built in Salt Lake City. He also lectured in various Eastern cities on the evils of Mormonism and appeared before the House Committee on Territories as part of the Gentile political struggle for control of Utah.

It was not until 1869 that both the Methodists and the Presbyterians were officially sent by their respective mission boards to confront the Mormon establishment. The Methodist church built by Rev. Gustavous Marshall Pierce in Corinne in 1870 was, in 1912, the oldest Gentile church building still in use in Utah.[75] The building of churches for these Protestants was not simply to supply their membership with religious services but to establish, on the strength of missionary funds, a basis for converting Mormons to the dominant American religion. To this end, a campaign to establish Christian schools throughout the territory was undertaken in the 1870s and the 1880s primarily by Methodists, Congregationalists, and Presbyterians, and to a lesser extent by Episcopalians and Baptists. Not unlike the Protestant mission schools established in New Mexico to convert Catholics, this project coincided with the increased establishment of Catholic schools in Utah and throughout the region. One reason that the mission school system succeeded so well was because the territorial public school system was inadequately supported by taxes and forced to charge tuition, while the sectarian missionary schools were supported by Eastern contributions and remained tuition free.

While several Protestant ministers made Mormon enemies by means of their preaching, several Catholic clergymen were remembered in the Gentile cities they served for the extension of their goodwill ministries to Protestants, Mormons, and Jews. These early inter-faith relations in Utah, and throughout the region, reflect the broader national thrust of Protestants to extend the dominant form of American Christianity, an exercise of the hierarchical principle. But, because of a well-established Catholic presence in the Southwest and the invincibly resolute Mormon Zion in Utah, the balance of religious power in the history of the Intermountain West has given the development of Catholic parish life a unique complexion that includes mutual respect.

During the first three decades of the twentieth century, the growth of Catholic parish life in the Intermountain West was irregular and uneven. In some instances, new developments in political and economic geography brought a localized stability to parish life. But, more often, even after the Church in the United States was removed from the jurisdiction of the Congregation of the Faith in 1908, terminating the mission status of the American Church, parish life in this region continued to be dealt with in a missionary approach to widely dispersed populations.

In the Southwest, despite the arrival of the railroad at the turn of the century, much of the area remained isolated. In 1900, in the Archdiocese of Santa Fe, there were nearly nine times as many parishes without priests as there were parishes with priests. (See Appendix A.) Even the achievement of statehood in 1912 failed to generate an increase in industry or population for New Mexico. In Arizona, however, the nation's first federal reclamation project, a dam on the Salt River, in 1911 created more water for irrigation. As a result, agriculture began to flourish in central Arizona, and Tucson and Phoenix became urbanized. Between 1900 and 1930, the Catholic population of the Tucson Diocese more than doubled, as did the number of parishes with priests. (See Appendix A.) Still, the problems of isolation and missionary status continued to complicate clerical ministry to the area. In 1923, more than 82,000 Catholics in the Tucson Diocese were served by thirty-three urban parishes and sixty-two priests, who also ministered to the many outlying areas still on missionary status.[76] This seemingly incongruous combination of urban growth and continued missionary conditions is illustrated in the arrival of Bishop Daniel Gercke in Tucson on December 3, 1923. Traveling by train from New Orleans in a party of ecclesiastical dignitaries from the East, the bishop asked one of the porters what the people of Tucson might think at their arrival. The porter looked at the Eastern clerics dressed in formal black suits, long black overcoats, and silk high hats and answered, "They ain't never seen anything like this before."[77] Forty years later, the bishop would recall that meeting of East and West in the "small, sleeping, western town" of Tucson and realize the crossroads at which his diocese stood.[78]

Changes were taking place, too, in the mining communities of Utah. In Carbon County at the turn of the century, a labor strike could be the means of upward social mobility for immigrants, the most assertive among coal miners in pushing for wage increases, better benefits, and union recognition. As a result of the 1903 to 1904 miners' strike in Carbon County, Utah, many Italians were evicted from coal company houses and 120 were arrested.[79] Some of the dispersed miners returned to Italy, while others took up farming on the Price River or entered into business in the nearby town of Helper. This economic change was instrumental in establishing St. Anthony's Church in Helper, with a predominantly Italian congregation and an Italian pastor, as a new kind of parish for Intermountain mining communities, a stable one.

In the Northwest, new economic opportunities as well as changes in mining or railroad enterprises often caused a sudden increase or decrease in a settlement's population, affecting the size and/or status of a local church. When St. Richard's was established at Columbia Falls in 1891 as the first Catholic church in northwest Montana, it was served from Frenchtown and then, in 1894, from Kalispell. But, in 1900, with the construction of a sawmill at the southern outlet of Whitefish Lake, the town of Whitefish began to grow. Then, when the Great Northern Railroad changed its right-of-way and made Whitefish a division point for the transcontinental railroad, Whitefish began to outgrow Columbia Falls. By 1907, St. Charles at Whitefish completed construction of a church, received its first resident pastor, and achieved parish status. By 1916, the sawmill and railroad had so sufficiently increased the population of Whitefish that St. Richard's was downgraded to a mission attached to St. Charles, until 1941.

Also in Montana, the mining boom begun in the 1880s (which had increased the population by 265%), as well as a homestead boom begun in 1910, came to an end in the 1920s.[80] These two abrupt changes, accompanied by years of drought, caused a 2% decline in the general population of the state during the 1920s, a 2% decline in the Catholic population of the Great Falls Diocese from 1920 to 1930, and a 45% decline in the Catholic population of the Helena Diocese during that same decade.[81] In 1932, Bishop O'Hara of the Diocese of Great Falls outlined some of the problems faced by Catholics of his jurisdiction:

> With 60 zealous priests ministering amid genuine hardships to small groups of the faithful assembled in 130 little churches scattered from 30 to 60 miles apart along different roads over the vast area of eastern Montana, it requires little imagination to draw the main lines of the picture.[82]

After naming the maintenance of mission churches as the first diocesan priority, Bishop O'Hara continues:

> But our need goes much further than the building of churches. Twenty-five of our pastors have received no salary whatever during the past year. With the drought which has so severely hit our dry land farmers for the past three years, we have scores of priests . . . (and missions) . . . without operating funds. There is no lack of generosity among the people, but they are so few and scattered and so stricken by drought that it is impossible for them to support the church.[83]

This example of the clear relationship between economic geography and Catholic parish life illustrates the pattern of irregular growth experienced by the Church in this region. Official establishment did not necessarily imply prosperity and growth.

In Nevada, although territorial status was achieved in 1861 (only two years after the Comstock Lode was discovered) and statehood came in 1864 (when President Lincoln needed a free state to "enrich an impoverished Union treasury in the Civil War"), economic and demographic instability based on mining booms and busts prevented the Church from passing beyond a pioneer stage until the turn of the century.[84] At that time (despite the general decline of mining), the legalization of prizefighting, new discoveries of gold and silver, the development of copper mining, the growth of Las Vegas as a railroad and freight center, and the launching of Reno as a divorce center all boosted a depressed Nevada economy.[85] These developments affected Catholic life in such centers as the copper mining town of Ely (whose population increased from 525 in 1900 to 2,090 in 1920), the gold and silver mining town of Tonopah (whose population increased from a handful of people in 1900 to nearly 4,000 in 1910), and the railroad center of Las Vegas, where St. Joan of Arc Parish flourished as the Las Vegas population increased from thirty people in 1900 to more than 5,000 in 1930.[86] By 1931, not only had the Nevada state legislature reduced the waiting period for a divorce to six weeks and legalized gambling, but papal authority had created the Diocese of Reno, making Nevada the last state in the Union to gain independent ecclesiastical jurisdiction. During the 1930s, the Great Depression, the droughts, and the Dust Bowl of the Southwest combined to slow progress in parish life, but did not stop it. In the rural town of Belen, New Mexico, the introduction of conservancy by the state and federal governments improved the ancient irrigation and flood control measures that had traditionally been handled by each community. These improvements brought expansion to the rural parish of Our Lady of Belen.

However, in the more isolated villages of northern New Mexico, land losses to the U.S. government and unscrupulous Anglo investors paved the way for increased dependence on a cash economy. As residents of such villages as Chamisal and Penasco were forced to seek migratory wage labor outside the area, the traditional pastoral/agricultural lifestyle of self-sufficiency was all but lost.[87] The Great Depression and local drought increased the poverty and dependence on government aid. Still, the people dug deep into a communal tradition of cooperation and compassion and clung to the land. They continued to live in *el estilo antiguo* (the old way), still devoted to the "feasts, processions, and wakes that celebrated God's and the saints' protection of flocks and fields and that symbolized community solidarity."[88] Gradual encroachment on this lifestyle would climax with the industrialization and individualism of a post-World War II Intermountain society.

In Utah, "the Depression, defense spending, and the proliferation of government agencies had hastened the exodus from country to city," and, by 1930, the state's population was more urban than rural.[89] This migration built upon the Mormon tendency to concentrate settlement along the Wasatch Front, and the Gentile immigrant tendency to seek jobs in the urban industries of Salt Lake City and Ogden, as well as in the coal mines and on the railroad in rural Carbon County. The creation of the Diocese of Reno, in 1931, had reduced the size of the Salt Lake Diocese and eliminated many of the remote missions in the mining camps of Nevada from the circuits of Utah clergymen. Despite hard times, efforts were concentrated upon fund-raising to reduce the debt on the Cathedral of the Madeleine, clearly an urban concern. When Utah Catholics had exhausted all means of fund-raising available at the time, Bishop Kearney announced:

> On Saturday, the 28th of November [1936], we shall consecrate the Cathedral. . . . During the period of preparation for this event, the debt on the Cathedral has been reduced to a few thousand dollars . . . whatever remains of the debt after this collection and the offerings on the day of the Pontifical Mass, I shall undertake to solicit somewhere.[90]

Like the Mormons, by whom they were surrounded, Utah's Catholics struggled to concentrate their energies in order to survive and build a solvent religious community under trying economic conditions.

In Colorado, as gold and silver mining declined, irrigation systems were expanded for increased agricultural activity. Between 1900 and 1940, Colorado became a major producer of food for the country. By 1930, more of Colorado's population was found in urban than rural areas, and, by 1941, the population in the southern portion of the state had grown sufficiently; thus, the Diocese of Pueblo was erected.[91]

The 1940s marked the beginning of industrial growth for most of the Intermountain region. Manufacturing for World War II and the establishment of military bases throughout the region boosted the economy and increased the population. At the end of the war, many servicemen returned with their families to the area, and in the 1950s people rushed in to seek jobs with the new governmental defense and science industries, particularly in such urban areas as Denver, Phoenix, and Albuquerque. By 1950, population in the states of Arizona, New Mexico, and Nevada had become more urban than rural.[92] These changes affected Catholic life by increasing significantly the Catholic populations and the number of parishes with priests in the archdioceses of Denver and Santa Fe and the Diocese of Tucson between 1950 and 1960; in each of the other dioceses of the region, the increase in Catholic population during that decade was approximately 20,000, except for Wyoming, which registered an increase of fewer than 250 Catholics. (See Appendix 2.)

By 1960, population in the states of Montana and Wyoming was more urban than rural.[93] Thus, with the exception of Idaho, whose population did not shift from predominantly rural to predominantly urban until 1970, the entire Intermountain region had experienced dramatic urbanization in a thirty-year period.[94] Missionary ventures among Native Americans had prepared foundations for white settlement. Shifting populations caused by early mining and railroad building had stabilized. New methods of controlling water, the region's most important economic asset, had contributed to the growth of agriculture and industry. Government contracts for military installations, defense laboratories, and forestry management boosted a slowly developing economy. Still, because of geographic determinants, much of the region remained rural and dependent both economically and ecclesiastically on outside support. It would not be until the energy crisis of the 1970s that the Intermountain West and its Catholic population could use its own resources as a tool for self-determination.

Notes

1. P. J. De Smet, S.J., *Letters and Sketches: With a Narrative of a Year's Residence Among the Indian Tribes of the Rocky Mountains* (Philadelphia: M. Eathian, 1843); reprint in Reuben Gold Thwaits, LL.D., *Early Western Travels 1748–1846*, Vol. 27 (Cleveland: The Arthur H. Clark Co., 1906), 159.
2. Neal R. Pierce, *The Mountain States of America: People, Politics, and Power in the Eight Rocky Mountain States* (New York: W. W. Norton and Co., Inc., 1972), 15.
3. *Fifty Years of Growth, 1904–1954*, Eastern Montana Catholic Register, Vol. XXX, No. 49, 11.
4. Dean Harris, *The Catholic Church in Utah, 1776–1909* (Salt Lake City: Intermountain Catholic Press, 1909), 102.
5. Fabiola Cabeza de Baca Gilbert, *We Fed Them Cactus* (Albuquerque: University of New Mexico Press, 1954), 11–14.
6. Father P. J. De Smet, of the Society of Jesus, *Oregon Missions and Travels Over the Rocky Mountains in 1845–46* (New York: Edward Dunigan, 1847); reprint in Ruben Gold Thwaits, LL.D., *Early Western Travels 1748–1846*, Vol. 29 (Cleveland: The Arthur H. Clark Co., 1906), 115.
7. De Smet, *Letters*, 159.
8. Odie B. Faulk, ed., *John Baptist Salpointe, Soldier of the Cross* (Tucson: The Diocese of Tucson, 1966), 7–8.
9. Paul Horgan, *Lamy of Santa Fe: His Life and Times* (New York: Farrar, Straus, and Giroux, 1975), 66.
10. In that same year, Utah became a territory of the United States.
11. Henry W. Casper, S. J., *History of the Catholic Church in Nebraska: The Church on the Northern Plains, 1838–1874* (Milwaukee: The Bruce Publishing Co., 1960), 61; and Rev. William O'Ryan and Rev. Thomas H. Malone, *History of the Catholic Church in Colorado* (Denver: C. J. Kelly, Art Printing, 1889); reprint ed. (Denver: Denver Catholic Register, 1961), 35.
12. Horgan, 319.
13. Rev. Wilfred P. Schoenberg, S.J., *A Chronicle of the Catholic History of the Pacific Northwest, 1743–1960* (Portland, Oregon: Catholic Sentinel Printery, 1962), 62. See also Casper, *Plains*, 219–224.
14. Henry W. Casper, S.J., *History of the Catholic Church in Nebraska: The Church on the Fading Frontier, 1864–1910* (Milwaukee: The Bruce Publishing Co., 1966), 283.
15. Most Rev. Patrick A. McGovern, S.T.D., LL.D., *History of the Diocese of Cheyenne* (Cheyenne, Wyoming: *Wyoming Labor Journal*, 1941), 9.
16. *Fifty Years*, 11.
17. James S. Olson, "Pioneer Catholicism in Eastern and Southern Nevada, 1864–1931," *Nevada Historical Society Quarterly*, 26 (Fall, 1983), 160.
18. David J. Weber, *Foreigners in their Native Land* (Albuquerque: University of New Mexico Press, 1973), 19–21.
19. Luis de Velasco, "Oñate's Appointment as Governor of New Mexico," trans. George P. Hammond, *New Mexico Historical Review*, 13, No. 3 (July, 1938), 246–48; in Weber, 23–24.

20. Father Eusebio Francisco Kino, S.J., *Favores Celestiales*, trans. Herbert Eugene Bolton, Ph.D., *Kino's Historical Memoir of Primeria Alta* (Berkeley: University of California Press, 1948), 100.

21. Herbert Eugene Bolton, *The Padre on Horseback* (Chicago: Loyola University Press, 1963), 64.

22. Pedro Bautista Pino, *Exposición* in. H. Bailey Carroll and J. Villansana Haggard, trans. and ed., *Three New Mexico Chronicles* (Albuquerque: The Quivera Society, 1942), 36.

23. *Ibid.*, 51.

24. Richard Santos, "The Organization of the Church on the Frontier," *Fronteras: A History of the Latin American Church in the USA Since 1513*, ed. Moíses Sandoval (San Antonio: Mexican American Cultural Center, 1983), 95–98.

25. Weber, 19–21.

26. Rev. Wilfred P. Schoenberg, S.J., *Jesuits in Montana, 1840–1960* (Portland, Oregon: The Oregon Jesuit, 1960), 15.

27. *Ibid.*

28. *Ibid.*, 21–22.

29. Rev. Kenneth J. Arnzen, *The First Hundred Years: A Centennial History of St. Mary's Church, Moscow, Idaho* (Moscow, Idaho: n.p., 1982), 5; and Schoenberg, *Chronicle*, 13–14, 34.

30. *Our Lady of Guadalupe, Taos, New Mexico* (White Plains, New York: Monarch Publishing, Inc., 1976), 4.

31. Rev. Kiernan McCarty, O.F.M., "Our Desert Under Spain," in *Shepherds in the Desert*, ed. Silver Jubilee Committee (Tucson: Diocese of Tucson, 1978), 22.

32. General Stephen Watts Kearney in *From Where the Sun Now Stands*, ed. W. D. "Dick" Crisso (Santa Fe: Stagecoach Press, 1963), 48–49.

33. Father Salvatore Persone, Lettera, in Marianne L. Stoller and Thomas J. Steele, *Diary of the Jesuit Residence of Our Lady of Guadalupe Parish Conejos, Colorado, December 1871–December 1875*, The Colorado College Studies, No. 19 (Colorado Springs: The Colorado College, 1982), 181.

34. Faulk, 54, 57.

35. Arnzen, 20.

36. Schoenberg, *Chronicle*, 50.

37. *Ibid.*, 111.

38. O'Ryan and Malone, 41.

39. *Diamond Jubilee*, Cathedral Parish, Denver, Colorado, 27.

40. Mary Ellen Gilliland, *Century of Faith: St. Mary's, Breckenridge, Colorado* (n.p., 1981), 6.

41. *Ibid.*

42. Arnzen, 12–13.

43. *Ibid.*, 16.

44. Schoenberg, *Chronicle*, 54.

45. *Fifty Years*, 13.

46. "St. Bartholomew's," 1983 (Xeroxed), 1; and "Story Is Told of New Church," *Meagher County News*, 19 June 1957, vertical file, Cushwa Center for the Study of American Catholicism, University of Notre Dame, Indiana.

47. Rev. Louis J. Fries, S.T.B., *One Hundred and Fifty Years of Catholicity in Utah* (Salt Lake City: Intermountain Catholic Press, 1926), 21.
48. *Ibid.*, 25.
49. Olson, 162.
50. *Ibid.*
51. *Ibid.*
52. *Encyclopedia Americana*, 1983 ed., s.v. "Nevada."
53. Olson, 161.
54. A section is 640 acres. Melville Bell Grosvenor, ed., *We Americans* (Washington, D.C.: National Geographic Society, 1975), 178.
55. McGovern, 7. See also Casper, *Plains*, 207.
56. Robert Joseph Dwyer, *The Gentile Comes to Utah*, revised 2nd edition (Salt Lake City: Publishers Press, 1971), 63.
57. Casper, *Frontier*, 44.
58. T. Harry Williams, *The Union Surrendered*, Vol. 5: 1849–1865: *The Life History of the United States* (New York: Time-Life Books, 1963), 36.
59. Williams, 37.
60. Myra Ellen Jenkins and Albert H. Schroeder, *A Brief History of New Mexico* (Albuquerque: University of New Mexico Press, 1974), 51.
61. Page Smith, *The Rise of Industrial America*, Vol. 6 (New York: McGraw-Hill Book Co., 1984), 806.
62. Winthrop S. Hudson, *Religion in America*, third edition (New York: Charles Scribner's Sons, 1981), 133.
63. *Ibid.*
64. Faulk, 10.
65. R. Douglas Brackenridge and Francisco O. Garcia-Treto, *Iglesia Presbyteriana: A History of Presbyterian and Mexican-Americans in the Southwest* (San Antonio: Trinity University Press, 1974), 38–39.
66. *Ibid.*, 34.
67. Archdiocese of Santa Fe, *The Old Faith and Old Glory, 1846–1946* (Santa Fe: Santa Fe Press, 1946), 13.
68. *Ibid.*
69. Thomas J. Steele, S.J., *Works and Days* (Albuquerque: The Albuquerque Museum, 1982), 100.
70. *Ibid.*
71. *Encyclopedia Americana*, 1983 ed., s.v. "Idaho," 736.
72. Dwyer, v.
73. Fries, 20.
74. Dwyer, 188.
75. *Ibid.*, 163.
76. Silver Jubilee Committee, *Shepherds in the Desert*, 90.
77. *Ibid.*, 87.
78. *Ibid.*
79. Philip F. Notarianni, "Helper—the Making of a Gentile Town in Zion," *Carbon County: Eastern Utah's Industrialized Island*, ed. Philip F. Notarianni (Salt Lake City: Utah State Historical Society, 1981), 159.

80. *Encyclopedia Americana*, 1983 ed., s.v. "Montana."

81. *Official Catholic Directory* (New York: P. J. Kenedy and Sons, 1920), 366, 395; and *Official Catholic Directory* (New York: P. J. Kenedy and Sons, 1930), 385, 413.

82. *Fifty Years*, 15.

83. *Ibid.*

84. Robert Laxalt, *Nevada: A Bicentennial History* (New York: W. W. Norton and Co., Inc., 1977), 38.

85. *Ibid.*, 95.

86. Olson, 166–167.

87. Charles L. Briggs, "Two Villages in Crisis," *Albuquerque Journal*, 24 September 1985, Impact, *passim*.

88. *Ibid.*, 9.

89. Charles S. Peterson, *Utah: A History* (New York: W. W. Norton and Co., Inc., 1977), 150, and U.S. Department of Commerce, Bureau of the Census, *United States Census of Population: 1980*, Vol. 1, *Characteristics of the Population*, 46, Utah.

90. Bernice Mooney, *The Story of the Cathedral of the Madeleine* (Salt Lake City: Lithografics, Inc., 1981), 118.

91. U.S. Department of Commerce, Bureau of the Census, *United States Census of Population: 1980*, Vol. 1, *Characteristics of the Population*, pt. 7, Colorado; and "A History of the Diocese," *The Southern Colorado Register*, 9 October 1959, 27.

92. U.S. Department of Commerce, Bureau of the Census, *United States Census of Population: 1980*, Vol. 1, *Characteristics of the Population*, pt. 4, Arizona, pt. 33, New Mexico, and pt. 30, Nevada.

93. U.S. Department of Commerce, Bureau of the Census, *United States Census of Population: 1980*, Vol. 1, *Characteristics of the Population*, pt. 28, Montana and pt. 52, Wyoming.

94. U.S. Department of Commerce, Bureau of the Census, *United States Census of Population: 1980*, Vol. 1, *Characteristics of the Population*, pt. 14, Idaho.

CHAPTER TWO
The Local Church

In taking a close look at local church life in the Intermountain West, one is aware of two distinct modes of religious conduct: an expressive style and an organizational style. While some differences between the two can be explained in terms of historical and geographic conditions, the most basic difference is ethnicity. In the southwestern portion of the region (Arizona, New Mexico, and southern Colorado), Catholic parish life was from the beginning an expression of Hispanic politics and culture in an isolated and undeveloped desert frontier. In the northwestern portion (Montana and Idaho) and the intermediate states (Nevada, Utah, Wyoming, and Colorado) nearly 300 years later, Catholic parish life was (with the exception of early Indian missions and a very few national parishes) an extension of Americanization and of U.S. ecclesiastical organization. The separate development of these two religious paths might have gone unnoticed, but for their abrupt interface in 1850 when Southwestern Hispanic and Indian Catholics came under the jurisdiction of an American Catholic Church. As one considers the roles of clerical and lay leaders, building and religious education programs, funding and donated services throughout the region's religious history, this distinction becomes apparent. The contrast in religious conduct can be traced through three developmental periods: (1) the gathering of congregations, (2) the strengthening of parish foundations, and (3) expansion and rebuilding. In the Intermountain West, the earliest period lasted nearly 300 years; the second corresponds to the first half of the twentieth century; the third, for purposes of this study, is focused on the 1950s. But, for many Intermountain Catholics, the struggle between these two forms of the faith is an ongoing one. For Hispanics, events in the history of specific parishes point to the contrast. For Native Americans, a more complex struggle with civil regulation, which complicates this contrast, will be presented in a later chapter.

Clerical leadership in the Southwest during the sixteenth and seventeenth centuries was characterized by a commitment on behalf of both church and state to Christianize Indians. Thus, in New Mexico, according to Fray Angelico Chavez, "the Franciscans, deeming themselves missionaries to the Indians primarily, had regarded the Hispanic faithful in a more or less casual manner outside the Sacraments of baptism and marriage."[1] Is it any wonder, then, that these isolated Catholics, deprived of regular clerical ministry, would develop a form of parish life in which the Sacraments became secondary to a personal/communal piety that could count on lay leadership? A faith totally integrated with one's daily life was centered in the home, where parents (particularly mothers) saw to it that prayer and religious education were part of the activities of each day. Only rarely is credit given to these spiritual leaders by scholars of Hispanic culture in America. And yet:

> the religious and familiar feeling, the concept of duty and of humor, the cult of decorum and honor, the profound piety which Spain left in America owes itself in great part to the women who from the beginning guided and oriented the spirituality of the foundations.
>
> When one speaks of the glory of the *conquistadores* and the missionaries who civilized all the world, one ought to associate always in the same memory the women who went with them.[2]

These early Spanish laywomen were entrusted, as were Anglo Protestant women later, with the spiritual and moral qualities of a civilization, while simultaneously relegated to a status within the institutional structures of church and society subordinate to and dependent on patriarchal organizations.

The policy of secularization, which had been adopted by all Spanish colonies in America, was to replace missionary order priests with secular clergy, subject to a bishop, as soon as a frontier area had enough domesticated Indians and Spanish colonists to support a priest and parish. This policy endorsed and implemented the unifying tendency of the Council of Trent by placing more emphasis on bishops who could exercise territorial power, and less emphasis on orders with the varying charisms of their respective founders. In Arizona, secularization seems to have proceeded smoothly, if ineffectively. Even before the Jesuit expulsion of 1767, two parishes in northern Sonora had been founded and manned by diocesan priests from Durango, San Juan Bautista de Sonora and Nuestra Señora del Rosario de Nacozari.[3] The arrangement was to staff each parish with two clergymen, one whose role was pastor, and another whose role was ecclesiastical judge and vicar for the bishop; while one priest was always in residence, the other rode the circuit from one Spanish settlement to another.[4] These diocesan priests faced the same dangers and difficulties as earlier religious missionaries and often died just as dramatically in the execution of their ministry. On April 16, 1754, Father Pedro Rodríguez Rey was killed by Apaches while responding to a sick call; in February of 1767, Father Francisco Ildefonso Felix died with a crucifix in his hand during the Cerro Prieto rebellion; and in October of 1843, Father Francisco Alday was killed by Apaches attacking the Santa Cruz presidio.[5] The ecclesiastical tendency to exert territorial control through organization did not entirely succeed in Indian-dominated Arizona.

In New Mexico, secularization was not successful for additional reasons. Unlike the Arizona martyrs just mentioned, many of the secular clergymen sent to

New Mexico were discouraged by the poverty and ruggedness of Church life there and returned to Durango, aggravating the pre-existing problem of insufficient clerical services for Hispanics. Early conflicts between friars and local political leaders became intertwined with conflicts over Franciscan and diocesan jurisdiction, further complicating secularization. In 1747, when Don Antonio de Orendal y Maza arrived in New Mexico as presidial inspector, he joined the faction of Governor Tomas Velaz Cachupen, and, composing an unfavorable report to the Franciscan administration, proposed secularization as a deliberate shift of ecclesiastical and secular power, rather than as a pastoral decision.[6] By 1789, the three New Mexico towns of Santa Fe, Santa Cruz, and Albuquerque (as well as El Paso, Texas) were diocesan parishes of Durango manned by secular clergymen. Regular celebration of Mass and legitimate administration of the Sacraments by clergymen were then joined to the folk religious practices of the people in those villages, temporarily combining both organizational and expressive forms of Catholicism. But, in 1821, Mexico declared its independence from Spain and in 1827 issued a decree exiling all Spanish-born residents of the United States of Mexico. This left missions and Hispanic parishes in Arizona much more vulnerable to Apache attack, and those in New Mexico vulnerable to physical and spiritual neglect on the part of clerical leadership. Again, lay leadership emerged, this time in the form of a *cofradia* called *La Fraternidad Piadosa de Nuestro Padre Jesus Nazareno*—the Penitentes. While details of their contributions to Hispanic Catholic life will appear later, it is important to note here their importance in continuing communal parish functions, such as funerals and Holy Week services, just as *santeros* continued to create devotional images and women continued to encourage personal devotions, religious education, and the use of such sacramentals as blessings, pious sayings, and blessed objects. Cleofas Jaramillo recalls how her Aunt Dolores awakened the family early in the morning with her hymn at dawn, greeted people in the name of God, knelt at a home altar for prayer, and blessed the family children at the end of the day as they kissed her hand in respect.[7] These memories of an expressive faith are more vivid for her than those of official Church functions directed by clergymen.

In the Northwest, although examples of lay initiative in the establishment of Catholic parish life have been recorded, clerical leadership was the dominant pattern in a U.S.-sponsored civil and ecclesiastical campaign to civilize the wilderness. While Jesuit missionaries here made it clear (as had Franciscans in the Southwest) that they had come primarily to work with Indians, in actuality they extended their ministry to whites as well. In 1853, a temporary log chapel at De Smet, Idaho, served both traders and Indians; and it was Jesuits from St. Ignatius Mission who built and manned the first churches for whites in the territory at Hell's Gate and Frenchtown.[8] Although some of these Indian missionaries later objected to staffing more new parishes for whites, the late dates of Jesuit replacement at other white parishes in both the Northwest and Southwest testify to the value of Jesuit ministry in bringing stability to the early establishment of white parishes in the Northwest.

The Jesuits of the Rocky Mountain Indian missions extended their ministry to serve not only the Catholics at Helena, but those scattered within a hundred-mile radius around that town. They visited stations at settlements where the number of Catholics ranged from seven or ten to as many as 125.[9] It was not the numbers of the faithful but the distances to be covered and the prior commitments to running Indian missions that made it impossible to visit some places more often than quarterly. In 1866, the resident pastor who came to Cottonwood was the first diocesan clergyman to reside in Montana. By 1884, Frenchtown received its first pastor, but it was 1905 before the Jesuits who had served St. James Parish at Plains were replaced by diocesan clergy.

Other than the early example of the Flatheads being evangelized and baptized by Iroquois laymen before setting out to obtain black robes for their tribe, few incidents are recorded of laypeople taking the initiative in the establishment of Catholic life in this portion of the region. In the rural, mobile settlements of white immigrants, cut off from their European roots and from Eastern ethnic ghettos, it is likely that the expression of one's faith was not as intimately bound to one's entire cultural complex as it was for isolated communities of Hispanics with hundreds of years of a lay tradition. It may be also be true that immigrant European Catholics had become aware in America of how the centrality of an elaborate sacramental system in their religion made for greater dependence on clerical leadership than they observed in American Protestants. Thus, these early white Catholic settlers came west for individual reasons, confident that their clergymen would follow to minister to what they saw as their basic spiritual needs. Even before Catholic miners and railroad workers began to come into the region, Catholic military men stationed at forts throughout the Northwestern and intermediate states were visited by passing clergymen or Indian missionaries eager to extend the grace of the Sacraments to whites on a somewhat lawless frontier. When Father Nicholas Point, S.J., spent the winter of 1846 to 1847 at Fort Benton, Montana, he insisted on validating the marriages between white men and Indian women and on baptizing their children.[10] Perhaps European immigrants, more easily Americanized than Native Americans or Hispanics, were seen as "civilizing" agents by the American institutional Church.

In the intermediate Intermountain states, where missionary work had not accustomed clergymen to the great distances and difficulties of frontier life, diocesan priests were the first to bring their ministry to Catholic settlers. These clergymen were often foreign born and frequently Irish. Like order and secular clergymen in both the Northwest and the Southwest, the few priests assigned to a diocese or vicariate regularly covered large areas as circuit riders. When the two Frenchmen, Rev. John B. Raverdy and Rev. Joseph P. Machebeuf (later to become Colorado's first bishop), were assigned to Colorado, Montana, and Utah in

1860, they visited many villages in that territory. In Utah and Nevada, small mining camps with predominantly Catholic populations were scattered throughout huge areas of wilderness. The geographical conditions of such an apostolate required men with physical and psychic endurance.

Many of the first clergymen sent to these areas were Irishmen from the San Francisco Diocese. Reports indicate that they got along well with both their Catholic parishioners and the Mormon leaders of the day, in their attempt to supply the spiritual need for Mass and the Sacraments. An outstanding member of the Irish clergy was Rev. William Kelly, sent to Wyoming in 1867 to care for all the Catholics from Sidney, Nebraska, to Wasatch Canyon, Utah. This robust pioneer had been a Christian brother in Ireland and was forty years old when he received holy orders.[11]

The nineteenth-century efforts of a foreign-born U.S. clergy to bring ecclesiastical order to the West were not limited to the Northwestern and intermediate states of the Intermountain region. With the 1848 Treaty of Guadalupe Hidalgo, their influence came as a culture shock to Hispanic and Indian Catholics in the Southwest. When French missionary priests under the leadership of Bishop Jean Baptist Lamy arrived in the newly established Vicariate of Santa Fe in 1851, they did so in the name of U.S. ecclesiastical authority. Ignorant of the circumstances that both Spanish and Mexican neglect had wrought in the American Southwest, these foreigners were appalled at the state of decline in which they found Church affairs. From their point of view, "the general disarray was the fault of the clergy. . . . The people went to Mass, observed the feast days, kept their sodalities active enough, but for the most part failed to adhere to the Sacraments."[12]

It would be some time before Lamy could see why the Sacraments were not central in these people's faith. Meanwhile, his campaign was to reform or replace the Mexican priests he considered at fault.

Of the ten priests that Lamy found in his new vicariate (which included New Mexico, Arizona, and, soon, parts of Colorado, Utah, and Montana), not all of them accepted his authority as legitimate. Among them was Antonio José Martínez, native of New Mexico, trained in Durango. The conflict between these two priests over tithes, clerical responsibility, and ethnic custom is a well-known topic of debate. One of the nonverbal elements in this cultural clash was Lamy's repeated appeal to France to obtain more clergymen for his growing diocese. Only after two sets of recruits arrived from Europe did Lamy see fit to ordain four native New Mexicans.[13]

Despite earnest efforts to man his diocese with secular clergymen from France, Lamy was also forced by necessity to obtain order priests. In 1867, five Neapolitan Jesuits (three priests and two brothers) in exile from Italy were assigned to Bishop Lamy's diocese. They stationed themselves in Bernalillo, temporarily took charge of two other parishes and seven Indian pueblos, and soon moved

The Local Church

downriver to Albuquerque's San Felipe de Neri Church, from which they spread into other parts of the territory.

In Colorado, Bishop Joseph P. Machebeuf was at first supplied with French priests from the Santa Fe Diocese; but soon he, like Lamy, was forced to seek order priests to supplement an insufficient number of secular clergy. In 1879, he wrote to his brother:

> We have a church at Leadville, but it is much too small. The Catholics come but the crowd is such that one-half of the people strive to hear Mass kneeling in the cold and snow outside the church in the street. I have only one priest there, one whom I ordained in 1872, and he is badly in need of an assistant, but I have none to send him.[14]

In 1871, Jesuits had taken over Our Lady of Guadalupe Parish at Conejos, and, in 1872, the same order had established St. Ignatius Parish in Pueblo. In the same letter to his brother, Machebeuf explained:

> I have also a Prussian exile priest to whom I have given the care of the Germans in Denver, and I have applied to the Franciscans for two priests to establish a house under their order and a parish here, and then, too, I expect two Jesuit Fathers soon to found a parish in Denver and later to build a college.[15]

Father John Wagner was the refugee from Bismarck's Kulturkampf who gathered Denver's German Catholics into the congregation that would become St. Elizabeth's Parish.[16] In 1879, he was succeeded by Father Frederick Bender; it was not until Father Francis Koch arrived as pastor in 1887 that the Franciscan Fathers of Paterson, New Jersey, answered Machebeuf's request. However, Sacred Heart Parish in Denver was established by Father John Guida, S.J., on September 12, 1879, and, in 1884, Sacred Heart College was founded.

In 1897, the Franciscans returned to Indian missions of the Southwest at the request of Tucson's Bishop Peter Bourgade. At St. Michael's in Arizona, they established the first mission for Navajo Indians, which later added a mission to Chinle and a station at Lukachukai. In 1900, they took over the parish at Pena Blanca, New Mexico, and, in 1902, returned to Jemez Pueblo.

Not all requests for parish priests came from bishops. Sometimes, laypeople made their needs and desires known, particularly in the Northwest, where clerical leadership was viewed as a necessary condition for parish life. In the spring of 1866, after a year of periodic services administered by Jesuit missionaries in their rounds of white settlements and mining camps, the Catholics of Helena presented a petition to Father Urban Grassi, S.J., requesting that two priests be stationed at Helena.[17] Although Grassi had only eight priests in all of Montana, and they were dedicated primarily to working with the Indians, he recognized that the 1,000 Catholics in Helena and 2,000 more in the vicinity were seriously in need of attention, and sent Father Kuppens and Father D'Aste there.[18]

In Idaho, the tradition of bishops who were also active on a pastoral level is large. Belgian-born Archbishop Charles Seghers is remembered in the Northwest for his stamina and energy:

> In his official visitations to the northern section of the Idaho Vicariate in 1879 and 1882, Archbishop Seghers traveled by horseback, camping along the trails. Father Cataldo, his constant companion in visiting the Indians, recalled Seghers' traveling habits. "Like everyone else in the group, the Vicar Apostolic insisted on taking his turn at cutting and carrying the wood, bringing water from the creek, and cooking supper or breakfast."[19]

Archbishop Seghers retired from the bishopric, returned to Vancouver, B.C., and enjoyed a missionary career in Alaska until he was murdered in his bed by a deranged lay missionary at Nulatto.[20]

Another pastorally oriented prelate, Bishop Alphonsus Joseph Glorieux, spent seven months in 1888 as pastor of St. Charles Borromeo Parish at Hailey, Idaho, when Father Emanuel M. Nattini retired because of poor health, and when his replacement "found the far-flung parish too much for his powers of endurance and resigned and went back east."[21]

These examples of episcopal ministry are probably not what Pope Leo XIII had in mind in 1895 when he addressed an encyclical to the American Church. In *Longingua Oceani,* there are praises for "the young and vigorous American nation, in which we plainly discern latent forces for the advancement alike of civilization and Christianity."[22] Lauding "the prosperous condition of Catholicity," the Pope gives credit "to the virtue, the ability, and the prudence of the bishops and clergy" with the "main factor, no doubt" being "the ordinances and decrees of your synods."[23] Clearly, the institutional aspects of the American Church are his primary concern. His expressed belief that the Catholic Church had greater opportunity for prosperity in a country where it was supported by the state rather than "as in America, dissevered and divorced" was not well-received by Protestant Americans.[24] There is no doubt that ecclesiastical organization contributed greatly to the stability of clerical leadership in the immense wilderness of the Intermountain West, but it was not the only force at work in the development, preservation, and celebration of the Catholic faith in that region.

Building programs for Intermountain parishes, like clerical and lay leadership traditions, suggest some differences between early Southwestern and other approaches. In the Southwest, Bishop Benito Crespo of Durango noted at Santa Cruz in 1730 that the church had been built not by Indians under the direction of friars with royal subsidies, but "at the expense of its Spanish citizens."[25] The phrase "at their own expense" became a common way of describing local lay initiative for the building of churches in Southwestern Hispanic villages.

In the Northwest, the construction of church buildings was often an essential part of creating a new town. Thus, it reflected secular as well as religious efforts to organize and "civilize" the frontier. This was true in Pocatello, Idaho, from 1871 to 1897, and in White Sulphur Springs, Montana, during the 1880s. Despite the national economic depression of 1893, Intermountain Catholics continued their pioneering struggle to provide what they considered the essentials for a proper parish life. After gathering for months or years in schools, homes, hotels, halls, saloons, stores, log cabins, or courthouses for the celebration of Mass and the Sacraments, these immigrant Catholics were eager to worship in what they considered a more sacred space.

In the intermediate states, as elsewhere, churches for whites were built only after subscription lists of pledged financial supports were collected. Bishop Machebeuf wrote in 1867:

> I came home yesterday from Golden City. . . . Our little church there is almost finished although there are but two Catholic families in the town, and these represent four different nationalities. They have each subscribed $100, and some of the farmers have subscribed $100 also, and the Americans help us liberally.[26]

In Idaho, the same Bishop Glorieux who thought it not beneath himself to take over pastoral duties at a parish suddenly bereft of its priest bought lots for churches at several towns where sufficient funds could not be gathered. As communities grew along with these early parishes, their hastily constructed churches usually needed to be replaced with more permanent structures either because of size, loss due to fires in wooden buildings, or damage due to weathering of adobe walls.

Once arrangements had been made by circuit-riding clergymen to provide Intermountain Catholics with celebration of the Sacraments on a regular basis and to build churches, some consideration was given to religious education. When Bishop John Baptist Lamy assumed the direct care of the Vicariate of New Mexico in 1851 he concluded

> that the education of the people, except in some rich families, had been very limited, if not entirely neglected in many instances. There was, however, a branch of learning and this indeed, the first among all others was, the teaching of catechism and of the Christian prayers, which had been kept alive in the Mexican families since the time of the Franciscan missionaries.[27]

Several years later, Bishop John Baptist Salpointe commented that this home education was of such value to missionaries that even after parochial school had been established, "these schools [could] accomplish very little in inculcating religion in the hearts of the young if the work [had] not been commenced at home."[28]

A complementary socializing activity in some Hispanic homes was the Christian education of Indian servants, an important obligation that the Spanish family took very seriously. These *criados,* both children and adults, were prepared for baptism and sponsored by the families with whom they lived.

Institutionalized programs of Catholic education in the Intermountain West can be best understood in a national context that includes both civil and ecclesiastical attitudes toward education and the role of women in it. One of the beliefs growing out of American Puritan society was that without education (both secular and religious) a person would retain a greater tendency toward evil than toward good and, thus, for the sake of social order, instruction in Godly living was essential. This attitude was deepened by the experience of the American Revolution and the fear of freedom generated by an irrevocable break with traditional authority. How would this newly liberated people create and maintain social order in a new governmental form? "Whig ideology stressed that liberty depended upon popular virtue; the American people must be pious, disinterested, and unworldly if the Republic were to survive."[29] And it was women who were entrusted with the responsibility of passing this piety on to their sons and, thus, preserving the republic. For Protestant women, this role was fulfilled not only through motherhood, but also by their conspicuous participation in revivals and prayer meetings and by individual evangelizing efforts. The principle that evangelical activity proved the authority of one's conversion experience applied to Protestant women as well as to men.

But how did Catholic women whose religious experience did not include emphasis on personal conversion share in this national belief? Hispanic women in the Southwest seemed to possess a similar sense of responsibility as culture bearers for an ancient code of honor that blended religion with personal refinement. Among white Catholic women in America, religious women (usually representing European congregations) carried the visible social responsibility for bringing civilization, refinement, and a sense of American culture to Native Americans and whites alike, via formal institutions for learning. In the Northwestern section of the Intermountain region, Jesuit missionaries wasted no time in obtaining the services of religious women for their Indian mission schools. In 1864, the Sisters of Charity of Providence came to Montana to run the Indian boarding school at St. Ignatius Mission, and, in 1884, the Ursulines came to eastern Montana to open missions among the Cheyennes.

Since most Catholic schools for Indians were established as private mission schools, primarily for boarders, they are not discussed here in the context of local parish life, but will be later in the section on religion and ethnicity.

Several of the Provincial Councils of Baltimore (held between 1829 and 1849), but especially the three Plenary Councils of Baltimore (held in 1852, 1866, and 1874), urged the erection of parochial schools. Certainly, part of the rationale for such schools had to do with the conflicts between European and American ways of life and between Catholic and Protestant social goals. These conflicts characterized the transitional period in America's religious history when two great waves of European immigration created serious social, political, and economic problems in this country. Catholic fears over the loss of the faith outside Catholic schools conflicted with Protestant resolve to create a public school system designed to pass on the faith of America's Protestant "beginnings." Whichever of these considerations was uppermost in the minds of the council fathers, by the time the mandate was carried to the Western frontier, it bore the marks of the old Protestant fear of barbarism. When Bishop Lamy attended the First Plenary Council of Baltimore in 1852, he resolved to bring a community of sisters back to Santa Fe. His assistant, Father Machebeuf, wrote to his sister from Pena Blanca, expressing some of that concern for Christian piety, especially in women:

> As the source of evil here is the profound ignorance of the people, the first necessity must be instruction, and for this we need Christian schools for the youth of both sexes, but especially for young girls. The means of forming them to virtue and to good example, which is rare in New Mexico, is the establishment of religious houses conducted by persons devoted to their calling, and filled with the spirit of self-sacrifice.[30]

The Sisters of Loretto who returned with Lamy to the Santa Fe Diocese first opened their own academies between 1852 and 1885. In 1894, they were asked to teach in the Taos public school. On their arrival in Denver, in 1864, to open St. Mary's Academy, this same community of sisters received the following tribute in the *Rocky Mountain News:*

> This new Seminary under the care of the Sisters of Loretto will be opened here on the first of August, and will be conducted in the successful style of the first class schools of the states. Apart from peculiarity of tenants connected with Catholic seminaries in our country, oft-times obnoxious to parties holding to the Protestant policy, it cannot be denied that schools such as the above is intended to be, have accomplished and are still accomplishing an immense amount of good in the cause of thorough and accomplished education. We hail good schools everywhere and of every kind as one of the most cheering signs of American civilization. . . . The highest ideal of a well ordered State or Territory should be realized in advanced and advancing conditions of female refinement. We should sustain to the utmost all the institutions whose object is to develop the charming qualities of modest intelligence, grace, generosity of character, and geniality of temper, which are calculated to adorn, protect, and dignify.[31]

In this single article, we see summarized the national WASP attitude toward education in relation to which Catholic education in America (especially on the frontier) was also understood.

In the Southwest, schools run by white missionaries, both Catholic and Protestant, were instruments not only of civilization, but of acculturation in a very particular American mode. Hispanic boys often attended Protestant schools "out of sheer necessity of learning English, for in these parts it is necessary for trade with Americans of the United States that the Spanish people make great and protracted sacrifices to send their boys to schools where it is taught."[32]

In the Northwest and intermediate states, congregations of sisters, like the orders of priests who preceded them, gradually extended their teaching apostolate to white as well as Indian Catholics. Small schools, often set up in spare rooms of church basements, were begun, sometimes by laypeople in anticipation of the arrival of religious women. In 1863, Father Machebeuf bought a vacant building, which he had moved next to the church and equipped as a school. He then hired a Miss Steele to conduct classes for pupils, not all of whom were Catholic. Other Catholic day schools were conducted by lay teachers during the next twenty years in such places as Tucson, Arizona; Bozeman, Montana; and Ogden, Utah. Although it is not always clear whether or not these early schools were intended to serve a particular parish or a much larger area, they are distinguished from academies and other sorts of private boarding schools established by communities of sisters or brothers at the request of a bishop.

Because territorial governments were slow in establishing public school systems in parts of the Southwest, members of religious orders were often asked to conduct these schools. In 1878, Sister Blandina Segale, a Cincinnati Sister of Charity, went to Trinidad, Colorado, to open a public school. But, in 1874, the Jesuits at Conejos could not accept an offer to run the county school as none of them could teach English. In commenting on this disappointment in a letter, Father Raffaele Baldassarre, a French Jesuit, laments in much the same disparaging tone used by many other Anglos, "Thus our ignorance of this language removes the means of instructing this miserable people so unlearned and superstitious."[33] Despite the willingness of Intermountain Catholics to cooperate with the bishops in council by building and supporting parochial schools, the services of religious and lay teachers in academies and public schools seem to have been more common. By 1900, only the Diocese of Denver had more than ten parochial schools. (See Appendix 2.)

Although religious education programs have always been a valuable element in parish life, either where a parochial school was unfeasible or where many Catholic students did not attend the parochial school, they grew in number and improved in quality dramatically as parochial schools struggled to survive and sometimes failed. Early parishes in newly developed towns often could not afford a building or could not obtain teachers for a parochial school, and so, as was done at Cheyenne and Laramie, Wyoming, organized Sunday schools for the first ten or twenty years of their existence. At the village of Duranes in New Mexico, the Jesuits who ran a school for boys in Albuquerque's Old Town also provided Mass and Catechism every Sunday for the students at the Albuquerque Indian School run by the Bureau of Indian Affairs. It appears that this religious education program extended itself to more than the Native American students, as it soon became the general children's Mass. These nineteenth-century beginnings of religious education programs in the Intermountain region may have seemed second best to parochial schools at the time, but they set precedent for what has become a nation-wide twentieth-century priority.

Perhaps the most common, but unavoidable, concern of most Catholics at any time has been fund-raising. Most often, the funds are raised for the construction of buildings and other organizational expenses. During the 1850s, Bishop Lamy in New Mexico energetically reinstituted the earlier tradition of tithing. In a circular letter of 1854, he stated in Spanish:

> The faithful of this territory, having no pretext for complaining of the parish taxes, nor of the collection of tithes; [they] will know that we have withdrawn from Pastors the facility of administering the Sacraments [nor may they] give ecclesiastical burial to the heads of families who refuse to pay their share of the tithes.[34]

This early tithing system was more diocesan than parochial; however, in later years, when pastors could not collect the amount of contribution they felt was suitable, they appealed to the bishop to use his influence in forcing payment of tithes.[35] At San Felipe Parish in Albuquerque:

> [i]n addition to the tithes, which they split with parish and bishop, and the first fruits, which they retained, the priests could also keep the income from fiestas, Holy Week sermons, and other such special ceremonies, and the stipend offerings for Masses. . . . A large portion of their income was spent in building and rebuilding.[36]

At Santa Cruz Parish in the same diocese, parishioners paid either the *diezmo* or the *primicias*. The former was a 10% tithe paid in different commodities or with manual labor; the latter was a commitment by parishioners to designate some portion of their hay or grain producing land, and the harvest from it, to the church.

However, finances for rebuilding and other parish projects came from a variety of sources. Often, the religious order serving Indians in the area built the first churches for whites. At other times, a local secular clergyman or even a visiting bishop bought the land and paid for the first simple structure. In the period of early settlement, railroad companies, power companies, or wealthy civic leaders frequently donated land or money for the construction of a church. In 1895, at Wilbax, Montana, Mr. Wilbax paid the entire cost of the church building and furnishings for St. Peter's.[37]

In Colorado, Father Machebeuf was less dependent on agricultural/pastoral Hispanics for financial support. He recognized the potential for income in white miners and military men. Still, he, like Lamy, knew how to be forceful in getting what he wanted.

> This winter I collected $1,600 for our convent from the Americans, who gave with good grace. I often state the sum that I expect them to give, and they smile and pay it to me. Then I show this to others and they give their share too. . . . I once got $100 from a Methodist preacher for the convent, but he was a public man, a Colonel Chivington of the army. Thus, Providence is assisting us in all sorts of ways.[38]

The last mentioned assistance from Providence came through the hands of the same Colonel Chivington who commanded the Sand Creek massacre in 1864.

Despite help from secular and ecclesiastical sources, the laity of most parishes in the region assumed the major responsibility for the building and continued maintenance of its churches. As evidence of their commitment to the congregation and its building program, parishioners often signed subscription lists professing their intention to financially support the project. Frequently, it was the women (particularly in Idaho) who devoted their time and talents to collecting funds for the building. In the fall of 1891, the Catholics of Idaho Falls decided to build a church. The women of the parish ran a concession at the county fair for six years, and, by 1897, the congregation was able to begin construction of a frame church.[39] While the women were busy collecting funds, the men were occupied in volunteering hours of labor to build the churches themselves. Assumption Church at West Broadview, Montana, was financed in an unusual way. Parishioners donated a section of land to the church, grew grain on the land, sold the grain to pay for building materials, then did the construction work themselves.[40]

In many parishes, pew rental was a regular means of raising funds. When names of parishioners accompanied by a statement of amounts given for this purpose and for special collections were published in church announcements or bulletins, negligent or poor parishioners must have been shamed into further efforts to contribute.

Happier ways of raising funds involve special projects that have a social as well as an economic goal. In 1873, although there was only one church in the entire territory of Utah, it was encumbered with a heavy debt. One of the first efforts of Rev. Lawrence Scanlon, third pastor of Salt Lake City, on assuming charge of his parish was to liquidate that debt. One project contributing to the elimination of the debt was a four-day fair held by the women of the parish at Hussey's Hall in December.

Special fund-raisers have frequently involved the domestic talents of Catholic women. But, public relations skills were also important when religious women went begging for funds to build schools. In 1875, two Holy Cross Sisters who had come to Salt Lake City, Utah, to open a school appealed not only to citizens of Salt Lake but to miners in mining camps and smelters, from whom they received substantial support. While this particular school was to be a private academy rather than a parochial school, its importance as the first Catholic school in the entire Salt Lake parish was seen by parishioners as a fund-raising priority. Both clergy and laypeople needed to use ingenuity in gaining financial support for frontier parish needs.

In addition to monetary contributions, personal contributions of time and talent were vital to the establishment of most Intermountain parishes. The two most common societies in most parishes (because they fulfilled necessary functions on the parish level) were the Altar Society for women and Holy Name Society for men. Sometimes called Altar and Rosary Society, the women's group was committed to the upkeep of the sanctuary, altar decorations, vestments, and altar linens. The Holy Name Society often served simply as the Men's Club, focusing on building and overall maintenance efforts.

While not much mention is made of either of these societies in parish histories of the region before the turn of the century, a sort of predecessor of these voluntary groups existed and continues to exist in parishes without priests among Hispanic Catholics in the Southwest. The *mayordomos* are one couple or more who commit themselves for a year to care for the church. "It is always considered a high honor to be entrusted with the keys to the church."[41] So dependable were the parishioners who served these ongoing material needs of the congregation that they often were in complete charge of a church that found itself without a resident pastor.

In a diary detailing one of his many trips throughout Colorado, Bishop Machebeuf made this entry on January 29, 1878: "I was surprised last week to find a neat church and residence at Boulder, due partly to the generosity of a pious lady convert, who also sings in the choir and plays the organ."[42] This type of generous, energetic, and talented layperson must have been highly prized on the frontier, especially since her piety also met the social expectations of one who could truly contribute to the civilization of the West.

Often, parish societies served ethnic, national, or material needs, but some confraternities (or *cofradias* as they are known among Hispanic Catholics) served primarily spiritual needs. In addition to the well-known *Hermanos de Nuestro Padre Jesus* (the Penitentes), whose own prayers and penances are supplemented by spiritual and corporal works of mercy, *La Cofradia de Nuestro Senora del Carmel* served parishioners in Santa Cruz de la Cañada, New Mexico. Founded in 1710 "under Fray Juan Mingues, with proper license from Fray Miguel de Santa Teresa, Father Provincial of the Carmelites of New Spain," the *cofradia* later built a chapel for their devotions and today boast a substantial membership, which holds an annual fiesta on July 16th.[43] These pious societies will be discussed later in greater detail in the context of religion and ethnicity.

During the first half of the twentieth century, the slow transition from missionary priests to secular clergy necessitated requests for more religious order priests to serve the region's parishes. Sometimes, leadership was even assumed by laypersons. Early churches were rebuilt while many parishes constructed their first churches. Parochial school development experienced an ebb and flow as other religious education programs grew in popularity. The founding of national benevolent societies gave vital support to Catholic efforts in a region where vast distances and insufficient clergy strained existing financial resources. During this period, parish societies and parish sponsored activities for youth became more popular as a growing need for better social bonds between parishioners became evident.

The twentieth century found this region still much in need of priests, especially to serve the previously converted Indians and the traditionally Catholic Hispanics. At the turn of the century, the Franciscans returned to the Archdiocese of Santa Fe after a long absence. Twenty-three friars were responsible for 33,648 people in eight parishes covering 56,000 square miles: 1,200 Anglos in thirteen towns and settlements; 800 Croatians in four mining camps; 11,000 Hispanics in sixty-four towns, villages, or ranchitos; three tribes of Pueblo Indians on nine reservations in twenty different villages numbering 6,670; 878 Jicarilla Apaches; and 23,000 Navajo.[44] When Fray Albert T. Daeger, O.F.M., was appointed Archbishop of Santa Fe in 1919, he invited the Sons of the Holy Family to administer a New Mexico parish where Spanish-speaking priests were needed.

Supplementing early missionaries and diocesan clergymen in parish life were the Salvatorians, the Benedictines, the Marists, the Nobertines, the Redemptorists, and the Capuchins, among others. The number of priests in all Intermountain dioceses increased significantly during these decades. (See Appendix A.) But, still, there were examples of lay leadership in areas where priests no longer or irregularly served.

From 1900 to 1912 in Provo, Utah, St. Peter's Church had been closed because of a decline in Catholic population. It was a layman, Joseph Gendron, who in 1912

> found the keys of the church, had it thoroughly cleaned, and gathered the few Catholics in the community together. He acted as a sort of deacon, instructing the children and saying the Rosary for the people. He then made application to Bishop Scanlon for a priest.[45]

In 1910, Sarah "Killarney" Reynolds, an Irish immigrant to the mining community of Helper, Utah,

> "transformed the dilapidated wooden Catholic church on a hill east of the railroads; it had no heat, water, or electricity. With pails of water carried up a steep hill, she, Vera Lizette, and Catherine Verdi, daughters of Italian immigrants, scrubbed, painted, polished and made the church a parish for the miners of the county."[46]

This church bridged the gap in pastoral care between that established in the company town of Castle Gate and that built by Rev. Anthony Petillo at Helper in 1914.

More permanent buildings to replace early churches were constructed from 1910 to 1940. Often, as at the mining camp of Bingham, Utah, in 1902, the decision to build a larger church was made by the Catholic population at a formal meeting. If the congregation disbanded because of fluctuations in mining ventures, sometimes the churches were disassembled and rebuilt on another site. While some parishes had to postpone rebuilding because of World War I or the Great Depression, others, like St. Mary's in Moscow, Idaho, did not. This parish (with some savings and the help of the Catholic Church Extension Society) replaced forty-four year old Holy Trinity Church with a brick building in 1930.

In the Southwest, those old Hispanic parishes in locales where economic developments began to draw new citizens joined in the general building movement. At Belen, New Mexico, which began to prosper in 1907 when it became a railroad center and shipping point, Our Lady of Belen Church was rebuilt in 1917, using the tower and roof of the old church as part of the new cement block building. Financing this project did not appear to be an extreme hardship, as the achievement of statehood for New Mexico in 1912 seems to have given a new boost to agriculture in its Rio Grande Valley. In the small, rural villages of northern New Mexico, however, a lack of economic development, combined with traditional Hispanic sentiments about one's parish church structure and site, often complicated and prolonged rebuilding projects. In 1928, at the village of Los Ojos, the church building was in danger of collapsing. Whether faulty construction was responsible, or neglect during the financially difficult years of building a parochial school and supporting the sisters was to blame, a new church was needed. Services were temporarily moved into the basement of the school in October of that year, but did not emerge until 1936. The economic hardships of the Great Depression were only part of the reason for the eight year struggle. Another economic difficulty was the severe winter of 1931, which devastated the sheep industry in the Tierra Amarilla area.

> Early snows caught many shepherds with their flocks still in summer pasture. Losses of 50% were common, and many lost everything they had before the flocks could be moved to winter pastures. The severe weather persisted through . . . [s]pring, creating havoc on the sheep industry. This "año de la nevada" dealt a severe blow to the area's main livelihood. . . . Many found themselves with no sheep and limited prospects for employment.[47]

In addition to these economic woes, two issues relating to Hispanic religious tradition created factions within the parish. The people's fondness for their church building and for many of its old furnishings caused resentment when the building was abandoned and the furnishings were placed either in the school basement or in storage. Letters of complaint from parishioners to the archbishop did not succeed in reversing the pastor's decision on this occasion. But, later, when construction plans for the new church called for a full basement that would function as a community center, and parishioners opposed the plan because of the complete excavation of the *camposanto* (graveyard) that it required, the next pastor tactfully decided to compromise and excavate only for the heating system and access to it.[48] Here, again, we have evidence on the parish level of the conflict between a Roman/American Catholic organizing tendency to modernize and expand ecclesiastical establishments and the ancient Hispanic Catholic expressive tendency to preserve sacred objects in particular environments.

At the beginning of the twentieth century in this region, the number of parochial schools fluctuated. Reasons for this trend seem to vary from diocese to diocese. In Santa Fe and Denver, decreases in the number of parochial schools are accounted for by the erection of the Gallup and Pueblo dioceses in 1939 and 1941, respectively. From 1930 to 1950, the Helena Diocese lost only two schools and the Boise Diocese only three; however, the Salt Lake Diocese lost five out of nine parochial schools. (See Appendix A.) The most probable explanation for the latter fact is the severity of the economic problems of the Great Depression throughout Utah, which suffered the unemployment of one-third of its work force by 1932 and increased migration from the state.[49] While close-knit Mormon communities in the state could afford to reject federal relief programs in favor of their own self-help programs, neither the number nor the organization of Catholics in the state warranted such independence, and so they suffered doubly.

In some parishes, high schools grew out of existing elementary schools. This, however, was an immense burden for the already overtaxed parishes, which had neither sufficient funds nor teachers to extend beyond their elementary schools. Some twelve-grade schools like St. Joseph's, opened by Redemptorists in Denver at the turn of the century, endured for some time. Others, like St. Patrick's in Butte, Montana, were discontinued when bishops opened central high schools. Today, few parochial high schools in the Intermountain region remain.

In 1947, the socioeconomic climate that had encouraged and allowed religious men and women to conduct the first public schools in parts of the Southwest came to an abrupt halt. A civil suit was filed against the Archdiocese of Santa Fe by some residents in Dixon, New Mexico, opposing the presence of religious brothers and sisters in public schools on the basis of the First Amendment. By the time the Dixon case had proceeded through the First District Court and was settled by the Supreme Court in 1952, most parishes affected by the issue had already established their own parochial schools.

Summer vacation school for religious education grew in popularity during the first decades of the twentieth century. Sometimes, as in the rural parish of Sacred Heart of Mary in Boulder, Colorado, the program included merely an hour of Catechism instruction three mornings a week with occasional Catechism tests in lieu of the Sunday sermon. Many years later, in looking back on these tests that were taken before the entire assembly, one student in the program recalled:

> The older people probably welcomed this, but for us culprits in the front pews it was sheer agony—sort of like a catechetical spelling bee. If we missed twice we were out—humiliated and dreading the admonition from our parents when we got home. . . . This spectacle, thank God, was a short-lived affair.[50]

In other settings, programs were more extensive. At Price, Utah, in the heart of the coal mining district, a summer school of 300 children was conducted by the Daughters of Charity of St. Vincent de Paul during the summers of 1924 and 1925.[51] At Salt Lake City's Guadalupe Mission and Parish, in addition to Sunday schools, religion classes were attended by children at the end of the regular school day. At a summer school started in 1928, besides religion, the boys were taught printing, glass painting, woodwork, and carving, while the girls were taught crocheting, sewing, and needlepoint.[52] This particular program became so popular that even Greek Orthodox and Mormon children began to participate. In Moscow, Idaho, during the episcopate of Bishop Edward J. Kelly (1928 to 1956), improved religious education programs included, in addition to religious vacation schools in the summer, correspondence courses for the children who lived in isolated areas. The growth that these examples suggest is reflected in statistics on the number and enrollment of vacation schools in the state of Colorado in the ten year period from 1931 to 1941. In 1931, there were 2,010 students enrolled in twenty-five religious vacation schools; by 1941, there were 9,129 students enrolled in 132 schools, a substantial increase.[53]

Such dramatic expansion was encouraged in the region by the foundation of religious communities dedicated specifically to catechetical work. In 1922, the Missionary Catechists of Our Lady of Victory were founded in the Archdiocese of Santa Fe to teach Catechism and to train lay catechists. As their efforts extended into other Western dioceses, the Holy Ghost Youth Center at Holy Ghost Parish in Denver was established in 1947 under their direction.

The fear of public schools expressed by Catholics during the nineteenth century was evident, too, on the level of higher education during the twentieth century. As the Newman Club movement grew, Catholics in the largely Mormon communities of Utah and Idaho saw in these organizations a preparation for "young men and women to refute calumnies against the Church, which are uttered by certain professors."[54] In 1911, at Moscow, Idaho (nineteen years after the founding of the University of Idaho there), Father Remigious Pecoul created the De Smet Club for Catholic students. This club was a ministry of St. Mary's Parish rather than an independent Catholic organization on campus, and it was not until 1940 that it became affiliated with the national organization of Newman Clubs. Father Pecoul's interest was supported by Bishop Gorman, and the De Smet Club flourished. By 1932, priests from St. Mary's were teaching religious classes for university students. By 1949, the number of Catholic students on campus seems to have been an issue. It was noted that:

> the Catholic Church had the fourth largest representation among students at the University. It had 301 students and the Methodists, 485. Presbyterians had 419; Mormons, 305. . . . During the second semester of 1954–1955, the Catholic Church was the second largest group with 359 students—second to the Methodists who had 656.[55]

In addition to parochial schools, religious education programs, and activities for Catholic college students enrolled on secular campuses, regularly scheduled social events for youth have served to include them in parish life. In 1927, in the isolated mining town of Park City, Utah, an annual Christmas tree celebration was held for the Catholic children. In addition to a decorated Christmas tree and the appearance of Santa with candy, fruit, nuts, and gifts for all, "[t]he Bobsled which had been kept over from the children's bazaar . . . was raffled off and the five dollar gold pieces given the boy and girl winners of the voting contest."[56] Even though the proceeds from this bazaar, given on December 13 by the pupils of the school, were to be used exclusively for the school, the project extended its activities to socialize others outside the school.

During these decades, an emphasis on providing recreational activities for youth often corresponded with the years of building, rebuilding, and expanding. When Monsignor Edward R. Cody became pastor at St. Mary's in Moscow, Idaho (1931 to 1937), he not only introduced new youth groups into the parish program, but, also remodeled the old Holy Trinity Church building in the town into a meeting room and gymnasium.

Social events as money raisers continued to be important to Intermountain Catholics into the twentieth century. At St. Bartholomew's in White Sulphur Springs, Montana, during the 1930s, the women sponsored bridge parties with boxes of groceries as prizes. They also sponsored election day and St. Patrick's Day dances. In addition to donating their time and energy to these activities, they also became actively involved in clergy sponsored raffles and turkey dinners. The nineteenth-century reality of church women (both Protestant and Catholic) being the financial backbone of local congregations seems to have carried over into the twentieth century as well, particularly in the rural parishes of the Intermountain West.

This appears to have been true in Hispanic parishes of the Southwest as well. During the eight year struggle of San José Parish in Los Ojos, New Mexico, to raise enough money for the construction of a new church, box socials and dances continued to supplement private donations from friends of the clergy in Eastern states and a $1,435 loan from the Franciscan Provincial House in Cincinnati, as part of a slowly accumulated building fund.[57] In 1931, when the church had already been housed in the school basement for three years, the pastor devised a plan to make the most of what little money had been accumulated, to use the dormant energies of those unemployed by the Great Depression, and to build up the spirit of *communidad* through cooperative labor. Padre Luis put all the building funds into materials, and through volunteer labor, parishioners made all the bricks necessary for construction of the new church (with a surplus of 105,000 adobes).[58] This example of reliance on locally donated labor and outside financial support is typical of the Intermountain West's struggle, in general, to outgrow a dependent economy.

From the first decade of the twentieth century, the benevolent Catholic Church Extension Society of the United States of America has supported, in part or entirely, the building of many churches in the Intermountain region. Founded in Chicago in 1905 by Father Francis Clement Kelley, the Extension Society "launched the home-mission movement in this country" for Catholics, pledging to serve "those areas of the United States where the work of the Church is seriously handicapped by a lack of personnel, organization, finances, etc."[59] Throughout the Southern and Western states, as well as Alaska, Hawaii, Puerto Rico, and the Philippines, the Extension Society helped build more than 7,000 churches, and, in addition, supported needy clergymen, seminarians, and missionary work of all kinds.[60] At a time in this country's history when Protestant denominations were experiencing great evangelizing success on the American frontier (due in great measure to the support of their own home mission societies), Catholic parish life might not have been as firmly established in this region had it not been for the aid of this society.

Because of peace treaties made with some of the Plains Indians, the U.S. government was responsible for the building of a few churches on reservations. The Marquette League, too, helped support Indian missions, mission schools, and chapels after its 1904 founding in New York. However, it was Mother Katherine Drexel who was most responsible for financing the establishment and rebuilding of Indian missions after their Jesuit beginnings in this region. In New Mexico, Arizona, and Wyoming, her generous contributions helped to lay the foundation for Native American parishes that continue to serve today.

Another development in parish life during the first half of the twentieth century, which gives evidence of a growing need for social bonds between parishioners, was the proliferation of societies. In addition to the Holy Name Society and the Altar and Rosary Society, whose functions were primarily practical, the establishment of ethnic societies and local chapters of national societies marks this period.

At Denver's Mount Carmel, an Italian parish, ethnic societies predate and outnumber other parish organizations. At St. Joseph's, a Polish parish in Denver, St. Casmir's Society, founded in 1910, seems to have been "somewhat atypical for the period, since the majority of such societies were linked to one or the other sex."[61] National societies like the Knights of Columbus, founded in New Haven, Connecticut, in 1882, and federations like the National Council of Catholic Women, founded in 1920, maintained exclusive meetings although their services were extended to Catholics of both genders. In 1913, Peter Pasino, S.J., with Amos Afraid of Bear and John Eagle Man, Sr., organized the St. Mary and St. Joseph Societies for Indians at West Poplar, Montana. Comparable to the Altar Society and the Holy Name Society, these two associations became the nucleus of a mission that was organized in 1919 by Father Nicholas Rauh, O.S.B.[62]

Building projects and other internal affairs were not the only concerns of Intermountain parishes during the first half of the twentieth century. During the war years, many parishes noted with pride the names of parishioners and priests serving in the armed forces, and most scheduled daily prayers for peace.

Although it may be true, in general, that American Catholics during the 1930s moved up the economic ladder and joined the ranks of non-Catholics, who were gaining personal prosperity by means of the capitalist system, in the Intermountain West this movement seems to have been limited to those urban areas where the success of businesses and the development of complex social systems permitted such progress. In the many undeveloped sections of this predominantly rural region, struggles with physical and economic geography still characterized the individual and communal lives of Catholic parishioners.

The national postwar enthusiasm for religion that characterized the decade of the 1950s in America was paralleled in the Intermountain region by an unprecedented period of industrial and population growth. This growth made possible within the Church a great amount of energy and economic support for the expansion of existing plants and the rebuilding of outdated facilities, as well as the construction of entirely new churches.

At Mount Carmel Church in Denver, the years between 1940 and 1960 were seen as an era of boundless opportunities. A building program at that time resulted in Mount Carmel High School in 1951, a new grade school in 1955, and a new convent in 1962. St. Joseph's Parish at Anaconda, Montana (site of a new copper boom), followed the building of a church in 1957 with the completion of a parochial school in 1958. But, in some areas, industrial growth was not always permanent. And, then, parishioners were challenged to discover new ways of financing or to continue their dependence on gifts and fund-raisers. In 1954, St. Charles Borromeo Parish at Hailey, Idaho, built a new hall. Materials abandoned at the nearby mines were used in its construction. In 1957, the money paid to the parish by the public school hot-lunch program housed in St. Charles Borromeo's hall helped to pay for the building.[63] During that same year at White Sulphur Springs, Montana, the establishment of the lumber industry brought prosperity to the area and a new church to St. Bartholomew's. This large A-frame structure of native rocks and cedar timbers, incorporating several unique works of art, replaced the sixty-six year old church. The combination church and rectory, unlike the hall at Hailey, carried a debt that was not lightened by extra income, but rather made heavier by a decrease in parish population. From 1955 to 1965, the number of families in St. Bartholomew's Parish dropped from 103 to sixty-five.[64] Consequently, it took more than sixteen years to repay this debt.

Because of such fluctuating economic and demographic conditions, and because of the continuing rural need for social activities, fund-raising for Catholic parishes in the region continued. On May 3, 1947, a meeting was held by Catholic women in Eden, Idaho, to organize in promoting the building of a church; soon, they had raised over $2,500.[65] This, plus a gift from the Extension Society and a generous donation from a pioneer family in the parish, made the building of St. Patrick's Church possible.

Frequently, these fund-raisers were meals, which in rural areas fulfilled a need for social activity as well. In Hailey, Idaho, the annual Basque dinners were in-

The Local Church

itiated in the 1950s by St. Charles Borromeo Parish. Today, at Boulder, Colorado's Sacred Heart of Mary, originally a rural parish, the most well-attended activities are meals sponsored for fund-raising.[66]

This corporate sense of church as community, which had always been present in the Hispanic Catholic Church, became more commonly manifest in all rural parishes during the first half of the twentieth century in the form of parish fund-raising events. But, it was given theological expression and more conscious attention after promulgation of the papal encyclicals *Mystici and Corporis* in 1943 and *Mediator Dei* in 1947. The impact of these two documents was not felt on a pastoral level in most places until the 1950s, when concern for the lay apostolate and liturgical interest became visible in the formation of local social action groups and the celebration of dialogue Masses. These changes encouraged wider use of the vernacular in the liturgy and greater flexibility in church architecture.

In Intermountain parishes, evidence of this international encouragement to broaden one's notion of church as hierarchical institution with a new understanding of the corporate nature of ecclesia seems to have been limited to church architecture, especially in the new buildings required for burgeoning suburban parishes. In the many rural sections of the region, more dramatic change was delayed until the startling revelations and revolutions of the 1960s.

Although it is generally held that the parochial school system experienced its most rapid expansion after World War II, it is hard to prove that this was so in the Intermountain region. Each diocese in the region shows an increase in the number of schools between 1950 and 1960, but only in the archdioceses of Denver and Santa Fe are these increases significant. (See Appendix A.) Finally, the building of a Newman Center by the Diocese of Boise affected the life of the parish, which had supplied services for Catholic students up to that time. When a Newman Center was built on the University of Idaho campus in 1959, Holy Trinity-St. Mary's was relieved of its forty-eight years of dedicated service to college students through the De Smet Club.

Despite the difficulties of insufficient clergy, isolation, and persistent financial concerns, local parishes in the Intermountain region documented some growth from 1850 to 1960. From initial goals of simply supplying Catholics with access to the Sacraments, to the building and maintenance of physical plants and the development of religious education programs, these predominantly rural parishioners, along with their priests, organized societies and sponsored frequent fund-raisers to sustain what the economic growth of the 1940s and the continued charity of national benevolent societies could not do alone. These frontier conditions, dramatized in some sections of the region by the interplay of expressive and organizational styles of clerical and lay leadership, have allowed the missionary spirit that launched the Church in the Intermountain West to endure and to serve as a historical basis for the evolution of parish life.

Notes

1. Fray Angelico Chavez, *My Penitente Land: Reflections on Spanish New Mexico* (Albuquerque: University of New Mexico Press, 1974), 208.
2. Nancy O'Sullivan-Beare, *Las mujeres de los conquistadores; La mujer espanda en los comienzo de la colonizacion america* (Madrid: Compania Bibliografica Espanola, 1956), 301.
3. Rev. Kiernan McCarty, O.F.M., "Our Desert Under Spain and Mexico: The Diocesan Story, 1691–1860," in *Shepheds in the Desert,* ed. Silver Jubilee Committee (Tucson: Diocese of Tucson, 1978), 18.
4. *Ibid.,* 18–19.
5. *Ibid.,* 19.
6. Henry W. Kelly, *Franciscan Missions of New Mexico, 1740–1760* (Albuquerque: University of New Mexico Press, 1941), 57–60.
7. Cleofas M. Jaramillo, *Shadows of the Past* (Santa Fe: Seton Village Press, 1941), 24–25.
8. Rev. Wilfred P. Schoenberg, S.J., *A Chroncle of the Catholic History of the Pacific Northwest, 1743–1960* (Portland, Oregon: Catholic Sentinel Printery, 1962), 34, 50, 54.
9. Henry W. Casper, S.J., *History of the Catholic Church in Nebraska: The Church on the Fading Frontier, 1864–1910* (Milwaukee: The Bruce Publishing Co., 1966), 49.
10. *Fifty Years of Growth, 1904–1954, Eastern Montana Catholic Register,* Vol. XXX, 38.
11. Henry W. Casper, S.J., *History of the Catholic Church in Nebraska: The Church on the Northern Plains, 1838–1874* (Milwaukee: The Bruce Co., 1960), 108. See also Most Rev. Patrick A. McGovern, S.T.D., LL.D., *History of the Diocese of Cheyenne* (Cheyenne, Wyoming: *Wyoming Labor Journal,* 1941), 29.
12. Paul Horgan, *Lamy of Santa Fe: His Life and Times* (New York: Farrar, Straus and Giroux, 1975), 107.
13. Archdiocese of Santa Fe, *The Old Faith and Old Glory, 1846–1946* (Santa Fe: Santa Fe Press, 1946), 7–8.
14. Rev. W. J. Howlett, *Life of the Right Reverend Joseph P. Machebeuf, D.D.* (Pueblo, Colorado: The Franklin Press, Co., 1908), 388.
15. *Ibid.*
16. Paul H. Hallett, "German Immigrants Helped Build Colorado," *The Denver Catholic Register,* 28 September 1983, 13.
17. Casper, *Plains,* 218.
18. Rev. Wilfred P. Schoenberg, S.J., *Jesuits in Montana, 1840–1960* (Portland, Oregon: The Oregon Jesuit, 1960), 99.
19. Rev. Kenneth J. Arnzen, *The First Hundred Years: A Centennial History of St. Mary's Church, Moscow, Idaho,* 1982, 46.
20. *Ibid.,* 47.
21. [Rev. Donald D. Fraser], *Humilitas* (Hailey, Idaho: n.p., 1983), 8.
22. Sidney E. Ahlstrom, *A Religious History of the American People* (New Haven: Yale University Press, 1972), 836.
23. *Ibid.*

24. *Ibid.*

25. John Kessell, *The Missions of New Mexico Since 1776* (Albuquerque: University of New Mexico Press, 1980), 82.

26. Howlett, 329.

27. Odie B. Faulk, ed., *John Baptist Salpointe: Soldier of the Cross* (Tucson: The Diocese of Tucson, 1966), 15.

28. *Ibid.*, 15–16.

29. Rosemary Radford Reuther and Rosemary Skinner Keller, gen. ed., *Women and Religion in America*, Vol. 1: *The Nineteenth Century* (San Francisco: Harper and Row, Publishers, 1981), 2.

30. Sister M. Lilliana Owens, S.L., Ph.D., *Loretto on the Old Frontier, 1823–1864* (St. Louis: Khowry Bros., Inc., 1965), 86.

31. *Rocky Mountain News*, 20 July 1864 in Owens, 128.

32. Thomas J. Steele, S.J., *Works and Days* (Albuquerque: The Albuquerque Museum, 1983), 100.

33. Marianne L. Stoller and Thomas J. Steele, S.J., *Diary of the Jesuit Residence of Our Lady of Guadalupe Parish, Conejos, Colorado, December 1871–December 1875*. The Colorado College Studies, No. 19 (Colorado Springs: The Colorado College, 1982), 188.

34. Archives of the Archdiocese of Santa Fe, Loose Documents, Diocesan, 1850–1900, Circular to the Clergy, 14 January 1854.

35. Steele, 66–67.

36. *Ibid.*, 67.

37. Schoenberg, *Chronicle*, 179.

38. Howlett, 329.

39. Schoenberg, *Chronicle*, 158.

40. *Ibid.*, 331.

41. *Our Lady of Guadalupe, Taos, New Mexico* (White Plains, New York: Monarch Publishing, Inc., 1976), 32.

42. Howlett, 380.

43. 250th Anniversary Book Committee, *La Iglesia de Santa Cruz de la Cañada, 1733–1983*, n.p., 1983, 52.

44. "The New Kingdom of St. Francis," in *The Franciscan Missions of the Southwest* (St. Michael's, Arizona: n.p., 1913), 41.

45. Rev. Louis J. Fries, S.T.B., *One Hundred and Fifty Years of Catholicity in Utah* (Salt Lake City: Intermountain Catholic Press, 1926), 106. See John Henry Kessler III, "The Original Peculiar People at Latitude 40° 13': A History of Catholicism in Provo, Utah" (Xeroxed), 14.

46. Helen Z. Papanikolas, "Women in the Mining Communities of Carbon County," *Carbon County: Eastern Utah's Industrial Island*, ed. Philip F. Notarianni (Salt Lake City: Utah State Historical Society, 1981), 82.

47. Robert J. Torrez, *El Primer Siglo: A Centennial History of San José Parish, Los Ojos, New Mexico, 1883–1983* (Los Ojos, New Mexico: San José Parish Council, 1983), 24.

48. *Ibid.*

49. *Encyclopedia Americana*, 1983, s.v. "Utah."

50. Therese S. Westermeier, *Centennial of a Country Church* (Boulder: Johnson Publishing Co., 1973), 20–21.

51. Fries, 104.

52. Jerald H. Merrill, "Fifty Years with a Future: Salt Lake's Guadalupe Mission and Parish," *Utah Historical Quarterly,* 40 (Summer 1972), 250–251.

53. William H. Jones, *The History of Catholic Education in the State of Colorado* (Washington, D.C.: The Catholic University of America Press, 1955), 301.

54. Fries, 138.

55. Arnzen, 104–105.

56. "Parish Notes," *Intermountain Catholic,* 1 January 1927, 44.

57. Torrez, 25.

58. *Ibid.,* 24.

59. James P. Gaffey, *Francis Clement Kelley and the American Catholic Dream.* Vol. 1 (Bensenville, Illinois: The Heritage Foundation, Inc., 1980), xi.

60. *New Catholic Encyclopedia,* 1967 ed., s.v., "Catholic Church Extension Society."

61. Stanley L. Cuba, *St. Joseph's Polish Roman Catholic Church,* n.p., 8.

62. Schoenberg, *Chronicle,* 298–299.

63. Fraser, 15.

64. Diocese of Helena, Annual Report of Rev. Lawrence D. Simons, Pastor of St. Bartholomew's Church, White Sulphur Springs, Montana, 1 January 1955 to 31 December 1955; Diocese of Helena, Annual Report of Rev. George B. Gerner, Pastor of St. Bartholomew's Church, White Sulphur Springs, Montana, 1 January 1965 to 31 December 1965.

65. Schoenberg, *Chronicle,* 428.

66. Rev. Edward J. Vollmer, O.S.B., personal letter.

CHAPTER THREE
Religion and Ethnicity

The struggle of the Intermountain West's diverse people to express and establish a meaningful religious life is nowhere more dramatic than in the ongoing encounter of one ethnic tradition with another. The national interplay of hierarchical tendencies (to place one unit in a position of superiority over another) with prophetic tendencies (to affirm different ways of being) has consistently characterized American life. In this region's Catholic history, it has surfaced in an emphasis on the "official establishment" of churches by an Eastern-based hierarchy and a frequent disregard for culturally integrated religious traditions. The imposition of organizational efficiency has often offended those for whom expressive celebration is a greater value. Yet, encouragement from a few order missionaries and secular clergymen in the region has enabled some Native Americans to resist the exclusion of tribal traditions from Catholic life, and Hispanics to resist the loss of folk religious practices from their cultural tradition. Conversely, the national religious customs of European immigrants in the Intermountain West succumbed, by and large, to Americanization. Even during the days before World War I, when American Catholicism defined itself primarily as an immigrant Church, Catholics of recent European extraction were widely dispersed in this region. Their only major urban concentrations were in Denver and Pueblo, Colorado, where, after some initial conflicts among themselves, they were gradually assimilated into the great American melting pot.

But Indians and Hispanics, particularly in the Southwest, have made themselves known as "the melting pot that wouldn't."[1] Objects of alternating Anglo disdain and pride, these two ethnic groups have the distinction of being the first and most consistently expressive Intermountain Catholics. For this reason, and because they have become essential elements in the region's spiritual self-image, they deserve careful consideration. The following presentation of ethnic Intermountain history falls into three time periods: (1) pre-twentieth century, (2) the first half of the twentieth century, and (3) the 1950s.

Native American Catholics have made a distinct contribution to the Intermountain Church since the sixteenth century. Not only did Indians attract the Church to particular locales, creating a social center for further settlement, but many have demonstrated in a variety of ways a more expressive approach to Church life than that commonly established among white settlers. Unfortunately, most ecclesiastical histories have overlooked this contribution. Although the limits of this study preclude a systematic examination of Native American Catholicism, a brief look at selected events in American Indian history, which affected the Intermountain Church, raises some important questions. It also illustrates the limitations of a primarily institutional approach to religion and suggests the rediscovery of some of the expressive elements in our own tradition. For Indians, as for most primal cultures, religion is not an experience or activity separate from one's economic, social, or political life; it is an integral part of one's whole cultural complex. Thus, Christian "conversion" for Indians has most often not meant a total abandonment of past religious traditions, despite American civil and ecclesiastical attempts to effect such a rejection. Yet, how much encouragement in this syncretistic exercise Native Americans can expect from official Catholic sources is still to be determined.

The first Native American converts to Catholicism in the Intermountain region were the Pueblo Indians of New Mexico and Arizona. Catholicism was imposed on them by the Spanish *conquistadores* in the sixteenth century. While the friars' strict control of Pueblo life during that century may have given the impression that the Indians were passive converts, the Pueblo Revolt of the seventeenth century proved that they were not. Social scientists today agree that although Catholic elements were added to Pueblo religion, nothing of traditional religious meaning was lost or replaced. A sort of spiritual compartmentalization enabled those cultures to adopt Christian ceremonies, rituals, and symbols without changing their native world view. "Converts to Christianity, though they were, old religious loyalties were far from dead; and the medicine men did all in their power to keep these sparks alive. The Revolt of 1680 was the end product of cultural clash on all levels—material, personal, and religious."[2]

The friars had attempted to replace one religion with another. They had made excessive demands on the Indians' time, energy, and loyalties to support the mission system, had even "persecuted their Indian leaders, destroyed sacred paraphernalia, and denounced certain ceremonies . . . as works of the devil."[3] But they could not destroy native religious traditions. Nor could their oppression provoke the revolting Pueblos to reject those aspects of Christianity they had made their own. Not all Pueblo churches were destroyed in the 1680 rebellion.

> Whether they brought them down or let them stand, the Pueblo patriots of 1680 were expressing in the extreme a feeling their descendents still share, a feeling of complete possession. The mission churches belonged to them. They had built them, they maintained and repaired them, and when free of constraint, they chose whether they stood or fell. No matter that architect-construction boss-priest acted as if he were the owner. He was an outsider. If he wanted to keep the people's good will he came to the *principales* first with his plans to expand the nave, add a steeple, or restore the flat roof. To this day, the Archdiocese of Santa Fe does not hold legal title to most Pueblo churches.[4]

Syncretistically, Pueblos have accepted part of the Catholicism imposed upon them. Those aspects of the Catholic calendar of celebrations that fit into pre-existing Pueblo beliefs and values, especially the saint's day fiesta, have become part of Pueblo life. These celebrations frequently are related to the cycle of natural seasons, and so to a particular place at a particular time. Another element of these celebrations that emphasizes the importance of place is the procession that serves as the transition from the church to the plaza, from the sacred place where the Catholic hierarchy officiates to the sacred place where a native spiritual leader presides.

In addition to the 1680 Pueblo Revolt, and earlier conflicts between Spanish friars and military officials that scandalized and victimized the Indians, recurring conflicts occurred in the Southwest between the raiding Ute, Comanche, Navajo, and Apache, and the sedentary Pueblo. While in some instances these raids encouraged alliances between the Pueblo Indians and Hispanic settlers (such as that at Taos, New Mexico), in other instances they caused further divisiveness even in Church life. *Genisaros* (nomadic Indians who had been taken captive by Spaniards and kept as servants in their households) were often separated from the dominant ethnic group in their religious lives. Santa Fe's left-bank church, San Miguel, was built in 1620 for the Indian servants of Hispanic Catholics and for others considered lower class who lived south of the Rio de Santa Fe. These Indians were not accepted by either the Spanish or the Pueblo Indians.

In Arizona, all mission work among the Hopi came to an end with the Pueblo Revolt of 1680. While, today, St. Joseph's Indian Mission at Keams Canyon stands on the Hopi Reservation, this parish is twelve miles away from the mesa pueblos that make up the heart of Hopiland, and it serves more than one Indian tribe.

Hopi disdain for Christian ways is an old tradition that soon became manifest in tribal factions, one friendly to outsiders and one hostile to them. In her autobiography, Polingaysi Qoyawayma recalls some of the roots of these sentiments. She speaks of the Mennonite church built in 1901 in the same way that she speaks of earlier Catholic missions.

> [I]t stood on the edge of the mesa beyond the flat-topped buildings, a foreign thing with not one feature to blend with the rest of the village. It did not belong there. It was a thing to be ignored, or to be looked at and rejected by the offended eyes of the Hopis.
>
> No doubt it brought to mind that other church of long ago, the San Francisco Mission of the invading Spanish, and the Franciscan priests whose presence stirred the *Orabians* to revolt and finally to murder. A mound marked its former location, but its stones had long since been scattered and its heavy beams used in kiva construction, and in the minds of the village people there was a consciousness of those days of hot rebellion against an imposed religion.[5]

These memories are not those of an individual, but of an indigenous non-Christian community whose attitude continues to affect Catholic life in the multi-cultural complex of the American Southwest. How can a universal church appeal to non-Western Europeans if it diminishes the spiritual potential of other cultures?

Because of their settled lifestyle, the Pima, Papago, and Yuma of Arizona attracted missionaries earlier than their nomadic brothers, the Apache and the Navajo. Padre Kino's work among the sedentary Pima, begun in 1687, was continued after the Pima Revolt of 1751 in the Tucson area, where the addition of a presidio in 1754 helped keep the peace. Their migrating Papago relatives seem to have moved into the San Xavier del Bac area around 1848, and, in 1876, the Papago agency was consolidated with that of the Pima by government order.[6] While the Pima lost their earlier attachment to Catholicism and eventually yielded to the evangelizing efforts of the Presbyterian Church, the Papago continued to combine Spanish Catholic practices with Indian traditions in a meaningful expression of their faith. One example of this syncretism is the fiesta Magdalena de Kino, the celebration of the Feast of St. Francis in the church of Magdalena de Sonora. Although held on the Mexican side of the U.S. border, this celebration blurs political boundaries as it brings together Native Americans whose ethnic solidarity and cultural bonds are stronger than those of U.S. citizenship. Originally a harvest festival held in early October by the Pima and Papago, this event became, in the hands of the early missionaries, a Christian celebration as well. The focal image of St. Francis documents the succession of early missionary orders that served there by combining characteristics of St. Francis Xavier, introduced by the Jesuits, St. Francis of Assisi, introduced by the Franciscans, and Padre Kino himself, considered a holy man.[7] While the harvest motif continues to be manifest at the fiesta in the sale of such items as corn, red chiles, striped squash, and quinces, the healing powers of San Francisco are recalled in the extensive sale of medicinal herbs, some of which are the same as those described by the first missionaries in the area.

Missionary work among the Yuma began in earnest with two establishments in 1778, Immaculate Conception, at the confluence of the Gila and Colorado; and St. Peter and St. Paul, nine miles further downriver. No longer considered a Yuma mission, Immaculate Conception became a parish in 1866, twelve years after the founding of the town originally called Colorado City and now known as Yuma, Arizona.

The nomadic Navajo, less threatening to Anglo, Hispanic, and Indian alike than the Apache, followed the Pueblos in receiving Catholic missionaries. When the Franciscans returned to the Southwest in 1897, they established St. Michael's Mission for Navajo Indians in northern Arizona. Unlike the early Franciscans who were frequently criticized for not learning the native Pueblo tongues, these friars accepted the challenge of mastering the difficult Navajo language, and during their first years there composed and printed a catechism, a bible history, a small dictionary, and part of a Navajo grammar. They also established a second mission at Chinle and a station at Lukachukai on the Navajo Reservation. Today, all three of these missions serve as parishes in the Gallup Diocese.

In the Northwest, the visionary leadership of Father De Smet was followed by the practical accomplishments of Fathers Gregory Mengarini, Nicholas Point, and others who saw in the plurality of highly differentiated types of Native American traditions concrete opportunities to minister. Father Mengarini mastered the Flathead language, composed a Selish grammar, and recorded anthropological data from the ancient beliefs of the people. Father Point, an artist, painted portraits of many of the Indians, preserving images of their native dress for a later age. At St. Ignatius Mission near Helena, Montana, Father Urban Grassi adapted Church ritual to local tradition when he administered the Sacrament of Reconciliation to an elderly Indian in the following way:

> The Father moved his chair to where the Indian was squatting and seated himself beside him. The penitent produced from under his blanket a bunch of little sticks held together by a bit of buckskin. He untied the bunch and placed the sticks, which were of different lengths and sizes, on the floor, one by one, under the Father's eyes. . . . Having gathered the sticks and thrown them into the stove, our good man left the room looking very happy.[8]

This concrete expression of a human psychological need and multi-sensory celebration of a Catholic sacrament combined perhaps the best of both Native American and Christian traditions in an effective religious ritual. It was this sort of willingness to appreciate and work with indigenous tradition that characterized the early ministry of Jesuit missionaries in the Northwest. But this was soon to change.

An advancing U.S. immigration through Indian lands soon became a full-scale invasion of whites moving westward with military and political might to support their advances. The Indians were clearly the losers. From the time of "The Great Smoke" held near Fort Laramie in the fall of 1851, sincere efforts were made by Father De Smet and other Jesuits to arbitrate between the Indians and the government, but in the end the Church, too, would act as an agent of U.S. domination in the Americanization and Christianization of the Native Americans.

Tired by ineffective treaties and drained by the economic cost of numerous military campaigns intended to subdue the American Indians, President Grant created in 1870 a Peace Policy that enlisted the aid of religious institutions in acculturating these indigenous peoples. Christianization became the means of Americanization and the reservation boarding school its method. Not only were the many U.S. churches (both Protestant and Catholic) asked to participate in this cultural domination, but they were arbitrarily assigned particular tribes as their charges, regardless of the religious faith or preference of the Indians themselves. Consequently, Indians who had learned to accept one form of Christianity were suddenly expected to adopt another. This caused not only interdenominational conflict, but a loss of continuity in developing a religious stance that could include both native tradition and an imposed culture.

Bishops throughout the country protested this aspect of Grant's policy, and, in 1873, organized the Bureau of Catholic Indian Missions to deal more effectively with the injustices they perceived. However, in some areas of the Intermountain region the ethnocentric attitude underlying the policy continued to characterize a Catholic approach to Indian boarding schools. One missionary historian wrote:

> Experience has amply proven that the Indian cannot be civilized except on Christian principles, through Christian schools, by Christian teachers; or in the very words of U.S. Senator Davis: "The education of the Indian cannot be accomplished but by a Sunday school which will last seven days in the week."[9]

In theory, on every Indian reservation, either existing missionary schools were to receive government aid or new schools were to be established at government expense. In practice, there were many disappointments to add to the trail of broken promises.

In the Northwest, boarding schools were conducted by the Jesuits, the Ursulines, and the Sisters of Charity of Providence at Montana Indian missions as early as 1864. In Wyoming, arrangements made by Bishop James O'Connor with the federal government and the Buffalo, New York, Mission of the Society of Jesus to open a new school on the Wind River Reservation at Fort Washakie were quashed in 1884, when Father John Jutz, S.J., arrived at Lander only to discover that the proposed school for Shoshoni had been assigned to an Episcopal minister, Rev. John Roberts. Father Jutz then moved to the far eastern end of the reservation among the Northern Arapaho and began St. Stephen's Mission. In 1888, the Sisters of Charity of Leavenworth took charge of that school.

In the Southwest, early Indian education was part of the Franciscan mission system. As the decrease in Franciscan clergymen became greater than the increase in secular clergymen from Durango, Mexico, Indian education suffered. During the episcopacy of Bishop Lamy, attempts were made to transfer pueblo schools from administration by the War Department, which insisted on conducting classes in English, to the Diocese, which would instruct in the more familiar Spanish; but it was not until 1886, during the episcopacy of Archbishop Salpointe, that a contract was made with the U.S. government for seven day schools and one boarding school. Although data on these schools are sparse, it appears that this contract fell under the provisions of President Grant's Peace Policy, was affected by the disintegrative Dawes Act of 1887, and then, as federal moneys dwindled, suffered the fate of many other government agreements with, and for, the Indians. Four of the seven proposed day schools were set up, but they lasted only a few years. St. Catherine's, the boarding school for boys begun at Bernalillo and then moved to Santa Fe, received the last of its federal aid in 1894.[10]

Just as Anglo attitudes toward and administrative success with Indian education have been mixed, so has Native American criticism of the system. Childhood memories of cultural shock are vivid as Indian adults recall being rounded up by government officials and forced to go to school, having their hair cut, their clothing changed, receiving a new name, and suffering intense loneliness.

But testimonies to the value of education for Indians forced to live in a white man's world are plentiful, too. Some see their formal education as a necessary extension of the traditional education they received at home, both necessary for survival in society. Myrtle Begay, a Navajo, says:

> My opinion is that traditional education and Anglo education are similar in many ways. . . . Getting involved in home activities gives a young person knowledge of Navajo family life. Then in school he must be involved in all the activities to learn, advance, and constantly be a better student.[11]

Many of the activities Myrtle Begay mentions were practical rather than scholarly. Most Indian boarding schools ran large farms to sustain themselves economically. Indian students often spent half the school day learning domestic and agricultural skills that simultaneously supported the mission, especially during those times when government assistance failed to materialize.

Other boarding school graduates express not only gratitude for their own education, but hopes that their children will not neglect this essential bridge from the Indian to the white world. Frequently, these testimonies came from Indians who have been converted to Mormonism or Protestantism. What are the sentiments of the Indian graduates of Catholic boarding schools? What of those Native Americans not fluent in English who participate in Catholic life? Few of them have been heard. Can the Church encourage them to tell their stories? Can the conservative function within Catholicism tolerate their prophetic voice? "By ignoring or denying the spiritual legacy left to us by the Indians we have contributed to their impoverishment, and we have cut ourselves off from the possibility of an enrichment we desperately need."[12]

Whether the beginnings of Native American Catholicism in the Intermountain West were founded on Spanish colonization in the Southwest or Indian initiative in the Northwest, both came to be dominated by U.S. civil and ecclesiastical efforts to Americanize the indigenous non-Christian. The beginnings of Hispanic Catholicism in the region were also modified by the imposition of a different mode of religious conduct—the Americanized and Americanizing institutional Church.

This contrast/conflict between two forms of the same faith can be seen in the ancient interplay of two traditions within Church life, one called the "great tradition," the other the "little tradition." According to some anthropologists and religious historians, a distinction can be made between the formal structures of the official institution, which tend to be "abstract, universalistic, and often historically grounded" (the great tradition), and the informal traditions of common people in their everyday lives, which tend to be "more immediate, ahistorical, and particularistic" (the little tradition).[13] Although originally "Catholicism embraced a dialectical interchange between its great and little traditions," the Council of Trent inaugurated a period of "centralization, rationalization, and literacy" in the Church, which emphasized the primacy of the great tradition over the little tradition.[14] Spanish Catholicism, despite the Council of Trent in 1545 and the promulgation of the Roman Ritual in 1614, continued to be influenced by the national character of the Rite of Toledo. And it was this form of Catholicism, a type of little tradition, that came to America with the friars and *conquistadores*. Somewhat later, a form of Catholicism more representative of the one universal great tradition developed in the Eastern and Midwestern portions of the United States. It was this "minority group along the Atlantic coastline . . . from which the mainstream of American Catholic life took its rise . . . that set the pattern for future Catholic development."[15] And (with the exception of some religious order missionaries), it was this emphasis on the great tradition that so often characterized the approach of an American secular clergy to the establishment of the Church in the Intermountain region. Among Hispanic Catholics isolated in Southwestern villages the meeting of these two traditions made for fierce ethnic and religious conflict. The great tradition frequently manifested itself in a concern with Church authority, organization, doctrine, official establishment of jurisdiction, and adherence to the streamlined, universal, official way of administering the Sacraments, subordinating (if not condemning) the little tradition.

In the Southwest, the little tradition flourished for Hispanics during the geographic and cultural isolation of both the colonial and the Mexican periods. When Bishop John Baptist Lamy and his party of U.S. sponsored churchmen arrived in 1851, Lamy came into conflict not only with the few Hispanic clergymen serving his new vicariate, but also with the folk religious customs these Catholics had developed during nearly 300 years of separation from institutional influence. In writing to Bishop John Baptist Purcell of Cincinnati, under whom Lamy and Machebeuf had first served the American Church, the new bishop of New Mexico spoke of the Mexican clergy. He hoped

> to keep them under fear. Perhaps that will change them, but I doubt it. . . . I must be patient and catch them doing wrong. . . . I suspended one of the senior clerics . . . perhaps that will serve as an example for the others.[16]

Although Lamy later sought to encourage the ordination of native clergy, his initial approach to the New Mexican priests as wayward subordinates, and his repeated importing of European clergymen to take over their duties, had sufficiently offended the local Catholic Hispanics to prevent their filling the clerical ranks of the institutional Church in New Mexico.

Lamy judged as inferior not only the New Mexican clergy, but also the religious expression of the people. He perceived that

> the people were well disposed and showed a strong attachment to their religion . . . on the surface. The people went to Mass, observed the feast days, kept their religious sodalities active enough, but for the most part failed to adhere to the Sacraments, upon which all else depended.[17]

A series of diocesan regulations pertaining to proper administration of the Sacraments stressed instruction for the recipients, clearly a function of the great tradition's emphasis on intellectual knowledge and literacy. A highly visible opponent in both of these arguments was Padre Antonio José Martínez, pastor, politician, man of learning, and champion of Hispanic Catholicism in America. As leader of the Hispanic secular clergymen whom Lamy criticized and disciplined, Martínez was able to find fault also with the French bishop's friend and right-hand man, Machebeuf, and to refer to Canon law in doing so.

> Most Reverend Lord Bishop of Agathonica . . . and Vicar Apostolic of New Mexico, Don Juan Lamy: The undersigned pastors, in due form and as best defined by law, declare before your Reverence that on the 5th of January of the current year [1853] we submitted to you a written complaint denouncing your Vicar Don Preyecto Machebeuf for unruly behavior which he practices in the churches of New Mexico, now vexing the clergy, now exercising jurisdiction and taking possession of obventions with the infraction of Canon law.[18]

But not all encounters between the two cultures were based on mistrust or ethnocentric vindictiveness.

One boost to ethnic identity and cultural expression was granted his Spanish faithful by Lamy: his insistence on foreign-born clergy learning and using the Spanish language or English. Lamy wrote most of his own pastoral letters in Spanish and even used that language in official documents when Latin was not required. The majority of parishes in his jurisdiction continued to use Spanish in all parts of their services, as many throughout the Southwest continue to do today.

Of the many Hispanic parishes in New Mexico and Colorado, most of which use the Spanish language frequently, if not primarily, only St. Cajetan's in Denver has been designated a national foreign language parish. Most rural Hispanic parishes in this region express their ethnicity as an unbroken tradition without national recognition.

In southern Colorado, too, the Hispanic settlement at Conejos had grown while clerical attention dwindled. "Without leadership and visited only sporadically, the villagers' religious practices inevitably underwent local developments that varied, sometimes widely, from official ritual."[19] When Joseph P. Machebeuf was made Vicar Apostolic of Colorado in 1868, he found himself in a different relation to conflicting ethnic groups than did Lamy in New Mexico.

Whereas Lamy had always to deal with the problems of a Hispanic Catholic majority population vis-à-vis an Anglo (and mostly Protestant) power structure, Machebeuf could afford some benign tolerance of his Hispanic parishioners in the San Luis Valley, who were seen, regrettably, as only of minor and marginal importance in the developing history of this state.[20]

Left for so long to their little tradition, then criticized by representatives of the great tradition, Hispanic Catholics in the Southwest depended on the family, on the community, and on lay *cofradias* (those brotherhoods that simultaneously sought to fulfill the people's religious needs and to help them maintain a sense of cultural identity). In New Mexico and southern Colorado, the people participated in public rituals under the leadership of the Penitentes, expressed privately and publicly their devotion to particular saints, and communally celebrated feasts of the liturgical year and major rites of passage with elaborate local custom.

During the time when Hispanic villages were most isolated from the regular care of clergymen, the Penitente Brotherhood conducted funerals and Holy Week services for local Catholics who would otherwise have gone without the consolation of religious support and an appropriate expression of their faith. In ministering to the dying, villagers under the leadership of the Penitentes would pray with the dying person, prepare the body and the grave, keep vigil (*velorio*) with the family, lead the singing of *alabados* composed for the occasion, conduct the funeral procession, and even conduct the interment. The Requiem Mass and the blessing of the plot could wait for the next visit of the priest, but the deference shown the departed, the consolation afforded his family, and the public expression of communal religious values could not.

During Holy Week, *Los Hermanos de Nuestro Padre Jesus* (Penitentes) often participated with the townspeople in public and non-penitential dramatizations based on the Stations of the Cross, but they also held their own private penitential "re-enactment of Christ's crucifixion on Good Friday, when one of the Brothers was tied on a full-size cross he had carried to the Calvario, raised up on it, and left for some time, frequently until he fainted."[21] In the parish dramatization, Christ was portrayed by a great bulto, a life-size image with movable limbs, often referred to as the *Santo Entierro*.

> The primary purpose of the passion plays was never dramatic excellence; instead it was always the involvement of the people, both performers and congregation, in a gripping religious ceremony. By cutting spoken lines to a minimum and drawing the congregation away from aesthetic contemplation and into reciting prayers of the Stations of the Cross and singing the *alabados* characterized by narrative structures and portions of the dialogue of the sacred personages themselves, the New Mexico passion play erased as nearly as it could the distinction between actors and audience. It joined them all into a performance, which, while it did not fail to be a play, displayed the features of a religious ceremony.[22]

Cleofas Jaramillo, daughter of a wealthy merchant in Arroyo Hondo, New Mexico, during the territorial period, remembers her visit to a Penitente *morada* (combined chapel and meeting place) with a mixture of pride and fear that represents her status as a religious and cultural syncretist. The Hispanic *rico* is simultaneously in sympathy with the folk customs of her people and a member of the modernized, Americanized ruling class that disdained them.

> Moved by curiosity to see the inside of the *morada*, I once asked *a penitente's* wife, who was going to pay a votive debt to the *santos* at the *morada*, if I might accompany her. We climbed the hill on which the *morada* stood in the upper town and were admitted to the chapel. On the wall of the hall dividing the chapel from the secret room hung a row of whips. The woman crawled on her knees from one statue to another, placing lighted candles before each. I was left kneeling before the statue of the Crucifixion. Paralyzed with fear, I could not move, for there before me on the mud altar stood the statue of *La Muerte*, Death.[23]

Both Archbishop Lamy and his successor, Jean Baptist Salpointe, denounced the *Cofradia de los Hermanos* for the severity of their penitential practices, another example of cultural conflict between the great tradition and the little tradition. "Salpointe was a determined enemy of the Penitentes, and it could be that during his regime anything that smacked of New Mexico folk religion . . . was put aside in favor of official services and French and Italian devotional practices."[24] Nevertheless, many believe that without the constancy of this *cofradia*, Catholic parish life among Hispanics in the Southwest might well have been lost to neglect or to aggressive Protestant evangelization.

The fact is that the problems of neglect and Protestant evangelization were aggravated by the ecclesiastical condemnation of Hispanic folk religious practices, so that disillusionment with the official Church led many either to ally themselves with what some historians call Padre Martínez's schismatic church, or to convert to some form of Protestantism. One administrative response to these defections was to conduct what was becoming in the second half of the nineteenth century "a commonplace experience in the Catholic community"—the parish mission; Padre Martínez's "schismatic" church survived his death in 1867, but ended with a mission preached by Father Donato Gasparri in Taos during January of 1869.[25] Subsequent missions served as counter-evangelizing efforts to Presbyterian conversions in the traditionally Catholic areas of Santa Fe, Las Vegas, and Taos, New Mexico, and southern Colorado. By this means, then, American Anglo clergymen "shaped the piety of the people and strengthened the institutional Church."[26] The great tradition exerted its domination over the little tradition. The Penitentes and Padre Martínez fell into disfavor, but not all elements of Hispanic folk religion were condemned. Since devotion to particular saints and to Mary, Queen of Saints, had popular appeal among many ethnic groups and had some doctrinal foundation, Church officials permitted related customs.

It was a nearly universal custom that Catholics would build shrines to particular saints who might intercede for them in obtaining favors. In the isolation of Hispanic villages, these shrines contained not plaster statues imported from Europe but wooden *santos* or *retablos* crafted by a local artisan. Since the goal of making a santo

> was to create an instrument of holiness and power rather than an artifact for detached contemplation, the connection between the saint in the picture and the saint of reality was a matter of great importance. . . . [T]he artifact is intrinsically holy not merely because of what may be done with it (prayer) but because it was made by a holy santero working within this multiple holy tradition.[27]

Cleofas Jaramillo recalls, again as she claims solidarity with both the masses and the ruling hierarchy, the treatment of *santos* in her family hacienda and chapel. A shoemaker from Taos came to her village to make

> lovely tin frames for Grandma's collection of *santos,* donated to her by the [Mexican] bishop and priests who stopped at the house during the year.
>
> There wasn't space left for another frame of the sanctuary wall of the *capilla,* so thickly was it covered with frames of all sizes. And when Bishop Chapelle came to administer confirmation, he told one parish priest that there were too many *santos.*[28]

La Conquistadora, Our Lady of the Conquest, has been associated with Hispanic history and cultural conflict in the Southwest. Originally brought to New Mexico in 1625 by Fray Alonzo Benavides, Franciscan Superior of the Missions of the Kingdom of New Mexico, this little statue of Mary immediately attracted the veneration of colonists and Indians who visited Santa Fe.[29] A Marian Society was formed, which quickly grew into a confraternity. Many Santa Feans and even those from the *estancias* joined. These devotees honored her as the Queen of Heaven, our Lady of the Rosary, and the Queen of their new Kingdom of New Mexico and their Villa de Santa Fe.[30]

At the time of the Pueblo Revolt, the fleeing Spaniards took the statue with them to El Paso del Norte, and when they returned twelve years later, reconquered the land in her name. A chapel was built for her until she was enthroned in the Santa Fe parish church, later the cathedral. Today, both the cathedral's Lady Chapel and Rosario Chapel, maintained by *La Cofradia de La Conquistadora,* are her shrines. Each year since the reconquest the ceremony of repossession takes place in Santa Fe.

Another way of showing veneration to Our Lady was by using pious salutations that included the name of Mary.

> The way to introduce oneself in a house was to say, on opening the door: *"Deo gratis"* (Thanks be to God) or *"Ave Maria Purisima"* (Hail Mary Immaculate) and the answer received was: *"Para Siempre bendito sea Dios la Siempre Virgin Maria: pasa adelante"* (forever blessed be God and the Holy Virgin Mary: come in). . . .

Another kind of pious and interesting salutation was used by persons at a distance from each other. The one who could first address the other by the words "Ave Maria" had the right to be answered by the recitation of the whole Hail Mary for his intention.[31]

In addition to private devotions to saints, public celebrations in honor of a local patron saint have been common among Hispanics of the Southwest. Cleofas Jaramillo remembers the nineteenth-century celebration of the feast of San Geronimo at Taos, New Mexico, as both an Indian and a Spanish fiesta.[32] Participants moved from pueblo to village and back again as the events for the day indicated.

In the Hispanic villages not attached to Indian pueblos, *la funcion,* the parish fiesta in honor of their patron's feast, was, and perhaps still is, the most significant expression of popular piety. These were usually extended celebrations consisting of Vespers with a procession around the plaza on the opening evening, and a High Mass followed by an even larger procession on the next morning. In some parishes, the *cofradias* carried the *estandartes* and chanted the traditional *alabados.* Then, the day was given over to visiting, eating, games, and, sometimes, the special *Matachines* dance. *La funcion* would usually close with a large dance. Not only members of that parish, but villagers for miles around still travel to neighboring parishes to share in this celebration. The *funciones*

> are the complete and valid self-expression of a traditional group . . . not so formal as the Latin rituals of the Roman Catholic Church, of course, but taken nearly as seriously. And with good reason, for this public or semi-public ritual activity flows from the people's true sense of its place among the other inhabitants of the cosmos, and each ceremony in its turn serves as a proclamation of the village's selfhood, which teaches and reinforces its common being.[33]

In addition to the ability of a particular saint to give a particular village a sense of identity, sometimes a saint associated with one's ethnicity or one's cultural history evoked expressions of popular piety. Accordingly, Santiago, the patron saint of horsemen, and, in colonial New Mexico, the protector from wild Indians, is still honored on his feast in many Hispanic villages. In addition to Mass and processions in his honor, an abbreviated version of the medieval drama, *La Danza de Los Moros y Cristianos,* has been revived at the Santa Cruz parish as part of the fiesta.

Ethnic and historic ties to a particular saint can project personal devotion beyond the private realm to the public sphere, and, yet, the celebration remains part of the little tradition. It is also true that personal rites of passage transformed by Catholic Sacraments can gather a variety of communal folk customs, illustrating the interplay of the little tradition and the great tradition in a single celebration. This is particularly evident in those circumstances where lack of clerical leadership breeds an independent attitude toward celebration, and where a traditional emphasis on ceremony and ritual is not curtailed by staunch representatives of the great tradition's streamlining, modernizing trend. Both weddings and funerals in Hispanic villages in the Southwest are examples of elaborate expressions of popular piety surrounding a clearly regulated Roman ritual.

Hispanic weddings, both within the central ceremony and in the preparatory and concluding celebrations, contain several blessings of persons and objects. At the *prendorio* (engagement party), in the days before engagement rings were included in the gifts given to the bride, a jeweled rosary was placed over the heads of the couple by the bride's oldest uncle or godfather.[34] This gesture combines the use of a sacramental with a personal blessing given by a significant family member.

The wedding itself was divided into two separate ceremonies, the first for the proposal and vows, the second for the nuptial blessing.[35] Sometimes, between these two ceremonies, a set of coins and rings was blessed by the priest for the couple in the church vestibule before approaching the altar for the nuptial blessing.[36]

Between the wedding ceremony and the reception, formal processions often formed to mark the transition from the church to the home or hall. This custom might be seen as one way in which popular piety recognized the difference between the places in which one most often conformed to the great tradition or felt free to express the little tradition. Another expression of popular piety surrounding Hispanic weddings took place in the home or reception hall. Cleofas Jaramillo describes the *entriega*, "the delivery of the wedded couple to their parents by the *padrinos* (sponsors) for a final blessing before departure," as a "long string of impromptu verses that the guitarist was addressing to the newlyweds, their parents, and *padrinos* (attendants), verses of advice, of parting, and blessings."[37] Whether celebrating weddings or funerals, Holy Week or the feasts of the saints, Hispanic Catholics in North America employed a little tradition that linked their religion to their culture. Faced with the imposition of a great tradition by an ecclesiastical institution that was unwilling to be mutually influenced, many surrendered the institutional Church in order to preserve an expressive one.

Less enduring or influential in this region than either Native Americans or Hispanics, separate communities of European immigrants contributed to the history of ethnicity and religion in the Intermountain West in a variety of ways. Irish and German Catholics were representatives of the earlier waves of immigration that added millions to the population of the country and thousands to the Intermountain region. Initially attracted by the mining and industrial enterprises, many turned to agriculture and business. Italian Catholics seem to have come in two separate groups, those from the northern provinces first, followed by those from the southern provinces. It was the second great wave of European immigration that added not only larger numbers of Catholics to the U.S. population, but also new ethnic groups from east European countries. Before assimilation obscured their distinctive features, most of these ethnic groups experienced cultural conflict even within parishes. Representatives of both waves of European immigration have been found in parishes scattered throughout the Intermountain West, but more prominently, more permanently, and more formally in the Pueblo Diocese and the Denver Archdiocese.

The Irish established Catholic congregations in many mining towns throughout Utah, Nevada, and Colorado as early as 1859. Despite the changing fortunes of these boom and bust communities, Catholic life among the Irish (frequently organized by Irish clergymen) flourished with a high degree of nationalism as bond. Because maintaining an ethnic identity in a largely WASP society was essential to these nineteenth-century immigrants, "[t]he parish (as well as the station and mission) was the center of their lives, and they sacrificed a great deal of their surplus resources to build chapels and rectories in their neighborhoods. . . . The local church was the center of the community, surrounded by homes, taverns, stores, and shops."[38]

In Montana, an 1865 attempt by an Irish layman to colonize the area with Irish Catholics resulted in an 1866 appeal to the Second Council of Baltimore to name Montana a Vicariate Apostolic. Consequently, in 1868 the first Vicariate of Montana was prematurely created and then returned (divided) to its earlier jurisdictions.

In a letter written by Archbishop John Ireland in 1912, the dream of General Thomas Francis Meagher was recalled:

> It was, he repeatedly said, his wish to colonize the territory with Catholics—drawing principally from Irishmen in Ireland and Irishmen in America with whom naturally his influence was potent. He would at once take steps to secure priests and would write to All Hallows' College in Dublin to engage there ten students for whose tuition he would make himself responsible. He would furthermore, he added, take steps to have a Bishop in Montana. . . . With those purposes of General Meagher I was quite conversant, having heard him time and again and having encouraged him very much to go forward and become the great founder of the Church in Montana.[39]

These sentiments were expressed by the same "outspoken and enormously energetic archbishop of St. Paul . . . [who] irritated Eastern bishops by advertising Western opportunities and even by arranging colonization projects with the railroads."[40] But Meagher was not to see his dream come true; on July 7, 1867, the general, who had taken a steamer east on business, disappeared. No evidence ever appeared to substantiate whether foul play, suicide, or an accident claimed the Irishman's life. It could well be that the loss of this layman's leadership resulted in the unsuccessful attempt to create a vicariate in Montana a year later. If his plan had succeeded, what would it have been like to see an Irish Catholic state established within two hundred miles of a Mormon state?

After the Irish came the Germans. Active in farming communities throughout the Intermountain region, German Catholics are probably most visible in Idaho and Colorado, where they were drawn originally by mining or steelworks. In 1878, Denver's second church, St. Elizabeth's, was established on the west side of Cherry Creek, but it was not until 1887 that the parish was divided by Bishop Matz (coadjutor to Bishop Machebeuf), gathering all the German Catholics of Denver into a single congregation.

> One of the principles of Catholic, Lutheran, and other German religionists of the nineteenth century was that the preservation of the German language and culture was essential to their religious identity.
>
> Charges were made—probably greatly exaggerated—that as many as 20,000,000 German Catholics were lost to the Church by the fact that the German language was not perpetuated in German parishes.[41]

The importance of language in maintaining ethnic identity was at the heart of the Kulturkampf, or clash of values, experienced between German and Irish Catholics in Denver. English-speaking Catholics at St. Elizabeth's were involved in conflicts over language until 1889, when St. Leo's Church was opened for the Irish. This local friction between Irish and Germans in Colorado was part of a larger cultural conflict between two nationalistic groups in America. Although German immigrants were economically better off than Irish immigrants after the Civil War, the former resented the fact that the majority of hierarchical positions in the American Church were filled by Irishmen. "Bishop Nicholas Matz (1889–1917) attributed much of the strife that plagued his rule to the mistaken impression of the Irish that he favored the Germans over them."[42] In 1871, the St. Raphael Society was organized to aid and protect German immigrants. This international organization gave support to American Germans whose self-conscious, militant effort weathered Protestant resistance in founding German-language parochial schools, and in generally seeking to change their subordination to Irish Catholics in the American hierarchy and in parish life.[43] This conflict was waged in the arena of the great tradition's hierarchical understanding of the Church and contributed further tension to the already highly charged debate between Catholic Americanists and anti-Americanists, which was not solved until 1899 when Pope Leo XIII condemned Americanism.

In South Boulder, Colorado, a rural community of farmers and miners was made up of immigrants of Belgian, German, Irish, Austrian, English, and Scotch descent. The German element began to prevail when, in 1887, Bishop Machebeuf granted previously purchased diocesan land to the Benedictines for the establishment of a monastery with jurisdiction over Boulder County. This establishment was an extension of the 1855 papal authorization of a self-governing Benedictine congregation in America, which gave added impetus and prestige to German Catholicism in this country. However, as with the Franciscans and the Diocese of Durango in seventeenth-century New Mexico, overlapping jurisdictions of order and secular clergy caused tension when hierarchical principles prevailed. In 1890, the Benedictine priests and sisters who had established a church and school in Breckenridge left that mountain mining town for Pueblo and Canon City in southern Colorado. Although the Benedictines retained the farm and part of the monastery building at South Boulder, their ministry was transferred primarily to Pueblo, known locally as "The Pittsburg of the West," and, in 1896, the courthouse record of their jurisdiction was changed from "The Benedictine Society of Boulder County" to "Benedictine Society of the State of Colorado and Benedictine College in Pueblo."[44] This shift in Benedictine ministry coincides with ethnic changes at St. Mary's Parish in Pueblo. Established in 1891 for a combined congregation of Slovenians, Germans, and Slovaks, St. Mary's was designated as a German parish from 1895 until 1901, when St. Boniface Church specifically for Germans was built.[45]

During the final decades of the nineteenth century, Polish immigrants, part of America's second great wave of immigration, came from partitioned sections of Poland and settled, among other places, in the Denver area. They were attracted by the prospect of employment in local smelters, while in search of better economic opportunities or of an escape from serving in the czarist army.[46] By the mid-1880s, there were two dozen Polish families in Globeville, and, by 1888, two local groups of national Polish societies were founded. These organizations were characterized as much by economic and social need as by religious piety. They were an expression of self-help in an era without welfare programs or social security.

Polish folk religious practices frequently included blessings of special foods. Christmas for the Polish parishioners of St. Joseph's in Denver included the traditional *Wigilia*. At this Christmas Eve supper, family members shared the *opatek*, the unleavened wafer embossed with seasonal religious pictures, before departing for caroling and Midnight Mass.[47] At Easter, Polish Catholics had their buffets blessed by the priest.

Our Lady of Mount Carmel is the patron for three Colorado parishes that at one time or another have served Italian Catholics. In Denver and in Pueblo, these immigrants were members of parishes in which Jesuits specifically assigned to care for them continued the old religious customs and rituals that had served as a source of cultural identity in the Old Country, an expression of the little tradition. In 1891, Father Mariano Felice Lapore was assigned to work with the Italians in Denver, and, by 1894, his congregation had its own church. However, in 1899 that church burned to the ground.

Between 1880 and the first part of the twentieth century, Italians became the largest group of foreign born citizens in Nevada.[48] While this may not be reflected in any special way on the parish level, it is evident today in a prominent Italian Catholic Federation on the diocesan level. Because distinct groups of Irish, German, Polish, or Italian immigrants in this region became so quickly acculturated or were obscured by urban growth in the areas where they settled, their cultural conflicts as well as their ethnic contributions to Catholic parish life were short-lived and minimally influential in the Intermountain West.

At the turn of the century, the U.S. government's reorganization of Indian life and its trail of broken promises continued to affect Catholic Indian missions, involving the Church in new economic and organizational approaches. As federal funds were promised and then withdrawn from many mission schools, Catholic institutions became more dependent on the Marquette League, the Bureau of Catholic Indian Missions, and the continued support of Mother Katherine Drexel. Without the magnanimous gifts of this wealthy Philadelphia heiress, who founded her own religious community (The Sisters of the Blessed Sacrament for Indians and Colored People), several missions in this region would not have survived to serve as ethnic parishes today. Some, in fact, did not survive. Others, like the six San Solano missions of Topowa, Arizona, joined in 1908 to serve Indians of several different tribes. In that same year, when the Arapaho and Shoshone realized that the government had failed to give St. Stephen's Indian Mission the money promised to run a school on the reservation, the General Council of the two tribes gathered to ratify the transfer of title to St. Stephen's Indian Mission (Catholic) and to the Roberts Mission (Episcopalian) at Fort Washakie.[49] This gift of land, so precious to the Indians, was a rare show of confidence in an equally rare Anglo system that encouraged both assimilation and cultural expression. A clear awareness of the energy invested in attempting to integrate the little tradition with the great tradition is evident in the testimony given by Arapaho and Shoshone leaders at that meeting:

> I am always very pleased to see our children going to the two mission schools, as they are taught to be honest there. I should be very glad to have the schools have their lands forever. We are here to take something old and make it new.[50]

In 1908, Lone Bear, Chief of the Arapahos, wrote a letter in which he praised the ongoing tradition of Indian and Anglo influences in worship and education at St. Stephen's.

> We gave the land of our own to them to put up a school for our children. We sent our children to that school because they took good care of them. All learn to talk English; all learn to speak about God. We see them and how they pray in Church. And they also learn to pray in their own language. I feel good about that. When the government gave nothing for these children in school we did not know about it.[51]

Also during this decade, new parishes served new combinations of Indian, Hispanic, and Anglo Catholics. In 1912, the Gallup Parish, surrounded by a number of coal mines and serving as one of the main divisions of the Santa Fe railroad, covered 11,000 square miles and served 300 American, English, and Italian Catholics, 800 Slovenians, 4,220 Hispanics, and fourteen Indian villages.[52] In this situation, the ethnic variety as well as distances and numbers made for a demanding ministry.

It was during this period that many Indian missionaries began to attack Indian culture as an obstacle to Americanization and Christianization. Among tribes like the Blackfeet, who had resisted Christian advances for decades, such an approach created only further antagonism. Among others, missionary attempts to transform once nomadic Indians into farmers met with failure. Meanwhile, extreme poverty and ill-health were common.

But there were some successes, too. Since 1910, the Gros Ventres have been almost 100% Catholic.[53] And at St. Stephen's in Wyoming, the tremendous increase in baptisms between 1904 and 1924 is attributed to the consecutive nine-year assignments of two priests who were also fluent in the Arapaho language.[54] In stark contrast to the approach of his predecessor among the Blackfeet, Rev. M. J. Halligan expressed an appreciation and tolerance of that tribe's culture. Despite the obstacles of past history, great distances, the failure "of several idealistic government ventures designed to contribute to [Blackfoot] civilization," droughts and severe winters, Father Halligan was able to "make headway and be loved by the people."[55]

> When Little Flower Chapel was dedicated [in 1932], participation by both the Indians and the [official hierarchical] Catholic Church was significant. Four bishops joined in the dedication. . . . And the fact that Indians had responsibility for arranging ceremonies at the dedication shows the indigenous nature of Little Flower Church.[56]

Once again, the great and the little traditions were joined. This parish, which replaced old St. Michael's (built in 1904), serves the Helena diocese today with two missions and many stations of its own.

With the passage of the Indian Reorganization Act in 1934, under the leadership of John Collier, Commissioner of Indian Affairs in the Roosevelt administration, Native Americans could exercise more control over their own secular affairs and religious practices. But this federal legislation did not have an immediate impact on Catholic missionary ventures. In some cases, continuing financial difficulties, misfortunes, and misunderstandings were irreversible. Such was the case at Holy Family Mission for the Blackfeet, which closed its doors in 1940.

In those tribes where Christianity failed to present a meaningful faith and where ancient religious traditions were being lost, a "vacuum [was] created by the cultural disintegration that was the result of the impingement of aggressively modernizing Western cultures on the traditional societies of . . . North America."[57] One of the movements that arose to fill this vacuum among Native Americans is the Peyote Cult. Based on practices used by Mexican Indians for many centuries, the cult spread to certain plains groups and was given its accomodationist form by the Comanche or Kiowa in the 1880s. Peyotism appealed to those people suffering oppression and deprivation who could neither return completely to the old ways nor totally accept Anglo culture. It came through the Utes to the Navajos in the 1930s, when the federal stock reduction program on their reservation deprived the people of their native economy and offered passive dependence as an alternative. Despite active hostility from the majority of the tribe, Peyotism spread among the Dine until in 1951 more than one out of every seven Navajo families had joined the cult.[58] The pan-Indian nature of this movement led in 1906 to the formation of a loose organization covering several states. As opposition to the cult increased, the federation grew and came to be known as the Native American Church. In 1945 and 1946, chapters of the Native American Church were incorporated in New Mexico, Utah, and Arizona.[59] The Utah and Arizona groups were composed entirely of Navajo while the New Mexico group included, in a rare exception to the Pueblo Indian pattern, the Native Americans of Taos Pueblo.

> Peyotists regard the institutional forms of Catholicism and Protestantism as a white person's faith, appropriate for whites but not meant for Indians. Instead, they conceive of themselves as relating to the same god through a different mediator. The Peyote Spirit encountered in the ritual is sometimes identified with Jesus or the Holy Spirit and serves the same mediating functions as do the Christian figures. It is the spiritual means through which divine power comes into contact with and can be assimilated by human beings.[60]

During the 1940s, St. Stephen's Indian Mission became a diocesan parish in its own right. This shift in status not only signaled an increased focus on Catholic education, celebration of the Sacraments, and involvement in diocesan life, but it also spawned a change in attitude toward native culture, creating conflict between parish policy and the people.

> For most of its long history St. Stephen's had exercised a qualified tolerance of its parishioners taking part in the Native American religious ceremonies, such as the Sun Dance and Peyote practices. This policy radically changed in the 1940's when it was felt that such a "dual practice" was impossible. Many St. Stephen's parishioners were, in effect, forced to make a choice between the practice of their Catholic ways and their Indian ways. . . . Sadly it would take almost two generations for the hurt begun at this time to heal.[61]

What has been the history of the institutional Church's openness to Native American religious traditions? Does a preference for hierarchical principles preclude an appreciation of non-Christian spirituality? Is it possible for the "officially established" Church to consider the appeal of the Peyote cult and other Indian practices and, in doing so, to clarify an understanding of its own ministry? Can a primarily institutional approach to religion be enriched by a rediscovery of the expressive, prophetic element within its own tradition?

While Native Americans were experiencing a variety of missionary approaches at the turn of the century, a dramatic change in the Hispanic-American population was just beginning. Until 1900, the Spanish-speaking population of the United States was centered largely in the American Southwest. Several economic and political events converged to swell their numbers and to disperse that ethnic group throughout the country; still, the heart of their Catholicism would remain communal, expressive, and allied with the little tradition. In 1882, the Chinese Exclusion Act created a labor shortage in the country; in 1887, the Dingley Tariff encouraged development of sugar beet growing, a new agricultural industry requiring manual labor; in 1907, the Gentleman's Agreement with Japan limited immigration from that country; and throughout that period, the increased use of irrigation for agriculture in the western desert created the need for more laborers.[62] The Spanish-American War of 1898 brought Christian missionaries to the Philippines, Cuba, and Puerto Rico where U.S. occupation and a sense of Manifest Destiny encouraged migration to the mainland. The Mexican Revolution drove many refugees northward while U.S.-supported mining and railroad ventures in Mexico brought others across the border. Finally, World War I created a labor shortage in many urban areas of the United States, which attracted Spanish-speaking migrants. Details and interpretations of these events as they affected Hispanic Catholics in the U.S. Church lie beyond the scope of this study, but it is important to note here that they did not, by and large, change the ethnic tension that had always characterized Hispanic Catholicism in North America. Like early Hispanic Catholics of the Southwest, these twentieth-century migrants were without sufficient clerical leadership. Unlike the European immigrants of the nineteenth century, the Hispanic migrants of the twentieth century did not bring with them priests of the same ethnic group to share their struggles. Instead, foreign-born clergymen encouraged the same kind of assimilation their countrymen ultimately chose, while the little tradition among Hispanics prevailed.

> Noninstitutional religion is the response of a religious people not adequately served by the institutional Church. . . . But the people did not forget to practice their beliefs simply because priests were not around. . . . [they] continued to practice their *religion casera* [home or do-it-yourself religion]. More accurately, it was a community religiosity of mutual help organizations and devotional groups growing out of the home-nurtured faith of the people.[63]

Mexican and other Spanish-speaking migrants began moving into Utah after 1900. As Greeks and Italians moved out of mining and railroad work in this state, Hispanics moved in. Of those who did not enter these two enterprises, most found work as manual laborers. There is evidence that some intermarriage with other ethnic groups took place at this time. As the social visibility of European immigrants decreased, the visibility of Hispanic migrants increased.

In 1920, an Italian mission was founded as part of St. Patrick's Parish (the second Catholic parish in Salt Lake) to serve those of Italian, Mexican, Syrian, and Armenian descent. After three changes of location, the mission stabilized as the assistant pastor of St. Patrick's, Hispanic himself, was given special charge of these ethnic groups. In 1930, when Father James Earl Collins, "was appointed 'Administrator of the Mexican Chapel of Our Lady of Guadalupe,' " the mission was given independent status.[64]

> For twenty-seven years the people of this mission, and later the parish, saw in the figure of Father Collins their church in action and their "Lord among them." Living in poverty—his only extravagance was the mission—Father Collins patched his suits and glued composition soles to his shoes. His salary was shared with his people. Each year, in order to visit his mother in Albany, New York, he borrowed on his insurance and repaid the loan month-by-month in the following year.[65]

Such extraordinary dedication to a traditionally neglected ethnic minority gave institutional support to the Catholic faith of the people and kept them within the religious tradition of their culture. But this kind of Catholic ministry was rare. It was not until the 1940s that the Catholic Councils for the Spanish-speaking began to do organized work with migrants. By 1944, Our Lady of Guadalupe Parish in Salt Lake City had grown sufficiently to be given parish status.

During these decades of Hispanic migrations, Protestant evangelizing efforts were quick to include the Spanish-speaking in their plan to convert the world to Christianity. But, in addition to the appeal of the mainline Protestant denominations, Pentecostalism and other sects began to attract large numbers of disaffected Hispanic Catholics, especially in the post-World War I years. While a thorough study of the Pentecostal appeal among Hispanics lies beyond the scope of this study, it is important to realize that this twentieth-century outgrowth of the Holiness Movement most often appealed to those people who found themselves in the interstices of society, neither in the mainstream nor outlawed. Like the disoriented Native Americans who turned to the Peyote cult, black immigrants to urban areas, poor rural whites, and Puerto Rican immigrants to New York City all found themselves among the socially dispossessed who hungered for an unmediated religious experience expressed in a spontaneous, unstructured way.[66] Except for those involved in the Charismatic Movement, the American Catholic Church has yet to come to terms with this growing socio-religious movement into the Pentecostal churches.

World War II brought an end to Hispanic isolation in the United States. In 1940, the country's Hispanic population was 15% urban and 85% rural; by the early 1950s, those proportions were reversed.[67] Spanish-speaking U.S. soldiers, sailors, and marines (the most highly represented of any ethnic group in the armed forces during World War II) returned from overseas imbued with a new consciousness. This spirit became evident on a national level in their organizing such groups as the G.I. Forum and in strengthening such pre-existing groups as the League of United Latin American Citizens (LULAC) and Sociedades Mexicanas.[68] The war also led Hispanics to question their status within the Catholic

Church. This new militance is seen by some as the roots of the Chicano movement of the 1960s.

By the turn of the century, many close-knit Irish communities were challenged by the need to cope with other ethnic groups. Italian, Slavic, and Basque settlers were all instrumental in provoking Irish resentment, rivalry, and wrath. This conflict was often as visible in the local churches as it was in more secular settings. Nevertheless, as the twentieth century progressed, "the more overtly Irish aspects of parish life became less visible. . . . In the second and third generations, some of the Old World passions became considerably less intense."[69] Shifting settlement patterns and gradual assimilation into a multi-ethnic society contributed to the fact that the Irish have never had a national foreign language parish in the Intermountain region. Of the three national foreign language parishes designated in the Colorado Diocese in 1900 (the only three in the entire region), two were German and one was Polish. (See Appendix A.)

Like Irish Catholics in America, German Catholics, too, exhibited a high degree of nationalism. In 1900, there were forty-five German societies in Denver; in 1910, Germans comprised 43% of the Colorado population.[70] With a higher level of education than other major immigrant groups of their time, Germans became assimilated by the dominant culture more rapidly than other ethnic groups. Sacred Heart of Mary Parish in Boulder, Colorado, with its large percentage of German farmers, had for some time a series of German pastors who gave sermons in both English and German. One old-timer recalls:

> It was bad enough to listen to one in English, but the ordeal of another one in German was unpardonable . . . his sermons were long. It took him some time to get going, and even longer to stop. . . . When World War I came along, this German business ended abruptly.[71]

Nonetheless, the parish was never designated specifically for Germans.

By 1902, the Polish community in Globeville had collected enough money to begin building their own church. In that same year, they received their first pastor through the efforts of Bishop Matz. Rev. T. Jarzynski, a Holy Cross priest educated at Notre Dame, Indiana, encouraged his parishioners to celebrate (in addition to important moments in life such as baptisms, weddings, and funerals) religious and national holidays that had been part of their lives in the Old Country.

Just as Catholic immigrants of other ethnic backgrounds often experienced cultural conflict, the Polish parish at Globeville was tested by a separatist movement by Slovenian and Croatian parishioners who wanted their own church. By 1920, they succeeded, and Holy Rosary was built one block from St. Joseph's, where it functioned for at least a decade as a Slovenian parish before losing that special designation.[72]

Always conscious of their political roots, the Polish immigrants of Globeville were active during the 1940s in the Polish War Relief.[73] The period following

World War II was a transitional one for Globeville's Polish residents as many second and third generation Americans of Polish descent moved to residential areas in other parts of Denver. Simultaneously, Polish displaced persons arrived in the city. Although they may have resided in other parts of the city, they joined St. Joseph's Parish for the same spiritual and social benefits that Polish immigrants had two generations earlier, ethnic identity and the freedom to celebrate rites of passage in culturally meaningful ways.

Parishes designated for Slovaks and Slovenians in Denver and Pueblo seem to have satisfied a temporary need. Holy Rosary in Denver served that purpose for slightly more than a decade; St. Mary's in Pueblo was designated as a Slovenian parish from 1920 through 1943.[74] Although St. Joseph's in Leadville, Colorado, was designated an Austrian parish from 1901 through 1918, since 1919 it has served as a Slovenian parish; and from 1913 through 1943, St. Anthony of Padua in Pueblo served as a parish designated for Slovaks.[75]

Slavic parishioners at Sts. Cyril and Methodius in Rock Springs, Wyoming, and Catholic Croatians who came to the coal mines of Gallup, New Mexico, while noted as loyal parishioners and significant ethnically, were never sufficient in numbers or influence to establish national foreign language parishes.

Another ethnic group without parishes of its own, but with a living Catholic tradition, is the Basque community of southern Idaho. By the turn of the century, the well-established sheep industry in Idaho attracted a good number of Basque herders. By 1910, Boise served as the center of the Basque community of Idaho. In 1918, Good Shepherd Church at Boise was built for this ethnic group, and Father Bernardo Arregui was appointed first pastor for all the Basques in southern Idaho and the Jordan Valley of Oregon. In 1922, Good Shepherd lost its resident pastor and was attended from the Boise cathedral until it was incorporated into the cathedral parish in 1928.[76]

The twentieth century brought to Our Lady of Mount Carmel Parish in Denver a new church to replace the one that burned, along with some cultural conflict. With the new structure in progress, a faction in the parish, based on ethnic tensions between northern and southern Italians, demonstrated its discontent by attempting to build a separate chapel with the hope of getting its own pastor. In the midst of this conflict, Father Lepore was murdered on the night of November 18, 1902.[77] This incident may have reflected the anti-clericalism that characterized many poor Italians in the home country.

Since two Jesuits had been assigned to help out at the parish, another one, Father John Guida, was sent to take over the administration until the Servite Fathers came in 1904. Their arrival was due to the intervention of Mother Cabrini, founder of the Missionary Sisters of the Sacred Heart, who had responded to Father Lepore's request for sisters by inaugurating a house for her community in Denver in 1902. Once Father Julius M. Piccoli, O.S.M., was in charge, the political, financial, and moral conditions of the parish improved.[78] During the thirty-four years of his pastorate, the Italian population was transformed from poor, illiterate, and unskilled workers to professionals and civic leaders.

In Pueblo and Trinidad, Colorado, during the first decade of the twentieth century, Our Lady of Mount Carmel parishes served both Italians and Spanish-speaking Catholics. While the Pueblo parish was designated as Italian, the Trinidad parish was designated simultaneously for both groups. Italian Catholics settled also in Butte, Montana, and in East Pocatello and Priest River, Idaho, but parishes in those places were never designated as national foreign language parishes.

It was during the first few decades of the twentieth century that the number of parishes specifically for European immigrants in the Intermountain region was at its highest. In 1930, the *Catholic Directory* listed eleven national foreign language parishes for the Denver Diocese. (See Appendix A.)

During the 1940s, as industrialization and urbanization began to change the demographics of the Intermountain West, many ethnic parishes in the region began to lose their enclosed neighborhood character and, instead, became gathering places for members of a particular ethnic group throughout a growing urban area. Some even lost their official designation as national foreign language parishes. By 1944, three years after the Pueblo diocese was erected, all national foreign language parishes in that diocese no longer carried that special designation.

The Apaches, a notorious threat to all from the sixteenth through the nineteenth centuries, gave up their nomadic marauding in the twentieth century, but had no Catholic parish of their own until San Carlos Apache Mission was established in 1950 in the Tucson Diocese. A second Apache mission, St. Francis, today serves with parish status at Whiteriver, Arizona, in the Gallup Diocese.

It was the Native American congregation at St. John Berchman's Church of the Jocko Reservation in Montana that became the experienced cultural and religious revival of the early Flathead/Catholic tradition. It began with the renovation of the church buildings by members of the tribe for a formal rededication on October 19, 1952. At that ceremony, a commemoration of the arrival of the last Flathead chief at the Jocko Reservation was accompanied by a sermon in the Indian language and a retelling of the Flathead history. Father Neil Byrne, on behalf of his parishioners, had served not only as a counselor but also as a public relations department and organizer of protest committees and meetings.

> Periodically, he appeared before government committees. His people caught fire. They began to take a more active part in the various phases of parish life confirming their pastor's thesis that Indians can and will accept the full responsibilities of parochial life and that they should be taught to do this without cutting them loose from their Indian background and customs.[79]

Further evidence of Flathead initiative was the artistic decoration of the renovated church with two life-sized portraits, one called "Christ As An Indian Chief," the other the "Indian Madonna."[80] Unfortunately, the church at Jocko was destroyed by fire in December of 1960, and today St. John Berchman's Church holds the status of a mission attached to St. Ignatius Parish in the Helena Diocese.

During the 1950s, the migration of new Spanish-speaking parishioners into areas where earlier Hispanics had settled seemed to give new impetus to old customs in some sections of the region. Although not designated as a national foreign language parish, Our Lady of Guadalupe Church for Spanish-speaking people was established in Billings, Montana, in 1954. It succeeded an earlier mission founded in 1925 and closed some time later. And, in 1950, the parishioners of St. Charles Borromeo Parish in Hailey, Idaho, began the tradition of sponsoring an annual Basque dinner, an event that continues to draw large numbers of people from surrounding communities.

While European immigrants have had some ethnic influence on the quality of Catholic parish life in the Intermountain West, that influence has often been temporary and always limited. Native Americans and Hispanics, however, have not only been among the earliest Catholics in the region, but have also allowed the cultural expressions of their faith to become obvious elements of the region's multi-cultural self-understanding. The interplay of ethnicity and religion in the Intermountain West is a dynamic in American Catholic life that reveals an official preference for a hierarchical approach and, thus, an Eastern attitude of superiority over the "uncivilized" West. But, it also suggests the possibility of reclaiming a prophetic appreciation of diversity and the inclusion of regional distinctions that can enrich the American Catholic experience.

Notes

1. Bernard Fontana, "The Melting Pot That Wouldn't: Ethnic Groups in the American Southwest Since 1846," *American Indian Culture and Research Journal*, 1 (1974), 18–24.

2. John Francis Bannon, *The Spanish Borderlands Frontier, 1513–1821* (Albuquerque: University of New Mexico Press, 1974), 80.

3. Edward T. Nash, "New Faces of Isleta Catholics," (Ph.D. dissertation, University of New Mexico, 1981), 3.

4. John Kessell, *The Missions of New Mexico Since 1776* (Albuquerque: University of New Mexico Press, 1980), 11.

5. Polingaysi Qoyawayma, *No Turning Back* (Albuquerque: University of New Mexico Press, 1964), 38.

6. Alice Joseph, M.D., Rosamond B. Spicer, and Jane Chesky, *The Desert People: A Study of the Papago Indians* (Chicago: University of Chicago Press, 1949), 22; and Odie B. Faulk, ed., *John Baptist Salpointe: Soldier of the Cross* (Tucson: The Diocese of Tucson, 1966), 120.

7. Gary Paul Nabhan, *The Desert Smells Like Rain: A Naturalist in Papago Country* (San Francisco: North Point Press, 1982), 114–115.

8. L. B. Palladino, S.J., *Indian and White in the Northwest: A History of Catholicity in Montana, 1831–1891* (Lancaster, Pennsylvania: Wickersham Publishing Co., 1922), 154–155.

9. *Ibid.*, 111.

10. Joe L. Montoya, *Isleta Pueblo and the Church of St. Augustine* (Isleta Pueblo, New Mexico: St. Augustine Church, 1978), 30.

11. Twenty-two Navajo Men and Women, *Stories of Traditional Navajo Life and Culture* (Tsaile, Navajo Nation, Arizona: Navajo Community College Press, 1977), 126.

12. Joseph Epes Brown, *The Spiritual Legacy of the American Indian* (New York: Crossroads Press, 1982), 29.

13. Peter W. Williams, *Popular Religion in America* (Englewood Cliffs, New Jersey: Prentice-Hall, Inc., 1980), 64.

14. *Ibid.*, 70, 72.

15. John Tracy Ellis, *American Catholicism* (Chicago: University of Chicago Press, 1969), 41.

16. Luciano Hendren, "The Church in New Mexico," *Fronteras: A History of the Latin American Church in the USA Since 1513,* ed. Moisés Sandoval (San Antonio: Mexican American Cultural Center, 1983), 201.

17. Paul Horgan, *Lamy of Santa Fe: His Life and Times* (New York: Farrar, Straus and Giroux, 1975), 106–107.

18. Fray Angelico Chavez, *But Time and Chance: The Story of Padre Martinez of Taos, 1793–1867* (Santa Fe: Sunstone Press, 1981), 117.

19. Marianne L. Stoller and Thomas J. Steele, S.J., *Diary of the Jesuit Residence of Our Lady of Guadalupe Parish, Conejos, Colorado, December 1871–December 1875,* The Colorado College Studies, No. 19 (Colorado Springs: The Colorado College, 1982), xxv.

20. *Ibid.*, xxvii–xxviii.

21. Thomas J. Steele, S.J., *Santos and Saints: The Religious Folk Art of Hispanic New Mexico* (1974; reprint, Santa Fe: Ancient City Press, 1982), 54–55.

22. Thomas J. Steele, S.J., "The Spanish Passion Play in New Mexico and Colorado," *New Mexico Historical Review*, 53 (July 1978), 241.

23. Cleofas M. Jaramillo, *Shadows of the Past* (Santa Fe: Seton Village Press, 1941), 69.

24. Steele, "Passion Play," 257.

25. Jay P. Dolan, *Catholic Revivalism: The American Experience, 1830–1900* (Notre Dame: University of Notre Dame Press, 1978), 57; and Stoller and Steele, 52.

26. Dolan, xvi.

27. Steele, *Santos and Saints,* 46.

28. Jaramillo, 41.

29. *Our Lady of Guadalupe, Taos, New Mexico* (White Plains, New York: Monarch Publishing, Inc., 1976), 8.

30. *Taos,* 8; and Steve Sandoval, "Rosario Chapel: Renovation Changing Looks, Not Essence," *Albuquerque Journal,* 3 September 1983, C11.

31. Faulk, 16–17.
32. Jaramillo, 43–47.
33. Thomas J. Steele, S.J., "Funciones of a Village," in *Funciones: Communal Ceremonies of Hispanic Life*, n.p., 5.
34. Jaramillo, 31–32.
35. Carol Jensen, "Cleofas M. Jaramillo on Marriage in Territorial Northern New Mexico," *New Mexico Historical Review*, 58 (April 1983), 164.
36. Carol Jensen, "Cleofas Jaramillo's View of Marriage: An Example of the Interplay of Folk Religion and Institutional Religion in Territorial Northern New Mexico" (Thesis: Indian University, 1981), 81.
37. Jensen, *New Mexico Historical Review*, 167; Cleofas M. Jaramillo, *Romance of a Little Village Girl* (San Antonio: The Naylor Co., 1955), 62.
38. James S. Olson, "Pioneer Catholicism in Eastern and Southern Nevada, 1864–1931," *Nevada Historical Society Quarterly*, 26 (Fall 1983), 168–169.
39. Palladino, 501.
40. Sidney E. Ahlstrom, *A Religious History of the American People* (New Haven: Yale University Press, 1972), 829.
41. Paul H. Hallett, "German Immigrants Helped Build Colorado," *The Denver Catholic Register*, 28 September 1983, 12.
42. *Ibid.*, 13.
43. Ahlstrom, 830.
44. Therese S. Westermeier, *Centennial of a Country Church* (Boulder, Colorado: Johnson Publishing Co., 1973), 15–16.
45. "Converted Broom Factory Served as First Church for 'Grove' Area," *The Southern Colorado Register*, 9 October 1959, Sec. 3, 45; *Hoffman's Catholic Directory and Clergy List* (Milwaukee: Hoffman Brother Co., 1895), 289; and *The Catholic Directory, Almanac, and Clergy List* (Milwaukee: H. W. Wiltzius and Co., 1901), 262.
46. Stanley L. Cuba, *Saint Joseph's Polish Roman Catholic Church, Diamond Jubilee*, 20 November 1977, n.p., 7.
47. *Ibid.*, 10–11.
48. *Encyclopedia Americana*, 1983 ed., s.v. "Nevada."
49. (Rev. Anthony Short), "The Beginnings," *The Wind River Rendezvous* 14 (April/May/June 1984), 8.
50. *Ibid.*
51. *Ibid.*
52. "The Parish and Missions of Gallup, New Mexico," in *The Franciscan Missions of the Southwest*, 45.
53. *Encyclopedia Americana*, 1983 ed., s.v. "Montana."
54. Short, "Beginnings," 9.
55. Howard L. Harrod, *Mission Among the Blackfeet* (Norman: University of Oklahoma Press, 1971), 103–106.
56. *Ibid.*, 105.
57. Williams, 23.
58. David Friend Aberle, *The Peyote Religion Among the Navajo* (Chicago: Aldine Publishing Co., 1966), 3.
59. *Ibid.*, 123.

Religion and Ethnicity

60. Williams, 37.
61. (Rev. Anthony Short), "Mission Centennial, 1884–1984," *The Wind River Rendezvous* 14 (July/Aug./Sept. 1984), 8.
62. Edwin Sylvest, Jr., "Hispanic American Protestantism in the United States," *Fronteras,* 317.
63. Moíses Sandoval, "Mexican Migration to the Midwest and East," *Fronteras,* 261, 263.
64. Jerald H. Merrill, "Fifty Years with a Future: Salt Lake's Guadalupe Mission and Parish," *Utah Historical Quarterly,* 40 (Summer 1972), 49.
65. *Ibid.,* 251.
66. Williams, 143–144.
67. Moíses Sandoval, "Effects of World War II on the Hispanic People," *Fronteras,* 341.
68. *Ibid.,* 342–343; and Moíses Sandoval, "The Church and El Movimiento," *Fronteras,* 378.
69. Olson, 170.
70. Hallett, 12.
71. Westermeier, 21.
72. Cuba, 11; *Official Catholic Directory* (New York: P. J. Kenedy and Sons, 1931), 332.
73. Cuba, 14; and *The Denver Post,* 12 December 1982, "Metro," vertical file, Archives of the Archdiocese of Denver, Denver, Colorado.
74. *Official Catholic Directory,* 1920, 306; 1931, 332; 1913, 376; 1919, 350; 1920, 309; and 1943, 592.
75. *Catholic Directory,* 1901, 266; *Official Catholic Directory,* 1919, 350; *Catholic Directory,* 1912, 376; and *Official Catholic Directory,* 1943, 592.
76. *Official Catholic Directory,* 1922, 236; and Schoenberg, *Chronicle,* 334.
77. *Our Lady of Mount Carmel* (South Hackensack, New Jersey: Custombook, Inc., 1975), 10.
78. *Ibid.,* 21.
79. Rev. Wilfred P. Schoenberg, S. J., *Jesuits in Montana, 1840–1960* (Portland: The Oregon Jesuit, 1960), 34.
80. *Ibid.*

CHAPTER FOUR
The Post-Vatican II Period

During the more than two decades since Vatican Council II, several economic, social, and political changes have taken place in the Intermountain West that affect the quality of Catholic life, and, in some cases, the ways in which the directives of the council have been implemented on a local level. A general movement toward greater economic development has led to continued urbanization and to growth in both the general and the Catholic populations in six of the region's eight states. But, this growth is tempered by a subsequent concern for maintaining a certain quality of life. In the face of an environmental dilemma created by the country's growing energy needs, this historically dependent region is determined to have a voice in deciding its own future. Meanwhile, Native American self-determination and a revival of Hispanic culture are prophetically influencing the region's social, political, and religious life. On the parochial level, these conditions lead some to question the limits of traditional parish structures in meeting the individual and communal needs of members, and to ponder the place of the "little tradition" in the renewal of Catholic life in the Intermountain West.

ECONOMIC, SOCIAL, AND POLITICAL CHANGES

As it did in the region's early history, geography continues to play a central role in the region's economic, political, and ecclesiastical development. "Once distance, space, and remoteness were our . . . curse. Now they are our blessing."[1] Open spaces, unique landscapes and land forms, and an abundance of untapped mineral wealth have encouraged governmental defense and science industries, manufacturing (especially of agricultural products), development of wilderness and recreation areas, and, most recently, the exploitation of energy resources.

By the 1960s, both Colorado's and Arizona's government defense contracts and manufacturing industries had created thriving urban centers in Denver and Phoenix, where high population density resulted in ecclesiastical growth. In the Denver area, the founding of St. Jude's suburban parish in 1967 gives evidence of that growth. "Nestled between the foothills of the Rocky Mountains and Southwestern Denver, [this] new parish covered approximately eighteen square miles

The Post-Vatican Period

of rapidly expanding territory."[2] According to a parish census taken on November 12, 1967, 1,151 families of 4,604 parishioners resided there.[3]

The continued concentration of Colorado's population along the eastern Front Range in cities and suburbs eventually resulted in the creation of the Colorado Springs Diocese in 1983, combining only one county from the Pueblo Diocese with nine counties from the more urban Denver Archdiocese. In Arizona, urban growth resulted in the 1969 establishment of the Phoenix Diocese, whose Catholic population is now increasing more rapidly than that of the Tucson Diocese. "But a rising standard of living has brought increased sophistication . . . and the old Arizona is vanishing as the cities take on the face of the southern California megalopolis."[4] This characterization of urban growth in the Intermountain West reflects a sort of regional fear that a valued reality may soon be lost and raises the issue of how or why it should be preserved.

In Idaho, the last of the region's eight states to have more of its population in urban rather than rural areas, it is the development of irrigation for agriculture and the transformation of ski resorts into all-season recreation and convention centers that account for most of the state's growth.[5] By 1978, Boise had three times its 1960 population; by 1980, Hailey's population increased 50% over the 1970 census figures; and between 1960 and 1980, Catholic population in the Boise Diocese grew from 42,234 to 70,416.[6] (See Appendix 2.)

In Utah, as in Colorado, population growth has been concentrated in an urban/suburban area (along the Wasatch Front). Between 1960 and 1970, the population of Salt Lake County grew from 383,000 to more than half a million.[7] Such growth reflects primarily the facts that the Mormon's Zion is located there and that a high birth rate is an integral part of Mormon life. But, an increase in Catholic population parallels these facts. Between 1960 and 1980 in the Diocese of Salt Lake City, Catholic population increased from 40,541 to 59,744. (See Appendix A.)

Nevada's unique status as a gambling center accounts for its growth. Between 1960 and 1970, the state's population increased 71.3%.[8]

> In 1972, the gaming business filled Nevada's coffers to the tune of $657.7 million. It is the largest employer in the state, and to some extent fills the need for employment and income usually covered by more typical major industries.[9]

The Catholic Church does not seem to be a significant influence in the state, and it is difficult to get information about its past or present. Still, Catholic population in the Reno-Las Vegas Diocese more than doubled between 1960 and 1980. (See Appendix 2.)

In New Mexico, federal laboratories employing scientists and technicians, as well as Bureau of Indian Affairs contracts and U.S. highway projects, have made the U.S. government the largest contributor to the state's economy.[10] Between 1960 and 1980, Catholic population in the Santa Fe Archdiocese grew from

275,000 to 324,357. (See Appendix 2.) These figures support the fact that New Mexico's economic and population growth have remained far below those of Arizona and Colorado. With the lowest per capita income in the region, New Mexico reflects, as does Wyoming, the undeveloped condition that has characterized this region for so long. With the federal government as the major landowner in the Rocky Mountain states (controlling 43% of the land in 1975) and a history of supplying the rest of the country with raw materials, it is no wonder that some claim that this region has been economically and politically discriminated against.[11] During the 1960s, Intermountain states clearly attempted to attract economic and industrial development.

> Then [in the 1970s] the market developed. The nation recognized that its oil and natural gas resources were dwindling rapidly, that its energy intensive economy demanded a doubling of energy consumption each decade, and that low sulphur coal was needed to meet air quality standards in the cities. . . . Today, the region is the nation's most richly endowed energy frontier.[12]

The energy market has given the region the economic and political opportunity it needed, but this development has not been an unmixed blessing. Wyoming and Montana present dramatic examples of the environmental dilemmas faced by the Intermountain states. As Wyoming's economy shifted from cattle to oil and natural gas, many began to wonder if the state was not prospering at its own expense. Between 1960 and 1980, the Diocese of Cheyenne's Catholic population decreased by 2,000. (See Appendix A.) By the early 1970s, unplanned-for booms in the towns of Rock Springs and Gillette resulted not only in inadequate services (doctors, teachers, housing), but also in a transient population with high rates of prostitution, narcotics, and crime. But, by 1975, Wyoming expressed a change in attitude. In a legislative session early in that year, three land use bills were passed, giving Wyoming "some of the most comprehensive environmental management powers in the nation."[13]

Montana, too, experienced economic changes during the 1960s and the 1970s from which it has emerged as the region's "peer group leader in enacting strong laws to enhance the state's control over energy development."[14] During the 1970s, farms increased in size and mechanization but decreased in number and in the amount of workers they employed. Montana's youth began immigrating to seek jobs outside the mining and agriculture industries. Farm and ranch population dropped 22% between 1960 and 1970.[15]

While ranching continues to be for Montanans a business and cherished way of life, mining continues to be a fluctuating enterprise. A depressed copper industry, in the late 1970s, caused the closing of several Anaconda Copper Company mines and the closing of five parishes in the Helena Diocese. St. Joseph's at Anaconda closed in 1977, and at Butte, Holy Savior, Sacred Heart, St. Helena, and St. Mary's were closed.[16] Between 1960 and 1980, the Catholic population of the Helena Diocese decreased by 19,000 while that of the Great Falls Diocese-Billings decreased by 2,884. (See Appendix 2.) Changes in the mining industry are also responsible for population decreases in the Gallup and Grants areas of New Mexico, evident in a decrease in the Catholic population of the Gallup Diocese between 1960 and 1980. (See Appendix 2.)

These failures in traditional economies of agriculture and mining have forced Montana ranchers to face the current environmental dilemma caused by the energy crisis. In Montana, because the Federal Bureau of Land Management owns the mineral rights beneath much of the state's most valuable privately owned ranch land, the state government has enacted some of the strongest environmental impact and reclamation legislation in the country. Montana's fears are shared by Idaho and Colorado. The former, with only hydroelectric and geothermal possibilities for energy needs, advocates some growth but wants no environmental damage that could threaten its thriving recreation industry.[17] In Denver, where the general population increased by 65% between 1970 and 1978, the question is, "How long will it be before 'progress' creates another Los Angeles, San José, or Newark here?"[18]

But not all the Intermountain states have this attitude. At the present time, it appears that the desire for economic development in Arizona, New Mexico, and Utah has placed growth higher in priority than environmental issues. This contrast seems to be most obvious in Utah where the lunch bucket argument that power plants mean jobs and jobs will keep the children at home is closely allied to the Mormon ideal of a cohesive society; Utah is more favorably inclined to industrialization than any part of the region, except the Denver area, and wants to go further yet.[19]

Nevertheless, all eight states are aware of the reality that energy issues in this region involve three separate sovereignties and a fourth interested party: the federal government, state government, Indian lands, and the "big-money power of the energy companies."[20] The tension created by this power play has united the region in an attempt to direct its own future. These energy producing states are attempting to work together through new political institutions to help meet the nation's energy needs while protecting environmental and other values of the West. Such groups as the Western Governors' Policy Office (WESTPO) and the Federation of Rocky Mountain States witness to a changing relationship with a federal government that in the past has imposed a national perspective on the economy of this region. "If there is one underlying theme of the people of the Rocky Mountain West, it is that those who live and work here are determined to play a strong role in shaping their future."[21]

Such "voluntary regionalism," concerned with economic and cultural progress and quality of life, is bound to affect the quality of Catholic life in the region as well.[22] It seems to have already done so in the Denver area.

The population of southern Boulder County has experienced phenomenal growth in the past two decades, mostly because of the simultaneous increases in the number of high technology firms and in student enrollment at the University of Colorado (located in Boulder). "This process . . . funneled large amounts of new economic activity into the region, and dramatically transformed its previously rural economic base."[23] What this has meant to the Church in that area is that both clerical and lay members of local parishes tend to ignore territorial boundaries in attempting to offer a specialized ministry: only one local parish runs a parochial school, while a second concentrates on university students and faculty, and a third focuses on young adults and their small children.[24] Is such specialization an important trend in rapidly growing urban areas? Does it express both the limitations of traditional parish structures in meeting the needs of parishioners and an impulse toward a sort of voluntary congregationalism?

Newman Centers that have become parishes are also drawing members from students, faculty, and other Catholics who live outside their geographical boundaries. Lively liturgies and comprehensive religious education programs are often the reasons given for the attractiveness of such parishes. But, perhaps, another reason is the need to integrate more approximately one's religious affiliation with the realities of one's daily life.

A second example of the effect of regional economic changes on Catholic life is based on an impending financial crisis in a rural area of Montana. While many communities founded on mining and railroad enterprises have disappeared or are, at least, greatly reduced in size from their peak years, others have remained, and are dependent primarily on the logging industry and ranching. Recently, however, a sawmill owner has decided to leave one of these towns. Unemployment for some 100 to 150 employees and total dependence on the ranching industry will result.[25] What this means to the town's Catholic parish is hard times. Some parishioners "see money as the number one issue affecting the continued survival of the parish."[26] Their concern is based on some old problems as well as new developments. A new church building and rectory constructed in 1957 created a parish debt that had immediate as well as long-term repercussions. "Because the buildings were not designed or insulated for Montana winters, the ongoing cost of heating the buildings has placed a large financial burden on a small parish."[27] These financial problems, combined with a rapid turnover of priests and the absence of a priest for a six-month period, have caused some to ask if they might not be better off without the financial costs of having a priest. The lack of continuity and confusion resulting from the several priests' differing styles in worship and interpretations of Church teachings has not made it easy for a large number of full-time cattle ranchers to enter enthusiastically into parish life. Not only is ranching "a seven-days-a-week job," but it "also requires vast expanses of land. Many parishioners drive 30 to 40 miles to church each week."[28] With the seeming indifference of assigned clergy to the local lifestyle and economic base, it is not surprising that "[t]he Church is a part of their lives but it is really not the center.

... The Church is thus left with a background role, one of value, but not indispensable."[29]

At the same time, the role of pastor at this parish has been one that continues to require a rural missionary spirit. One pastor concluded his 1979 parish profile with the following remarks:

> Yes, this is a one man parish where the priest keeps house, cooks, maintains the office, gathers firewood, mows the lawn, and is the main operational force. The country here is for an outdoor person. I would strongly suggest sending someone here who is very self-sufficient and likes the outdoors. The priest definitely has to make a life for himself, since it can be very lonely.[30]

Recent national concern over the health and stress level of American priests, especially as their numbers decline, may be an indicator of changes that need to be made in parish structure because of geographic and socio-economic conditions.

Is it possible that similar situations threaten the survival of other rural parishes in the region? Are the basic issues of lifestyle and economics so vital to rural Intermountain Catholics that they must question the role and necessity of clerical leadership in striving to shape an authentic and meaningful parish life? With the current national concern over the declining number of priests (perhaps as few as 25,000 by the year 2000), a chronic shortage in this area, and a regional history of large numbers of priestless parishes, this may become a very important question for the entire region.[31]

THE LOCAL CHURCH

In this region, where enlightened citizens struggle to shape their own future and post-Vatican II Catholics seek an authentic relationship between religious affiliation and the realities of daily life, the universal changes initiated by Vatican II have been accepted with varying degrees of success and enthusiasm. The early national euphoria surrounding the election of Pope John XXIII as successor to Pope Pius XII, the election of John F. Kennedy as President of the United States, and the initial proceedings of the council were followed, however, by both vacillation and dissidence in the American Church.[32] The Intermountain Church was not unaffected by those mood swings. A close look at changing parish styles and structures during the past two to three decades in this region reveals some new developments, some unresolved tensions, and an increased voice for the laity in Catholic parish life.

Perhaps the most obvious renewal of all those ushered in by Vatican II was the new liturgy. Changes in the rituals of the Mass and the Sacraments were accompanied by structural changes in church buildings and by social changes in the degree to which lay ministers helped administer the Sacraments. A greater variety in the style of local liturgies began to give individual parishes a greater sense of communal personality and in some instances a greater sense of spiritual unity.

Liturgical teams in many Intermountain parishes consist of Eucharistic ministers, lectors, music ministers, ushers, and altar boys and girls. Holy Family Parish in Pueblo, Colorado, states that its team

> directs their efforts to aid the priest-celebrants in planning and sharing the responsibility of providing the parish with meaningful and effective means to unite our worshiping assembly for real prayer, and provide a personality to our worship, unique to our parish.[33]

While this structural change has extended liturgical leadership in a parish to a wider circle of laypersons, it has not always extended it equally to both sexes. An old patriarchal bias is still evident on the parish level, if one looks to the equal representation of boys and girls as altar servers or of men and women as Eucharistic ministers or lectors. Of fifty parishes responding to a 1982 questionnaire, seven (14%) have no male Eucharistic ministers, while nine (18%) have no female Eucharistic ministers.[34] Unless only religious women are permitted to act as Eucharistic ministers in some parishes, it is hard to see how these figures could represent parishes where women, rather than men, filled that role. Of the same fifty parishes, only one (2%) did not in 1982 have any male lectors, but eight (16%) did not have any female lectors.[35] The implications of this data are not overlooked by a growing number of men and women who are concerned about the status of women in the Church and in society. On a national level, 2,100 priests who are members of Priests for Equality are in the process of preparing a formal statement entitled "Toward a Free and Equal Sharing." In a preliminary draft of that statement they say:

> The question of equality is not a "women's issue." It is a basic question for our total community, both men and women. Indeed, the call to equal sharing, while raised most forcefully by women, is raised with vigor by many men, including bishops and priests.[36]

This hunger for a less hierarchical, more egalitarian Church is not only a practical element in local parish life, but also an international issue, as we shall see later.

Music, with an emphasis on congregational singing, has received a great deal of attention on the part of parish liturgical committees. At some Intermountain parishes, it is considered so important that a full-time organist and liturgist/music director is a paid staff member. Some also have large adult choirs. Others emphasize a youth Mass with volunteer musicians and song leaders. Some of these parishes have become so dependent on youth initiative and commitment that when these students graduate, they are hard pressed to replace them with experienced music ministers.

At St. Charles Borromeo Parish in Hailey, Idaho, it has been noted that "the

Sunday Mass is perhaps the most unifying experience" of the parish, ". . . enhanced by the liturgical planning and participation of the laity."[37] However, such formally organized planning is not that common throughout the region. A 1982 questionnaire revealed that only 64% of those Intermountain parishes responding had organized liturgical planning.[38] If it is true that "[m]any today are disappointed with the superficial adjustments effected so far by the council" and that "many local liturgies continue to be only translations of the Roman liturgy," then perhaps greater involvement in local liturgical planning could create more authentic religious expression for Intermountain Catholics.[39] With the energy and imagination of a dedicated liturgy committee, perhaps such regionally relevant images as water, mountains, frontier life, economic dilemmas, energy resources, and indigenous ethnic groups could enliven parish celebrations and renew a sense of the little tradition in Church life. Ideas for such relevant celebrations can be found in the Church's sacramental system of blessings. An example of a regionally appropriate public blessing took place in Pierce, Idaho, on November 30, 1965. The lumber and logging industry at Pierce had expanded and with it the Catholic population of Our Lady of the Woodland, a mission of St. Catherine's in Kamiah. The invocation at the opening of the new Jaype mill two miles north of Pierce included the following:

> O Almighty Creator, Thou made the trees of the forest in this beautiful woodland region and created men to match these mountains in our loved state. Look with a smiling face on the beginnings of the Jaype mill. . . .
> May the workers appreciate the new job opportunities and see the dignity of their labor in the finished product.
> O Lord, help us to understand from the beginning what this mill means in the support of families, the development of Pierce and neighboring villages, and what the production means for homes and buildings throughout America and the world.[40]

Parish structure in the Intermountain West has changed during the past twenty-five years as staffs are expanded in many instances to include lay or religious members (including permanent deacons) and as parish councils add a new dimension to collegial authority. In many parishes, standing committees answerable to the parish council produce works that preserve parish history, provide important links to the larger community, or provide a sense of direction for the parish as a whole.

In the Intermountain region, 58% of the parishes responding to a questionnaire on parish life stated that their parish staff consisted simply of the pastor (and the pastoral associate).[41] While 34% of the respondents said that they had a "clearly understood team but not formally designated as such," only 12% stated that they had a "formally designated team" that consists "of clergy and laity or religious," with another 4% who stated that they had a "formally designated team of clergy plus other staff."[42] Of the region's eight states, New Mexico indicated the highest percentage (27.3) of parishes whose staffs consisted of clergy and laity or religious.[43] There is no clear data to indicate whether this trend is in any way connected to the Hispanic tradition of lay leadership, to a declining number of priests in the Santa Fe Archdiocese, or to a greater number of religious women included on parish staffs in that state.

While less than half of Intermountain parishes indicate that they have expanded the structure of their staffs, many parishes have added permanent deacons. And the number of permanent deacons in a state seems to correspond to the Catholic population of that state. Arizona, which had the largest Catholic population of all the Intermountain states in 1980, had also the largest number of deacons.[44] In that same year, Colorado ranked second in Catholic population and number of permanent deacons, while New Mexico ranked third in both those areas.[45] These states are also the sixth, eighth, and fifth largest in area in the United States, with long distances between some parishes and their missions or stations. In such settings, the restoration of this ancient order serves the purpose of ministering more often to more parishioners in less time. While some parishes in the region have found that the ministry of a permanent deacon helps to create continuity when clerical turnover is high, or when the parish is without a resident pastor for a number of months, they also realize that strengthening the lay power in a parish (especially if there is a strong parish council as well) can be perceived as a threat by some priests newly assigned to such a parish. On a national level, recent debate over the role of the permanent deacon (one of function or one of witness) seems to indicate that these lay "link[s] in the hierarchical chain" are not yet fully understood.[46]

In the small town of Buckeye, Arizona, two men, one an ordained deacon, the other a candidate in the Phoenix deaconate program, consider the impact of their role on the Church. Both admit that the official status the deaconate bestows opens doors for them, but wonder about the ways in which their work interfaces with that of trained lay ministers. John Bilinski, ordained in December of 1984, is concerned about elitism. " 'I don't want to distance myself from all these people I've known for 15 years.' . . . In Bilinski's view the deacon is saying to the people, 'Hey, I'm one of you . . . but I'm willing to make this commitment to be of service to you.' "[47]

Anthony Scarabino, a deacon candidate who works with primarily Hispanic inmates at a nearby medium-security prison, is also concerned about clerical elitism for deacons. He laments:

> The more education they get, the more they separate the deacon from the people. You learn to talk with better words . . . with more polish, more psychology, and so you're no longer part of the laity, because you don't talk like them and you don't act like them. Once they do that to the deacon, he's more priest than deacon.[48]

Scarabino's interest in the image projected by highly educated deacons to those less sophisticated is an important one in this multi-cultural region and recalls the attitude of an Americanized European clergy at mid-nineteenth century in the Southwest. The restoration of the permanent deaconate in 1968 may have broadened the base of representation on parish staffs and may provide necessary service, but it is still not clear just how this position fits into local parish life.

One of the most dramatic changes in parish structure during the past twenty-five years has been the establishment of parish councils. In the Intermountain West, 78% of the parishes responding to a questionnaire in 1982 indicated that they have a parish council, while another 12% said that they had one in formation; only 10% indicated that they never had or did not, in 1982, have a parish council.[49] In both Montana and New Mexico, 100% of the respondents said that they had a parish council.[50]

Some parish councils in the region not only compose formal statements of purpose with clearly defined functions and methods of election, but also seem to assume a genuine share of the responsibility for administering the parish. This appears to be the case in Our Lady of Guadalupe Parish in Taos, New Mexico, where the parish council "provide[s] a vehicle for encouraging and facilitating constructive discussion of parish policy, programs, and progress among and between laity, religious and clergy."[51] As it sets working priorities and serves as a clearinghouse for parish organizations, this group gives evidence of active involvement at the decision-making level and in keeping open channels of communication.

At Moscow, Idaho, another effective parish council provides unity and vitality for a variety of parish groups. The School Board, the Religious Education Board, the Liturgy Committee, and any ad hoc committees are responsible to an elected council. Evidence of its efforts can be seen in a well-written parish history published in conjunction with the parish centennial celebration and in its open appeal for suggestions in extending parish facilities. In a parish bulletin dated May 20, 1973, the council announced:

> Our parish council has been studying various plans for change and extension of our parish facilities, and they have reached certain conclusions. They want all the parishioners to be in on the decision-making process, and they need your ideas and suggestions and approval soon after, when final plans are determined.[52]

The list of ideas that followed contained rationale for each proposal, projection of costs, and a statement of volunteer needs. The tone of this notice suggests that the council feels responsible for both the decision making and the actual construction work, and that it wants all the parishioners to share in both of these functions.

In larger parishes, such as Most Precious Blood in Denver, more elaborate diagrams of the parish council's structure indicate a sophisticated interaction of standing committees that act as "the coordinating and unifying body" of an impressive array of parish activities.[53] This council also advertises a regular meeting date and states a procedure by which parishioners can bring their ideas to the attention of the parish council.

But parish councils sometimes deal with more than internal affairs. At Santa Cruz de la Cañada in New Mexico, a special committee appointed by the parish council was created to supervise the restoration of a historically and architecturally valuable artifact of the state, their own church. The Restoration Committee first

> researched the history of the church. These historical findings were submitted to the State Cultural Properties Review Committee and resulted in the Santa Cruz Church receiving a State Historical Site rating in December of 1972. Further documentation was then submitted to the Department of the Interior and, in July of 1973, the church was rated a National Historical Site.[54]

Additional phases of the project included hiring an architect and an art conservator and arranging with a museum for the return of a valuable *retablo* to its original location in the church. The entire project resulted in a restoration that has been celebrated in pride by an entire state.

But, all parish councils are not so effective. Either in their composition, their obscure method of selection of members, or their statement of purpose, they seem to operate more as the pastor's helpers than as a representative body for the entire parish. In 1974, one parish council of a national foreign language parish had five members, all men.[55] At another parish in the region, although a parish council exists, "[t]he decision-making processes in the parish are one-dimensional and one-sided. The pastor makes the decisions."[56] Not only does this pastor decide when the parish council should meet, but he also feels free to disregard its suggestions. The council itself seems satisfied with this arrangement; the president of the council "describes the council's purpose as being 'to help Father out.' "[57] Such a mode of operation seems to deny what the formal structure of a parish council suggests—shared decision making. At another parish the pastor admits, "We haven't had much luck with elected parish councils."[58] Closer study reveals that although the pastor is extremely successful in providing economic security for the parish, in effectively computerizing important parish data, and in implementing innovative liturgies, his dictatorial style and dependence on the initiative and creativity of a core group of lay leaders are more confusing than encouraging to a separately organized parish council.[59]

While the largest percentage of Intermountain parishes that have parish councils seem to use popular elections or a combination of election and appointment to select their councils, a significant percentage, responding to a 1982 questionnaire, neglected to specify the basis for election of council members.[60] Such "missing" information suggests, if not deliberate secretiveness about this procedure, at least a careless attitude toward the process by which a potentially vital element of parish structure is formed. Perhaps they do not realize, as other Intermountain parishes do, that a good parish council, like a permanent deacon, can provide essential continuity and leadership when clerical leadership changes or disappears.

A recent custom of some Intermountain parishes, which reflects collegial authority and a communal self-image as the People of God, is the composition of a written proclamation or covenant. At St. Charles Borromeo in Hailey, Idaho, a 1983 parish assembly produced a candid statement of the parish's history, its hopes for the future, and its immediate plans to implement those dreams. The language of this proclamation is both realistic and idealistic, theoretical and practical:

> St. Charles Borromeo Parish has a history which combines success and failure, struggle and achievement, doubt and hope. There have been difficult times when the parish was weak; yet the moments of personal connection have strengthened its members and kept them together. We know that our dreams must be sought after as well as trusted. Therefore, we wish to design plans to help the dreams unfold.[61]

In 1982, St. Michael the Archangel Parish in Denver marked the third anniversary of its parish covenant by renewing that commitment at all Masses on October 2; the covenant, which "identifies the goals and concerns of the entire parish . . . social life, education, services, community and liturgy . . . was ratified by 850 parish families in October of 1980. In 1982, 1,740 families renewed the covenant," and, in 1983, 1,900 families renewed it.[62] Such a custom may be one way in which to integrate the abstract symbols of a communal church and the concrete realities of a particular gathering of unique individuals.

A shift in emphasis during the past twenty-five years from parochial schools to sophisticated religious education programs has been evident in the Intermountain region as well as in the entire American Church. The rationale for such a shift was the rediscovered value of family centered religious education, but a practical basis for the change has been an economic one.

As costs for construction, maintenance, and staffing of parochial schools have increased over the past century, many parishes, after evaluating the total effectiveness of their schools, have had to close them. Others, despite the need to subsidize one-third of the costs coming from tuition with another third from parish support and the final third from individual contributions and fund-raisers, see an economic liability as a "valuable Catholic influence in the parish."[63]

National studies show that as enrollments in parochial schools dropped and the number of religious faculty members decreased during the 1960s, the increased economic burden "was aggravated by a questioning of the value and quality of parochial education, some arguing that the whole system should be phased out."[64] In the Intermountain West, a decrease in the number of parochial schools between 1960 and 1980 may have several other causes as well. In the Helena Diocese, the dramatic drop from twenty-two parochial schools in 1960 to four in 1980 coincides with a decrease of 19,000 in the Catholic population of the diocese and a decrease of three-fourths in the number of religious women.[65] These dramatic statistics can be explained partially by changes in the mining industry, which (as in the early boom and bust days of the region) affected the fortunes of large numbers of Catholics. In Pueblo, Colorado, "[t]he year 1971 found the parochial school system . . . in dire financial stress, forcing the closing of all Catholic schools in the city," but, by 1985, the diocese had seven parochial schools operating.[66] Among those parishes in the region, which, after deliberation, chose to maintain their schools, some decreased the number of grades while others increased the number of fund-raisers necessary to subsidize such a costly commitment.

The only two dioceses in the Intermountain region demonstrating an increase or at least maintenance in the number of parochial schools during the last two decades are those of Reno-Las Vegas and Salt Lake City.[67] In the Salt Lake Diocese, the vulnerable status of Catholics in a predominantly Mormon society necessitates the continued commitment to Catholic education as a balance to Mormon evangelization. Even if it means that parochial schools must be supported by more than one parish and students must travel greater distances to attend them, Utah Catholics are determined to keep them.

While some would explain the decrease in the number of parochial schools elsewhere as a result of similar consolidation of smaller schools, such a theory requires further investigation in this region. Those pursuing the matter might also consider the change in Catholic attitudes toward authority spawned by Vatican II, and how such changes may affect their response to the general mandate requiring all Catholic parents to send their children to Catholic schools unless excused by the bishop. The general mandate from the Third Plenary Council of Baltimore may still be held as an ideal by the institutional Church, but it may not carry much weight with post-Vatican II Catholics for whom "loyalty to organizations in the traditional sense of submission and self-sacrifice is not a priority."[68]

Fortunately, parochial school buildings, whether used for their original purpose or not, have helped accommodate growing numbers of students enrolled in religious education programs. At Holy Family Parish in Pueblo, Colorado, a new parochial school (completed in December of 1963 and closed just eight years later) "provided space for the crowded parish school of religion, conducted for children attending public schools in the area. At that time, 518 students attended the junior and senior high division. . . . More than 900 attended the elementary division."[69] At St. Mary's Parish in Moscow, Idaho, in 1969, "a decision was reached to have only six grades in St. Mary's School. Many Catholic seventh and eighth graders were attending Moscow Junior High School, and the thought was that it was best to concentrate on even better quality in the first six grades."[70]

Consequently, the parish council postponed an old plan to build a new parish hall and rectory in favor of remodeling the two empty classrooms into a multi-purpose room.[71]

A declining parochial school system and an expanding religious education program occurred at the same time that a variety of administrative changes were taking place on the parish level. Official directors of religious education were appointed to work with lay boards responsible to the parish council. In 1972, a Confraternity of Christian Doctrine Coordinator was introduced at St. Mary's in Moscow, Idaho, and, in 1974, a "Religious Education Board was set up to supervise all teachings of religion and [to work] closely with the CCD Coordinator, who is now titled the Religious Education Director."[72] Such administrative changes at the parish level were often accompanied by changes at the diocesan level. Resource centers and directors of regional offices of religious education helped parishes train lay volunteers, suggested updated curricula, and initiated adult education classes as a new element in parish religious education.

An updated comprehensive religious education program on the parish level includes many new elements and emphases, such as adult and pre-school classes and the Catechumenate or Rite of Christian Initiation for Adults. In the large, well-organized parish of Most Precious Blood in Denver, the Education Commission, a standing committee of the parish council, supervises eleven different programs for parishioners of all ages.[73] At St. Charles Borromeo in Hailey, Idaho, as at many other Intermountain parishes, a family based religious education program presents a common topic on several different age levels with follow-up materials to be used by the family at home.[74]

A recent study of parishes in the Intermountain West reveals that 70% of those parishes responding have an adult religious education program, but only 48% have a catechumenate program for adults.[75] It is interesting to note that Colorado had the highest percentage of all states in the region for both programs.[76]

Perhaps the most dramatic change in parish structure and style during the past twenty-five years has been the growth of lay ministry. Encouraged by Vatican II's emphasis on personal responsibility for the quality of one's individual and communal life within the Church, laypersons throughout the world have felt free not only to criticize but to actively build up the local parish. As a response to this movement, many parishes and dioceses have initiated workshops and training programs for specific ministries. In 1984, the National Association for Lay Ministers Conference was attended by 275 people from sixty-three dioceses.[77] In March of 1985, a national institute for pastoral life was initiated in Kansas City, Missouri, where participants will earn a certificate or degree as lay ministers. "That the center will be in a former seminary, . . . which had been closed for lack of vocations, speaks volumes about the personnel resources the U.S. Church now has—and what it needs."[78]

In Intermountain parishes, a growing array of ministries (once officially carried out on a full-time basis by religious women no longer teaching in parochial schools, or by individual parishioners unofficially serving the needs of their neighbors) is now available to laypersons.

> However, the bulk of those active in ministry see themselves as caring for needs within the church or in the world, rather than as carrying out directives from above. . . . This more independent course of action is often made easier and more effective because of support and encouragement from the clergy with whom the laypeople are working.[79]

In the Intermountain West, three of the most highly developed ministries are those to youth, to the sick, and to those who are grieving. According to a 1982 questionnaire, 70% of the Intermountain parishes responding had some form of youth or young adult ministry to which some staff time is devoted.[80] While these parishes may include Newman Centers (whose original purpose, despite growing family membership, is to serve Catholic students at secular universities), they also include traditional parishes, both rural and urban, whose concern is to provide youth an opportunity to grow through spiritual, social, and service-oriented activities. Some of these parishes employ a paid youth minister. At Aquinas Newman Center in Albuquerque, New Mexico, a student night is scheduled once a week, at which a discussion of appropriate Scriptures precedes the celebration of a 9 P.M. Mass, followed by refreshments.[81] In many parishes, these same students are involved as teachers in religious education programs for children on a regular basis, and they provide opportunities periodically for youth-oriented retreats.

According to the same 1982 questionnaire, 56% of the Intermountain parishes responding indicated that they had a formally organized ministry to the sick.[82] In addition to two groups that regularly extend such ministry on behalf of Most Precious Blood in Denver, that parish has organized an Emmaus Grief Ministry. This is "a pastoral care and service team working with those who are experiencing grief . . . due to death, illness, disability, or any of the many other events in our lives which need to be talked about and shared."[83] This team extends spiritual, psychological, and physical help to the grieving and offers workshops several times a year to train parishioners for active service in grief ministry.[84]

Some see the growth of lay ministry as one means of integrating the sacred and the secular, a spiritual life and a socio-political life. But, if this is to bring about "an authentic inner response to present realities," that spirituality will have to be based on more than group liturgies or the recitation of private prayers.[85] There will be a consequent need for contemplative prayer, that silence in which the prophetic call to ministry can be heard.

One architectural feature that symbolizes the expanded program of ministries and activities in many contemporary parishes is the family center or parish center. While these structures are often costly both to build and maintain, there is not the same pride in the structure and its impact on the local environment that characterized so many building projects of earlier decades. Instead, one senses the satisfaction that a local parish has a facility that allows for and encourages a wide variety of parish activities. Often, these centers can be rented by individuals and non-parishioners, a service to the public and a bonus to building and maintenance costs. At Most Precious Blood in Denver, the parish center facility accommodates over twenty parish related organizations on a regular basis.[86] At St. Mary's in Moscow, Idaho, the family center, completed in 1981, was the result of much donated time and work, a unity of spirit that parishioners hope will help make the fruits of their labor a place "to build up the Catholic community."[87]

There is no doubt that the changes of Vatican II have been difficult for some American Catholics. Many still cling to passive roles as obedient followers, more concerned about being saved than building the Kingdom. They "still expect their pastor or the bishop to make all the decisions, to do the organizing and to shoulder the responsibility. . . . They do not wish to be shaken out of their apathy."[88] Others, long active in the Church as "volunteers," simply miss "the old-time religion," the old hymns, the ornate high altars, side altars, the solemnity of organ music, and "the statues representing dear old friends who gladdened [them] in joy and consoled [them] in sorrow."[89] Where is the middle ground to be found between a religion of consolation and one of constant challenge? Perhaps, in looking beyond specific changes in parish structure and style and in recovering the prophetic spirit that inspired them, Intermountain Catholics can (like their Native American brothers and sisters) rediscover something old and, in the light of current circumstances, make it new.

RELIGION AND ETHNICITY

If the post-Vatican II Church, "[w]hile denying its historical roots, . . . is becoming truly a world Church . . . recogniz[ing] its duty to enculturate Christianity into divergent societies," then this region's Native Americans and Hispanics must call for the kind of exploration that will make diversity and pluralism within the Church once again fruitful.[90] To consider the status of Indian mission parishes and schools is only the first step in understanding the history of the Church's attitude toward them, the meaning of the political and economic changes that are revolutionizing their communal lives, and the possibilities for spiritual integration they seek. To consider the current statistics on Spanish-speaking immigrants to this country is only the first step in understanding the history of their invisibility in the American Church, recent attempts on the part of the Church to address their needs, the impact of the Chicano movement on Hispanic Catholic life, the appeal of disaffected Protestant evangelists, and the prophetic voice communicated by three national *Encuentros*.

Throughout the Intermountain West, a good number of Indian missions do not have parish status. Of the nineteen Pueblos existing in New Mexico now, thirteen bear the institutional status of mission, but six have become parishes with multiple missions of their own. San Esteban at Ácoma, San José at Laguna, and San Antonio at Zuñi belong to the Diocese of Gallup; San Augustín at Isleta, San Diego at Jémez, and San Juan De Los Caballeros at San Juan (the oldest of the Franciscan missions) belong to the Archdiocese of Santa Fe. The only Indian mission with parish status in the Helena Diocese is St. Anne's, the Heart Butte Indian Mission on the Blackfoot Reservation established in 1911; however, in the Great Falls-Billings Diocese, there are five Native American parishes today. They serve the Crow, Cheyenne, Gros Ventre, and Assiniboine.

It is difficult to classify Catholic Indian communities as either mission or parish. In a sense, most are both. Father Chuck Cichanowicz, O.F.M., pastor of Christ the King in Shiprock, New Mexico, has recently changed the name of his congregation from mission to church. He reasons that although the congregation is not self-supporting and has no native clergy, its members are a stable community rather than part of an evangelizing effort by Franciscans.[91] On the other hand, the Pastoral Policy at St. Stephen's Indian Mission in Wyoming states, "It is a parish in the full canonical sense of the word. Nevertheless, the Missouri Province of the Society of Jesus recognizes it as a mission, in that it is not locally supported and operated by its own people as a fully operating parish in the diocese."[92]

Determining the status of Catholic Indian schools is equally problematic. The only parochial school that exists today among the Pueblo, Navajo, or Apache in Arizona and New Mexico is at Zuñi in the Gallup Diocese. In addition, a parochial school is conducted at the Papago Indian Mission, San Xavier del Bac, in Tucson, heir of more than a century's Catholic education at that site.[93] In the Northwest, one of Great Falls-Billings' eighteen parochial schools is conducted by St. Paul's Indian Mission for the Gros Ventre and Assiniboine. No parochial schools are conducted for Indians in either the Helena or Boise diocese. St. Stephen's Indian School for the Shoshone and the Arapaho in the Cheyenne Diocese, once considered a parochial school, is now a separate corporation owned and controlled by native people, while St. Michael's School for the Navajo in the Gallup Diocese is considered a private rather than a parochial school, despite the fact that it is attached to a church given parish status.

In some Catholic Indian communities, it is difficult to determine just how many of those who claim to be Catholic are so and by what standard. Father Cichanowicz in Shiprock describes a wide range of Navajo parishioners along the continuum of five distinct acculturation levels and wonders at what point one is more Catholic (Christianized? Americanized?) than another.[94] While it is difficult to estimate what percentage of the Navajo Nation can be considered Catholic, it is estimated that nearly 60% claim membership in the Native American Church.[95]

As the practice of native religious tradition declines among the Navajo, many of that tribe consider the Peyote way their traditional religion; membership in any Christian churches or affiliation with such Pentecostal evangelists as Boots Wagner is considered a rejection of the old way in order to embrace the new.[96]

In the Phoenix Diocese, Father Jim O'Brien, S.J., estimates that 100% of the Yaqui are nominal Catholics, 95% of the Papago, and 25% of the Pima.[97] Only four parishes in the Phoenix Diocese are exclusively Indian, while St. Michael Church at Gila Bend has a mixed congregation of Native Americans, Anglos, and Hispanics.

As we have seen, the early history of these missions was filled with problems of all kinds.

> In the past, religious policy frequently followed secular guidelines. Indians were supposed to adapt themselves to the majority culture, the majority legal system, the majority religion. In this campaign, the missionary was often a willing partner.[98]

Attacks upon the Indian's culture and, thus, his religion "diminished the Indian's inner world at a time when his outer world was disappearing."[99] These problems continued into the 1960s. At Isleta Pueblo, during the controversial pastorate of the German-born Frederick A. Stadtmueller, insistence on Catholicism with no elements of native tradition echoed too clearly those early policies and angered the Isletas.

> They charged him with gross disrespect for "the Indian way of Life." By early 1964, a petition for Stadtmueller's removal was circulating. One visible bone of contention was the 30-foot slab of concrete poured in the church yard during the 1959–1960 renovation and designated by the priest a dance platform. The Isletas, whose ceremonial dances were meant to take place on Mother Earth, refused to use it. Matters had come to such a pass by June of 1965 that the Pueblo's governor, Andy Abeita, threatened to evict Stadtmueller if he did not leave. Stadtmueller did not.[100]

After the pastor's dismissal by the Pueblo governor, Archbishop Peter Davis said a farewell Mass at the church of San Augustín de la Isleta and had the church locked up. It was nine years before Archbishop Robert F. Sanchez re-elevated Isleta to parish status, and a resident priest removed the concrete slab.[101]

Reflecting on this incident nearly twenty years later, a parishioner at San Augustín says that he feels that Father Stadtmueller's challenge to native tradition "by calling it 'pagan' and by saying that there was 'only one God' " revealed his ignorance of Indian religion but, more important, was responsible for splitting the Isleta community into factions.[102]

> Lorenzo recalls how he was instrumental in alerting the Pueblo leaders to this fact and urged them to expel this priest from the village. Lorenzo continued to pursue this problem even after his college graduation. He felt prompted while working in

Washington, D.C., to notify the Apostolic vicar (the Catholic Church's Roman delegate to the United States) of this problem between the Church and his Indian people. Lorenzo became even more exasperated with the Catholic institutional Church when the vicar told him this dispute was a local problem.[103]

Was this rebuff simply a matter of bureaucratic fumbling, or did it express the kind of ignorance that contributes to the ongoing tension between an organizational style and an expressive style, the great tradition and the little tradition in Catholic life?

On the Blackfoot Reservation in Montana, it was noted at the end of the 1960s that despite overwhelming poverty and related social problems, neither Catholic nor Protestant missionaries had "historical traditions which nurtured new movements toward social justice."[104] But, by the mid-1970s, things began to change.

On January 4, 1975, President Ford signed into law the Indian Self-Determination Act—PL 93-638. This act clearly supported and encouraged Indian people to contract with the federal government for the operation and control of their own institutions—especially schools, and to determine their own futures.[105]

At St. Stephen's Indian Mission in Wyoming, in March of 1976, the control and operation of St. Joseph's School was turned over to the Indian people. Fortunately, this occurred at about the same time that the Arapaho and Shoshoni began to receive royalties from land leases for mineral rights.[106] Economic and educational self-determination are becoming a reality on the reservation according to Louis Headley, a thirty-six-year-old Arapaho, who is superintendent of St. Stephen's School. He says of the Indian students:

My aim is to build them up academically, socially, utilizing all the domains: including the affective and the cognitive. You begin building up a child inside, letting him know who he is, showing that he has a faith and pride in himself, in his heritage, in his family, in his culture. . . . We are trying to build a well-rounded student.[107]

The attempt of St. Stephen's all-Indian administration to combine both cognitive and affective modes of behavior is a goal that could enhance Church life as well; it is a style that those in touch with the natural images and resources of their region could easily learn to exercise on the parish level. In the Phoenix Diocese, the Indian Self-Determination Act changed the pastoral approach of those working with Native Americans in that greater emphasis was placed on lay ministry and local decision making.[108]

Today's Indians still struggle. They, too, want quality of life as well as economic security based on energy exploitation (for which they must wrestle with the federal government, state governments, big energy companies, and their own sense of reverence for the land). In response to drastic national cutbacks in tribal-funding, several New Mexico Pueblos have joined in the national rash of Indian bingo operations. At Ácoma Pueblo in the Gallup Diocese, bingo revenues are being earmarked for development projects, which include a sophisticated full-service tourist stop adjacent to the Pueblo on I-40, and a manufacturing plant for solar hot-water tanks.[109] It is hoped that these projects will not only be profitable, but that they will help the longest continually inhabited community in the United States deal with:

> a 66% unemployment rate, a per capita income 60% below the national average, a high school dropout rate of 40%, an average life span 20 years less than the national average, and an infant mortality rate two times higher than the national average.[110]

In the fall of 1985, ten years after the passage of Public Law 93-638, a series of suicides on the Wind River Reservation served as a reminder that the struggle for successful self-determination is not over.

Another federal law that has potential for helping Indians determine their own future and continue traditional reverence for their land is the American Indian Religious Freedom Act (AIRFA), which was signed into law by President Jimmy Carter on August 11, 1978.[111] Thus far, the law has not worked in Native Americans' favor. Richard Hughes, an Albuquerque attorney who represents Indian litigants, says that because "[t]he courts have not accepted the relationship of religion to land," most attempts on the part of Indian claimants to protect and preserve tribal land in the past several years have failed.[112] A new plan to invigorate the AIRFA would create a Religious Quality Council made up of federal land managers, Indian leaders, and theologians as advisors who could set guidelines for federal district courts acting on Indian religion cases. Catholic Indian missions that have kept track of their interactions (positive or negative) with native traditions, and that are aware of the strongly integral nature of tribal life, are in an excellent position to share special insights into "the inextricable linkages in preliterate cultures between religion and culture and between religion and land."[113]

It has been suggested that for some Native Americans, Catholicism is the bridge or buffer between two different cultures, tribal life and American society.[114] At Isleta Pueblo in the Santa Fe Archdiocese, a twenty-five-year-old social worker whose mother is Isleta Catholic and whose father is a Laguna Pueblo still active in the Kachina tradition gives herself to both forms of religion. "Each religion is relegated in a comparmentalized manner to its own distinct times, places, and ceremonies. There is little attempt to reconcile Christian monotheistic belief with Pueblo pantheistic and polytheistic belief."[115] She simply says, "I've never been bothered by two religions. I need both. . . . For me to be comfortable with myself, I need to go to church and also to participate in my Indian way."[116] For this Native American Catholic, living in the pueblo and working in the nearby city of Albuquerque, Catholicism is the meaningful system that eases the transition from one culture to the other.

In the last decade, mission policy on native culture and religion at places like St. Stephen's has stated that it

> respects the culture, language, and native religious customs of the Native American people. It honors the rights of . . . [its] people . . . to be both Roman Catholics in good standing and to practice the authentic elements of tribal religion.[117]

One Church program helping on a national level in the advancement of Indian Catholic life is the Tekakwitha Conference begun in 1939. Originally assembled to provide advice and support for ecclesiastical leaders, it remained for forty years primarily a gathering of missionary priests from the northern plains states.[118] But, by the mid-1970s, when so many other significant developments began for Native Americans, the conference members "became dissatisfied with the role of their meeting in the growing crisis of native Church affairs, and they decided either to develop or disband."[119] When Native American members were invited in 1976, the focus of the conference shifted to the relationship between native religious life and Christianity. It is this aspect of the conference that has had an enormous influence on Native American members' identity as Catholic Indians. And, perhaps, it is this aspect of the conference that can have some influence on future implementation of the AIRFA.

Native American participation in the Tekakwitha Conference has grown during the 1980s. The 1980 Denver conference drew 600 participants, half of whom were Indian; the 1981 Albuquerque conference drew over a thousand participants, two-thirds of which were Indians from the United States and Canada.[120] In 1985, the conference gathered east of the Mississippi River for the first time, at Syracuse, New York. Father Diego Mazon, a Franciscan of Peña Blanca, New Mexico, and a Zuñi Apache Mexican Indian, spoke of the conference in general and of the reasons for choosing the Syracuse site in 1985:

> There is the Catholic way and there is the Indian way and this is an attempt to work to bring the two together. . . . [It] is a chance to get together as Indian people to share things going on with the Church, and also to address continuous problems on reservations, specifically drug and alcohol dependency. . . . In the past, there have been many workshops, but this year is mostly a spiritual journey in Mohawk country, to be in Blessed Kateri Tekakwitha's land and be with her people.[121]

The current need for more local Tekakwitha meetings to address regional issues suggests the growth of faith in the conference as a positive force and the growing self-confidence of its members.

Despite the existence of federal regulations, national ecclesiastical support (the American Board of Catholic Missions, and the 1977 Statement of U.S. Catholic Bishops on American Indians), and a national conference of Catholic Indians (the

The Post-Vatican Period

Tekakwitha Conference), most efforts to incorporate Indian traditions regarding the earth and nature into Catholic liturgies for Indians have been those of imaginative, sensitive, knowledgeable individuals. The Pastoral Policy Statement of St. Stephen's Mission in Wyoming includes the following pledge:

> The mission welcomes and seeks advice as to the authentic "inculturation" of its worship and catechesis: that is in the grounding of worship and religious instruction in the culture of the native people. To this end, all available means should be employed to prepare mission personnel, both before coming to the mission and through on-site training, to understand native life and culture.[122]

While not all Native American missions or parishes demonstrate the willingness to go to these lengths in accommodating Catholicism to Indian ways, there is enough evidence of the Catholic use of Indian art, language, and natural symbols in liturgical life to indicate a trend in that direction. In New Mexico and Arizona, individual priests and religious do what time and circumstance allow to make worship meaningful. Examples of such inculturation are the increased use of water and chants in Navajo funerals at Christ the King, Shiprock, New Mexico; a reading from the history of the Papago Indians at the funeral of a Papago man educated by the Sisters of St. Joseph of Carondelet at San Xavier del Bac, and later employed by them; use of the Keres language in hymns sung at Laguna Pueblo's annual Feast Day Mass for San José. These and many other attempts to create meaningful Catholic liturgies for Native Americans take not an organizational approach, but one of a shared need to acknowledge and express the presence of God among us. As one missionary sister remarked, "Instead of saying to the Indian, 'Here is Jesus,' . . . we should be saying, 'Jesus is here. Let's find him together.' "[123] The Native American sense of the interrelationship of all things and the abiding presence of the Sacred at the center of all is a gift that can enrich the entire American Church. More concretely, the Native American reverence for the earth and for particular pieces of land in the Rocky Mountain West is a heritage that can enliven both the worship and the social justice concerns of all Catholics in this region.

While Hispanic Catholicism has been an important element in the multi-cultural history of the Southwest for 300 years, and in certain urban centers of the Intermountain West for the past eighty-five years, it is only within the past twenty-five years that an unprecedented infiltration of Spanish-speaking people and the impetus of the Chicano movement have made the Hispanic community of greater concern to the entire American Church. On national, diocesan, and parish levels, official organization of ministries and extended social services are attempting to reach the most rapidly growing group of Catholics in the United States. But other forces are at work as well. Militant Protestant evangelists and a growing number of disaffected Christians are appealing to these nominal Catholics and succeeding. Meanwhile, national gatherings of Hispanic Catholics are struggling to experience ownership of their Church.

Between 1961 and 1970, the number of Latin American immigrants entering the United States surpassed that of any other ethnic group, and between 1970 and 1980, the Hispanic population of the United States grew from nine million to 14.6 million; today, it is estimated to be twenty million.[124] Puerto Ricans, Cubans, Mexicans, and South Americans can be found throughout the country, but most settle in the Southwest. Here, they mix not only with other newcomers but also with descendants of sixteenth-century Hispanic colonists still struggling to preserve their culture in a modernized, Americanized society.

The influx of Hispanics, traditionally Catholic, has spurred the American Church into action. In an attempt to provide a broader ministry to these people, national, diocesan, and parish programs have multiplied. There are now on the national level a Secretariat for Hispanic Affairs with eight regional offices and four pastoral institutes; the oldest and most prestigious of the latter is the Mexican American Cultural Center in San Antonio, Texas. On the diocesan level, special offices for Hispanic affairs are the rule. In the Intermountain West, only three out of fourteen dioceses have not officially named offices, commissions, councils, or vicars for the *Cursillo* Movement, Spanish-speaking people, or the Chicano. The Archdiocese of Denver also specifies a director of Migrant Ministry, while New Mexico lists a formal organization of Hispanic clergymen, PADRES. Also on the diocesan level, there is an effort at St. Thomas Seminary in Denver to prepare priests for this special ministry. Father John Castro, new dean for the Hispanic Intercultural Program says that his

> main concern is that those studying for the priesthood be prepared to minister to the Hispanic population. . . . There will continue to be Hispanics who only speak Spanish and those who do not speak English well . . . we want to prepare men to become well versed in Spanish and have an awareness and appreciation of Hispanic culture.[125]

In addition to diocesan commitments, efforts at the parish level in extending social as well as religious services to Hispanics are evident in this region. The early history of Our Lady of Guadalupe Parish and Mission in Salt Lake City, presented elsewhere in this volume, indicates how successful its more traditional Catholic activities were in meeting the needs of Hispanic immigrants during the first half of the twentieth century. Its post-Vatican II history includes the creation of (1) education programs (an Early Learning Center and an adult education program, partially funded by federal and national grants); (2) economic programs (a storefront food co-op "supported by twenty-five Catholic and Protestant parishes and several private agencies in Salt Lake Valley," and the Utah Nonprofit Housing Corporation "formed by a group representing churches and cooperative associations"); and (3) social programs (particularly Guadalupe Center, "a gathering place for families, teenagers, and adults," of the parish as well "as a meeting place for Mexican Americans and people from the larger community to plan projects and organizations answering the needs of local Mexican Americans," and La Morena Cafe, "the principal source of revenue for the center and its projects."[126] While such a sophisticated and specialized extension of parish life is rare, it reflects the old Hispanic tradition of unifying one's sense of church with one's sense of *communidad* and may well serve as a model for additional parish outreach programs in other urban areas of the region.

In the Northwest, St. Nicholas Parish in Rupert, Idaho, has an extensive Mexican-American ministry. The parish "serves an irrigated farming district which also includes food processing plants; the Mexican-American parishioners who are permanent are mainly employed by these plants. They originally came as migrant workers, but soon became residents of the area."[127]

In the Southwest, parishes that have maintained the little tradition continue to reconstruct village history, revive ancient folk customs, restore old folk art objects and church buildings, and express their faith through celebration. In New Mexico, there is a growing concern for saving neighborhoods rich in ethnic and religious history. Los Griegos community, one of the oldest in the Albuquerque area, was once a separate village. Absorbed now by the city, it seeks to rediscover and maintain its special identity. Today

> [t]he Historic Landmarks Survey of Albuquerque is nominating part of Los Griegos [including the old chapel] to the State Register of Cultural Properties and the National Register of Historic Places as the only Spanish settlement in Albuquerque's North Valley which has kept its physical identity and cultural traditions.[128]

Parishioners at Our Lady of Guadalupe are energetically working as part of the Los Griegos history project to bring this about.

Throughout the Hispanic Southwest, restored folk customs include dramatizing *Los Pastores* and *Las Posadas* and dancing *Las Matachines*. At Christmastime, many churches and homes light *luminarias* or *farolitos* to commemorate "the shepherd campfires long ago outside the town of Bethlehem."[129] In some old Hispanic parishes, adaptation and renewal of the liturgy also have meant restoring old religious artifacts. Tradition-oriented parishioners at San José Parish in Los Ojos were delighted when the need to adapt an old altar to the new liturgy inspired its restoration, "retaining that which has been cherished and is familiar to our people."[130] Hispanic communal custom also includes an oral tradition of *cuentos* and *dichos,* which transmit Catholic values in folk religious form to the next generation.

In New Mexico, both Pueblo and Hispanic churches contain precious murals, altar screens, *santos, retablos,* and basic architectural features, all conceived and executed to enhance worship. The parish at Santa Cruz de la Cañada has recently completed a restoration of its artistically valuable altar screen and of its entire church. Parishioners take pride in the results of the project as they do in the historical fact that "a number of *santeros* [santo makers] have been associated with the Santa Cruz church" for the past hundred years.[131]

Some of the difficulties involved in preserving these ethnic art treasures include the dilemma of how to obtain funding and expertise for effective restoration. If federal funding is sought to employ professional art conservators, then the requirements for public access to the buildings must be met. Another problem is the conflict between museums

> concerned about the lack of security provided for irreplaceable religious images . . . and the local parishes' sensitivity to intrusions from the outside in the management of their churches. Parishioners venerate their churches, and this fervor extends to the art that is in them. After all, it is the parishioners who have done most of the work of maintaining those churches, and they have done an exemplary job.[132]

In 1983, the Rosario Chapel of La Conquistadora in Santa Fe was restored and redecorated for the September 9th De Vargas Fiesta Mass.[133] And, in 1984, Los Duranes Chapel's restoration was completed. After two and a half years and the donated funds and labor of 300 families, the one-hundred-year-old neighborhood structure is ready once again for the communal celebration of weddings, baptisms, and First Communions.[134]

At the Regional Encuento held in Salt Lake City during May of 1985, Bishop William K. Weigand praised such ongoing efforts to keep alive that expressive style of Hispanic Catholicism:

> The Hispanics of the Intermountain region are a most valuable element in the Church. You were the first to bring the faith to these mountains and you continue to be an example of faith.[135]

But as Bishop Ricardo Ramirez, ordinary of the newly formed Las Cruces Diocese, and Berna Facio, Director of the Office of Hispanic Affairs for the Santa Fe Archdiocese, suggest, there is still much work to be done. Many Southwestern Hispanics have become comfortable with their middle-class status and are not as aware of the needs of their own people as they might be. It is a long, slow process to establish *communidades de base* (basic Christian communities), to initiate religious instruction in Spanish (and from a Hispanic perspective), to address the economic needs of Spanish-speaking immigrants, and to welcome them warmly into parish life, even in this area of the country. Why so?

Some claim a history of Hispanic invisibility in the American Church has been the rule. Sabine R. Ulibarri, professor of modern languages at the University of New Mexico, says:

> A dynamic and aggressive Anglo culture has come between us (the Hispano) and his past and is uprooting him from the soil, cutting him off from his ancestors, separating him from his culture. Very little is being done to facilitate his transition from

the culture of his ancestors, whose voice is silent, to the culture of the majority, whose voice makes his laws and determines his destiny.[136]

What has been preserved of Hispanic Catholic culture has been due more to the resistance and persistence of an isolated people true to their little tradition than to any leadership on the part of the great tradition. Hispanic Catholic observers see this invisibility in three areas: in ecclesiastical leadership, in parish leadership, and in church attendance.

Until 1970, when Patricio Florez was consecrated Bishop of San Antonio, Hispanics were absent from the episcopacy of the American Church. And not until 1985 did the U.S. Church get its first Puerto Rican bishop, Jesuit Father Alvaro Corrada del Rio. Although the Intermountain West can now claim four of the nation's nine Hispanic ordinaries, Spanish-speaking people, who now make up one-third of the American Catholic population, complain that while Irish make up only 17% of the American Catholic population, they hold 56% of the episcopal posts.[137]

In addition to positions of national and diocesan leadership, Hispanics have also been invisible in positions of local church leadership. While parish councils in Southwestern areas may list several Hispanic surnames, many of them old, established families, nationally this is not the rule. Hispanics make up less than 3% of the nation's priests, sisters, and brothers; only among permanent deacons are Hispanics represented in nearly approximate proportions (20%).[138] Some credit the *Cursillo* Movement and Marriage Encounter (both imports from Spain) with the kind of leadership training needed to prepare mature Hispanics for this ministry.

Of greater concern than Hispanic invisibility in leadership positions is the lack of participation in religious services. National estimates indicate that as many as 30% to 40% of Catholic Hispanics are not involved in parish life.[139] Other studies find that religion seems to be important primarily to women, older Hispanics, and those of low socio-economic status.[140]

At St. Charles Borromeo Parish in Hailey, Idaho, while the Basques have for some time had high visibility in the community, a growing Mexican population keeps a low profile, as many of them do not have citizenship. "They have their children baptized, in private, at St. Charles, but they do not participate in parish activities nor do they attend Mass."[141] Clearly, this parish is called to offer a special program of ministry for this ethnic group. But, to do so requires meeting many challenges as well as facing the sanctuary issue.

While the Catholic Church struggles to face and to deal with these challenges, evangelists of other faiths are working hard to win Hispanic souls. Early Protestant evangelizing efforts in the Southwest by Presbyterians, Methodists, and Baptists succeeded in creating an indigenous leadership among Hispanic converts. Although still subordinate to Anglo leadership in most large Protestant denominations in this country, many educated Hispanics cling to these American mainstream churches, aware that these were the agents of their education and consequent higher status. Others are influenced by the new wave of conservatism in American religious life and find themselves attracted to fundamentalist, Pentecostal, millennialist, and other disaffected Protestant sects. By 1960, the number of disaffected Protestants (including fundamentalists) in the United States was estimated at 8,500,000, ranking this group third in the country (after Baptists and Methodists) in numerical strength.[142] Appealing generally to the socially disinherited, these sects frequently offer a religious affiliation that is simple, direct, personal, and emotional. Often independent neighborhood churches, they have no elaborate ecclesiastical structure or even a national organization to impose customs from the dominant culture. They are not representatives of the great tradition. Rev. Avery Dulles, professor of theology at Catholic University of America in Washington, D.C., says that

> for years Hispanics have been nominally Catholic. We have taken them for granted as always being good Catholics.
> Their first contact with a vibrant, emotional Pentecostal ministry, and they are convinced this is the way for them.[143]

In the largely Hispanic section of south Phoenix, many small independent churches are drawing new members from the Catholic parishes in the area. Rev. Antonio Sotelo, vicar of the Spanish Speaking Council for the Phoenix Diocese and assistant at St. Catherine of Sienna Catholic Church, says:

> There is a lot of defection from the church locally. . . . For many Hispanics, leaving the church is a defection from society and culture. . . . We have not taken Hispanic culture seriously in the church. We have often Americanized them . . . not given them the freedom to be Hispanic. This . . . is more of a cultural problem than simply a religious problem.[144]

Bill Hennaan, an elder with the Valley Jehovah's Witnesses in Phoenix, points to the disillusionment of Hispanics with Catholicism as one motive for their conversion to that sect:

> I think their main frustration comes from being told that the priest has all the answers and they do not need to know themselves. . . . When they start asking questions in the church, they find they can't get them. When they find out that the Bible has all the answers, they like it.[145]

Whether the attraction is being able to look for answers oneself or being given all the answers according to Witness interpretation, the old Protestant appeal of the Bible and the personal touch is here made new. Archbishop Robert Sanchez of Santa Fe, New Mexico, adds, "They're out there ringing doorbells and going into people's homes. That's hard to beat."[146]

While the flow of Hispanic immigrants continues, and the churches attempt to respond in their own ways, a third force (perhaps the most powerful of all) is consistently at work: *El Movimiento.* The Chicano Movement of the 1960s was actually a new name for an old struggle, one ongoing since 1836 in Texas, and since 1846 in the rest of the Southwest; but its most measurable successes can be attributed to the past twenty-five years. Although its leadership has often been inspired by religious roots, and aided by religious persons, its key organizers (unlike the black movement) have been laypersons. In the 1960s, these leaders succeeded gradually in getting the churches to support their economic struggles. In the 1970s and the 1980s, they have attempted to confront the churches as oppressive institutions. Some of them like Alberto Alurista, Dolores del Grito, and Armando Rendón have attacked the Church out of anger. Rendón counseled:

> When Chicanos deliberate about taking over institutions, they should not forget the churches. The churches belong to us, the people; so do the school buildings and the diocesan newspaper. The church bureaucrats can no longer operate their fiefs without regard for the needs of the poor.[147]

Others have left the Church and encouraged all Hispanics to do so, charging that the passivity it preaches buttresses the miserable condition in which Spanish-speaking people already find themselves. But a third branch of *El Movimiento* has also been active. A group of lay leaders formed by the experience of *Cursillos,* a group of priests called PADRES, and a group of religious and lay women known as *Las Hermanas* have formed national organizations that work through individuals at the local level as well. These Catholic Hispanics and others like them have confronted the Church, filled with hope that their efforts may succeed in making them "agents, missionaries, and constructors of the Church."[148]

This "ownership of the church" was a pervading theme in the Third National Hispanic Pastoral Encuentro held in Washington, D.C., August 15–19, 1985.[149] This Encuentro, convoked by the U.S. bishops with their 1983 Pastoral Letter on Hispanic Ministry ("The Hispanic Presence: Challenge and Commitment"), follows on the heels of two others.

The First National Encuentro, held in 1972, gathered 250 participants, who, as they began to draw a pastoral plan for Spanish-speaking people of the United States, acknowledged failure on the part of the Church.

> Generally Spanish-speaking Catholics in the United States feel isolated from the official structures and institutions of the Church and recognize a long history of lack of knowledge about and sensitivity toward Spanish-speaking traditions on the part of the American Church.[150]

The Second National Encuentro, convoked in 1977, drew 1,200 participants who produced a thoughtful set of recommendations as well as denunciations and affirmations. The concept of integration rather than assimilation prompted the sophisticated two-year effort "to find out what Hispanics think about their faith," which resulted in the Third National Encuentro.[151] How all of this will be implemented on the diocesan and parish level remains to be seen. Some plans include the institution of *communidades de base* within large parishes, revitalization of the role of the mayordomo, updating and expanding the techniques of *Cursillo,* and education with the materials produced by the Encuentros and the bishops' pastoral.

The national pastoral plan for Hispanics produced by these three Encuentros will not bind any bishops, but should give direction and encouragement to Church leadership. More important, the Encuentros illustrate the development of Hispanic leadership within the American Church. The emphasis has shifted from critique and request to responsibility and commitment. Delegates to the Third National Encuentro and the more than 600,000 Hispanic voices they represent have prepared a series of nine "prophetic pastoral thrusts" and an extensive list of "commitments" touching individual, national, and parish levels. Like Native American Catholics, self-determination is their goal. Will the institutional Church's support come too late?

CONTEMPORARY RELIGIOUS ISSUES

During the past twenty-five years, Intermountain Native Americans and Hispanic Catholics have reached beyond parish life to find a sense of identity and self-determination in national movements. Intermountain Anglos, too, have identified themselves with issues that go beyond parish concerns. Many find their commitment to world peace, the sanctuary movement, Central American crises, ecumenism, the Charismatic Movement, or the status of women in the Church more compelling than "internal" parish matters. This does not mean that these Catholics no longer find the parish a liturgical and social community or that parishes cannot address these issues. It does mean that some deeply held religious values motivate them to participate in a less parochial and more global Church.

The documents of Vatican II have called all Catholics

> "to seek the kingdom of God by engaging in temporal affairs and by ordering them according to the plan of God." . . . Following Vatican II, many papal encyclicals and bishops' pastoral letters have analyzed current world and national conditions and have interpreted ways that Christians can be of service to humankind.[152]

But current studies show that "parishes provide a limited range of opportunities for social welfare/social action; only 52% of American parishes have social service programs that serve needy individuals, and only 20% have social action programs."[153]

In the Intermountain West, involvement in world peace efforts has been intensified by the regional reality of nuclear weapons' labs in New Mexico and sanctuary trials in Arizona. Sandia Labs at Kirtland Air Force Base in Albuquerque, Trinity Site at White Sands (where the first atom bomb was tested), and Los Alamos National Laboratory (where that bomb was designed) are sites that frequently draw Catholic parishioners as well as people of all faiths to demonstrate and to pray for peace. Whether coordinated by local chapters of Pax Christi International, diocesan peace and justice commissions, or inter-faith groups, some attempt is made to work through and with local parishes. In September of 1985, Albuquerque Pax Christi members even sponsored a workshop entitled "Building Community in the Parish."[154]

In the Phoenix Diocese, Bishop Thomas O'Brien has found himself in the midst of a controversy over the plight of Central American refugees and the application of the Refugee Act of 1980 by the U.S. Immigration and Naturalization Service. Acknowledging sanctuary as "an important practical issue" in his diocese, he sees it as one of the many current concerns that can "put new questions to Christian tradition and stimulate a rethinking of that tradition."[155] The arraignment of four Phoenix women indicted with twelve others in January of 1985 inspired a prayer service at St. Mary's Church and a supportive march of 800 people through downtown Phoenix. One of the indicted women, Sister Darlene Nicgorski, said, "If I am guilty of anything, I am guilty of the Gospel."[156] Her witness and that of the other sanctuary workers have awakened many in this politically conservative area. Arizona is the only one of six Intermountain states to officially list Catholic communities as sanctuaries.[157] Those three listed in the Tucson Diocese are either monasteries or offices. All Saints Newman Center is affiliated with Arizona State University and is not officially listed as a parish in the Phoenix Diocese. Thus, the sanctuary movement in this region seems to be an extra-parochial activity.

A series of Central American crises has also called Intermountain Catholics to social action. In the fall of 1985, Aquinas Newman Center in Albuquerque sponsored an eight-week study series entitled "Central America: A Challenge to U.S. Christians." The Central American Awareness Festival held in conjunction with the study included a Mass, as well as a free evening of fun, food, live music, arts and crafts, exhibits, audiovisuals, raffles, and special guests, drawing a crowd that included many from outside the parish. Mary Helen Carroll, member of the Newman Committee on Central America, says:

> A world vision compels us as Catholics and Americans to do something about the plight of a people fighting for a minimal quality of life. The lessons taught us by the Central American people united in *communidades de base* inspire us to action, making the internal workings of U.S. parish life pale in contrast.[158]

Although there is some evidence of episcopal leadership in each of these issues, for the most part they are lay movements within, but far beyond, the vision of the official Church. In 1978, the Gallup Organization in its report on the Unchurched American concluded:

> Perhaps the most telling of all is the finding that 86% of the unchurched—and 76% of the churched—agree that "an individual should arrive at his or her own religious beliefs independent of any church or synagogue."[159]

In the Intermountain region, this confidence that the prophetic principle as well as the institutional Church can lead one to deeply held religious values is evident in interfaith encounters that may or may not be formally labeled ecumenical.

Both the documents of Vatican II and Pope John XXIII's early example of inviting non-Catholic observers to attend Vatican Council II have encouraged Catholics to learn about and interact with a variety of non-Catholic churches and sects. The early struggles between these competing groups in the Intermountain West (all attempting to save the frontier from "barbarism") have given way in the past twenty-five years to noticeable cooperation, with one exception, the Mormons. Official ecumenical efforts on a diocesan or parish level are only part of the story. Less formal interfaith encounters are frequent and may, in many cases, be more authentic and meaningful, both personally and communally, than those sponsored in the name of a particular church. A shared sense of fundamental human problems experienced in a particular geographic and economic setting is often the basis for this unity. Good examples of the mix of formal and informal ecumenism can be seen in some rural Montana and Colorado parishes.

Both the Helena and the Great Falls-Billings dioceses, in addition to having their own Ecumenical Commissions, belong also to the Montana Association of Churches, and the Helena Diocese belongs to the Anglican-Roman Catholic Dialogues in Montana. Although ten of fifty-seven of the state's counties in 1980 had Catholics making up more than 50% of reported church membership, and another twenty-nine counties had Catholics making up 25% to 49% of reported church membership, two counties had Lutherans making up more than 50% of reported church membership and another twelve counties had Lutherans making up 25% to 49% of reported church membership.[160] It is among this last group that White Sulphur Springs, a rural ranching town, serves as the political, educational, and religious hub of Meagher County.

> Although White Sulphur Springs has a population of only 1,200, it is the home of at least eight religions: Catholic, Assembly of God, Christian Missionary Alliance, American Lutheran, Presbyterian, Episcopalian, Lutheran Church Missouri Synod, and the Latter Day Saints. . . . The salaried clergy of the community—Catholic, Assembly of God, Christian Missionary Alliance, and Presbyterian-American Lutheran—meet for an "ecumenical dinner" once a month. The activities planned among the churches include a joint worship service on Thanksgiving Eve, a summer Bible school for children, and youth activities sponsored by one church, but open to all churches.[161]

Of the eight churches in White Sulphur Springs, the Catholic Church and the Christian Missionary Alliance were reported in 1983 as being the largest.[162] Either this means that most of the Lutherans are found in other parts of the county or that the Christian Missionary Alliance has dramatically increased in membership in the three years between 1980 and 1983. Reports of low morale among Catholics, juxtaposed with reports of Christian Missionary Alliance programs in the same town, suggest a relatively high number of Catholic parishioners involved in denominational cross-over.[163] What this says about ecumenism on a formal, diocesan level may not be significant; what it says about a basis for the spirit of rural, regional, or Christian unity in some locales may be.

In Colorado, Catholics made up more than 50% of reported church membership in thirteen out of sixty-two counties in 1980 and 25% to 49% in twenty-five counties; nevertheless, in twelve counties no church had 25% of the reported church membership, and Methodists, Lutherans, or Baptists made up the majority in twelve other counties.[164] While the Catholics of Sacred Heart in rural Peetz, Colorado, deal most directly with a town that is half Methodist, they are in a county that was in 1980 25% to 49% Catholic.[165]

At Peetz, the population of approximately 200 belongs primarily to two large families (one Methodist and one Catholic) who are friendly with each other. Two voluntary associations in the community (the Lions Club and the Fire Department—each with auxiliary clubs for women) seem to provide integration for the Peetz citizens who are not members of these two extended families, and seem to replace the Knights of Columbus and Holy Name Society for many Catholics. "Today, ecumenical youth groups and Bible study groups are organized by the people without any ministerial guidance."[166] But, the clergy are not uninvolved. "There are ecumenical services on Thanksgiving, ecumenical choir meetings on an irregular basis, and, whenever possible, the pastor of the Methodist church and the Catholic priest plan their liturgies together. Occasionally, the Methodist pastor brings his entire congregation to Mass on a Sunday. The present minister accepts many recent Catholic actions, especially the bishops' letter concerning nuclear arms control."[167]

In northern Arizona, eastern Nevada, southern Idaho, and throughout Utah, Catholics and Mormons continue to compete rather than cooperate. Jan Schuetz, daughter of an Idaho potato farmer, recalls that whatever German/Irish conflicts occurred in Holy Rosary Parish at Idaho Falls during her childhood were minimal compared to the constant tension of being Catholic in a Mormon community.[168] The same spirit continues today.

In Hailey, Idaho, during the 1980s

> ecumenical activity . . . is led by the laity of the churches and not by the paid clergy. . . . For instance, the Lutheran minister and the Catholic priest were uncertain whether a joint Advent Choir was a good idea, but the lay members were certain and would not be convinced otherwise.[169]

While many ecumenical efforts of a social or liturgical nature in this region are the result of diocesan direction or pastoral leadership, in some small agricultural towns it is the laypeople who extend a tradition of neighborly cooperation to an ecumenical level. Perhaps, the bond between people in this region on the basis of self-determination in economics and the quality of life is as influential in creating Christian unity as diocesan direction or the initiative of pastoral leadership.

In addition to social action and ecumenical interests that draw Catholics beyond the limitations of parish life, while simultaneously trying to work through parish structures, are spiritual movements that have national and international networks. Charismatic Renewal is one of these movements, primarily lay inspired, often ecumenical in nature, and usually operating beyond parochial boundaries.

The Charismatic Renewal formally began in this region shortly after its national beginnings at Duquesne University in 1967, and in a similar manner among small groups of students and faculty at Catholic colleges. As it spread, some groups affiliated themselves with a parish, but others met independently in homes. A recent study indicates that in this region only 38% of the parishes responding named Charismatic Renewal as "a formally organized program to which some staff is devoted," while 56% named prayer/reflection small groups in that category.[170]

By the 1970s, some renewal centers had been established in urban areas, but in many parts of the region a diocesan liaison became the coordinator for widely dispersed groups. Most groups in the region have between ten and twenty-five members, but one urban parish in Albuquerque has between 400 and 500 regular members who are subdivided into groups for youth and women, as well as mixed groups.[171] Most groups are characterized by lay membership. Some even lament that the clergy and religious have been so busy administering programs for the institutional needs of the Church that they have often not broadened their spiritual lives sufficiently to lead small prayer groups.[172] While national interest in the movement may be declining, in the Southwestern section of the country enthusiasm continues to be high, especially among Hispanics. Some reports of charismatic groups among Native Americans indicate that they are more divisive than supportive to parish life since native religious traditions seem not to be consistent with the Catholic Charismatic Movement.[173] In the Southwest, the renewal has engendered fears on the part of some clergymen that the movement is a substitute for Church membership, and, indeed, in some parishes, charismatics have broken away to form their own sect. Father Tom Zotter warns:

> In all things, we have to realize that the Charismatic Renewal is not the Church. It can never be an end in itself, nor a substitute for the Church. The Church, not the Charismatic Renewal, is the source of the full sacramental life, the full and authentic teachings of Christ; the renewal cannot have an existence separate from that of the Church.

> The long-term goal is not that all Catholics attend charismatic prayer meetings, but that the movement phase itself out in the sense that there be a complete renewal of Christian life in the power of the spirit.[174]

These fears are well-founded as American religious history points to the failure of the Holiness revival to reform the Methodist Church during the latter half of the nineteenth century, resulting in disaffection, the formation of numerous independent Holiness groups, and, ultimately, in the establishment of such sects as the Church of God, the Christian Missionary Alliance, and the Church of the Nazarene. Nevertheless, such movements give prophetic voice to the truth that not all the spiritual and social needs of Catholics are met by existing parish structures.

As a rule, however, Catholic members of charismatic groups tend to take an active part in parish life as liturgical ministers, religious education instructors, and even as fund-raisers or participants in social action ministries. In some parishes where the renewal program has been adopted, charismatics have been sought out as leaders for certain phases of the renewal process.[175]

Another issue that concerns Intermountain Catholics is the status of women in the Church. Not limited to matters of equal rights in the public institutional structures of the Church, this movement also includes an emphasis on spirituality. Although never as involved in formal Church leadership as Protestant women in nineteenth-century America, Catholic women were informally influential and visibly active in organizing the first Catholic congregations on the Intermountain frontier, in petitioning for formal clerical leadership, and in sustaining priests and parish plants through fund-raisers, particularly during times of economic crisis. In twentieth-century America, an increased consciousness of the effects of sexism in the churches as well as in society has moved some hierarchical leaders to reconsider past customs and to act.

Concerned with this issue, as with the issue of ethnic minorities in the Church, Bishop Charles A. Buswell of the Pueblo Diocese, in 1975, published a pastoral letter on Ecclesial Affirmative Action. Summarizing the history of the early Church in regard to discrimination, and calling for a reversal of racism and sexism within the Church "and a return to the early Christian ideal of true equality among all persons," Bishop Buswell proposed "a plan to bring about increased participation of all individuals and groups in decision making and other responsibilities within our parish and diocesan structure."[176] This plan was to be implemented in a form determined by each parish community following a four-step process.

A recent report by the University of Notre Dame Study of Catholic Parish Life suggests that women today, despite the lack of formal recognition or appropriate compensation, do more than men to lead and minister in U.S. Catholic parishes. In such roles as catechetical teacher, parish council member, leader of recreational programs and youth ministries, participant in prayer group, parish renewal, or spiritual growth programs, participant in Bible study or discussion groups, minister to the poor, sick, or others in need, the percentage of women committed exceeded the percentage of men.[177] When will the ministry of these women no longer be hidden? While a handful of U.S. bishops has addressed the role of women in pastoral letters and related documents during the past decade, most concerned women are not optimistic about the imminent eradication of sexism in a patriarchal Church. The process of preparing for a new pastoral letter on women indicates that many bishops are ignoring the request of the committee headed by Bishop Joseph Imesch to hold hearings and gather input from a broad spectrum of women in each diocese. While some Intermountain groups of women are gathering opinions on their own initiative and submitting them to their bishops unbidden, they are simultaneously strengthening their own spiritual lives in small gatherings where study, discussion, and prayer are building communities of faith. In Pueblo, Colorado, in June of 1985, a group of sisters and laywomen who are members of parish staffs gathered to discuss women's roles in shaping the future of the world and of the Church. One of those present expressed the hope "that those who attended the gathering will be able to facilitate women's discussion groups in their own parishes to enable more women to network with one another."[178] In Albuquerque, New Mexico, a group of laywomen and sisters, originally sponsored by Aquinas Newman Center but now ecumenical in nature, has been meeting weekly since 1983 for study, prayer, and discernment on the issues of women, religion, and spirituality. For these women, it is not merely a matter of gaining equal access to old or new positions in the same patriarchal structure, but of creating alternative avenues to authentic Catholic expression based on experiential as well as conceptual values. Many hope, along with the Leadership Conference of Women Religious (LCWR), that the U.S. bishops will "not issue a pastoral on women in society and in the Church or alternately that they will defer writing for several years."[179] The rationale for such a hope has been carefully stated by the national board of the LCWR:

> As a Church, all of us need conversion to justice in regard to women; all of us, given our socialization both culturally and religiously, stand in need of liberation from a patriarchal world view. . . . A conversion process is long and painful; the issuing of a written statement has a tendency to signal closure, solution.[180]

These women await not the hierarchical voice of the Church, but its prophetic voice.

On this issue, as on many others calling for a response from American Catholics, ecclesiastical leadership can be helpful, but it is not essential for understanding and commitment. In the Intermountain West as well as throughout the country, belief in the prophetic spirit is tempering the old dependence on hierarchical authority and leading faithful Catholics to search for the satisfaction of personal/social religious needs through, but also beyond, existing parish and diocesan structures. In Indian missions, *communidades de base,* retreat houses, contemplative prayer centers, and social action gatherings, parish-like communities (that in many cases are more profoundly rooted than parish membership) are allowing committed Catholics to experience and profess their faith in expressive rather than organizational ways.

While Vatican Council II encouraged individual Catholics to assume responsibility for their own religious lives, many members of the American Church took the message to heart. Although some still depend totally on hierarchical authority to guide them, and many still believe that the Spirit works primarily through ecclesiastical leaders, growing numbers of Intermountain Catholics have been influenced by recent movements for self-determination among Native Americans, Hispanics, and federations of Rocky Mountain states. Consequently, they question the limitations of traditional parish structures and involve themselves in more global issues. There is hope among these Catholics that as the Church surrenders its exclusive Western European form in the transformative process of becoming an inclusive world Church, the quality of parish life in this region, as well as across the globe, will be enriched.

Notes

1. Wallace Stegner and Page Stegner, "Rocky Mountain Country," *Atlantic Monthly,* April 1978, 48.
2. *St. Jude Church* (Lakewood, Colorado: n.p., 1967), 7.
3. *Ibid.*
4. *Encyclopedia Americana,* 1983 ed., s.v. "Arizona."
5. Stegner and Stegner, 46. See also Appendix C.
6. *Ibid.;* and Michael Ball, field notes on St. Charles Borromeo Church, Hailey, Idaho, Notre Dame Study of Catholic Parish Life, 7.
7. Stegner and Stegner, 75.
8. Federation of the Rocky Mountain States, Inc., *The Rocky Mountain Region: A Unity of Interests,* n.p., 1975, 23.
9. *Ibid.*
10. *Ibid.,* 25.
11. *Ibid.,* 3, 4; and Lynton R. Hayes, *Energy, Economic Growth, and Regionalism in the West* (Albuquerque: University of New Mexico Press, 1980), 55.
12. Hayes, 1–2.
13. *Ibid.,* 65.
14. *Ibid.,* 66.
15. Federation, 21.
16. *Official Catholic Directory* (New York: P. J. Kenedy and Sons, 1980), 400.
17. Stegner and Stegner, 56, 62.
18. *Ibid.,* 86.
19. *Ibid.,* 62, 80.

20. *Ibid.*, 51.
21. Federation, 4.
22. *Ibid.*, 9.
23. D. La Magdeleine, field notes on Sacred Heart of Mary Parish, Boulder, Colorado, Notre Dame Study of Catholic Parish Life, 1.
24. *Ibid.*
25. Roger Finke, field notes on St. Bartholomew's Parish, White Sulphur Springs, Montana, Notre Dame Study of Catholic Parish Life, 1.
26. Michael Ball, field notes on St. Bartholomew's Parish, White Sulphur Springs, Montana, Notre Dame Study of Catholic Parish Life, 4.
27. Finke, field notes, White Sulphur Springs, 4.
28. Ball, field notes, White Sulphur Springs, 5.
29. Ball, field notes, White Sulphur Springs, 6.
30. Rev. William A. Dornbos, "Parish Profile," St. Bartholomew Parish, White Sulphur Springs, Montana, 5 November 1979, 2.
31. Sean D. Sammon, *Growing Pains in Ministry* (Whitinsville, Massachusetts: Affirmation Books, 1983), 36.
32. Winthrop S. Hudson, *Religion in America,* 3rd edition (New York: Charles Scribner's Sons, 1981), 417–418.
33. *Holy Family Church, 1954–1974* (Pueblo, Colorado, n.p., 1974), 4.
34. "Parish Background Information," Notre Dame Study of Catholic Parish Life.
35. *Ibid.*
36. Priests for Equality, "Toward a Full and Equal Sharing," Draft, December 1984, lines 78–82.
37. Finke, field notes on St. Charles Borromeo Church, Hailey, Idaho, Notre Dame Study of Catholic Parish Life, 6.
38. "Parish Background."
39. Sammon, 43.
40. Rev. Kenneth J. Arnzen, *The First Hundred Years: A Centennial History of St. Mary's Church* (Moscow, Idaho, 1982), 121.
41. "Parish Background."
42. *Ibid.*
43. *Ibid.*
44. *Official Catholic Directory,* 1980, 703–972.
45. *Ibid.*, 269–270, 343, 745–746, 878.
46. Tim McCarthy "Deacons: To Be or What To Be," *National Catholic Reporter,* 15 March 1985, 26.
47. *Ibid.*
48. *Ibid.*, 27.
49. "Parish Background."
50. *Ibid.*
51. *Our Lady of Guadalupe, Taos, New Mexico* (White Plains, New York: Monarch Publishing, Inc., 1976), 31.
52. Arnzen, 118.
53. *Most Precious Blood Church, Parish Information Directory,* Denver, 1983, 6.

54. 250th Anniversary Book Committee, *La Iglesia de Santa Cruz de la Cañada, 1733–1983*, 37.
55. Stanley L. Cuba, *St. Joseph's Polish Roman Catholic Church*, 1977, 17.
56. Ball, field notes, White Sulphur Springs, 1.
57. *Ibid.*
58. Abbott Edward Vollmer, "Sacred Heart of Mary Church," 2.
59. D. La Magdeleine, *passim.*
60. "Parish Background."
61. "A Proclamation," St. Charles Borromeo Parish, Hailey, Idaho; vertical file, Notre Dame Study of Catholic Parish Life.
62. "St. Michael's Will Renew Its Covenant," *The Denver Catholic Register*, 28 September 1983, 7.
63. Arnzen, 72, 125.
64. Hudson, 418.
65. *Official Catholic Directory*, 1960, 475; 1980, 402.
66. *Holy Family*, 23.
67. *Official Catholic Directory*, 1960, 1970, and 1980, *passim.*
68. Sammon, 78.
69. *Holy Family*, 23.
70. Arnzen, 116.
71. *Ibid.*
72. *Ibid.*, 117, 123.
73. *Most Precious Blood Church*, 12.
74. Ball, field notes, Hailey, 2.
75. "Parish Background."
76. *Ibid.*
77. Jim McManus, "New Center Opens Where Lay Pastoral Ministers Can Learn," *National Catholic Reporter*, 15 March 1985, 24.
78. *Ibid.*
79. Bernard Cooke, "U.S. Lay Ministry Bouncing Over Old Boundaries," *National Catholic Reporter*, 15 March 1985, 17.
80. "Parish Background."
81. "Aquinas Newman Center—The Catholic Parish at UNM," Albuquerque, New Mexico, bulletins, passim.
82. "Parish Background."
83. *Most Precious Blood Church*, 11.
84. *Ibid.*
85. Cooke, 17; and Sally Cunneen, " 'Observe, Judge, Act': The First Words of Infant Lay Ministry," *National Catholic Reporter*, 15 March 1985, 24.
86. *Most Precious Blood*, Annual Report, 1982–1983.
87. Arnzen, 123.
88. Cooke, 17.
89. Therese S. Westermeier, *Centennial of a Country Church* (Boulder: Johnson Publishing Co., 1973), 30–31.
90. Sammon, 41.

91. Interview with Rev. Chuck Cichanowicz, Albuquerque, New Mexico, 20 September 1985.
92. "St. Stephen's Indian Mission Pastoral Policy Statement" (Xeroxed), 1.
93. Father Bonaventure, O.F.M., *Mission San Xavier Del Bac* (Topawa, Arizona: The Franciscan Fathers of Arizona, 1937), 31.
94. Cichanowicz interview.
95. *Ibid.*
96. *Ibid.*, and KNME, "No Turning Back."
97. Rev. Jim O'Brien, personal letter.
98. Rev. Carl F. Starkloff, S.J., "My Song Is a Good One," *The Wind River Rendezvous*, 10 (Jan/Feb 1980), 1.
99. Howard L. Harrod, *Mission Among the Blackfeet* (Norman, Oklahoma: University of Oklahoma Press, 1971), 188.
100. John L. Kessell, *The Missions of New Mexico Since 1776* (Albuquerque: University of New Mexico Press, 1980), 220–221.
101. *Ibid.*, 221.
102. Edward T. Nash, "New Faces of Isleta Catholics" (Ph.D. dissertation, University of New Mexico, 1981), 189.
103. *Ibid.*, 190.
104. Harrod, 180.
105. Rev. Anthony Short, S.J., "1975—The Year of Self-Determination," *The Wind River Rendezvous*, 14 (Jan/Feb/Mar 1984), 1–2.
106. Stegner and Stegner, 64.
107. Short, "1975," 5–6.
108. O'Brien, letter.
109. Talli Nauman, "Acoma Aims for the Sky," *Albuquerque Journal*, 27 May 1984, G-1.
110. *Ibid.*
111. Robert S. Michaelsen, "The Significance of the American Religious Freedom Act of 1978," *Journal of the American Academy of Religion*, 52 (March 1984), 93.
112. Leah Beth Ward, "Indian Religion Complex Issue," *Albuquerque Journal*, 30 June 1984, A-10.
113. Michaelsen, 104–105.
114. Nash, *passim*.
115. *Ibid.*, 126.
116. *Ibid.*, 128.
117. "Pastoral Policy," 1.
118. Rev. Carl Starkloff, S.J., "Arapaho Service at the Tekakwitha Conference," *The Wind River Rendezvous*, 13 (July/Aug/Sept 1983), 12.
119. *Ibid.*
120. Starkloff, "Tekakwitha Conference," 13.
121. Jim Murphy, "Conference 'Touches the Touches' of Tekakwitha," *People of God*, September 1985, 12.
122. "Pastoral Policy," 2.
123. Rev. Carl F. Starkloff, S.J., "The Spring Has Come," *The Wind River Rendezvous*, 10 (Jan/Feb 1980), 14.

124. Willi Paul Adams, "A Dubious Host," *The Wilson Quarterly*, 7 (New Year's, 1983), 114, and " 'Stew Pot,' Not 'Melting Pot' Means Latinization," *People of God*, August 1985, 6.

125. Julie Asher, "New Hispanic Dean at St. Thomas' Seminary Feels Challenged To Prepare Seminarians for Future Church," *The Denver Catholic Register*, 28 September 1983, 5, col. 1.

126. Jerald H. Merrill, "Fifty Years with a Future: Salt Lake's Guadalupe Parish," *Utah Historical Quarterly*, 40 (Summer 1973), 261–264.

127. Arnzen, 119.

128. "Proposed Los Griegos History District," 1.

129. Lorin W. Brown with Charles L. Briggs and Marta Weigle, *Hispano Folklife of New Mexico* (Albuquerque: University of New Mexico Press, 1978), 173.

130. Robert J. Torrez, *El Primer Siglo: A Centennial History of San José Parish* (Los Ojos, New Mexico: San José Parish Council, 1983), 62.

131. 250th Anniversary Book Committee, *Santa Cruz*, 97.

132. Raymond Sokolov, "Saving New Mexico's Adobe Churches," *The Wall Street Journal*, 30 September 1983, 26.

133. Steve Sandoval, "Rosario Chapel: Renovation Changing Looks, Not Essence," *Albuquerque Journal*, 3 September 1983, C-11.

134. Denise Tessier, "A Happy Ending," *Albuquerque Journal*, 15 May 1984, B-1.

135. Berna Facio, "Regional XIII Encuentro Held in Salt Lake City," *People of God*, June 1985, 3.

136. Sabine R. Ulibarri in Moíses Sandoval, "Effects of World War II on the Hispanic People," *Fronteras: A History of the Latin American Church in the USA Since 1513* (San Antonio; Mexican American Cultural Center, 1983), 363.

137. *Ibid.*, 370.

138. Moíses Sandoval, "Hispanic Catholics: A Problem or a Blessing," *People of God*, August 1985, 6.

139. Richard N. Ostling, "The Crusade for Hispanic Souls," *Time*, 8 July 1985, 78.

140. Sandoval, "Problem," 6.

141. Finke, field notes, Hailey, 3.

142. Hudson, 356–357.

143. "Growing Number of Hispanics Switching Churches," *Albuquerque Journal*, 17 August 1985, A-6.

144. *Ibid.*

145. *Ibid.*

146. *Time*, 78.

147. Armando Rendón in Moíses Sandoval, "The Church and El Movimiento," *Fronteras*, 394.

148. "Hispanic People; Prophetic Voice," *People of God*, September 1985, 6.

149. "Hispanics Are Urged To Accept Ownership of Church," *People of God*, September 1985, 6.

150. Sandoval, "World War II," 367.

151. "Encuentro Involves Hundreds of Thousands," *People of God*, September 1985, 7.

152. David C. Leege and Thomas A. Trozzolo, "Religious Values and Parish Partic-

ipation: The Paradox of Individual Needs in a Communitarian Church," Notre Dame Study of Catholic Parish Life, Report No. 5, June 1985, 5.

153. *Ibid.*

154. "La Paz," monthly newsletter of Pax Christi, Albuquerque Chapter, July 1985.

155. "Bishop O'Brien Recognizes Efforts of Those in the Sanctuary Movement," *People of God*, September 1985, 12.

156. Tim McCarthy, "Activists Meet Plan, in Sleepy Arizona," *National Catholic Reporter*, 1 February 1985, 1, 20.

157. Interview with Jane Bergquist, Albuquerque, New Mexico, 23 October 1985.

158. Interview with Mary Helen Carroll, Albuquerque, New Mexico, 18 October 1985.

159. Joseph Fitzer, "Historical Research in Religion: An Amplification," *The Council on the Study of Religion Bulletin*, 13 (October 1982), 99.

160. Glenmary Research Center, "Major Denominational Families by Counties in the United States: 1980," map.

161. Finke, field notes, White Sulphur Springs, 2.

162. *Ibid.*, 3.

163. *Ibid.*

164. Glenmary map.

165. *Ibid.*

166. Mike Meacham, field notes on Sacred Heart Parish, Peetz, Colorado, Notre Dame Study of Catholic Parish Life, 2.

167. *Ibid.*, 1.

168. Interview with Jan Schuetz, Albuquerque, New Mexico, 20 October 1985.

169. Finke, field notes, Hailey, 3.

170. "Parish Background."

171. Marge Sena, personal letter.

172. Interview with Sister Martha Jean McGarry, Albuquerque, New Mexico, 18 May 1984.

173. Nash, 215–217.

174. Father Tom Zotter, "Charismatic Renewal Is Not the Church," *People of God*, January 1984, 3.

175. McGarry interview.

176. Most Rev. Charles A. Buswell, D.D., "Ecclesial Affirmative Action," Pastoral Letter (Pueblo, Colorado: *Catholic Crosswinds, 1975*), 2.

177. "Women and Parish Life," *People of God*, June 1985, 7.

178. Mary Heer, "Women's Role Discussed," *Catholic Crosswinds*, 14 June 1985, 2.

179. "LCWR Board Urges Change of Course," *Origins*, 14 (21 March 1985), 655.

180. *Ibid.*

For Further Reading

Archdiocese of Santa Fe. *The Old Faith and Old Glory, 1846–1946.* Santa Fe: Santa Fe Press, 1946.
Arnzen, Rev. Kenneth J. *The First Hundred Years: A Centennial History of St. Mary's Church.* Moscow, Idaho: n.p., 1982.
Casper, Henry W., S.J. *History of the Catholic Church in Nebraska: The Church on the Northern Plains, 1838–1874.* Milwaukee: The Bruce Publishing Co., 1960.
Faulk, Odie B., ed. *John Baptist Salpointe: Soldier of the Cross.* Tucson: The Diocese of Tucson, 1966.
Fries, Rev. Louis J., S.T.B. *One Hundred and Fifty Years of Catholicity in Utah.* Salt Lake City: Intermountain Catholic Press, 1926.
McGovern, Most Rev. Patrick A., S.T.D., LL.D. *History of the Diocese of Cheyenne.* Cheyenne, Wyoming: *Wyoming Labor Journal,* 1941.
Schoenberg, Rev. Wilfred P., S.J. *A Chronicle of the Catholic History of the Northwest, 1743–1960.* Portland, Oregon: Catholic Sentinel Printery, 1962.
Schoenberg, Rev. Wilfred P., S.J. *Jesuits in Montana, 1840–1960.* Portland, Oregon: The Oregon-Jesuit, 1960.
Silver Jubilee Committee. *Shepherds in the Desert.* Tucson: Diocese of Tucson, 1978.
Steele, Thomas J., S.J. *Works and Days.* Albuquerque: The Albuquerque Museum, 1983.
Stoller, Marianne L. and Thomas J. Steele, S.J. *Diary of the Jesuit Residence of Our Lady of Guadalupe Parish, Conejos, Colorado, December 1871–December 1875.* The Colorado College Studies, 19, Colorado Springs: The Colorado College, 1982.
250th Anniversary Book Committee. *La Iglesia de Santa Cruz de la Cañada 1733–1983.* n.p.: n.d., 1983.

APPENDIX 2

Catholic Church Statistics in the Intermountain West

Appendix: Church Statistics in the Intermountain West

ARIZONA
Diocese of Tuscon (1897)

	1850	1880	1900	1930	1950	1960	1980
Parishes	—	—	16	39	53	80	56
Parishes without Priests	—	—	126	156	29	133	72
National Parishes	—	—	0	0	0	0	0
Parish Schools	—	—	7	8	27	35	17
Diocesan Priests	—	—	20	27	62	92	74
Religious Order Priests	—	—	5	53	59	67	86
Women Religious	—	—	3 comm.	246	401	551	348
Catholic Population	—	—	40,000	95,472	115,000	276,000	198,000
Total Population	—	—	122,931	435,573	—	1,625,000	862,200

ARIZONA
Diocese of Phoenix (1969)

	1850	1880	1900	1930	1950	1960	1980
Parishes	—	—	—	—	—	—	79
Parishes without Priests	—	—	—	—	—	—	42
National Parishes	—	—	—	—	—	—	0
Parish Schools	—	—	—	—	—	—	27
Diocesan Priests	—	—	—	—	—	—	101
Religious Order Priests	—	—	—	—	—	—	114
Women Religious	—	—	—	—	—	—	317
Catholic Population	—	—	—	—	—	—	269,710
Total Population	—	—	—	—	—	—	1,524,900

COLORADO
Archdiocese of Denver (1887)

	1850	1880	1900	1930	1950	1960	1980
Parishes	—	—	54	111	83	107	131
Parishes without Priests	—	—	197	144	61	88	49
National Parishes	—	—	3	11	5	5	4
Parish Schools	—	—	16	50	37	54	45
Diocesan Priests	—	—	45	123	124	148	158
Religious Order Priests	—	—	42	106	108	148	207
Women Religious	—	—	11 comm.	518	405	943	931
Catholic Population	—	—	60,000	132,887	100,299	202,206	309,839
Total Population	—	—	539,700	1,035,791	—	1,240,350	2,203,221

COLORADO
Diocese of Pueblo (1941)

	1850	1880	1900	1930	1950	1960	1980
Parishes	—	—	—	—	43	55	57
Parishes without Priests	—	—	—	—	122	108	75
National Parishes	—	—	—	—	0	0	0
Parish Schools	—	—	—	—	17	21	10
Diocesan Priests	—	—	—	—	53	70	75
Religious Order Priests	—	—	—	—	59	73	51
Women Religious	—	—	—	—	299	390	221
Catholic Population	—	—	—	—	89,397	107,152	101,706
Total Population	—	—	—	—	—	401,211	396,708

IDAHO
Diocese of Boise (1893)

	1850	1880	1900	1930	1950	1960	1980
Parishes	—	—	14	45	50	53	67
Parishes without Priests	—	—	97	173	117	100	48
National Parishes	—	—	0	0	0	0	0
Parish Schools	—	—	4	19	16	20	12
Diocesan Priests	—	—	10	44	61	77	74
Religious Order Priests	—	—	8	15	15	15	27
Women Religious	—	—	40	272	388	8 comm.	143
Catholic Population	—	—	10,000	19,027	27,701	42,234	70,416
Total Population	—	—	161,772	445,032	588,637	669,885	915,960

MONTANA
Diocese of Helena (1884)

	1850	1880	1900	1930	1950	1960	1980
Parishes	—	—	28	48	52	53	58
Parishes without Priests	—	—	109	197	211	209	72
National Parishes	—	—	0	0	0	0	0
Parish Schools	—	—	9	22	20	22	4
Diocesan Priests	—	—	28	87	90	100	99
Religious Order Priests	—	—	11	12	14	14	17
Women Religious	—	—	236	385	335	334	81
Catholic Population	—	—	40,000	41,204	65,000	83,500	64,500
Total Population	—	—	243,329	—	—	330,000	376,000

Appendix: Church Statistics in the Intermountain West

MONTANA
Diocese of Great Falls–Billings (1904)

	1850	1880	1900	1930	1950	1960	1980
Parishes	—	—	—	45	58	63	60
Parishes without Priests	—	—	—	243	138	115	83
National Parishes	—	—	—	0	0	0	0
Parish Schools	—	—	—	11	18	22	16
Diocesan Priests	—	—	—	51	64	80	65
Religious Order Priests	—	—	—	17	24	28	34
Women Religious	—	—	—	254	250	297	192
Catholic Population	—	—	—	32,425	48,875	68,676	65,792
Total Population	—	—	—	—	—	305,000	351,838

NEVADA
Diocese of Reno–Las Vegas (1931)

	1850	1880	1900	1930	1950	1960	1980
Parishes	—	—	—	—	25	29	38
Parishes without Priests	—	—	—	—	37	35	30
National Parishes	—	—	—	—	0	0	0
Parish Schools	—	—	—	—	2	8	11
Diocesan Priests	—	—	—	—	44	40	35
Religious Order Priests	—	—	—	—	0	12	45
Women Religious	—	—	—	—	56	119	131
Catholic Population	—	—	—	—	23,100	49,966	110,000
Total Population	—	—	—	—	160,083	261,004	650,000

NEW MEXICO
Archdiocese of Santa Fe (1950)

	1850	1880	1900	1930	1950	1960	1980
Parishes	10	30	39	56	71	90	95
Parishes without Priests	50	175	340	390	374	302	265
National Parishes	0	0	0	0	0	0	0
Parish Schools	0	0	8	35	30	47	21
Diocesan Priests	10	52	51	52	108	125	113
Religious Order Priests	0		10	52	80	120	94
Women Religious	0	28	124	215	600	610	410
Catholic Population	60,000	111,000	133,000	142,934	205,000	275,000	324,357
Total Population	61,547	119,565	195,310	423,317	—	600,000	780,000

NEW MEXICO
Diocese of Gallup (comprising part of Arizona, as well) (1939)

	1850	1880	1900	1930	1950	1960	1980
Parishes	—	—	—	—	20	25	56
Parishes without Priests	—	—	—	—	124	136	87
National Parishes	—	—	—	—	0	0	0
Parish Schools	—	—	—	—	7	13	8
Diocesan Priests	—	—	—	—	12	26	32
Religious Order Priests	—	—	—	—	50	60	57
Women Religious	—	—	—	—	138	161	163
Catholic Population	—	—	—	—	40,606	54,511	48,099
Total Population	—	—	—	—	—	200,000	323,028

UTAH
Diocese of Salt Lake City (1891)

	1850	1880	1900	1930	1950	1960	1980
Parishes	—	—	7	19	25	32	37
Parishes without Priests	—	—	26	56	70	38	21
National Parishes	—	—	0	0	0	0	0
Parish Schools	—	—	3	9	4	8	8
Diocesan Priests	—	—	10	29	34	39	41
Religious Order Priests	—	—	6	1	20	43	44
Women Religious	—	—	96	117	173	200	110
Catholic Population	—	—	7,600	17,248	23,392	40,541	59,744
Total Population	—	—	276,749	507,847	688,862	850,000	1,367,000

WYOMING
Diocese of Cheyenne (1887)

	1850	1880	1900	1930	1950	1960	1980
Parishes	—	—	12	21	28	37	38
Parishes without Priests	—	—	80	60	49	44	40
National Parishes	—	—	0	0	0	0	0
Parish Schools	—	—	4	3	6	8	7
Diocesan Priests	—	—	12	25	40	53	47
Religious Order Priests	—	—	2	6	8	6	7
Women Religious	—	—	3 comm.	26	57	115	89
Catholic Population	—	—	6,000	24,466	48,263	48,500	46,500
Total Population	—	—	92,531	225,565	290,529	320,000	425,000

APPENDIX 3

Number of parishes in various locales of the Intermountain West. Taken from the 1980 *Catholic Directory* and the 1980 United States Census

State	Diocese	Rural	Small Town	Small City	City	Large City	Suburb
Arizona	Tucson	8	21	7	0	20	0
Arizona	Phoenix	11	13	12	16	25	0
Colorado	Denver	25	20	4	20	39	26
Colorado	Pueblo	24	16	5	17	0	0
Idaho	Boise	32	20	15	5	0	0
Montana	Helena	27	11	21	0	0	0
Montana	Great Falls	49	10	1	15	0	0
Nevada	Reno-Las Vegas	13	10	5	15	0	0
New Mexico	Santa Fe	39	14	14	0	26	0
New Mexico	Gallup	32	14	9	0	0	0
Utah	Salt Lake City	5	7	7	12	0	0
Wyoming	Cheyenne	10	15	12	2	0	0

APPENDIX 4

Date when states in the Intermountain West became more urban than rural in population

1930	1950	1960	1970
Colorado	Arizona	Montana	Idaho
Utah	Nevada	Wyoming	
	New Mexico		

PART THREE

The Cities and the Plains, A Home For God's People: A History of the Catholic Parish in the Midwest

Stephen J. Shaw

Contents

Preface	279
CHAPTER ONE: The Establishment of Parish Life in the United States, 1604–1914	282
CHAPTER TWO: The Consolidation of Parish Life, 1914–1962	327
CHAPTER THREE: The Reorganization of Parish Life Since Vatican II, 1962–	355
For Further Reading	380

Preface

The history of the Catholic Church in the United States has traditionally been defined in terms of the hierarchy. John Gilmary Shea, the father of American Catholic history, saw the Church as a hierarchical institution, with the laity taking a subordinate role. Succeeding Catholic historians like Peter Guilday and John Tracy Ellis also emphasized the hierarchy at the expense of the laity.[1] Vatican Council II, however, redefined the Church in terms of the people themselves. Instead of restricting its definition to an exclusively hierarchical Church, the council fathers stressed that "the laity, by their very vocation, seek the kingdom of God by engaging in temporary affairs and by ordering them according to the plan of God. They live in the world, that is, in each and in all of the secular professions and occupations. They live in the ordinary circumstances of family and social life from which the very web of their existence is woven."[2]

To study the people of God, we must study the parish. For it was the parish that was and still is the fundamental institution around which Catholics gather. And while not ignoring the hierarchy—indeed, it is impossible to do so—I intend to highlight the role of the men, women, and children who made up the history of so many parishes in the Midwest. How did they see the parish and how did the parish see them? What devotions, societies, or other institutions made the parish a focus of their lives? And how did all of this change after Vatican Council II? These are the questions I wish to address.

But the history of a people must be put into the context of a certain time and place. In 1790, the United States was a rural nation, with only three out of one hundred Americans living in the city. American Catholics, who numbered only 35,000, were scattered across the villages and farmlands of the original thirteen colonies. Bishop John Carroll presided over a Church that has often been described as an Anglo-American minority. By 1815, when Carroll died, there were fewer than 200,000 Catholics in the entire country. But all this dramatically changed in the ensuing decades, as Catholicism became the largest denomination in the United States, with well over 3 million adherents by 1860.[3] For it was the large-scale migrations from northern Europe that brought about this change and transformed Roman Catholicism from a mere minority to a multi-ethnic denomination.

Between 1830 and 1860, some 2 million Irishmen came to the United States. Driven out by overpopulation, an unequal land system, and the potato famine of 1845 to 1849, the Irish settled in the emerging cities of the East and the Midwest.

They were soon joined by more than a million Germans from Württemberg, Baden, and Bavaria. Up to 1850, Irish immigrants exceeded Germans by 18.1%. But, from 1850 to 1860, Germans superseded them as the leading ethnic group. They came for many reasons—overpopulation, crop failure (a potato famine in southwest Germany and a wine failure in Württemberg), but most of all, for better economic opportunities, as newer methods of production forced farmers out of business.[4]

By 1860, 4,136,000 Americans were foreign born. And most were tied to the city, as nearly half of the populations of New York, Chicago, Milwaukee, and Detroit were foreign born. It is no accident that by the end of the Civil War the "face of American Catholicism had changed, and the Anglo-American Catholic Church of 1815 was gone . . . in its place was an Anglo-Irish-German-French-Italian-American Catholic Church." And to a large extent it was an urban Church. As Jay P. Dolan has pointed out: "The city was the stage on which the American Catholic Church was formed . . . the institutional Church which emerged in the city became a prototype for other Catholic communities both on the parochial and extra-parochial level and it remained as a model for almost one-hundred years."[5]

The period between 1865 and 1962, when Vatican Council II began, was a period of building, constructing, and consolidating what had already begun before. America welcomed its immigrants, a large majority of whom were Catholic; and the Church responded by establishing parishes for their needs. Germans, Irish, Poles, and Italians filled up the empty spaces of the Midwest. By 1900, Illinois numbered 332,169 Germans and 114,563 Irish; it was the leading foreign-born state in the Midwest. Wisconsin and Ohio followed, with 242,777 and 204,160 foreign-born Germans, respectively.[6] Church spires of all nationalities dotted the plains and valleys of the Midwest, from Ohio in the east to Nebraska and Kansas in the west. The parishes of the Midwest were a mosaic of many nationalities and races, bound together by a common faith and belief. How these parishes developed—and what they meant to the men and women who belonged to them—is the focus of the first part of this story.

Notes

1. Shea's monumental opus, *A History of the Catholic Church in the United States* (4 Vols., Merscham Co. Press, 1886–1892), is primarily institutional Church history. Guilday's and Ellis' ecclesiastical biographies essentially follow the same pattern and break no new ground. For a more modern history, see James Hennesey, S.J., *American Catholics* (Oxford: Oxford University Press, 1981).

2. Walter Abbott, S.J., ed., *The Documents of Vatican II* (New York: The Guild Press, 1966), 57–58.

3. Jay P. Dolan, "Urban Catholicism: New York City, 1815–1865" (Ph.D. dissertation, University of Chicago, 1970), 1–4.

4. Albert B. Faust, *The German Element in the United States* (2 Vols., New York: Houghton Mifflin, 1909), I:585. Between 1851 and 1860, 951,667 Germans arrived in the United States.

5. Dolan, "Urban Catholicism," 282, 277–278.

6. Faust, *German Element,* I:578.

CHAPTER ONE

The Establishment of Parish Life in the United States, 1604–1914

THE MISSIONARY ERA, 1604–1865

The rocky and forbidding Northeast Coast of North America seemed most inhospitable to the first European voyagers, while the forested Appalachians to the west proved no less an obstacle to travel. But the St. Lawrence River lured many a European into the vast continent's interior. French fur trappers came first, as they followed the path of Jacques Cartier to Canada's back-country. And French religious, who first arrived at Ile. Ste.-Croix, Maine, in 1604, soon brought God's Word to the Algonquians and Iroquois. By 1632, the Blackfriars, or Jesuits, had converted the Hurons north of Lake Erie, and within a few years, had converted most of the Indians of the area. The French, who laid claim to the entire Great Lakes and Mississippi River regions, soon dotted the landscape with trading posts and missions. They left their names and imprint on the entire region. In 1641, Father Charles Raymbaut, S.J., and Father Rene Jogues, S.J., planted the cross at St. Ste. Marie. In 1661, Fathers Rene Menard, S.J., and Claude Allouez, S.J., set up the Ottawa mission for "the Chippewas, the Beavers, the Crees, the Ottawas, and refugee Hurons on Lake Superior, the Menominees, Potawatomies, Sacs, Foxes, Winnebagoes, Miamis, Illinois, and those of the Sioux who live on or near the banks of the Mississippi."[1] In 1663, they established the mission of La Pointe de Saint Esprit on the west side of Lake Superior. Fathers Claude Dablon, S.J., James Marquette, S.J., and others established further missions at Michilimackinac (Mackinac) and Green Bay.

Father Jacques Marquette, S.J., a master of the Algonquin and Huron languages, arrived at St. Ste. Marie in 1668 and established the St. Ignatius Mission at Michilimackinac the same year. After France took over the entire Upper Lakes region in 1671, Marquette, with the French explorer Louis Jolliet, set sail for the then unknown upper Mississippi Valley. Entering the Mississippi by way of Wisconsin, they traveled as far south as the Arkansas River, and returned to their mission by way of "Chicagou." Marquette, who returned to this "place of wild garlic" in 1674, ministered to the needs of the Potawatamies and wintered over there until 1675.² The first recorded European to stay in the area, Marquette died near Ludington, Michigan, in October of 1676.

Father Louis Hennepin, a Recollect Franciscan, established a series of missions in the lower Illinois and Mississippi region around 1680. Canoeing down the Illinois and Mississippi rivers, he was captured by Sioux near the Turkey River in Iowa and returned to Quebec by way of the Michilimackinac Mission. Although he never returned to the Midwest, Hennepin wrote many books describing his adventures for eager Europeans. In 1699, French members of the Seminary of Foreign Missions built a chapel at Cahokia, the oldest permanent settlement in Illinois, which later became an important trading post on the Mississippi. In 1696, Father François Pinet, S.J., established the Mission de L'Ange Guardien de Chicagou near Lake Calumet. It became a favorite stopping-off place for early pioneers. These missions were very primitive, and "when brandy was opened and the drunkenness and brawling started, missionary protest to both Indian and trader was less than the passing wind."³ Political struggles in France soon limited the number of French missions, so that by 1700 French activity switched to the lower Mississippi south of the Missouri River. The beaver trade also aroused intense competition between France, Spain, and England, as a series of struggles culminated in the French and Indian War (1754–1763). Quebec's surrender to the British in 1759, and the Treaty of 1763, effectively ended the French era in Midwestern history. For the British, unlike the French, were uninterested in befriending or Christianizing the Indians. But hundreds of families and towns in Indiana, Illinois, Missouri, and Iowa trace their origins to this era.⁴

The earliest missions in Indiana, at Vincennes, Ouiatenon (near Lafayette), and Ft. Miami (Ft. Wayne), were French.⁵ Established by the Sieur de Vincennes in 1730, Vincennes was still considered a French town in the 1780s. Stern French priests frowned on the Frenchmen's love of dance and festivity (especially the annual King Ball celebration, a secular combination of Christmas, New Year's, and Epiphany). For the French, religion was as essential as civil government, and while the earliest pioneers were simply interested in eking out their daily lives, they looked to the Church for spiritual sustenance. Father Pierre Gibault, who assisted the American takeover of Vincennes in 1786, set up a new church and home for missionaries, instructed the children of the village, and made a sincere effort to keep the frontiersmen in line. The departure of Gibault in 1789 marked the end of French influence in the territory. But the city remained an important outpost as the capital of the vast Indiana territory from 1800 to 1813.

The Northwest Ordinance of 1787 opened the future states of Ohio, Michigan, Indiana, and Illinois to rapid development. The boom was on, as Englishmen, Scots, Germans, and New Englanders went west to seek their fortunes. The history of Ohio began in the south, as towns such as Cincinnati, Chillicothe, and Marietta sprung up overnight. Cincinnati began as a small fortress in 1789, and, by the 1820s, was the hub of the Ohio Valley. Popularly known as Porkopolis, the meat-packing center of the Midwest, Cincinnati soon grew to 160,000 (1860). Chillicothe, the capital of the Northwest Territory in 1800, was twice state capital before 1820. The city boomed with the growth of the Ohio and Erie Canal in the 1830s. And Marietta, Ohio's oldest permanent settlement, grew with the shipbuilding industry of the early nineteenth century. Speculative land companies such as the Ohio and the Scioto lured Europeans to the Midwest with tales of newfound wealth. Some, like the Gallipolis settlement on the banks of the Ohio, failed when the investors took the money and ran.[6] Organized religion was carried on through Methodist camp meetings, small Baptist congregations, and itinerant Protestant and Catholic preachers. The earliest Roman Catholics were Marylanders, who crossed the Cumberland Gap into Ohio by way of Kentucky. The first permanent chapel can be traced to Somerset, where, in 1818, Father Edward Fenwick, O.P., organized St. Joseph Parish; as he noted, "the congregation consisted of ten families. A humble convent was built nearby, and its inmates were one American . . . one Irishman . . . and one Belgian."[7] From this early settlement, the Church in southern Ohio grew to such an extent that Cincinnati was named its first diocese in 1821. The entire territory had only five or six organized parishes. By 1835, Fenwick, who was named the first bishop, noted that "my diocese in Ohio and Michigan is flourishing. It contains 24 priests and missionaries, 22 churches, and several more congregations without churches, whereas 14 years ago there was not a church and I the only missionary in the state of Ohio."[8]

Irish and Germans played a prominent role in Ohio's early development. The former began to migrate into the state in the early 1830s, as the state legislature decided to build two canals linking Cleveland and Toledo in the north, with Marietta and Cincinnati in the south. Germans, who first arrived in Cincinnati around 1830, were attracted to the area by the promises of the *Leopoldinen Stiftung* in Vienna. But most tended to settle in the small towns and villages that had arisen across the hilly Ohio landscape. The story of (New) Lancaster is typical of the era. Founded by Colonel Ebenezer Zane, a veteran of the American Revolution, in 1800, Lancaster soon grew with the influx of German settlers from the East. The first newspaper, *Der Ohio Adler,* was established in 1807, and the town was formally incorporated in 1831. The Lancaster Lateral Canal opened the town to new markets from the East, and with these new markets came money and more settlers. By 1841, the Hocking Canal (as it was called) extended to Athens, and the first canal boats unloaded cargoes of coal in 1840. Lancaster was predominantly German, as trades- and craftsmen made their home there. The Duke of Saxe Weimar, who visited his co-nationals in 1825, was enthusiastically received by his fellow Germans in the town square. Lancaster soon became a home for the state's most renowned lawyers, as men such as Thomas Ewing and John Sherman settled there.[9]

The Church responded to these groups by sending English- and German-speaking priests to their own people. Archbishop John Baptist Purcell of Cincinnati (1833–1883) visited Columbus in 1836 and "announced the object of his visit to be the consulting with the Catholics of Columbus in relation to the building of a church . . . during his stay in the city the Bishop visited the different families and ministered to the spiritual wants of the English-speaking Catholics, and promised to send a German priest as soon as possible to do a like service for the German Catholics."[10] Mass was said in private homes until 1833, when a lot was donated for the purpose of building a church. Germans and Americans contributed, a committee was established, and soon St. Remigius (Holy Cross) Church was erected as Columbus' first German church. These parishes relied heavily on trustees to administer the finances of the parish. But this arrangement often led to conflict with the resident pastor. For example, a priest in Norwalk, Ohio, quarreled so often with his German parishioners that he was thrown out of the parish. When Archbishop Purcell intervened on his behalf, the parishioners reluctantly took him back. But the differences continued to grow to such an extent that the tired priest was forced to retire to Baltimore. Bishops also had their financial problems. Since they did not own the parish property outright, they often ventured into purely secular affairs for financial gain. Archbishop Purcell came to the "queen city" when there was only one Catholic church in the entire city and only sixteen churches in the entire state. Purcell entrusted the affairs of the diocese to his brother, Rev. Edward Purcell. Although such a move was not uncanonical, it did prove disastrous for the archdiocese as a whole. Purcell persuaded hundreds of poor Irish, German, and Italian immigrants to entrust their life savings to him; he, in turn, invested it in several companies, including Jay Cooke and Co. But when the latter failed and the "investors" demanded their money back, vital diocesan resources had to be sacrificed to pay back the debts. Much more seriously, "many became despondent and many fell away from the faith . . . the ecclesiastical seminary had to be closed until 1887. Growth in parishes ceased automatically."[11] The above episode points out the chaotic financial arrangements that often existed in early dioceses and the tragic consequences that often ensued.

While the 1840s have often been characterized as anti-Catholic (and anti-ecumenical), the frontier often softened these harsh battle lines. Settlers of all faiths found themselves next to each other on the Ohio frontier and worked together to build their new towns and churches. Indeed, Protestants often contributed significantly to the building of Catholic churches. Father Joseph Machebeuf, an early Ohio pioneer, dressed "a little better in town so as not to give occasion to disrespectful comments, which might be made by the Protestants if they were to see a Catholic priest shabbily dressed." A Father James Mullon, standing on the steps of the Lisbon County Courthouse, won over many Protestant listeners with a stirring discourse on Christian charity. And, in 1837, Archbishop Purcell debated the noted Baptist minister, Alexander Campbell, with such success that he won over many a hardened Protestant.[12] But these instances do not belie the fact that the Irish were often hated for their Catholicity, while Germans, in general, were distrusted for their accents and strange ways.

Parish life, such as it was, existed only on the most primitive level. Itinerant clergy, traveling from one county to the next, would settle among a group of Catholics for a time and then move on. And while they did rely on the local bishop for financial aid, they were relatively free to move from one diocese to the next. Father Machebeuf, who came to Ohio in the early 1820s, was one of these priests. He traveled the Ohio valleys with a long black bag containing a chalice, vestments, and other necessary items. News of his arrival often preceded him, as Catholics quickly gathered for Mass and the Sacraments. Since there were few established parishes at this time, many Catholics went for years without the Sacraments. Father Machebeuf baptized the children, blessed marriages, and heard confessions for these early pioneers. By the time he left Ohio to become the first bishop of Denver, Colorado, the Church was already a nascent urban community, as the frontier quickly moved west.[13]

While new settlers pushed west into the Ohio Valley through the Cumberland Gap, older settlements to the north reawakened and grew considerably. The Church in Detroit dates to 1701, when the parish of St. Anne was formally dedicated with a staff of Recollect priests.[14] By the dawn of the nineteenth century, Detroit was still a military post and numbered approximately 2,000 predominantly French Catholics. In 1796, Bishop Carroll sent the Sulpician Father Michael Levadoux to renew the Church's position in that city. He was soon joined by Father Gabriel Richard, one of the most remarkable priests of his time. Ordained in Paris in 1791, Richard, who first served at Prairie du Rocher and Kaskaskia, Illinois, arrived at Detroit in 1798. He at once made his presence felt by promoting the numerous Indian missions in the surrounding country, starting a seminary to foster vocations, and establishing a strong parochial school system in Detroit. He soon widened his efforts to the entire state of Michigan. He was one of the founders of the University of Michigan (1817) and taught in six of the thirteen departments offered at the time. He was elected a delegate to Congress from the Michigan Territory in 1823, and worked diligently for the interests of Michigan. When the territory passed to the jurisdiction of Bishop Fenwick in Cincinnati in 1822, Richard reported that there were approximately 6,000 Catholics, with five churches and two priests, in the entire territory. He died, most fittingly, serving others, as an epidemic of cholera swept through Detroit in 1832.[15]

Illinois became a territory in 1809.[16] Life was rough at the beginning of the eighteenth century, as a handful of French and American frontiersmen trapped foxes and beavers. The population of the entire state was no more than 12,282 by 1812. The state was slow to grow, as it was cursed with a lack of capital, inadequate banks, and poor land policy. But the western movement into the state could not be stopped, as settlers from the East arrived by flatboats or horse and wagon. Towns such as Kaskaskia, Vandalia, and Alton grew as men and women entered the new territory. Kaskaskia, an old French settlement on the Mississippi, served as state capital from 1818 to 1820. Vandalia, as the western terminus of the National Road, served as Illinois' capital from 1820 to 1839. Covered wagons took settlers and manufactured goods westward, and rumbled back east with raw materials and farm produce. Alton, laid out in 1817, was an important river town until eclipsed by nearby St. Louis. Wracked by anti-abolitionist violence in the 1830s, it still preserves the character of a small nineteenth-century Midwestern community.

Roman Catholicism grew with the state. Bishop Joseph Flaget of Bardstown, Kentucky, noted that "in the very midst of the Indians were four French congregations belonging to my diocese; one on the upper Mississippi, another in a place usually designated Chicagou, still another on the shores of Lake Michigan, and a fourth toward the source of the Illinois River; but lack of time and the prevalence of war have prevented me from visiting them." Chicago, the future giant of the Midwest, remained a relatively isolated outpost until 1816.[17] A detachment of U.S. soldiers erected a fort at Michigan and Wacker in July of 1803. Named after Henry Dearborn, the fifth Secretary of War, the compound spawned a thriving settlement that attracted many immigrants from the East. But the Battle of Tippecanoe (1811) was a harbinger of bad times. The War of 1812 left Fort Dearborn far beyond the American line of settlement, a week's march from the closest fort. On August 15th, a band of Indians, attacking a group of retreating soldiers and civilians, killed fifty-two and captured forty-two as prisoners. They burned Fort Dearborn the same day.

But Chicago rose like a phoenix from the ashes of war. Soldiers rebuilt the fort in 1816; Illinois became a state in 1818; and Chicago, which received a town charter in 1833, became a city on March 4, 1837. The town first attracted real-estate speculators as well as Irish and German immigrants. The Irish, who were the largest foreign-born group through the first half of the century, numbered 6,096 by 1850. The majority, who were Catholic, soon supplanted the French as the most important ethnic group within Catholicism. Germans numbered 5,035 by mid-century with the majority coming from the upper Rhine Valley. A Yankee who came to Chicago in 1847 noted the "Dutch, who talk bad English . . . you could understand them about as well as you could a flock of cackling geese." While the Irish worked as laborers, the better-educated Germans opened shops and businesses. The English, Welsh, and Scotch, who numbered 2,493 in 1850, completed the ethnic mix of the city.[18]

Catholicsm grew with Chicago from its very beginning.[19] A group of Chicagoans petitioned Bishop Joseph Rosatti, of St. Louis, Missouri, for a permanent clergyman:

> We, the Catholics of Chicago, Cook Co., Ill., lay before you the necessity there exists to have a pastor in this new and flourishing city. There are several families

of French descent, born and brought up in the Roman Catholic faith, and others quite willing to aid us in supporting a pastor, who ought to be sent before other sects obtain the upper hand.[20]

Bishop Rosatti answered their letter by appointing Father John Mary St. Cyr as Chicago's first permanent pastor. Conditions were primitive—there was no permanent church, money was scarce, and few had but a rudimentary knowledge of the faith. But St. Cyr managed to build Chicago's first Catholic church in 1837. Americans, Irishmen, French, and Germans met at a common altar for the first time. As more and more immigrants inundated the city, ecclesiastical authorities wisely made it a diocese in its own right in 1844.

Rt. Rev. William Quarter, Chicago's first bishop, arrived in the city on May 5, 1844. The diocese included the entire state of Illinois, with only twenty-three native and foreign-born priests in residence. The new bishop was particularly concerned for the Irish and Germans within his community. He appealed to the Leopoldin association in Germany for financial assistance. German Catholics, who numbered about 1,000, were in dire need of German-speaking priests. Rev. C. H. Ostlangenberg was sent to Chicago and another priest to Quincy, Illinois, for the German communities in the respective cities. Quarter established two German-speaking parishes in Chicago at this time; St. Joseph's to the north and St. Peter's to the south. But his premature death in 1848 robbed the city of a young and dynamic leader. The youthful bishop left a diocese of 80,000 Catholics, forty priests, and fifty-six churches.[21]

Rt. Rev. James Oliver Van de Velde, Chicago's second bishop, reflected on the missionary nature of the Church at mid-century in his illuminative diary:

> In general, the immigrants who come to these parts and who make up almost the entire Catholic population are not in a position to supply even their own wants. Poverty is so great that there is not a single parish . . . which is provided with the necessary equipment for the celebration of the sacred rites. A single priest has sometimes eight parishes to attend and he has for those various stations only one chalice, one missal, one chasuble, one alb, one altar-stone; he must perforce carry all these articles with him, however long and distressing be the way.[22]

His successor, Anthony O'Regan, soon found himself embroiled in a controversy with his nationalist clergy. Writing to a friend in 1857, O'Regan noted: "For the last nine years this diocese has been grievously afflicted by bad priests, Irish, French, and German. My predecessor was frustrated and tried to resign; he could not live here. I am suffering far, far more, and do not know what I shall do." When a dissident Frenchman even threatened his life, O'Regan exclaimed that "this has been more than once threatened and they are wicked enough to do it." But despite these difficulties, the Church in Chicago and Illinois continued to grow, as new parishes were established not only in Chicago, but even in such remote towns as Edwardsville, Rockville, Woodstock, and Buffalo Grove.[23]

While Chicago was emerging from the prairies as *the* center of urban Catholicism in the Northwest Territory, the upper Mississippi Valley states also began to emerge from their primitiveness.[24] The Jesuits had briefly visited the region in the eighteenth century; Augustine de Langlade, often called the "father of Wisconsin," opened a warehouse in Green Bay in 1764. But the area did not develop until the American government opened forts at Prairie du Chien, Portage, and Green Bay in the early 1800s. The territory was still wide-open at the beginning of the century, as "there were no laws enforced in this country. The marriages that took place at that time were according to the Indian laws and customs. There were no priests or magistrates in the country."[25]

Perhaps the history of this region is best exemplified by the life of Father Charles S. Mazzuchelli, O.P., a true "pathfinder in the wilderness."[26] Born in Milan, Italy, in 1806, Mazzuchelli answered the call of Bishop Fenwick to minister to the needs of Midwestern America. Ordained in 1830, this intrepid missionary was first assigned to Mackinac, where he worked among the scattered settlers of the Upper Peninsula and northeastern Wisconsin. Mazzuchelli designed and built hundreds of churches in Wisconsin, northern Illinois, and Iowa. At Green Bay, he designed and built a combination church/school. Arriving at Galena, Illinois, in 1835, he ministered to 200 Catholics and collected funds for a church. He designed, contracted, and supervised the construction of St. Michael Church and the Galena County Courthouse in 1842. But Mazzuchelli became convinced that the future of the region was in Dubuque, and so he resolutely pushed for the erection of a diocese in that city. His mission was accomplished in 1837, as the Dubuque Diocese encompassed not only the present state of Iowa, but all the land between the Mississippi and Missouri rivers north to the Canadian border. The diocese was small, with only Dubuque and Davenport having congregations; the Catholic population was approximately 500. In alliance with Bishop Matthias T. Loras, the first bishop of Dubuque, Mazzuchelli bought up hundreds of acres of land in Iowa "in order to lay a good foundation for religion . . . I shall have many deeds in the territory if I am given time." Their plan was to buy property first, and then wait for Catholics to fill it up. Between 1839 and 1855, Loras spent $15,482.00 on real estate alone. But not all priests agreed with this policy. Father Jean A. Pelamourques, one of the first priests in Iowa, consistently opposed Loras' policy. He noted:

> I have always been against building churches in places where there are not Catholics enough to pay the expenses of the priest who visits them . . . a few congregations well-attended will do more good than a great number of them which the means of the priest do not afford to visit. We injure old congregations by establishing new ones around them; we by that means induce people to scatter and at the end, there is no congregation able to support a priest.[27]

Mazzuchelli continued to serve the Iowa diocese as vicar general until a serious illness forced him to return to Milan in 1853. But we cannot underestimate his contribution to the development of the Church in the Midwest. If he had not been there, the Church in the upper Mississippi Valley would not have developed as fast as it did. And the fact that Mazzuchelli was a religious also made a difference. Like Fenwick of Ohio, Mazzuchelli was a Dominican, who was subject only to his superiors in Rome. As such, he was able to move freely from one diocese to the next without being subject to the sole authority of a particular bishop. He paved the way, as so many religious order priests before and after him, for the local diocesan clergy.

It was not uncommon at this time for priests to move from one diocese to another. Diocesan boundaries were often ill-defined, and geography, more than anything else, determined who took care of whom. Bishop Quarter of Chicago sent Father Alexander Hattenberger, an Alsatian, to Ft. Madison, Iowa, to minister to the needs of the German Catholics in that diocese. Hattenburger, pastor of the entire Des Moines Valley, later became vicar general for all Germans until his death in 1899. And Bishop Loras ministered to not only his own people, but parishioners in southwestern Illinois and Wisconsin as well. Prairie du Chien, the site of Wisconsin's only battle in 1812, became an important Catholic center by 1839. Loras journeyed extensively through southern Wisconsin in 1841 and 1842, as he confirmed Catholics in Green Bay, Little Chute, Kenosha, and Milwaukee. Parishioners in East Dubuque, Illinois, often crossed the Mississippi to attend services in Dubuque itself. During the winter of 1866, more than a hundred Catholics were returning from Mass in Dubuque when the ice gave way and the intrepid parishioners floated down the river until the ice was stopped by a sandbar; fortunately, all were saved.[28]

The story of Father John G. Alleman is an interesting example of interfaith cooperation.[29] Alleman chose Ft. Madison, on the Iowa side of the Mississippi, as the locus of his work with German Catholics. Across the river, on the Illinois side, was Nauvoo, a community of Mormons that had reached 20,000 by 1843. Alleman cultivated Joseph Smith's friendship, and Smith often called on Alleman to translate French and German documents. Smith offered Alleman the use of his barge and several strong men to cross the river whenever he wanted because "those days there was a sort of cable ferry across the river, with a bell at each side. If the skiff or boat was at the opposite side, Father Alleman had the privilege of ringing and the boat was brought posthaste to convey him across." Smith even gave Alleman space in his temple to offer Mass and administer baptism. But this kind of cooperation was limited to the frontier, where harsh conditions forced settlers to band together for their own good. In urban areas, where Catholicism was stronger, and there was no need for such cooperation, there were fewer attempts to cross denominational lines.

The Establishment of Parish Life, 1604-1914 291

The vast reaches of the northern Great Lakes remained relatively unpopulated until the first Frenchmen arrived from the East.[30] Father Claude Allouez, S.J., often called "a second Xavier," baptized more than 10,000 Chippewas around Lake Superior in the early seventeenth century. Daniel Greysolon, Sieur de Lhut, was the first explorer to reach the area in 1679. Pierre de la Verendrye led a successful expedition across Lake Superior as far north as the Lake of the Woods in 1731 to 1732. But as Britain took control of the region, Catholic activity ceased until after the War of 1812. The Treaty of Ghent, which ceded the northwestern territory to the United States, opened the way for American settlement. Even before the war ended, a group of dispossessed Scotch and Irish peasants established a settlement at Pembina, in the northeastern corner of North Dakota. Father George A. Belcourt traveled extensively through the region, built a chapel and school at Pembina, and founded a religious community of women for half-breeds.

Father Pierre De Smet, S.J., born in Belgium in 1801, was a leading figure in the early history of the Dakota Territory. He was perhaps the best friend the Indian ever had, and, as his biographers noted of him, "the history of the native races of North America can never be written without consulting the writings of Father De Smet."[31] Setting off for the Rocky Mountain country in 1840, the young black robe soon established a mission on the Columbia River and made peace with the menacing Blackfeet. His almost inexplicable ability to be accepted by all the tribes he met, and his numerous writings on the territories he visited, brought him to the attention of the U.S. government. He brought peace to the Oregon Valley in 1851, effectively intervened between the Sioux and the government in 1862 and 1867, and, on the most important mission of his career in 1868, effected a peace treaty with Sitting Bull in the Badlands of South Dakota. Described as a short and rather corpulent man, De Smet almost became an Indian himself, as he traveled from one tribe to another. It is said that during one of his visits to the Sioux a young brave put a knife to his throat and threatened his life, but De Smet only took the brave's hand and placed it over his heart. Such was De Smet's fame that he could walk unarmed into any Indian camp and come out alive. It somehow seems ironic that his last years were spent pushing papers as procurator of the St. Louis Province of the Jesuits, a post he held until his death in 1873.

The establishment of the Territory of Minnesota in 1849, along with successive Indian treaties in 1851, 1854, and 1855, opened this vast area to settlement. Hordes of Easterners and Europeans began to arrive at St. Paul; and a third of these newcomers came from England, Ireland, Germany, and Scandinavia. By 1857, 1,025 steamboats were docking at St. Paul alone. While rivers provided the main means of navigation, new roads pushed toward Iowa and the wooded interior; a network of roads to the south opened the southern portion to even more settlement. New towns such as St. Cloud, Winona, and New Ulm began to rise from the Minnesota forests. And the Church was there from the beginning. The

Diocese of St. Paul, established in 1850, encompassed more than 166,000 square miles. By 1857, there were twenty-nine churches, thirty-five missions, and more than 50,000 Catholics in the territory. The Irish gave their names to such towns as Derrynane and Green Isle, while the Germans of St. Paul established a church of their own in 1855.[32] New parishes were soon organized in St. Anthony Village (German), Wabasha, and Chaska, while new churches were built in Hastings and Marysburg. But life was rough and primitive, and most immigrants were pathetically poor.

The lives of Father Frederick Baraga and Father Francis X. Pierz stand out as exemplars of the era. Both were born in Carniola, Slovenia (later part of Yugoslavia), and both showed a profound interest in the American Indian. Baraga came to the United States through the Leopoldinen-Stiftung, and was soon sent to the Ottawas of Arbre Croche (Harbor Springs), Michigan.[33] By 1843, he had established several missions for the Chippewas around Lake Superior and a mission on Keweenaw Bay for newly arrived immigrants from the East. He was appointed vicarate apostolic of the entire Upper Peninsula in 1853 and became that area's first bishop in 1857. Baraga was responsible for the establishment of the Church in upper Michigan, and his voluminous writings are still valued as an aid to the study of Indian languages. Pierz came to the United States in 1834 to work with his countryman, Baraga. From 1835 to 1871 he labored among the Indians of Michigan, Wisconsin, and Minnesota. From a base at Crow Wing, Minnesota, Pierz worked unceasingly for the conversion and betterment of the Chippewa Indians. He encouraged German and Slovene Catholics to fill up the land vacated by the Indian, to "bear out the opinion that Germans prove to be the best farmers and the best Christians in America."[34] He also brought the Benedictines to Minnesota, an order that would soon devote itself entirely to the German Catholics of that region. Pierz, who outlived Baraga by more than fourteen years, died in Slovenia at the age of eighty-eight in 1880.

BUILDING AND CONSOLIDATION, 1865–1914

General Developments

By 1865, the Catholic Church had emerged as a distinctive force in the United States. Parishes, missions, and stations had been established in all parts of the Midwest. The history of this era is one of building and consolidation—building the vital institutions that were needed at this time and consolidating the parishes that had already been established. The clergy itself was a mosaic of nationalities often working under several bishops. Some succumbed to the dreariness and harshness of the times and left the priesthood; others became drunkards or adventurers. Bishop Martin Marty, O.S.B., the first Vicar Apostolic of the Dakota

Territory, noted that "I do not want anything to do with a drinker, for I have always had bad luck from such people . . . it is my wish to give the clergy enough time so that they will enter upon the ministry fully equipped for liturgical and pastoral duties." Bishops such as Marty had to be astute psychologists in dealing with such an amalgam of different personalities. For example, of the thirty-nine priests active in South Dakota in the 1880s, more than half were foreign born.[35] Thus, the Church that emerged after the Civil War was a predominantly immigrant Church. National parishes dotted the hills and plains of Midwest America. Indeed, the history of the Midwestern Church is largely a history of these parishes.

But the Church that emerged after the Civil War was also an urban Church, for it was the towns and cities of the Midwest that most attracted the immigrant. Ohio, Indiana, Michigan, and Illinois changed from predominantly frontier states to economic powers.[36] Let us look at the history of Illinois and Chicago as an example of this change. Between 1848 and 1871, the railroads crossed Illinois like a giant web. The state's population grew from 851,470 in 1850, to 2,539,891 in 1870. Towns such as Springfield, Alton, Peoria, Cairo, Quincy, Belleville, Beardstown, and Ottawa became thriving cities during these decades. But it was Chicago that grew the most.[37] The city numbered 29,963 in 1850; it was a metropolis of 109,260 by 1860. Foreign-born immigrants were 50% (54,586) of the total population. Germans were the largest foreign-born element, with 22,230 inhabitants; the Irish followed with 19,889. Chicago was still a frontier town in the sense that dysentery and tuberculosis claimed hundreds of victims. But native and foreign born alike literally raised the streets out of the mud in 1857; they built sewers and public works to make life more amendable; and they manned the factories and warehouses that made Chicago the packing center of the country by 1860.[38]

The decades between 1870 and 1900 were critical for Illinois and Chicago. The state as a whole changed from a largely rural area to an urban manufacturing center. Twenty-eight farm counties lost population between 1870 and 1890, as more and more immigrants were drawn to Chicago. By 1890, 28.7% of the total state population lived in Chicago. The city grew from 298,977 in 1870, to 1,698,575 in 1900. The immigrant population continued to flow into the city: Germans, Poles, and Italians. Chicago was America for these immigrants, a place where they could nourish their own traditions, but, at the same time, find the dream that was America. Germans increased from 52,316 in 1870, to 170,738 in 1900. Czechs, Slovaks, and Hungarians were also present at the beginning of the twentieth century. By 1910, first- and second-generation immigrants accounted for 77% of Chicago's total population.[39] Max Weber noted the "maddening mixture of Chicago's peoples" in 1904: "The Greek shining the Yank's shoes for five cents, the German acting as his waiter, the Irishman managing his politics, and the Italian digging his dirty ditches."[40]

The Church grew with the city—new parishes sprang from older ones, as Chicago's Catholic immigrants filled up the vacant prairies and farmlands of this expanding metropolis. By 1870, Chicago numbered twenty-seven parishes averaging 11,074 per parish. Irish communities spread north and south, as the men of Eire and their families bettered their lives. St. Patrick's begot St. Jarlath's on the West Side, while St. Columbkille's spawned Annunciation Parish on the North Side.[41] There were 39,988 foreign-born Irish in Chicago by 1870. Germans, who numbered 52,316 the same year, were now the leading foreign-born nationality.[42] They already boasted five national parishes—St. Joseph, St. Peter, St. Francis of Assisi, St. Michael, and St. Boniface. Other ethnic parishes included Notre Dame de Chicago (French, 1865) and St. Wenceslaus (Bohemian, 1866).

Rt. Rev. Patrick A. Feehan guided Chicago Catholicism through the 1880s and 1890s. His greatest accomplishment was to reconcile the various ethnic and national forces in his archdiocese. Feehan was an American pragmatist, who sought practical solutions to Chicago's problems.[43] While Pope Leo XIII decreed that ethnic parishes could only exist for the *first* generation immigrant, Feehan, recognizing their necessity, supervised the establishment and continuance of a vast network of ethnic communities. He managed to placate the three most powerful immigrant groups within his city—the Irish, the Germans, and the Poles. For the Irish, he supported nationalistic societies devoted to the liberation of Ireland. And for the Germans and Poles, he established fifty-three ethnic parishes on the North and South sides of the city. Feehan described his immigrant Church on the Silver Jubilee of his episcopal ordination in 1890:

> But though speaking many tongues and representing many races there is one common language which you all speak . . . I believe in the Holy Catholic Church. . . .
> As the mountain streams uniting form at length the broad, deep river, so those streams of population coming from many sources will make great people. Strong, free, intelligent, Catholic. . . . They will be always found among the best and most devoted of our citizens.[44]

This speech, like many others on this occasion, shows us a Church that was in the very first stages of Americanization. Immigrant groups were still strong and vital, as they fostered their own languages and traditions. Germans, Frenchmen, and Italians all vied for a place in the Catholic Church. Archbishop Feehan, who recognized these differences, allowed each nationality to develop its own brand of Catholicism. But he also realized that these groups could not remain separate forever; that they would one day merge into a united American people. Feehan's genius, which lay in his ability to recognize these differences, effectively reconciled disparate and often feuding elements. When Feehan died in 1902, he left Chicago a legacy of 137 parishes, 566 priests, and over a million Catholics. These parishes included sixty-one national communities—twenty-seven German, fifteen Polish, eight Bohemian, four French, four Italian, and three Lithuanian.[45]

Chicago remained a city of immigrants through World War I. Immigration reached a four-year peak from 1911 to 1914, when 29,813 foreign-born people entered Chicago. In 1910, first- and second-generation immigrants accounted for 77% of Chicago's population; the foreign born alone were 35% of the total number. And Catholics were more than a third of the total population. German foreign stock (33% of whom were Catholic) accounted for approximately 25% of the total population in 1890. In the same year, Irish stock (76% Catholic) accounted for 13%, and Polish ancestry (97% Catholic), 5.5%.[46] By 1900, German parishes averaged 7,302 members per parish, while Italian parishes were somewhat behind with 4,002 parishioners per parish.[47] Indeed, at the turn of the century, ethnic parishes were the strongest component of Chicago Catholicism.

Rt. Rev. James Quigley led the Chicago Archdiocese through the first decades of the new century.[48] Educated in Austria and Rome, Quigley understood better than most bishops the plight of the newcomer. He always took a deep interest in ethnic minorities, and preached to them in German, Italian, Polish, or French. As he said, "a young people, a people of composite stock, we have kinship with many different nations, but we are not identical with any of them, and are developing a separate national life." While recognizing the need for temporary separation, Quigley also encouraged Americanization:

> Undoubtedly temporary segregation has its advantages; it protects to some extent, religion and race. It is impossible, however, that such a status could continue. The friction resulting from association with other races will gradually disintegrate these colonies . . . the importance of having all nationalities touch at certain points with the great Catholic body is apparent.[49]

Quigley consistently opposed immigration restrictions prejudicial to all foreigners. He headed the Catholic Colonization Society, which attempted to direct immigrants to agricultural communities. He was a member of the national Liberal Immigration League, which sought to counteract prejudice against foreigners.

Chicago remained an immigrant city throughout Quigley's twelve-year episcopate. Rev. M. J. Madaj noted that "Chicago Catholics boasted that the archdiocese had more Irish Catholics than Dublin, more German Catholics than Berlin, more Polish Catholics than Warsaw, more Bohemian Catholics than Prague, and more Italian Catholics than Pisa."[50] Indeed, Quigley was a builder of immigrant churches. The city, which numbered 211 ecclesiastical communities by 1915, included numerous ethnic communities. There were thirty-six German parishes, thirty-three Polish, ten Italian, nine Lithuanian, and eight Slovenian parishes by the end of his episcopate.[51] While Quigley did establish two new German parishes in Chicago, it was the Italians whom he understood best. Having lived in their country for four years, he sympathized with their varying problems and understood their need to continue ethnic traditions. He erected twenty new Italian churches within the archdiocese during his episcopate alone. He also established numerous organizations, societies, and educational institutions to support parish life. He established parish boards, which included lay trustees, to supervise parish finances. He also divided larger parishes into smaller ones, as he founded seventy-four new parishes between 1903 and 1915. It was an episcopate marked by growth and consolidation, a time when Chicago Catholicism welcomed its immigrant flocks, and made them a part of the city and the Church.

The story we have traced in Illinois and Chicago was repeated again and again across the Midwest. Strong bishops, who governed at times even stronger priests, built the churches, schools, convents, and rectories needed at that time. The history of Holy Rosary Parish, in Darlington, Wisconsin, is illustrative of the entire period.[52] Laid out in 1859, Darlington was a village of no more than one-hundred in 1865. Holy Rosary, which began as an Irish mission of Willow Springs Church, received its first pastor in 1864. Rev. A. T. David immediately set out to build a church, rectory, and school. But it was Rev. Dean Hannon, from County Kerry, Ireland, who put his personal stamp on the parish for the next thirty-five years. Educated at Notre Dame and ordained in 1852, Hannon "was a commanding figure among our group of either priests or laymen—tall, sturdy, dignified . . . he kept the reigns of the parish in his own hands until the end." Hannon was typical of the priests of his time, men who would risk everything to establish God's church in the wilderness. Hannon once rode a railroad handcar all night just to reach a mission station in time. He built the church institutions that were vitally needed for this era. A 1905 expense report noted that $1,194.50 came from pew rent, with $800.00 going for the pastor's salary. Lay societies were minimal, with only the Altar Society and a branch of the Catholic Knights extant in 1904. Indeed, the laity, both men and women, played a subordinate role under Hannon's direction. Hannon celebrated his fiftieth ordination anniversary in 1902, "and the very high esteem in which he was held by his fellow citizens, non-Catholic as well as his own people, was shown by the active part they took in making this event a success."[53]

The history of Holy Rosary Parish is typical of the late nineteenth century. Strong pastors governed people who were mostly concerned with establishing new lives in the Midwest. Minnesota continued to develop as railroads connected it with Chicago and the Great Lakes. Most of the Irish, Germans, Poles, and Bohemians who came to the state were Catholic. The Chicago Land Society sent a group of thirty Germans west of St. Paul, to a region near Le Sueur. Disappointed with the site, they settled in present-day New Ulm, a city that would later become an important German Catholic center in its own right.[54] Northern Minnesota, the "land of a thousand lakes," grew as well. The area around the upper Mississippi and St. Croix valleys filled with Poles, Irishmen, Germans, and Scandinavians. By 1888, there were more than 20,000 Catholics in Duluth alone, with 2,000

Catholic Indians scattered across the vast north. By 1889, when the region became an autonomous diocese, there were thirty-two parishes and ten stations, with five parochial schools numbering 500 pupils. National parishes flourished, as each ethnic group set up its own parish to perpetuate its language and culture. For example, Father Elie Theillon led a group of French Canadians for forty-seven years at Gentilly, Minnesota. Not content with pastoral duties alone, he began a diary association, built a cheese factory, and made his parish one of the wealthiest in Polk County.[55]

Although John P. Ireland, the first Archbishop of St. Paul, was more known as a national spokesman for American causes, he did not leave his own diocese unattended.[56] Consecrated coadjutor bishop of St. Paul in 1875, Ireland immediately began a policy of buying up railroad lands (more than 75,000 acres) and colonizing Catholics on them. The towns of De Graff and Clontarf in Swift County began as just such colonies, with Ireland supplying a priest, a church, and even an immigration house for temporary shelter. Such was Ireland's zeal that he once had five carloads of lumber railed to Morris, and then overland to Graceville, to build a church. One of his most successful colonies was Ghent, a town settled in the early 1880s by Belgian immigrants. The Belgian farmers proved so successful that their descendents now own most of Lyons County. Indeed, the entire state of Minnesota grew enormously during Ireland's tenure (1875–1918). In 1889, five dioceses were carved out of Ireland's original domain—St. Cloud, Duluth, and Winona, in Minnesota; and Jamestown and Sioux Falls in the new states of North and South Dakota, respectively. New churches were hurriedly built (". . . if the truth be told, without always the highest aesthetic standards. . . .") as the population surged forward. By 1910, Minnesota numbered more than 2 million inhabitants.[57]

But Ireland's policy of buying land before Catholics were actually settled on it was not always conducive to growth. Churches were often built before there were enough parishioners to support them. In South Dakota alone, there were more than 1,600 congregations for a population of only 328,000 (1890). Towns of 600 boasted six or more churches. It was not uncommon to find a German Lutheran, a Danish Lutheran, and a Swedish Lutheran church within blocks of each other (or even on the same block). And while Catholic parishes did not show the same degree of fragmentation, they did divide according to language and nationality. The experience of the Dakotas was that a church with no priest did little good, while a priest on Sunday with no church did much good. And the ideal was a priest, a church, and a school.[58]

The Dakota Territory opened up as well.[59] Indian treaties between 1851 and 1873 opened the region to further settlement. And while the Sioux continued to cause problems, the railroads inched westward until they crossed the Missouri River in 1879. The Great Northern pushed further west during the 1880s, as new settlers established themselves in Jamestown, Bismarck, and the smaller towns of Minot, Williston, and Mandan. The discovery of gold in the Black Hills brought thousands to South Dakota. Yankton served as principal supply depot, with the towns of Custer, Deadwood, Lead City, and Rapid City growing quickly at this time. Twenty-four million acres of farmland were opened to settlers in the southeastern part of the territory by 1878, as the population increased from 135,000 in 1880 to 350,000 in 1885. When both states entered the Union on the same day (November 2) in 1889, North Dakota numbered 190,000 (excluding the Indian population), while South Dakota numbered 325,000.[60]

The Church grew with the territory. Bishop Martin Marty, appointed first vicar of the Dakotas in 1880, found himself in a wild and sparsely populated land. There were but a few national Catholic communities in the entire territory. But immigration soon changed this situation. The Irish were one of the first to arrive. Father Jeremiah Trecy founded Saint John's City (Jackson), South Dakota, in 1855. Ministering to the needs of a large Irish colony at Fort Randall, Trecy heard confessions, baptized, and noted that "I have never yet . . . seen a single quadruped, save a wolf, and of fowls, none." The Irish were also among the first settlers of Mandan, Dickinson, Bismarck, and Minot, North Dakota. German Catholics came from as far east as Ohio, settling in Glenn Ullin and Richardton in the 1880s. A colony of fifty Austrians recreated their picturesque village of Zell on the grassy plains of Redfield, South Dakota.[61] When Bishop Marty visited the parish in 1886, the townsfolk erected a triumphal arch three miles outside the city to greet him. Young men rode prancing horses while bells rang and guns fired.

But it was the German-Russians who had the greatest impact on the territory. They were Germans who had settled around the Lower Volga River and the Black Sea in Russia during the late eighteenth century, but were forced from their homes about one hundred years later by Czar Alexander II.[62] Some went to South America, while others headed for America's heartland—the Dakotas, Kansas, Nebraska, and Missouri. The largest contingent occupied the triangle of land between Aberdeen (South Dakota), Hettinger (North Dakota), and Rugby (North Dakota). Bishop Marty secured the services of the Benedictines to minister to these largely Catholic people. Between Mandan and Medora alone, there were forty-four stations extant in 1881. The Benedictines served a scattered immigrant flock throughout the 1880s, from Richardton and Minot in North Dakota, to Hettinger and Aberdeen in South Dakota.

Father Vincent Wehrle, a Swiss-born Benedictine, was the apostle to these German people.[63] Wehrle came to North Dakota in 1888, and began a series of missions at Richardton, Glenn Ullin, Crown Butte, and a number of settlements in Emmons and MacIntosh counties. He built Saint Gall's monastery at Devil Lake, to provide more missionaries for the German-Russians of North Dakota. Writing to Bishop John Shanley, the first bishop of Fargo, he noted that "it is too bad these Catholic people (German-Russians) cannot have a priest residing permanently among them. If taken care of, they will become a pillar of your diocese.'' Wehrle thus became Shanley's troubleshooter, a man who often intervened between German Catholics and their pastors. He was sent to Richardton in 1898 to settle a dispute between a non-German pastor and his German flock. Shanley persuaded Wehrle to move his monastery to Richardton, "where you will be in the midst of these people." Such was Wehrle's influence that he and his fellow Benedictines established fifty-five parishes and serviced more than 115 by the turn of the century. The Church grew enormously, from five parishes with resident pastors in 1889, to thirty in 1910; from three mission chapels, to forty-seven mission chapels; and from fourteen mission stations, to forty-two stations. Between 1907 and 1908, fifty-eight churches were dedicated in North Dakota alone.[64]

German-Russian parishes clung too tenaciously to their ethnicity. Both young and old alike spoke German through the nineteenth and twentieth centuries. A typical home was brightly colored with framed baptismal and Confirmation certificates on the wall; marriage celebrations lasted for days, while burials attracted large crowds. But unaccustomed to paying pew rent or supporting the church in any way, they often wreaked havoc on parish finances. Catholic congregations with a large percentage of *Russlanddeutsche* often needed the skills of a diplomat to maintain normalcy between these "eastern" immigrants and ther Irish or Bohemian neighbors. Some parishes agreed to give half the church to the German-Russians, if they would contribute half of the annual funds to maintain the church. But this did not always work; for example, in Mandan, Father Daniel V. Collins found that "it is simply financially impossible (to build a new rectory) unless I have the aid of the entire congregation. The English-speaking people are not very enthusiastic about the matter. The seventy Russian-German families of the congregation refuse to pay any pew rent this year."[65]

The German population of North and South Dakota grew to such an extent that they were given a "diocese" of their own. When Bishop Shanley died in 1908, Archbishop Ireland and the other bishops of the metropolitan region decided to create a separate diocese for the German-Russian people. The reasons were essentially ethnic, for "this division of the regions seems most fitting both by reason of the railroads that run there and by reason of the language which the settlers there use." Now Abbot Wehrle noted that "we need a bishop who has a warm heart for these German-Russians and Hungarians. It may not be necessary for him to know the language, but he must be able to love and understand them." Thus, it happened that the Bismarck Diocese was created in 1910, with approximately 25,000 Catholics and Abbot Wehrle as its first bishop. And while the English-speaking clergy feared his appointment, the people welcomed him as one of their own. One of Wehrle's first acts was to summon the Ursaline Sisters from Ahrweiler, Germany, to open more parochial schools. The bishop wrote to them: "Dakota is a rich field of labor and great promise; it does not offer natural scenery, but if one seeks souls, one finds in our German-Russian and German-Hungarian people a race of men that has a capacity for the good and the best. Under the severest tests, these people have been true to their Catholicism and their German character."[66] German newspapers were established to promote German culture (*Der Volksfreund* in 1904, and the *Nord Dakota Herald* in 1907), and allowed Wehrle to keep in touch with his immigrant flock. At the dawn of a new age, the Bismarck Diocese was a uniquely German diocese.

The Church in Nebraska and Kansas developed as well.[67] While Nebraska was known for its "treelessness and lack of water," Kansas had no roads "except those which lead to Oregon, to California, and to the different forts." Between 1854 and 1857, Nebraska became prey for Eastern speculators, while Kansas was the stage for abolitionists and slave holders. Most of the early inhabitants of Nebraska were native born: of 28,826 inhabitants in 1860, 22,475 were native born. And most of the foreign born came from Iowa and Illinois to the east. Kansas was considerably larger, with 107,206 inhabitants in 1860.[68] But most foreigners (particularly Germans) preferred the more attractive states of Iowa, Missouri, and Illinois to the east.

The *Catholic Almanac of 1855* reported no more than 3,000 Catholics scattered across the vast plains of the Kansas-Nebraska territory—a small Irish colony near Omaha City, a German settlement in the South Platte, and a French outpost in the southeast. The same year, Bishop John B. Miege, first vicar of the Kansas-Nebraska territory, moved his residence from St. Louis to Leavenworth, Kansas. There were few Catholics and Miege found it extremely difficult to attract priests to his vicarate. Leavenworth, the largest city in the territory, remained the most significant Catholic center, a "mixture of all nations, colors, and so-called religions."[69] By 1857, there were more than 1,200 parishioners in Meige's parish, and, by 1858, there were enough Germans in the city to establish a separate parish for them. Like most new churches of the day, the Germans built a combination church/school, with the church on the second floor and a school/rectory on the first.

While Catholicism was a distinctive minority in Kansas and Nebraska, the parishes that did arise were predominantly ethnic. Father Henry Lempke, O.S.B., believed that the Church should first organize colonies and then establish parishes. He led a group of German Catholics to Doniphan, Kansas, where he immediately set up a church and residence on lots built from credit. By 1860, there were four small parishes in Doniphan alone.[70] Indeed, Germans settled throughout the territory in the years preceding the Civil War, and where there were Germans there were parishes as well. Of the fourteen priests in the vicariate in 1859, ten were Germans, with one Italian, a Savoyard, a Frenchman, and an Irishman completing the lot. The tenuousness of Catholicism at this time was succinctly expressed by Bishop Miege:

> What a sad spectacle . . . that so many thousands of Catholics should be abandoned to the mercy of the enemy without instruction, without encouragement in the midst of Protestants whose every effort tends solely to pervert the parents by ridicule and the children though their school . . . zealous priests and a great number will be necessary. Those who are zealous do not wish to risk their vocation in a country where they have to remain five or six months without confession; adventurous or suspended priests who are never lacking it seems present themselves in great number—but experience has already proved to me that it is better not to have any than to have scandalous ones.[71]

And when gold fever struck the territory in the 1850s, Miege did all in his power "to dissuade the Catholic from going, convinced as I am that peril to soul and body is almost inevitable there, and that for one who will succeed, there are at least fifty who will be ruined forever."[72]

Kansas entered the Union in 1861, and was followed (albeit unwillingly) by Nebraska in 1867. New settlers spread through the vast plains, and despite the prairie fires, the hordes of locusts and grasshoppers, and the fierce winters, they made the land their own. As the railroads inched across the vast prairie, homesteaders brought their own languages and traditions with them. Native Americans, like William Sheridan, returned to Kansas even though he had made good money in Ohio, for, as he put it, there was "no future for a large family there—no chance to get lands and homes."[73] Saint Mary's, in Kansas, was the hub of Catholic activity—scores of missions were established around it. A Father A. Cumortier, an early Kansas missionary, had to ride more than a hundred miles to visit all the stations around St. Mary's, the largest being a group of 200 Catholics at Solomon. By 1870, the Kansas missions stretched from St. Bridget's on the Nebraska line to Junction City, Humboldt, and Fort Scott. Omaha was the hub of Catholic activity in Nebraska, with scores of missions established around it. A young German cleric noted that "the majority of Catholics here [Columbus, Nebraska] know only English. But in the missions I have found various languages and heard confessions in English, German, French, Italian, Bohemian, and even Dutch." By 1874, there were eleven parishes in the South Platte region of Nebraska alone, with resident pastors in Nebraska City, Plattsmouth, Falls City, Lincoln, and Crete. Both states continued to develop until the end of the century. By 1874, Kansas had more than 2,000 miles of railroad, and, by 1885, all railroad lands in Nebraska were sold. Catholicism developed accordingly, bringing with it new parishes and missions. By 1885, Nebraska numbered forty-nine parishes, stretching from the North Platte region to the southern part of the state. Kansas, which was raised to a diocese in 1877, numbered thirty-five parishes, forty-five missions, sixty priests, and 45,000 Catholics that very year. Nebraska, which developed more slowly, numbered forty-nine parishes and sixty-four priests in 1885.[74]

The story of St. Philip Neri Parish, in Osawatomie, Kansas, is indicative of Catholic life on the Western frontier.[75] Potawatomi Indians, who had moved to Kansas from Indiana around 1837, were the first Catholics in the area. They built the first church in what was to become the town of Osawatomie. New Englanders organized the town in 1855, but there were a few Catholics among the first settlers. Father Ivo Schacht said the first Mass at the home of a Mrs. Remington in 1858. The town fathers donated land for a church, but the plot remained unclaimed for three decades. During that time, Osawatomie was simply a station of Paola. But, in 1889, Catholics and non-Catholics alike contributed to the establishment of St. Philip's Church. A 30 × 60-foot frame building was erected with an altar from Knox County, Illinois. The first families of the parish included such names as the Franklins, Dolans, Hanleys, and Browns. In fact, "to the women of Osawatomie goes most of the credit for the first church in that town. Little by little they got the money for necessities." They sponsored raffles and gave balls to secure the success of St. Philip's. Indeed, it was the laity that kept the church going for decades; as one contemporary described them: "These good people, busy about many things, cheered the drooping spirits of the lonely and weary priest who had not whereon to lay his head." But the "parish" remained without a permanent pastor until 1918. Priests came to St. Philip's from Paola for thirty years, first by horse and buggy, and then by the Missouri Pacific Railroad. But, as Father Kinsella noted in 1914: "Catholics will multiply; they will come from the farms around and the industries within your town. The grime and sweat and tears of eight years will have their reward some day." Indeed, the plains and wide-open spaces of Kansas and Nebraska were filled with such stories of men and women who gave all to keep their faith alive.

Both plains states were inundated with Germans and Bohemians from the Old World. There were numerous German settlers in Nebraska and Kansas after statehood. The first distinctly national church in Nebraska was a German church built in Omaha in 1868. Unlike most native Americans, Germans were wary of having Mass said in homes, and immediately set out to build churches and schools. In 1876, Bishop James O'Connor of Omaha noted that "the Germans, Bohemians, and Poles need immediate attention. I have no need just now of an Irish community." Thus, it was that the Franciscans of Teutopolis, Illinois, came to Nebraska. They immediately built a monastery in Columbus and established parishes throughout Platte County. Indeed, Columbus resembled a small European village, with four national parishes within four miles of each other. A young German cleric described Columbus as an English-speaking town, but "in the missions I have found various languages and hear confessions in English, German, French, Italian, Bohemian, and even Dutch." And a Father P. J. Erlach noted that "my church is frequented by all kinds of Protestants, Mormons, Methodists, etc., for all without exception are accustomed to go to sermons no matter by whom they are preached."[76]

Bohemians began to arrive north of the Platte River shortly after the Civil War. Unused to the drabness of Western life, they often migrated from one settlement to another. It wasn't until 1871 that the first Bohemian priest, Father Francis Bobal, came to Nebraska. Unlike the Germans who often lived next to them, Bohemians shunned organized parish life. Most were pathetically poor and balked at the idea of contributing to the church. In Wilbur, Nebraska, fourteen families left the parish congregation when a missionary preached that God's laws had to be kept in the New World as well as the Old. By the time the controversy was over, practically all the Bohemian families had left the Catholic parish for a separatist sect.[77]

The development of the Church in the Midwest was as varied as its cities and plains. The eastern states, Ohio, Indiana, Michigan, and Illinois, changed from predominantly agricultural to industrial powers, while the western states, like the Dakotas, Kansas, and Nebraska, remained primarily agricultural. And parish life developed accordingly. In the east, the Church became an urban Church, as parishes quickly spread through such cities as Cincinnati, Cleveland, and Detroit. Chicago was an exemplar of all, as parochial life increased from twenty-seven parishes in 1870, to 211 in 1915. And almost half of these communities were ethnic parishes. Irish, Germans, Poles, and Italians made this city their own, a place to make roots and establish their own local societies and congregations. Farther west, the Church was a loose network of diocesan and ethnic parishes, spread across the vast wilderness that was then the heartland of America. But these states also beckoned the newcomer, as Easterners, Germans, Bohemians, and many others, following the advice of Horace Greeley, went west to seek (if not fame and fortune) a better life for themselves and their families.

Clergy, Laity, and Youth

The bishops of the Midwest were often pioneers, who accepted the challenges of the frontier and were willing to adapt to it. They realized that for the Church to survive, it must first root itself firmly in the soil of the Midwest. Bishops such as Foley of Chicago, Ireland of St. Paul, Richard Gilmour of Cleveland (1872–1891), and John Lancaster Spalding of Peoria (1877–1916) encouraged the laity to further its own self-awareness. A group of laymen in St. Paul formed the Catholic Truth Society to respond to attacks against the Church.[78] And hundreds of laymen and laywomen were involved in holding two Catholic Lay Congresses in 1889 and 1893, respectively. Further out on the frontier, Bishop Martin Marty initiated several Indian congresses and established Catholic Action groups of men and women in the late 1880s. The St. Joseph and St. Mary societies proved so successful that they were imitated on other reservations. But Marty's ideas were years ahead of their time and would only reach fruition in the post-Vatican II era.[79]

By the end of the century, the gap between cleric and lay had only widened. In 1888, an anonymous layman asked: "Is there not a certain exaggerated feeling of condescension toward the laity, a certain feeling of exclusive possession in the Church displayed among a large number of the priesthood?" Papal condemnations of Americanism (1899) and Modernism (1907) stifled any lay initiative. And, as Bishop Spalding noted in 1902: "Our great sees are largely in the hands of men who have lost their vigor of mind and body." Indeed, the great leaders of the nineteenth century had given way to mediocre bishops of the twentieth. The *Catholic World* noted that "priestly happiness consists in being let alone by the people and promoted by the bishop."[80] The actions of Bishop John Shanley in North Dakota echo the period. Shanley had been bothered for some time by pastors who insisted that he, an Irish bishop, was opposed to German and French ethnics. To respond to these accusations, he called a laymen's convention in Fargo in 1895. With more than 600 attending, Shanley essentially lectured the parish delegates on their place in the Church, and "from the convention dates the growth of the diocese of Fargo. Priests and people knew . . . that order must be preserved."[81]

Statistics indicate that there was an ethnic factor in lay participation. Germans relied heavily on lay trustees to administer the finances of the parish. Reliable data from the Midwest indicate that Germans were much more likely to establish such a system than the Irish surrounding them. While less than 50% of Irish parishes had trustee systems, more than 72% of German parishes did. From 1860 to 1900, German parishes having trustees ranged from 49% to 46%, while those not having such a system dropped to only 25%. We can conclude that Germans were unique among all ethnic groups in establishing a strong trustee system wherever they established parishes. It was often the laity who organized a parish, staffed its ever-present school, and ran the financial affairs of the parish. More than the Irish who preceded them, German pastors often had to contend with a vocal and sometimes belligerent laity.[82]

Another indicator of lay involvement is parish societies. Between 1800 and 1860, more than 70% of all parish societies were devotional, with the vast majority (95%) being women's groups. On the other hand, mutual-aid societies, which were present in one form or another in all parishes, were exclusively male (100%). It is interesting to note that of all the women's devotional groups, more than 21% were for young girls. These statistics indicate a male-dominated laity, with women (and young girls) occupying a subordinate position. Woman's place was clearly in the home, with her work in the church limited to devotional and charitable pursuits. These statistics remained fairly constant, although women did begin to move into mutual-aid societies by the end of the century (17% of the total membership by 1890). As the new century dawned, the development of the Holy Name and St. Vincent de Paul societies changed these figures dramatically. Men began to move into devotional and charitable work, and for the first time surpassed women in these endeavors. There was an ethnic factor here as well, for Germans had a much greater organizational life than the Irish or other ethnic groups. While Germans were more inclined to devotional and mutual-aid societies, Irish showed a greater interest in instructional and social justice groups. The statistics simply confirm that the Irish, with a built-in knowledge of English, became "Americans" much faster than their Teutonic neighbors.[83]

Catholic schools were *the* primary means of keeping the young faithful to the Church. The tone was set in 1829, when the First Provincial Council of American Bishops stated that "it was absolutely necessary that schools be established in which the young may be taught the principles of faith and morality, while being instructed in letters." This theme, re-echoed for more than 150 years, went unchallenged until the Vatican Council II seriously undermined it.[84] Not until the development of the Catholic Youth Organization (CYO) in the 1930s was there a comparable force for youth within American Catholicism. Bishop James Trobec, of St. Cloud, Minnesota, noted that "moral training, or the education of the will, is one of the fundamental aims of the Christian school . . . in public schools, which are frequented by pupils of different creeds, religion cannot be taught. It is simply impossible, hence the necessity of private schools for those who wish to receive a Christian education."[85]

Catholic schools were often the first schools in a district. The laity often took the initiative in organizing such schools and employed reputable laymen to teach in them. But as religious orders became more available after the Civil War, nuns soon replaced these early lay leaders. Most priests realized that without a parochial school there would often be a corresponding loss of faith. A priest in Yankton put it well when he said: "Don't say a word about a new church until every child in this parish is a regular attendant of the parochial school. *That* is the church we are building."[86] Indeed, the school often became the center of parish life, and it was often the need for school boundaries that led many bishops to establish definitive parish limits.

The story of the parochial school system in Kansas is illustrative of all the parochial school systems in the Midwest.[87] Even before it had become a state, the Benedictines built a college and seminary at Doniphan to provide a continuous supply of priests for the territory. The parish connected with the seminary erected a parochial school, a day school, and a boarding academy by 1863. As white settlers moved in after the Civil War, they replaced Indian missions with their own schools. Bishop Miege asked his priests to establish Sunday schools at every station, with lay associates often assigned to carry on the program. The *Ludwig Missionsverein* and other immigrant organizations helped finance schools in Lawrence and Topeka. Where a school district was entirely Catholic, as in Atchison and several missions around Osage, Catholic teachers were hired for the district school. Bishop Ludwig Fink, O.S.B., the first bishop of Leavenworth, was so eager for parochial schools that he placed resident pastors in missions so that schools could be organized. By 1878, there were thirteen parochial schools in Kansas, ranging in size from 600 at the Cathedral in Leavenworth, to thirty in Salina.

Bringing with them a rich educational heritage, Germans practically established the parochial school system in the Midwest.[88] They were so concerned for the establishment of such schools that they usually built them before their churches. It was particularly important that religious subjects be taught in German. As early as 1853, the parochial schools of New York adopted this method of instruction. German parochial schools flourished through the nineteenth century, as over 95% of German parishes had such institutions by 1914. Midwestern statistics clearly indicate that German parishes had the greatest commitment to parochial schools. More than 65% of all German parishes had established such schools within two years of the founding of the parish; and after ten years, 86% of all such parishes had established schools. This contrasts sharply with the fact that only 27.5% of Irish parishes had schools two years after their founding. By the outbreak of World War I, more than 60% of all parishes surveyed had constructed parochial schools.[89]

The Ethnic Parish

The history of the Catholic parish in the Midwest is to a large extent (although not exclusively) the history of the ethnic parish. For as we have just seen, the first parishes in many states were ethnic parishes. It is my thesis that these parishes served as "way-stations" of ethnicity and Americanization.[90] The parish was the focus of immigrants' daily life and the principal institution that carried on their native traditions, but it was also the indispensable force that pushed its members into mainstream American life. The language of priests and teachers, the parish bulletins, the extensive network of elementary and high school education, all served to affirm the past, but, at the same time, helped the immigrant accept the society in which he had settled. Bishops such as Feehan and Quigley of Chicago, Marty of the Dakotas, and Gilmour of Cleveland accepted the ethnic parish as a necessity of the day. It was within the ethnic parish that immigrants struggled to keep what they had and learn from the new. The dioceses of the Midwest pushed them to be both American and Catholic—and the parish was the way-station.

The Irish. As we have seen, the Irish were among the first immigrants to settle in the Midwest. They helped build the railroads that connected Ohio in the east to Kansas and in the west to Nebraska. Census data in 1900 indicate that Illinois had by far the greatest number of Irish foreign born, 114,563; in fact, Illinois was the fourth largest Irish state in the Union at that time. And Chicago, the second city of the nation, accounted for 73,192 of these Irish.[91] But with their reputation for drink and their Catholicism, the Irish were not always welcome. The *Chicago*

Tribune asked in 1855: "Who does not know that the most depraved, debased, worthless, and irredeemable drunkards and sots within the community are Irish Catholics? . . . Who does not know that the influence of the Church of Rome is always directed in favor of drunkenness?"[92] Indeed, Catholicism and Irish ethnicity fused into an almost indivisible unity. As Thomas Brown noted, there is difficulty "in differentiating between the specifically Irish and specifically Catholic aspects of their lives. They had emerged into the modern world from a past in which Catholicism had played a stronger role than among any other people of Western Europe."[93]

It is no wonder then that one of the principal institutions of the Irish was the ethnic parish. We have already seen that Irish settlements dotted the Midwest at mid-century. But Chicago alone had a significant number, for it was in the cities of the Midwest that the Irish principally settled.[94] One of the first Catholic communities in Chicago was St. Patrick's, at 718 West Adams Street. As families moved southwest along Archer Avenue, the city's earliest bishops established more and more Irish parishes: St. Bridget, St. John, and St. James sprang up from older parishes. The South Side attracted the largest number, as the Union Stock Yards provided work and security for thousands. Between 1880 and 1886, six Irish parishes were established in the twenty-ninth, thirtieth, and thirty-second wards; more than 100,000 lived in this area alone.

Although the Irish parish was not a national parish, it functioned just like one. In fact, the Irish clung to their parishes long after they had left their original ghettos, for the parish provided a "sense of belonging," a place where friends, mates, and other Irishmen met and kept friendships.[95] The parish supported such organizations as the Ancient Order of Hibernians and the Friends of Irish Freedom. Irish-born pastors tried to organize Irish Catholics through the parish. By 1893, 10% of Chicago's registered voters were Irish born. The Irish also supported the parochial school, which was a means to enter American life as well as a source of Irish history. Irish "high schools" evolved to provide even greater access to the American dream. In 1891, the Irish Christian Brothers established De La Salle Institute as an originally Irish institution. By 1897, St. James, St. Elizabeth, and St. Gabriel parishes had established their own parochial high schools. These schools provided a ready corp of public school teachers, for, by 1910, Irish-Catholic public school teachers were a common sight. And, finally, the Irish parish was the locus of the first St. Patrick's Day parade, an event that later became a unique urban phenomenon.

But since the Irish were English speaking, their parishes were canonically open to anyone. The most susceptible to change, they quickly became "American" parishes. The history of Holy Rosary Parish clearly demonstrates this tendency.[96] Holy Rosary, at 351 East 113th Street, was first settled by Irishmen who worked at the huge Pullman works on the Southeast Side. When the strikes of 1894 forced many of the original settlers to leave, French, Germans, Dutch, and Italians moved in. The parish declined from 157 baptisms in 1888, to seventy-seven in 1895. Newer national parishes, which were carved out of Holy Rosary's original territory, left the community a mere shell of its original glory. By 1900, Holy Rosary was no longer an Irish parish, but a small collection of Italians and Lake Shore elite.[97]

The Germans. Germans and their descendants represent the most important northern European nationality to come to America.[98] By 1910, they and their descendants numbered 8,282,618.[99] Statistics indicate that approximately 35% of these immigrants were Catholic. Some 40,000 came to the United States during the 1830s, a number that tripled in the 1840s. By 1842, Cincinnati had 20,000 Catholic Germans; New York, 18,000; Philadelphia, 12,000; and St. Louis, 7,000.[100] These Germans, proud of their Catholicity, had to defend themselves against Know-Nothings and nativists, who attacked them vehemently during the 1840s. They also had to defend themselves against the Irish, who did not always understand them. Bishop Shanley of Fargo was accused of being unsympathetic toward his German and Bohemian flock. Conversely, Bishop Loras of Dubuque was accused of being pro-German and of not spending enough money on the Irish.[101]

Germans tended to settle according to the province they came from—Northern Germans from Saxony and Schleswig-Holstein settled in Pennsylvania, Ohio, and Michigan, while Swabians and Prussians settled in Indiana in the 1840s. A contemporary noted that "the Saxon does not like the Swabian, nor the Prussian the Bavarian, and the Westphalian would . . . devour the poor Badenser alive, and so conversely." In rural northern Ohio, Germans from Alsace fought Hessen-Darmstadters over which hymns to sing in church; the discussion heated up to the point that one group burned down the church! At St. Michael's in Chicago, the trustees refused to accept six pastors between 1852 and 1860; they even locked the church doors against Bishop James Duggan when he tried to hand the church over to the Redemptorists.[102]

The shape of German Catholicism was largely formed by mid-century. The ethnic parish stood at the heart of their daily lives:

> For the Germans, as for most other Catholic immigrant groups, the national parish was the most important ethnic institution not only because it met their deepest religious needs but also because it furnished the social nucleus around which all voluntary associations clustered.[103]

The German parish emerged from the laity itself, since it was the laity that often took the initiative in asking bishops for ethnic parishes. Most of the priests who serviced these parishes were German-born and belonged to such German orders as the Redemptorists or Franciscans. The people admired and respected their priests, as huge crowds attended first Masses and pastoral funerals. Germans, who loved magnificent churches, populated the Midwest with beautiful Gothic edifices. Taking pride in elaborate ceremonies and pageantry, Germans filled their churches with *lustige Gesang* (hearty singing). The parish mission was a central event in German-Catholic life, as German missionaries stressed baptism, confession, and a return to the Sacraments. One of the most important characteristics of the parish was the *Vereinswesen,* or societal life, which grew up around the parish. While the Irish fostered societies outside the parish, Germans tended to gather their associations within it. These voluntary groups were either devotional or mutual-aid societies, the former devoted to local devotions and pious works, the latter acting as insurance agents for the newly arrived immigrant.

The German ethnic parish arose out of an intense desire to preserve the German language. It preserved religion, language, and nationality for thousands of German Catholics. Loss of language meant loss of faith, for it was *die deutsche Sprache* that held Catholicism and German tradition together. The German did not claim that his language was *the* language of faith, but he did stress that faith could best be kept through that language. A letter from Friedrich von Held to the Director of the *Ludwig Missionsverein* amply illustrates this point:

> The erection of new missions for German Catholics becomes more urgent and pressing each day. German immigration will increase each day, yes, considerably every night and every week. Thus, the problem is for the Germans to preserve German, and this can only come about if they are snatched from the pernicious influence of American morals and habit of life through religious unity under the direction of German priests. Unfortunately, experience teaches only too well that where there is no German priest, the German parents preserve only very poorly those good civil and religious qualities, which, in a more pious German fatherland, they sucked in with their mother's milk. The children in every respect are lost, and soon, without Catholic German services and schools, they necessarily succumb to the American spirit.[104]

Leading German Catholics spoke out for the preservation of German culture, customs, and language, under the slogan, "Language saves faith." King Ludwig I of Bavaria exhorted his fellow Bavarians: "I shall not forget you, but stay, German, German! Do not become English."[105]

German pastors were often appointed for life, and it wasn't unusual for a pastor to head a parish for more than forty years. They were strong-willed and stubborn men, but were needed to build a church in the urban wilderness. The story of Father Aloysius J. Theile illustrates the type of pastor common to the ethnic parish.[106] A Germanizer par excellence, Theile became pastor of St. Aloysius Parish in Chicago in 1884. He actively supported the efforts of Feehan and Quigley to establish German parishes. Becoming the voice of the German clergy for forty years, he took an active interest in Guardian Angel German Orphanage, established the German cemetery of St. Joseph in River Grove, Illinois, and brought the German Sisters of Christian Charity to teach in his own school. When Theile died at the age of eighty-seven in 1935, the Chicago *New World* called him "an outstanding figure in the religious and civic life of Chicago, being a tremendous spiritual and material life of the city."[107] He was succeeded by another Germanophile, Rev. Bernard Laukemper of Westphalia, Germany. Father Laukemper, a liturgical innovator, was active in the Kolping Society, a German lay organization, throughout the 1940s. Indeed, it was common practice to appoint German priests to German parishes, long after they had ceased to be German.

German religious orders also played a prominent role in fostering German ethnicity. The Benedictine Fathers played a prominent role in the establishment of the Church in Minnesota and the Dakotas. Their efforts were so successful that by 1875 a vicariate had been established in northern Minnesota. But their work was not always appreciated by the local diocesan clergy. Indeed, the power of the Benedictines in Minnesota was so great that newly elected bishops often had to deal with them before they could deal with local problems. Otto Zardetti, a native of Switzerland and the first bishop of St. Cloud, Minnesota, wrote to a friend that when he first came to Minnesota "the diocese was nearly in the power of the Benedictines. There were but fifteen secular priests in the poorest missions . . . I could hope to destroy the prevalent impression that the St. Cloud Diocese was but a dominance of the Benedictines." By 1892, Zardetti could report that "all counties except Stearns are now free from the religious."[108] The Franciscans of Teutopolis, Illinois, established German parishes throughout Ohio, Indiana, Illinois, Missouri, and Nebraska. The Redemptorist Fathers, who established St. Michael's in Chicago, made it "one of the largest and most admired German-Catholic parishes in the city of Chicago. Mrs. Henry Hahn, a life-long resident of Chicago, recalled that St. Michael's pastor was "as German as they came."[109]

Ethnic parishes also built up a following through weekly bulletins, or *Pfarrbote,* which disseminated information about parish happenings. Although they were usually written by laymen, they reflected the thoughts and ideals of the clergy itself. Publishing articles exclusively in German through World War I, these bulletins relayed news from Germany, told what was happening among local Germans, and were advertisers for German products and businessmen. The *Pfarrbote* of St. Boniface Parish in Chicago is a prime example of the kind of information found in these bulletins. St. Boniface strongly resisted the introduction of English into parish life, as "it was no blessing or grace for religion." It encouraged younger Germans to join local *Vereine* and read German newspapers. The bulletin also urged its readers to attend meetings of the Federation of German Catholic Societies "to demonstrate that the German Catholic citizens are firmly united . . . and that they endeavor to further the Catholic cause." But the *Pfarrbote* also interpreted America for the German immigrant. St. Boniface's monthly bulletin deplored the loss of esteem felt for the church, school, and society. It decried the growing tendency of young people to delay marriage. And it also decried such contemporary fads as the tango ("Twenty-two Wedding Guests

Wounded by the Tango'') and the theatre (''no believing Christian businessman would hire an employee because he is a theatre friend to the employer'').[110]

Germans delighted in the theatrics of Church liturgy and their churches reflected this love of ceremony. Many of the most prominent ecclesiastical edifices in Chicago (St. Boniface, St. Martin, and St. Paul, for example) were designed by the noted church architect, Henry J. Schlacks, who delighted in duplicating an Old-World magnificence that cannot be built today. In Johnsburg, Illinois, German settlers built three roadside chapels, which duplicated the roadside shrines of Germany—places to pray for good crops, propitious weather, or the sick and needy.[111] But it was the liturgies themselves that held the people together as Germans. Most services were conducted *auf Deutsch* (in German) through World War I. The Franciscans of St. Augustine's preached and held evening devotions in German through the 1930s, and the Redemptorists of St. Alphonsus in Chicago continued to say High Mass in German as late as 1935.

Ethnic parishes also held special religious devotions and celebrations that cemented their people together. Parish missions brought in outstanding German clergy, who preached the word and revived the faith. At St. Boniface Parish, the Precious Blood Fathers held a mission in 1912 to attain ''luck and peace'' for all; they conducted Masses every hour from 5 A.M. to 9 A.M., and held confessions in German for the duration of the mission. Southern Germans brought the feast of the Ascension (*Christi Himmelfahrt*) to the United States in the early 1800s. Bavarians who introduced the feast of Corpus Christi (*Fronleichnamsfest*) in the late eighteenth century, brought the traditional processions to American parishioners. In Hermann, Missouri, in the foothills of the Ozarks, the thrifty German farmers who settled the region made the Corpus Christi processions the center of parish life.[112] St. Augustine's *Pfarrbote* noted that ''it is a feast right for the German spirit, because it came from a German heart and German soil, and first took hold in Germanland.'' The cities of Cologne, Würzburg, and Augsburg popularized the processions; as the *Pfarrbote* reported: ''The Corpus Christi processions, which take place in spring under the clear-blue sky and in front of flower-bedecked homes, are such a rich experience to nature-loving Germans that whoever participates once—in a spirit of faith and prayer—never wants to miss them again.''[113]

The ethnic parish also provided the milieu around which the rituals of life and death took place. Funerals were social occasions for most Germans, as they were for Irish and other immigrant groups. Many rural superstitions came to America by way of Germany; in some towns of Wisconsin, the people believed that the dead remained in the houses where they lived for forty years, and that women who died in childbirth came back to feed their babies every six weeks. Mrs. Theresa Krutz, an astute observer of the German scene, recalled that it was common at St. Aloysius to hold funerals in the home. A wreath of black crepe was put in front of the house, furniture was placed in the living room, and the coffin put in front of a window. As she remembered, "that was common practice—I don't know when it happened that people started going more to chapels—at that time—the neighbors would all provide food—it was just more community than it is now."[114]

Of all the nationalities that came to America, Germans were the most prolific in establishing local societies to perpetuate their peculiar culture. Germans developed their associational life around the parish, which provided a focus for their personal, religious, and ethnic needs. The earliest societies were mutual-aid organizations, which provided insurance and burial expenses in case of death. Others were devotional, devoted to a particular saint or devotion within the Church. Many of these societies joined together to form the Federation of German Catholic Societies of Illinois, which tried "to interest the members in the study of the social question . . . with a vow to advancing the interests of the laboring class."[115] Members often clashed with clergy over goals and methods, although much of this friction diminished in the twentieth century. The *Pfarrbote* of St. Boniface noted that "we see in that the dawn of a better time, a better understanding between priest and societies" (August 1910).

Many societies sponsored community plays and choral societies. St. Boniface's *Junglings Verein* presented *Was einem Schusterjunger passieren kann,* while the Young Ladies' Society presented *Drei Räuber auf Maria Kulm* in 1902 (*Pfarrbote,* February 1902). St. Augustine's established a Dramatic Club (*Deutsche Dramatische Gesellschaft*) in 1904, to promote German literature, drama, and entertainment. The *Verein* presented *Die beiden Reichenmüller* in 1918, and the *Goldene Spinne—eine deutsche Vorstellung* in 1916. It celebrated its twenty-fifth anniversary with a sold-out presentation of *Muttersegen* in 1929. Singing societies (*Sängerbund*) were also present from the very beginning. Parishes often sponsored such clubs, which later became local institutions. The Chicago Symphony began its history as the Theodore Orchestra in 1892, while the German-American Singers of Chicago, established in 1935, continues to maintain the German tradition of "song and *Gemütlichkeit.*" Through all these activities, German *Vereine* furthered the ethnic ties of their members.

We have now seen that German parishes were active centers of German ethnicity for more than seventy years. German religious orders like the Redemptorists and Franciscans nurtured America's *Deutschtum* through local celebrations, parish *Vereine,* and numerous publications and sermons. Parish *Pfarrbote* encouraged the retention of German on the family level, reported on happenings in Germany, and advertised German products and services. Parish anniversaries brought out the most noted German clergy of the day, while German *Vereine* carried on such traditional Teutonic concerns as singing, drama, and *Gemütlichkeit.* But the parish was more than this, for it was the focus of the family, a place where members gathered for the important celebrations of life. It was even a way-station for the primordial rituals of life and death.

But the ethnic parish was not only a way-station of ethnicity—it was also a focus of Americanization. Through a variety of institutions and organizations, the parish actively encouraged this painful process. Some of the primary institutions that furthered Americanization were the same *Vereine* that encouraged ethnicity. German priests established local societies that directly or indirectly encouraged contact with other nationalities. In Chicago, St. Augustine's organized a Young Men's Society in 1887 to promote "the moral, physical, and social welfare of its members." It provided space for recreational reading, bowling, pool, and gymnastics, as well as operating a library and baseball team. Through these facilities and activities, the Young Men's Society promoted contact with other young men in Chicago. The parish also founded a Young Ladies' Society in 1891 for the same purposes. The members helped America's soldiers during World War I by knitting socks and sweaters for the "boys over there." They also introduced English plays, which further expanded their neighbors' horizons during the 1920s. Both groups contributed significantly to the support of the parish.[116]

We have now seen that German parishes were not only way-stations of ethnicity, but active centers of Americanization. Through local organizations, they actively supported American customs and morals. But it was the parochial school, more than any other institution, which firmly planted German Catholics on American soil.[117] The parochial school was a microcosm of the parish as a whole—while it nurtured German ethnicity, it also fostered Americanization. The school, like the parish as a whole, was a way-station of German ethnicity and Americanization, as it nurtured German traditions and encouraged assimilation for six decades. First staffed by German laity, the parochial schools soon hired German sisters to train children—the School Sisters of Notre Dame, the Franciscans, Benedictines, and Holy Cross Congregations all had German branches to work in German parishes. German schools often rose next to Irish ones, as both immigrant groups settled in the same community. Germans established St. Francis of Assisi and Holy Trinity schools on the Near West Side, while Chicago's Irish established five schools in Holy Family Parish at the same time; there were only 900 students in both German schools in 1890, while there were over 5,000 students in Holy Family's five schools the very same year.[118] The situation was reversed on the North Side, where German schools outnumbered Irish two to one.

Parish bulletins continuously stressed the need for German parochial schools. St. Augustine's *Pfarrbote* succinctly described the dual purpose of these schools:

Children not only learn religion, but also reading, writing, arithmetic, history, and geography; in short, all those things which are necessary to succeed in this world. . . . In the German parish school, the children also learn their German mother tongue next to the language of the country—which is important not only for daily conversation but also for business and religious life.[119]

German schools encouraged ethnicity through the continued use of German in the classroom. Mrs. Henry Hahn recalled that all the subjects at St. Michael's High School were taught in German (except English grammar), while students presented German plays through the 1920s. As she recalled: "The nuns would insist that students only speak German during recess; if someone started to speak English, they would tell them 'Du musst Deutsch sprechen' ('You must speak German')." A German father at St. Michael's complained that his children weren't learning enough English, for "if the teachings in St. Michael's School or the preference can't be English more than German, I am sending three children to this school and they tell me they insist they have to learn German." Theresa Krutz remembered her days at St. Alphonsus in the 1930s, where "until I was in third grade we had German readers—I think everybody in the school knew the Christmas chorales in German—we read and talked German—not on a regular basis, there were just some people who went to this class."[120] The school set aside special hours for German reading (in Gothic print!) and German literature. In this way, German schools nourished a sense of ethnicity in their young Germanic pupils.

But German schools also prepared their students for Chicago life. St. Augustine's introduced English-language curricula as early as 1912. Other parishes established commercial schools as early as 1910, to prepare young women for the business world. At St. Alphonsus, "hundreds of graduates of St. Alphonsus Grammar School learned business skills which enabled them to obtain jobs in downtown Loop offices." St. Martin's commercial program, which continued until 1950, prepared scores of young women for secretarial work; a 1926 graduate wrote, "I learned much that will profit me while seeking my fortune out in the big business world."[121] German parishes also established high schools, which became commonplace in the United States by 1930. St. Michael's set up separate boys' and girls' high schools in the early teens, and expanded its facilities to two separate school buildings by 1929. St. Augustine's, St. Gregory's, and St. Benedict's also erected high schools in the 1920s. Many parishes introduced auxiliary courses, which further prepared their children for daily life. St. Augustine's Parish Souvenir reflected the success of these programs in a 1937 article:

> The pastors of St. Augustine's Parish left no stone unturned or overlooked any opportunity to promise the standard of education inasfar as the demand of the parish warranted. This is seen in their manifold efforts, for instance, to enlarge the school buildings, to improve the educational methods, to extend the curriculum of studies, adding grade after grade, a commercial high school, a kindergarten; by encouraging sewing classes for the girls, the music, of courses in hygiene and physical culture.[122]

It is clear, then, that the ethnic school consciously encouraged Americanization through specialized courses, commercial schools, and high schools. Indeed, the

The Establishment of Parish Life, 1604-1914

ethnic school was a microcosm of the parish as a whole—a way-station of ethnicity and Americanization, a place where German immigrants could foster their own traditions while preparing to enter the larger American society.

But there is one more point to be made. German Catholics were more tolerant of Protestants than their Irish and American co-religionists. While most Catholics feared Protestantism, German Catholics welcomed them as fellow Germans. Parish bulletins and sermons consistently praised Luther, Zwingli, and Calvin. St. Boniface's *Pfarrbote* noted Luther's veneration of Mary ("Luther über die Marienverehrung," May 1897), while St. Augustine's *Pfarrbote* praised Zwingli for the same devotion ("Zwingli über die Verehrung Mariens," December 1911). St. Boniface's bulletin called a certain Dr. Forster "a believing Protestant" (November 1907, p. 23). But it was the lives of the parishioners themselves that exhibited an open-mindedness toward Protestants in general. Mrs. Louise Venn Juhnke of St. Boniface Parish was a friend and confidante of many Protestants.[123] Her life demonstrates a constant openness to other nationalities and creeds. Her grandfather, Joseph Dinet, was born in Granville, France, in 1812; her grandmother, Adele Dedier, a Frenchwoman, came to America in the mid-1800s. Coming to Chicago by covered wagon, the Dinets settled at Clark and Randolph and set up an apothecary in the immediate neighborhood. Mrs. Dinet could even remember the days when Indians came to the back porches of Chicago. Mrs. Juhnke's personal diary reflects an openness to Protestants for the most part unknown among her Catholic contemporaries. In a revealing episode of her life, Mrs. Juhnke recalled how she became close friends with a Mrs. Splitthoff, who first introduced her to St. Boniface Parish. When an usher was about to throw Mrs. Juhnke out of the church because she did not have a paid pew, Mrs. Splitthoff came up and led her to her own pew. Although the latter only spoke German and the former French, they became friends for life. The life of Mrs. Juhnke reflects an acceptance of Protestants unknown in other parts of Chicago. While ethnics like the Irish and Italians feared Protestant converts, Germans who lived next to them for centuries accepted them as fellow co-nationals. Although there are no statistics to indicate the extent of this acceptance, Mrs. Juhnke's diary, as well as numerous citations in German *Pfarrbote,* indicates a general tolerance of Protestants unknown among Chicago's other Catholic elements.

St. Boniface Parish, at 921 North Noble Street, in Chicago, offers a glimpse of the ethnic parish as it really was. By following its history through seven decades of growth and decline, we get an impression (if not a photographic image) of what the national parish was and what it meant to the immigrants who made it their home. As one of Chicago's leading German parishes, St. Boniface's history is a paradigm of all German parishes.[124] The area that encompassed St. Boniface was swampy, as sidewalks rose and dipped with the elevation, and floods covered the primitive streets with annoying regularity. A group of German laymen who lived in the community met with the pastor of St. Joseph's and Bishop James

Duggan to discuss the possibility of a new parish west of the Chicago River. Rev. Ferdinand Kalvelage, pastor of St. Francis of Assisi, investigated the possibility and recommended the establishment of St. Boniface. The Benedictine Fathers, who had guided a primitive mission as early as 1862, relinquished the parish to diocesan clergy in 1865. Bishop Duggan appointed Rev. Philip Albrecht as St. Boniface's first pastor. There were only twenty-five families in the parish at the time, with seventy-two baptisms and nine weddings recorded the first year. When Albrecht was transferred to another parish in 1867, Bishop Duggan appointed Rev. James Marschall as St. Boniface's second pastor. Although he spoke German, English, and Polish fluently, Marschall could not adapt to the needs of his parishioners. Duggan was forced to appoint a new pastor.

Rev. Clement Venn, born in Westphalia, Germany, guided St. Boniface to the end of the century. Father Venn served at various parishes in McHenry County, Illinois, before coming to St. Boniface. Encountering trustee problems, Venn had to oust a disreputable member of the *Unterstützungs Verein* for conducting drunken picnics at parish outings. He then founded the St. Boniface Fraternal Society (St. Bonifacius Liebesbund) to counteract the *Unterstützungs Verein's* influence. A battle ensued over which society would prevail in the parish, and reached a dramatic conclusion when a member of the mutual-aid society knocked Father Venn down in the middle of the church. This altercation marked the end of the *Verein's* influence, for most parishioners were shocked by the episode. Joseph Reisel, a prominent member of the *Liebesbund,* told a defeated *Unterstützung* member that he would die miserably, for "he had stepped on an ordained minister behind his back."[125] Father Venn soon consolidated his position, as he led St. Boniface to the dawn of the new century. During his long tenure as St. Boniface's third pastor, Father Venn established numerous parish societies, founded St. Boniface Cemetery on the far North Side, and left the parish $4,000.00 when he died in 1895. St. Boniface had grown to be the largest German parish in the city at the time of his death.

Archbishop Feehan appointed Father Albert Evers as Venn's successor in 1895. Born in Warburg, Germany, in 1863, Evers served in Aurora and Kankakee, Illinois, before becoming St. Boniface's fourth pastor. By this time, the parish was growing rapidly and there was an acute need for a new church and school. Father Evers met these needs by building a new school in 1896 (including twelve classrooms, an auditorium, a small meeting hall, a kitchen, and a bowling alley), and a new church in 1903. Indeed, the highlight of Father Evers' career was the consecration of St. Boniface's magnificent church. The *Pfarrbote* commented: "The Church is a magnificent structure. Large, stately, and imposing, it compares in architectural beauty with the finest churches in the West. . . . The main tower of the belfry is over 150 feet high. The interior of the church is 160 feet deep, 40 feet wide, and 52 feet high, and has a seating capacity of 900. The windows and altars are temporary and will be removed in the near future to be replaced by new ones to be imported from Munich'' (June 1904). The church, designed by the noted church architect Henry Schlacks, measured 80 feet wide and 218 feet long. The *Chicago Examiner* noted that ''through the crowded streets decorated with flags, banners, evergreens, 30,000 men marched yesterday at the dedication of St. Boniface . . . it was one of the most impressive spectacles in the history of Chicago'' (June 5, 1904).

Father Evers' pastorate was not altogether happy, for he saw his beloved parish change from a predominantly German parish to a community of Poles, Slovaks, and other eastern Europeans. He did what he could to stop this process. The *Pfarrbote* continually exhorted its parishioners to stay within the parish: ''It is important for our community that those who live within the parish stay there. Don't leave your mother church; don't leave the holy St. Boniface Parish'' (September 1902, p. 13). And again: ''It is wise and smart for every good German Catholic to maintain a home in the neighborhood, to buy goods in the shadow of the old and worthy St. Boniface Church'' (June 1907, p. 7). The parish, acting as a real-estate agency, even listed good homes for sale as it encouraged parishioners to sell to Germans alone. The *Pfarrbote* remained optimistic through 1907, despite the appearance of ''foreign elements.'' It was optimistic because the parish had grown to 750 families, Poles were joining the parish, and the new church seemed to strengthen the devotion of the old German members. But Father Evers was not so optimistic, for he could not accept the Poles and Slovaks who were weakening his parish. He called St. Boniface a ''wasted city.'' Many parts of Chicago, ''which stood earlier in highest bloom, in this way have been robbed of their best supports and their most beautiful jewels.'' Evers, who intensely disliked these newcomers, urged his parishioners to stay in the parish and keep ''the dirty and unsightly elements far from our home.''[126]

Statistics show that St. Boniface did decline during Father Evers' pastorate. The school decreased from 1,200 children in 1901, to twenty children in 1916 (half of whom were Slovaks from another parish). Jews began to move into the neighborhood from 1913 to 1915. Father Evers decided to turn the church over to a German order, but a group of laity became so incensed that it forged a number of signatures on a letter to Archbishop Mundelein and insisted that there were enough Germans to keep St. Boniface a national parish. The aging pastor, who could not keep up with the strain of a changing neighborhood, resigned on June 16, 1916. As the world turned to ''a war to end all wars,'' St. Boniface lost forever its Germanic character. The world (and St. Boniface!) would never be the same again. For while World War I irrevocably changed the way all men saw the world and themselves, the very fact that Germany was the enemy made it impossible for a truly German parish to survive. The rise and decline of St. Boniface was a microcosm of the world as a whole.[127]

Notes

1. *Jesuit Relations and Allied Documents,* Vol. 1, n. 32, cited by Sister Madeleine M. Schmidt, C.H.M., *Seasons of Growth, History of the Diocese of Davenport, 1881–1981* (Davenport, Ia.: The Diocese, 1981), 3. In addition to numerous works in French, the following books provide an excellent introduction to the French period in Midwestern history: Cornelius Janen, *The Role of the Church in New France* (New York: McGraw-Hill, 1976); J. H. Kennedy, *Jesuit and Savage in New France* (New Haven, Conn.: n.p., 1950); and H. H. Walsh, *The Church in the French Era: From Colonization to the British Conquest* (Toronto: Ryerson Press, 1967).

2. An excellent bibliography on the early history of Illinois is found in Theodore C. Pease's *The Story of Illinois* (Chicago: University of Chicago Press, 1925; rev. ed. by Marguerite J. Pease, 1965).

3. Schmidt, *Seasons of Growth,* 12.

4. England acquired title to the French territory east of the Mississippi River in 1763. On the transition from British to American rule, see Robert I. Schuyler, *The Transition in Illinois from British to American Government* (New York: Columbia University Press, 1909). On the growth of St. Louis as a major Catholic center, see John Rothensteiner, *History of the Archdiocese of St. Louis,* 2 Vols (St. Louis: Blackwell Wielandy Co., 1923); and William B. Faherty, S. J., *Dream by the River: Two Centuries of St. Louis Catholicism, 1766–1967* (St. Louis, 1971).

5. Thomas T. McAvoy, *The Catholic Church in Indiana, 1789–1834* (New York: Columbia University Press, 1940), 50–61.

6. Theodore Roemer, *The Catholic Church in the United States* (St. Louis: B. Herder Book Co., 1950), 118–119.

7. J. J. Hartley, ed., *The History of the Diocese of Columbus, 1868–1943,* 2 Vols. (Columbus: The Diocese, 1918, 1943), I, 1.

8. Albert Hamilton, *The Catholic Journey through Ohio* (St. Meinrad, Ind.: Abbey Press, 1976), 5; R. E. Brennan, *Cradle of the Faith in Ohio, 1818–1968* (Columbus: Privately printed, 1968); V. F. O'Daniel, *The Rt. Rev. Edward Dominic Fenwick, O.P. . . . First Bishop of Cincinnati* (Washington, 1920).

9. "The Lancaster Story," compiled by the Lancaster Fairfield County Chamber of Commerce; *Lancaster Eagle-Gazette* (Sesquicentennial Edition), June 3, 1950, Sec. B, 2.

10. *Diocese of Columbus,* I, 3–6.

11. Hamilton, *Journey through Ohio,* 55.

12. *Ibid.,* 8, 17–18.

13. *Ibid.,* 8–15. The state was divided into two dioceses in 1847, when Cleveland was created a diocese in its own right, with Rev. Amadeus Rappe appointed first bishop. The new diocese, which included the northern counties of the state, numbered approximately 1,000 Catholics, 42 churches, and 25 priests. By 1870, when Rappe resigned his office, the Cleveland Diocese had grown to 100,000 Catholics, 160 parishes, and 90 parochial schools. See J. J. Hynes, *History of the Diocese of Cleveland, 1847–1952* (Cleveland, 1953).

14. The Diocese of Detroit, established in 1833, consisted of not only the state of Michigan, but the entire "northwestern territory." Roemer, *Catholic Church,* 180–182.

See George Pare, *The Catholic Church in Detroit, 1701–1888* (Detroit: Gabriel Richard Press, 1951).

15. See F. B. Woodford and A. Hyms, *Gabriel Richard: Frontier Ambassador* (Detroit, 1958).

16. The history of Illinois during the early part of the eighteenth century is very limited. Inadequate census data indicate that there were only 2,500 inhabitants in Illinois in 1800. (Pease, *Illinois,* 70). See also Clarence Wl. Alvord, *The Illinois Country, 1673–1818, The Centennial History of Illinois,* Vol. I (Chicago: A. C. McClurg & Co., 1918–1920.). Some of this history is also related in John J. Hogan, *On the Mission in Missouri, 1857–1868* (Glorieta, N. M.: Rio Grande Press, 1976).

17. Primary sources for the early history of Chicago remain Alfred T. Andreas, *History of Chicago,* 3 Vols. (Chicago: A. T. Andreas, 1884–1860); John Moses and Joseph Kirland, *History of Chicago,* 2 Vols. (Chicago: Munsell & Co., 1895); and the classic work by Bessie L. Pierce, *A History of Chicago,* 3 Vols. (New York: A. A. Knopf, 1937–1957). On the early history of Catholicism in Chicago, the work by Gilbert J. Garraghan, *The Catholic Church in Chicago, 1673–1837* (Chicago: Loyola University Press, 1921), remains fundamental.

18. Pierce, *History of Chicago,* I: 185. Native Americans were not always friendly to Chicago's immigrants; Chicago's first mayor, William E. Ogden, called them "poor and vicious foreigners." (*Ibid.,* 186.)

19. Besides Garraghan, see Shea, *History Catholic Church,* Vol. 4.

20. Andreas, *History Chicago,* I: 189, quoted in Garraghan, *Catholic Church Chicago,* 45.

21. *Ibid.,* 108–136. Quarter also established St. Patrick's Church for the Irish, and St. Ann's, at Bourbonnais Grove, for the French, in 1847.

22. December 13, 1849; see Garraghan, *Catholic Church Chicago,* 137–166, for a complete summary of Van de Velde's ministry.

23. Tired out by strife and illness, O'Regan died at Brompton, England, on November 23, 1866. (*Ibid.,* 169, 173.)

24. On the Upper Mississippi Valley states, see Schmidt, *Seasons of Growth,* 21–53; Leo Rummel, *History of the Catholic Church in Wisconsin* (Madison; Knights of Columbus Press, 1976), 1–33; Robert R. Miller, *That All May Be One: A History of the Rockford Diocese* (Chicago: Lakeside Press, 1976), 185–205; James P. Shannon, *Catholic Colonization on the Western Frontier* (New Haven: Yale University Press, 1957); and the classic work by M. M. Hoffmann, *The Church Founders of the Northwest* (Milwaukee: Bruce Publishing Co., 1937).

25. Alice E. Smith, *The History of Wisconsin from Exploration to Statehood* (Madison: n.p., 1973), 607, cited by Rummel, *Catholic Church Wisconsin,* 33; see also A. L. Johnson, *Crosier on the Frontier: A Life of John Martin Henni* (Madison, 1959).

26. See Samuel S. Mazzuchelli, *Memoirs* (Chicago: Priory Press, 1967); Rosemary Crepeau, *Un apotre dominicain aux Etats-Unis* (Paris: J. de Gigord, 1932); and Theodore Maynard, *Great Catholics in American History* (Garden City, N.Y.: Hanover House, 1957), 171–181.

27. Schmidt, *Seasons of Growth,* 37, 53. Mazzuchelli was an architect and general contractor as well, as he supervised the design and construction of hundreds of churches throughout the Midwest.

28. Miller, *History Rockford Diocese,* 185.
29. Schmidt, *Seasons of Growth,* 57–63.
30. An excellent survey of this region is found in Patrick H. Ahern, ed., *Catholic Heritage in Minnesota, North Dakota, and South Dakota* (St. Paul: H. M. Smyth Co., 1964), 1–5, 62–71.
31. On the life of Father Pierre De Smet, see E. Laveille, *The Life of Fr. De Smet, S.J.* (New York: P. J. Kenedy and Sons, 1915), as well as numerous writings by the author himself.
32. Ahern, *Catholic Heritage Minnesota,* 6–16, 20–23.
33. On Bishop Fredrick Baraga, see Joseph Gregorich, *The Apostle of the Chippewas* (Chicago: Bishop Baraga Association, 1932), and Maximilijan Jezernik, *Frederick Baraga* (New York: Studia Slovenica, 1968).
34. Ahern, *Catholic Heritage Minnesota,* 53.
35. Sister M. Claudia Duratschek, O.S.B., *The Beginning of Catholicism in South Dakota* (Washington, D.C.: Catholic University of America Press, 1943), 222–223.
36. The Diocese of Columbus, Ohio, was established in 1868 to provide for the state's growing population. As the chronicler of the diocese noted in 1914, "in its early days the diocese was largely an agricultural district, the first settlers from Pennsylvania and Maryland . . . later came the immigrants from Ireland and Germany, who were followed by priests of their native land . . . immigration has also added to the variety of races among the Catholic population . . . Poles, Hungarians, Greeks, Lithuanians, and Slavs." (*Diocese of Columbus,* I, 25–26.)
37. Statistical data for the city of Chicago are concisely summarized in *The People of Chicago: Who We Are and Who We Have Been* (Chicago: Department of Development and Planning, 1976); see also *Historic City* (Chicago: Department of Development and Planning, 1976); and Pierce, *History of Chicago,* Vol. II: 1848–1871.
38. See Pierce, *History of Chicago,* Vol. III: 1871–1893.
39. Pease, *Illinois,* 186–187.
40. Silvano M. Tomasi and Madeline H. Engel, eds., *The Italian Experience in the United States* (Staten Island, N.Y.: Center for Migration Studies, 1970), 163.
41. Garraghan, *Catholic Church Chicago,* 90.
42. *People of Chicago* 13–15.
43. See Charles H. Shanabruch, "The Catholic Church's Role in the Americanization of Chicago's Immigrants: 1833–1928" (Ph.D. dissertation, University of Chicago, 1975), 190–230; John P. Walsh, "The Catholic Church in Chicago and the Problems of an Urban Society, 1893–1915" (Ph.D. dissertation, University of Chicago, 1948), 1–6; and W. J. Madaj, "The First Archbishop of Chicago," *New World,* August 16, 1974, 7–9.
44. James J. McGovern, *Souvenir of the Silver Jubilee in the Episcopacy of His Grace, the Most Rev. Patrick Augustine Feehan* (Chicago: Privately printed, 1891), 196–201.
45. Madaj, "First Archbishop," 9.
46. Catholic statistics taken from Gerald Shaughnessy, *Has the Immigrant Kept the Faith?* (New York: Macmillan Co., 1925), *passim.*
47. François Houtart and Jean Remy, *Milieu Urbain et Communaute Chretienne* (Tours: Mame, 1968), 143, 181.

48. On the life of Archbishop Quigley, see Walsh, "Catholic Church Chicago," 280–320; Shanabruch, "Catholic Church Chicago," 300–325; W. J. Madaj, "The Second Archbishop of Chicago," *New World,* August 23, 1974, 7–10; and various issues of the *New World,* the Archdiocesan newspaper, 1903–1915.

49. *New World,* March 14, 1983, 14; November 26, 1904, 3.

50. Madaj, "Second Archbishop," 7. Quigley's 1913 report to Rome included the following statistics on Chicago's Catholics: English-274,686; Polish-174,642; German-75,951; Italian-56,200; Bohemian-32,700; Lithuanian-24,600; Slovak-9,224; Croatian-8,000; and Hungarian-1,600. (*Ibid.*)

51. Joseph Parot, "The American Faith and the Persistence of Chicago Polonia, 1870–1920" (Ph.D. dissertation, Northern Illinois University, 1971), 301.

52. *Holy Rosary Parish, One Hundred Years* (Darlington, Wisc.: Privately printed, 1964); and other material now kept in the Archives of the University of Notre Dame (hereafter cited as AUND).

53. *Ibid.,* 12, 14.

54. Noel Iverson, *Germania, U.S.A., Social Change in New Ulm, Minnesota* (Minneapolis: University of Minnesota, 1966).

55. Ahern, *Catholic Heritage Minnesota,* 108–109. Conditions were harsh in northern Minnesota, as winters and Indian uprisings took their toll. A Father Lawrence Lautishar froze to death during a cold winter's night in 1858, as he returned home from a mission call. But the Church continued to grow, as new dioceses were established in Duluth (1889) and Crookston (1919).

56. *Ibid.,* 126–131. On the life of John P. Ireland, see James H. Moynihan, *The Life of Archbishop John Ireland* (New York, 1953). On the series of controversies known as "Americanism," see Thomas T. McAvoy, *The Great Crisis in American Catholic History 1895–1900* (Chicago: Henry Regnery Co., 1957).

57. Ahern, *Catholic Heritage Minnesota,* 31. See also J. M. Reardon, *The Catholic Church in the Diocese of St. Paul* (St. Paul, 1952).

58. Duratschek, *Catholicism South Dakota,* 110. See also Andrew M. Greeley, *The Catholic Experience* (New York: Doubleday & Co., 1969), 152–218.

59. A complete history of the Church in North and South Dakota remains to be written. The best treatments so far are Ahern, *Catholic Heritage Minnesota, passim;* Duratschek, *Catholicism South Dakota, passim;* and Louis Pfaller, *The Catholic Church in Western North Dakota, 1738–1960* (Mandan, N. Dak: Crescent Printing Co., 1960).

60. Ahern, *Catholic Heritage Minnesota,* 141–145.

61. *Ibid.,* 154–155; Duratschek, *Catholicism South Dakota,* 160–165.

62. On the German-Russians of North America, see George P. Aberle, *From the Steppes to the Prairies* (Bismarck, N. Dak.: n.p., 1963); Ahern, *Catholic Heritage Minnesota,* 35–44; and Richard Sallet, "Russlanddeutsche Siedlungen in den Vereinigten Staaten von Amerika," *Deutsch-Amerikanische Geschichtsblätter,* 31 (1931), 5–126.

63. On the life of Abbot Wehrle, see Ahern, *Catholic Heritage Minnesota,* 208–22, and Pfaller, *Western North Dakota,* 35–50.

64. Ahern, *Catholic Heritage Minnesota,* 214–215.

65. Duratschek, *Catholicism South Dakota,* 41–42, 168–174.

66. Ahern, *Catholic Heritage Minnesota,* 216–218. We cannot understate the value

of the Benedictines and other religious orders that single-handedly established and solidified the position of the Church in the vast Northwest. If it were not for them, the Church would never have arrived on the frontier until much later; but the fact that they were there when they were assured the continuance of Catholic life for generations to come.

67. The classic work on Nebraska Catholicism remains Henry W. Casper, *History of the Catholic Church in Nebraska*, 3 Vols. (Milwaukee: Bruce Publishing Co., 1960); see also Sister M. Aquinata Martin, *The Catholic Church on the Nebraska Frontier, 1854–1885* (Washington, D.C.: Catholic University of America Press, 1937). For Kansas, see Peter Beckman, *The Catholic Church on the Kansas Frontier, 1850–1877* (Washington, D.C.: Catholic University of America Press, 1943); Gilbert J. Garraghan, *Catholic Beginnings in Kansas City, Missouri* (Chicago: Loyola University Press, 1930); and T. H. Kinsella, *A Century of Catholicity in Kansas, 1822–1922* (Kansas City, 1921).

68. Martin, *Catholic Church Nebraska*, 2, 20; Beckman, *Catholic Church Kansas*, 1, 70.

69. *Ibid.*

70. *Ibid.*, 40–43.

71. Martin, *Catholic Church Nebraska*, 46–47.

72. Beckman, *Catholic Church Kansas*, 58.

73. *Ibid.*, 78.

74. Martin, *Catholic Church Nebraska*, 50–53. The earliest missionaries noted the demoralizing effect of the frontier on religious life, for "the West is young, vigorous, strong, but it is self-willed, speculative, and material in its inner life and tendencies . . . it cannot be doubted that too many Christians are 'demoralized' by coming to the West and not willing to sacrifice either through the purse or personal effort as they would amid old associations and old surroundings." (*Ibid.*, 127.)

75. M. Charles McGrath, "History of Churches in Miami County," 1976 (unpublished manuscript); and "Osawatomie, Miami County" (unpublished manuscript).

76. On ethnicity in Nebraska, see Martin, *Catholic Church Nebraska*, 50–52, 100–105, 158. On the extensive contributions of the Franciscans to parish life, see Marion A. Habig, *Heralds of the King* (Chicago: Franciscan Herald Press, 1958). Franciscan parishes extended from Ohio and Michigan in the east, to Nebraska and Missouri in the west.

77. Martin, *Catholic Church Nebraska*, 170–174. There are few histories of the Bohemian Church in the United States. See Joseph Chada, *Czech American Catholics, 1850–1920* (Lisle, Ill.: Center for Slav Culture, 1964).

78. Daniel Callahan, *The Mind of the Catholic Layman* (New York: Charles Scribner's Sons, 1963), 63–76.

79. Pfaller, *Western North Dakota*, 26–28.

80. Callahan, *Catholic Layman*, 62, 72.

81. Ahern, *Catholic Heritage Minnesota*, 181.

82. Parish History Project, Notre Dame University, 1977. Jeffrey M. Burns compiled data from the 894 parish histories collected at the Archives of the University of Notre Dame and then ran the significant data through a computer. His statistics are particularly useful for this history, since more than 53% of the data were taken from Ohio, Wisconsin, Illinois, and Indiana. Of the 894 parishes surveyed, 104 were Irish and 287 German. As Mr. Burns notes, "the use of the survey as an indicator in regards to the lay-clerical balance of power

is problematic." ("The Parish History Project: A Descriptive Analysis of the Data," mimeographed report, 2).

83. Burns, "Parish History Project," 8–9.

84. *Concilia Provincialis,* 1829, as cited in Duratschek, *Catholicism South Dakota,* 84. This theme was re-echoed at the First and Second Plenary Councils (1852, 1866), and given definitive form at the Third Plenary Council in Baltimore (1884). For a concise summary of these conciliar decrees, see Peter Guilday, *A History of the Councils of Baltimore, 1791–1884* (New York: Macmillan Co., 1932), and idem, *The National Pastorals of the American Hierarchy, 1792–1919* (Washington: National Catholic Welfare Conference, 1923).

85. Ahern, *Catholic Heritage Minnesota,* 56.

86. Duratschek, *Catholicism South Dakota,* 201. The situation in Iowa is illustrative of the entire Midwest. Seven district public schools were staffed by Catholic sisters from as early as 1855 to as late as 1959, when state laws finally forbade such a practice. (Schmidt, *Seasons of Growth,* 156.)

87. Beckman, *Catholic Church Kansas,* 72–97. An analogous situation existed in Ohio, where parochial schools began to emerge after 1860. As anti-Catholic sentiment began to grow against Irish and German immigrants, Ohio's bishops began to encourage the establishment of parochial schools. The First Ohio Provincial Council in 1855 warned that public schools taught "false maxims," and that "the erection of Catholic schools is . . . as important an object as the building of new churches." The Second Provincial Council of 1861 argued that "the only system that would be fair and equitable to all would be that which would make education . . . entirely free." But Catholics continued to pay taxes "for the support of schools which are thus virtually closed against us [and] to erect others, at enormous expense, for the Christian education of our children." Bishop Richard Gilmour of Cleveland denied the Sacraments to any Catholics who failed to send their children to parochial schools. He increased the number of grammar schools from 50 in 1872, to nearly 150 in 1892. The school became the center of congregational life, and it was often the need to establish reasonable school boundaries that led to parish territorial boundaries. (Hamilton, *Journey through Ohio,* 29–40, 62–63.)

88. Germans introduced the kindergarten system to America in 1855; American high schools were modeled after similar institutions in Prussia; and German universities were the basis of the American graduate school system. German educators devoted their lives to improving the quality (and quantity) of education in the United States. A number of secular German institutes arose in the middle of the nineteenth century, including the German-English Academy in Milwaukee. The Milwaukee public schools introduced German in 1867, while a bilingual public school was established in Baltimore in 1873. By 1900, there were six such bilingual schools in the United States, with more than 7,000 students attending. See Robert H. Billigmeier, *Americans from Germany* (Belmont, Calif.: Wadsworth Publishing Co., 1974). For a general survey of a particular school system, see the excellent work by James W. Sanders, *The Education of an Urban Minority: Catholics in Chicago, 1833–1965* (New York: Oxford University Press, 1977). It is interesting to note that German Lutheran schools had the same objectives as Catholic parochial schools, namely, the retention of German as a viable language and the nurturing of German culture. Chicago's Missouri Lutheran schools reached their peak in 1927–1928, when the Synod

operated forty-five such schools in the Chicagoland area alone. See Dean Wayne Kohlhoff, "Missouri Synod Lutherans and the Image of Germany, 1914–1945" (Ph.D. dissertation, University of Chicago, 1973), 118–161.

89. Burns, "Parish History Project," 6.

90. Stephen J. Shaw, "Chicago's Germans and Italians, 1903–1939: The Catholic Parish as a Way-Station of Ethnicity and Americanization," (Ph.D. dissertation, University of Chicago, 1981), 1–2.

91. Faust, *German Element,* I: 578. The next most-Irish state was Ohio, with 55,018 native-born Irishmen. This compares to New York's 425,553 Irishmen the same year (1900).

92. February 26, 1855; quoted in Shanabruch, "Catholic Church Chicago," 55–56.

93. *Irish-American Nationalism, 1870–1890* (Philadelphia: J. B. Lippincott, 1966), 34–35.

94. For Chicago's Irish, see Michael Funchion, "Chicago's Irish Nationalities, 1881–1890," (Ph.D. dissertation, Loyola University of Chicago, 1962); Joseph H. Thompson, "The Irish in Chicago," *Illinois Catholic Historical Review* 2 (April 1920): 458–473; and, in particular, Ellen Skerrett, "Irish Catholic Parish: Schools, Politics, Parades," *New World,* February 6, 1976, 15; "St. Anne's, St. Cecilia's—Distinctly Irish," *New World,* March 19, 1976, 15; and "Irish Twins: Holy Angels, St. Elizabeth," *New World,* May 7, 1976, 27.

95. Skerrett, "Irish Catholic Parish," 15.

96. Houtart, *Milieu Urbain,* 208–209.

97. The history of Holy Rosary Parish in Chicago was repeated throughout the Midwest. For example, in Niles, Michigan, St. Mary's Parish went through four successive nationality changes. The Irish arrived first (1840s) as workers on the Michigan Central Railroad; the Germans came next (1840s) as farmers, teamsters, carpenters, and tradesmen; then came the Italians (1890s) as fruit vendors and shoe repairmen; and finally Slovacs arrived in the early 1900s as tanners. (*St. Mary's Catholic Church, Niles, Michigan, 1870–1970.* (Niles: Privately printed, 1970).

98. The classic work on German-Americans remains Albert Faust's *German Element;* the major work on German Catholicism remains Colman Barry's *The Catholic Church and German-Americans* (Milwaukee: Bruce Publishing Co., 1953). Philip Gleason's *The Conservative Reformers* (Notre Dame: University of Notre Dame Press, 1968) takes the Germany Catholic story into the twentieth century, with a history of the German Catholic Central Verein.

99. Richard O'Connor, *The German-Americans* (Boston: Little-Brown, and Co., 1968), 200.

100. Joseph Salzbacher, *Meine Reise nach Nord-Amerika in Jahre 1842* (Vienna, 1845), quoted in Emmet H. Rothan, *The German Catholic Element in the United States, 1830–1860* (Washington, D.C.: Catholic University of America Press, 1946), 14.

101. Schmidt, *Seasons of Growth,* 63. But Germans could be just as unsympathetic toward their English-speaking contempories. Nicholas Goner, editor of the Dubuque *Katholischer Western,* claimed that German stock was superior to "the consumptive Yankee," and that Germans "lived close to God on farms." (*Ibid.,* 123.)

102. Gleason, *Conservative Reformers,* 19–23.

The Establishment of Parish Life, 1604-1914

103. *Ibid.,* 9. Dolan, in "Urban Catholicism," maintains that the German parish was more central for Germans than it was for the Irish, since among "German Catholics the local parish was the center around which much of their community activities revolved" (215).

104. Barry, *German Americans,* 9–12.

105. *Ibid.*

106. Shanabruch, "Catholic Church Chicago," 291–292.

107. *New World,* September 9, 1935, 1.

108. Ahern, *Catholic Heritage Minnesota,* 48–52.

109. *Centennial, St. Michael Church, 1864–1964* (Chicago: Privately printed, 1964), 16; Interview with Mrs. Henry Hahn, Chicago, Illinois, May 30, 1978.

110. St. Boniface *Pfarrbote,* July 1907, 21; June 1902, 11; December 1914, 3; October 1914, 12.

111. Miller, *History Rockford Diocese,* 235–236.

112. Habig, *Heralds of the King,* 246–250.

113. *Der Pfarrbote,* "Fronleichnam," June 1920, 3; LaVern Rippley, *Of German Ways* (Minneapolis: Dillon Press, 1970), 126–127.

114. Interview with Mrs. Theresa Krutz, Chicago Historical Society, Chicago, Illinois, August 20, 1978.

115. St. Boniface *Pfarrbote,* June 1902, 11.

116. *Der Pfarrbote,* February 1930, 36; *Golden Jubilee, St. Augustine's Parish, 1886-(1881)-1936* (Chicago; Privately printed, 1936), 175–179.

117. For a general survey, see the excellent work by Sanders, *Education Urban Minority,* 55–60.

118. *Ibid.,* 61.

119. *Der Pfarrbote,* September 1911, 6.

120. Interview, Mrs. Henry Hahn; Sanders, *Education Urban Minority,* 109; and Interview, Mrs. Theresa Krutz.

121. *St. Aloysius Parish, Diamond Jubilee, the Seventy-five Years of St. Aloysius Parish, 1884–1959* (Chicago: Privately printed, 1959), 36; *St. Martin Parish, Diamond Jubilee, 1886–1961* (Chicago: Privately printed, 1961), 28–32. St. Benedict's commercial program was designed to make stenographers of young women by the age of sixteen; when the government refused to accredit it, Monsignor Fasnacht decided to supplant its courses with a regular four-year high school (*Golden Jubilee Celebration, St. Benedict Parish, 1902–1952* (Chicago: Privately printed, 1952), 40.

122. *Der Pfarrbote,* September 1911, 9.

123. Mrs. Louise Venn Juhnke, personal diary, Chicago, Illinois (Handwritten).

124. Primary source material for this section is found in F. L. Kalvelage, *The Annals of St. Boniface Parish, 1862–1926* (Chicago: Privately printed, 1926); *Centennial, St. Boniface Church, 1864–1964* (Chicago: Privately printed, 1964); and the *Pfarrbote der St. Bonifacius Gemeinde,* which provided invaluable information on Chicago's German community through the 1930s.

125. Kalvelage, *Annals St. Boniface,* 49. Venn also encountered the wrath of some die-hard Germans, who accused him of making the parish Irish, since he occasionally preached in English for the sons of his immigrants.

126. *Der Pfarrbote*, January 1907, 11.

127. *St. Boniface Church*, n.p. It was the Poles, symbolically, who took over the membership of St. Boniface Parish during the war years. Father F. L. Kalvelage summarized the situation succinctly: "But while the census proved the insufficiency of the German element, it also showed that a large percentage of the Polish population was not affiliated with any parish. . . . Most of them were born and raised in this country, scarcely understanding Polish. Others, though born abroad, have become lax in the performance of their religious duties. . . . And it is from these that the parish has grown." (*Ibid.*, 103.)

CHAPTER TWO

The Consolidation of Parish Life, 1914–1962

WORLD WAR I AND BEYOND

The story we have traced so far both ends and continues with World War I. On the one hand, "it was World War I that brought great changes . . . to the nation in very radical ways . . . beginning in 1917 [when the United States entered the war] and the years that followed, the whole world experienced changes still too recent to be viewed with clear perspective."[1] Indeed, when the United States entered the war, America, which had left the frontier at the beginning of the century, became a world power. But in religious terms, the Church simply continued to build on what had gone before. As we have already seen, papal decrees against Americanism and Modernism effectively tempered any real reform. Pioneer bishops such as Marty, Feehan, Gilmour, and Loras were true innovators, who responded to the times and built the Church to fit those times. But their successors were less hardy men, their enthusiasm tempered by the papal decrees. They were mainly concerned with building new churches, rectories, convents, and schools, and, above all, keeping their dioceses in the red. For while the country was in a "progressive" mood, the Church lost its innovativeness and adaptability. The laity exercised little influence in civic affairs and accepted this subordinate position within the Church. Woman's place was still "in the home." Indeed, at a time when most political leaders were advancing women's suffrage, the Church encouraged its members to avoid the movement. Even after the Nineteenth Amendment was passed, Church leaders simply advised their parishioners to "use the ballot wisely."[2]

As the world prepared for war in 1914, the German community was at the height of its powers.[3] Catholic Germans had built up a strong and flourishing *Deutschtum*, with numerous societies (*Vereine*) and schools to nourish ethnic life. But paradoxically, as the world was plunged into war, the German community suffered the most. Many Americans were openly anti-German. Theodore Roosevelt said that "our bitter experience should teach us for a generation . . . to crush under our heel every movement that smacks in the smallest degree of playing the German game."[4] The German language disappeared from schools and universities; orchestras even banned Beethoven and Bach from their repertoire. Chicago's newspapers, which were generally anti-German, lashed out at "the disloyal Dachshund," while publishing inflammatory articles against all German Americans. Aliens suspected of sympathizing with the enemy were summarily interred and their property confiscated.

But most Catholics were sympathetic toward the German cause. The *Davenport (Ia.) Messenger* noted that the "Germans especially are victims of gross misrepresentation by the press." The Chicago *New World,* although officially neutral, described events in Germany with such articles as "Germany is Little Disturbed," "Germany's Case Stated," and "Letters of a German Chaplain." Bishop Vincent Wehrle of Bismarck fearlessly defended his German people from 1914 to 1917. As he said: "In these hard times of the old Fatherland, and especially when the American press fights a war of misrepresentation against Germany and German culture, it is natural that the national spirit is mightily aroused in many Germans of this country. This is praiseworthy. On the other hand . . . it is necessary that our German Catholics be cautious and do not readily give confidence to anyone who cries 'Deutschland über alles.' " Wehrle waged an unceasing battle against ruthless politicians who feared him; he distributed more than 10,000 pamphlets decrying those "who are really guided by the infidel and revolutionary ideas."[5]

After continued attacks by German submarines, the United States declared war on Germany on April 6, 1917. From that moment on, everything German was anathema. Sauerkraut became liberty cabbage, while the frankfurter became the hot dog. As William O'Connor observed: "Within the hours it took to bring the United States into war, German Americanism disappeared forever. It could no longer exist. In those febrile times, the German American had to make his decision to be either German or American. With startling few exceptions, the choice was made instantly for Americanism." After 1917, German Americans found themselves "on an irreversible downward course as a cultural force in American life."[6] After 1918, they had to prove loyalty again and again. America's *Deutschtum* was never the same, for although remnants remained through the 1920s and the 1930s, German America never regained the vitality it had before 1914.

The postwar Church grew enormously during the next two decades. By 1930, there were five archdioceses and thirty-three dioceses within the Midwest region. Chicago, which numbered 1,250,000 Catholics, was the second largest diocese in the country, with 387 parishes and 1,267 priests. Detroit, the second largest diocese in the region, numbered 635,764 Catholics, with 298 parishes and 603 priests. And Cleveland, with 540,193 Catholics, was the third most-populous diocese.[7] But some areas, especially those in the Northwest, declined, as the ravages of weather and depression depopulated the area. In Crookston, Minnesota, the diocese lost 9,000 Catholics between 1920 and 1940. By 1938, the rural problem was so severe that Bishop John H. Peschges organized the Catholic Rural

Life Conference and a Farmers' Placement Bureau in his diocese. The Church in North Dakota was still in the missionary stage as late as the 1920s and the 1930s, as dusty roads, driving rains, and frisky horses were the usual accoutrements of the missionary. One missionary had his sled catch fire when a charcoal foot-warmer blew up; the horses, running crazily from fright, strewed charcoal all over the North Dakota landscape! And in Sioux Falls, South Dakota, scores of missions and schools had to be closed because of the ravages of the Great Depression. Parishes in Turton, White Lake, Geddes, and De Smet could not meet their obligations and went heavily into debt during this period. Bishop Aloysius Muench of Fargo established the Catholic Church Expansion Fund to save mortgaged parishes and provide credit for future parish development.[8]

The trend toward consolidation in Catholic life increased during the war, as forty-two bishops and representatives from twenty-seven prominent Catholic societies met in 1917 to form the National Catholic War Council, an organization that later emerged as the National Catholic Welfare Conference (1919). While it is a strictly voluntary organization, the NCWC has inspired the foundation of forty-two national bishops' conferences and operates seven distinct departments from its national headquarters in Washington, D.C. How this organization affected diocesan and parish life can best be illustrated by its influence in the Davenport diocese.[9] Bishop Henry Rohlman, installed as Bishop of Davenport in 1927, immediately asked the Social Action Department of the NCWC to analyze the rural and urban population of the area in order to better appropriate diocesan funds. The immediate result was the establishment of a Catholic Charities Office, which provided family welfare services, health needs, care of the aged, recreational and protective programs for children, care for unmarried mothers, and special services to newly arrived Mexican immigrants. The Diocesan Council of Catholic Women, a branch of the National Council of Catholic Women, was instrumental in assessing the needs of the diocese. In 1932, at the height of the Great Depression, Catholic Charities became associated with the Community Chest, and its objectives were expanded to include various family and child care programs and an adoptive service for both native- and foreign-born children.

The National Catholic Rural Life Conference, an association of Catholics dedicated to the spiritual and material well-being of rural people, was formed in 1923 at a meeting convened by Edwin V. O'Hara, later Bishop of Kansas City. O'Hara had become head of the Rural Life Bureau of the NCWC in 1920, and from contacts thus gained, laid the foundation for the NCRLC.[10] The Davenport Diocese established its own branch of the conference to learn and discuss farm problems, as well as develop the spiritual life of farm families through days of reflection, prayer, devotions, and the building of shrines. The conference presented a "Back to the Land" program on radio in 1932, and explained to Iowans the Subsistence Homestead Plan of colonization. The Rural Life Conference of the diocese continued to grow through the 1940s, as the department helped youth, displaced persons, and the needy throughout the world.[11] Indeed, the Rural Life Conference was a distinctly Midwestern contribution to the NCWC.

But one thing remained the same, whether in Columbus, Ohio, or Kansas City, Missouri, namely, the social and devotional life of the Church. The story of St. Cecilia Parish in Detroit is typical of the era. The devotional life of the parish revolved around frequent Communions, Holy Hours, devotions to the Sacred Heart, the Blessed Mother, and St. Theresa, as well as various retreats for men and women. The Parish Holy Name sponsored a CYO, a Young Men's Club, an Ushers' Club, and a Junior Holy Name. While the Altar and Rosary Society provided for the needs of married and older women, a Young Ladies' Sodality and a girl scout troop served the younger crowd. The social life of the parish revolved around various affairs, for "these were the days of anniversary dinners, parish excursions, choral concerts . . . Thanksgiving dances, hard-time socials, and even bazaars . . . they served as perhaps nothing else to weld the people into one great family."[12] Parish life thus revolved around certain pietistic and social practices. One's degree of participation in the parish was strictly determined by participation in such practices. The spirituality so-described was highly individualistic and sacramental. Parishioners considered themselves Catholic insofar as they participated in the cultic and pietistic practices of the parish. This type of spirituality, which can be traced to the Counter Reformation of the sixteenth century, went unchallenged until Vatican Council II reintroduced a more biblical style of piety, one that was actually truer to the earlier Church than that practiced for nearly 500 years.

Parochial education remained the principal means of influencing youth. But statistics between 1900 and 1930 demonstrate that while some were willing, the majority were simply unable to keep up with the financial demand for parochial schools. While the overall number of elementary schools increased from 3,812 to 7,387 during this period, the number of parishes increased from 6,127 to 12,475. By the end of the Great Depression, the number of schools increased to 7,660, but the overall school population dropped to 2,017,094. More progress could be seen in secondary education, as the number of Catholic high schools rose to 2,123 by 1930. By 1947, there were 1,637 diocesan and parochial high schools, and 795 private Catholic high schools, in the United States. But the trend here was toward more diocesan and religious order high schools than strictly parochial ones.[13]

While Pius X did revive the Confraternity of Christian Doctrine (CCD) in 1905 by his encyclical, *Acerbo nimis,* it was not until 1934 that a committee on the CCD was established with the NCWC.[14] Several innovative programs were devised in the Midwest to reach those children not attending Catholic parochial schools. In North Dakota, sisters and seminarians spent their summers preparing non-parochial school children for Holy Communion and Confirmation. Traveling from one parish to the next, these volunteers helped prepare more than 5,000 children for their First Holy Communion (1947).[15] Bishop Francis J. Schank of Crookston, Minnesota, became nationally known for the establishment of Catholic summer schools for migrant children in Moorehead (1945) and Crookston itself (1949).[16] And in Davenport, Iowa, more than 3,000 summer vacation schools were established for children not attending parochial schools. Indeed, there seemed to be no end to the practical solutions offered by these Midwestern farmers.[17]

The postwar Church is epitomized by the life of George Cardinal Mundelein, who became Chicago's third Archbishop in 1915.[18] Mundelein was the quintessential bishop of the 1920s and the 1930s. While Quigley essentially favored ethnicity through a vast network of national parishes, Mundelein merely tolerated it. While Quigley actively supported ethnic schools and institutions, Mundelein hastened their Americanization. One of his first acts as archbishop was to reform and reorganize the parochial school system. Ethnic schools were required to teach the ordinary subjects in English, while standardized tests were chosen for all schools. Mundelein saw the parish school as "an anchor that steadies and holds the boat. A school will ensure the continuation of a parish more than anything else . . . more than that, it is the junior church."[19] The parochial school was the principal means of keeping the young within the influence of the Church.

Archbishop Mundelein encouraged Americanization through numerous archdiocesan organizations and societies. He elevated the Holy Name Society to one of the principal sodalities for men. Originally founded in France in 1274, the society was largely a loose federation of parochial units until Mundelein made it a laymen's militia, for "the personal sanctification of the individual members." He entrusted it with the care of juvenile delinquents through the Big Brother movement. He built Holy Name Technical School in Lockport, Illinois, to care for young men sent from Boy's and Juvenile Court. By 1921, there were over 200 Big Brother groups that cared for more than 4,000 boys. The Holy Name Society also operated an employment bureau for young men, a lecture circuit, and a subscription service for the *New World*. By joining the Holy Name Society, ethnic parishes became more American and more Catholic. The records of the *New World* indicate that membership in the Society increased dramatically during the 1920s and the 1930s; by 1943, there were over 15,000 members.[20] Indeed, Mundelein's efforts to coordinate parish activities through the Holy Name Society were largely successful.

A small group of French Catholic laymen founded the St. Vincent de Paul Society in 1833. Frederick Ozanam, a spokesman for the society, described its goals in an 1830 article: "The visitation of the poor in their homes, if carried out prudently, would have a more salutary influence on themselves. If you are to serve the poor, turn your charity to the moral and spiritual improvement of the families visited."[21] The society came to the United States in 1845, where it organized its first conference in St. Louis, Missouri; by 1883, there were 4,000 conferences with 45,000 members; by 1911, there were 7,500 conferences, with 100,000 members. Mundelein saw the society as one of the two great spiritual organizations in the Church—while the Holy Name offered personal sanctification, St. Vincent de Paul followed the example of the Good Samaritan. As the archbishop stated: "In the church today we have societies, sodalities, confraternities . . . but I have ever maintained that there is no body of laymen in the Church more Christian, more Catholic, more charitable, than the St. Vincent de Paul Conference."[22] Acting through the parish, these conferences brought immigrants into archdiocesan activities. Parish records clearly indicate that ethnic communities were active in the society—and their activity gradually Americanized them. But it was Mundelein who made the society a moving force in Catholic life. When the threat of Nazism was spreading throughout Europe, he called on all Catholics to support the St. Vincent de Paul Society:

> I have repeatedly said that one of our great assets, not only in the parish, but also in the diocese, is a flourishing St. Vincent de Paul Society . . . it would be disastrous indeed if through fault of ours, negligence or indifference, the field of the volunteer worker were restricted . . . Vincentians continue to be apostles of Christian charity in a selfish, unbelieving world; you belong to an army which has its corps, its companies, its regiments in the Church Triumphant as well as our Church Militant.[23]

The St. Vincent de Paul Society would play a prominent role in Catholic life for decades to come.

The Knights of Columbus was a national organization that also fostered Americanization on the parish level.[24] Founded in 1882 by Father Michael J. McGivney, the Knights of Columbus was a predominantly Irish society that accepted all men between the ages of eighteen and forty-five.[25] Its rituals and ceremonies stressed charity, fraternity, and patriotism. With $8 million at the end of World War I, the society set up free employment bureaus, evening schools, and correspondence courses to help servicemen adjust to peacetime life; some 500,000 veterans received free academic, commercial, and technical training through the Knights of Columbus. The society, which increased steadily during the 1920s and the 1930s, gave thousands of dollars for charitable relief during the Great Depression. Mundelein himself said that "It needs no particular elaboration on my part to bring home to them [i.e., the Knights of Columbus] the great need of charitable assistance at this time in the general depression that exists in our midst."[26] Like the Holy Name and St. Vincent de Paul societies before them, the Knights of Columbus acted admirably to alleviate the general suffering of the 1930s.

The Catholic Youth Organization (CYO) was the most significant youth organization to be established in the United States since the establishment of the parochial school system. Organized by Bishop Bernard Sheil (an auxiliary to Mundelein) in 1930, the CYO Americanized thousands of immigrant children in scores of American parishes. The *Chicago Herald-American* praised its efforts on its tenth anniversary in 1940:

> The Catholic Youth Organization, ten years old tomorrow, is and has always been a completely, unwaveringly, proudly American youth organization.
> It has helped to shape the lives of hundreds of thousands of boys and young men in the past ten years, and it has shaped them into thoroughly American ways of life.
> It has provided education and opportunities for those who lack them . . . it has combined, in perfect balance, practical help with training in the finest ideals of Christianity and Americanism . . . instead of helplessly fearing for the future of America, it has gone practically to work to ensure a good future for America by training thousands of boys and young men into Good Americans . . . Following that policy, CYO has become, in ten short years, *one of the most powerful influences for good citizenship in Chicago and one of the great forces for Americanism* in America.[27]

The organization operated a Working Boys' Home, at 1140 West Jackson Boulevard, where young men provided a Motor Delivery Service, a garage, a candle factory, and a mimeograph and stencil-cutting business. Summer schools were set up in the city parks to provide recreation for Chicago's children. The St. Rose of Lima CYO enrolled 1,600 boys and girls in its varied program of gymnastics, arts and crafts, and education at Sherman Park on the South Side. But it was boxing that became the most popular event sponsored by the organization. Parishes from north, south, and west participated in the annual Christmas Fund Boxing Tournament at the International Amphitheatre. Germans, Poles, Irishmen, and, especially, Italians were well-represented at these events. A series of matches between the CYO and the national team of Ireland drew over 38,000 fans to Soldier Field. The fights continued to draw enormous crowds to the lakefront facility as well as the Chicago Stadium during the 1930s and the 1940s. The CYO also sponsored parish Boy Scout units, which brought hundreds of young men into contact with other nationalities. Through scouting, summer schools, boxing, and numerous other activities, the CYO effectively encouraged Americanization for thousands of immigrant children. Together with the Holy Name Society, the St. Vincent de Paul Society, and the Knights of Columbus, the Catholic Youth Organization was an effective way-station of Americanization.[28]

THE ETHNIC PARISH REVISITED

Chicago's ethnics were highly enthusiastic when Mundelein became Chicago's third archbishop. The *New World* stated: "When he came from Brooklyn to Chicago, the Poles, Italians, Germans, Irish, Bohemians, and other racial groups . . . lauded him to the skies for his wisdom and energy and the sympathetic attitude he maintained toward each and all of them."[29] And, yet, the new Archbishop would eventually disappoint them, for he was not as compassionate toward ethnics as his immediate predecessor. During his twenty-year tenure in Chicago, Mundelein established only one new German parish, St. Williams, in 1915; and only one new Italian parish, St. Callistus, in 1919. Although he was willing to maintain existing national parishes, Mundelein refused to establish new ones. He stated: "My purpose in the formation of these new parishes is to make them largely territorial, i.e., to give them certain limits." In 1916, he refused to see a delegation of Poles, who were pressing him to establish a new Polish parish in Summit, Illinois. He wrote the following note: "I advised you, therefore, that you allow the matter to rest where it properly belongs, in the judgment of the archbishop, who has his own reasons for action."[30] Slovaks also pressured the archbishop for parishes of their own, but Mundelein adamantly refused to establish them. In 1927, he was still "as much opposed to the making of a Slovak bishop to look after the interests of the Slovak resident here as I was to the making of a Polish bishop or a German bishop for the same reason."[31] Lithuanians, who had fought for control of church property under Quigley, continued to trouble Mundelein through the first four decades of the century. They opposed all attempts to introduce English into their churches and schools. A group of hard-line nationalists distributing anti-English pamphlets outside the doors of Lithuanian churches in 1925 urged parishioners to resist any attempt at Americanization. The Catholic newspaper *Draugus* observed: "Our Lithuanian Church is the only stronghold for our Lithuanian nationality in America. Let us defend it from Americanization. Away with the English sermons from Lithuanian churches, and, you traitors, and Americanizing priests, get out from our Lithuanian parishes."[32]

The fate of "the German oak tree" is best illustrated by the fate of St. Boniface Parish. Father Charles A. Rempe took charge of St. Boniface in July of 1916. He faced monumental difficulties since the average Sunday attendance was only 400 and the average collection was $55.81. The parish debt stood at $128,392. The Centennial History of the parish noted that "Father Rempe soon realized that it would be impossible for him to be pastor of a German parish in the old tradition." Since he spoke Polish, he tried to attract the unchurched people of this newer immigrant group. Father F. L. Kalvelage summarized the situation succinctly:

> But while the census proved the insufficiency of the German element, it also showed that a large percentage of the Polish population was not affiliated with any parish. Some of them had made their First Communion either in St. Boniface Church or some other non-Polish parish in the neighborhood . . . others had never been to confession or communion. There are literally thousands of these in our neighborhood. Most of them were born and raised in this country, scarcely understanding Polish. Others though born abroad have become lax in the performance of their religious duties; among these are generally the parents of the children who make their

First Communion in our Church. Here was indeed a large and legitimate field of labor and recruits for St. Boniface Parish. And it is from these that the Parish has grown.[33]

But the growth did not take place overnight. A year after he came, Father Rempe complained to Archbishop Mundelein that the obstacles he met at St. Boniface were insurmountable. Mundelein insisted that Rempe continue his work, since "all that matters was gone over and thoroughly considered when St. Boniface was permitted to conserve its character as a German-speaking parish."[34]

St. Boniface gradually revived, but it lost much of its German flavor. Rempe sought new parishioners from the Poles directly north of St. Boniface, a move that angered both Germans and Poles. The Germans who remained in the parish were indignant about the new Polish members, while the Polish clergy accused the new pastor of stealing their parishioners. But the parish continued to attract new members from this unchurched group. Rempe started First Communion classes for public school children in 1916, classes that averaged 400 a year by 1917. Mass attendance rose from 400 a Sunday in 1916, to 1,400 a Sunday in 1926.[35] Parishioners reduced the parish debt to $105,806 by 1920. As America entered the 1920s, St. Boniface was once again a flourishing parish. But it was no longer a strictly German parish, for many of its parishioners were now Poles or Slovaks from eastern Europe. The history of St. Boniface Parish clearly demonstrates the rise and decline of an important German parish. But the parish did not die, for it continued to serve other immigrant groups through World War I and beyond.

But German traditions died hard. Father Rempe worked diligently to maintain the dignity of German Catholicism, even after the wreckage of World War I. Feeling that many Americans equated German Americanism with Protestantism, Rempe believed that German Catholics had to publicize their heritage and culture. He encouraged all parishioners, both past and present, to take part in an annual St. Boniface Day celebration (*St.-Bonifacius Tag*); he called this "a modest beginning toward the regaining of our self-respect" (*Pfarrbote,* June 1917).[36] At St. Michaels, "though the war caused a great change of attitude toward the use of the German language . . . St. Michael's still maintains its title of a German parish."[37] Parish anniversaries were special occasions when national customs could be fully displayed. St. Augustine's celebrated its fiftieth anniversary in 1936 with German songs and a traditional *Rathskeller.* And St. Benedict's Parish—the last Catholic parish in Chicago that could be called German—continued to function as a German parish as late as 1952, when Samuel Cardinal Stritch, Mundelein's successor, commended it on its fiftieth anniversary, for "that is the debt we owe in the United States to our Catholics of German origin."[38]

German traditions also continued in the rural Midwest. Walter Stahlke, of Skokie, Illinois, recalled that his own parents carried on Germanic traditions when he was grown up in rural Minnesota. "My parents had eleven children, and they taught us all German, which sort of demonstrates the pride they had in their cultural heritage—even though they had no acquaintances in Germany, never went there, and never corresponded with anybody there. Yet they sort of clung to this German language."[39] In Flush, Kansas, parishioners at St. Joseph's Parish continued to speak German through World War II. Father Biehler, the chronicler of the parish, noted that "when I visited some of my relatives at Ellis back in 1930, we went to church at Ellis on Sunday and I never heard any English outside of the church nor in the church. I attended Mass one Sunday in St. Joseph in Topeka in 1931 and it was the same story there. But World War II changed all of that in a hurry."[40] Indeed, there was an awareness on the part of the clergy that some parishes were "German" long after they had lost their distinctive language. In Menominee, Illinois, a succession of German pastors serviced Nativity of the Blessed Virgin Mary Parish until 1934, when "Father Joseph Lonergan was the first pastor . . . who was not of German descent."[41] Even as late as 1960, priests spoke of "the German league." And when Albert Cardinal Meyer, the fifth Archbishop of Chicago, died in 1965, many priests asked whether the new bishop would be Irish or German.

The Italian Parish. While the German oak tree merged into the American mainstream, Italians from southern Europe began to challenge their numerical superiority. Very few came before 1880, but between 1880 and 1900, 971,556 Italians left *l'Italia* for an uncertain future in America. While a few did settle in rural areas, the vast majority recreated their village life in the urban centers of the Midwest. And Chicago was the most significant, as it grew from 5,685 Italians in 1890, to 73,960 in 1930, making it the third largest Italian city in America.[42] Native Americans disdained these southerners for their crude and often illiterate ways. Catholicism struggled to provide the necessary priests and parishes to support them. But it was soon obvious that these new immigrants could not be treated like the Irish and Germans before them. The "Italian Problem," as it came to be called, was a combination of poor education in matters of faith and religion, few Italian priests and few churches to accept and provide for their peculiar style of Italian Catholicism. The first attempt to deal with the problem was the duplex parish, which allowed Italians to celebrate their own liturgies at already existing parishes. But this experiment soon failed, as Irish priests complained that Italians failed to support the Church and that Italian men did not attend Mass regularly.[43]

While the Italian parish was not as central to the lives of its parishioners as the Irish or German parish, it was an important way-station of ethnicity and Americanization. Italian religious orders like the Servite and Scalabrini Fathers encouraged Italianization through local *feste,* parish societies, and numerous bulletins and sermons. The parishioners supported the priests through active participation and local contributions to the parish. They kept their ties to the Old Country by encouraging the continuation of the Italian language at all levels of parish activity—*feste,* local societies, and ordinary worship. Italian officials acknowledged their presence by attending local activities and even soliciting their vote.[44]

One of the most significant Italian parishes in the Midwest was St. Philip Benizi, established by Archbishop Quigley of Chicago in 1904.[45] By following its history through two World Wars, we get a glimpse of ethnicity that remained vital through four decades of war, prosperity, and depression. St. Philip's parishioners were Sicilians from Alto Villa, Baglieria, Santa Christina, and Mezzoniso. They tended to settle with their own compatriots to such an extent that individual streets were often occupied by Sicilians from the same small village. By 1918, when a sociological study of St. Philip's had been made, "the Italians [still] hold together with more tenacity than any other racial group in the ward."[46] False priests and bishops took advantage of their ignorance by swindling them out of their money, while Protestant proselytizers tried to lure them away from the faith. But these attempts at proselytization were largely unsuccessful, as Catholicism was a way of life to most Italians and to abandon it was unthinkable.[47]

St. Philip Benizi was an active center of *Italianità* (Italianness) for more than four decades. Its second pastor, Father Luigi Giambastiani, was an Italianizer par excellence. He was a leading figure on the Near North Side for fifty years. When friction arose between the Italian Servites and those born in America, Giambastiani sided with the Italians. He insisted that Italian couples be referred to St. Philip's for marriage, as "Italian families are to be given service by their own Italian priest, in the Italian churches as in the past. To do otherwise means to confuse the mind of the people, to bring discord in the families, to break the unity of the parish, to lessen the authority of the pastor."[48] Speaking through the parish bulletin, *Il Calendario Italiano,* Giambastiani cajoled his parishioners to attend St. Philip's Church: "Don't say that you live near the German, the Irish, or the Polish church; friends know no distance, and besides the German church was built by and for the German people, the Polish church by and for the Polish people, the same way the Italian church of St. Philip was built by and for the Italian people." But the inevitable fact was that Italians left their national parishes and moved to American churches. Writing "to our faraway friends" (i.e., those who had moved away from St. Philip's), Father Giambastiani claimed that Italian Americans forgot their ethnicity when they moved to more cosmopolitan parishes. They were ashamed of their origins and preferred to give their money to American churches. Father Giambastiani repeatedly reminded his readers that "St. Philip has been made for the Italians; and it is just that Italians help it; and if they don't help it, who will? . . . Italians, do not be afraid to honor your Catholicism with a sentiment of Italianness."[49]

It was the traditional *feste* that most appropriately expressed the peculiar brand of Catholicism that came from Italy. Father Giambastiani described these festivals in an interview with the Chicago Historical Society in 1928:

> In Sicily each town, which is usually located on top of a mountain, has its own festival, one town having its festival in May, the next in June, etc. This had a tendency to bring the people of Sicily together. And so it is in Chicago.[50]

Father Giambastiani noted that St. Philip's retained the meaning of these festivals through the 1920s and the 1930s, in particular, the Feast of Our Lady of Loretto. He called it the "loveliest festival" of the year, as it retained "almost all of the significance and beauty which it had in Sicily." *Il Calendario Italiano* gave a detailed account of this *festa* in a 1926 issue.[51] The festival began on September 4th as a group of bands marched through the streets of the Near North Side for an hour and a half; the *Carro Triunfale* (Triumphal Float) left the church with a band atop at 6 P.M. to entertain the parishioners until Solemn Vespers at 7:30 P.M. The bands then gathered together for a concert immediately afterward, until midnight. On September 5th, a huge procession formed in front of the church, with floats, torches, and parish societies joining in. The Solemn Feast in honor of Our Lady started at 10:30 A.M., with an orchestra and fireworks accompanying the festivities. The Great Procession followed at 2 P.M., as parishioners carried Our Lady of Loretto through the streets of Chicago. The procession wound its way through Milton Avenue to Oak Street, Oak Street to Cambridge, and finally stopped in front of St. Philip's, where it saluted the crowds that had gathered. The bands, which continued to serenade the neighborhood, marched through the streets of the Near North Side until midnight. The festival concluded with bicycle races and other athletic events the following day. A final procession concluded the solemnities at 8 P.M., and the statue of Our Lady was then put away until another year.

Like their German counterparts, Italians fostered a host of societies and organizations.[52] Most of these societies, which centered around the town from which the immigrants came, carried on a good part of their activities through the local parish. St. Philip's principal society was the *Società di S.S. Lauretana di Altavilla* (Society of Our Lady of Loretto from Altavilla). It sponsored the parish festival of the year, the Feast of Our Lady of Loretto, on September 5th. But there were other societies as well. *Le Madre dei Dolori* was established when the parish began in 1904; *the Figlie di Maria* (Daughters of Mary) also began at the beginning of the century. Many of these associations were devotional, such as the *Società del Crocifisso di Ciminna* (Society of the Crucifix Ciminna), which held various Masses and processions during this period.[53] An annual banquet of all the Italian societies on the North Side was held during the 1920s and the 1930s, an event that attracted twenty-four societies in 1941. Parishioners soon established the Ladies of St. Philip Benizi Guild as "one of the largest groups of Italian ladies (over 1,100) to support the work of the parish school."[54]

Ethnic parishes, however, were not only way-stations of ethnicity; they were also a focus of Americanization. National parishes actively encouraged this process through parish institutions and societies, bulletins and sermons, as well as constant cooperation with archdiocesan-wide activities and organizations. Father Luigi Giambasiani felt that the ethnic parish had done everything possible to Americanize the immigrant. *Il Calendario Italiano* observed that "all should be Americans and there should be no distinction of nationalities . . . you can be just as good Americans at St. Philip as in any other church, German, Irish, Polish, or whatever nationality it might be."[55] Various institutions and organizations furthered Americanization. Monthly bulletins, which began English-language announcements in 1916, continued bilingual publication through the 1930s. Servite missionaries conducted English missions "for the young people of the parish." Indeed, pastors and laity, conscious of Americanization, did everything possible to further assimilation.[56]

Ethnic parishes also established sodalities and organizations for the betterment of the young men and women of the community. St. Philip's founded two public school sodalities in the 1920s, as well as a band for girls and a Junior Holy Name for boys. Both groups, which numbered over 500 members by 1926, adequately served the public school children of the area. The Third Order of Servites, a Choral Society, a Sewing Club, and Social Club also brought many young men and women together under the patronage of the parish. A Mother's Club cooperated with the parish sisters for "the *civic* and *Christian* formation of our children, the Chicago citizens of tomorrow."[57] During the 1930s, St. Philip's cooperated with the North Side Civic Center in providing all the facilities of a modern Boys Club—a game room, arts and crafts equipment, and numerous sporting events. Our Lady of Pompeii also sponsored a variety of athletic teams that were supported by local politicians or tavern owners. In addition, it operated a summer camp in Wisconsin for the enjoyment of the entire parish.[58] Through all these activities, ethnic parishes fostered Americanization for the youth of the early twentieth century. Instead of alienating them, the national parish actively supported them and provided societies and organizations for their economic and social betterment.

Ethnic parishes also supported naturalization efforts. Both priests and laity actively encouraged this process. Our Lady of Pompeii conducted Americanization classes where Italians learned to read and write English. Later on, "doctors and lawyers would tutor them [the immigrants] and go down and sponsor them for their papers. They helped each other out quite a bit years ago. You wouldn't hesitate to go to your doctor to ask for guidance . . . it wasn't just for medicine . . . you would go for advice in investments . . . when they had banquets they would honor these professional men. They looked up to them quite a bit."[59] But it wasn't just the professionals who commanded respect—it was the priests as well. They were consulted for legal advice, sought after by politicians, and guided the parish as one of the principal socializers of the period. Mr. Anthony Serritella recalled that "if a person had anything to do with courts at all the priests would go along to see that they were treated right. And they would be the first ones they would call on as character witnesses. . . . They went to the priests for a lot of things. The Italian people used to get pushed around, so they got better treatment."[60]

We have now seen that Chicago's Italians, unhindered by the cultural shock of World War I, effectively continued their ethnicity through years of war, prosperity, and depression, while German Americans quietly merged into the general population after 1918. Italian Americans kept their identity as Italians well past World War II. And it was the ethnic parish that provided the focus for this dual culture and loyalty. But the Poles, who came to America at the same time as the Italians, also kept their identity, and—more than the Italians—made the parish the center of their daily life. While the Italians gradually merged into an Irish-dominated Church, the Poles staunchly maintained their parishes as ethnic parishes. And while the Italians only became Italian in America, the Poles brought with them a deep sense of being Polish, a feeling that led to the formation of hundreds of Polish parishes in the Midwest.[61]

The Polish Parish. Poles began to arrive in the New World shortly after the Civil War. Most were peasants, who had no intention of settling permanently in the United States, but saw America as "the land of opportunities for advancing in the Old Country."[62] By 1875, there were more than 200,000 Polish foreign-born in America, with fifty established parishes. By 1890, their numbers had increased to 800,000, with 132 churches, 126 priests, and 122 schools. Buffalo, Pittsburgh, Cleveland, Detroit, Chicago, and Milwaukee had emerged as important Polish centers. And while Wisconsin had the largest number of settlements, Chicago had the largest population.[63] St. Stanislaus Kostka, established in 1867 as Chicago's first Polish parish, grew to such an extent that, by 1899, it was reported to be the largest Catholic parish in the world, with more than 50,000 parishioners and fifty extant societies. Polish immigration peaked during the prewar decades, as more than 100,000 Poles came to America each year between 1901 and 1914. They generally settled north of the Ohio River, and east of the Mississippi, to such an extent that Chicago became the capital of these new *okolica* (communities) with 250,000 Polish residents by 1905, and 400,000 by 1910. In the Midwest, Milwaukee and Detroit each numbered 100,000 Poles, with Cleveland and Toledo also having significant populations. By 1920, the number of Polish Americans reached 3 million.[64]

The national parish was "the most important Polish-American institution" in the United States.[65] It recreated the narrower village life from which most Poles had come. Thomas and Znaniecki, authors of the classic *The Polish Peasant in the United States,* noted that the ethnic parish helped break down the anonymity of American life and provided a center for the organization and unification of the community. The societies and organizations grouped around the parish helped to affirm and give an identity to each of its members. And the festivals and celebrations that sprang from each parish deepened his religious sense.[66] At the heart of each parish was the pastor, who "embodied religion, language, and national culture in his own person."[67] The Congregation of the Resurrection established a large network of Polish-American communities throughout the Midwest; by 1899, nine of the fifteen parishes established in Chicago were Resurrectionist parishes.[68]

By studying the growth of the Polish Church in Wisconsin, we get a glimpse of what the Polish parish was really like. For not only did Wisconsin have the largest number of Polish settlements, but it was also the battleground for the forces of ethnicity and Americanization within the Polish community in the Midwest. The first Pole to settle in Wisconsin was Count Vincent Djewanewski, who came to the Northwest shortly after the revolt of 1830. Poles soon began to dot the Wisconsin landscape with small rural communities.[69] The most significant was in Portage County, where Poles first arrived in 1857 to work at the Wisconsin Lumber Company. By 1870, in the town of Sharon, all but fifty of the 948 families in the town were Polish. Father Joseph Dabrowski was a leading figure of the times. Dabrowski, who came to Portage County in 1870, was assigned to the remote town of Polonia. But the young pastor soon found himself embroiled in a controversy at Ellis. Poles in that town were clamoring for a church of their own, since they had to occupy pews in the German church. And even when Bishop Matthias Henni of Milwaukee established for them a parish of their own, they continued to complain of unsympathetic German pastors. The dispute was finally resolved when Father Dabrowski had the entire parish moved to Polonia and renamed Sacred Heart Parish in 1872. Dabrowski was also involved in another controversy. Parishioners at his own parish were angered when Dabrowski proposed to move the church from a saloon-infested crossroad to a quieter location. The disgruntled parishioners subsequently sabotaged the pastor's woodpile with gunpowder-filled sticks of wood. Fortunately for Dabrowski, he left the room after throwing only one stick into the fire. This early pioneer soon invited the Sisters of St. Felix (Felicians) to come to Polonia and teach in his school. Dabrowski became known as the "father of the Polish-American parochial school system" and later established a seminary for the training of Polish-American priests.[70]

The real center of Polish life in Wisconsin, however, was Milwaukee.[71] The first Polish family came about 1855, and as new settlers arrived, they settled on the West and East sides of the city. In 1866, Poles established St. Stanislaus Parish, at Grove and Mineral Streets, for their growing community. By 1872, the old church had outgrown its capacity, and two new ones were built—St. Stanislaus, on the corner of Grove and Mitchell, and St. Hedwig's, at Franklin and Brady. A strong Polish enclave arose south of the Menominee River, as Poles slowly became the second largest immigrant group in Milwaukee. By 1903, there were 65,000 in Milwaukee alone, with seven established parishes scattered throughout the city. Bayrd Still, a Milwaukee historian, observed that "the Polish settlement in Milwaukee is largely a chronicle of the expansion of their Catholic parishes." Poles became more and more a factor in Milwaukee life, as the predominantly German city slowly changed its character to a more cosmopolitan metropolis. By 1939, Milwaukee numbered 120,000 Poles, with seven new parishes established after World War I. Indeed, Poles became such a factor in Milwaukee life that five of the eight city aldermen elected that year were Polish.[72]

The story of St. Josephat Parish is indicative of the growth of Milwaukee's Polish community.[73] The original church, built in 1888, burned down a year later, and a second one was erected for $30,000. But the pastor had more grandiose plans, so he bought stone columns from the old Chicago Federal Building for $13,900. The Chicago and Northwestern Railroad laid a special track to the east end of the Kinnickinnic River so that the five-hundred flatbeds carrying the stone could be brought to the construction site. Work began in 1896, and was completed in 1901, at a cost of $1 million. The imposing edifice was a symbol of Polish solidarity in the service of God in a new land. But the debts on the structure grew to such an extent that hundreds of parishioners who had mortgaged their homes to build the structure went bankrupt. Archbishop Sebastian Messmer was forced to intervene, and even journeyed to Rome, hat in hand, to find help for St. Josephat. The Franciscans finally guaranteed a loan of $200,000 to save the structure. Pope Pius XI honored the Polish community by raising St. Josephat to the rank of basilica in 1927.

While Poles soon gained access to Wisconsin's democratic process—and took their place alongside German Americans in countless city and village halls—they found themselves on the outside of a German-controlled Church.[74] The Germans, who had a strong foothold in Wisconsin, were unwilling to grant Polish Americans the same consideration they granted themselves—namely, the selection of native bishops. And the Poles, who had come to America with a long tradition of anti-Germanism, had reasons to distrust the German clergy. As Thomas I. Monzell put it, "in the eyes of [the Poles], Americanization was synonymous with the . . . Germanization they had known in Europe."[75] The protagonist in these so-called "church wars" was Sebastian Messmer, Archbishop of Milwaukee (1903–1930), who found the Poles aloof, their pastors independent and greedy, and their finances a constant source of worry. The financial chaos at St. Josephat only hardened his attitude toward all Poles. Like Archbishop Ireland of St. Paul, Messmer believed in the rapid Americanization of his immigrant flock. In order to accomplish this goal as quickly as possible, Messmer encouraged the use of English in all parishes and parochial schools. And he was very reluctant to establish any new Polish parishes. By insisting that these new immigrants learn English as quickly as possible, Messmer believed that they would soon become American. The controversy centered around the request for a Polish-American bishop. Messmer outlined his attitude on the subject in 1905, in a letter written to Cardinal Gibbons:

> Now the paper brought the news today that the Polish are going to make new efforts to get one of their men elected bishop for the new diocese. The longer I think it over the more it seems to me a dangerous experiment at this stage to give the Polish people a bishop for the very reason that he will be considered the bishop for all the Poles of the United States. . . . The Polish are not yet American enough to keep aloof too much from the rest of us.[76]

Later, in 1912, Messmer noted that "the agitation for Polish bishops in the United States had assumed such a character, especially in our province, that it becomes positively subversive and destructive of Catholic faith, loyalty, discipline, and order."[77] Ultimately, Messmer gave the Poles what they wanted, for with the appointments of Bishop Paul Rhode, as the first Polish-American bishop in 1908, and Edward Kozlowski, as auxiliary bishop of Milwaukee in 1914, the controversy subsided and peace was restored. As an historian of this controversy noted, "he [Sebastian Messmer] made it possible for Poles to fulfill some of their most crucial aspirations within the Church."[78]

The antagonists in this war were Wenceslaus and Michael Kruszka, brothers in blood, religion, and nationality.[79] Wenceslaus came to Milwaukee in 1895, and in his spare time prepared the first comprehensive history of the Polish people in America. For Kruszka, the appointment of a Polish bishop in the United States was of paramount importance, for it reflected his pluralistic view of Catholicism in a multi-denominational society. In 1901, in the *Freeman's Journal,* he argued that bishops should know the principal languages of their dioceses or risk losing a good part of the flock. At the Polish Catholic Convention in Buffalo, the very same year, Kruszka noted that "the schismatics have the popular side of the affair . . . they have so-called Polish bishops, whereas they accuse the Polish Roman Catholic clergy of treason to their nation when holding allegiance to Irish and German bishops, as they say."[80] To the exasperation of Kruszka and large numbers of Polish Catholics, the selection of a bishop was painstakingly slow. Under Archbishop Messmer, Kruszka was exiled to a small parish in Ripon, but did not give up his fight to obtain Polish-American bishops. Michael Kruszka supported his brother as editor of the *Kuryer Polski,* a Polish-American weekly that constantly criticized the role of the Church in Polish-American life. Though attacked personally by Messmer, Kruszka staunchly defended the rights of his people and won office to the Wisconsin Assembly. Through both brothers, Wisconsin's Poles discovered that they could be good Catholics, but Poles, nonetheless.[81]

Parochial schools were a key element in the growth of Polish parishes. The schools, like the parish, preserved Polish ethnicity, but, at the same time, fostered Americanization.[82] And parochial schools were more important to Polish parishes than Irish ones, for the school fostered a distinctive national language. The first formal Polish school opened at St. Stanislaus Parish in Milwaukee in 1868. By 1898, there were seven parochial schools, with 4,605 pupils, in Milwaukee alone; St. Josephat's even opened a high school, or "business college," for seventy-eight boys. By 1910, American Poles numbered approximately 3 million, with 530 parishes and 330 schools. But the era of greatest growth came after World War I. By 1921, Polish schools numbered 511, with an enrollment of 220,000 students. By 1933, the number had risen to 4 million Poles, 800 parishes, and 530 schools.[83]

Most Polish Americans agreed that parochial schools were absolutely necessary to preserve and maintain the culture and language of Poland. Walery Jasinski expressed the sentiment of many when he said: "You want to study the Polish language and the culture of Poland because you want to be a useful citizen of the United States. . . . How can one who does not know the treasures of Polish culture himself . . . enrich America with them?"[84] For this reason, a typical parochial school conducted classes in Polish and English, with special courses on Polish grammar and composition, history and literature, and music. The traditional three R's were conducted in English. But despite the large amount of time devoted to Polish, most school children preferred to speak English. As an early Polish priest observed, "not two boys out of twenty employ Polish in their conversation with another . . . the girls are slower in abandoning Polish as a medium of conversation. The boys' games . . . make the boys think in English, and think quickly."[85] The Polish school, therefore, helped the second and third generation adapt to their host culture and quickly enter the American mainstream.

By the 1920s, many children knew little or no Polish. Despite the pluralistic view of the Kruszkas and other Polish leaders, Polish communities slowly assimilated into the larger culture—without a complete rejection of their ethnic past. The Felician Sisters, in cooperation with the Polish societies and press, inaugurated or promoted programs to revive interest in things Polish. From 1932 to 1952, the Felicians held ten provincial meetings to discuss the relative problems attached to teaching Polish in parochial schools. Shortly after the first meeting, the Sisters began publishing a series of Polish readers, grammar books, and workbooks, all of which enjoyed thirty years of popularity.[86] But the parochial school rapidly Americanized the children of these immigrants, and the use of English quickly spread throughout the entire system. The teaching *of* Polish and *in* Polish gradually diminished, so that, by 1971, fewer than 15% of the schools offered Polish language instructions as part of the curriculum. The total number of Polish schools had fallen to 310 by that time.[87] Nevertheless, Polish schools did reinforce family bonds and instill in students a pride in being Polish. Indeed, recent research has shown that Polish involvement within the Church has increased over the past several generations. Perhaps this is the greatest legacy the Polish parish has left to the Church.[88] For Polish Catholics have maintained a strong loyalty to Catholicism, but a loyalty that has been highly influenced by its ties to Polish nationalism.

THE END OF AN ERA

When George Cardinal Mundelein died on October 1, 1939, the Chicago Archdiocese numbered over 1,400,000 Catholics. With 1,836 priests to guide them, Mundelein had supervised the establishment or continuance of 422 parishes, 388 elementary schools, eighty-five high schools and academies, twenty-three hospitals, thirteen seminaries, eight universities and colleges, seven orphanages, and thirty-six other institutions.[89] This figure represents the culmination of more than one-hundred years of work by the Catholic Church in the Midwest. Dioceses throughout the twelve-state region grew enormously during this period. By 1950, nine of the twenty-three archdioceses in the United States were located in the Midwest. These included Chicago, Cincinnati, Detroit, Dubuque, Indianapolis, Milwaukee, Omaha, St. Louis, and St. Paul. Chicago was the largest, with 1,691,681 Catholics, followed by Detroit, with 950,000 Catholics, and St. Louis, with 433,422 Catholics. Cleveland was the largest diocese, with 519,336 faithful.[90]

The end of World War II brought hundreds of servicemen into parish life. Wartime industry had brought prosperity to thousands of Americans, and the return of industry to peacetime production meant good jobs and good pay for veterans and non-veterans alike. It was "the best years of our lives," as Americans enjoyed a hitherto unknown prosperity. Older urban parishes began to decline, as parishioners moved centrifugally from the downtown areas to new parishes. At Holy Cross Parish, in Columbus, Ohio, the number of parishioners declined to 500 by 1943. But in northern Illinois, the number of Catholics increased to such an extent that the Joliet Diocese was created to accommodate their growing numbers. In the far west, pioneer structures were soon replaced by more permanent buildings, as the Church in the Dakotas, Kansas, and Nebraska slowly entered the American mainstream. But life within the parish resembled a sleeping giant that had grown to such an extent that it was unable to move or act.

By mid-century, the pattern of parish life had been set. Pastors ruled their territory with varying degrees of benevolent dictatorships. And they used their power to uphold traditional moral and doctrinal teachings. The laity, both male and female, continued to occupy a subordinate position. But within this hierarchy men were dominant over women. By 1940, male devotional societies exceeded female by some 8% (54.7% to 45.3%).[91] Through such organizations as the Holy Name and St. Vincent de Paul societies, men dominated parochial life during the 1940s and the 1950s. And no one challenged the supremacy of the parochial school as *the* means of keeping the young within the Church. Although the CCD had already been established for non-parochial school children, the program's effectiveness was limited by time and lack of general support.[92]

By the late 1940s, the Holy Name Society was the principal organization in all parishes of the Midwest. At St. Thomas More in Chicago, the society grew to be the "largest society of all the parishes in the Chicago Archdiocese." It promoted an annual Mother's Day parade, which featured the cub scouts and boy scouts, altar boys, Knights of Columbus, the school band, and, of course, the Holy Name men, "proclaiming by deed . . . their allegiance to the Roman Catholic Faith." The Holy Name also promoted social and athletic activities, such as golf outings, parish picnics, bowling and softball leagues, and, above all, the booster club, which brought in thousands of dollars to support these activities. The Altar and Rosary Guild was established as a feminine counterpart to the Holy Name Society. Established at St. Thomas More in 1947, the guild was dedicated to "the care of Church and Altar; assistance to the pastor in developing his parish; spiritual, educational, social, and financial activities for the well-being and happiness of all parishioners."[93] The guild sponsored many parish gatherings (Las Vegas Nights, parish musicals, bake sales, etc.) as well as performing more spiritual duties (an annual retreat, an evening of recollection, holy hours, etc.). But in all these activities, women were subordinate to men, and both were subordinate to the pastor's veto.

Devotional life also reached a peak in the early 1950s, as the highly individualistic type of piety described above reached its zenith. St. Alphonsus Parish, in Dearborn, Michigan, is typical of the period.[94] Established by Wesphalian farmers in 1852, St. Alphonsus maintained a strong sense of Germanity until the 1920s, when "this German exclusiveness finally gave way to the great tide of the American melting pot." Rev. A. Buechsenmann, who guided the parish after World War I, gradually introduced English sermons and announcements and led the parish through two world wars. By 1940, St. Alphonsus was a strictly American parish, with 5,000 parishioners and an average income of $60,000. Devotions included a novena to Our Mother of Perpetual Help, a weekly Holy Hour, a monthly hour of reparation in honor of the Immaculate Heart of Mary, a nightly Rosary, and daily confession. In addition, the block Rosary was "spreading through the parish . . . in many homes the Our Fathers and Hail Marys of the Rosary storm Heaven for Peace." Thus, by the Centennial of its History (1852–1952), St. Alphonsus represented the typical devotional life of most Midwestern parishes. Its devotional program was repeated in countless parishes throughout the Midwest.

The spirituality of this era was highly individualistic, and often Marian, in character. One of the most significant devotions of the 1940s and the 1950s was the perpetual novena to Our Sorrowful Mother.[95] Conceived by Father James Keane, O.S.M., at our Lady of Sorrows Parish in Chicago, in 1937, the devotion quickly attracted thousands of men and women to weekly Friday night services. By 1938, 70,000 people attended the novena at thirty-eight separate services. The novena soon spread throughout the United States and the world, to such an extent that Our Lady of Sorrows became a National Shrine raised to the status of a basilica in 1956. The rapid success of this devotion gives credence to the belief that most Catholics were Catholics insofar as they actively participated in the devotional life of the Church. The spirituality of this period was succinctly described by Bishop Hilary B. Hacker, the fourth Bishop of Bismarck, North Dakota, in a letter addressed to his flock on the occasion of the fiftieth anniversary of the diocese. He said:

> The doctrine of the Holy Eucharist is a basic and fundamental part of Catholic teaching . . . other religions are vague and indefinite in regard to their interpretation of the Eucharist. The Catholic Church does not quibble, but states firmly and positively that the Eucharist is the Body and Blood of Christ . . . the changing of the bread and wine into the Body and Blood of Christ comprises the essential part of the Eucharist sacrifice. This is the tremendous action around which the other ceremonies of the Mass are clustered. They form the ceremonial background, the liturgical setting for this great act of worship . . . the Church encourages us to develop love for the Eucharist through processions, devotions, and Benediction . . . we encourage our people to make private visits to the Blessed Sacrament as a source of spiritual strength.[96]

Meanwhile, ethnic parishes lost old members, but gained new ones. As the twentieth century turned fifty, German Americans drifted into the American middle-class, or what Richard O'Connor called "the great white whale, a stolid and often lethargic creature which moves in the deeps of the subconscious."[97] Some turned to local societies to further their ethnicity, but, with a few exceptions, the German parish had died a slow but inexorable death. On the other hand, Polish and Italian parishes continued as way-stations of ethnicity through the mid-century.[98] Our Lady of Mount Carmel, in Melrose Park, Illinois, continued to function as a major Italian center. But it is significant that no new national parishes were established after the original settlements were abandoned. While most returned to ethnic churches for marriages and funerals, they did not bring these traditions to newer parishes in the suburbs. Recent studies indicate that Italian Catholics largely abandoned their Old-World attitudes in favor of an American-style Church. But this Church was largely Irish-orientated, with Irish priests and nuns imparting a Jansenistic and conservative viewpoint on themselves and their children. But the Poles, despite Americanization, retained a set of habits, attitudes, and values that were distinctly Polish. The Americanization of the Polish immigrant has tied him even closer to the Catholic Church.[99]

While the Church as a whole remained predominantly hierarchical, seeds of reform began in Indiana, Illinois, and Minnesota.[100] The monks of St. John's Abbey, in Collegeville, Minnesota, initiated a series of liturgical reforms that antedated the council by more than four decades. Rev. Reynold Hillenbrand, rector of St. Mary of the Lake Seminary in Mundelein, Illinois, from 1935 to 1944, was a charismatic leader who influenced a generation of clergy and laity. Basing his vision of the Church in the modern world on the social encyclicals, Hillenbrand sought to form a modern Christian community through liturgy and social consciousness. He soon became acquainted with John Egan, still a seminarian, and James O'Shaughnessy, a Chicago layman, and quickly tried to adapt such European Catholic Action groups as the JOC (*Jeunesse Ouvriere Chretienne*) to the United States. Egan and the Servite, Hugh Calkins, were also a tremendous influence on the beginnings of the Cana Conference, a movement initiated in 1944 to make good marriages even better. From Cana came pre-Cana, a series of evenings devoted to sharing ideas with engaged couples. The movement reached a peak in the 1960s, as every diocese in the United States made pre-Cana a prerequisite for marriage.

Meanwhile, in the late 1940s, a group of Catholic professionals actively involved in Catholic Action questioned the wisdom of maintaining separate men's and women's groups. By 1947, the wives of many of these professionals actively pushed for a merger of male and female groups. Under the leadership of Patrick and Patricia Crowley, the Christian Family Movement (CFM) was first organized in Chicago, and from there spread throughout the country and even beyond.[101] By 1957, there were 25,000 CFM units in forty-four states and 150 dioceses. Patricia Crowley observed that "the whole concept of CFM began with the neighborhood and went out from there . . . we stressed the idea that as a family you lived in the midst of a community, and all that happened in that community affected your family, the parish, the community, and the country and the world. I think this notion is missed in many movements today—too many are ingrown and they don't reach out to issues that exist in the world."[102] The irony of this statement is that when the movement began this was precisely the criticism against it. Namely, that by focusing most of its energies on the family, CFM limited its effectiveness to the world beyond. In retrospect this was true, for most members were white middle- or upper-class professionals, who were more interested in bettering their family relationships than changing the world as a whole. But notwithstanding these qualifications, the Christian Family Movement was—and still is—a tremendous success, and represents the zenith of an age that symbolically ended in 1962. But like the Holy Name Society that preceded it, the Christian Family Movement was able to bridge the gap between the old and the new, between the pre- and post-Vatican II Church.

Notes

1. *Historic City*, 77.
2. Philip Gleason, *Catholicism in America* (New York: Harper and Row, 1970), 81–91.
3. For a general survey of German Americans and World War I, see O'Connor, *German-Americans*, 348–413; Hermann Hagedorn, *The Hyphenated Family* (New York: Macmillan Co., 1960), *passim;* Andrew J. Townsend, "The Germans of Chicago" (Ph.D. dissertation, University of Chicago, 1927), 113–177, and Rudolf Hofmeister, *The Germans of Chicago* (Champaign, Ill.: University of Illinois Press, 1976), 60–70.
4. William E. Leuchtenburg, *The Perils of Prosperity, 1914–1932* (Chicago: University of Chicago Press, 1956), 44–45.
5. Schmidt, *Seasons of Growth*, 165–166; *New World*, January 8, 1915, 3; Pfaller, *Western North Dakota*, 55.
6. O'Connor, *German-Americans*, 405–406; Philip Gleason, "Frederick P. Kenkel," *New World*, August 3, 1976, 6.
7. *Official Catholic Directory* (New York: P. J. Kenedy & Sons, 1886–   ).
8. Ahern, *Catholic Heritage Minnesota*, 115–118, 162–164, 186–187. For a discussion of the problems of a rural parish, see Emerson Hynes, "The Parish in the Rural Community," in *The Sociology of The Parish*, eds., C. Joseph Nuesse and Thomas J. Harte (Milwaukee, 1950), 100–132.
9. Schmidt, *Seasons of Growth*, 189–197.
10. On the NCRLC, see R. P. Witte, *Twenty-Five Years of Crusading* (Des Moines, 1948); and E. W. O'Rourke, "The Catholic Church in the Rural Midwest," in *Catholic Church, U.S.A.*, ed., L. J. Putz (Chicago, 1956), 202, 210.
11. Schmidt, *Seasons of Growth*, 198.
12. *St. Cecilia Silver Jubilee, 1921–1946* (Detroit; Privately printed, 1946).
13. Roemer, *Catholic Church*, 373–376.
14. *Ibid.*, 377–378.
15. Pfaller, *Western North Dakota*, 100.
16. Ahern, *Catholic Heritage Minnesota*, 113–115.
17. Schmidt, *Seasons of Growth*, 205. Many public school districts in the far Midwest were staffed by Catholic sisters. In Hague, North Dakota, six Benedictine sisters were assigned to teach in the public school, and did so from 1941 to 1957. (Pfaller, *Western North Dakota*, 94.)
18. For the life of George Cardinal Mundelein, see Paul R. Martin, *The First Cardinal of the West* (Chicago: New World Publishing Co., 1934); George W. Mundelein, *Letters of a Bishop to His Flock* (New York: Benziger Brothers, 1927); George W. Mundelein, *Two Crowded Years* (Chicago: Extension Press, 1919); Shanabruch, *Catholic Church Chicago*, 400–430; Edward R. Kantowicz, *Corporation Sole: Cardinal Mundelein and Chicago Catholicism* (Notre Dame: University of Notre Dame Press, 1982); and various issues of the *New World*, 1916–1939.
19. *Two Crowded Years*, 54–55.
20. *New World*, January 10, 1936, 1; March 22, 1921, 3; May 2, 1943, 4.
21. See Patrick Mallon, "The Society of St. Vincent de Paul," *Messenger of the*

Sacred Heart, 67, No. 9 (September 1929): 11–15; and Walsh, "Catholic Church Chicago," 63–94.

22. Mundelein, *Two Crowded Years*, 203.

23. Address to Annual Meeting of St. Vincent de Paul Society, Palmer House, December 12, 1937 (*New World*, December 17, 1937, 5). Chicago conferences numbered 212 in 1937, with 2,594 members; they visited 64,689 families, and spent $526,765.59 for depression relief.

24. Christopher J. Kauffman, *Faith and Fraternalism: The History of the Knights of Columbus* (New York: Harper and Row, 1982); and Elmer Von Feld, "Knights of Columbus," *New World*, May 28, 1976, 6.

25. The society was first established to counteract the influence of early unions, which were quasi-religious and anti-Catholic societies. The Knights gained national attention during the Mexican Campaign of General John J. Pershing, when the society established nineteen Catholic centers from Brownsville to El Paso, Texas.

26. Ethnic parishes also joined the Knights of Columbus, as they contributed thousands to general relief. *New World*, June 26, 1931, 4.

27. *Chicago Evening American*, July 12, 1940.

28. There is no adequate history of the Catholic Youth Organization, nor is there an adequate history of the St. Vincent de Paul or Holy Name societies.

29. *Catholic Herald*, St. Louis, Missouri, October 6, 1939.

30. Cited in Shanabruch, "Catholic Church Chicago," 478.

31. Mundelein to Most Rev. P. Fumasoni-Biondi, Apostolic Delegate, Washington, D.C., March 7, 1927; quoted in Sanders, *Education Urban Minority*, 52.

32. February 6, 1925, quoted *ibid.*, 53.

33. *St. Boniface Church*, n.p.; Kalvelage, *Annals St. Boniface*, 103.

34. Mundelein to C. A. Rempe, August 25, 1917; Archives Archdiocese of Chicago 4 1917 20.

35. *St. Boniface Church*, n.p.

36. Joseph Thompson, in *The Archdiocese of Chicago, Antecedents and Development* (Des Plaines, Ill.: St. Mary's Training School Press, 1920), notes that "a list of German Catholics who have attained prominence in the social, political, and commercial life of our city and the state of Illinois sounds like the roster of St. Boniface. Almost all the German Catholic families of Chicago have at one time or other worshiped there . . . it is this fond association with the great past that has made St. Boniface so dear to all the German Catholics of Chicago" (361).

37. *St. Michael Diamond Jubilee*, 24.

38. *Historic City*, 66; Archives Archdiocese of Chicago 5 1919 M 34.

39. Jack Hurst, "Ja, Chicago Still Has Lots of German Soul," *Chicago Tribune Magazine*, October 30, 1977, Sec. 9, 23–52.

40. "The German-Russians," Flush, Kansas, 1974. (Mimeographed—AUND).

41. Miller, *History Rockford Diocese*, 109.

42. Wayne Moquin and Charles Van Doren, eds., *A Documentary History of the Italian Americans* (New York: Praeger Publishers, 1974), 37–38. Other significant studies of Italian Americans include: Silvano M. Tomasi and Madeline H. Engel, *The Italian Experience in the United States* (Staten Island, N.Y.: Center for Migration Studies, 1970); Luciano Iorizzo and Salvatore Mondello, *The Italian Americans* (New York: Twayen Pub-

The Consolidation of Parish Life, 1914-1962 351

lications, 1971); and, on Chicago's Italian community, Humbert Nelli, *Italians in Chicago, 1880–1930* (New York: Oxford University Press, 1970).

43. Tomasi-Engel, *Italian Experience*, 196–197. New York's St. Patrick's Cathedral accommodated hundreds of Italians from 1882 on, when the parish celebrated an Italian Mass in the church basement.

44. The Italian Consul General often visited Chicago's Italian parishes as an official representative of the Italian government. For example, Consul Carosi noted that St. Anthony de Padua Parish was "a thriving Italian center for religion as well as patriotism. . . . I also sincerely wish that all Italians may always gather around the church, because it and the fatherland, especially abroad, represent the two greatest directors of our moral and material life" (*New World*, September 18, 1936, 3).

45. St. Philip's institutional history is recorded in *The Silver Book, by the Servite Fathers, for the 25th Anniversary of St. Philip Benizi Church* (Chicago: Privately printed, 1929); *Golden Jubilee Celebration* (Chicago: Privately printed, 1954); and the Archives of St. Philip Benizi Parish, at Assumption Parish, 323 West Illinois Street, Chicago, Illinois (hereafter cited as ASPBP).

46. Vivien M. Palmer, "History of Communities," Vol. 3, Document 61, Chicago Historical Society, 1928 (Mimeographed).

47. Presbyterians and Methodists were particularly militant in trying to win converts from Italian districts. But their efforts eventually failed since the illiterate immigrant was irrevocably tied to Roman Catholicism, for "the Church the Italians love is the Church of their fathers, the Church of their native Italy, the Holy Roman Catholic Church" (*Il Calendario Italiano* [ICI], April 1924).

48. ASPBP, October 2, 1935, II, VI, 41; September 20, 1935, II, 41; August 15, 1936, II, 41.

49. *ICI*, June 1922, 9; May 1925, 8–10.

50. Palmer, "History of Communities," 3: Document 27.

51. *ICI*, September 1926, 12. The thousands of dollars spent at these festivals give an indication of the appeal and strength they had through the 1920s and the 1930s. The financial records of St. Philip Benizi indicate that parish income increased from $2,902.87 in 1915, to $45,103.49 in 1927 (ASPBP, I, II, 6; II, V, 29).

52. St. Philip Benizi alone supported twenty-two separate societies in 1937 (ASPBP, IV, V, 29).

53. *Ibid.*

54. *Ibid.* St. Philip also supported such extra-parochial societies as Italica Gens, a Federation for the Assistance of Immigrants over the Oceans and in the East. It sought to support the Catholic faith of the immigrant and also to maintain his culture through gainful employment, the support of Italian agricultural communities, a legal committee to defend poor Italians, promotion of Italian newspapers, and continual efforts to retain the Italian language in parochial schools.

55. *ICI*, December 1926, 14–16.

56. Americanizing efforts at St. Philip Benizi included a kindergarten and day nursery, and a community center that sponsored three Boy Scout troops, a sewing school, a manual training course, a dramatic club, boxing facilities, and civic classes (ASPBP, II, X, 96).

57. ASPBP, II, V, 29.

58. Interview with Anthony Serritella, Chicago, Illinois, October 13, 1978.

59. *Ibid.*

60. *Ibid.* But ethnic parishes did not function as entities unto themselves. St. Philip's actively cooperated with Cardinal Mundelein's plan of Americanization by participating in such societies as the Holy Name, St. Vincent de Paul, and Catholic Youth Organization.

61. On Polish Americans, see Paul Fox, *Poles in America* (New York: George H. Dorn Co., 1952), and Joseph A. Wytrwal, *America's Polish Heritage* (Detroit: n.p., 1961).

62. William I. Thomas and Florian Znaniecki, *The Polish Peasant in Europe and America* (2nd ed; New York: Octagon Books, 1974), 2:203.

63. Anthony J. Kuzniewski, S. J., "The Catholic Church in the Life of the Polish Americans," in *Poles in America, Bicentennial Essays,* ed., Frank Mocha (Stewart Point, Wisc.: Wonzalla Publishing Co., 1978), 400–401.

64. *Ibid.,* 401. Outside the Midwest, New York City was the largest Polish settlement, with 200,000 Polish Americans by 1920; Buffalo numbered 100,000 by that date, with other large concentrations in Philadelphia, Baltimore, and Boston.

65. Thomas and Znaniecki, *Polish Peasant,* 1:41–42. But, as Edward R. Kantowicz has noted, "the American Polonia was not a tightly knit geographical entity . . . the reality was a series of isolated immigrant colonies scattered across the American continent." (*Polish-American Politics in Chicago, 1880–1940* (Chicago: University of Chicago Press, 1975), 10.

66. See Thomas and Znaniecki, *Polish Peasant,* 2:1521–1524; Kantowicz, *Polish-American Politics,* 26–27; and Arthur E. Woods, *Hamtramck* (New Haven: Yale University Press, 1955), 178–179.

67. *Ibid.,* 30–31. See Daniel S. Buczek, *Immigrant Pastor: The Life of the Rt. Rev. Monsignor Lucyan Bojnowski of New Britain, Connecticut* (Waterbury: Hemingway Corp., 1974).

68. John Iwicki, *The First One Hundred Years: A Study of the Apostolate of the Congregation of the Resurrection in the United States* (Rome: Gregorian University Press, 1966). Undoubtedly the greatest individual to emerge during the Resurrectionist era was Vincent Barzynski, pastor of St. Stanislaus Kostka Parish in Chicago from 1874 to 1899. He was the guiding spirit of the Polish Roman Catholic Union, and his policies and principles largely determined the development of the Polish community in Chicago and beyond. See Victor R. Greene, *For God and Country: The Rise of Polish and Lithuanian Consciousness in America, 1860–1910* (Madison: The State Historical Society of Wisconsin, 1975), 75–78, 87–88; Kantowicz, *Polish-American Politics,* 11–33; and Joseph J. Parot, *Polish Catholicism in Chicago, 1850–1920* (De Kalb, Ill.: Northern Illinois University Press, 1981), 59–94.

69. On Poles in Wisconsin, see Rummel, *Catholic Church Wisconsin,* 90–95; Ladislaus J. Stiekaniec, "The Poles in the Diocese of Superior," *Polish-American Studies* (1958), 15; and idem, "The Poles of Northern Wisconsin," *Polish-American Studies* (1957), 14.

70. Kuzniewski, "Catholic Church," 404, 406.

71. Boleslaus A. Goral, "The Poles of Milwaukee," in Jerome A. Watrous, ed., *Memoirs of Milwaukee County,* 3 Vols. (Madison: Western Historical Association, 1909), 1:612–633; Thaddeus Borum, *The History of the Milwaukeeans of Polish Descent and a*

Record of Their Contributions to the Greatness of Milwaukee (Milwaukee, 1965); and Rummel, *Catholic Church Wisconsin,* 90–92.

72. Bayrd Still, *Milwaukee: The History of a City* (Milwaukee, 1965), 269. On the early history of Poles in Milwaukee, see Frank H. Miller, "The Polanders in Wisconsin," in *The Badger State, A Documentary History of Wisconsin,* eds., Barbara and Justus Paul (Grand Rapids: A. B. Eerdmans Publishing Co., 1979), 291–295.

73. Rummel, *Catholic Church Wisconsin,* 93–95.

74. See Anthony J. Kuzniewski, *Faith and Fatherland: The Polish Church War in Wisconsin, 1896–1918* (Notre Dame: University of Notre Dame Press, 1973).

75. "The Catholic Church and the Americanization of the Polish Immigrant," in *Polish-American Studies* (January–June 1969), 15.

76. Barry, *German Americans,* 275, quoted in Monzell, "Americanization Polish Immigrant," 4. See also Benjamin J. Blied, *Three Archbishops of Milwaukee* (Milwaukee, 1955), 116–117.

77. *Ibid.*

78. Monzell, "Americanization Polish Immigrant," 4.

79. Kuzniewski, "Catholic Church," 406–408; idem, "Faith and Fatherland," 160–413.

80. *Ibid.,* 407.

81. Kuzniewski, *Church War Wisconsin,* 126.

82. Ellen Marie Kuznicki, "The Polish-American Parochial Schools," in *Poles in America, Bicentennial Essays,* ed., Frank Mocha (Stewart Point, Wisc.: Wonzalla Publishing Co., 1978), 435–460; Kuzniewski, "Catholic Church," 409–415; Monzell, "Americanization Polish Immigrant," 9–13.

83. *Ibid.,* 9–10.

84. Quoted in *ibid.,* 10.

85. Quoted in *ibid.,* 12.

86. Kuznicki, "Polish-American Parochial Schools," 455–456. We cannot underestimate the value of the Felicians and other religious orders in the development of the Polish parochial school system. There were about 5,500 religious women teaching in Polish schools during the 1920s and 1930s. A 1943 survey showed that 5,400 of the 9,300 Polish sisters in America were teachers. (Kuzniewski, "Catholic Church," 416.)

87. *Ibid.,* 415.

88. Harold J. Abramson, *Ethnic Diversity in Catholic American* (New York: John Wiley and Sons, 1973), 176–177. Will Herberg, in *Protestant, Catholic, Jew* (rev. ed.; Garden City: Doubleday Anchor Books, 1960), argued that religious identity was strengthened by the third generation's search for ethnic roots. For studies on Cleveland's Polish community, see Monzell, "Americanization Polish Immigrant," 13–15; J. J. Grabowski, J. Z. Zak, et al., *Polish Americans and Their Communities of Cleveland* (Cleveland: Cleveland State University, 1976); and Michael J. Hynes, *History of the Diocese of Cleveland* (Cleveland: The Diocese, 1953).

89. W. J. Madaj, "The First Cardinal of the Archdiocese of Chicago," *New World* August 30, 1974, 8.

90. *Official Catholic Directory,* 1950. By the early 1950s, many urban parishes were in decline, as parishioners moved from the downtown to the periphery or suburban areas of the city. At Holy Cross Parish in Columbus, the parish enrollment decreased to 500

parishioners between 1918 and 1943. (*Diocese of Columbus,* II, 9.) Meanwhile, in the far West, the missionary era was practically over, as such remote dioceses as Duluth and Bismarck "marked the transition from the status of missionary to a well-organized parish diocese." (Ahern, *Catholic Heritage Minnesota,* 75.)

91. Burns, "Parish History Project," 9.

92. It is interesting to note that of the seven Iowa women honored with the Pro Ecclesia et Pontifice Medals in 1960, all occupied professions "subservient" to men—one was a bishop's secretary, another a church organist, and a third a housekeeper (Schmidt, *Seasons of Growth,* 355).

93. *St. Thomas More Parish Anniversary Album, 1967* (Chicago: Privately printed, 1967).

94. *A Century of Conquest, 1852–1952, St. Alphonsus Parish* (Kingsport, Tenn.: Kingsport Press, 1952), 177.

95. Harry C. Koenig, ed., *A History of the Parishes of the Archdiocese of Chicago,* 2 Vols. (Chicago: The New World Publishing Co., 1981), I: 736–737.

96. Pfaller, *Western North Dakota,* 119–225.

97. O'Connor, *German-Americans,* 400.

98. Koenig, *Archdiocese of Chicago,* II: 612–622.

99. See Tomasi-Engel, *Italian Experience in United States,* 190. Nicholas J. Russo, in his study of "Three Generations of Italians in New York City: Their Religious Acculturation," found that Italians gradually approached the Irish ideal of attending Mass every Sunday, contributing to the church, and taking upon themselves the identity of Irish-Catholic Americans. (As found in Tomasi-Engel, *Italian Experience in United States,* 195–209.) On Polish Americans, see p. 85 above.

100. Virgil Michel, O.S.B., brought the liturgical movement from Europe to Minnesota in the mid-1920s, and immediately launched the publication *Orate Fratres* (since 1951, *Worship*) as a monthly review of liturgical reform. See L. Bouyer, *Liturgical Piety* (Notre Dame: University of Notre Dame Press, 1955) and L. C. Sheppard, ed., *The Liturgical Movement* (New York, 1964). On the general movement known as Catholic Action, see T. M. Hesburgh, *The Theology of Catholic Action* (Notre Dame: University of Notre Dame Press, 1946) and J. Newman, *What Is Catholic Action?* (Dublin, 1958). And on the Cana Movement, see A. H. Clemens, *The Cana Movement in the United States* (Washington D.C., 1953). On "The Chicago Experience," see Greeley, *Catholic Experience,* 251–279.

101. There is no definitive history of the Christian Family Movement. See "An Interview with Pat Crowley," *U.S. Catholic,* May 1981, 25–29.

102. *Ibid.,* 26.

CHAPTER THREE

The Reorganization of Parish Life Since Vatican II, 1962–

David J. O'Brien, in *The Renewal of American Catholicism,* states that the election of John F. Kennedy in 1960 and the reforms of Vatican II in 1962 changed American Catholicism forever. No longer was Catholicism an alien force in an alien land, concerned with its own survival, but an essential part of the American mosaic. And no longer could the traditional structures be accepted, as centuries of shared beliefs and practices were shattered by Vatican II.[1] The parish would experience all these changes because it is "for Catholics the single most important part of the Church . . . this is where for them the mission of Christ continues."[2] In America, the parish became a voluntaristic phenomenon, an institution that had to compete for its own membership. As the Irish, Germans, Poles, and Italians became more American, and felt accepted by Americans, they joined parishes that suited their needs. But as Americans, Catholics could not escape the milieu in which they lived, for they were no longer outsiders to these happenings, but an essential part of them. The indisputable fact was that American Catholics had become as much American as Catholic, and were just as much influenced by the forces shaking their country as their Protestant and Jewish compatriots. American Catholics could not escape the turbulence of the 1960s and the 1970s. But the times, both secular and religious, had different effects on different parts of the country, for the Midwest was not a homogeneous whole, but a sum of its individual parts.

THE RURAL, URBAN, AND SUBURBAN PARISH

The plight of rural America has been dramatically portrayed recently in such films as *Places in the Heart* and *The River* (both 1984). In many areas of the Midwest, the family farm has given way to larger agricultural corporations. Rising debts and governmental price controls have forced many farmers to mortgage what they own and move to non-rural locations. While there have been some attempts to deal with this problem on an institutional level, these have been sporadic, at best. But rural parishes continue to exist throughout the Midwest as centers of one unique type of parish life. The Des Moines, Iowa, Diocese is typical of rural America. In 1981, the diocese numbered 81,000 Catholics (less than 13% of the total population), eighty-four parishes, and ninety-four priests. Father Leonard Kayser, the director of the National Rural Life Conference, who also worked in a small South Dakota parish, noted that the rural parish "has a sense of place . . . these people attend the same Mass each Sunday, sit in the same pews. They identify with the place, it's theirs."[3] Rural parishes tend to be "open and sensitive to families on an individual basis, rather than a production line method of hatch, match, and dispatch." Participation in the Sacraments is higher, youth involvement greater, and the pageantry of the Mass more important. However, rural priests feel a greater sense of isolation than their urban counterparts. Some have gathered together in team ministries to overcome this problem. And while such nationwide movements as the *Cursillo* and Marriage Encounter have affected rural life, they haven't been able to adjust to the rural time schedule. As one farmer put it, "Why not divide the [Marriage Encounter] weekends up into five days of programs. It's hard to get people to do your chores."[4]

The parish of St. Joseph in Flush, Kansas, is typical of rural parish life.[5] Father J. E. Biehler established the parish more than fifty years ago, and continues to maintain the same type of control he exercised in the 1930s. Although parishioners seem to like it that way, the parish council is purely advisory. Many seem to be afraid that when Biehler retires no resident pastor will be appointed to take his place. However, there is a great deal of cooperation between pastor and parishioner, as Biehler obviously understands his rural flock. Like many rural parishes, St. Joseph's has no parochial school, but the pastor compensates for this lack by conducting high school marriage courses at the local public school. Young couples also seem to be at home in the parish. St. Joseph's is typical of hundreds of small parishes scattered across the valleys and plains of the Midwest. Often governed by the same pastor for decades, the rural parish needs no parish council, but is comfortable with this somewhat autocratic type of leadership. Parish life often revolves around bazaars, picnics, and other social activities, which bring an often disparate flock together. For hundreds of rural Catholics, the parish is the focus of their social and religious lives.

Another type of parish emerged in suburbia. These are parishes on wheels, whose members do not have the same roots as their rural counterparts.[6] They are the exact antithesis of the ethnic urban parish, for the suburban parish has neither a common ethnic background nor a sense of oneness. The problems of the suburban parish range from extensive territorial boundaries to a broad range of cultural pluralism. Since the parish is not the focus of all activities, it has to rely on voluntary efforts to keep its programs going. As one suburban parishioner put it: "Programs pull people together and make them familiar with one another. The adults here [St. James, Arlington Heights, Illinois] . . . have many social activities, such as an annual play."[7] In New Hope, Minnesota, a Minneapolis suburb, the parish has been broken up into thirteen regions of thirty families, each of which has been further broken down into groups of ten. Members get together to prepare the Sunday liturgy, staff the nursery, and act as ushers on Sunday. Such programs seem rare, however, for most suburbanites are so preoccupied with their own families and jobs that they have little time for involvement in church activities.

Located in Dupage County, Illinois, the richest per capita county in the state, St. Michael's Parish in Wheaton is the prototypical suburban upper-middle-class parish.[8] Father James Lynch (1949–1979), the third pastor, maintained a traditional pre-Vatican II parish until his retirement in 1979. Ecumenical activities were practically non-existent (a startling fact when one considers the importance of Wheaton to evangelical Christians), and there were no attempts to maintain a parish council. Rev. Daniel Ryan, who succeeded Lynch as pastor, began some reforms, while Rev. John Kloepfer, who assumed the pastorship in 1982, developed a post-conciliar style of leadership, in which everyone in the parish had "a piece of the wisdom." His present objective is to build a new parish center, which can accommodate a variety of social and religious activities. In Father Kloepfer's own words, St. Michael's Parish is "many different people engaged in a variety of activities . . . we are unique because of the wide range of people engaged in so many different ministries."[9]

Suburbanites are particularly interested in quality education. But since many suburban school districts are among the best in the country, the need for parochial education is often eliminated. Schaumburg, Illinois, is an interesting example of suburban Catholicism in action. Located in northwestern Cook County, Schaumburg has grown from a small unincorporated village in 1960, to a suburban giant of 53,805 in 1980. As *Chicago* magazine noted in 1978, "Schaumburg is the place where you can see rural America fade. The cornfields, silos, hayracks, and truck farms are still there, but . . . across from the cornfields lies the future: the paved landscaped industrial parks; the rows of single family dwelling units; and, of course, Woodfield Mall, the world's largest shopping center."[10] Three parishes have been established in Schaumburg since Vatican II (St. Marcelline, 1966; Holy Spirit, 1974; and St. Matthew, 1976). Most significantly, all three do not have a parochial school. Parishioners have opted instead for an energetic religious education program, which has enrolled more than 1,750 children in St. Marcelline Parish alone. Holy Spirit Parish is notable for its dynamic adult education program, which encourages adult preparation in First Holy Communion and first confession, small group discussions, as well as liturgical and spiritual renewal. The situation in Schaumburg is typical of many suburban parishes throughout the Midwest where new parishes do not automatically mean new parochial schools. On the one hand, archdiocesan authorities are reluctant to build such schools, while on the other, parishioners do not always want them. And the cost of building such facilities is practically prohibitive.

The urban parish is similar to the rural in that it represents a tight insular community. As Father Leonard Kayser points out, the real distinction in Catholic communities is between rural and urban parishes, vis-à-vis suburban parishes. St. John Fisher in Chicago represents the typical urban parish, a community of largely Irish Americans.[11] Organized in 1948 by Samuel Cardinal Stritch, St.John Fisher occupies a perfect square mile of land. The parish developed with the community, as nothing but tomato farms existed when the parish began. Between 1948 and 1950, the parish increased from 371 to 591 families; a twelve-room school was dedicated in 1950. The area proved to be extremely attractive to Chicago residents because it allowed them to remain in the city while enjoying a suburban-like atmosphere (in fact, one-fourth of the parish lies in Evergreen Park, one of Chicago's older suburban communities). Single-family dwellings dominated the area, with very few apartment buildings in sight. The parish school was an immediate success, as enrollment reached a peak of 1,565 in 1962. For the people of St. John Fisher, "the neighborhood is the parish and the parish is the neighborhood."[12]

St. John Fisher enthusiastically welcomed the reforms of Vatican II. Rev. John Kane (1951–1966) immediately instituted the liturgical changes of the council in 1963, and Rev. Monsignor Francis McElligot (1966–1984) continued these changes until he retired. Monsignor McElligot made the parish a real community because his style of leadership recognized the advantages of consulting others on major decisions. A twenty-five-member advisory board, all of whom were appointed by the monsignor, has a real voice in parish affairs. Monsignor McElligot proved to be such an effective post-Vatican II leader that many parishioners feared his eventual retirement. The new pastor now has to deal with providing more responsibility to lay parishioners in a parish so long dominated by a highly competent pastor.

One of the central focuses of this Irish-Catholic area is the parish school, which has remained financially viable since its inception in 1950. The school board evolved as a "policy-making body dedicated to insuring quality education for all the children in the parish." But, "the responsibility to promote or 'sell' the school belongs to every person in the parish . . . our school is very much alive. Finances are tight, to be sure . . . we have supporting parents; let's build on all that by spreading the good news."[13] School tuition has remained comparatively stable, ranging from $505 for one child to $800 for three or more. This compares with a low of $392 for one child at St. Christina Parish, to $850 for one child at St. Ethelreda.[14] Hence, despite national losses since Vatican II, St. John Fisher has managed to maintain its school as an integral part of the parish community.

From the history of the above disparate parishes, one fact stands out: namely, that a parish is made or broken by the type of pastor who leads it. Men such as Biehler and McElligot have proven to be effective leaders precisely because they understood their respective parishioners; and the parishioners, in turn, respected them. But where the pastor was weak or unwilling to implement the changes of Vatican II, like Father Lynch of St. Michael's, the parish remained stagnant and dormant. As Gregory Friedman has stated: "The foremost leader of the parish remains the pastor. He is the crux to whether or not parish councils work."[15] As we have seen from the above histories, parish councils have had, at most, an advisory capacity. Many parishes do not have them, while others function on a purely consultative level. Their effectiveness and real decision-making powers have yet to be realized in the majority of parishes.[16] Indeed, for most parishes, the pastor remains the key element of the parish's success, for without his support and encouragement very little can be done.

One of the key elements to a successful parish is strong preaching. A 1983 survey noted that 20% of the parishioners surveyed felt that sermons were excellent, 35% rated them good, while the remaining group rated them fair, or even poor. A man from New Middletown, Ohio, said: "Don't worry about being a great speaker . . . be sincere." Geri Wurth from Kansas asked her priests to "illustrate a message through a small story or incident." Most parishioners were appalled at sermons that attacked people who did not attend church, or those that were highly conceptual. Many wanted an open pulpit, "to hear from others besides the clergy. What's more inspiring than a layman or laywoman who would speak to us not out of obligation but out of a deep spiritual commitment to Christ and his church?"[17]

Dissatisfaction with sermons or pastors had led to a number of officially voluntaristic parishes, which have been set up to appeal to a more discriminating laity. John Cardinal Cody, the sixth Archbishop of Chicago, established the Ford City Catholic Center in 1969 as an alternative parish for those in the Ford City shopping area.[18] The parish has no territorial boundaries, but attracts 1,500 people weekly to its three Sunday Masses, and is notable for its pioneering efforts at lay decision-making. Both laity and religious sisters head meetings and make decisions with regard to liturgy, spirituality, and parish policy. Without any parish buildings to act as a focus (Masses are held in a basement room at Chicago's largest shopping center), the bond between pastor and parishioner is much more personal than at traditional parishes. But the success of such parishes is questionable, for many parishioners maintain a dual loyalty to their own territorial parish and Ford City Center. Some parishioners have "returned" to their local communities for the sake of their children who attend the parochial school, while others simply do not wish to contribute to two parishes. The financial strain has taken its toll, for the future of Ford City Center (and other such parishes) remains problematic, at best.

Two innovative programs for parish renewal have spread extensively throughout the Midwest. Christ Renews His Parish, begun in Parma, Ohio, in 1969, has had great success in major metropolitan areas. Couples go on separate weekend retreats to discuss personal renewal, parish needs, conversion, and reconciliation.

Most pastors agreed that the program brought about subtle, if not dramatic changes. Edward Prendergast of St. Christopher Parish in Rocky River, Ohio, noted that since the program began "it's given people a more personal relationship with Christ . . . we've had a lot of marriages strengthened and saved because of Christ Renews." At Blessed Sacrament Parish in Cleveland, Ohio, two brothers made up after not speaking with each other for twelve years.[19] And at St. Benedict's Parish in Chicago, Terry and Karen Fisher noted that "for the first time I really saw the Lord in action. Jesus was there in all the men and I felt it . . . my marriage has a new and much deeper meaning."[20] More dispassionately, of the 300 parishes involved in Christ Renews His Parish since 1982, only three did not continue the program the following year.

Renew began as a diocesan program in Newark, New Jersey, in 1976. The heart of the program is small groups formed for several six-week sessions, with the entire process taking from three to five years to complete. Renew helps build a personal relationship with Jesus, thus making the parish a more spiritual and prayerful place. Father Robert Gosma, pastor of St. Mary's Parish in Burlington, Wisconsin, notes that Renew takes "average armchair Christians and energizes them to be more effective Christians who grapple with issues such as social justice and peace." And a parishioner at St. Mary of the Woods Parish in Chicago noted that "our goals are to build community . . . people are friendlier in even their normal parish activities."[21] As of 1983, more than thirty-three dioceses had adopted Renew as a means of renewal. Together with Christ Renews His Parish, these two programs have effectively brought the reforms of Vatican II into the parish itself.

Of all the institutions to face intense scrutiny after Vatican Council II, the parochial school was the most important.[22] As we have seen from the first two chapters of this work, the parochial school system was often the first school system in a district, and the parochial school was often built before the church itself. Germans, Poles, Italians, and many other ethnic groups built up a vast system of nationalistic schools. And bishops like Cardinal Mundelein reformed and consolidated them into one parochial school system. But since Vatican II, the leaders of the Church seem to have given up on this important institutional structure. It is a paradox of the 1980s that while the American bishops as a whole have given only lip service to solving the financial crisis of Catholic schools, American Catholics (and even non-Catholics) have shown a renewed interest in parochial school education. This was not the case ten years after the council. A 1972 survey showed that only 36% of the priests and 29% of the laity interviewed were in favor of Catholic schools. As one parishioner noted, "the school is pushing the parish under . . . separate the school from the parish so people are parish-centered, not school-dominated . . . we take care of the privileged few and use up all the parish funds for the minority." Sister Joan Cook, S.C., of Cincinnati, observed that if the parish spends most of its resources on the school "one runs the risk of having a parish whose adults . . . are eighth-grade Christians."[23]

But as the twentieth century turned eighty, the pendulum swung back in favor of parochial education. Andrew Greeley, a pioneer in the study of parochial schools and their effectiveness, found a renewed interest in them by 1976. And eight years later, *U.S. Catholic* noted a distinct shift in lay opinion. While none of the respondents felt that Catholic schools would disappear altogether (77%), a large number (31%) did believe that the U.S. bishops had turned their backs on Catholic schools. Sixty-three percent thought that the Catholic schools in their area provided better education than the public schools, while a corresponding 62% believed that CCD programs could not be as effective as Catholic schools. An overwhelming 86% thought that Catholic schools were worth saving. It is ironic that at this writing a group of Philadelphia businessmen (many of them non-Catholic) is helping raise money ($28 million, so far) for that area's Catholic schools because it is convinced that the parochial school system is indeed worth saving. Not only does the system save its taxpayers from $350 million to $450 million a year, but, more important, it provides well-educated and disciplined citizens for the community.[24]

In many rural areas, such as Flush, Kansas, parochial schools have closed altogether because of the lack of students. But in smaller towns, such as Darlington, Wisconsin, the school has managed to survive. The parish actively seeks students by emphasizing its "sixty-seven years' tradition in Catholic education, the only Catholic school in Lafayette County. . . . Help us keep a good thing going." In a letter addressed to all parishioners, the principal noted that "Catholic school education is needed more than ever. Catholic schools assist parents in instilling values and moral principles in their learning." A similar situation exists in Lancaster, Ohio, where a massive effort to save the local Catholic high school was apparently highly successful. Parishioners were asked to contribute a certain percentage of their income toward an endowment fund that would keep the school running into the next century. The drive was so successful that the school's existence seems assured for the next two decades. The success of such drives indicates the laity's continued willingness to support the parochial school system, even when the hierarchy is lukewarm at best.

The history of the parochial school system in Davenport, Iowa, is indicative of the history of most rural dioceses.[25] Parochial school education, which took off immediately after World War II, reached a peak of 12,000 students in 1965. But the boom was short-lived, as decreasing enrollment reduced the number of elementary schools from fifty-one in 1966 to thirty-eight in 1980; high schools dropped from twenty-five in 1944 to eleven in 1966. The gradual decline of the school system took place in four steps. First, rural public school districts staffed by Catholic sisters were gradually closed because of a succession of Iowa court cases that refused them public aid. Second, several high schools were consolidated between 1953 and 1980. Third, twenty-two elementary schools were closed entirely between 1967 and 1983. And fourth, beginning in 1968, several schools were merged into one. The Davenport Synod of 1974 noted that the problem in Catholic education was the lack of clear-cut goals, and the lack of general support for the parochial school system. And the lay council of the diocese noted that there was much more concern for adult education and youth ministry among the laity than there was for the parochial school system.

While rural and small town parochial schools are disappearing, the urban Catholic school remains strong and viable. As we have just seen, the parochial school in many white urban areas (such as St. John Fisher) continues to be a focus of parish activity despite rising costs. The school is highly regarded in the community and serves as a drawing card for attracting young families with children into the parish. Its principal serves on the parish advisory council and holds other positions that tie her to the parish. But while St. John Fisher is in many ways a unique success story, other urban schools have been forced to close their doors for lack of general support. The consolidation and closure of many parochial schools in the Chicago area, particularly in the inner city, have met with widespread but unsuccessful opposition. Joseph Cardinal Bernardin, in closing three more such schools in 1984, seems unwilling (or unable) to substantially support the parochial school system in the manner of his predecessors.[26]

In many inner-city parishes, the school acts as an attractive alternative to poor public school education. At St. Basil's in Chicago, the parish itself is 75% Polish, but the school is 85% black—and more than half the students are non-Catholics.[27] At St. Clara/St. Cyril in Woodlawn, one of the poorest communities in Chicago, the parish spent $182,749 on the operation of the school alone ($150,000 of which went for school salaries).[28] As only $67,871 came from tuition, the rest had to come from the diocese or fund-raising activities. By 1983, an elaborate tuition schedule had been arranged ranging from $635 to $895, depending upon one's willingness to participate in parish fund-raising activities. But these figures simply demonstrate the overwhelming odds of continuing such a school, for the parish numbers no more than a hundred families, most of which are among the poorest in the city. As a recent study noted: "The parish is a community hub in a burnt-out region of virtually no economic viability."[29] Its future as a parish, let alone the future of the school, is highly in doubt.

It is not our intention in this work to trace the history of the ecumenical movement, but, rather, to see its impact at the parish level.[30] We have already seen that ecumenism was often practiced on the frontier, where harsh conditions and practicality forced Protestants and Catholics to cooperate. The nativism of the 1840s and beyond was more characteristic of the cities than the plains. And Germans, in general, were more tolerant of their Protestant co-nationals than their

Irish compatriots. Vatican Council II raised ecumenism to an official status, but its effects at the parish level have been sporadic, at best.

A survey of several parishes throughout the Midwest indicates a limited number of ecumenical activities. Thanksgiving Day services, common youth and senior citizen programs, and ministerial associations are the only thread running through the responses. Indeed, as one layperson put it: "We have all the documents now and we just keep them in the drawer until the churches are ready for them."[31] It would seem that of all the parishes surveyed the suburban parishes are most responsive to ecumenical programs. At St. Mary Parish in Riverside, Illinois, Catholics have joined with Protestants to sponsor a blood drive and an adult education program offering eighty-nine courses. And at St. Iraneaus Parish in Park Forest, Illinois, church facilities are freely shared with Jewish confirmation classes and Protestant youth groups.[32] But these are exceptions more than the rule, as ecumenism has had more effect at the hierarchical than the parochial level.[33]

THE LAITY, MALE AND FEMALE, YOUNG AND OLD

On May 14, 1955, in St. Louis, Missouri, John Tracy Ellis, the dean of American Catholic historians, bitterly indicted the Catholic hierarchy for not recognizing the inherent talents of its laity. He maintained that American Catholics had not developed the intellectual skills needed to be effective leaders, and that those who did have such skills did not participate in the financial and educational projects of the Church.[34] Ellis' speech rang true, for in the mid-1950s there was little call for lay participation in Church affairs. There was no national organization uniting the various ethnic groups nor were there any significant lay writers of note. And yet, there was a yearning for more. As Gustave Weigel, S.J., put it: "The situation of 1960 is revolutionary . . . the relationship of the action of the laity and the hierarchy must be seen in the light of the new world . . . the laity have manifested an eagerness to do something more than to assume the layman's posture of 1900 . . . they want a program of responsible action."[35]

Vatican Council II gave them that program, for it redefined the laity in terms of the "people of God." But many Catholics were unwilling or unable to accept these changes, as the following "lament" from Darlington, Wisconsin, testifies:

> Latin's gone, peace is too; singin' and shoutin' from every pew. Altar's turned around, priest is too; Commentators yellin': "Page 22." Communion rail's gone, stand up straight! Kneelin' suddenly went out of date . . . rosary's out, psalms are in; hardly ever hear a word against sin. Listen to the lector, hear how he reads; Please stop rattlin' them rosary beads . . . I hope all changes are just about done; That they don't drop Bingo, before I've won. (Holy Rosary Bulletin, January 31, 1965).[36]

But in the very next bulletin, a "liberal" had the last laugh, for "Sleep is gone, dozing is, too. Wakeful participation is forced upon you . . . Communion is a meal, no magic feast. I say 'Amen' at least. I hope the changes are barely begun—because to the living improvement's fun."[37] Underneath these poetic musings, however, lies a significant truth—that the changes of Vatican II sorely divided Catholicism for decades to come. At Santa Maria del Popolo in Mundelein, Illinois, the liberal element took such control of the parish that by 1972 the conservative members had "dropped out." Church attendance and financial support decreased to such an extent that the continuance of the parochial school was seriously in doubt. The situation was repeated in many parishes, as traditionalists or progressives left their respective parishes for greener pastures.[38]

Thomas Sweetser, a noted Jesuit sociologist, has extensively surveyed the mood of the post-conciliar Church in two significant works. A 1972 survey of Chicago parishes found that while the clergy was unanimously in favor of the changes brought by Vatican II, the laity was sorely divided about the future of the Church, with 42% expressing difficulties with renewal.[39] The survey also found that more than 30% had dropped out of parish life altogether, while 28% considered themselves only marginal or nominal members, at best.[40] Eleven years later, in 1983, after surveying 13,000 Catholics in twenty states, Sweetser found that the Church was just as divided as it was when the council began. The significant question for many Catholics was "who owns the parish—the clergy or the laity?"—and the overwhelming response was the laity. But pastors still hold the decision-making powers, and, as Sweetser noted: "Many Catholics are unhappy with the liturgy and preaching, unwilling to accept the teachings of the Church, and at least skeptical that the parish pertains to the circumstances of their lives."[41] In many parishes, the gap between cleric and lay has become an impossible bridge to cross.

Many new forms of lay ministry have arisen in the post-Vatican II era—in particular, the lay diaconate and lay associate programs. While the diaconate is quite extensive throughout the Midwest, its ultimate goals are confusing, at best. Where the program is going and what its exact function is in relationship to the entire parish remain to be answered. Much more promising is the phenomenon of religious sisters or laymen going by the title "associate pastor." The impetus has come from rural and small-town areas where pastors are desperately short-handed and simply accept the role of laymen or sisters in the running of the parish. One 52-year old nun preaches Mass at her small rural Midwestern parish every Sunday. But what ultimately "seems to matter the most is how a pastor feels about sharing his work in a parish with others . . . if he believes a brother, nun, or layperson can do just as well in the job, then he might take that person as an associate, not giving a thought to canonical titles or trappings."[42] But where the pastor is opposed, there is little chance for success.

The role of women in the Church has virtually exploded onto the ecclesiastical scene during the last few years. While most laywomen were content with their position in the Church before Vatican II, the laywomen of the 1970s and the 1980s are quite different. Sister M. Theresa Kane, R.S.M., has noted that "until the institutional Catholic Church undertakes a serious critical examination of its mode of acting toward women, it cannot . . . give witness to justice in the world." A Chicago laywoman observed that "there is a lot of sexism in most parishes . . . women have to be persistent."[43] Indeed, even though women make up the majority in most Catholic parishes, they exercise little control in the actual running of the parish. A two-day conference in Chicago, on November 13–14, 1983, addressed these issues for the National Conference of Catholic Bishops. Professor Elizabeth Schussler-Fiorenza warned that some of its most creative members would leave the Church if it did not alter its "patriarchal and hierarchical structure." Susan Kline observed that "among younger women there is a good deal of disenchantment with the Church. Many are falling off the edge."[44] While many sisters and laywomen are crying for actual ordination, others are simply concerned that women take their rightful place in parish life. But their present role seems limited to purely perfunctory duties—lectors and commentators (which are still not allowed at all parishes), song leaders and choir members, and membership in all-female societies. While the banning of altar girls by Pope Paul II may seem insignificant, it symbolizes the second-class citizenship that women endure even today. Joseph Cardinal Bernardin, certainly the leading figure in American Catholicism today, has upheld the ban and not spoken publically against it.[45]

Perhaps most notable for their absence are parish programs for the family as a whole. Most parish organizations are neatly divided into male and female, young and old. But there are no specific programs for married couples (with children). As we have seen earlier, devotional and mutual-aid societies accounted for the largest percentage of parish organizations in the pre-Vatican II Church. Membership in the Holy Name Society made that organization the leading male society of the twentieth century; and membership in the Altar and Rosary Society made it the leading female society. By 1960, athletic clubs, such as the CYO, grew to 5.7% of the total, while social justice groups, like the CFM, accounted for 9.2% of the total.[46] Sweetser's 1972 survey simply reiterates these statistics. He found that 75% of the laity surveyed chose "recreational" groups as the most popular type of parish organization. This category includes all those societies that carry on some type of recreational activity (e.g., picnics, bazaars, cake sales, etc.). But none of Sweetser's categories includes any organizations for the family as such.[47] Some Catholics have simply left the Church and joined more familial Protestant denominations.

In 1978, the National Conference of Catholic Bishops called together forty of the most significant Catholic organizations in the country to act as a continuing task force on lay activity. The list is illustrative of those societies—both pre- and post-Vatican II—that continue to affect parish life in a major way.[48] The core group included the Knights of Columbus, Serra International, the Catholic Daughters of America, National Marriage Encounter, *Cursillo,* Christian Life Communities, Teams of Our Lady, Retreats International, and the North American Conference of Separated and Divorced Catholics. A correspondence group, which reacted by phone and mail, included the National Association of the Holy Name Society, the National Catholic Society of Forestors, the National Conference of Catholic Women, Pax Christi, Worldwide Marriage Encounter, the Catholic Charismatic Movement, the Christian Family Movement, and the Focolare Movement. Groups such as the Holy Name and the Knights of Columbus continue to play a prominent role in parish life. But many post-Vatican II groups have emerged to stand beside them.[49] Two movements are particularly Midwestern in flavor and success.

The Catholic Charismatic Movement began in the fall of 1966, among faculty and students at Duquesne University in Pittsburgh. The movement soon spread to the University of Michigan, Michigan State University, and Notre Dame University. A 1980 survey estimated that 252,014 Catholics considered themselves to be charismatics, with 6,364 prayer groups across the country. The Charismatic Renewal is theologically conservative and incarnational because, while it sees the world negatively, it does not deny the possibility of changing it. The movement also began as an ecumenical endeavor, although this aspect is diminishing. As Father Edward O'Connor put it: "The encounter of Catholics and Protestants is good, but it is harmful if Catholics lose doctrine or the Sacraments of the Church."[50] Bishop John Riordan of Detroit noted that "the most promising sign of growth within the movement is a deepening interest in contemplative prayer forms."[51]

One of the key questions concerning the charismatic revival is its relationship to the local parish. It is a tenuous relationship at best because most prayer groups seem to meet outside the local parish. But there are exceptions. Kathleen Riley of Chicago found St. Tarcissus receptive to her charisms; and six women in Auburn, Massachusetts, made St. Philip Parish *the* charismatic community. Even some dioceses have experienced the spirit on a diocesan-wide level; e.g., the Steubenville (Ohio) Diocese ran a charismatic renewal for all its priests.[52] But while individual charismatics take part in a large number of parish activities, the parish itself does not openly welcome such piety. It seems ironic that while a large number of parish volunteers come from such post-Vatican II movements as the Charismatic Renewal, they are not accepted by their own pastors or contemporaries.

The Charismatic Movement has experienced serious losses since its peak membership of 720,000 in 1978. One former charismatic noted that "we've seen a lot of people going back to the parishes." And many groups have disbanded altogether, such as the prayer meeting at St. Bernard Parish, in Eureka, Kansas. But

Matt Lanz of Fargo, North Dakota, observed that "we've hung in a long time—the renewal isn't dying, its deepening."[53] An interesting development in the movement is its ties to Hispanic Catholicism. The National Service Committee, a twelve-member governing body for the movement, has joined with Hispanic Catholics to support a television series entitled "Send Forth Your Spirit." St. Aloysius Parish in Chicago has become the center of the largest Spanish prayer group in the city (1978). Attracting from 300 to 600 Puerto Rican teenagers to weekly bilingual prayer meetings, St. Aloysius has become a focus for the Spanish Charismatic Movement.[54] While Anglos seem to be leaving the movement in record numbers, Hispanics are reinforcing its ranks to make it a significant force within Hispanic Catholicism.

Marriage Encounter, both national and international, is a movement that has been particularly successful in the Midwest.[55] Rev. Gabriel Calvo, a Spaniard from Barcelona, conceived the idea in 1952, when he realized that the institutional Church had little to offer married couples. As a local parishioner put it: "many of us are tired because the Church and priests are separating us into different organizations, such as men's clubs and women's club. . . . There is nothing for couples." Based on the principle of "mutual confiding" (*confianza mutual*), Marriage Encounter quickly spread to the New World through the efforts of Patrick and Patricia Crowley of the Christian Family Movement.[56] In fact, the first International CFM Conference in the United States, which was held at the University of Notre Dame in 1973, was preceded by a Marriage Encounter. But the two groups soon split over the issue of "going out into the world." As Patricia Crowley put it: "The philosophy of CFM reaching out to the world . . . is missing in Marriage Encounter . . . there is indeed a place for Marriage Encounter, but also for the CFM method . . . injustices affect family life, so they must all be part of our concerns."[57]

A 1978 survey of National Marriage Encounter enumerated 114 separate groups in the United States. Of these 114, almost 50% were located in the Midwest—ten of each from Minnesota and Iowa, eight from Michigan, seven from Wisconsin, five from Ohio, four from Indiana, two each from Missouri and Illinois, and one each in Nebraska and South Dakota.[58] One of the most interesting aspects of Marriage Encounter is its ecumenical overtones. Marriage Encounter includes various faith expressions, such as the Baptist, Episcopal, Lutheran, and United Church of Christ. In Joliet, Illinois, the former regional coordinators, Bob and Donna Haan, are Reformed Christians, but the majority of the couples in the region are Catholic. In Worldwide Marriage Encounter, separate weekends are held for United Church of Christ members, where the team couples and the minister on the weekend are United Church of Christ members. But many participants have questioned the true ecumenical nature of the movement, since many chapters refuse to allow interfaith weekends. As one writer put it: "We have seen little coming together of various Marriage Encounter faith expressions at the local level, and we feel the loss because our lives could be enriched by their presence."⁵⁹

While Marriage Encounter did not begin as a specifically parish organization, its links at the local level seem to be growing. The Family Life Commission of the Diocese of Columbus (Ohio) recognized Marriage Encounter when it stated that "the need for marriage support is continual, for marriages face difficulty in early years as well as in later years." A survey of ninety-six Marriage Encounter groups showed that more and more "encounters" were being held at local parishes rather than the traditional retreat center. In Frasur, Michigan, the individual sessions were held at the parish from 8 to 10:30 P.M. once a week for four consecutive weeks.⁶⁰ At Our Lady of Knock Church, in Calumnt City, Illinois, Marriage Encounter became an integral part of parish life, as "twelve couples from this parish participated in a Marriage Encounter weekend and returned as apostles of this important movement in Christian Family life. Their enthusiasm and zeal are typical of the openness of Our Lady of Knock parishioners who enjoy and share in the fruits of Vatican II."⁶¹ But many pastors remain wary of Marriage Encounter, even refusing to publicize its events. It is a paradox of the modern parish that those who want to take an active part in parish life are often put off or frustrated by pre-Vatican II pastors. But the definite thrust of the movement is to bring Marriage Encounter into the parish, and through the parish, to better the lives of all married couples.

Sweetser's 1972 survey showed that 77% of the clergy queried believed that there was a definite decline in involvement of youth in the parish. A similar study of Catholic college students noted that while 93% attended church regularly while growing up, only 52% attended Mass at college.⁶² Many parishes in the Midwest have developed innovative programs to meet the challenge of youth. St. John Fisher has attracted hundreds of teenagers to its high school program entitled Quest. At St. Philip Parish, in Osawatomie, activities are specifically designed to bring youth into the parish. St. Cajetan's Parish in Chicago formed a Catholic Youth Ministry at neighboring Morgan Park High School, where courts decreed that the school must be 50% white and 50% black. St. Jane de Chantal Parish on the southwest side of Chicago "is very much a youth-orientated parish," with such organizations as the Junior Holy Name, the Knights of the Altar, and the Lumen Club especially designed for young people.⁶³ And at Northern Illinois University, in De Kalb, Bishop Loras Lane raised the Newman Center to the status of a parish, so that the "fuller sacramental life of the Church will enhance the Newman apostolate" of the university. The "parish" is specifically designed for university students with discussion groups, retreats, counseling, and small group liturgies.⁶⁴ With the decline of the parochial school system in much of the Midwest, programs such as these will decide whether or not the youth of the country will remain involved in the parochial life of the Church.

We have now seen that Vatican Council II sorely divided the clergy and laity on several important points of doctrine and morals. While the clergy was unanimously in favor of the conciliar decrees, the laity split along liberal and traditionalist lines. Many Catholics either left the parish altogether, or became marginal members, at best. Others adopted a policy of "pick and choose," i.e., while they did not entirely abandon the parish (usually for the sake of the children attending the parochial school), they themselves opted for more creative forms of worship on Sundays. Sweetser's latest survey indicates that 66% of all Catholics do not feel they have to follow the teachings of the Church, for "the majority of parishioners are not willing to give precedence to the pope's teaching over their own assessment of what is right and wrong."[65] The future of the Catholic parish largely lies in the ability of Church leaders to close this gap. Pastors must account for a new and enlightened laity in their midst, and be willing to truly lead their flock into the post-Vatican II era.[66] The recent Synod of Bishops in Rome (November–December 1985) did not rebuke these reforms, but called for further implementation of these changes. The course of the Church is to sail forward with the changes of Vatican II, and not to drift with the tides of uncertainty and doubt. There can be no turning back to the pre-conciliar forms of institution and spirituality.

THE ETHNIC PARISH, REDIVIVUS

While some scholars have declared ethnicity dead, it seems that this "sense of belonging" cannot be so easily buried.[67] The Irish have kept a sense of identity well into the fourth and fifth generation. And even German Americans have continued their *Deutschtum* at the parish level. St. Benedict's continues to remember its past with an annual Oktoberfest filled with *Gemütlichkeit;* and St. Augustine's celebrated its Centennial (1979) with a trilingual Mass in English, German, and Spanish.[68] But it is the eastern and southern Europeans who have steadfastly maintained their ethnicity more than any other group.

Chicago's Lithuanians have stubbornly preserved their language and culture on Chicago's Southwest Side for more than eighty years.[69] In fact, the entire area has been renamed Lithuanian Plaza, with many streets rerouted to accommodate this staunchly nationalistic group. And it is the parish that remains the focus of many ethnic activities. Nativity of the Blessed Virgin Mary Parish is considered the largest Lithuanian parish in the free world, with well over 2,500 registered families (1981). Liturgies are conducted in Lithuanian, with appropriate music to further reinforce a sense of "Lithuanianness." Even though many parishioners have moved to the suburbs, they continue to return to Nativity for Sunday Mass, baptisms, and weddings. A parochial school further strengthens this process by teaching Lithuanian history, music, folk dances, and, above all, the Lithuanian language. Indeed, Chicago's Lithuanian community is the second largest in the world, and it is the Lithuanian parish that continues to function as a way-station of ethnicity. But while eastern and southern Europeans continue to maintain their ethnic ties through the parish, black and Hispanic Catholics have developed a "national" parish of their own.[70]

The Black Parish. The history of blacks and the Catholic Church begins immediately after the Civil War, when the institutional Church accepted the color line and chose to relegate its black members to separate parishes.[71] Brother Cyprian Rowe, former executive secretary of the National Office for Black Catholics, noted that from that time "black Catholics were sort of like second-class citizens within the religious structure."[72] The first attempt to organize black Catholics came in 1889, when a series of congresses urged the end of discrimination in Catholic schools and better equality for its members. But discrimination continued, as few blacks were allowed to enter the seminary to become priests. Blacks were even refused admittance to the Catholic University of America.

The color line continued after World War I, as most bishops were unable to escape the Jim Crow mentality of the time. Even George Cardinal Mundelein, one of the most influential clerics of his day, could not bridge this gap. Addressing a group of black Catholics at St. Monica Church in Chicago, in 1917, he observed:

> Because of the circumstances that exist in this city I am convinced that our colored Catholics will feel themselves very much more comfortable, far less inconvenienced and never at all embarrassed if, in a church that is credited to them, they have their own sodalities and societies, their own church and choir, in which they alone will constitute the membership. . . . It would be puerile for us to ignore the fact that a distinction as to color enters very often into the daily happenings of our city. I am not going to argue as to the reasons for or against this line of distinction which causes so much bitterness, nor will I say anything as to the justice or injustice of it. It is sufficient to say that it does exist and that I am convinced that I am quite powerless to change it.[73]

By 1930, the Black Belt of Chicago grew to 233,903 inhabitants. The history of St. Elizabeth Parish, at 24 East Forty-first Street, is illustrative of the times.[74] Archbishop Patrick Feehan established the parish in 1881 for the Irish Catholics who could not attend Mass at St. Maes (Twenty-ninth and Wabash) or St. Anne's (Fifty-fifth and Wentworth). But as blacks filled up the area after World War I, St. Elizabeth's devised a dual system of education, with the Sisters of the Blessed Sacrament conducting classes for black students and the Mercy Sisters teaching the whites. In 1924, the parish merged with St. Monica's, the first black parish in Chicago, and "soon became the center of Chicago's black community." In many respects, the black parish simply imitated its white counterparts. Traditional societies such as the Holy Name, the Knights of Columbus, and Ladies' Sodality were established to maintain a sense of Catholicity. The parochial school was particularly important, as blacks saw education as the primary means of getting ahead. St. Elizabeth's School increased from 505 pupils in 1925 to 1,016 pupils in 1928. Parishioners even established a high school that provided quality education for boys and girls until 1962. But there was little attempt to establish black culture at these parishes, since, as a minority in the Church, blacks were simply content to imitate their Irish-American co-religionists.[75]

Between 1940 and 1970, black Catholics grew from 2.3% to 4% of the total black population. Black priests increased from six in 1935, to 285 in 1981.[76] And the number of black Catholics stabilized at about one million by that time. But there was now a new awareness that blacks were unique or, as one parishioner put it, "this is my church and nobody's talkin' me out of it or putting me out of it." African music and symbols began to appear in many black parishes. Even some names changed, as St. Anne's in Chicago became St. Charles Llwanga. Father George Clements, pastor of Holy Angels Parish on Chicago's South Side and one of America's leading black spokesmen, insists that the black parish must "justify its very existence in the black community . . . I would rather see the . . . Church fade into oblivion instead of having it play little games with white America." Father Clements, who gained nationwide attention for adopting two black children, has made his parish one of the most well-known in the country. Insisting upon strong discipline and a firm hand, Clements has achieved remarkable success in educating lower-income children. He feels that the Catholic parish has a significant role to play in the black community, since "our church is one of the few churches that remain in the black community when the whites move out and blacks move in."[77] Indeed, Clements has made Holy Angels a living testament to the enduring vitality of the Catholic parish.

Black parishes also tend to give the laity a greater role in the running of the parish. As Rev. Michael Pfleger, pastor of St. Sabina Parish in Chicago, noted: "They are the parish and therefore must feel ownership. They decide together our direction and rejoice in our accomplishments and accept our failures." And Rev. John Eaton, O.F.M., pastor of Corpus Christi Parish in Chicago, observed that "Corpus Christi exceeds many parishes in regards to lay involvement." Several organizations exist to critique parish progress and suggest improvements on a regular basis. A recent Volunteer Appreciation Dinner honored 140 people, "which is a lot of volunteers for a parish of only 550 people."[78] While the parish council was disbanded a number of years ago, decisions are made collectively by a parish staff. And four parishioners have participated in the archdiocesan lay leadership training program. It would also seem that black Catholic women have a more significant role in their parishes than women in corresponding white parishes. For example, at St. Clara/St. Cyril, thirteen laywomen hold administrative posts, from the School Board to the Liturgy Committee.[79] Perhaps this phenomenon is simply a reflection of the large number of single-family households in the black community.

The focus of black parish life is the Sunday liturgy. There seems to be a real effort at most black parishes to make it the center of worship. Father Clarence Rivers, a nationally known Cincinnati liturgist, observed that black liturgy is unique, but it does not require constant noise and mounting hysteria. And Cyprian Rowe, director of the National Office for Black Catholics, noted that "a good liturgy is a family celebration, all brought together around the Eucharist."[80] While a few black devotions do exist (e.g., to St. Martin de Porres), most piety is directed toward such traditional devotions as the Stations of the Cross and the Sacred Heart.[81] Much more notable is the degree of ecumenical activity at black parishes. Community organizations such as Senior Citizens are often coordinated between adjoining Catholic and Protestant churches. St. Clara/St. Cyril's Parish operates an interfaith soup kitchen for the needy of the entire Woodlawn area. Many churches have joined together to provide relief for the poor and indigent of the inner city. Indeed, because of their minority position in the community, black parishes often coordinate their activities with Protestant congregations. And very often, the black parish is the only station for the poorest of the poor in the inner city.[82]

The Hispanic Parish. While black parishes represent a hybrid between true ethnic and Irish-American parishes, Hispanic congregations are vital way-stations of ethnicity and Americanization. They have taken the place previously occupied by Irish and German parishes. Hispanics have been part of Midwestern history for more than seventy years. Mexican-Americans, or *chicanos,* began to arrive in Ohio, Michigan, Illinois, Wisconsin, and Iowa shortly after World War I. Some came to Toledo and southern Michigan as migrant workers, while others were attracted to the steel mills of Chicago and Milwaukee.[83] They soon established parishes of their own, very often in honor of Our Lady of Guadalupe. But these congregations remained relatively isolated until the Hispanic population began to boom after World War II. Illinois' Hispanic population, largely concentrated in the Chicago area, makes it the fifth in the nation, larger than that of either Arizona or New Mexico. And it is a mixed group of Hispanics, with 400,000 from Mexico, 200,000 from Puerto Rico, 70,000 from Cuba, and 130,000 from Central and South America (1980). As Mario Aranda, executive director of the Latino Institute in Chicago noted: "we have been an invisible community. There is a perception that we are transient, that we are not here to stay. But we are here to stay."[84]

Language remains central to the Hispanic experience. As Father Virgil Elizondo, president of the Mexican-American Cultural Center in San Antonio, Texas, observed: "We don't want to see Spanish in place of English but rather to show that people can easily handle both languages and feel its enrichment."[85] The Church has always recognized the connection between language and faith and has fully incorporated the Spanish language into all Hispanic parishes. Music, prayer, and culture are fully intertwined in all parish liturgies. And the parochial school continues the tradition of offering bilingual education and fostering a sense of ethnicity. In the Archdiocese of Chicago, approximately fifty Catholic schools are participating in either English as a Second Language program or bilingual education.[86] Indeed, like its German and Italian predecessors, the Spanish school functions as a true way-station of ethnicity and Americanization.

The history of Our Providence of God Parish, at 717 West Eighteenth Street, amply illustrates that the ethnic parish continues to function in Chicago's Hispanic neighborhoods.[87] Originally established as a Lithuanian Parish, Providence of God turned Mexican in the early 1960s. Yoland Zapian notes that "this neighborhood is united. It has good families. We're strong, and we have lots of dreams." On the one hand, the parish fosters traditional Spanish *fiestas,* with most liturgies in Spanish, but on the other hand, it acts as a "focus for political and social action, it sustains the hearts and souls of its residents." The parish school operates both day and night, with 280 students during the day, and adult education and bilingual teachers' programs at night. The *chicanos* of this neighborhood are particularly devoted to the priests who serve them. When Rev. James Colleran, pastor of St. Vitus Church, was transferred to the West Side, more than 600 turned out to say good-bye, for Father Colleran had led his people against unauthorized search-and-seizure procedures by the local police. As Rev. Frederick Branstrader noted, it is the Church that welcomes them and cares for them; and it is the Church that "stands as the focal point of independent duchies, bands of politically unsophisticated men and women."

One of the unique aspects of the Hispanic ministry is its emphasis on family life. It is the core of the Hispanic community. Values of family proximity, cohesiveness, and respect for parental authority continue throughout a Hispanic's life. Liturgies and *fiestas* are also times to deepen family relationships. And perhaps it is this deep sense of family that has made the diaconate program particularly successful in the Spanish community. In the Davenport (Iowa) Diocese, "each man's family was made a part of the training process. Wives could attend the weekly study sessions and siblings and children also attend the 'family formation weekends.' "[88] The Hispanic parish has also been successful in dealing with the young. Movements such as the Charismatic Renewal and *Cursillo* have been particularly successful in the Spanish community and have far outdistanced their Anglo counterparts.[89] In a population that is 54% twenty-five years of age and under, the Church must actively seek out and influence this segment, or risk the loss of the fastest-growing minority in the country.

The history of the parish in the Midwest is a history of the men, women, and children who made it a focus of their daily lives. It is not only a tale of the bishops and pastors who founded the parishes, but a story of the parishioners who lived and died in these communities. Overriding all this history is the ethnic parish—from the Irish and German parishes of the nineteenth century, to the Polish and

Italian parishes of the twentieth, to the black and Hispanic parishes of today. For all these groups, the ethnic parish was a way-station of ethnicity and Americanization. While national communities throughout the Midwest nurtured ethnic languages and culture through innumerable societies, devotions, and parochial schools, they also encouraged Americanization through the gradual introduction of English into all activities and an active participation in such national organizations as the Holy Name and St. Vincent de Paul societies. The history of the Midwest is to a large extent the history of the immigrants who made these parishes their own.

But there is one more point to be made. Of all the regions in the United States, the Midwest was the most significant in terms of nurturing the reforms of Vatican II. The Benedictines of Minnesota encouraged liturgical reform as early as 1926; the University of Notre Dame was a leading center for the lay apostolate during the 1940s and the 1950s; and the Cana Movement began in St. Louis, Missouri, in 1944. Perhaps, most symbolically, the Christian Family Movement, the leading pre-Vatican II movement in the United States, began and had its greatest impact in the Midwest. Even after Vatican II, the Midwest continued to lead the reforms of Pope John XXIII. The Charismatic Movement, which began in Pennsylvania, quickly spread throughout the Midwest and beyond. And Marriage Encounter, which began in Spain, had its greatest impact in Minnesota, Iowa, Michigan, and Wisconsin. Perhaps Joseph Cardinal Bernardin of Chicago represents the best attributes of the Midwest. Speaking at the ordination of four new auxiliary bishops for Chicago, he noted that "today authority is exercised more through our caring presence than through counsel and directives—a presence which demonstrates our love and concern even when we may not have an immediate solution for the problems that threaten to overwhelm us."[90] With a rich and long tradition behind it, the Church in the Midwest seems poised to meet these challenges.

Notes

1. New York: Oxford University Press, 1972, 9–10.
2. Gregory Friedman, "What's Happening to the American Catholic Parish?" *St. Anthony Messanger,* June 1982, 29. Friedman maintains that there are four key elements to a successful parish: (1) good liturgy and preaching; (2) a democratic style of leadership; (3) a practical concern for the people; and (4) a sense of vitality.
3. Robert T. Reilly, "Rural Catholics: They Know They Belong To the Land and the Land They Belong to Is Grand," *U.S. Catholic,* April 1981, 35–40; and E. W. O'Rourke, "The Catholic Church in the Rural Midwest," *Catholic Church, U.S.A.* (Chicago: n.p., 1956), 202–210.

4. *Ibid.*, 38.

5. J. E. Biehler, "How It Came About," Flush, Kansas, n.d. (Mimeographed); and other material now kept in the Archives of the University of Notre Dame.

6. James Brieg, "Suburban Catholics: They Are Driven," *U.S. Catholic*, April 1981, 52–56; Andrew Greeley, *The Church and the Suburbs* (New York: Sheed and Ward, 1959).

7. *Ibid.*, 53. Dr. Mary Durkin, a Chicago theologian and parishioner, notes that suburban parishioners try to recreate their urban ethnic parishes through weekend retreats, CCD classes, discussion groups, fund-raisers, Marriage Encounter, the Christian Family Movement, and other such activities.

8. "A History of St. Michael Church," Wheaton, Illinois, 1982 (AUND). The parish itself dates back to 1882, when Rev. William De la Porte was appointed first permanent pastor of this early German mission.

9. Father John Kloepfer, Pastoral letter, 1982. Kloepfer developed a Rite of Christian Initiation of Adults at St. Michael's for the entire Diocese of Joliet in 1983–1984.

10. Koenig, *Archdiocese of Chicago*, II: 1521–1527.

11. *Ibid.*, I: 493–496. *Saint John Fisher Parish, Silver Jubilee, 1948–1973* (Chicago: Privately printed, 1973), and other archival material at AUND.

12. "Ethnographic Impressions, St. John Fisher, Chicago, Illinois," 1983 (Mimeographed).

13. "Contact," Parish School Newsletter, March 1981; April 1983.

14. "Survey of 1982–1983 School Year Income and Expenses—Southwest Cluster," Chicago, Illinois. School expenses have obviously increased since these data were accumulated. For example, at St. Thomas More Parish, in Chicago, tuition rose a dramatic 27% during the 1985–1986 school year, from $550 to $750 for one child.

15. Friedman, "American Catholic Parish," 33. Statistics indicate that diocesan pastors ruled their parishes longer than religious order priests, and urban pastors remained at their posts longer than their rural counterparts. After 1900, 70% of all city parishes had pastor tenureships of more than 7.5 years. And we have already seen from the above histories that it was not unusual for pastors to stay from twenty to fifty years at the same parish (Burns, "Parish History Project," 7–8).

16. Bishop Peter Muldoon of Rockford encouraged parish councils as early as 1921, for "the organizing of parish councils . . . will be of incalculable value to the country and the Church" (Miller, *History Rockford Diocese*, 59). But these earliest "councils" had little authority and merely performed such perfunctory duties as promoting religious retreats and supplying Catholic literature for the church vestibule. The real thrust toward authoritative councils came in the post-Vatican II era, for the parish council "should be the means of achieving full participation by the whole parish in its mission by giving all voice in encouraging, guiding, and directing the various aspects of religious life" ("Parish Council, Objectives and Vision," Elmhurst, Illinois, 1981, 8).

17. James Brieg, "What U.S. Catholic Readers Think about Sermons," *U.S. Catholic*, March 1983, 17–23.

18. Koenig, *Archdiocese of Chicago*, I: 276–279.

19. James Brieg, "How to Heat Up a Lukewarm Parish," *U.S. Catholic*, March 1983, 17–23.

20. *Parish Community of St. Benedict,* October 2, 1983, 17. Thomas Sweetser notes that while Christ Renews His Parish has been quite successful at establishing core groups, it depends upon new members to keep it going.

21. Brieg, "Lukewarm Parish," 22–23. The parish mission, "an old tool, dusted off," has also been updated to include such topics as "Worries, Anxieties, and the Power of Spiritual Surrender," "The Challenge of Christian Parenting and Family Life," and "Life is Worth Living." This program has proved quite successful in the Chicago area (Office for Chicago Catholic Evangelization).

22. On the growth of the Catholic School system in the United States, the classic work remains James A. Burns, *Principles, Origin, and Establishment of the Catholic School System in the United States* (New York, 1908), and idem, *Growth and Development of the Catholic School System in the United States* (New York, 1912). The works of Joseph Fichter, S.J., in *Dynamics of a City Church* (Chicago: University of Chicago Press, 1951) and *Social Relations in the Urban Parish* (Chicago: University of Chicago Press, 1954) are illuminative for the pre-Vatican II Church.

23. Thomas P. Sweetser, *The Catholic Parish* (Chicago: Center for the Scientific Study of Religion, 1974), 18; and *U.S. Catholic,* December 1981, 16.

24. Andrew Greeley and Peter Rossi, *The Education of Catholic Americans* (New York, 1968); and, by Greeley himself, *The Catholic Priest: Sociological Investigations* (Washington D.C., 1972); idem, *Catholic Schools in a Declining Church* (New York, 1976); and idem, *The American Catholic: A Social Report* (New York: 1977). For 1984 survey, see Dan Herr, "Stop Killing Catholic Schools," *U.S. Catholic,* October 1984, 13–16. For the Philadelphia experiment, see Casey Banas, "Philadelphia Sets Pace for Catholic School Funding," *Chicago-Tribune,* December 22, 1985, Sec. 2, 1–2.

25. Schmidt, *Seasons of Growth,* 260–275. On Darlington, see "Would You Consider Sending Your Child to Holy Rosary School?" (Mimeographed.)

26. The debate over parochial schools was graphically played out in several issues of *U.S. Catholic.* William McCrady, in "Let's Support Catholic Schools at Any Price" (November 1981) argued that Catholic schools are effective bargains for the entire Church, since they trained future Church leaders. But in the very next issue, several readers took him to task, for "today . . . it's just as likely that 'good' Catholics are a product of 'good' Catholic families instead of 'good' Catholic schools" (December 1981, 16).

27. Koenig, *Archdiocese of Chicago,* I: 109.

28. Archival material on St. Clara/St. Cyril at AUND. Additional material taken from D. LaMagdeline, "Ethnographic Report: St. Clara/St. Cyril," Chicago, Illinois, 1983 (Mimeographed).

29. *Ibid.*

30. On the ecumenical movement in general, see Robert McAfee Brown and Gustave Weigel, *An American Dialogue: A Protestant Looks at Catholicism and a Catholic Looks at Protestantism* (Garden City, 1960) and Robert McAfee Brown, *The Ecumenical Movement* (1960).

31. Friedman, "American Catholic Parish," 33. On December 1, 1983, 1,400 Lutherans and Catholics joined to celebrate the 500th anniversary of Martin Luther's birth. But the majority of those participating were Church leaders, not the ordinary parishioner.

32. Koenig, *Archdiocese of Chicago,* II: 1468; 1503.

33. Sweetser's 1972 survey indicated that bishops were more active in ecumenical work than the local clergy, and that the clergy, in general, were more favorable toward ecumenism than their parishioners.

34. John Tracy Ellis, *American Catholics and the Intellectual Life* (Chicago: n.p., 1956), from a paper given in St. Louis, Mo., on May 14, 1955.

35. *Act,* January 1961, 3, as quoted in McAvoy, *History Catholic Church,* 460.

36. "A Conservative's Lament," *Holy Rosary Bulletin,* January 31, 1965.

37. *Ibid.,* February 7, 1965.

38. Koenig, *Archdiocese of Chicago,* II: 1359–1360. But the majority of Catholics seem to vacillate between the two extremes of "liberalism" and "conservatism," as they make their own choices on theology and morality. A fifty-year old grandmother says that she's conservative when she prays the Rosary at Mass, but is quite liberal when she declares "all I know is that birth control avoids a lot of fights in marriages." (Sister Mary A. Walsh, "Conservative Catholics: Somebody Has to Keep the Faith," *U.S. Catholic,* April 1981, 17.)

39. Sweetser, *Catholic Parish,* 38.

40. Joseph Fichter, in *Urban Parish* (17), constructed a model of lay involvement that was used by Sweetser in his 1972 survey. In a descending order of participation, parishioners were classified as: (1) nuclear members—those who went to church once a week and took part in two church activities; (2) model members—same as above, but only one church activity; (3) marginal members—those who went to church once or twice a month; and (4) nominal (dormant) members—those who attended Mass only a few times a year and participated in church activities. For a thorough discussion of this topic, see Sweetser, *Catholic Parish,* 40–77.

41. Thomas R. Sweetser, *Successful Parishes* (Chicago: Winston Press, 1983), as quoted in Bruce Buursma, "American Catholics Reshape their Church," *Chicago Tribune,* Sec. 1, September 24, 1983, 7. Martin E. Marty notes that recent polls point to "pick-and-choose" Christianity, a kind of a la carte religion where difficult doctrines and moral positions are repudiated" (quoted in Bruce Buursma, "Poll Finds U.S. Faith in Religion Growing," *Chicago Tribune,* September 17, 1983, Sec. 1, 8).

42. Brian Baker, "Are Lay Pastors a Perishable Breed?" *U.S. Catholic,* August 1981, 33.

43. Margaret Murphy, "Why Catholic Women Have Stopped Skirting the Issues," *U.S. Catholic,* October 1983, 25–26.

44. Roy Larson, "Church Reform Urged for Women," *Chicago Sun-Times,* November 14, 1983, 9.

45. Linnet Myers, "Bernardin Supports 'Radical Equality' for Women in Church," *Chicago Tribune,* September 11, 1983, Sec. 2, 1. Bernardin represents a new, dynamic type of bishop that has emerged in the post-Vatican II Church. J. T. Ellis, the dean of American Catholic historians, calls this change "a major turning point" in the development of U.S. Catholicism. (See Marjorie Hyer, "Cardinal's Death May Be Turning Point for U.S. Church," *Chicago Sun-Times,* October 7, 1983, 11.)

46. Burns, "Parish History Project," 8–11.

47. Sweetser, *Catholic Parish,* 49. The laity's preference for recreational groups contrasts sharply with that of the clergy. Only 59% of the clergy surveyed put recreational

groups at the top of their list. The clergy were also more in favor of religious ed programs (96% to 72%), liturgical groups (91% to 70%), and administrative groups (82% to 62%). Some parishes are attempting more familial activities. At Sacred Heart Parish in Palos Hills, Ill., the parish has introduced such activities as Lovin' Links (for couples only), monthly religious education family activities, and a referral service for more serious marital problems.

48. This list was found in the official magazine for *Marriage Encounter*, February 1979, 34.

49. For a further discussion of those groups not treated here, see *Ultreja*, the magazine of the *Cursillo* movement.

50. James Bradley, "Are the Charismatics Losing Their Spirit?" *U.S. Catholic*, August 1983, 24; and Daniel Cohen, *The New Believers* (New York, 1975), 53–62.

51. *U.S. Catholic*, November 1983, 43.

52. Bradley, "Charismatics," 19, 24. Bishop Arthur J. O'Neill, of Rockford, Illinois, authorized the establishment of the Community of the Holy Spirit, a non-territorial parish that does not own property in its own name and which specifically meets the needs of the charismatic community. (Miller, *History Rockford Diocese*, 99.)

53. Bradley, "Charismatics," 19, 22.

54. Koenig, *Archdiocese of Chicago*, I: 53.

55. Resource material on the history of Marriage Encounter was found in *Marriage Encounter*, the official journal of National Marriage Encounter, as well as numerous discussions with several Marriage Encounter members from Joliet, Illinois.

56. Jerry and Marilyn Sexton, "Confianza," *Marriage Encounter*, September 1978, 8; Tom Hill, "Vivencia," *ibid.*, 11–13.

57. *Marriage Encounter*, July 1979, 4.

58. *Marriage Encounter*, September 1978, 16–21. There are nine ME groups that are not affiliated with either Worldwide Marriage Encounter or National Marriage Encounter; they include one from Joliet, Illinois, and one each from Indiana and Minnesota.

59. *Marriage Encounter*, August 1979, 5; June 1979, 4.

60. *Marriage Encounter*, September 1983, 7.

61. Koenig, *Archdiocese of Chicago*, II: 1064.

62. Sweetser, *Catholic Parish*, 28, 112. It is interesting to note that Protestant and Jewish congregations showed a 61% increase in the involvement of youth. This underscores the assumption that non-Catholic congregations are more family orientated than Catholic parishes.

63. Koenig, *Archdiocese of Chicago*, I: 159, 464.

64. Miller, *History Rockford Diocese*, 84, 147–149.

65. Sweetser, *Successful Parishes*, as quoted in Buursma, "American Catholics," 7.

66. Sweetser's 1972 survey indicated that only 37% of the clergy surveyed were satisfied with diocesan administration and policies. Indeed, "the condition of the associate pastor is poor. Job satisfaction in this group . . . is generally lower than that of unskilled workers" (20). See Sweetser, *Catholic Parish*, 14–34.

67. On recent ethnic studies, see Andrew M. Greeley, *Why Can't They Be Like Us?"* (New York: Institute of Human Relations Press, 1969); Herbert J. Gans, *The Urban Villagers* (New York: Free Press of Glencoe, 1962); and Herald J. Abramson, "Ethnic Di-

versity within Catholicism: A Comparative Analysis of Contemporary and Historical Religion," *Journal of Social History,* 4 (Summer 1971), 359–388.

68. Parish Bulletin of St. Benedict Community, October 2, 1983; Koenig, *Archdiocese of Chicago,* I: 96.

69. *Ibid.,* I: 652–653. On Chicago's Lithuanians, see Joseph Krisciunas, "Lithuanians in Chicago" (Master's thesis, DePaul University, 1935).

70. We would be remiss in not mentioning Native American and Asian parishes—parishes that indeed are way-stations of ethnicity and Americanization. On Native Americans, see Joanne T. Asperheim, "Native American Catholics: Blending Traditions," *St. Anthony Messenger,* January 1982, 28–34. And at St. Thomas of Canterbury Parish in Chicago, more than two hundred Vietnamese families have made the parish community their own, by offering settlement services, social get-togethers, and obtaining scholarships for Vietnamese children. (Koenig, *Archdiocese of Chicago,* II, 942.)

71. Bernadette J. Hayes, "The Black Catholic," *Dollars and Sense,* June–July 1981, 40. See also William A. Osborne, *The Segregated Covenant: Race Relations and American Catholics* (New York, 1967).

72. *Ibid.,* 42.

73. Mundelein, *Two Crowded Years,* 59–60.

74. Koenig, *Archdiocese of Chicago,* I: 245–252.

75. This observation was confirmed by an informal discussion with Rev. Rollins Lambert, a former Chicago priest now serving on the African Affairs Committee of the NCBC.

76. Robert McClory, "Black Catholics: Souls on Ice?" *U.S. Catholic,* April 1981, 23.

77. Hayes, "Black Catholic," 49. See also Koenig, *Archdiocese of Chicago,* I: 353–358.

78. Responses to a survey taken of Midwestern Catholics by the author, 1983–1984.

79. "Alumni Sunday Ad Book," June 7, 1981. Resource material on St. Clara/St. Cyril Parish at AUND.

80. McClory, "Black Catholics," 27.

81. From 1937 to 1968, the parishioners of Corpus Christi Parish in Chicago presented the "living stations," a dramatized version of the traditional Catholic devotion, the Stations of the Cross. The one-hour presentation attracted thousands of whites and blacks to this black parish, and many felt that its success was due "to the cultural heritage of blacks—that fathomless depth of feeling and endurance characteristic of the black race" (See *Corpus Christi Parish, Our History, 1901–1977* (Chicago: Privately printed, 1977).

82. See archival material at AUND.

83. On the early history of Hispanics in the Midwest, see Virgilio Elizondo, *Galilean Journey, The Mexican-American Promise* (Maryknoll: Orbis Books, 1983); Hamilton, *Journey through Ohio,* 71–73; and Rummel, *Catholic Church Wisconsin,* 114–115.

84. Jim Yuenger, "Power Struggle," *Chicago Tribune Magazine,* August 28, 1983, Sec. 9, 13–21.

85. Virgilio Elizondo, "Hispanic Catholics: They Don't Fit into the Melting Pot," U.S. Catholic, October 1981, 21.

86. Yuenger, "Power Struggle," 13.

87. *Ibid.,* 15–20.

88. Schmidt, *Seasons of Growth*, 292–294.
89. See Michael P. Hamilton, ed., *The Charismatic Movement* (Grand Rapids: Eerdmans Publishing Co., 1975), and John F. MacArthur, *The Charismatics: A Doctrinal Perspective* (Grand Rapids: Zondervan Publishing House, 1978).
90. *New World*, December 16, 1983, 1.

For Further Reading

Ahern, Patrick H., ed. *Catholic Heritage in Minnesota, North Dakota, and South Dakota*. St. Paul: H. M. Smyth Co., 1964.

Elizondo, Virgilio. *Galilean Journey: The Mexican-American Promise*. Maryknoll, N.Y.: Orbis Books, 1983.

Gleason, Philip. *The Conservative Reformers*. Notre Dame: University of Notre Dame Press, 1968.

Hamilton, Albert. *The Catholic Journey through Ohio*. St. Meinrad, Ind.: Abbey Press, 1976.

Iverson, Noel. *Germania, U.S.A., Social Change in New Ulm, Minnesota*. Minneapolis: University of Minnesota, 1966.

Kuzniewski, Anthony J. *Faith and Fatherland: The Polish Church War in Wisconsin, 1896–1918*. Notre Dame: University of Notre Dame Press, 1973.

McAvoy, Thomas T., C.S.C. *The Great Crisis in American Catholic History, 1895–1900*. Chicago: Henry Regnery Co., 1957.

Nelli, Humbert. *Italians in Chicago, 1880–1930*. New York: Oxford University Press, 1970.

Parot, Joseph J. *Polish Catholics in Chicago, 1850–1920*. DeKalb, Ill.: Northern Illinois University Press, 1981.

Sanders, James W. *The Education of an Urban Minority, Catholics in Chicago, 1833–1965*. New York: Oxford University Press, 1977.

Schmidt, Sister Madeleine M., C.H.M. *Seasons of Growth, History of the Diocese of Davenport, 1881–1981*. Davenport: The Diocese, 1981.

Sweetser, Thomas, S.J. *Successful Parishes*. Chicago: Winston Press, 1983.

APPENDIX 5
Catholic Church Statistics in the Midwest

OHIO
Archdiocese of Cincinnati (1821; archdiocese, 1850)

	1850	1880	1900	1930	1950	1960	1980
Parishes	70	195	143	201	219	232	235
Parishes without Priests (i.e., Missions)	—	18	85	31	30	22	21
National Parishes	5	5	5	7	4	4	4
Parish Schools	12	140	100	144	150	159	121
Diocesan Priests	38	121	159	302	371	459	467
Religious Order Priests	20	47	100	207	419	486	444
Women Religious	—	—	—	—	2,956	3,286	1,890
Catholic Population	75,000	200,000	190,000	220,000	294,493	472,000	505,666
Total Population	—	—	—	—	1,576,283	2,250,000	2,668,300

Source: The Metropolitan Catholic Almanac and Laity's Directory (Baltimore: Fielding Lucas, 1849); *Sadlier's Catholic Directory Almanac and Ordo* (New York: D. & J. Sadlier & Co., 1880); and *Official Catholic Directory* (New York: P. L. Kenedy & Sons, 1900-1980).

OHIO
Diocese of Cleveland (1847)

	1850	1880	1900	1930	1950	1960	1980
Parishes	36	190	188	236	206	232	244
Parishes without Priests (i.e., Missions)	—	20	74	23	2	22	12
National Parishes	1	18	34	31	51	45	40
Parish Schools	—	64	140	186	146	179	160
Diocesan Priests	20	134	227	436	462	582	642
Religious Order Priests	35	161	41	135	209	278	288
Women Religious	—[a]	623	—	—	2,867	3,374	2,516
Catholic Population	26,000	21,000	275,000	540,193	519,336	757,875	979,300
Total Population	—	—	—	—	1,851,834	2,467,300	2,758,337

[a]Complete figures are not provided by the directories.

Appendix: Church Statistics in the Midwest

OHIO
Diocese of Columbus (1868)

	1850	1880	1900	1930	1950	1960	1980
Parishes	—	77	71	125	88	100	107
Parishes without Priests (i.e., Missions)	—	40	35	32	19	2[a]	1[a]
National Parishes	—	2	3	3	0	0	0
Parish Schools	—	32	40	71	53	57	52
Diocesan Priests	—	41	83	142	167	209	235
Religious Order Priests	—	20	24	56	99	96	72
Women Religious	—	—	—	—	1,375	1,017	703
Catholic Population	—	40,000	60,000	140,186	105,500	161,341	204,816
Total Population	—	—	—	—	1,169,061	1,597,358	1,901,100

[a]1960 and 1980 data reflect parishes without resident pastors; data prior to 1960 reflect traditional category of "missions."

OHIO
Diocese of Steubenville (1944)

	1850	1880	1900	1930	1950	1960	1980
Parishes	—	—	—	—	57	70	70
Parishes without Priests (i.e., Missions)	—	—	—	—	14	—	4
National Parishes	—	—	—	—	0	0	0
Parish Schools	—	—	—	—	27	32	17
Diocesan Priests	—	—	—	—	85	143	166
Religious Order Priests	—	—	—	—	11	14	14
Women Religious	—	—	—	—	210	279	151
Catholic Population	—	—	—	—	61,451	50,390	53,578
Total Population	—	—	—	—	503,224	485,735	545,060

OHIO
Diocese of Toledo (1910)

	1850	1880	1900	1930	1950	1960	1980
Parishes	—	—	—	127	131	144	136
Parishes without Priests (i.e., Missions)	—	—	—	22	—	16	—
National Parishes	—	—	—	13	11	11	12
Parish Schools	—	—	—	140	99	103	88
Diocesan Priests	—	—	—	204	233	262	281
Religious Order Priests	—	—	—	54	71	120	129
Women Religious	—	—	—	—	1,454	1,658	1,531
Catholic Population	—	—	—	—	163,204	265,182	347,594
Total Population	—	—	—	—	994,332	1,307,735	1,438,800

OHIO
Diocese of Youngstown (1943)

	1850	1880	1900	1930	1950	1960	1980
Parishes	—	—	—	—	98	110	115
Parishes without Priests (i.e., Missions)	—	—	—	—	7	—	2
National Parishes	—	—	—	—	12	11	10
Parish Schools	—	—	—	—	53	72	63
Diocesan Priests	—	—	—	—	168	243	264
Religious Order Priests	—	—	—	—	42	79	72
Women Religious	—	—	—	—	540	712	510
Catholic Population	—	—	—	—	149,436	275,000	281,439
Total Population	—	—	—	—	784,374	935,198	1,281,917

INDIANA
Archdiocese of Indianapolis (1834; archdiocese, 1944)

	1850	1880	1900	1930	1950	1960	1980
Parishes	52[a]	151	112	150	118	135	130
Parishes without Priests (i.e., Missions)	—	—	49	37	32	27	12
National Parishes	2	10	9	2	1	1	1
Parish Schools	5	151	92	130	87	104	74
Diocesan Priests	37	83	129	230	219	259	235
Religious Order Priests	5	39	55	106	200	191	192
Women Religious	—	—	—	—	2,466	2,645	1,913
Catholic Population	45,000	85,000	112,388	135,775	119,195	184,281	202,087
Total Population	—	—	—	—	1,287,813	1,505,527	2,022,366

[a]Diocese of Vincennes until 1898.

Appendix: Church Statistics in the Midwest

INDIANA
Diocese of Evansville (1944)

	1850	1880	1900	1930	1950	1960	1980
Parishes	—	—	—	—	66	67	74
Parishes without Priests (i.e., Missions)	—	—	—	—	7	1	8
National Parishes	—	—	—	—	—	—	—
Parish Schools	—	—	—	—	45	53	30
Diocesan Priests	—	—	—	—	84	105	132
Religious Order Priests	—	—	—	—	22	23	21
Women Religious	—	—	—	—	616	378	448
Catholic Population	—	—	—	—	57,258	70,910	91,701
Total Population	—	—	—	—	392,389	417,327	435,177

INDIANA
Diocese of Ft. Wayne-South Bend (1857)

	1850	1880	1900	1930	1950	1960	1980
Parishes	—	108	102	155	118	78	66
Parishes without Priests (i.e., Missions)	—	20	39	25	—	7	3
National Parishes	—	6	9	14	15	10	—
Parish Schools	—	50	73	118	94	56	44
Diocesan Priests	—	66	107	216	205	120	125
Religious Order Priests	—	31	62	170	238	313	270
Women Religious	—	—	—	—	1,963	863	887
Catholic Population	—	80,000	72,000	183,977	192,252	139,015	147,438
Total Population	—	—	—	—	1,103,496	740,526	980,952

INDIANA
Diocese of Gary (1957)

	1850	1880	1900	1930	1950	1960	1980
Parishes	—	—	—	—	—	81	83
Parishes without Priests (i.e., Missions)	—	—	—	—	—	1	3
National Parishes	—	—	—	—	—	20	20
Parish Schools	—	—	—	—	—	60	41
Diocesan Priests	—	—	—	—	—	149	141
Religious Order Priests	—	—	—	—	—	79	79
Women Religious	—	—	—	—	—	581	325
Catholic Population	—	—	—	—	—	154,349	190,033
Total Population	—	—	—	—	—	603,833	782,300

INDIANA
Diocese of Lafayette (1944)

	1850	1880	1900	1930	1950	1960	1980
Parishes	—	—	—	—	47	56	58
Parishes without Priests (i.e., Missions)	—	—	—	—	11	5	4
National Parishes	—	—	—	—	—	—	—
Parish Schools	—	—	—	—	31	37	17
Diocesan Priests	—	—	—	—	56	89	110
Religious Order Priests	—	—	—	—	72	79	63
Women Religious	—	—	—	—	403	452	119
Catholic Population	—	—	—	—	39,088	62,860	86,540
Total Population	—	—	—	—	687,212	772,494	986,880

ILLINOIS
Archdiocese of Chicago (1843; archdiocese, 1880)

	1850	1880	1900	1930	1950	1960	1980
Parishes	78	194	214	387	386	425	444
Parishes without Priests (i.e., Missions)	—	—	51	—	—	3	—
National Parishes	3	29	69	168	120	98	35
Parish Schools	—	60	130	337	341	416	380
Diocesan Priests	41	142	334	767	1,040	1,264	1,264
Religious Order Priests	1	64	125	500	1,076	1,549	1,289
Women Religious	—	—	—	—	6,891	9,235	3,050
Catholic Population	53,100	200,000	700,000	1,250,000	1,691,681	2,073,616	2,406,728
Total Population	—	—	—	—	4,200,000	4,976,989	5,750,405

ILLINOIS
Diocese of Belleville (1887)

	1850	1880	1900	1930	1950	1960	1980
Parishes	—	—	75	109	115	119	111
Parishes without Priests (i.e., Missions)	—	—	27	30	23	20	19
National Parishes	—	—	1	1	1	1	1
Parish Schools	—	—	58	82	83	82	57
Diocesan Priests	—	—	86	138	144	179	164
Religious Order Priests	—	—	5	16	36	39	50
Women Religious	—	—	—	—	792	779	434
Catholic Population	—	—	50,000	69,842	82,970	114,465	122,147
Total Population	—	—	—	—	789,488	799,594	807,682

Appendix: Church Statistics in the Midwest

ILLINOIS
Diocese of Joliet (1948)

	1850	1880	1900	1930	1950	1960	1980
Parishes	—	—	—	—	72	98	110
Parishes without Priests (i.e., Missions)	—	—	—	—	16	—	1
National Parishes	—	—	—	—	9	5	4
Parish Schools	—	—	—	—	46	64	67
Diocesan Priests	—	—	—	—	79	154	205
Religious Order Priests	—	—	—	—	183	238	181
Women Religious	—	—	—	—	948	973	1,100
Catholic Population	—	—	—	—	93,229	201,081	411,000
Total Population	—	—	—	—	355,573	597,979	1,191,000

ILLINOIS
Diocese of Peoria (1877)

	1850	1880	1900	1930	1950	1960	1980
Parishes	—	100	110	159	148	154	158
Parishes without Priests (i.e., Missions)	—	—	90	77	60	3	12
National Parishes	—	4	1	1	—	—	—
Parish Schools	—	20	58	82	81	82	58
Diocesan Priests	—	60	123	194	218	274	252
Religious Order Priests	—	5	31	64	114	144	113
Women Religious	—	—	—	—	1,397	1,098	699
Catholic Population	—	—	—	—	117,742	149,648	200,006
Total Population	—	—	—	—	1,108,051	1,210,591	1,434,428

ILLINOIS
Diocese of Rockford (1908)

	1850	1880	1900	1930	1950	1960	1980
Parishes	—	—	—	84	85	92	100
Parishes without Priests (i.e., Missions)	—	—	—	21	12	3	2
National Parishes	—	—	—	10	9	7	—
Parish Schools	—	—	—	45	47	62	48
Diocesan Priests	—	—	—	140	128	179	175
Religious Order Priests	—	—	—	18	81	102	82
Women Religious	—	—	—	—	59	669	470
Catholic Population	—	—	—	—	60,063	78,534	146,833
Total Population	—	—	—	—	407,718	610,424	934,938

ILLINOIS
Diocese of Springfield (1853)

	1850	1880	1900	1930	1950	1960	1980
Parishes	—	76[a]	90	128	136	142	126
Parishes without Priests (i.e., Missions)	—	—	46	35	40	—	18
National Parishes	—	—	1	3	1	—	—
Parish Schools	—	96	61	63	70	71	62
Diocesan Priests	—	114	112	194	222	236	181
Religious Order Priests	—	12	30	37	124	143	106
Women Religious	—	—	—	—	1,145	1,250	988
Catholic Population	—	—	75,000	94,117	110,303	152,030	183,639
Total Population	—	—	—	—	934,975	969,006	1,091,191

[a] Diocese of Quincy until 1857; Alton until 1923.

MICHIGAN
Archdiocese of Detroit (1833; archdiocese, 1937)

	1850	1880	1900	1930	1950	1960	1980
Parishes	39	203	122	298	243	298	335
Parishes without Priests (i.e., Missions)	—	—	76	60	20	—	2
National Parishes	2	2	2	37	38	28	21
Parish Schools	—	58	64	185	180	255	160
Diocesan Priests	26	114	174	511	572	724	619
Religious Order Priests	1	13	44	92	286	409	432
Women Religious	—	—	—	—	5,360	2,645	3,050
Catholic Population	75,000	180,000	177,905	635,764	950,000	1,324,951	1,190,042
Total Population	—	—	—	—	3,378,212	4,526,800	4,425,800

MICHIGAN
Diocese of Gaylord (1971)

	1850	1880	1900	1930	1950	1960	1980
Parishes	—	—	—	—	—	—	57
Parishes without Priests (i.e., Missions)	—	—	—	—	—	—	2
National Parishes	—	—	—	—	—	—	—
Parish Schools	—	—	—	—	—	—	19
Diocesan Priests	—	—	—	—	—	—	61
Religious Order Priests	—	—	—	—	—	—	21
Women Religious	—	—	—	—	—	—	153
Catholic Population	—	—	—	—	—	—	84,425
Total Population	—	—	—	—	—	—	419,700

Appendix: Church Statistics in the Midwest

MICHIGAN
Diocese of Grand Rapids (1882)

	1850	1880	1900	1930	1950	1960	1980
Parishes	—	—	65	130	103	126	87
Parishes without Priests (i.e., Missions)	—	—	3	0	5	—	5
National Parishes	—	—	13	10	5	4	3
Parish Schools	—	—	12	91	66	79	46
Diocesan Priests	—	—	80	188	151	183	163
Religious Order Priests	—	—	12	20	35	47	40
Women Religious	—	—	—	—	760	1,035	669
Catholic Population	—	—	95,000	145,000	111,759	155,501	148,128
Total Population	—	—	—	—	1,000,000	1,297,561	899,238

MICHIGAN
Diocese of Kalamazoo (1971)

	1850	1880	1900	1930	1950	1960	1980
Parishes	—	—	—	—	—	—	46
Parishes without Priests (i.e., Missions)	—	—	—	—	—	—	—
National Parishes	—	—	—	—	—	—	—
Parish Schools	—	—	—	—	—	—	21
Diocesan Priests	—	—	—	—	—	—	58
Religious Order Priests	—	—	—	—	—	—	38
Women Religious	—	—	—	—	—	—	306
Catholic Population	—	—	—	—	—	—	93,340
Total Population	—	—	—	—	—	—	796,812

MICHIGAN
Diocese of Lansing (1937)

	1850	1880	1900	1930	1950	1960	1980
Parishes	—	—	—	—	71	93	84
Parishes without Priests (i.e., Missions)	—	—	—	—	19	—	—
National Parishes	—	—	—	—	2	—	—
Parish Schools	—	—	—	—	41	63	40
Diocesan Priests	—	—	—	—	104	169	153
Religious Order Priests	—	—	—	—	31	28	59
Women Religious	—	—	—	—	602	904	560
Catholic Population	—	—	—	—	90,000	180,436	221,338
Total Population	—	—	—	—	1,001,640	1,533,420	1,511,910

MICHIGAN
Diocese of Marquette (1857)

	1850	1880	1900	1930	1950	1960	1980
Parishes	—	27[a]	56	74	81	93	89
Parishes without Priests (i.e., Missions)	—	—	24	58	40	5	—
National Parishes	—	1	33	10	6	4	—
Parish Schools	—	—	20	25	24	31	12
Diocesan Priests	—	19	59	82	139	151	129
Religious Order Priests	—	1	8	15	25	24	24
Women Religious	—	—	—	—	315	353	156
Catholic Population	—	—	65,000	70,693	90,984	106,135	98,528
Total Population	—	—	—	—	323,544	300,407	304,347

[a]Diocese of Sault Ste. Marie until 1865; Sault Ste. Marie-Marquette until 1937.

MICHIGAN
Diocese of Saginaw (1938)

	1850	1880	1900	1930	1950	1960	1980
Parishes	—	—	—	—	86	109	95
Parishes without Priests (i.e., Missions)	—	—	—	—	30	—	10
National Parishes	—	—	—	—	—	—	—
Parish Schools	—	—	—	—	46	61	35
Diocesan Priests	—	—	—	—	120	156	143
Religious Order Priests	—	—	—	—	15	25	28
Women Religious	—	—	—	—	395	493	261
Catholic Population	—	—	—	—	112,867	152,337	168,397
Total Population	—	—	—	—	443,900	499,927	613,443

WISCONSIN
Archdiocese of Milwaukee (1843; archdiocese, 1857)

	1850	1880	1900	1930	1950	1960	1980
Parishes	53	263	195	256	221	255	264
Parishes without Priests (i.e., Missions)	—	24	90	67	—	3	2
National Parishes	28	14	26	57	40	30	15
Parish Schools	—	261	150	187	169	215	178
Diocesan Priests	35	185	264	395	516	621	646
Religious Order Priests	8	38	51	138	336	421	515
Women Religious	—	—	—	—	4,820	4,466	3,720
Catholic Population	65,000	195,000	237,900	310,000	421,308	594,336	706,712
Total Population	—	—	—	—	1,260,553	1,700,000	2,039,217

Appendix: Church Statistics in the Midwest

WISCONSIN
Diocese of Green Bay (1868)

	1850	1880	1900	1930	1950	1960	1980
Parishes	—	111	123	176	174	184	187
Parishes without Priests (i.e., Missions)	—	—	79	66	45	—	7
National Parishes	—	91	101	15	25	15	—
Parish Schools	—	32	73	121	110	119	99
Diocesan Priests	—	60	131	207	219	301	295
Religious Order Priests	—	4	20	69	143	173	219
Women Religious	—	—	—	—	1,060	1,634	965
Catholic Population	—	65,000	125,000	175,000	273,953	273,236	337,139
Total Population	—	—	—	—	535,427	573,639	736,053

WISCONSIN
Diocese of La Crosse (1868)

	1850	1880	1900	1930	1950	1960	1980
Parishes	—	40	101	155	150	159	161
Parishes without Priests (i.e., Missions)	—	56	120	74	51	3	13
National Parishes	—	3	11	5	3	1	—
Parish Schools	—	22	72	89	89	104	76
Diocesan Priests	—	45	105	196	216	315	266
Religious Order Priests	—	5	27	40	55	79	43
Women Religious	—	—	—	—	1,391	1,431	718
Catholic Population	—	46,000	86,000	120,123	142,609	172,519	218,754
Total Population	—	—	—	—	577,206	655,000	667,849

WISCONSIN
Diocese of Madison (1946)

	1850	1880	1900	1930	1950	1960	1980
Parishes	—	—	—	—	—	111	113
Parishes without Priests (i.e., Missions)	—	—	—	—	—	24	25
National Parishes	—	—	—	—	—	—	—
Parish Schools	—	—	—	—	—	67	47
Diocesan Priests	—	—	—	—	—	182	209
Religious Order Priests	—	—	—	—	—	57	55
Women Religious	—	—	—	—	—	900	727
Catholic Population	—	—	—	—	—	140,587	215,255
Total Population	—	—	—	—	—	606,029	861,020

WISCONSIN
Diocese of Superior (1905)

	1850	1880	1900	1930	1950	1960	1980
Parishes	—	—	—	65	73	85	80
Parishes without Priests (i.e., Missions)	—	—	—	87	73	2	7
National Parishes	—	—	—	23	5	4	4
Parish Schools	—	—	—	26	31	37	22
Diocesan Priests	—	—	—	72	63	113	105
Religious Order Priests	—	—	—	24	42	33	19
Women Religious	—	—	—	—	537	496	241
Catholic Population	—	—	—	58,920	67,552	75,469	88,937
Total Population	—	—	—	—	312,219	291,229	341,904

MINNESOTA
Archdiocese of St. Paul-Minneapolis (1850; archdiocese, 1888)

	1850	1880	1900	1930	1950	1960	1980
Parishes	—	168	250	211	283	208	208
Parishes without Priests (i.e., Missions)	—	—	63	46	24	4	9
National Parishes	—	16	26	28	28	20	10
Parish Schools	—	—	79	139	142	161	109
Diocesan Priests	—	90	184	362	475	431	396
Religious Order Priests	—	25	36	63	82	124	221
Women Religious	—	—	—	—	1,976	2,227	1,642
Catholic Population	—	118,000	215,000	281,435	335,880	423,869	554,662
Total Population	—	—	—	—	1,406,365	1,302,174	2,017,225

MINNESOTA
Diocese of Crookston (1909)

	1850	1880	1900	1930	1950	1960	1980
Parishes	—	—	—	45	53	53	47
Parishes without Priests (i.e., Missions)	—	—	—	39	34	1	2
National Parishes	—	—	—	4	1	1	—
Parish Schools	—	—	—	10	11	12	11
Diocesan Priests	—	—	—	38	55	63	50
Religious Order Priests	—	—	—	16	21	27	23
Women Religious	—	—	—	—	—	313	320
Catholic Population	—	—	—	24,991	32,170	36,679	41,925
Total Population	—	—	—	—	231,263	238,700	220,132

MINNESOTA
Diocese of Duluth (1889)

	1850	1880	1900	1930	1950	1960	1980
Parishes	—	44[a]	36	65	69	84	74
Parishes without Priests (i.e., Missions)	—	—	31	46	50	2	4
National Parishes	—	1	4	9	4	4	2
Parish Schools	—	—	9	18	19	21	15
Diocesan Priests	—	14	27	89	79	107	101
Religious Order Priests	—	28	13	18	29	40	35
Women Religious	—	—	—	—	468	367	334
Catholic Population	—	21,500	24,000	64,000	89,646	100,917	101,487
Total Population	—	—	—	—	381,256	381,256	421,400

[a] Vicariate of Northern Minnesota until 1889.

MINNESOTA
Diocese of New Ulm (1957)

	1850	1880	1900	1930	1950	1960	1980
Parishes	—	—	—	—	—	86	73
Parishes without Priests (i.e., Missions)	—	—	—	—	—	—	21
National Parishes	—	—	—	—	—	—	—
Parish Schools	—	—	—	—	—	39	28
Diocesan Priests	—	—	—	—	—	103	114
Religious Order Priests	—	—	—	—	—	3	10
Women Religious	—	—	—	—	—	264	179
Catholic Population	—	—	—	—	—	68,432	71,039
Total Population	—	—	—	—	—	282,939	279,054

MINNESOTA
Diocese of St. Cloud (1889)

	1850	1880	1900	1930	1950	1960	1980
Parishes	—	—	64	116	126	126	133
Parishes without Priests	—	—	25	23	13	9	15
National Parishes	—	—	4	6	—	—	—
Parish Schools	—	—	25	47	45	37	52
Diocesan Priests	—	—	58	118	152	178	160
Religious Order Priests	—	—	42	68	28	142	170
Women Religious	—	—	—	—	1,252	1,474	1,129
Catholic Population	—	—	41,500	65,900	90,882	114,741	151,162
Total Population	—	—	—	—	326,334	322,542	349,853

MINNESOTA
Diocese of Winona (1889)

	1850	1880	1900	1930	1950	1960	1980
Parishes	—	—	55	86	92	98	95
Parishes without Priests (i.e., Missions)	—	—	47	39	36	31	29
National Parishes	—	—	4	—	—	—	—
Parish Schools	—	—	20	38	37	45	23
Diocesan Priests	—	—	63	119	129	184	172
Religious Order Priests	—	—	7	6	16	20	17
Women Religious	—	—	—	—	734	1,389	744
Catholic Population	—	—	40,000	68,800	73,044	98,905	119,753
Total Population	—	—	—	—	447,082	464,708	516,382

IOWA
Archdiocese of Dubuque (1837; archdiocese, 1893)

	1850	1880	1900	1930	1950	1960	1980
Parishes	16	160	218	184	196	198	190
Parishes without Priests (i.e., Missions)	—	125	45	54	34	4	—
National Parishes	6	5	8	—	—	—	—
Parish Schools	—	76	118	102	107	117	60
Diocesan Priests	17	176	271	277	331	426	378
Religious Order Priests	—	14	12	11	39	96	101
Women Religious	—	—	—	—	1,682	1,882	1,467
Catholic Population	7,050	120,000	150,000	119,424	147,412	169,684	242,744
Total Population	—	—	—	—	794,565	840,658	956,078

IOWA
Diocese of Davenport (1881)

	1850	1880	1900	1930	1950	1960	1980
Parishes	—	—	92	94	99	93	95
Parishes without Priests (i.e., Missions)	—	—	50	31	—	32	24
National Parishes	—	—	2	—	—	—	—
Parish Schools	—	—	42	52	46	50	38
Diocesan Priests	—	—	107	142	188	209	196
Religious Order Priests	—	—	9	9	17	21	18
Women Religious	—	—	—	—	722	716	457
Catholic Population	—	—	70,000	62,126	72,655	92,506	105,000
Total Population	—	—	—	—	589,361	660,500	687,000

Appendix: Church Statistics in the Midwest

IOWA
Diocese of Des Moines (1911)

	1850	1880	1900	1930	1950	1960	1980
Parishes	—	—	—	63	66	68	65
Parishes without Priests (i.e., Missions)	—	—	—	30	31	2	19
National Parishes	—	—	—	—	—	—	—
Parish Schools	—	—	—	29	27	33	22
Diocesan Priests	—	—	—	96	92	122	126
Religious Order Priests	—	—	—	15	21	11	10
Women Religious	—	—	—	—	322	319	205
Catholic Population	—	—	—	38,724	48,053	70,434	80,427
Total Population	—	—	—	—	597,400	598,541	512,883

IOWA
Diocese of Sioux City (1902)

	1850	1880	1900	1930	1950	1960	1980
Parishes	—	—	—	117	121	122	117
Parishes without Priests (i.e., Missions)	—	—	—	29	27	20	—
National Parishes	—	—	—	4	2	—	—
Parish Schools	—	—	—	72	69	73	39
Diocesan Priests	—	—	—	156	167	203	208
Religious Order Priests	—	—	—	12	15	16	220
Women Religious	—	—	—	—	651	682	333
Catholic Population	—	—	—	67,725	83,393	103,000	112,758
Total Population	—	—	—	—	556,224	548,301	512,883

MISSOURI
Archdiocese of St. Louis (1826; archdiocese, 1847)

	1850	1880	1900	1930	1950	1960	1980
Parishes	56	216	175	258	268	225	237
Parishes without Priests (i.e., Missions)	—	51	77	60	52	7	9
National Parishes	4	16	30	7	3	4	5
Parish Schools	13	110	138	212	231	196	171
Diocesan Priests	9	162	240	385	501	508	575
Religious Order Priests	50	98	178	313	479	489	527
Women Religious	—	—	—	—	3,944	3,205	3,395
Catholic Population	—	145,872	262,380	440,000	433,442	451,958	531,108
Total Population	—	—	—	—	1,960,606	1,152,746	1,924,220

MISSOURI
Diocese of Jefferson City (1956)

	1850	1880	1900	1930	1950	1960	1980
Parishes	—	—	—	—	—	87	80
Parishes without Priests (i.e., Missions)	—	—	—	—	—	4	14
National Parishes	—	—	—	—	—	—	—
Parish Schools	—	—	—	—	—	53	36
Diocesan Priests	—	—	—	—	—	124	127
Religious Order Priests	—	—	—	—	—	20	14
Women Religious	—	—	—	—	—	325	157
Catholic Population	—	—	—	—	—	62,525	79,905
Total Population	—	—	—	—	—	595,000	670,706

MISSOURI
Archdiocese of Kansas City-St. Joseph (1880, 1868)

	1850	1880	1900	1930	1950	1960	1980
Parishes	—	30[a]	27	56	61	87	90
		55[b]	85	101			
Parishes without Priests (i.e., Missions)	—	—	31	46	24	11	7
			13	25	32		
National Parishes	—	—	—	—	—	—	—
				3	2		
Parish Schools	—	9	14	34	32	62	44
			41	59	62		
Diocesan Priests	—	11	28	64	74	175	158
			48	106	142		
Religious Order Priests	—	15	18	36	48	146	166
			42	52	106	1,401	640
Women Religious	—	—	—	—	407		
					919		
Catholic Population	—	18,000	20,000	46,274	32,063	135,822	137,766
			45,000	80,000	85,000		
Total Population	—	—	—	—	633,987	1,030,247	1,271,000
					1,216,239		

[a]Diocese of St. Joseph, established 1868,
[b]Diocese of Kansas City, established 1880; dioceses combined in 1956.

Appendix: Church Statistics in the Midwest

MISSOURI
Diocese of Springfield-Cape Girardeau (1956)

	1850	1880	1900	1930	1950	1960	1980
Parishes	—	—	—	—	—	56	60
Parishes without Priests (i.e., Missions)	—	—	—	—	—	3	1
National Parishes	—	—	—	—	—	—	—
Parish Schools	—	—	—	—	—	31	22
Diocesan Priests	—	—	—	—	—	72	74
Religious Order Priests	—	—	—	—	—	47	41
Women Religious	—	—	—	—	—	302	227
Catholic Population	—	—	—	—	—	33,817	48,989
Total Population	—	—	—	—	—	900,000	833,669

NORTH DAKOTA
Diocese of Bismarck (1909)

	1850	1880	1900	1930	1950	1960	1980
Parishes	—	—	—	64	80	89	69
Parishes without Priests (i.e., Missions)	—	—	—	91	58	2	4
National Parishes	—	—	—	2	—	—	—
Parish Schools	—	—	—	17	19	27	19
Diocesan Priests	—	—	—	48	73	96	76
Religious Order Priests	—	—	—	33	33	62	66
Women Religious	—	—	—	—	28	420	298
Catholic Population	—	—	—	49,326	54,905	67,302	76,817
Total Population	—	—	—	—	233,062	243,794	244,777

NORTH DAKOTA
Diocese of Fargo (1889)

	1850	1880	1900	1930	1950	1960	1980
Parishes	—	20[a]	43	102	115	122	98
Parishes without Priests (i.e., Missions)	—	—	75	85	62	2	4
National Parishes	—	12	—	1	—	—	—
Parish Schools	—	—	12	24	12	15	14
Diocesan Priests	—	—	38	127	123	161	144
Religious Order Priests	—	—	16	6	22	26	29
Women Religious	—	—	—	—	617	646	249
Catholic Population	—	—	27,000	69,871	75,734	85,449	109,111
Total Population	—	—	—	—	408,873	391,107	372,960

[a] Vicariate of Dakota until 1888; Diocese of Jamestown until 1897.

SOUTH DAKOTA
Diocese of Rapid City (1902)

	1850	1880	1900	1930	1950	1960	1980
Parishes	—	—	—	77[a]	75	62	52
Parishes without Priests (i.e., Missions)	—	—	—	111	81	5	4
National Parishes	—	—	—	—	—	—	—
Parish Schools	—	—	—	9	13	11	1
Diocesan Priests	—	—	—	84	68	78	38
Religious Order Priests	—	—	—	20	32	38	41
Women Religious	—	—	—	—	224	188	100
Catholic Population	—	—	—	39,865	43,360	40,355	40,138
Total Population	—	—	—	—	151,109	158,099	178,208

[a] Diocese of Lead until 1920.

SOUTH DAKOTA
Diocese of Sioux Falls (1889)

	1850	1880	1900	1930	1950	1960	1980
Parishes	—	—	70	120	112	115	100
Parishes without Priests (i.e., Missions)	—	—	132	69	61	4	22
National Parishes	—	—	—	—	—	—	—
Parish Schools	—	—	10	35	33	42	24
Diocesan Priests	—	—	62	126	111	145	144
Religious Order Priests	—	—	14	8	38	65	69
Women Religious	—	—	—	—	666	859	487
Catholic Population	—	—	35,000	60,745	74,294	85,219	100,245
Total Population	—	—	—	—	491,852	491,878	484,000

Appendix: Church Statistics in the Midwest

NEBRASKA
Archdiocese of Omaha (1885; archdiocese, 1945)

	1850	1880	1900	1930	1950	1960	1980
Parishes	—	42[a]	83	138	132	137	134
Parishes without Priests (i.e., Missions)	—	—	63	46	—	2	2
National Parishes	—	2	1	1	—	—	—
Parish Schools	—	12	36	84	80	88	63
Diocesan Priests	—	16	88	178	241	215	223
Religious Order Priests	—	42	22	63	73	151	180
Women Religious	—	—	—	—	895	1,294	844
Catholic Population	—	39,000	61,050	94,400	125,842	151,614	216,779
Total Population	—	—	—	—	529,078	543,656	758,125

[a]Vicariate Apostolic of Nebraska until 1885.

NEBRASKA
Diocese of Grand Island (1912)

	1850	1880	1900	1930	1950	1960	1980
Parishes	—	—	—	50	53	54	50
Parishes without Priests (i.e., Missions)	—	—	—	50	38	—	—
National Parishes	—	—	—	—	—	—	—
Parish Schools	—	—	—	6	13	17	9
Diocesan Priests	—	—	—	14	70	81	82
Religious Order Priests	—	—	—	2	16	3	2
Women Religious	—	—	—	—	225	240	144
Catholic Population	—	—	—	24,629	30,432	42,076	51,846
Total Population	—	—	—	—	296,076	295,000	299,012

NEBRASKA
Diocese of Lincoln (1887)

	1850	1880	1900	1930	1950	1960	1980
Parishes	—	—	54	90	98	100	86
Parishes without Priests (i.e., Missions)	—	—	48	50	—	—	—
National Parishes	—	—	2	—	—	—	—
Parish Schools	—	—	15	35	32	35	24
Diocesan Priests	—	—	59	97	117	149	117
Religious Order Priests	—	—	3	14	21	24	28
Women Religious	—	—	—	—	222	254	170
Catholic Population	—	—	22,150	41,132	39,695	50,736	66,517
Total Population	—	—	—	—	426,147	527,947	511,400

KANSAS
Archdiocese of Kansas City (1877; archdiocese, 1952)

	1850	1880	1900	1930	1950	1960	1980
Parishes	—	120[a]	50	102	107	106	92
Parishes without Priests (i.e., Missions)	—	—	48	23	—	3	27
National Parishes	—	1	1	4	4	4	4
Parish Schools	—	24	35	70	75	72	38
Diocesan Priests	—	50	53	96	99	141	125
Religious Order Priests	—	27	60	118	211	247	138
Women Religious	—	—	—	—	1,495	1,709	1,225
Catholic Population	—	70,000	30,000	86,413	80,000	120,500	145,000
Total Population	—	—	—	—	594,289	641,477	882,028

[a] Diocese of Leavenworth until 1947.

KANSAS
Diocese of Dodge City (1951)

	1850	1880	1900	1930	1950	1960	1980
Parishes	—	—	—	—	—	50	44
Parishes without Priests (i.e., Missions)	—	—	—	—	—	—	2
National Parishes	—	—	—	—	—	—	—
Parish Schools	—	—	—	—	—	23	11
Diocesan Priests	—	—	—	—	—	64	56
Religious Order Priests	—	—	—	—	—	10	11
Women Religious	—	—	—	—	—	296	190
Catholic Population	—	—	—	—	—	25,850	37,174
Total Population	—	—	—	—	—	201,758	218,907

Appendix: Church Statistics in the Midwest

KANSAS
Diocese of Salina (1887)

	1850	1880	1900	1930[a]	1950	1960	1980
Parishes	—	—	30	65	66	70	65
Parishes without Priests (i.e., Missions)	—	—	52	32	—	30	33
National Parishes	—	—	—	—	—	—	—
Parish Schools	—	—	16	34	32	19	12
Diocesan Priests	—	—	30	64	69	86	79
Religious Order Priests	—	—	9	31	40	50	44
Women Religious	—	—	—	—	490	542	345
Catholic Population	—	—	20,000	44,118	40,848	53,410	60,145
Total Population	—	—	—	—	316,821	338,809	327,903

[a]Diocese of Concordia until 1944.

KANSAS
Diocese of Wichita (1887)

	1850	1880	1900	1930	1950	1960	1980
Parishes	—	—	39	94	118	169	141
Parishes without Priests (i.e., Missions)	—	—	60	59	42	4	7
National Parishes	—	—	1	2	—	—	—
Parish Schools	—	—	25	62	80	52	28
Diocesan Priests	—	—	44	105	160	169	141
Religious Order Priests	—	—	10	38	47	58	28
Women Religious	—	—	—	—	1,122	840	451
Catholic Population	—	—	21,690	61,137	68,849	78,477	97,350
Total Population	—	—	—	—	904,927	924,247	846,792

General Index

"Active spirituality," 38
Adult education, 107–109, 181–182
Advent, 36
AIRFA (American Indian Religious Freedom Act), 247
Alaskan Gold Rush, 14
Albrecht, Philip, 316
Alday, Francisco, 175
Alemany, Joseph Sadoc, 15, 19–20, 22, 80–81
Alleman, John G., 290
All Hallows College (Ireland), 20–21
Allouez, Claude, 282, 291
Altar Society
   in Alaska, 124
   and fund-raising, 29
   and parish life, 40–41, 186–187
   and women, 365
Alurista, Alberto, 255
Amat, Thaddeus, 20, 81
American Dream, 17
American Indian Religious Freedom Act (AIRFA), 247
American Protective Association (APA), 16
American Revolution, 1
Americanization
   of German Americans, 313–315
   of Italian Americans, 63–64, 338–339
   of Mexican Americans, 87–88
Amos Afraid of Bear, 193
Ancient Order of Hibernians (AOH), 55–56, 307
Angelic Warfare, 36
Anti-Catholicism, in Pacific states, 15–17
AOH (Ancient Order of Hibernians), 55–56, 307
APA (American Protective Association), 16
Apache Indians, 202, 223
Apostleship of Prayer, 36
Aranda, Mario, 372
Arapaho Indians, 216, 246
Athletics, 46–47

Bachelot, Father, 122
Baltimore Catechism, 125

Baptism, 100
Baptists, 162. *See also* Protestants
Baraga, Frederick, 292
Barrioization, 83
Basque Americans, 222, 253
Battle of Tippecanoe, 287
Bavarian Americans, 311
Bazaar, 28–29
Begay, Myrtle, 205
Belcourt, George A., 291
Benavides, Alonzo, 151, 210
Bender, Frederick, 179
Benedictines
   in Colorado, 214–215
   and devotions, 37–38
   in Intermountain West, 188, 214–215, 310
   and liturgy, 374
   in Minnesota, 310
Benediction, 33
Bernabo, Alessandro Cardinal, 147
Bernardin, Joseph Cardinal, 362, 365, 374
Biehler, J. E., 356
Bilinski, John, 236
Bishops, 180, 204, 303. *See also* Clergy; specific names of
Black Americans, 74, 370–372
Blackfeet Indians, 217, 246, 291
Black robes, 142–143. *See also* Priests
Blanchet, Francis, 147
Blessed Imelda Confraternity, 36
Blessed Sacrament procession, 35, 122
Blessing, Patrick, 54–55, 57
Bobol, Francis, 303
Bohemian Americans, 302–303
Bolton, Eugene, 150
Bouchard, James, 21
Bourgade, Peter, 179
Bradley, Charles, 71
Breton, Albert, 72
Brondel, John B., 148
Brotherhood of the I.D.E.S. (Irmandade do Divino Esanto), 67

General Index 403

Buddy, Charles, 82
Building, 26–27
Burchell, R. A., 54–56, 58
Bureaucracy, 118–119
Bureau of Catholic Indian Missions, 216
Burke, Maurice F., 147–148
Buswell, Charles A., 261

Cabrini, Mother, 222
Cachupen, Tomas Velaz, 176
Californian Gold Rush, 10–11
Calkins, Hugh, 348
Calvo, Gabriel, 367
Camarillo, Albert, 79, 83
Campbell, Alexander, 285
Cana Conference, 38
Cana Movement, 374
Cantwell, John J., 35, 49, 51, 74, 87
Capuchins, 188
Carroll, John, 279, 286
Carroll, Mary Helen, 257
Carter, Jimmy, 247
del Castillo, Richard Griswold, 79
Castro, John, 250
Catechism, 44, 125. *See also* CCD
Catholic Almanac of 1855, 300
Catholic Charismatic Movement, 366–367
Catholic Charismatic Renewal, 104–105
Catholic Charities Office, 329
Catholic Church. *See also* Catholicism; Local church; Parish life
　and agricultural settlements, 153–155
　building, 26–27
　and capitalism, 161
　and Civil War, 160
　conflict in, 161–162
　and ecclesiastical boundaries, 145–148
　and economics, 148–149
　and First Great Awakening, 161
　and Indian missions, 150–153
　in Intermountain West, 141–169
　and mining settlements, 155–158
　and Mormons, 163–165
　in Pacific states, 12
　and physical geography, 141–144
　and political geography, 144–145
　and Protestants, 161–163
　and railroad, 158–160
　and science, 160–161
　and Second Great Awakening, 161
　and Spanish colonization, 149–150
　statistics on
　　in Intermountain West, 271–276
　　in Midwest, 382–401
　　in Pacific states, 128–133
　women in, 261–262
Catholic Daughters of America, 41–42
Catholic Directory, 223
Catholic Evidence Guilds, 16
Catholicism. *See also* Catholic Church; Parish life
　in 1980s, 117–119
　in Alaska, 124–125
　American, 2–3
　in California, 11, 15
　charitable organizations of, 42–44
　disadvantaged in, 103
　and ecumenism, 105–106
　and ethnic groups, 4, 111–113
　and family enrichment programs, 103–104
　in Florida, 5
　folk, 53
　in France, 3
　in Hawaii, 121–124
　history of, 1–2
　in Intermountain West, 4
　in Ireland, 3
　and Irish Americans, 55, 57–58
　in Italy, 3
　maturing of, 113
　and Mexican Americans, 79–80, 85–86
　in Midwest, 4
　in Northeast, 4–5
　in Pacific states, 4, 11–12, 15, 74–75
　in post-Vatican II period
　　in Intermountain West, 243–256
　　in Pacific states, 103–106, 114
　prejudice against, 15–17
　Progressive reformers in, 43–44
　and Sanctuary Movement, 117–118
　social outreach of, 103, 256–258
　in South Carolina, 5
　in South Central states, 5
　Southern, 5
　in Spain, 3
　and spiritual movements, 104–105
　in U.S., 2–3
　in Washington, 15
Catholic Ladies' Aid Society, 42–43
Catholic Order of Foresters, 41

Catholic Rural Life Conference, 328–330
Catholics. *See also* specific ethnic groups of
  in Arizona, 236
  in California, 11, 13
  and charity, 42–44
  in Colorado, 236, 259
  "communal," 111
  "cultural," 52–53
  in Hawaii, 11
  and history, 1–2
  in Illinois, 295
  and immigrants, fear of, 50
  indifferent, 34
  in Intermountain West, 193–194
  in Kansas, 300
  lapsed, 34
  in Minnesota, 296–297
  mission, 53
  in Nebraska, 300
  in New Mexico, 235–236
  in Oregon, 14–15, 51
  in Pacific states, 10–11
  "practical," 52
  and Protestants, 105–106, 285–286
  and religious education, 183
  in Washington, 14–15
Catholic Total Abstinence Union, 57
Catholic Truth Societies, 16
Catholic Truth Society, 303
Catholic Women's Union, 58
Catholic Youth Organization (CYO), 46–47, 305, 332–333
Catolicos por la Raza, 118
Cayuse Indians, 16
CCD (Confraternity of Christian Doctrine). *See also* Catechism
  in 1950s, 45
  effectiveness of, 361
  and Mexican Americans, 87
  in Midwest, 330–331
  in post-Vatican II period, 106–107
  in suburban parishes, 109
Cerro Prieto rebellion, 175
CFM. *See* Christian Family Movement
Chan, Anthony, 71
"Chapel car" program, 23
Charisma in Missions, 105
Charismatic Movement, 256, 347
Charismatic Renewal, 260, 373
Chavez, Angelico, 174

Chavez, Cesar, 90–91, 103, 118
Cherry Creek gold strike, 156
Chicano Americans, 118. *See also* Hispanic Americans; Mexican Americans
Chicano Movement, 255
Children's mission, 33
Children of Mary, 45
Chinese Americans
  and Cian, 49
  parish life of, 72
  parish organizations of, 72–73
  priests serving, 72
Chinese Language School, 71
Chippewa Indians, 292
Christian Family Movement (CFM)
  in 1960s, 103–104, 365
  Conference, 367
  and German Americans, 60
  organization of, 348
  and parish life, 38
  in post-Vatican II period, 374
Christmas Fund Boxing Tournament, 333
Christ Renews His Parish, 359–360
Church of Jesus Christ of Latter-Day Saints. *See* Mormons
Cian, Thomas, 49, 70–71
Cichanowicz, Chuck, 244
Circuit riding, 181
Civil War, 1, 5, 160
Clark, N. H., 51–52
Clements, George, 371
Clergy. *See also* Bishops; Priests
  circuit-riding, 181
  Irish, 56
  and local church, 174–177
  in Midwest, 303–306, 368–369
  in post-Vatican II period, 368–369
Cody, Edward R., 192
Cofradia de los Hermanos, 209
Collier, John, 217
Collins, James Earl, 220
Comanche Indians, 217
Comhair, 55
Communal Catholics, 111
Communion, 35–36, 65, 101, 364
Concjos, 154–155
Confessions, 34
Confirmation, 100–101
Confraternities, 36, 187
Confraternity of Christian Doctrine, *See* CCD

General Index

Confraternity of the Blessed Sacrament, 36
Confraternity of the Rosary, 36
Congregationalists, 162. *See also* Protestants
Cook, Joan, 360–361
Corpus Christi procession, 35, 122, 311
Corrada del Rio, Alvaro, 253
Council of Trent in 1545, 206
Covenants, written, 239
Crespo, Benito, 180
Croatian Americans, 221–222
Crowley, Patricia, 348
Cuban Americans. *See* Hispanic Americans; Latin Americans
Cultural Catholics, 52–53
Cultural Exchange Committee, 113
Cumortier, A., 301
Cursillo Movement
  in 1960s and 1970s, 104
  in Hawaii, 124
  and Hispanic Americans, 250, 253
  origin of, 90
  in post-Vatican II period, 356, 373
  in rural parishes, 356
CYO (Catholic Youth Organization), 46–47, 305, 332–333

Dablon, Claude, 282
Dabrowski, Joseph, 341
Daly, Marcus, 161
Daughters of Charity, 190
David, A. T., 296
Davis, Peter, 245
Dawes Act of 1887, 204
Deacons, 236
Decker, Peter, 40
Dedier, Adele, 315
De La Salle Institute, 307
Depression, Great, 12, 80, 168, 189, 329
Devotions. *See also* Parish life; Spirituality
  and Benedictines, 37–38
  and Dominicans, 37
  and Filipino Americans, 114
  and Franciscans, 37
  and German Americans, 58, 60, 311
  and Irish Americans, 55
  and Italian Americans, 63
  and Jesuits, 37
  Marian, 37, 86, 109
  and Mexican Americans, 86
  non-liturgical, 37

  in Oregon, after World War II, 37
  Our Lady of Fatima, 37
  Our Lady of Guadalupe, 37
  in post-Vatican II period, 101
  private, 37
  and Redemptorists, 38
  and religious orders, 37–38
  after World War II, 345–346
Dialogue Mass, 38
Dinet, Joseph, 315
Diocesan Council of Catholic Women, 329
Divine Word Fathers, 72
Djewanewski, Vincent, 341
Dodds, Gordon, 15, 51
Dolan, Jay P., 280
Dominguez, Francisco Atanasio, 164
Dominicans, 34, 37
Dominican Sisters, 44
Dowling, Patrick J., 159
Drexel, Katherine, 193, 216
D'Aste, Father, 179
Duggan, James, 308, 315–316
Duggan, Ralph, 89
Dulles, Avery, 254
Dust Bowl, 168

Eaton, John, 371
Ecclesial Affirmative Action, 261
Ecumenism, 105–106, 125, 362–363
Education. *See* Adult education; CCD; Parochial schools
Egan, John, 348
Elderly
  in inner-city parishes, 109
  in Midwest, 363–369
  in suburban parishes, 110–111
Elizondo, Virgil, 113, 372
Ellis, John Tracy, 363
El Movimiento, 255
Emmaus Grief Ministry, 241
Encomienda system, 151
England, John, 161
English missal, 38
Erlach, P. J., 302
de Escalante, Silvestre Velez, 164
Eskimo Americans, 125
Ethnic groups. *See also* specific groups
  in Alaska, 125
  in California, 52
  and Catholicism, 4, 111–113

and "cultural" Catholics, 52–53
fear of, by Catholics, 50
in Hawaii, 122–123
in Intermountain West, 199, 223–224
in Midwest, 306, 333–336
and Mission Catholics, 53
in Oregon, 51
in Pacific states, 49–53
and parish life, 50–51
in post-Vatican II period
in Intermountain West, 243–256
in Midwest, 373–374
in Pacific states, 111–114
and "practical" Catholics, 52
in Washington, 51–52
Ethnicity, 4, 50–51. *See also* Ethnic groups
Evers, Albert, 316–317
Extension Society of America, 22–23, 192–193

Family First Communion, 104
Farmers' Placement Bureau, 329
Favores Celestiales, 150
Feast of St. Francis, 202
Feehan, Patrick A., 294, 370
Felician Sisters, 344
Felix, Francisco Ildefonso, 175
Fenwick, Edward, 284, 286
Fernandes, Manuel Francisco, 66
Festival of the Holy Ghost, 66–67
Festivals, 66–70. *See also* Bazaar
Filipino Americans
and devotions, 114
in Hawaii, 123
and Knights of Columbus, 68
parish life of, 68–69
parish organizations of, 68
prejudice against, 69
priests serving, 68
processions of, 69
and Protestants, 69
and Santo Niño de Cebu festival, 69–70
"Filling station mentality," 110
Finance committees, 30–31
Financing. *See* Fund-raising
Fink, Ludwig, 305–306
First Great Awakening, 161
First National Encuentro, 255
Fisher, John, 358
Fisher, Karen, 360
Fisher, Terry, 360

Flaget, Joseph, 287
Flatheads, 142–143, 152–153, 223–224
Flores de Mayo, 69
Florez, Patricio, 253
Foley, James B., 143, 303
Folk Catholicism, 53
Forty Hours' Devotions, 37
Franchi, Carlo, 62
Franciscans
and devotions, 37
and German Americans, 310–311
missions of, 179
in Nebraska, 302
in Southwest, 149, 151
Fraternal associations, 40, 60
Fraternal insurance societies, 41–43
French Americans, 73–74
French Canadian Americans, 2, 74, 282–283
Friedman, Gregory, 359
Friends of Irish Freedom, 307
Fund-raising
and Altar Society, 29
events, 28–29
in Intermountain West, 185–187, 194–195
lay involvement in, 27, 30–32
and local church, 185–187, 194–195
organizations, 29
in Pacific states, 25–32
parish organizations for, 29
priest involvement in, 28
and rebuilding, 185
in suburban parishes, 109

Gadsden Purchase, 145
Gaffey, James, 118
Garcia, John, 89
Gasparri, Donato, 209
Gendron, Joseph, 188
Gercke, Daniel, 166
German Americans
Americanization of, 313–315
assimilation of, 215–216
in California, 52, 58–60
in Chicago, 287–288, 295
and Christian Family Movement, 60
and devotions, 58, 60, 311
and Franciscans, 310–311
and fraternal insurance societies, 41
fraternal societies in, 60
influence of, 212–215, 308

General Index

and Irish Americans, 214
in Kansas, 300–303
and laity, 304–305
and liturgy, 311
and marriage, 60
nationalism of, 221, 310
national parishes of, 49
in Nebraska, 302–303
in North Dakota, 298–300
in Ohio, 284–285
parishes of, 49, 308–312, 315–317
parish life of, 60
parish organizations of, 60, 312–313
and parochial schools, 58, 306, 313–315
in present times, 369
priests serving, 309–310
and Protestants, 315
religious orders of, 310
and sodalities, 58
in South Dakota, 298–300
in St. Paul, 292
before World War I, 327–328
after World War I, 333–336
after World War II, 347
German Catholic Central Verein, 58, 312
German-Russian Americans, 298–299
Giambastiani, Luigi, 337–338
Gilbert, Fabiola Cabeza de Baca, 144
Gilmour, Richard, 303
Gleason, Philip, 112
Glorieux, Alphonsus Joseph, 180–181
Gold Rush, 10–11, 14
Gosma, Robert, 360
Grassi, Urban, 179, 203
"Great Smoke, The," 203
Greeley, Andrew, 111, 119, 361
Greysolon, Daniel, 291
Griswold del Castillo, Richard, 79
del Grito, Dolores, 255
Guida, John, 179, 222

Haan, Donna, 367
Hacker, Hilary B., 347
Hahn, Mrs. Henry, 310, 314
Halligan, M. J., 217
Hanna, Archbishop, 27, 35
Hannon, Dean, 296
Hattenberger, Alexander, 290
Headley, Louis, 246
Held, Friedrich von, 309

Hennaan, Bill, 254
Hennebery, Patrick, 21
Hennepin, Louis, 283
Henni, Matthias, 341
Hermanos de Nuestro Padre Jesus, 187
High Mass, 33
Hillenbrand, Reynold, 348
Hispanic Americans
in 1950s, 224
agricultural settlements of, 153–155
and community, 208
and *Cursillo* Movement, 250, 253
and family, 208
and fiestas, 211–212
and laity, 208–209
and Lamy, 146, 206–207
and Marriage Encounter, 253
national parishes of, 49
and Native Americans, 205
population changes in, 218–220
in post-Vatican II period, 249–256
in present times, 372–374
and Protestants, 220, 253–254
and saints, 210–212
and Sanctuary Movement, 117–118
and shrines, 210
and Southern Catholicism, 5
and tradition, 206–209
and weddings, 212
and World War II, 220–221
Holy Family Mission, 71
Holy Name Society
in 1940s, 346
and men, 365
and parish life, 40–41, 186–187
Homstead Act, 154–155
Hopi Indians, 149, 201–202
Huerta, Dolores, 90
Hunger Sunday, 103

ICF (Italian Catholic Federation), 64–65, 215
Immaculate Heart Confraternity, 36–37
Immigrants. *See* Ethnic groups
Indian Reorganization Act of 1934, 217
Indians. *See* Native Americans; specific tribes of
Indian Self-Determination Act, 246
Inner-city parish, 108–111
Intermountain West. *See also* Post-Vatican II period; specific ethnic groups in
Benedictines in, 188, 214–215, 310

Catholic Church in, 141–169
Catholic Church statistics on, 271–276
Catholicism in, 4
Catholics in, 193–194
ethnic groups in, 199, 223–224
fund-raising in, 185–187, 194–195
local church in, 174–195
parish life in, 139–140, 165–169
parish organizations in, 187
parochial schools in, 189–190, 195
Protestants in, 141, 161–163
Ireland, John P., 213, 297, 303
Irish Americans
and alcohol, 57
assimilation of, 215–216
in California, 11, 52
and Catholicism, 55, 57–58
in Chicago, 287, 295
and devotions, 55
and fraternal insurance societies, 41
and German Americans, 214
and immigrants, other, 57–58
influence of, 212–213, 306–307
and Italian Americans, 61–62
and laity, 304–305
nationalism of, 56–57, 221
in Nebraska, 300
negative image of, 57
in North Dakota, 298
in Ohio, 284–285
parishes of, 307–308
parish life of, 56
and parochial schools, 56, 306, 313
prejudice against, 57
and sodalities, 55–56
in South Dakota, 298
in St. Paul, 292
after World War II, 347
Irish Christian Brothers, 307
Irish Race in California, The, 56
Italian Americans
Americanization of, 63–64, 338–339
assimilation of, 215–216
in California, 12, 61
conflict among, 222–223
and devotions, 63
and fraternal insurance societies, 41
and ICF, 64–65, 215
and Irish Americans, 61–62
and Jesuits, 215

and marriage, 62–63
nationalism of, 62–63, 340
national parishes of, 49
and naturalization, 339–340
parish life of, 64
parish organizations of, 64–65, 339
priests serving, 62
and Protestants, 62
turnover rates of, 61
waves of, 212
after World War II, 347
youth of, 339
Italian Catholic Federation (ICF), 64–65, 215
"Italian Problem," 336

J.O.Y. (Jesus Over You), 102
Japanese Americans
parish life of, 72–73
parish organizations of, 71–72
priests serving, 70–72
Jaramillo, Cleofas, 176, 209–212
Jarzynski, T., 221
Jesuits
in Alaska, 124
and devotions, 37
and Italian Americans, 215
in Midwest, 289
missions of, 176–177, 179, 203–204
and preaching, 34
and de Smet, 152
in Southwest, 150–153
Jeunesse Ouvriere Chretienne (JOC), 348
JOC (*Jeunesse Ouvriere Chretienne*), 348
Jogues, Rene, 282
John Eagle Man, Sr., 193
John XXIII, 233, 374
Juhnke, Louis Venn, 315
Jutz, John, 204

Kalispels, 153
Kalvelage, Ferdinand L., 316, 334–335
Kane, John, 358
Kane, M. Theresa, 365
Kayser, Leonard, 356, 358
Keane, James, 346–347
Kearney, Stephen Watts, 154, 168–169
Kelley, Francis Clement, 192–193
Kelly, Edward J., 191
Kelly, Francis, 23
Kelly, William, 159, 178

Kennedy, John F., 233
Kino, Eusebio Francisco, 150, 202
Kinsella, Father, 302
Kiowa Indians, 217
KKK (Ku Klux Klan), 16
Kline, Susan, 365
Kloepfer, John, 357
Knights of Columbus
    and Filipino Americans, 68
    founding of, 193
    and Mexican Americans, 88
    in Midwest, 332
    and parish life, 41–42, 193
Koch, Francis, 179
Kootenais, 153
Kozlowski, Edward, 343
Kruszka, Michael, 343
Kruszka, Wenceslaus, 343
Ku Klux Klan (KKK), 16
Kulturkampf, 214
Kuppens, Father, 179

La Cofradia de La Conquistadora, 210
La Cofradia de Nuestro Senora del Carmel, 187
Ladies' Auxiliary, 41–42
La Fortune, Bellarmine, 125
La funcion, 211
Laity
    and building of local churches, 186
    and fund-raising, 27, 30–32
    and German Americans, 304–305
    in Hawaii, 122
    and Hispanic Americans, 208–209
    in local church, 176–177
    in Midwest, 303–306
    and parish, 97
    and peace movement, 257–258
    in post-Vatican II period, 363–369
    and priests, 97–98
    and Sanctuary Movement, 257–258
    spiritual involvement of, 38
    and spirituality, 38
    in suburban parishes, 109–110
    teaching by, 107
La Mousse, Ignace, 143
Lamy, John Baptist
    at First Plenary Council of Baltimore, 183
    and Hispanic Americans, 146, 206–207
    in New Mexico, 146, 162, 178, 181
    and tithing, 185

Lancaster, John, 303
Lane, Loras, 368
Langlade, Augustine de, 289
Lanz, Matt, 367
Lapore, Mariano Felice, 215
Las Hermanas, 255
Latin Americans, 117–118
Laukemper, Bernard, 310
Lay council, 97
LCWR (Leadership Conference of Women Religious), 262
Leadership Conference of Women Religious (LCWR), 262
League of Cross Cadets, 57
League of the Sacred Heart, 36
League of United Latin American Citizens (LULAC), 220
Lee, Daniel, 163
Lee, Jason, 163
Legion of Mary, 37–38, 108–109
Lempke, Henry, 300
Lent, 36
Leo XIII, 214
Lepore, 222
Lithuanian Americans, 334, 369–370
Liturgical committee, 101–103
Liturgical teams, 234
Liturgy
    and Benedictines, 374
    and German Americans, 311
    in post-Vatican II period
        in Intermountain West, 233–235
        in Pacific states, 100–103
    after World War II, 348
Local church. *See also* Catholic Church; Parish life
    adult education in, 181–182
    bishops serving, 180
    building programs for, 180–181, 188, 193
    changes in, 195
    clergy serving, 174–177
    and fund-raising, 185–187, 194–195
    growth of, 194–195
    in Intermountain West, 174–195
    and laity, 176–177
    parish organizations in, 187
    parochial schools in, 182–185, 189–190, 195
    in post-Vatican II period, 233–243
    priests serving, 177–179, 187–188
    and religious communities, 191

and secularization, 175–176
and social events, 191–193
and styles of religious conduct, 174
summer vacation schools in, 190–191
Lone Bear, 216
Longingua Oceani, 180
Loras, Matthias T., 289–290, 308
Louisana Purchase, 144
Lucey, Robert, 88
LULAC (League of United Latin American Citizens), 220
Lynch, James, 357, 359

Machebeuf, Joseph Priest
in Arizona, 155
and building of churches, 181
and Christian piety, 183
in Colorado, 156, 177–179, 187, 207, 214
in Ohio, 285–286
Madaj, M. J., 295
Magnet parishes, 110–111
Marian devotions, 37, 86, 109
Marian Visitors, 103
Marist Fathers, 73–74, 188
Marquette, James, 282–283
Marquette League, 193, 216
Marriage, 60, 62–63
Marriage Encounter
in 1960s, 104
in Hawaii, 124
and Hispanic Americans, 253
in post-Vatican II period, 356, 367–368, 374
in rural parishes, 356
Worldwide, 367
Marschall, James, 316
Martínez, Antonio Jose, 162, 178, 207
Marty, Martin, 292–293, 298, 303
Mary's Igloo, 125
Maryknoll Fathers, 68, 72
Mass, 33–34, 38
Maternity Guild, 60
Matz, Nicholas, 214
Mayordomos, 187
May procession, 36–37
Mazon, Diego, 248
Mazzuchelli, Charles S., 289–290
McCullough, Thomas, 89–90
McDonnell, Donald, 89–90
McElligot, Francis, 358
McGucken, Joseph T., 118

McIntyre, James Francis, 88, 118
McLeod, Norman, 165
Meagher, Thomas Francis, 213
Mediator Dei, 195
Men
and Holy Name Society, 365
in Midwest, 304–305
in parochial life, during 1940s and 1950s, 345–346
in post-Vatican II period, 363–369
Menard, Rene, 282
Men's Club, 45
Mengarini, Gregory, 203
Men religious. *See* Bishops; Clergy; Priests; Religious orders
Mesplie, Toussaint, 156
Messmer, Sebastian, 342–343
Methodists, 162–163. *See also* Protestants
Mexican Americans
Americanization of, 87–88
and barrioization, 83
in California, 12, 79–82
and Catholicism, 79–80, 85–86
and CCD, 87
and *Cursillo* Movement, 90
and devotions, 86
failure of ministry to, 85
and family, 86–87
and Knights of Columbus, 88
neglect of, 83–84
in Oregon, 51, 90–91
and Our Lady of Guadalupe, 85–86
parish life of, 82–83, 86–87
and parochial schools, 87
and patron saints, 87
prejudice against, 16
priests serving, 84, 89–90
problems of, 84–86
and Protestants, 84–85, 90, 162
rituals of, 82
rural, 88–89
and socialization of children, 86
and social outreach, 91
and Spanish Mission Band, 89–90
successful ministry to, 91–92
and UNO, 91
urban, 87–88
"Mexican problem," 84–86
Mexican Revolution, 12, 80, 219
Meyer, Albert Cardinal, 336

General Index

Midwest. *See also* Post-Vatican II period; specific ethnic groups in
  Catholic Church statistics in, 382–401
  Catholicism in, 4
  CCD in, 330–331
  clergy in, 303–306, 368–369
  elderly in, 363–369
  ethnic groups in, 306, 333–336
  Jesuits in, 289
  Knights of Columbus in, 332
  laity in, 303–306
  men in, 304–305
  parish life in
    building and consolidating of, 292–303
    clergy in, 303–306
    history of, 279–280
    laity in, 303–306
    missionary era of, 282–292
    after World War II, 327–333, 345–346
    youth in, 303–306
  parochial schools in, 305–306
  women in, 304–305
  after World War I, 327–333
  after World War II, 345–348
  youth in, 303–306
Miege, John B., 300–301, 305
Missionary Catechists of Our Lady of Victory, 191
Mission Catholics, 53
Mission Revival, 15, 35
Missions, parish, 33–35
Mitty, John, 89
Monzell, Thomas I., 342
Mormons, 141, 163–165, 259
Morning Star, 72
Mother's Club, 29, 45
Muench, Aloysius, 329
Mullon, James, 285
Mundelein, George Cardinal, 331–334, 345, 360, 370
Mystical and Corporis, 195

National Association for Lay Ministers Conference, 241
National Catholic War Council, 329
National Catholic Welfare Conference, 329
National Conference of Catholic Bishops, 365–366
National Council of Catholic Women, 193
Nationality, 4. *See also* Ethnic groups

National Opinion Research Center, 119
National parishes, 49–50, 340–341
National Service Committee, 367
Native Americans. *See also* specific tribes of
  in 1950s, 223–224
  Apache, 202
  contribution of, 199–200
  conversion of, 19–20, 142–143
  education of, 204–205
  first converts, 200
  Flatheads, 223–224
  and Hispanic Americans, 205
  Hopi, 201–202
  missions to, 150–153, 216–217, 282–283
  Navajo, 202–203
  Papago, 202
  parochial schools for, 244
  and Peace Policy of 1870, 203–204
  persecution of, 16
  and Peyote Cult, 217–218
  Pima, 202
  in post-Vatican II period, 243–249
  and Protestants, 163
  Pueblo Indians, 200–201
  and tradition, 205–206
  and white immigration, 203
  Yuma, 202
Nattini, Emanuel M., 180
Navajo Indians
  and inculturation, 249
  missions for, 179, 202–203
  parochial schools for, 244
  and Peyotism, 218, 245
Newman Centers, 111, 195, 232, 242
Newman Clubs, 47, 191
Nicgorski, Darlene, 257
Nobertines, 188
Northeast region, 4–5
Northwest Ordinance of 1787, 283
Notre Dame Study of Catholic Parish Life, 1, 5
Novenas, 37, 60, 101, 346–347

O'Brien, David J., 355
O'Brien, Jim, 245
O'Brien, Thomas, 257
O'Connell, Eugene, 22
O'Connor, Edward, 366
O'Connor, James, 147–148, 160, 204
O'Connor, Richard, 347
O'Connor, William, 328

O'Dea, Archbishop, 68
O'Gorman, Bishop, 146, 158–159
O'Hara, Edwin V., 167, 329
de Oñate, Don Juan, 149
O'Regan, Anthony, 288
O'Reilly, Charles, 25
de Orendal y Maza, Don Antonio, 176
O'Shaughnessy, James, 348
Ostlangenberg, C. H., 288
Osuna, Luciano, 19–20
Our Lady of Fatima devotions, 37
Our Lady of Guadalupe, 85–86
Our Lady of Guadalupe devotions, 37
Our Lady of Sorrows, 346–347
Our Lady of the Conquest, 210
Ozanam, Frederick, 331

Pacific states. *See also* Post-Vatican II period; specific ethnic groups in
　anti-Catholicism in, 15–17
　Catholic Church in, 12
　Catholic Church statistics in, 128–133
　Catholicism in, 4, 11–12, 74–75
　Catholics in, 10–11
　concerns of, in 1980s, 117–119
　ethnic groups in, 49–53
　frontier mission parishes in, 19–23
　fund-raising in, 25–32
　immigrants to, 10
　parish life in, 10–12, 27
　parish organizations in, 29, 40–44
　socialization of children in, 44–47
　spirituality in, 33–38
PADRES, 250, 255
"Pag-Asa," 109
Papago Indians, 143–144, 150, 202, 245, 249
Parent-Teacher Guild, 45
Parish councils, 97, 99, 237–238
Parish Education Plan (PEP), 110
Parish festival, 28–29
Parish life. *See also* Devotions; Spirituality
　in 1980s, 117–119
　in Alaska, 124–125
　and Altar Society, 40–41, 186–187
　and American Catholicism, 2–3
　and American Dream, 17
　and bazaar, 28–29
　in California, 14
　of Chinese Americans, 72–73

　and Christian Family Movement, 38
　communication in, 31–32
　of cultural Catholics, 52–53
　and ethnicity, 50–51
　of Filipino Americans, 68–69
　finance committees in, 30–31
　in France, 3
　of French Canadians, 2–3
　on frontier, 19–23
　fund-raising events in, 28–29
　of German Americans, 60
　in Hawaii, 121–124
　and historian, 3–4
　and history, 1–2
　and Holy Name Society, 40–41, 186–187
　and immigrants, 47
　inner-city, 108–111
　in Intermountain West, 139–140, 165–169
　in Ireland, 3
　of Irish Americans, 56
　of Italian Americans, 64
　in Italy, 3
　of Japanese Americans, 72–73
　and Knights of Columbus, 41–42, 193
　and Legion of Mary, 38
　in magnet parishes, 110–111
　mass in, 33–34
　men in, in 1940s and 1950s, 345–346
　of Mexican Americans, 82–83, 86–87
　in Midwest
　　building and consolidating of, 292–303
　　clergy in, 303–306
　　history of, 279–280, 306
　　laity in, 303–306
　　missionary era of, 282–292
　　after World War II, 327–333, 345–346
　　youth in, 303–306
　of mission Catholics, 53
　Notre Dame study of, 1, 5
　in Pacific states, 10–12, 27
　of Polish Americans, 2–3
　of Portuguese Americans, 66–67
　in post-Vatican II period
　　in Intermountain West, 235–239
　　in Pacific states, 96–98, 108–111
　of practical Catholics, 52
　and retreats, 38
　and socialization of children, in 1950s, 44–47
　in Spain, 3

suburban, 108–111
tithing in, 29–30
in U.S., 2–3
Parish mission, 33–35
Parish organizations. *See also* Parochial schools; specific names of
in Alaska, 125
and Altar Society, 40–41
and athletics, 46
and Catholic Daughters of America, 41–42
and Catholic Ladies' Aid Society, 42–43
and CCD, 45
charitable, 42–43
of Chinese Americans, 72–73
concerns of, 40
of Filipino Americans, 68
and fraternal associations, 40
and fraternal insurance societies, 41–43
for fund-raising, 29
of German Americans, 60, 312–313
in Hawaii, 123–124
and Holy Name Society, 40–41
and immigrants, 44
of Italian Americans, 64–65, 339
of Japanese Americans, 71–72
and Knights of Columbus, 41–42
in local church, 187
and Newman Clubs, 47
in Pacific states, 29, 40–44
and parochial schools, 44–46
of Polish Americans, 73
of Portuguese Americans, 67
in post-Vatican II period
in Intermountain West, 242–243
in Midwest, 365–368
and sodalities, 46
and St. Vincent de Paul Society, 42–43
and teen clubs, 46
and YCS, 47
and YCW, 47
and YLI, 41–42
and YMI, 41–42
"Parish plant," 26, 31
Parish Worship Committee, 102
Parker, Samuel, 163
Parochial schools
in 1950s, 44–47
and athletics, 46–47
building, 26

in California, 44–45
and CCD, 44–45
and German Americans, 58, 306, 313–315
in Intermountain West, 189–190, 195
and Irish Americans, 56, 306, 313
in Kansas, 305–306
in local church, 182–185, 189–190, 195
and Mexican Americans, 87
in Midwest, 305–306
for Native Americans, 244
for Navajo Indians, 244
in Oregon, 44
organizations of, 109
and parish organizations, 44–46
and Polish Americans, 343–344
in post-Vatican II period
in Intermountain West, 239–242
in Midwest, 358, 360–362
in Pacific states, 106–110
and public school law, 16
and public schools, 163
sisters teaching in, 44
and socialization of children, 44–47
and sodalities, 46
in suburban parishes, 110
and teen clubs, 46
in Washington, 44
after World War I, 330
Pasino, Peter, 193
Pastoral Letter on Hispanic Ministry, 1983, 255
Pastors. *See* Priests
Patron saints, 87
Pauwelyn, Cyril, 157
Pax Christi International, 257
Peace movement, 256–257
Peace Policy of 1870, 203–204
Pecoul, Remigious, 191
Pelamourques, Jean A., 289
Pend d'Oreilles, 153
Penitente Brotherhood, 208
PEP (Parish Education Plan), 110
Persone, Salvatore, 155
Peschges, John H., 328–329
Petillo, Anthony, 188
Pew rents, 28
Peyote Cult, 217–218
Peyotism, 217–218
Pfleger, Michael, 371
Philipps, Charles, 89

Piccoli, Julius M., 222
Pierce, Gustavous Marshall, 165
Pierce v. Society of Sisters, 16
Pierz, Francis X., 292
Pima Indians, 150–151, 202, 245
Pima Revolt of 1751, 202
Pinet, François, 283
Pino, Don Pedro Bautista, 151
Pious Fund, 27
Pitt, Leonard, 19
Pius X, 330
Pius XI, 342
Plains Indians, 193
Plate collections, 28
Plenary Councils of Baltimore, 182
Point, Nicholas, 177, 203
Polingaysi Qoyawayma, 201
Polish Americans
  in Chicago, 295
  nationalism of, 344–345
  national parishes of, 340–341
  parish life of, 2–3
  parish organizations of, 73
  and parochial schools, 343–344
  priests serving, 73
  waves of, 340
  in Wisconsin, 341–343
  after World War II, 347
Polish War Relief, 221–222
Poor Soul's Day, 34
Portuguese Americans
  in California, 65
  festivals of, 66–67
  and fraternal insurance societies, 41
  and I.D.E.S., 67
  parish life of, 66–67
  parish organizations of, 67
  priests serving, 66
  and Sociedade Portuguesa Rainha Santa Isabel, 67
  societies of, 67
Post-Vatican II period
  in Intermountain West
    and Catholicism, 243–256
    concerns of, 256–263
    economic changes, 228–233
    and ethnic groups, new, 243–256
    and Hispanic Americans, 249–256
    and liturgy, 233–235
    and local church, 233–243
    and Native Americans, 243–249
    and parish organizations, 242–243
    and parish structure, 235–239
    and parochial schools, 239–242
    political changes, 228–233
    and religion, 243–256
    social changes, 228–233
    and women, 261–262
  in Midwest
    changes, 355
    and Christian Family Movement, 374
    clergy, 368–369
    and *Cursillo* Movement, 356, 373
    elderly, 363–369
    implementation of changes, 374
    laity, 363–369
    and Marriage Encounter, 356, 367–368, 374
    men, 363–369
    parish renewals, 359–360
    parochial schools, 358, 360–362
    priests serving, 358–359
    rural parish, 355–363
    suburban parish, 355–363
    urban parish, 355–363
    women, 363–369
    youth, 363–369
  in Pacific states
    and Catholicism, 103–106
    and CCD, 106–107
    concerns of, 103–106
    and demographic shift, 108–111
    and devotions, 101
    and ethnic groups, new, 111–114
    and liturgy, 100–103
    and parish life, 96–98, 108–111
    and parochial schools, 106–110
    and priests, 98–100
Poulin, A. Z., 156
Poverty Sunday, 103
Practical Catholics, 52
Preaching, 34–35
Pre-Cana Conference, 38
Prendergast, Edward, 360
Presbyterians, 162. *See also* Protestants
Presentation Sisters, 44
Priests. *See also* Bishops; Clergy; specific names of
  and Chinese Americans, 72
  and Filipino Americans, 68

General Index

and fund-raising, 28
and German Americans, 309–310
Irish, 56
and Italian Americans, 62
and Japanese Americans, 70–72
and laity, 97–98
and local church, 177–179, 187–188
and Mexican Americans, 84, 89–90
missionary, 20–21
in Pacific states, 20–22
and Polish Americans, 73
and Portuguese Americans, 66
in post-Vatican II period
  in Midwest, 358–359
  in Pacific states, 98–100
Priests for Equality, 234
Processions, 35–37, 64–65, 69
Progressive reformers, 43–44
Protestants
  and anti-Catholicism, 16
  in California, 13
  and Catholic Church, 161–163
  and Catholics, 53, 105–106, 285–286
  and cultural Catholics, 53
  and Filipino Americans, 69
  and First Great Awakening, 161
  and German Americans, 315
  in Hawaii, 121
  and Hispanic Americans, 220, 253–254
  in Intermountain West, 141, 161–163
  and Italian Americans, 62
  in Los Angeles, 13
  and Mexican Americans, 84–85, 90, 162
  and Mormons, 164–165
  and Native Americans, 163
  and religious education, 183
  in San Francisco, 13
  and Second Great Awakening, 161
Provincial Councils of Baltimore, 182
Public Law 93–638, 247
Public schools, 163, 184, 190–191
Pueblo Indians, 154, 200–201
Pueblo Revolt in 1680, 149–151, 200–201, 210
Puerto Rican Americans. *See* Hispanic Americans
Purcell, John Baptist, 206, 285

Quarter, William, 288, 290
Quigley, James, 295–296, 337
Quigley, Thomas, 56

Ramirez, Ricardo, 252
Raverdy, John Baptist, 146, 156, 177–178
Ravoux, Augusting, 147
Raymbaut, Charles, 282
Reciprocal cooperation, 55
Redemptorists, 34, 38, 188, 190, 310–311
Refugee Act of 1980, 257
Reisel, Joseph, 316
Religious communities, 191
Religious Education Task Force, 96–97
Religious orders, 53, 310. *See also* specific names of
Religious Quality Council, 247
Rempe, Charles A., 334–335
Rendón, Armando, 255
Renew, 360
Renewal of American Catholicism, The, 355
Retreat movement, 38
Retreats, 104
Reynolds, E. V., 159
Reynolds, Sarah "Killarney," 188
Rhode, Paul, 343
Richard, Gabriel, 286
Right to Life, 103
Riley, Kathleen, 366
Riordan, John, 57, 366
Rischin, Moses, 13
Rite of Toledo, 206
Rizal Day, 69
Roberts, John, 204
Robinson, Henry, 156
Rodriguez, Richard, 86
Rohlman, Henry, 329
Roman Ritual in 1614, 206
Romo, Richard, 79
Rosary, 33, 346
Rosary Society, 365
Rosati, Bishop, 145
Rosatti, Joseph, 287–288
Roualt, Father, 121–122
Rowe, Cyprian, 372
Royce, Josiah, 13
Rubio, Gonzalez, 79
Ryan, Daniel, 357

Sacred Hearts Fathers (SS.CC.), 121
Salesian Boys Clubs, 47
Salpointe, John Baptist, 181, 209
Salvatorians, 188
Sanchez, Robert, 254

Sanctuary Movement, 117–118, 257–258
Santo Niño de Cebu festival, 69–70
Scalabrini Fathers, 336
Scanlon, Lawrence, 157, 186
Scarabino, Anthony, 236–237
Schank, Francis J., 331
Schlacks, Henry J., 311
Schuetz, Jan, 259
Schussler-Fiorenza, Elizabeth, 365
Schweninger, Florian, 59
Second Great Awakening, 161
Second National Encuentro, 255
Secularization, 175–176
Segale, Blandina, 184
Seghers, Charles John, 157, 180
Senior citizens. See Elderly
Serrano, Gabriel, 81
Serritella, Anthony, 339–340
Servite Fathers, 336
Shanley, John, 298–299, 304, 308
Shea, John Gilmary, 279
Sheil, Bernard, 332
Sheridan, William, 301
Shoshone Indians, 216, 246
Sieur de Vincennes, 283
Simbang Gabi, 69
Sioux Indians, 297
Sisters, 44, 313
Sisters of Charity, 44, 204
Sisters of Loretto, 183
Sisters of Mary, 44
Sisters of St. Joseph of Carondolet, 44
Sisters of the Holy Name, 44
Slovak Americans, 73, 215, 222, 334
Slovenian Americans, 215, 221–222
de Smet, Pierre Jean
  in Dakota Territory, 291
  and Flatheads, 145
  and Jesuits, 152, 164
  and negotiations with Native Americans, 203
  and Oregon Indians, 19
  and physical geography of Intermountain West, 141–142, 164
De Smet Club, 191
Smith, Joseph, 290
Smith, Truman, 145–146
Sobaipuri Indians, 150
Social events, 191–193
Socialization, 44–47, 86
Social outreach, 91, 103

Sociedade Portuguesa Rainha Santa Isabel, 67
Sociedades Mexicanas, 220
Society for the Propagation of the Faith, 27
Sodalities, 36, 46, 55–56, 58
Sodality of the Blessed Virgin Mary, 55
Sotelo, Antonio, 254
South Americans. See Hispanic Americans; Latin Americans
South Central region, 5
Southern California Renewal Conference (SCRC), 104
Spalding, Henry, 163, 304
Spanish-American War of 1898, 219
Spanish mission, 11
Spanish Mission Band, 89–90
Spirituality. See also Devotions; Parish life
  activist, 38
  and confraternities, 36–37
  and indifferent Catholics, 34
  lay involvement in, 38
  and mass, 33–34
  and Mission Revival, 35
  in Pacific states, 33–38
  and preaching, 34–35
  and processions, 35–36
  and sodalities, 36
  after World War II, 346–347
Sporting events. See Athletics
St. Casmir's Society, 193
St. Cyr, John Mary, 288
St. Francis Guild, 60
St. Francis Xavier Mission, 72
St. Joseph's Benevolent Society, 55, 125
St. Mary's Ladies' Society, 55
St. Raphael Society, 214
St. Turibius Indian Mission, 20
St. Vincent de Paul Society, 42–43, 68, 109, 331–332
Stadtmueller, Frederick A., 245
Stahlke, Walter, 335–336
Stark, Ignatius, 71
Starr, Kevin, 43
Stations of the Cross, 36
Stoeke, William, 73
Stritch, Samuel Cardinal, 358
Suburban parishes, 108–111
Summer vacation schools, 190–191
Sunday Benediction of the Blessed Sacrament, 37
Sunday bulletin, 31

Sunday envelope, 28
Sweetser, Thomas, 364–365

Tavares, Joao Manuel, 66
Teen clubs, 46
Tekakwitha Conference, 248
Territorial parish, 49–50
Theile, Aloysius J., 309–310
Third National Hispanic Pastoral Encuentro, 255
Third Plenary Council of Baltimore, 163, 240
Tithing, 29–30, 185
Tobin, John, 30
"Toward a Free and Equal Sharing," 234
Transcontinental railroad, 12
Treaty of Ghent, 291
Treaty of Guadalupe Hidalgo, 79, 145, 178
Trecy, Jeremiah, 298
Triduums, 37, 60
Trobec, James, 305

Ulibarri, Sabine R., 252–253
United Neighborhoods Organization (UNO), 91
UNO (United Neighborhoods Organization), 91
Ursulines, 204
Ute Indians, 218

Valentin, 62
de Vargas, Diego, 149
Vatican II Council. See Post-Vatican II period
de Velasco, Luis, 149
Van De Velde, James Oliver, 288
Venn, Clement, 316
de la Verendrye, Pierre, 291
Vietnamese Americans, 111–112
Vigilance Committees, 16, 20, 57
Volpi, Sylvia, 46

Wagner, John, 179
Walsh, Henry, 20
Walsh, Patrick, 164
War of 1812, 287
Weber, Max, 293
Wehrle, Vincent, 298–299, 328
Weigand, William K., 252
Weigel, Gustave, 363

Whitman, Marcus, 163
Whitman massacre, 16
Wolf, Sebastian, 59
Women
    and Altar Society, 365
    in Catholic Church, 261–262
    in Midwest, 304–305
    in post-Vatican II period
        in Intermountain West, 262–263
        in Midwest, 363–369
    and World War I, 327
Women religious. See Religious orders; Sisters
Working Boys' Home, 333
World War I
    German Americans after, 333–336
    German Americans before, 327–328
    parochial schools after, 330
    and women, 327
World War II, 73, 220, 345–348
Worldwide Marriage Encounter, 367
Wurth, Geri, 359

Yaqui, 245
YCS (Young Christian Students), 38, 47
YCW (Young Christian Workers), 38, 47
YLI (Young Ladies' Institute), 41–42, 68
YMI (Young Men's Institute), 41–42
Yorke, Peter C., 16, 35, 56–57
Young, Brigham, 163–164
Young Christian Students (YCS), 38, 47
Young Christian Workers (YCW), 38, 47
Young Ladies' Institute (YLI), 41–42, 68
Young Ladies' Society, 313
Young Men's Institute (YMI), 41–42
Young Men's Society, 313
Youth
    of Italian Americans, 339
    in Midwest, 303–306, 363–369
Yuma Indians, 150, 202
Yzermans, Vincent A., 124

Zane, Ebenezer, 284
Zapian, Yoland, 373
Zardetti, Otto, 310
Zotter, Tom, 260–261

Index of Places and Parishes

Alaska, 11, 124–125, 134
   Anchorage, 125, 135
   Fairbanks, 124–125, 135
   Juneau, 125, 134
   Nome, 125
   St. Joseph's Parish, 124
   Wrangell, 124
   St. Rose Parish, 124

Arizona, 142–144, 147, 150, 154–155, 200–202, 228, 236, 244, 249, 276
   Buckeye, 236
   Fort Washakie, 216
   Gallup, 203, 215
   Keams Canyon
   St. Joseph's Indian Mission, 201
   Magdalena de Sonora Church, 202
   Phoenix, 166, 229, 245–246, 254, 257, 271, 275
   St. Mary's Church, 257
   San Bernardo, 149
   St. Joseph's Indian Mission, 201, 216
   St. Michael's Mission for Navajo Indians, 202
   Topowa
   San Solano missions, 216
   Tucson, 148, 155, 166, 229, 271, 275
   All Saints Newman Center, 257
   San Carlos Apache Mission, 223
   St. Michael's Parish, 179
   Whiteriver
   St. Francis Apache Mission, 223

California, 10–12, 17, 19, 27, 37, 42, 44–45, 47, 51–53, 58–59, 61, 65, 79–80, 90, 106–107
   Anaheim
   St. Boniface Parish, 20, 26, 58
   Berkeley, 27, 89
   St. Joseph's Parish, 36
   Daly City
   St. Andrew's Parish, 113
   Fresno, 130

   Grass Valley, 21
   Los Angeles, 13, 20, 43, 82–84, 88, 128
   El Christo Rey Parish, 73
   Loyola-Marymount Parish, 105
   St. Basil's Church, 118
   St. Columban's Parish, 68
   St. Francis Xavier Chapel, 72
   St. Odilia Parish, 74
   St. Peter's Italian Church, 62
   St. Victor Parish, 74
   Monterey, 13, 129
   Oakland, 30, 97, 100, 130
   Cathedral Parish, 96, 111
   St. Elizabeth's Parish, 59–61
   St. Francis de Sales Parish, 96–97, 105
   St. Joseph's Parish, 66
   St. Mary's Parish, 43, 89
   Orange County, 92, 106, 130
   Blessed Sacrament Parish, 105
   Richmond, 89
   Riverside
   St. Andrew's Newman Center, 111
   Sacramento, 129
   San Bernardino, 130
   San Diego, 31, 130
   San Francisco, 10, 12–13, 16, 20–21, 28, 30, 103, 105, 112, 128
   Corpus Christi Italian Parish, 34, 49–50, 62
   Immaculate Conception Parish, 62
   Notre Dame des Victoires Parish, 49, 73–74
   Our Lady of Guadalupe Parish, 49, 62
   Sacred Heart Parish, 34
   SS. Peter and Paul Parish, 62
   St. Anthony Parish, 59–60
   St. Benedict the Moor Parish, 74
   St. Boniface German Parish, 42, 49, 59–60, 101
   St. Brigid's Parish, 55
   St. Cecilia's Parish, 30
   St. Dominic's Parish, 101
   St. Elizabeth's Parish, 96
   St. Francis of Assisi Parish, 55, 62, 81
   St. Gabriel's Parish, 101

Index of Places and Parishes

St. Ignatius Parish, 37
St. Joseph Parish, 42, 55
St. Mary's Parish, 55, 118
St. Patrick's Parish, 42, 55, 108
St. Paul's Parish, 29, 31, 103
St. Philip's Parish, 30–31
St. Thomas the Apostle Parish, 29
St. Xavier Mission, 72
Star of the Sea Parish, 101
  San Jose, 83
Five Wounds Parish, 66
Our Lady of Guadalupe Chapel, 85
St. Julie's Parish, 102–103
St. Patrick's Parish, 85
  San Mateo
Our Lady of the Pillar Parish, 81
  Santa Ana
Southwest Community Center, 106
  Santa Rosa, 130
  Stockton, 130

Colorado, 142, 144, 147, 156, 169, 185, 214, 228, 236, 276
  Boulder, 231–232
Sacred Heart of Mary Parish, 190, 195, 221
  Colorado Springs, 229
  Conejos
Our Lady of Guadalupe Parish, 154–156, 179
  Denver, 148, 156, 190, 193, 199, 229, 271, 275
Holy Rosary Parish, 222
Most Precious Blood Parish, 237–238, 241–243
Our Lady of Mount Carmel Parish, 193–194, 222–223
Sacred Heart Parish, 179
St. Cajetan's Parish, 207
St. Elizabeth's Parish, 179, 214
St. Joseph's Parish, 190, 193, 215, 222
St. Jude's Parish, 228–229
St. Leo's Church, 214
St. Mary's Parish, 156, 183
St. Michael the Archangel Parish, 239
  Globeville, 215, 221–222
  Leadville
St. Joseph's Parish, 222
  Peetz
Sacred Heart Parish, 259
  Pueblo, 169, 199, 223, 229, 240, 262, 272, 275
Holy Family Parish, 240

St. Anthony of Padua Parish, 222
St. Boniface Church, 215
St. Mary's Parish, 215, 222
  San Luis Valley, 154
  Trinidad, 184, 223

Florida, 5

France, 3

Hawaii, 11, 121–124, 133
  Honolulu, 123
Holy Family Parish, 123

Idaho, 142, 146, 155, 186, 195, 213, 229, 276
  Boise, 148, 153, 156–157, 190, 229, 272, 275
Good Shepherd Church, 222
St. Patrick's Parish, 157
  Coeur d'Alene River
Sacred Heart Mission Church, 153
  Eden, 194
  Hailey, 229, 259
St. Charles Borromeo Parish, 180, 194, 224, 234–235, 239, 241, 253
  Kamiah
St. Catherine's Parish, 235
  Lewiston, 156
St. Stanislaus Parish, 156
  Moscow, 191, 237
St. Mary's Parish, 191–192, 240–241, 243
  Pierce, 235
  Pocatello, 181, 223
  Priest River, 223
  Rupert
St. Nicholas Parish, 251
  St. Joe River, 153
  Wood River Valley
St. Charles Parish, 157

Illinois
  Alton, 286–287
  Belleville, 386
  Calumnt City, 368
Our Lady of Knock Church, 368
  Chicago, 2–3, 287–289, 293–296, 328, 386
Corpus Christi Parish, 371
Holy Rosary Parish, 307–308
Our Lady of Pompeii Parish, 339
Our Lady of Sorrows Parish, 346–347
Our Providence of God Parish, 373

SS. Clara and Cyril Parish, 362
St. Aloysius Parish, 367
St. Alphonsus Parish, 311, 314
St. Augustine's Parish, 311, 313–314
St. Basil's Parish, 362
St. Benedict's Parish, 314, 360
St. Boniface Parish, 310–312, 315–317, 334–336
St. Bridget Parish, 307
St. Cajetan's Parish, 368
St. Callistus Parish, 334
St. Elizabeth Parish, 307, 370–371
St. Gabriel Parish, 307
St. Gregory's Parish, 314
St. James Parish, 307
St. Jane de Chantal Parish, 368
St. John Fisher Parish, 358, 362, 368
St. John Parish, 307
St. Martin's Parish, 314
St. Mary of the Woods Parish, 360
St. Michael's Parish, 308, 314
St. Monica Church, 370
St. Patrick's Parish, 307
St. Philip Benizi Parish, 337–339
St. Philip Parish, 368
St. Stanislaus Kostka, 340
St. Tarcissus Parish, 366
St. Thomas More Parish, 346
St. Williams Parish, 334
Galena
St. Michael Church, 289
Joliet, 345, 367, 387
Kaskaskia, 286–287
Mundelein
Santa Maria del Popolo Parish, 364
Park Forest
St. Iraneaus Parish, 363
Peoria, 387
Prairie du Rocher, 286–287
Riverside
St. Mary Parish, 363
Rockford, 387
Schaumburg, 357
Holy Spirit Parish, 357
St. Marcelline Parish, 357
Springfield, 388
St. Louis, 287
Vandalia, 286–287
Wheaton
St. Michael's Parish, 357

Indiana
Evansville, 385
Fort Wayne, 385
Gary, 385
Indianapolis, 384
Lafayette, 386
South Bend, 385
Vincennes, 283

Intermountain West region. *See* specific states in

Iowa
Davenport, 289, 361–362, 373, 394
Des Moines, 356, 395
Dubuque, 289, 394
Sioux City, 395

Ireland, 3, 21

Italy, 3

Kansas, 300–303, 305–306
Dodge City, 400
Doniphan, 300, 305
Eureka
St. Bernard Parish, 366
Flush, 361
St. Joseph Parish, 336, 356
Kansas City, 400
Leavenworth, 300
Osawatomie
St. Philip Neri Parish, 302
Saline, 401
St. Mary's Parish, 301
Wichita, 401

Massachusetts
Auburn
St. Philip Parish, 366

Michigan
Dearborn, 287
St. Alphonsus Parish, 346
Detroit, 286, 328, 388
St. Anne Parish, 286
St. Cecilia Parish, 330
Gaylord, 388
Grand Rapids, 389
Kalamazoo, 389

Index of Places and Parishes 421

Lansing, 389
Marquette, 390
Saginaw, 390

Midwest region. *See* specific states in

Minnesota
Clontarf, 297
Crookston, 328, 331, 392
Crow Wing, 292
De Graff, 297
Duluth, 297, 393
Minneapolis, 392
Moorehead, 331
New Hope, 356–357
New Ulm, 393
St. Cloud, 297, 310, 393
St. Paul, 291–292, 296–297, 392
Winona, 297, 394

Missouri
Cape Girardeau, 397
Hermann, 311
Jefferson City, 396
Kansas City, 396
Springfield, 397
St. Joseph, 396
St. Louis, 395

Montana, 142–144, 146, 177, 213, 230, 232–233, 237, 276
Anaconda
St. Joseph's Parish, 194, 230
Billings, 159–160, 231, 244, 258, 273, 275
Our Lady of Guadalupe Church, 224
Bitterroot Valley
St. Mary's Mission, 152–153
Butte, 223
Holy Savior Parish, 230
Sacred Heart Parish, 230
St. Helena Parish, 230
St. Mary's Parish, 230
St. Patrick's Parish, 190
Columbia Falls
St. Richard's Parish, 166–167
Frenchtown, 155
Great Falls, 167, 231, 244, 258, 273, 275
Havre, 160
Helena, 148, 155, 157, 167, 177, 179, 190, 230–231, 258, 272, 275

St. Ignatius Mission, 153, 155, 203
Hell's Gate Church, 155
Jocko Reservation
St. John Berchman's Church, 223–224
St. Louis Church, 155
West Broadview
Assumption Church, 186
White Sulphur Springs, 157, 181, 258–259
St. Bartholomew's Parish, 192, 194
Wilbax
St. Peter's Parish, 185

Nebraska, 159, 300–303
Columbus, 302
Grand Island, 399
Lincoln, 399
North Platte, 301
Omaha, 399
South Platte, 301
St. Mary's Cathedral, 159
Wilbur, 303

Nevada, 142, 146–148, 158, 167–168, 229, 276
Battle Mountain, 159
Sacred Heart Parish, 159
St. John Bosco, 159
Carlin, 159
Sacred Heart Parish, 159
Elko, 159
St. Joseph's Parish, 159
Hamilton
SS. Peter and Paul Parish, 158
Las Vegas, 159, 168, 229, 240, 273, 275
St. Joan of Arc Parish, 159, 168
Pioche
St. Lawrence Parish, 158
Reno, 168, 229, 240, 273, 275
Tonopah, 168

New Hampshire, 2–3

New Jersey
Newark, 360

New Mexico, 142, 145–146, 176, 200, 229, 235–237, 249, 276
Acoma
San Esteban Indian mission, 244
Albuquerque, 153, 247, 262
Aquinas Newman Center, 242, 257

San Cruz Parish, 185
San Felipe Parish, 185
  Belen, 168
  Our Lady of Belen Church, 189
  Bernalillo
  St. Catherine's Parish, 204
    Doña Ana, 145
    Duranes, 184
  Los Duranes Chapel, 252
    Durango, 176, 214
    Gallup, 231, 244, 247, 274–275
    Grant, 231
    Isleta
  San Augustin Indian mission, 244
    Jemez
  San Diego Indian mission, 244
    Laguna
  San Jose Indian mission, 244
    Las Cruces, 145
    Los Griegos, 251
    Los Ojos
  San Jose Parish, 192
    Nuestra Senora de Guadalupe de Zuñi, 149
    San Juan
  San Juan De Los Caballeros Indian mission, 244
    San Juan Bautista, 149
    Santa Cruz, 153
    Santa Cruz de la Cañada, 187, 238, 251–252
    Santa Fe, 146, 153, 166, 183, 190, 229–230, 236, 244, 247, 273, 275
  Rosario Chapel of La Conquistadora, 252
    Shiprock
  Christ the King Parish, 249
    Taos
  Our Lady of Guadalupe Parish, 237
  San Geronimo Parish, 153–154
    Zuni
  San Antonio Indian mission, 244

New York, 5

North Dakota, 298
  Bismarck, 397
  Fargo, 304, 397
  Jamestown, 297
  Pembina, 291

Ohio
  Cincinnati, 283–284, 382
  Cleveland, 328, 382
    Blessed Sacrament Parish, 360
    Columbus, 285, 368, 383
    Holy Cross Parish, 345
    St. Remigius Parish, 285
    Lancaster, 284
    Parma, 359
    Rocky River
  St. Christopher Parish, 360
    Somerset
  St. Joseph Parish, 284
    Steubenville, 366, 383
    Toledo, 384
    Youngstown, 384

Oregon, 10–11, 14–16, 19–20, 22–23, 27, 42, 44, 47, 51, 90–91, 144–145
  Baker, 14, 131
  Eugene, 100
  Milwaukie
  Christ the King Parish, 29–30
  Portland, 14, 37, 51, 131
  Holy Redeemer Parish, 101, 103
  St. Brigitta's Parish, 29
  St. Ignatius Parish, 36
  St. Michael's Italian Parish, 51
  Richland
  St. William Parish, 23
  Verboort, 35

Pacific coast region. See specific states in

Pennsylvania, 5

South central region, 5

South Dakota, 297–298
  Rapid City, 398
  Sioux Falls, 297, 329, 398
  Yankton, 298

Spain, 3

United States, 3. See also specific states of

Utah, 142, 146–147, 168, 229, 276
  Carbon County, 166
  Corinne, 159
  Helper, 188
  St. Anthony's Church, 166
  Ogden

Index of Places and Parishes 423

Holy Family Parish, 159
  Park City, 191–192
St. Mary's, 157
  Price, 190
  Provo
St. Peter's Church, 188
  Salt Lake City, 148, 157–158, 168, 229, 240, 274–275
Cathedral of the Madeleine, 168
Our Lady of Guadalupe Parish, 250–251
St. Mary Magdalen Parish, 164
St. Patrick's Parish, 219–220

Washington, 10–11, 14–16, 20, 22–23, 27, 42, 44, 47, 51–52, 106–107
  Battle Ground
Sacred Heart Parish, 109
  Kenmore
St. John Vianney Parish, 98–99, 109
  Rockford, 100
  Seattle, 14, 41, 132
Our Lady Queen of Martyrs Parish, 68, 72
Sacred Heart German Parish, 58–59
  Snohomish
St. Michael's Parish, 98–99, 104
  Spokane, 14, 100, 132
St. Thomas More Parish, 98–99, 109
  Tacoma
St. Charles Borromeo, 110
St. Joseph's Parish, 73
  Tekoa
Sacred Heart Parish, 98, 100, 106
United Church of Christ, 106
  Yakima, 133

West coast region. *See* specific states in

Wisconsin, 341
  Burlington
St. Mary's Parish, 360
  Darlington, 363
Holy Rosary Parish, 296
  Green Bay, 289, 391
  La Crosse, 391
  Madison, 391
  Milwakee, 390
  Milwaukee, 341–342
St. Hedwig's Parish, 341
St. Josephat Parish, 342, 344
St. Stanislaus Parish, 341, 344
  Polonia
Sacred Heart Parish, 341
  Portage County, 341
  Prairie du Chien, 290
  Superior, 392

Wyoming, 142, 144, 230, 276
  Cheyenne, 148, 160, 184, 230, 244, 274–275
  Fort Laramie, 158
  Fort Washakie, 204
  Gilette, 230
  Laramie, 184
  Rock Springs, 230
SS. Cyril and Methodius Parish, 222
  St. Stephen's Indian Mission, 204, 244, 246, 249
  St. Stephen's Parish, 217